LOCKOUT

Dublin 1913

LOCKOUT
Dublin 1913

Pádraig Yeates

Gill & Macmillan

Gill & Macmillan Ltd
Hume Avenue, Park West, Dublin 12
With associated companies throughout the world
www.gillmacmillan.ie

© Pádraig Yeates 2000, 2001
0 7171 2891 1
First published in hard cover 2000
First published in paperback 2001

Print origination by Andy Gilsenan, Dublin
Printed by ColourBooks Ltd, Dublin

This book is typeset in Berkeley 10.5 on 12pt.

The paper used in this book comes from the wood pulp of managed forests. For every tree felled, at least one tree is planted, thereby renewing natural resources.

A CIP catalogue record for this book is available from the British Library.

5 4 3 2 1

For Pat and Jane (née Hanlon) Fagan, and all
the other unsung heroes and heroines of 1913

CONTENTS

PREFACE

IN March 1998 Dublin Airport was closed for the first time in its history. Thousands of SIPTU members took unofficial action in sympathy with fewer than fifty baggage-handlers, who were fighting for trade union recognition in Ryanair, one of Ireland's most profitable companies. The revival of the 'sympathetic strike' on such a scale seemed an appalling anachronism in a society feeling increasingly at home with 'social partnership'. The invocation by the strike's defenders of the lockout of 1913—when perhaps a third of the city's population starved in a fight over trade union recognition—appeared misleading or irrelevant to many people, and was probably incomprehensible to even more.

There was a time, not so long ago, when the great lockout was not only part of the collective memory of every Dubliner but part of their collective experience. Today trade unions are struggling to redefine their role in society. The development of 'social partnership' is part of that process; it has become the dominant model for Irish industrial relations, though the level of involvement by unions and employers at local level is hotly debated. Nevertheless social partnership is widely regarded as one of the fundamental building blocks of Ireland's remarkable economic growth in the nineteen-nineties, and it has certainly helped to save the trade union movement from the sort of marginalisation that has occurred in many parts of the English-speaking world.

The Dublin Airport dispute was a timely reminder, not just to the trade union movement but to employers and the Government, that social partnership is still a fragile growth. Above all, it showed that its institutions lack the capacity to deal effectively with trade unionists and employers when they behave badly. Such outbursts occur because we all carry bad habits in our baggage, to which we resort when provoked. Whether we like it or not, 1913 is part of that baggage.

The past does not have to be a burden. The sympathetic strike and social partnership are opposite sides of the same coin; both stem from that peculiarly Irish version of syndicalism known as Larkinism.

The main repository of Larkinism today is SIPTU, Ireland's largest trade union. That is no accident. SIPTU was formed in 1990 from the amalgamation of the Irish Transport and General Workers' Union and the Federated Workers' Union of Ireland, both of which were founded by the author of Larkinism, James Larkin.

The Dublin Airport dispute was only the most dramatic of a series of recognition disputes that punctuated industrial relations in the nineteen-nineties. Most of them involved SIPTU, partly because it has been one of the most active unions in organising the low-paid and weakest elements in the work force; but the SIPTU shop stewards who mobilised thousands of members in support of a handful of badly paid baggage handlers were also responding to Larkin's most fundamental dictum, 'An injury to one is the concern of all.'

SIPTU, as a union, was not officially involved. It was bound by national agreements—and the Industrial Relations Act (1990)—not to engage in, or support, unofficial strikes. But its general officers did not disown members at the airport. Indeed not alone SIPTU but the Irish Congress of Trade Unions was able to use the Ryanair dispute, and the eruption of workers' militancy provoked by the company's anti-union stance, to significantly improve their bargaining position in negotiations on new legislation in the Government's High-Level Group on Trade Union Recognition.

That too was in line with the Larkinite heritage. At the heart of Larkinism is the notion that the trade union movement is far more than a vehicle for improving the wages and conditions of workers. Its primary purpose is to create within the very infrastructure of capitalism its successor, socialism. Today Larkin's dream may seem no nearer than in 1913, but it still exerts a powerful influence. Trade unionists continue to pursue their own radical social and political agenda, convinced that politics is far too serious to be left to politicians. Arguably, social partnership is a more modern and more effective way of exerting industrial muscle and social solidarity on behalf of the weak and the marginalised than ever the sympathetic strike was.

This does not mean that the debate is over. Today supporters and opponents of social partnership within the trade union movement—not to mention the broader left—claim the mantle of 1913. They can do so partly because, at a time when most Irish historical myths are being deconstructed, that of 1913 has remained unsullied. The reason is simple: we have no basic record of what happened. The lockout is frequently referred to, often analysed—usually as a prelude to 1916 and all that—but never described.

Chronologically, 1913 was of course a prelude to 1916 and the triumph of militant nationalism. But to a far greater extent it was a response to a wider and potentially more benign world that beckoned to millions of European workers before they were blasted away by the guns of the First World War. It was an era in which trade unionists, employers and politicians were beginning to debate the internationalisation of capital and its consequences. Issues of globalisation, competition and the social wage are once more at the centre of political dialogue. Hopefully they will remain there long after the ghosts of 1914 have finally been exorcised.

The lockout is also the nearest thing Ireland has ever had to a socialist revolution, and it therefore provides a glimpse of an alternative Ireland that people strove for before competing nationalisms imposed their own social straitjackets, ones that proved immensely durable as well as restrictive. For all these reasons, the lockout deserves to be remembered as more than just an adjunct to other stories of Ireland's progress towards national statehood.

Of course, trying to disinter the facts from the myth carries its own risks. The myth has survived in large part because it has suited everyone. It gave the moral victory to the workers, while their material defeat underlined the comforting contention of the employers—and other defenders of conservative ideologies—that Larkinism, and by extension socialism, made for good rhetoric but was impractical.

For the most part the lockout was a far shabbier, bloodier and more mundane affair than the myth allows. It was also a much more closely run battle than the myth allows. Above all, it was an unnecessary dispute and probably would not have occurred but for the peculiarly perverse personalities of Larkin and the employers' leader, William Martin Murphy.

Few of the principals emerge well from this awful episode in Dublin's history. It was left to what Tom Kettle referred to as the 'second-class people on both sides' to pick up the pieces. Of course, individual Dubliners of all classes and creeds, acting on the impulses of common humanity, did what they could to mitigate the worst aspects of the tragedy. So did thousands of workers in Britain who contributed almost £100,000 (the equivalent of £10 million today) to help their locked-out brethren. Nevertheless the lockout raised passions that were by turn sectarian and nationalist. The help from Britain was often resented and, perversely, helped strengthen separatist tendencies within the Irish trade union movement.

I wrote this book from idle intellectual curiosity, but I hope that others might like to learn more from the lockout. Not only does it describe the furnace in which the Dublin working class and Irish industrial relations were forged but it shows what happens when the rich and privileged in any society deny to those less well off their birthright.

ACKNOWLEDGMENTS

Both my parents were born in 1912—my father in Buckingham Street and my mother around the corner in Gloucester Diamond, where some of the worst riots of the lockout occurred. I was born in 1946, a few months before the death of Jim Larkin, the principal workers' leader in the lockout. His funeral was the first public event I attended. I have no more memory of that bitter winter's day than my parents had of the lockout, but Larkin and the lockout were part of the family folklore, as they were in the homes of thousands of working-class people of that generation. The story told here would hold some surprises for them were they still alive to read it, but I hope it wouldn't disappoint them.

That the book exists at all is due to Fergal Tobin of Gill & Macmillan, who first suggested it. I also have to thank him for the ditty on Lady Aberdeen, and his secretary, Síofra Gavin, for printing out manuscript drafts when my own printer failed to meet the challenge. Deirdre Rennison Kunz was of immense help in organising the illustrations and tidying up the loose ends.

Special thanks are due to Theresa Moriarty, who started out on the venture with me and remained extremely supportive when the original plan didn't work and I pressed on alone. She continued to help with advice on sources, a copy of the TUC Food Fund list, and photocopies of other material from the Irish Labour History Society archive and library.

Nor would this book, written and researched in a little over a year, have been possible within such a short period without the co-operation of the Irish Times. I would like to thank the sabbatical committee and the editor, Conor Brady, for granting me two months' leave of absence. I would also like to thank my colleagues on the news desk and in the news room for putting up with my frequent disappearances, even when it plunged them unexpectedly into the arcane world of industrial relations.

Another advantage of working for the Irish Times is that it provided me with ready access to the best newspaper archive in Ireland. John Gibson and his colleagues in the library met all my requests for assistance uncomplainingly, and John Vincent made sure the photocopier survived frequent ill-usage at my hands. Raymond and Jonathan Reynolds came to my assistance in solving some pressing software problems.

One of the great pleasures of historical research is pottering around the archives. It would take too long to mention all those who helped, but I would particularly like to thank Éimear Ó Broin for access to the papers of his father, León Ó Broin; the Dublin city archivist, Ann Clark; the chief librarian of the Gilbert Library, Máire Kennedy; the late Commandant Peter

Young, founder of the Irish Army archive; the archivist of the Dublin Catholic Archdiocese, David Sheehy; the keeper of the manuscript room in Trinity College, Dublin, Bernard Meehan; the Guinness archivist, Theresa O'Donnell; Clifton Flewitt and Brendan Pender of the Railway Society; Cyril Ferris of CIE; Dolores Senior of RTE; the staff of the National Library of Ireland; the staff of the National Archives; and the Society of St Vincent de Paul for access to its records during the lockout period. Larry Donald and Michael Kelly of the ESB provided source material on the early history of the electricity industry in Ireland, for which I am grateful.

In Britain, those who assisted me in finding and obtaining access to important records included Richard Temple and Christine Woodland of the Modern Records Centre at the University of Warwick; Mary Doran of the British Library; Christine Coates of the University of North London; Margaret Messenger and other staff of the Bodleian Library, University of Oxford; the staff of the House of Lords Records Office; and the staff of the Public Records Office, London.

Among trade union colleagues I would like to thank the general secretary of Mandate, Owen Nulty, for access to records of the Drapers' Assistants' Association and Francis Devine of SIPTU and the Irish Labour History Society for his advice—not always taken—and his support and for the poem 'The Steamship Hare'. Shay Cody and Séamus Fitzpatrick of IMPACT shared their knowledge of Dublin trade unionism in the lockout years, and Martin Maguire drew the existence of Dublin's large Protestant working-class community in 1913 to my attention; if I failed to make better use of his pioneering work in this area the fault is entirely mine. Peter Rigney shared with me his enthusiasm for trains, trams and Dublin's labour history, and Hugh Geraghty gave me useful insights on William Partridge.

In Britain my old comrade from past battles in the National Union of Journalists, Eddie Barret, put me in touch with the former general secretary of the Transport and General Workers' Union, Jack Jones, who in turn helped me gain access to the union's records. The union's Irish secretary, Mick O'Reilly of the ATGWU, gave me a copy of Ken Coates and Tony Topham's magisterial history of the TGWU's formative years.

I must also thank the labour historian and leading pioneer of the inexact science of industrial relations, Father Tom Morrissey SJ, for his encouragement and advice.

This book was originally intended as a much shorter overview of the lockout. It would not have been possible to produce it in its present extended form without the generosity of a number of sponsors. I would like to thank the former director-general of the Irish Business and Employers' Confederation, John Dunne, for his prompt, generous and enthusiastic response to my request for funds, and also the general secretary of the Irish Congress of Trade Unions, Peter Cassells, for securing the support of Congress at a time when he and his colleagues were involved, like John Dunne, in difficult negotiations on the Programme for Prosperity and Fairness. The general secretary of IMPACT, Peter McLoone, the general secretary of SIPTU, John McDonnell, and the director-general of the Construction Industry Federation, Liam Kelleher, all supported sponsorship from their own organisations while facing similar distractions.

I would also like to acknowledge the generous contribution from FÁS and to thank the agency's former director-general, John Lynch, and its director of corporate affairs, Greg Craig, for their interest and support.

Finally I have to thank Geraldine and Simon for putting up with an absentee husband and father who, even when he was physically present, was often elsewhere in mind for the better part of the fifteen months this book took. Again, I hope they are not disappointed with the outcome.

ABBREVIATIONS

AOH	Ancient Order of Hibernians
ASE	Amalgamated Society of Engineers
ASLEF	Associated Society of Locomotive Engineers and Firemen
ASRS	Amalgamated Society of Railway Servants
DAA	Drapers' Assistants' Association
DMP	Dublin Metropolitan Police
DTPS	Dublin Typographical Provident Society
DUTC	Dublin United Tramways Company
GFTU	General Federation of Trade Unions
GSWR	Great Southern and Western Railway
IAOS	Irish Agricultural Organisation Society
ILP	Independent Labour Party
IRB	Irish Republican Brotherhood
ITGWU	Irish Transport and General Workers' Union
ITUC	Irish Trades Union Congress
IWFL	Irish Women's Franchise League
JLB	Joint Labour Board
LNWR	London and North-Western Railway
NTWF	National Transport Workers' Federation
NUDL	National Union of Dock Labourers
NUR	National Union of Railwaymen
RIC	Royal Irish Constabulary
SPI	Socialist Party of Ireland
TUC	Trades Union Congress
UBLTU	United Builders' Labourers' Trade Union
UCD	University College, Dublin
UIL	United Irish League
UVF	Ulster Volunteer Force

PROLOGUE

IN August 1913, all eyes were on the North. Ulster unionists were threatening to resist home rule by force. There had been four days of serious rioting in Derry; one man had been killed and dozens of people injured, some by gunfire. One of those critically wounded was a policeman, shot in the chest by a member of the Orange Order. The British army had been called out to clear the streets.[1] An uneasy peace hung over Belfast. Intensive drilling by the Ulster Volunteers kept unionist militants busy and prevented a repeat of the previous year's pogroms against the Catholic population.

Dublin, by contrast, was enjoying the unusually good weather and anticipating Horse Show Week, the social event of the year. There had been severe industrial unrest; but even the syndicalist leader of the Irish Transport and General Workers' Union, Jim Larkin, seemed to be taking a summer sabbatical. On 3 August the union opened a new recreation centre for its members at Croydon Park, Fairview, with a 'Grand Temperance Fête and Children's Carnival'.[2] Larkin was intent on using the leased house and its grounds 'to interest our people in the culture of vegetables and flowers.' Later a cow and calf would be purchased, 'to familiarise the Dublin slum dweller with another side of Irish life.' There were playing-pitches and a boxing-ring.[3] The union had also bought the head offices it had been renting in Beresford Place on the city's quays, close to the work-place of the dockers who made up the core of its membership. The dilapidated Royal Victoria Hotel cost the union £5,500; it was renamed Liberty Hall.[4] It remained to be seen whether these new acquisitions and the easing of industrial strife were signs of incipient respectability or a mere pause in the onward march of labour.

Dublin's middle classes expected that life would be different, and hopefully better, once the home rule assembly was established in the old Parliament House in College Green. With a nationalist renaissance in the offing, Ireland's deposed capital was, for once, a more contented part of the British Empire than either Belfast or Derry. The Derry riots had indeed been a sinister reminder of the different political topography of Ulster, and of the sectarian undertow that threatened to suck the whole country into civil war over the home rule issue.

Long promised by the British Liberal Party, some limited measure of self-government had seemed imminent since the second general election of 1910. Asquith's Liberal administration had clung to power only with the support of its Irish allies at Westminster, and now they must be rewarded.

The Protestant and unionist people of Ulster had no intention of accepting home rule. They threatened to resist the measure by force, on the grounds that they represented a majority of the population in the province. But Derry, the second-largest city in Ulster and one that had played a historic role in defending Protestantism in the past, had been captured by the nationalists. In a by-election early in 1913 the Irish Party had triumphed, by the tightest of margins, and now the province was represented in the House of Commons by seventeen MPs who supported home rule and only sixteen unionists. It was a cogent reminder that in the nine counties of Ulster there was in fact a small Catholic and nationalist majority.

Given the overlapping political and religious affiliations of the population, sectarian tensions had inevitably run high. The previous summer an attack by members of the Ancient Order of Hibernians on an outing for Presbyterian schoolchildren in Castledawson, County Down, had resulted in the most serious pogroms Belfast had seen for many years and in the mass expulsion of Catholic workers from the city's shipyards and factories. In September 1912, 250,000 Ulster Protestants signed the Solemn League and Covenant, pledging their lives to defend the union with Britain. They included 2,000 Protestants resident in Dublin, all of whom first had to prove they had been born in Ulster.[5]

*

This was a reminder that Dublin had its own unionist community. In fact it had the largest concentration of Protestants in the country outside Belfast. Altogether there were 92,328 living in Dublin city and county, and they dominated banking, the railway companies, and the larger manufacturing enterprises, such as Guinness's and Jacob's, as well as the higher professions. They had a smaller but significant presence in the lower social strata, comprising 16 per cent of the white-collar and manual work force. Well over half the Protestant workers in Dublin were clerks, sales assistants, or craftsmen. Soldiering was the only unskilled occupation in Dublin dominated by Protestants; however, most of the 3,100 soldiers hailed from across the Irish Sea.

While generally considered conservative in outlook, Protestants comprised 42 per cent of the skilled workers in Inchicore, site of the city's rail and tramway works. The district was a labour stronghold, and many of its skilled Protestant workers must have voted for socialist candidates in the municipal elections, even though most of the latter were devout Catholics.

There remained of course a strong Orange undercurrent. Lord Ardilaun aimed his *Evening Telegraph* at Protestant workers, and many were members of the City and County Dublin Conservative Workingmen's Club in York Street. In some streets, figurines of King Billy in the fanlight were almost as common as the Child of Prague. But it was a community in decline. Only in the middle-class townships in the southern suburbs, such as Rathmines, Pembroke, and Kingstown (Dún Laoghaire), did unionism remain a political force to be reckoned with. Just over half of Dublin's Protestants had fled the disease-infested metropolis for the suburbs, and they now constituted 27 per cent of the population of County Dublin.[6]

The most distinguished member of this beleaguered community was Sir Edward Carson, leader of the Unionists in the House of Commons. He may have spent the previous two years as a sort of political shuttlecock—part plenipotentiary, part rabble-rouser—hurtling between London and Ulster, but he represented that bastion of Protestant privilege, Trinity College, Dublin. He was a 'liberal Unionist': in other words, Toryism was not his spiritual home; however, he had no intention of being governed by nationalists of any hue.

Thirty years earlier Carson had built a reputation at the bar as a relentless Crown prosecutor. 'Coercion Carson' was the name given him during the Land Wars. The Conservative government of the day had been delighted to have a man whom no threats from Fenians, or public denunciations by home rulers (often the same people in those days), could deter from doing his duty. One of his legal opponents was John Redmond, who, as leader of the Irish Party at Westminster, had now become his antagonist once more. They never allowed political differences to affect their feelings of mutual respect; but there were younger, sharper men coming up on both sides who had no time for anything that smacked of compromise, including civilised behaviour towards one's opponents.

Since the early eighteen-nineties, Carson had been based in London, performing on the larger stage of the English bar. His most famous court victory had been over his Trinity contemporary Oscar Wilde in the Queensbury libel case. Like many southern unionists, Carson would find that the increasingly bitter political conflicts of the coming decade would make him a stranger in his native city; but until 1912 he had successfully combined the undemanding task of representing Trinity College in Parliament with a glittering legal career. It was his ability as an advocate that led to the invitation from unionists to lead them at Westminster, and by the following year he had been hailed as the saviour of Ulster. The death of his wife in April made the task of defending the Union, which he described as 'the guiding star' of his political life, less a burden than a distraction from his grief.[7] Dour, ruthless, and charming, Carson mesmerised the Orange masses. 'His tall body, his rather brutal face, the dark eyes brooding over the long jaw and heavy chin, put one in mind of a pirate … or was it a puritan? Or both?' a contemporary wondered.[8]

Violence, or at least the threat of violence, was the basis of Carson's defence of the Union. He understood its political value well from his days as a Crown prosecutor in the Land Wars. He had won the apparently unconditional support of his Tory allies in England for this somewhat alarming stance; they were only too happy to obtain any stick with which to beat the Liberals for allowing David Lloyd George to introduce the 'people's budget' in 1909, and then removing the legislative veto of the

House of Lords when they sought to block it. Carson warned the Liberal administration that any attempt to impose home rule on Ulster would meet with far sterner resistance than that of their lordships. The Tory leader, Bonar Law, predicted with some relish that using force against the Ulstermen was far more likely to result in British government ministers being lynched in Whitehall than loyal Ulstermen being shot by soldiers in the streets of Belfast. To be on the safe side, Carson had established the Ulster Volunteer Force in January 1913; by August they were 85,000 strong and willing to fight, if only they could obtain guns.

For the first time, an Irish leader, and a unionist at that, had made the advocacy of physical force respectable, potent, and therefore politically profitable. It was an odd vocation for a lawyer, and even odder that advanced nationalists and labour men should now regard him as a role model, even a hero, whose tactics should be emulated. It was fitting, if ironic, that Carson had revolutionary forebears. He was descended on his mother's side from John Lambert, one of Cromwell's most ardently anti-monarchist generals, who played a leading role in pacifying Ireland in the seventeenth century and was imprisoned for life by King Charles II after the Restoration.

*

In 1913, militarism was in the air, not just in Ireland but throughout Europe. Conscription was seen not as a burden to be avoided but as a badge of citizenship.[9] In Britain, where large standing armies were frowned on, young men volunteered for weekend soldiering with the Territorial Army, training to defend their country should it ever be threatened with war. The British military establishment baulked at the idea of extending the Territorial system to Ireland; but one of the first measures of the new Liberal administration in 1906 had been to end a 25-year embargo on the importing of arms into Ireland. It says much about the ambivalence of nationalists towards political violence that it was John Redmond who had campaigned for this confidence-building measure; it says even more about the confused state of Irish politics that it was Carson and the UVF who first availed of the change in the law.

It was inevitable that nationalists, inspired by Carson's example, would follow with their own Irish Volunteers by the end of the year. But before they could do so, Jim Larkin, publicly citing Carson's example, would establish his own workers' militia in order to wage class war. Not only were militarism, nationalism and unionism (arguably a variant of nationalism) in the air but also socialism and its twin, syndicalism. The Irish Citizen Army was thus a manifestation of both the wider infatuation with militarism that was sweeping Ireland and something very different. It would evolve into a body that was by turns socialist, nationalist, and internationalist. And it was to be all three in a uniquely Dublin way.

One did not have to look far to find the causes of labour militancy in Dublin. At the beginning of the twentieth century Dubliners shared little of the confidence and municipal pride that existed among even the poorest working-class denizens of other cities, including Belfast. For one thing, while the middle class built the magnificent municipal palaces of such cities as Manchester, Birmingham, and Belfast, their Dublin counterparts abandoned the capital for its more salubrious suburbs with their lower rates. The working class had been left in possession of the city's festering heart. Theirs was still an eighteenth-century metropolis, with all the opulence, poverty and filth that this entailed. An English visitor, James Johnson, wrote in 1844: 'Dublin—rent and split—worm-eaten, mouldering, patched and plastered—unsightly to the eye, unsavoury to the taste, and not very grateful to the olfactories—here there is but one step from magnificence to misery, from the splendid palace to the squalid hovel.'[10] Seventy years had changed little. In 1913 another English visitor, the *Westminster Gazette* correspondent Arnold Wright, described the stench more delicately as the 'scents which are not those of Araby.'

One reason the city still stank was that no adequate system of sewerage had been installed, though a supply of fresh water was now pumped from Dartry reservoir. Taps and water-closets galore had been installed in houses and courtyards, but the sewerage system was totally inadequate to the task of carrying away the resultant waste. A faecal sediment impregnated the city's subsoil, and its distinct smell complemented that of social decay and economic stagnation. Even Wright, who was reputedly paid £500 by the city's employers to record their version of the lockout, wrote scathingly that 'the Gothic pinnacles of St. Patrick's Cathedral ... look directly down upon the quarter of the Coombe where the degradation of human kind is carried to a point of abjectness beyond that reached in any city of the Western world, save perhaps Naples.' Hard by O'Connell Bridge, 'with its really magnificent vista of soaring monuments and magnificent buildings, is a maze of streets physically and morally foul.' For all that, Wright found Dublin 'a likeable city'. It was a common reaction of visitors.[11]

It is hard today to visualise the teeming, lurching tenements and poverty-ridden streetscapes of the early years of the twentieth century. The premier cause of poverty, as everyone recognised, was lack of employment. There was a vast surplus of labour, especially unskilled labour. The eminent historian and social scientist D. A. Chart estimated at the time of the lockout that

> 24,000 men, more than a quarter of the adult male population, were engaged in unskilled labour. As regards wages, naturally unskilled labour occupied an unfavourable position. The average wage was about 18s. a week, and even so low a figure as 15s. or 16s. had been recorded.[12]

Chart pointed out that a worker on 18s a week

> could not afford to pay more than 2s. 6d. or 3s. a week for the rent of his dwelling. Decent accommodation fit for the inhabitation of a family

could not be commercially supplied for this figure. The labouring man, therefore, in Dublin was driven to adopt the same policy with housing as he did with other necessities—the adaptation to his own use of the second-hand possessions discarded by his richer fellow-citizens. The great mansions of the eighteenth century aristocracy, forsaken by the class which designed them, had been occupied in quite a different manner … Instead of one family occupying a ten-roomed house, there was a family in every room.

Chart provides a typical budget of a 'labouring household' as follows:

Rent, 2s. 6d.; fuel and light, 2s.; bread, 4s.; tea, 9d.; sugar, 8d.; milk (usually condensed), 6d.; butter (dripping, margarine), 1s. 6d.; potatoes or other vegetables, 1s.; meat, fish, bacon etc., 2s.; leaving a balance of 3s. 1d.[13]

The health problems of a poor diet and the social stress caused by overcrowding were compounded by the refuge many tenement inhabitants, particularly men, found in the comparative comfort of the pub. Alcoholism was rampant.

Like their homes, the working class obtained their clothes from the cast-offs of the well-off.

Husband and wife probably wore second-hand clothes purchased in Little Mary Street or elsewhere for a few shillings. The children went hatless and barefoot, and were frequently dressed in the worn-out clothes of their parents, rudely cut down to fit, thus producing that characteristic figure, the street child with its tousled head, its bare legs, and the quaintly fluttering rags of its wardrobe.

Chart thought it a 'standing wonder' that families could survive in such conditions; and yet he found that the Dublin working class 'exhibited to a marked degree the social virtues of kindness, cheerfulness and courtesy.' They were also 'deeply religious, if prone to trades unionism … rather of the militant than the provident type.'[14]

Men worked long hours for subsistence wages. A coal-carter, for instance, might have to work fifty to sixty hours a week to earn 16s. In contrast, the coal he transported was dear. Horrified at the poverty he had encountered, Chart proposed a modest short-term measure to alleviate it. He suggested that if the price of coal was increased by 1¼d per ton, or 0.35 per cent, and the entire amount passed on to the carters, their wages could be increased from 16s to 20s a week, or 25 per cent.[15] Similar modest price rises could have a similar effect in other employments.

The notion cut little ice with the employers, or with middle-class consumers. Chart made his observations at a meeting of the Statistical and Social Inquiry Society of Dublin on 6 March 1914; this was less than a month after the collapse of the lockout. Father Thomas Finlay SJ responded to Chart's suggestion by saying that 'if it paid the employers of

Dublin to give higher wages they would give them.' However, he thought that an increase of 1¼d on a bag of coal would be 'burthensome' to the consumer and might even undermine the economy.

> The public were not given to acts of generosity of this kind on a large scale. They thought charity was charity, and business was business, and the law of business, as they understood it, was always to purchase in the cheapest market.[16]

He could have added that, having just fought a bitter five-month battle to smash trade unions, the employers were hardly going to increase the men's wages by 25 per cent on the whim of an interfering do-gooder. There had been more than enough such people making a nuisance of themselves during the dispute itself.

Perhaps the most striking aspect of the exchange between Chart and Finlay was how little the cataclysmic events of the previous few months had affected the attitudes of many of the well-off. They had vanquished the twin-headed beast of Socialism and Syndicalism and did not wish to be bothered by its sociological death rattle.

*

In Dublin at that time, socialism and syndicalism were synonymous, largely because the leading exponent of both was Jim Larkin, general secretary of the Irish Transport and General Workers' Union. By 1913 the term 'Larkinism' had become a catch-all to denote syndicalism, socialism, and any manifestation of either—most notably the sympathetic strike. This was because Larkin had used the sympathetic strike tactic to considerable effect to win improved pay and working conditions for the unskilled. It is estimated that his industrial blitzkrieg raised the pay of unskilled workers who joined the ITGWU by between 20 and 25 per cent in the first eight months of 1913. If so, it did little more than restore their purchasing power to what it had been at the turn of the century.[17] This fact would not have surprised Larkin. He accepted that strikes were a weapon of limited value. His real aim, one he repeatedly proclaimed to his followers, was the creation of 'One Big Union'. Such an organisation would have the industrial and political muscle to bring down capitalism and replace it with a co-operative industrial democracy.

Even stripped of its political baggage, the sympathetic strike had tipped the balance of forces in Dublin's industrial arena from the employers to the employed. Traditionally, employers had used the vast reservoir of labour to replace workers who were truculent or strike-prone. Larkin's great achievement had been to persuade thousands of unskilled workers to subscribe to the principle that an injury to one was an injury to all. If the unemployed refused to 'scab', by taking the jobs of those on strike, and if workers in other firms refused to handle the 'tainted' goods of the strike-bound employer, then the victory of the strikers was assured. In the first six months of 1913 Larkin had given his most powerful demonstration yet of the power he had harnessed. The worst dispute that spring had been at the

City of Dublin Steam Packet Company. A three-month battle ended in the firm's Dublin dockers winning similar rates of pay to those of their counterparts in Liverpool. That was in April. By May six other shipping lines in the port had agreed to the same terms, with 'constant men' earning 30s for a sixty-hour week. This was an increase of 25 per cent for some dockers.[18]

Altogether, between 29 January and 14 August 1913 there were thirty major disputes in Dublin, most of them involving the ITGWU. They included strikes at three of the biggest coal merchants in Dublin, Tedcastle McCormick, Heiton and Company, and S. N. Robinson; one at the main ironfounders, J. and C. McGloughlin; and another at Jacob's biscuit factory. In the lockout all these companies would be among Larkin's most implacable enemies.[19]

But that was in the future. On 8 July the Lord Mayor of Dublin, Lorcan Sherlock, called together representatives of the Dublin Chamber of Commerce and Dublin Trades Council to discuss how a system of conciliation could be created to reduce the number of strikes in the city.[20]

Sherlock was a leading member of the United Irish League, the political machine of John Redmond's Irish Party, which dominated the city council. Though Sherlock was only a tobacconist, he was representative of the powerful shopkeepers' and publicans' lobby within the UIL. He also had close personal links with the more moderate elements on the trades council, and his conciliation scheme was known to have the discreet backing of the Catholic Archbishop of Dublin, Dr William Walsh, who was widely respected by trade unionists and employers alike. Sadly, Dr Walsh was not in good health and was to spend much of the summer in France. The redoubtable William Martin Murphy, a firm opponent of Larkinism, was president of the Chamber of Commerce, but he too was ill for much of that summer. His absence from council meetings may have helped make other members more amenable to the Lord Mayor's peace initiative. In the week before the Horse Show the Chamber of Commerce selected its nominees to represent the employers on the conciliation board, and the Trades Council was planning to appoint its members shortly.[21] Even James Larkin seemed enthusiastic about the scheme.

*

By the summer of 1913, Larkin was thirty-nine years old and at the height of his power and influence. He had been born in the Liverpool slums of Irish parents from County Armagh. The family were part of the great post-Famine diaspora. Larkin left school at thirteen to help support the family, following the death of his father from tuberculosis. Larkin competed for work with other sons of the poor. At one stage he stowed away on a ship to South America in search of adventure as well as employment. On his discovery he was put to work as a fireman, and then placed in irons for demanding decent wages and conditions for the crew. He returned to Liverpool and became a foreman on the docks. He was a teetotaller and, like many early socialists, vehemently denounced the evils of drink. Though reared as a Catholic, he married Elizabeth Brown, the daughter of a Baptist lay preacher who managed a local cocoa bar. Characteristically, in choosing a wife Larkin did not allow himself to be bound by traditional sectarian constraints.

A socialist even before he became a trade union activist, Larkin had, like thousands of other workers, reached instinctively for an alternative to the obvious evils of capitalism. While on trial years later for treason in the United States he told the court:

> At an early age I took my mind to this question of the age—why are the many poor? It was true to me. I don't know whether the light of God or the light of humanity or the light of my own intelligence brought it to me, but it came to me like a flash. The thing was wrong because the basis of society was wrong.[22]

As with most socialists of his generation, the staple of Larkin's political education had been attending public meetings, reading pamphlets, and debating with friends. But, unlike many of his contemporaries, he did not reject his religion, or regard it merely as a totem of capitalist hegemony. He insisted that the children of his mixed marriage be reared as Catholics, and he was himself a member of the Catholic Socialist Society. This small organisation had been set up by an émigré Irish activist, John Wheatley, in Glasgow. It played a significant and largely unacknowledged role in winning many immigrant Irish workers to the cause of labour.[23]

Larkin at first regarded trade unionism as ancillary to politics in the struggle for workers' power. The Liverpool docks strike of 1905 changed all that. Though a foreman, he became heavily involved in the dispute, and was sacked as a ringleader. His organising talents were then channelled into the National Union of Dock Labourers, whose general secretary, James Sexton, recruited Larkin as a lieutenant. Sexton was also the son of Irish immigrants, a Catholic and a socialist. There the similarities ended. Sexton was much older than Larkin. While he had dabbled in Fenianism in his youth, he was by nature cautious and methodical. His socialism was of the peculiarly conservative kind to be found among many members of the British labour movement who came of Irish Catholic stock. Within four years the two men were to become sworn enemies; but in his memoirs Sexton could still recall Larkin having 'an energy that was almost superhuman ... Nothing could frighten Jim.' In the general election of 1906 Sexton stood as a candidate for the West Toxteth constituency in Liverpool; Larkin acted as his election agent and campaign manager. 'It was largely owing to Larkin's overwhelming labour that we reduced a Tory majority to five hundred, but I would rather not give an opinion on some of the methods he adopted,' Sexton wrote in his memoirs.[24]

Within two years, Larkin had breathed new life into the NUDL in Scotland and had been sent to Belfast to work the same miracle there. He soon had the city at a standstill and managed to unite Catholic and Protestant workers in a successful pursuit of better pay and conditions. He followed his Ulster triumph by expanding NUDL membership in the south of Ireland. Unfortunately his aggressive tactics, disregard for head office instructions and readiness to spend union funds on strike pay landed him in serious trouble.

At the end of 1908 Larkin was suspended. He decided to appeal over the heads of the NUDL leadership to the union's Irish members, and established his own union in January 1909, the Irish Transport and General Workers' Union. The addition of the word 'General' was apparently a suggestion of William O'Brien. The president of the 'progressive branch' of the Amalgamated Society of Tailors in Dublin, O'Brien was one of the younger generation of Dublin trade unionists converted to syndicalism and the aggressive 'new unionism', of which Larkin was now the leading exponent in Ireland.[25]

But the addition of the word 'General' to the union's title also reflected Larkin's syndicalist aim of building 'One Big Union'. As it happened, most contemporaries insisted on referring to the new body as the Transport Union. It quickly became a byword for militancy.

*

Sexton was not finished with his rebellious subordinate. He sought the return of NUDL funds, claiming that Larkin had 'misappropriated' significant sums to finance an unofficial strike by Cork dockers in the summer of 1908. When Larkin and some of his supporters were subsequently charged with fraudulent conversion, Sexton appeared as a witness for the prosecution. It was his testimony that secured Larkin's conviction.

The victory was a pyrrhic one. Sentenced to a year's imprisonment by what Larkin castigated as 'a jury of employers', he was immediately adopted by the trade union movement as a victim of capitalist oppression. This was deeply embarrassing to the more conservative elements within Irish trade unionism. Representatives of the old craft unions, outraged by Larkin's activities and apprehensive of an influx of unskilled workers into the movement under the leadership of this syndicalist wild man, had vigorously opposed the admission of the ITGWU to the Irish Trades Union Congress. The ITUC was a rather toothless imitation of the British TUC; nevertheless it was Irish labour's national forum, and moderates within the movement hoped it would assume greater significance once home rule had been granted. Larkin's ITGWU would jeopardise the respectability of the Congress; but his transformation into a martyr made continued opposition to ITGWU affiliation impossible. The Dublin Trades Council had launched a campaign for Larkin's release immediately after his conviction. Three months later the well-meaning and humane Lord Lieutenant, Lord Aberdeen, conceded their demand. Larkin was greeted on his release with a great torchlight procession through the city.[26]

How far Larkin's revolt against the NUDL was premeditated is hard to tell. He had certainly come to love Ireland, and especially Dublin, during his brief sojourn in the country. He must also have been attracted by the city's revolutionary potential and the opportunity it provided to spread his syndicalist gospel, uninhibited by more cautious counsels. And, unlike the more radical elements within Irish nationalism, he saw the role of Dublin's working class as the tinder that would ignite not only Ireland's revolution but that of Britain's workers as well.

Larkin's greatest asset was not his organising ability, considerable though that was, but his power as an orator. It was an era of great oratory, and the open-air public meeting was a significant source of free entertainment and education as well as political and social mobilisation. As a speaker, Larkin's power lay in his ability to establish an emotional bond with his audience rather than to persuade them by force of argument. He played on his listeners' grievances, which were many, and contrasted their abject state with the moral grandeur of their future, if they had the courage to seize it. He quickly became 'the idol of the Dublin working classes.'[27]

By the beginning of 1912 the ITGWU had over 18,000 members, and Larkin's allies—partly through the tactical expertise of the tailors' leader, William O'Brien—had seized control of both the ITUC and Dublin Trades Council.[28] O'Brien was president of the ITUC and vice-president of the more strategically significant Trades Council. Larkin now dominated the industrial life of the city like a new messiah. And, as a messiah, he attracted adulation and hatred in almost equal measure. Among his messianic traits was a tendency to be overbearing and arrogant. He was an impossible chairman of meetings because of his constant interruptions, and when he had disagreements with fellow trade unionists they often became personalised. Of course employers too felt the lash of his tongue. And though he frequently overstepped the bounds of decency and truth, he rarely apologised.

Iron-willed though he was, like most messianic figures Larkin was also subject to alternate moods of elation and profound depression. During the three-month battle with the City of Dublin Steam Packet Company, the ITGWU's Belfast organiser, James Connolly, told O'Brien that Larkin was 'looking and feeling bad ... and if the strain is not eased soon, I fear he will break down mentally and physically.' But Connolly could also depict his union boss as a bully 'forever snarling at me' and 'consumed with jealousy and hatred of anyone who will not cringe to him.' After two years with the ITGWU Connolly confessed: 'I am sick of this playing to one man, but I am prepared to advise it for the sake of the movement.' By the time this last letter was written, in September 1913, O'Brien too was having doubts about Larkin. However, he also kept them to himself 'for the sake of the movement.'[29]

Another of Larkin's collaborators, the revolutionary nationalist and feminist leader Maud Gonne, an exotic political animal in her own right, summed up the Liverpool Irishman well. 'Larkin has wonderful magnetic influence on the crowd,' she wrote to a friend, 'but I fear he is too vain and too jealous and too untruthful to make a really *great* leader.'[30]

However, these were members of a knowledgeable, and perhaps jealous, elite. The great mass of Dublin workers, and many more who had seen him in action, from Aberdeen to Cork and from Leith to Derry, viewed Larkin very differently. Over forty years later one of them could still write that 'this man, so great, so unselfish, so apostolic will live forever in the hearts and minds of those who knew him ... and all he did to bring security and decency and honour to a class that never knew of these things until Jim Larkin came.'[31]

*

Some contemporaries took a more detached view of Larkin and Larkinism. One of these was Tom Kettle, the former Irish Party MP for East Tyrone. Though widely regarded as the ablest of the younger generation of constitutional nationalists, he suffered bouts of melancholia, fuelled by alcohol as well as the country's depressing political state. He had given up politics to become professor of national economics at the Royal University in Dublin. It was a more congenial task for this affable sceptic—and a worrying sign that fighting Ireland's battles in Parliament had lost its appeal for younger patriots. Kettle saw Larkinism as no more than another twist in the evolving spiral of industrial relations. He believed that it could, and would, be tamed. Its more vociferous opponents he characterised as alarmists predicting that it would lead to 'a sort of blood-stained Bedlam, the plans of which have already been prepared by a number of unpronounceable foreign, and unspeakable home agitators, hideously devoted to the hideous cult of Syndicalism.' Lamentably, discussion of this cult had become 'the talk of the railway train, the club smoke room and the golf links, that is to say the three foci of middle class civilisation.' Like Chart, Kettle's only wonder was that labour was not more discontented at its lot.[32]

Unfortunately, Kettle's characterisation of the middle-class reaction to syndicalism proved all too accurate. An unprecedented wave of industrial unrest had generated this hysterical reaction. Not only Ireland and Britain were affected by the sympathetic strike but North America and Europe also, from Bourbon Spain to Tsarist Russia. In many of these countries the strike wave had been accompanied by specific political demands, as well as economic ones.

In Britain the rise of industrial militancy was accompanied by the growing electoral strength of the Labour Party. Lloyd George, the leader of the radical wing of the Liberal Party, argued that 'Syndicalism and Socialism are ... two totally different things.' He ventured to think that 'the microbe of Socialism ... may be a very beneficent one.' Lloyd George himself championed many 'socialist' demands, such as old-age pensions and a national minimum wage. He was of course trying to convince British workers that if they wanted to see the more positive aspects of socialism implemented without the mayhem of social revolution, they should keep voting Liberal. It remained to be seen whether they would heed his advice.

Meanwhile there was no denying the mayhem. Between the last era of industrial unrest in the early eighteen-nineties and 1909 the number of workers involved in strikes in the United Kingdom had hovered between 200,000 and 300,000 a year. But in 1910 the number jumped to over 515,000. In 1911 the number of workers taking industrial action was almost 962,000, and in 1912 it soared to 1.46 million. The Board of Trade's expert, F. H. McLeod, said there had 'never before been a series of three consecutive years … marked by such widespread industrial unrest.'

There were signs that the worst was over by 1913. The number of workers involved in strikes that year fell below 689,000, and the number of production days lost was 12 million, compared with a record 42 million in 1912. But the potential for serious renewed conflict in important sectors such as the railways, docks and manufacturing remained. Even before Dublin erupted, many feared that 1913 was simply a lull in the storm.

The reason for the militant upsurge in Britain had as much to do with economic conditions as the machinations of syndicalists. Prices had risen by 10 per cent since 1906, while wages had stagnated because of high unemployment. By 1910 unemployment among trade unionists, the only rate recorded in those days, had dropped to 2½ per cent, and workers' confidence had returned.[33] A similar pattern had emerged in Dublin, but its effect was muffled by the huge army of unemployed.

If Dublin had escaped the worst excesses of syndicalism, it was no thanks to Larkin. While his name may not have been foreign, he came from Liverpool, and that was even worse in the eyes of many. In 1913 Dublin and Liverpool were in most respects much closer neighbours than they are today. Even before the Famine of the eighteen-forties Liverpool had been the first landfall in England for thousands of Irish emigrants. It had a huge Irish population, and it shared with Dublin some of the worst poverty indices of the time. Indeed the two cities were like desperately poor provincial twins at the heart of the British Empire. And yet for the increasingly influential Irish-Ireland movement, keen to seek out the nation's ancient folk roots, the similarities between Dublin and Liverpool were a constant reminder of the threat industrialisation posed to the nationalist identity of Ireland's capital. Dublin may have been the seat of British power in Ireland for seven hundred years and therefore the most Anglicised part of the country—far more Anglicised than 'loyal' Ulster— but to Irish-Irelanders it was never British. They were revolted at the thought that the most beautiful and degraded capital city in the British Empire could sink imperceptibly to the same level as Liverpool.

For Irish-Irelanders, therefore, Larkin embodied everything that was most objectionable about British rule. He was the son of dispossessed emigrants returning to preach the brotherhood of man, a doctrine they associated with the cultural impoverishment that British capitalism brought in its wake. What was more, he used his alien socialist ideas to justify pay increases that undermined the competitiveness of native capitalism. It was no wonder that one of Irish-Ireland's most consistent champions, Arthur Griffith, denounced Larkin's 'English-made' strike weapon in his newspaper, *Sinn Féin*. Griffith warned readers against 'doctrinaires whose ultimate message to man is to give up his God, his country, his family and his property and be happy.'[34]

For once, moderate home rulers could agree with Griffith's analysis. By harping on class warfare and the evils of Irish capitalism, Larkin was contradicting their own claim that, but for a few recalcitrant Ulstermen, Ireland was a united nation yearning for the contentment that self-government would bring. What made Larkin's socialist diatribes even more annoying was that the Irish Party had to be careful about how it rebutted them. It needed not alone the good will of the Liberal administration but that of the forty Labour MPs to secure the passing of the Home Rule Bill. Even Dublin unionists had reason to dislike Larkin. Many of them were employers, and most of the rest were 'well to do'. Larkin's claim to support the notion of a home rule parliament in College Green, albeit one where the voice of the working class would be uppermost, also fanned their antipathy.

Despite the host of enemies Larkin had accumulated in Dublin, differences within the nationalist camp, and differences between nationalist and unionist, had so far prevented them from uniting effectively against him. In August 1913 most of the city's employers seemed to accept that the Lord Mayor's proposed conciliation system offered the best means of containing the Larkinite threat. It was Larkin's decision to organise one of the city's largest enterprises, the Dublin United Tramways Company, that inadvertently gave his enemies an issue on which they could come together and reverse his run of victories.

Part I

Stars in Their Courses

1

AT twenty to ten on the morning of Tuesday 26 August 1913 the trams stopped running in Dublin. Striking conductors and drivers pinned the Red Hand badge of the Irish Transport and General Workers' Union on their lapels and abandoned their vehicles. Dublin's transport system came to a halt.[1]

It had been feared for some time that the union might choose the first day of the Dublin Horse Show to take action. That very morning the *Irish Times* expressed concern that 'a rumoured dislocation of the city traffic by a strike among the servants of the Dublin United Tramways Company' might cast a 'cloud on the horizon.' This was most unfortunate, thought the *Times*, because everyone predicted that Horse Show Week would be an enormous success in 1913. It had been a glorious summer, with eight weeks of almost unbroken sunny weather, and the forecast was excellent. Improvements to the show-jumping arena in Ballsbridge promised to increase the enjoyment of participants, judges and spectators alike. Most important of all, a record number of foreign visitors was expected. Steamship companies said they were having difficulty accommodating the demand from first-class travellers, and the *Times* reported hotels turning away hundreds of disappointed guests. Unfortunately, the Horse Show appeared to be dogged by misfortune. In 1912 there had been an outbreak of foot and mouth disease that caused some events to be cancelled, and in 1911 attendances plummeted because of a rail strike that crippled train services throughout Ireland and Britain.

If the trams stopped this year, the fifty miles of track that linked Dublin with the middle-class suburbs of Clontarf, Rathmines, Blackrock and Kingstown (Dún Laoghaire) would be idle. In the circumstances it was reasonable for a liberal unionist newspaper like the *Irish Times* to warn prospective strikers that, whatever legitimate grievances they might have, they could only arouse the public's hostility if they pursued their threatened course of action. But reasonableness was a quality that would be noticeably lacking in the industrial convulsion that was about to engulf Dublin. It was certainly not a characteristic of the two great protagonists in the coming struggle, Larkin and the rather ascetic chairman of the Dublin United Tramways Company, William Martin Murphy.

*

Murphy was the antithesis of the flamboyant Larkin. He was a private man who was instinctively repelled by the sort of public notoriety in which Larkin revelled. Time spent with his family and sailing his 25-foot yacht *Eva* were Murphy's favourite forms of recreation. This did not mean he was a recluse. He had been the first captain of Milltown Golf Club and president of Rathmines and Rathgar Musical Society. He was also one of that peculiar breed of Irish businessmen who managed to combine extreme personal piety with utter ruthlessness in their commercial dealings. One admirer described him as a man 'who blends the milk of human kindness with an unswerving rectitude of conduct.'[2] A fellow Home Rule MP and long-time political ally, P. A. Chance, put it more pungently when he described Murphy as a man who carried a copy of the Companies Act in one hand and *The Imitation of Christ* in the other.[3]

Murphy was born in Bantry, County Cork, in 1847, the son of a small builder. He was educated by the Jesuits at Belvedere College in Dublin. His mother died when he was four, and at seventeen he had to abandon his studies and take over the family firm, following the sudden death of his father. He quickly showed an entrepreneurial talent rare for Ireland in that era and developed an expertise in constructing light rail and tramway systems. Ireland was full of cheap labour, and Murphy had the wit to pay well: he recognised that a well-fed labourer could work much harder than a hungry one. His marriage to Mary Julia Lombard happily furthered his career. She was the daughter of one of Cork's leading capitalists, James Fitzgerald Lombard, who had extensive investments in property, retailing, and railways. When Dublin's tram companies amalgamated to form the DUTC in 1880 it was under Lombard's chairmanship. Murphy succeeded his father-in-law in 1899 and ran the company until his own death in 1919. By then he had accumulated a fortune of over £250,000, had built railways and tramway systems in Britain, South America, and West Africa, and owned or was a director of many Irish enterprises, including Clery's department store, the Imperial Hotel and the Metropole Hotel in Dublin's premier thoroughfare, Sackville Street (O'Connell Street). But his primary interest remained the transport industry and ancillary enterprises such as electrical engineering and power generation. Partly through his father-in-law's influence, his role evolved from building railways to owning them. His early directorships were on light provincial lines, such as the West Clare Railway (immortalised in Percy French's song 'Are You Right There, Michael?'). But by 1904 Murphy had joined the board of the Great Southern and Western Railway, the principal railway company of Ireland. It represented a form of apotheosis in the Irish business world, for its chairman was Sir William Goulding, reputedly the richest businessman in the south of Ireland, after the head of the Guinness dynasty, Lord Iveagh.

Murphy reached the pinnacle of success with his election as vice-president of the Dublin Chamber of Commerce in 1911 and president the following year. His political stock in the business community rose considerably when he co-operated with Goulding in defeating an ITGWU strike at the GSWR with an early application of the lockout tactic. That was in 1911, and as a result of the year's labour troubles he founded the Dublin Employers' Federation. The lockout would ensure that the railway workers played a rather subdued role in the troubles of 1913.

However, the Dublin Employers' Federation itself fell moribund, as Murphy's attention was diverted by other issues. As president of the Dublin Chamber of Commerce he hosted meetings of the Association of Chambers of Commerce of the United Kingdom and the British Chambers in Foreign Countries during 1912. On a more practical note, he lobbied vigorously on behalf of the Chamber of Commerce against British government efforts to foist the more extravagant aspects of Lloyd George's social and health insurance schemes on Ireland. He argued that this would impose an unfair and disproportionate burden on the Irish taxpayer. He also led opposition to a proposal to build an art gallery in Dublin to house the collection that Sir Hugh Lane was offering to the city, on the grounds that the ratepayer—that is, the business and property-owning classes—would have to foot the bill. At a national level he lobbied the British government to prevent the Cunard line dropping Dublin and Queenstown (Cóbh) from its transatlantic schedules. The loss of such a service would be a blow to Irish ports—and, of course, the railways.[4]

In August 1913 Murphy, at sixty-eight, was very much an elder statesman of the Irish business community. 'Mr. Murphy enjoys the entire confidence of the citizens of the more substantial class,' an admirer enthused. 'Uncompromising Unionists and equally determined Nationalists sit under his presidency … in complete harmony.'[5] Murphy was nearly thirty years older than his adversary, and age had taken its toll. His tall figure had developed a slight stoop, his hair had turned silver, and his bewhiskered face suggested 'the typical family solicitor of the old school.' But this outwardly courtly capitalist was a formidable opponent, as many distinguished members of the Irish Party who had crossed him could testify. Behind the twinkling blue eyes 'dwelt a soul of iron.'[6] It was no accident that it was the wittily vituperative Timothy Healy who was Murphy's closest political confidant. Another vitriolic nationalist politician from County Cork, the rural radical William O'Brien, referred to them as 'Messrs. Healy, Murphy & Co., Moral Assassins'. It was a business in which 'Mr. Murphy bought the knives and Mr. Healy did the stabbing.' Though they worked closely together for forty years, Healy described Murphy as a 'cold man'. G. K. Chesterton detected the same reptilian quality, comparing Murphy to 'some morbid prince of the fifteenth century, full of cold anger, not without a perverted piety.'[7]

*

Piety and parochialism were the axis of the 'Bantry Band', the small group of influential west Cork politicians to which both Healy and Murphy belonged on the conservative and intensely Catholic wing of the nationalist movement. Though Healy was 'the more prominent and brilliant figure,' a fellow nationalist MP and shrewd observer of people, T. P. O'Connor, added that 'Murphy ... must be regarded as the most potent.'[8] Part of that potency rested in his control of the *Irish Independent* and its associated publications. They had been acquired during the bitter civil war within the Irish Party following the Parnell divorce case. If Healy was Parnell's bitterest and most articulate opponent in the public debate, it was Murphy who used his wealth to finance the anti-Parnellites. He regarded the divorce case as 'an interposition of divine providence' that released the nationalist movement from bondage to a Protestant landlord and adulterer.[9] It was a stance for which the predominantly Parnellite electorate of Dublin never forgave him. Though he had represented St Patrick's division of the city since 1885, he was defeated in 1892 by a Parnellite, William Field, who still held the seat in 1913.

Murphy's distaste for the forced camaraderie of the hustings and his poor speaking voice were no doubt contributory factors in cutting short his parliamentary career. Attempts by Healy to find his friend a safe seat in an anti-Parnellite constituency proved unsuccessful; Murphy's personality was voter-resistant. Yet the public perception of him was not entirely fair. While he was denounced as a philistine for his opposition to the proposed Hugh Lane gallery, he had earned almost universal praise for his organising of the International Exhibition of 1907, which was the high point of the visit to Dublin that year by King Edward VII and Queen Alexandra. Some of Murphy's enemies said that he only took on the job in the hope of winning a knighthood. Stung by the allegation, Murphy declared that in no circumstances would be accept a title, even if one were offered to him. Presumably one was, for the king proposed to knight Murphy on the spot at the exhibition grounds in Herbert Park. To everyone's surprise and embarrassment, Murphy refused it. With the characteristic attention to the niceties that marked all his dealings with polite society, Murphy wrote a letter to the king explaining that he intended no disrespect by his refusal of a knighthood. He said that he would not wish the king to leave Ireland 'thinking that he had left one churlish man behind him.'[10]

Knighthoods were tricky things for nationalists. Recruiting an existing knight like Roger Casement to the movement was a political coup; but for a nationalist to accept a knighthood was a very different matter. Murphy's action in 1907 showed that he still cherished his reputation as a nationalist, whatever the electorate thought of him. Indeed his nationalism was more substantial than that of many members of the Irish Party and was closer in many respects to that of Sinn Féin than to the rural activists who comprised the main weight of constitutional nationalism. He saw home rule less as an opportunity to seize the levers of state power and patronage than as a chance to develop Irish industry. His increasing criticism of Redmond's leadership of the Irish Party had less to do with the fact that Redmond had been a Parnellite than with his inability to gain greater fiscal powers from the Liberals for the proposed home rule parliament. Murphy believed that Ireland's salvation lay as much in economic discipline and fiscal rectitude as in political action. When Redmond compounded his mistake by vacillating over partition, which would exclude the country's industrial heartland from home rule, Murphy would be sick to his heart. In March 1914 he confided to Healy that he 'never lost a night's sleep during the tram strike; but was awake all night from humiliation' at the prospect of partition.[11]

This, then, was the man who planned Larkin's downfall. He did so with characteristic thoroughness, insisting all the while that he was not anti-union. As we have seen, the fact that his strategy would require locking out thousands of workers and starving a third of the city's population into submission never cost him a night's sleep. The courtly patriarch was by no means unsympathetic to the plight of employees, but he insisted that they 'must help employers to compete … They must put themselves in their employers' place, and see whether they are allowing him a margin … without which the shop must ultimately close.'[12] By 26 August the tramway men's actions had shown they were not that kind of employee; and the shop was about to close.

*

It was in July that Murphy learnt of Larkin's efforts to organise DUTC workers. Larkin was doing it discreetly, just as he had been doing in Guinness's brewery at St James's Gate. The tramway workers, and the Guinness carters and boat crews, were the elite of the city's transport employees in pay and conditions. The tramway workers were particularly important; a strike at the company could seriously disrupt the city's business. But the DUTC and Guinness's were not like other companies. Guinness's paid employees well and exercised a benevolent despotism over them in return for loyalty. The company had early hired a retired DMP sergeant, Michael Walsh, to monitor the activities of Larkin and his union so that it could minimise his inroads at the brewery. Only one in six of the workers had joined the ITGWU by the summer of 1913.[13]

Murphy had a simpler and harsher strategy. Like many transport magnates, he ran the tramways on military lines. Not only did tramcar workers have to wear uniforms but they were completely at the mercy of their immediate superiors, the inspectors. These, in turn, answered to office-based supervisors. 'Discipline is too severe for an industrial concern,' a confidential informant told the Archbishop of Dublin, Dr William Walsh, in a detailed memorandum.

> Promotion depends on favour and plasticity of employees' character rather than efficiency and seniority. Tenure of men's employment insecure owing to frequency and trivial nature of Inspectors' reports.

Hours too long and pay about 10s per week less than other big centres. Numerous stoppages from wages. No union tolerated … Regulations too numerous and unworkable and cars not kept in proper repair.

Conductors had to work between nine and seventeen hours a day, 'and a man may be reported for leaning or sitting while running a car; he must stand erect and keep a sharp look out.' There was an informer culture within the company, and passengers were encouraged to complain.

A conductor from Cabra depot did his duty in refusing to allow a man under the influence of drink to board the car. The passenger complained, and the Company suspended this Conductor until he went to the passenger's house and apologised. When he went the passenger expressed regret for his action and admitted the conductor had acted properly.[14]

Most employees were recruited on a temporary basis and might wait six years for a permanent post. Known as 'sparemen', new employees had to attend for work every day (including Sundays) and wait from seven o'clock until noon to see if they were needed. Sparemen often worked only two or three days a week and earned no more than 9s a week, at a time when most unskilled workers in the city expected to earn between 15s and 20s. If a spareman became permanent, however, wages would rise to 21s 6d for conductors and 28s for drivers.

There were several deductions from pay, including 2s a week for twenty weeks to defray the cost of the uniform, 6d for the company rule book, 6d a week for sickness benefit, 3d death benefit, 2s 6d for a licence to operate a tramcar, and a further 1s a year for renewal of the licence. For the first six weeks of training, employees were paid nothing. Worst paid of all were the cleaners: they worked an eleven-hour shift, seven nights a week, for 19s. Sixpence a week was deducted from all employees for contributions to a provident society, to cover them for accidents at work.

There was also a punitive schedule of penalties. Conductors were particularly vulnerable. As we have seen, a complaint from a passenger could lead to suspension but could also mean instant dismissal. Omitting to collect a fare, allowing passengers to exceed the distance paid for, or even talking to them, could mean the loss of a day's pay. Drivers could also lose a day's pay if they did not keep strictly to the timetable, as could a driver one minute late at Nelson's Pillar.

When the cars are unfit to make the maximum speed necessary on certain parts of the road to keep time the men have to drive them on all the other parts at a speed in excess of the regulations on their own responsibility with consequent risk of accidents. The hand-brake is often inefficient … The fitting is done by handy-men not tradesmen, and the drivers' reports about faulty cars are not always heeded. Drivers are suspended for three days with loss of pay for using the power-brake except in the last emergency. This is rigidly enforced and results in some saving to the Company, but serious danger to the general public.

Where lines met, drivers were instructed to give precedence 'to the cars that serve wealthier districts—Dalkey, Donnybrook, Terenure'—regardless of other factors. Dr Walsh's informant added that Murphy had refused to meet deputations of tramway men, telling them that if they had grievances they could present them to him as individuals. So far from tolerating unions, the company rules imposed a £15 bond for good behaviour on drivers and conductors. This would be forfeit if they went on strike, or if they left the company without giving fourteen days' notice. Two independent sureties of £10 would also be forfeit. It was no wonder the report to the archbishop concluded that the men believed 'the judicial methods of Venice in the Middle Ages are still in force in the Dublin Tram Company of today.'[15] It was little wonder either that there was a 25 per cent turnover of employees every year, or that Murphy did not want Larkin recruiting members in the DUTC.

*

Both sides prepared carefully for the coming battle. Despite his dislike of public speaking, Murphy arranged a meeting to address DUTC workers on Saturday 19 July. It was held at midnight so as not to interfere with tram schedules. Six known ITGWU activists had been sacked earlier in the day to help set the mood; but for the rest of the workers there was Bovril and sandwiches to guard against the chill night air as they arrived at the Antient Concert Rooms in Great Brunswick Street (Pearse Street). Each employee who turned up also received a half-day's extra pay. Murphy, who was accompanied by the other DUTC directors, told the seven hundred assembled workers that he was well aware of Larkin's efforts to recruit them. He assured them that he had 'not the slightest objection to the men forming a legitimate union,' provided they did not ally themselves with 'disreputable organisations' or become tools of

> the labour dictator of Dublin ... A strike in the tramway would, no doubt, produce turmoil and disorder created by the roughs and looters, but what chance would the men, without funds, have in a contest with the Company, who could and would spend £100,000 or more.

Making a point he returned to constantly when discussing industrial relations, whether with employees or his fellow-employers, Murphy told the tramway men that the company's shareholders 'will have three meals a day,' whether the strike succeeded or not. 'I don't know if the men who go out can count on this.'[16]

However, he was far from satisfied that he had convinced the workers of the dangers of associating with Larkin. In the following weeks, additional workers were hired by the DUTC. As was usual with Murphy, Christian sentiment and business acumen combined to help him reach his decision. Charlie Gordon, the DUTC's manager and acting company secretary, issued a statement that new recruits were needed to repair and re-lay tramlines. The work did not need to be done until 1914, but it was being brought forward to relieve the widespread hardship caused by the dearth of employment for casual workers.

> As they [the directors] believe that the prevailing distress among casual labourers is due to the effects of the operations of the Irish Transport Workers' Union, they will not employ anyone on these new works who will not undertake that he does not belong, and will not belong, to that Union as long as he remains in the company's employment. In taking this course my directors desire to say that they are not hostile to trade unions governed by the well-known rules of such associations, but that they do object to employing men in future that make themselves slaves of one man, who may order them to go on strike whenever it suits him.[17]

Larkin returned the compliment in kind. Through the columns of the *Irish Worker* he had been referring to Murphy as 'the most foul and vicious blackguard that ever polluted any country' and 'a creature who is living on the sweated victims who are compelled to slave for this modern capitalistic vampire.' The editor of the *Leader*, D. P. Moran, wrote: 'It is a pity that both Murphy and Larkin are not pugilists, as if they were they might have had it out on the stage of the Theatre Royal—tickets from one guinea upward … It is evident that both Larkin and Murphy are quite "mouldy" for a fight.'[18]

Though Murphy made light of the attacks in the *Irish Worker*, the stress of the impending battle appears to have made him ill. It was because of illness that he missed the meeting of the Chamber of Commerce on 30 July, where it was formally agreed to accept Sherlock's conciliation scheme. Murphy was enraged, but he kept his own counsel. He decided, regardless of what the council of the Chamber of Commerce had decided in his absence, to grasp the nettle of incipient Larkinism within his own commercial empire. On Friday 15 August he walked into the despatch and delivery department of the *Irish Independent* and told employees that they would have to choose between the ITGWU and their job. Some forty men and twenty boys were paid off on the spot. They placed pickets on the offices, and that afternoon the city's newsboys refused to sell the *Independent*'s sister publication, the *Evening Herald*.

The newsboys had been unionised by Larkin two years earlier.[19] Some of them were also members of Fianna Éireann, the militantly nationalist boy scout organisation founded by Constance Markievicz, a social and political maverick who recognised a kindred spirit in Larkin. When the Fianna was being established in 1911 Larkin had provided premises in which its members could train, and they reciprocated by joining the ITGWU. Such a move made great sense. Far from being street urchins, the newsboys tended to come from the homes of the better working-class families in the city. Children, including ten girls, accounted for over half the city's licensed street traders. A condition of their licence was that they attend school; if employers could recruit these workers there was no reason why the ITGWU should not do likewise. By organising the newsboys Larkin also ensured that his own newspaper had an effective distribution network. As it retailed at 1d, compared with ½d for the *Irish Independent*, the boys earned a higher commission—½d as opposed to ¼d. It is no coincidence that during the lockout newsboys were among the most frequent visitors to the police courts, where they were charged with a variety of offences, ranging from stone-throwing to assault and intimidation.[20]

*

The boycott of *Independent* publications quickly spread to ITGWU members in the DUTC parcels department and to Eason's, the newspaper distributors. That afternoon's editions of the *Evening Herald* had to be carried to the newsagents in the *Independent's* own vans under police escort. The rest of the day passed off relatively peacefully, with a small band of newsboys providing the only drama—an evening protest march through the city centre.

By Sunday 17 August, Murphy had dismissed two hundred tramway workers for refusing to handle his newspapers or to carry out other instructions. The same weekend the ITGWU won a signal victory. The County Dublin Farmers' Association agreed to pay their farm labourers 17s a week; for most of the workers concerned this represented an increase of 3s, or over 20 per cent.[21] As the association's chairman, James McGrane, told an emergency meeting of members in the Gresham Hotel on Saturday, they had little choice but to concede the claim if the harvest was to be saved. The strike by the six hundred members of the ITGWU had been brief and decisive. The outcome underlined the power the union now enjoyed among groups of workers previously unorganised and quiescent. Larkin's union appeared unstoppable.

At midnight on Tuesday 19 August a meeting was held in Liberty Hall for ITGWU members in the DUTC, including those who had already been dismissed. On Larkin's advice, the men decided to seek a weekly wage of 30s, one day off in every eight, and 'time and a half' for working on Sundays. They were reported to have voted overwhelmingly for strike action in a secret ballot, but it is unlikely that one took place.[22] Whatever happened that night, the demands amounted to a mutiny, and Larkin never had a chance to present them. Hours before the meeting began, the DUTC began circulating a document to conductors and drivers telling them that the company knew that Larkin was trying to organise a strike. They were warned that DUTC directors

> would not consider any communication from Mr. Larkin or his emissaries. They have no doubt about the loyalty of all but a small number of their men, and they have no apprehension that a strike will be attempted, and no fear at all, if it is attempted, that it will last a single day.

The directors sought 'an assurance of ... loyalty.' Each employee was required to give a written undertaking that, 'should a strike of any of the employees of the company be called for by Mr. James Larkin or the Irish Transport Workers' Union, I promise to remain at my post and to be loyal to the company.' They had until Wednesday morning to sign the undertaking. On Tuesday night the company issued a statement claiming that four-fifths of its tramcar operatives had already returned the signed forms.[23]

Earlier on Tuesday, Murphy had called to City Hall to request the assistance of the Dublin Metropolitan Police if the strike went ahead. Not only was the DMP available but the authorities made arrangements to bring contingents of the Royal Irish Constabulary, the armed national gendarmerie, into the city.[24]

For the next few days the dispute hung fire. Thirty employees of Eason's came out in sympathy with their sacked colleagues at the *Independent*, after their own company decided to renew the distribution of Murphy's papers. However, Murphy was still having difficulty persuading employees in the parcel delivery section of the DUTC to handle his papers. On Thursday 21 August he decided to suspend the section rather than see it distribute rival publications while his own were blacked.[25]

*

Larkin had problems of a different kind on the Thursday. An encounter took place that showed that not all his enemies were members of the capitalist class. At about six o'clock in the evening an unemployed clerk, Peter Sheridan, attacked him in North Frederick Street with a walking-stick. Larkin was on his way home to Auburn Street at the time. Sheridan lived nearby, in Eccles Street; he had followed Larkin from Sackville Street, constantly shouting.[26] Larkin had overpowered his assailant before the police arrived. Sheridan was charged with assault, and he cross-charged Larkin with the same offence. Both men were summoned to appear in the Northern Police Court on Saturday 23 August, a complication Larkin could well do without in the present crisis.

Sheridan was one of a small but intensely vocal group of Larkin's opponents within the labour movement who were almost certainly financed by Murphy. He had been a shipping clerk on the North Wall for twenty-seven years and claimed he had been sacked on Larkin's insistence because he was a friend of William Richardson.[27] Richardson was a member of Dublin City Council elected on the Labour ticket in 1912; he had been a member of the ITGWU at the time but later that year had been expelled for 'consorting with known blacklegs.' The group included a former secretary of the Irish Trades Union Congress, E. W. Stewart, and two other labour renegades, John Saturninus Kelly and Patrick J. McIntyre. Kelly was a city councillor and McIntyre a freelance journalist.

Stewart was by far the most significant member of the group. A former treasurer of the Amalgamated Union of Shop Assistants, he had been a committed socialist in his younger days, briefly succeeding Connolly as secretary of the Irish Socialist Republican Party in the eighteen-nineties. He had also been the most successful ISRP candidate in city council elections, though never winning a seat for the party. But he moved rapidly to the right after the ISRP collapsed. By 1903 he was part of the Dublin Trades Council establishment, and he seconded the council's motion of congratulations to Pope Leo XIII on his attaining the twenty-fifth year of his pontificate. Leo XIII had issued a seminal encyclical, *Rerum Novarum*, on the rights of workers.

During 1903 Stewart also began to concentrate on his activities in the ITUC, where his influence was considerable. He served as treasurer until 1908 and then as secretary. He consistently opposed Larkin's efforts to affiliate the ITGWU. When the union was finally admitted at the 1910 conference, Stewart suffered the indignity of being removed as ITUC secretary because he was no longer a paid-up member of a trade union. It was part of the revolution that was seeing advocates of the 'new unionism' assume control of the labour movement nationally as well as in Dublin. Stewart, who found a new home in the United Irish League, was an extreme example of the alienation that more conservative trade unionists felt at the Larkinite incursion. He had his revenge two years later when Larkin won a seat on Dublin City Council. Stewart mounted a successful legal challenge to Larkin's election, using the NUDL fraud case to argue that, as a convicted felon, Larkin was ineligible to hold public office. Later that year Stewart wrote a highly coloured *History of Larkinism*, in which he described Larkin as 'a foreign adventurer from the slum recesses of probably some clog wearing town' in England.[28] It showed that the xenophobia generated by Larkin's activities was not confined to Irish-Irelanders.

It was during the 1912 municipal elections, when the Trades Council tried to put forward a common front of candidates with firm socialist principles, that William Richardson fell foul of Larkin. With the help of McIntyre, who was an enthusiastic if rather unscrupulous scribbler, he fabricated an interview with a worker attacking Larkin and the ITGWU. When the ploy was exposed, the union took the unusual step of placing an advertisement in the national newspapers to announce details of Richardson's expulsion. The notice also named all Richardson's accomplices, effectively branding the group as traitors to the labour movement in the city.[29] Richardson retaliated by establishing the Irish National Workers' Union. It was Sheridan's membership of this organisation that had incurred Larkin's wrath and led, Sheridan believed, to his losing his job.

The Irish National Workers' Union was one of a number of 'yellow' unions set up with the backing of William Martin Murphy in the city; another was the Irish Railway Workers' Trade Union, financed by Murphy but fronted by John Saturninus Kelly. Neither proved an effective source of strike-breakers, and Kelly's union collapsed in October 1913, when

Murphy withdrew support. He was satisfied by then that the railway workers would not support the lockout and no longer needed Kelly's paper organisation.[30] It is hard to believe that Sheridan's assault on Larkin at a critical moment in the DUTC dispute was entirely fortuitous.

The assault case was quickly dealt with in the police court on Saturday morning. Independent witnesses supported Larkin's version of events, and Sheridan was sentenced to six weeks' imprisonment. Characteristically, Larkin appealed for clemency. He asked that Sheridan be bound over to keep the peace, saying that he was used to such harassment and well able to protect himself. But when Sheridan's solicitor praised Larkin for coming forward 'in the most manly way and asking for his former friend to be dealt with leniently,' Larkin snapped: 'He is not my friend and never was.'[31]

*

While Larkin was in court that morning there was a serious and unplanned escalation of the dispute. ITGWU dockers refused to unload a ship belonging to the British and Irish Steam Packet Company at the North Wall, the *Lady Gwendolen*, carrying goods for Eason's. Larkin, unwilling to extend the *Independent* dispute at this stage, persuaded his members to return to work. He told them their action was in breach of the agreement made with the company in May. However, when they walked off the job a second time that afternoon he told the management resignedly, 'When an army rebels, what is a commander to do?'[32] It was a comment that would be used repeatedly against him by the employers during the lockout as proof of his bad faith as a negotiator.

At this stage in the dispute Larkin wanted to use less direct methods than the sympathetic strike to pursue his war with Murphy. He mobilised ITGWU members to canvass newsagents throughout the city and to suggest strongly that they stop carrying Murphy's publications. By Monday morning a steady trickle of ITGWU members, particularly newsboys, was appearing before the police courts on charges of intimidation, stone-throwing, assault, and obstruction. The boycott of the *Independent* was obviously having an effect, because the newspaper's manager, W. T. Brewster, placed advertisements in his own and other newspapers offering a reward of £10 for information leading to the conviction of anyone guilty of intimidating newsagents.

Meanwhile Larkin's members in the DUTC were feeling the pressure from the company's reign of terror. Larkin was reluctant to move, however, until he was sure of the key group in the company, the workers who manned its power station at Ringsend. On Monday morning one of his ablest lieutenants, William Partridge, had been at the plant trying to persuade workers to back the tramcar men. Partridge was reckoned the best public speaker in Dublin after Larkin himself and had recently been re-elected to the city council on the Labour ticket. The ITGWU had already recruited many of the labourers at Ringsend, and if anyone could swing the rest it was Partridge.[33]

*

On Monday evening Larkin attended the regular fortnightly meeting of Dublin Trades Council. He had no desire to show his hand in the DUTC dispute, so he concentrated instead on seeking help for his locked-out members at Independent Newspapers. He immediately ran into resistance from the printing unions. Printers were Dublin's princes of labour. They were among the best-paid workers in the city, and—as with several other crafts—only the sons of printers could normally aspire to be printers themselves. It was the former secretary of the Dublin Typographical Provident Society, John Nannetti, who had founded the Trades Council. Nannetti, the son of an Italian sculptor, was a foreman in the *Freeman's Journal* before graduating to become Dublin's longest-serving MP and John Redmond's resident expert on trade union affairs. Ironically, he is remembered (to the extent that he is remembered at all) from his days of obscurity at the *Freeman's Journal*, for he features briefly in this capacity in James Joyce's *Ulysses*.[34]

Nannetti always advised trade unionists against forming a labour or socialist party of their own. Unlike the English workers, they were 'in the happy position' that they already had a labour party: 'the Irish Parliamentary Party are the Labour Party,' he told the ITUC delegates at Athlone in 1906; it had policies 'broad enough for any working man.'[35] In those days Murphy's relationship with the Trades Council had been extremely cosy. He had even helped Nannetti finance its launch.

When the delegates met at the council's offices in Capel Street that August evening, therefore, Larkin cannot have been surprised when James Nolan, a delegate from the bookbinders, said that the Printing Federation could not become involved in the disputes of other workers. Another printers' delegate called Timmons explained that under union rules his members could not withdraw their labour without two weeks' notice. An ITGWU member of the Trades Council, P. T. Daly, himself a printer and a former DTPS delegate, said that he could recall a printers' dispute in 1898 when no notice was served and the union still paid its members strike pay. Another Larkinite, Thomas Farren, who represented the stonecutters, said that every union was affected by Murphy's action. It might be the despatch men in the *Independent* today, but it could be carpenters or bricklayers tomorrow. The ITGWU was not asking for sympathetic strike action: it was asking other trade unionists not to work with blacklegs recruited to replace union men. The printers were unmoved by this Jesuitical argument; and Larkin did not help his cause by launching into an attack on Timmons for consorting with the management.

'The employing class have determined in the interests of themselves and all the capitalist class that one individual must be broken and the organisation he represents must be smashed into chaos,' Larkin said, with no hint of false modesty. Unfortunately, he growled, there was a handful of trade unionists opposed to the ITGWU. These were 'men who never understood the fundamental principles of trade unionism, that what injured one injured all.' He was confident that 97 out of every 100 workers did support that principle. His own understanding was that 28 out of 56 workers who attended a printers' chapel (section) meeting at the *Independent* had wanted to stop work immediately after the despatch men were dismissed, but they were dissuaded.

The printing delegates did not dispute the figures when Larkin challenged them to do so, but his speech cannot have helped the ITGWU cause.

Trades Council delegates were becoming familiar with Larkin's constant identification of every ITGWU dispute with an employers' conspiracy to destroy himself. As we have seen, even advocates of the 'new unionism', such as the vice-president of the Trades Council, William O'Brien, and Larkin's Belfast organiser, James Connolly, were complaining privately of Larkin's egomania. Not satisfied with castigating the printers, Larkin then accused the conservative leadership of the United Building Labourers' Union of offering to replace sacked tramwaymen at lower rates.

Larkin's performance almost split the Trades Council that night. The president, Thomas McPartlin of the Tailors' Society, had difficulty persuading the printers that a motion urging them to review their position in the *Independent* was not a vote of censure. The easy part of the meeting was a motion denouncing Murphy and calling on the public to support the tramway men. The company's treatment of workers 'exhibits a tyranny that is intolerable; and inconsistent with the most elementary rights of freemen.' The council pledged its moral and financial support to the strikers and passed the resolution by acclamation. Whatever the divisions that had emerged with some craft representatives at the meeting, Larkin could feel well pleased with the formal endorsement of Dublin's trade union leaders for his war with Murphy.[36]

*

Larkin then went to meet the tramcar men at Liberty Hall. They were impatient to know when the trams would be halted. He replied: 'When they will no longer move.' Partridge's report of the morning's meeting at the power station must have been an optimistic one, and Larkin was now obviously hoping that a power cut would win the battle with Murphy for him. But he had reckoned without the foresight of the 'capitalistic vampire'. Father Michael Curran, a rather priggish cleric, knew better. He was secretary to Dr Walsh and responsible for keeping the archbishop briefed on events at home during his convalescence in France. Curran was also a confidant of Murphy, and he now wrote to tell Dr Walsh that 'the power house men are working as usual and no trouble is anticipated from them, although it is said that half of them are in Larkin's union.' He added that the plant 'has six months' supply of coal' and that Murphy was 'very fierce and swore he would spend his last shilling in beating Larkin.'[37]

Probably unaware of Murphy's detailed preparations, Larkin decided on Monday night to bring the tramcar men out. It says something of his leadership style that the fatal decision appears to have been made by Larkin alone. The ITGWU had not been built on meticulous attention to procedure; and its leader probably felt that he had little choice. If he did not move soon, Murphy would have purged all the ITGWU members from the DUTC and won a bloodless victory. Besides, the mood of the dockers and newsboys and the series of victories in numerous pay disputes over the preceding months—culminating in the 20 per cent rise for the agricultural labourers the previous week—had boosted Larkin's confidence and that of the ITGWU membership generally.[38] Against any other employer in the city, Larkin's decision might well have been the right one. If he underestimated Murphy, so had Parnell and many others before him. And so, at twenty minutes to ten on Tuesday morning, the trams stopped running.

8/26/1913

2

CROWDS quickly gathered to see the spectacle of fifteen trams blocking the tracks in Sackville Street, north of Nelson's Pillar, and almost as many blocking routes to the south. Murphy, however, could take some satisfaction from hearing that only 200 of the 650 tram workers had left their jobs.[1]

It was not long before groups of strikers began to jeer the 'scabs' who stayed at their posts. The DUTC's offices were in Sackville Street, and the manager, Charlie Gordon, rushed over and ordered the police to arrest the ITGWU members for obstruction. It was a criminal offence to block the tramway, and six strikers were quickly bundled off to Store Street station after refusing to either return to work or take their trams to the depot. The *Freeman's Journal* reported:

> The vacant places on the deserted cars were in many cases quickly filled. The vast majority of the strikers seem to be conductors. Their places were taken by other officials of the Tramways Company. In some cases inspectors, who had probably been motormen [drivers] before promotion, took their places in guiding the cars.

Even so, about 70 trams out of almost 300 throughout the city remained abandoned. Some drivers immobilised their vehicles and avoided being charged with obstruction by simply removing the steering handle and leaving it at the company's offices. Conductors did likewise with ticket machines and cash. Until they were retrieved by emergency crews, the stately 'ships of the suburbs' remained becalmed.

Despite these delaying tactics, the *Freeman's Journal* reported that within forty minutes 'the tram service was again running pretty smoothly.' The strikers now pinned their hopes on the power workers. It was eleven o'clock before word of the stoppage reached Ringsend. Only nine boilermen walked out, followed by a couple of labourers and trolley boys. When Partridge arrived at the plant to address the ITGWU members still at work he found it ringed with police. Murphy had already replaced the strikers with new men, who were being given makeshift accommodation on the premises so that they would not be subjected to either Partridge's oratory or abuse from pickets.

By mid-afternoon the DUTC had ensured that tram schedules on routes serving middle-class areas, especially the coastal corridor south to Kingstown, were almost back to normal. The pattern of support among tram crews for the strike actually helped the company's strategy. While most of the men based at the Inchicore depot, which served the working-class Liberties and Kilmainham areas, had supported the strike, depots in middle-class areas, such as Donnybrook and Clontarf, were less affected. On the Drumcondra line only one worker struck.

*

Murphy's counter-measures had robbed the strike of the dramatic impact the workers had expected, and his consultations with the police during the previous week also quickly bore fruit. As early as ten past ten the DMP were out in force in Sackville Street, supplemented by a large contingent of RIC men, drafted into the city from surrounding counties and kept overnight at their depot in the Phoenix Park. They now occupied the city centre in force, helping the DMP to keep the crowds moving. Many people in Sackville Street, including a small boy with a bloody nose, were soon complaining of being roughly handled by policemen of both corps.

The overwhelming police presence could not suppress completely what the *Irish Times* described as an air of 'subdued excitement'. Hundreds of curious sightseers mingled with the strikers to await events. At eleven o'clock fifty members of the ITGWU decided to defy the police with a parade around Nelson's Pillar. Simultaneously a tram arrived from Kingstown. The driver was John Butler, an ITGWU man who lived in a DUTC cottage in Tramway Terrace, Blackrock. He immobilised his vehicle, once more blocking the northbound line; he offered to surrender his handle to Gordon but was bundled off to Store Street. Butler was the seventh union member arrested that day; before the dispute was over more than four hundred others would face the courts on charges arising from the lockout. The charges would range from obstruction to murder, and the union would pay out nearly £1,250 in legal fees defending them.[2] From the beginning, the Dublin United Tramways Company was making it clear that it would take a hard line with the strikers and use the full measure of the law to break their resolve.

There was nothing unusual in what the DUTC was doing. Employers regularly took employees to court for breach of contract. Only the day before, a Bray shopkeeper had been awarded 8s, with costs, against a messenger boy who left his employ without notice. The 8s penalty was equivalent to the youngster's weekly pay.

With the massive show of police force in Sackville Street, the strikers began to fan out along the tramlines, looking for vehicles to stop and for scabs to harry. In D'Olier Street an angry crowd gathered round one tram, whereupon the driver returned the compliment by jumping down, wielding his handle, and threatening to 'brain' anyone who came near. The police cleared the track and sent the driver on his way. At the other end of the city centre, in Rutland Square (Parnell Square), a crowd of youths tried to pull down the overhead cables that powered the trams. The police chased them back into the side streets and slums that lay a mere stone's throw away.

In Talbot Street, within sight of the Pillar, strikers enjoyed the spectacle of a Howth tram, driven by a ticket inspector, crashing into a lorry. Elsewhere there were isolated reports of tramcars being stoned; but these were not enough to deter the 'loyal' tramway crews, as Murphy dubbed them, or their passengers. Besides, the uniformed 'giants' of the DMP were usually on hand to provide escorts.

If the union was frustrated at the company's success in combating the strike, Larkin appeared to be counselling members to show forbearance. They could take solace from the thought that the abandoned trams had, temporarily, provided an alternative spectacle to the Horse Show for the city's less-favoured citizens. There was some satisfaction too when the company issued a statement at two o'clock that the trams would not run after dark; there were fears that the vehicles might be attacked. However, the company statement promised that any inconvenience to the travelling public 'will be of short duration.'

*

Larkin had been noticeable for his absence from the streets that morning. Again it was the work of one of Murphy's covert allies, Councillor William Richardson. Richardson had taken a leaf out of E. W. Stewart's book and used the courts to frustrate the 'Labour dictator of Dublin'. He had brought proceedings in the Court of Bankruptcy against William Henry Hunt, the printer of Larkin's newspaper, the *Irish Worker*. Richardson had won a libel award against the *Irish Worker* for £37. Larkin had since refused to pay Hunt any printing bills, for fear the money might go to Richardson, and the unfortunate Hunt, who was himself a socialist, now faced bankruptcy. He had offered to pay his debtors 10s in the pound, and all had agreed, except Richardson. Larkin admitted owing £227 to Hunt but candidly told the court that 'as long as I live Richardson will never get a penny.' The case was adjourned to hear further evidence.[3]

Despite its leader's temporary indisposition, the ITGWU was ready that morning with a statement strongly defending the actions of the tramcar men. It said that the union had no intention of doing 'anything to inconvenience the public during the present Horse Show Week.' If anyone was to blame for the strike it was Murphy. His employees had not struck for better wages or conditions but for the right to be members of a union.

However, it would be a rare strike that did not contain other demands besides union recognition. Though Larkin's plan to make pay demands on the company had been pre-empted by Murphy, the ITGWU now laid out the men's case. It stated that 'the Tramway servants of Dublin work 12 hours a week longer than the Belfast tram men and receive 20 per cent lower wages.' Murphy's tyrannical practices were possible only because of the company's monopoly of the tramway system, and the ITGWU compared his personnel policies to 'the foul methods of a Star Chamber.' The union summarised its demands as the 'reinstatement of the dismissed men unconditionally, more wages, shorter hours and [the] right of appeal against inspectors' secret reports.' The statement appealed 'with confidence to the citizens and lovers of fair play for sympathy and active assistance in the struggle for freedom.' It ended with the sharp injunction, 'Do not patronise the cars.'

That evening the city was full of rumours. Word had it that the military were only awaiting the word to place Dublin under curfew. Some said that Murphy was planning to import large numbers of tramway drivers from Bristol to break the strike, while others claimed that face-to-face talks were planned between Murphy and Larkin to resolve the dispute that very night. All were groundless, but all helped keep the crowds on the street in anticipation of some new drama.

It came at eight o'clock at the regular venue for trade union meetings, Beresford Place. The striking tramcar workers arrived in their uniforms, now sporting the Red Hand badge, to hear their leaders. A good-humoured crowd of seven thousand was there, watched by a mere forty policemen. William O'Brien, president of the Tailors' Society and vice-president of Dublin Trades Council, was the first to address the crowd. He told them they were in the midst of the greatest labour battle ever fought in Dublin. If the tramway men continued to show the same determination for another few days, they would smash the DUTC 'to smithereens.'

Larkin was the man the crowd had come to hear, and, as usual, he did not disappoint. One experienced reporter of class strife and revolution at the beginning of the century described Larkin as

> incomparably the finest orator I have heard, just as Chaliapin was the finest singer—and for the same physical reasons. Larkin was, I believe, actually taller than Chaliapin and could have outroared the Russian. There, striding about the platform, one beheld the whole of the sweated, starved, exploited working class suddenly incarnate in the shape of a gigantic Tarzan of all the slum jungles of the West.[4]

But it was Seán O'Casey who has left us with the best picture we can hope to have of a great artist at work, one whose power was every bit as much in his persona as in the words he spoke. Describing one of these late summer gatherings outside Liberty Hall, O'Casey wrote:

> Suddenly the window is raised and the tense anxious feelings of the men crowded together burst out into an enthusiastic and full-throated cheer that shatters the surrounding air, and sends up into the skies a screaming flock of gulls that had been peacefully drifting along the sombre surface of the River Liffey. Louder still swells the resonant shout as Jim Larkin appears at the window, with an animated flush of human pride on his strong rugged face, as he brushes back from his broad

forehead the waving tufts of dark hair that are here and there silvered by the mellowing influence of Time and the inexorable force of issuing energy from the human structure. Again the cheers ring out, and Larkin quietly waits till the effort to demonstrate their confidence and affection will give place to the lustful desire to hear what he has to say to them, while hidden under the heavy shadows of the towering Custom House a darker column of massive constables instinctively finger their belts, and silently caress the ever-ready club that swings jauntily over each man's broad, expansive hip.

Rumours had been circulated that Jim Larkin had forged a new weapon for the workers, some plan which, when developed, would make their resisting power irresistible, a power that would quickly change their disorganised, clumsy, incoherent units into a huge, immovable, unbreakable Roman phalanx.

Hope's ruddy flame was leaping in their hearts: this day would be an historic one in the happy annals of the Irish Labour Movement. Perhaps this lovely autumn sunset would be followed by the dawn of their social emancipation.

And the lusty cheers died away to a droning echo, which was followed for a few moments by a silence that was so strangely sincere that the mass of people resembled the upright figures of an assembly in the shady and silent regions of the dead.

And then, with a sweeping gesture of his arm, that seemed to pass around that tremendous gathering and make them one with himself in thought and hope and action, Jim Larkin began to speak.[5]

That night Larkin was not to make one of his great speeches, but it was certainly remarkable. He began by referring to the previous speaker.

My friend the chairman is always pessimistic. O'Brien believes that the Tramway Company is the 'Be-all' and the 'Do-all' of Dublin industrial life. But I believe we can smash the Tramway Company in a few days, if the same determination and spirit exists as was seen today.

He then turned his attention to Murphy and, inadvertently, gave the dispute the name it has carried ever since.

It is not a strike, it is a lockout of the men, who have been tyrannically treated by a most unscrupulous scoundrel. Murphy has boasted that he will beat Larkin. What a wonderful boast that was for the mighty man of Gath walking in fear of the Lord. He said he would spend £100,000 to break Larkin, a man who is going to lead you out of bondage into the land of promise.

William Martin Murphy has stated that the cars are running, but I would ask, how many are running? I hope that no workingman will go into them. The cars are taken off the street at seven o'clock. Murphy is a coward. If I had the same power behind me as Murphy, I would take the cars out night, noon and morning. Murphy talked of Larkin biting a file, but if it were not for Larkin the trams would be running until 12 o'clock tonight. Therefore, I won the first round.

Murphy had recruited the RIC, the military and 'the great Scotchman' (Lord Aberdeen, the Lord Lieutenant) to his cause. But Larkin reminded his audience that he had faced longer odds in Belfast during 1907. The workers 'had taught Murphy a lesson and they would teach him a greater one before he was many days older.' Larkin promised to organise 'the greatest demonstration that had ever been seen in Dublin' that weekend. They would march wherever they liked, no matter how many police and military were offered to Murphy by the Lord Lieutenant. The workers would go into O'Connell Street or any other street; in fact they would go wherever William Martin Murphy's cars were permitted to go.

So far Larkin had confined himself to the stock in trade of industrial disputes, but now he talked darkly of police violence that day on Dublin's streets.

I would advise the friends and supporters of this cause to take Sir Edward Carson's advice to the men of Ulster. If he says it is right and legal for the men of Ulster to arm, why should it not be right and legal for the men of Dublin to arm themselves, so as to protect themselves? You will need it. I don't offer advice which I am not prepared to adopt myself. You know me, and you know when I say a thing I do it. So arm, and I'll arm. You have to face hired assassins. If Sir Edward Carson is right in telling the men of Ulster to form a Provisional Government in Belfast, I think I must be right too in telling you to form a Provisional Government in Dublin. But whether you form a Provisional Government or not, you will require arms, for Aberdeen has promised Murphy not only police but the soldiers; and my advice to you is to be round the doors and corners, and whenever one of your men is shot, shoot two of theirs.

This sanguinary advice was greeted with cheers.

Inevitably the concluding speech of another ITGWU stalwart, Councillor Partridge, the man who had tried to bring out the Ringsend power workers earlier that day, was more prosaic. But he caught the spirit of Larkin's Ulster references with his advice that 'the cry should be no surrender, and no surrender in this fight means that each individual will use his best efforts to prevent the trams from running.'[6]

As the meeting concluded around ten o'clock, the union's fife and drum band arrived on the scene. It was followed by a small crowd that had meandered peacefully behind it as it played its way through the city streets, accompanied by a strong police escort. Thus the first day of the tram strike ended.

3

THE strike had no effect on the Horse Show. Lady visitors such as the Duchess of Beaufort, in her black broche dress with white lace ruffles and black tulle hat wreathed in water-lilies, had nothing more serious to contend with than a light breeze. The Marchioness of Headfort, Lady Arnott, Lady Goulding and other social luminaries were no more inconvenienced. The *Irish Times* reporters covering the show almost managed to avoid mentioning the strike altogether.

> News of unrest among tramway employees had aroused some anxiety, and in some parts of the city people experienced long and tedious delays in getting a car, but an excellent service was maintained to the very gates of the Show ground. Dublin would never forgive any trifling with transit facilities in regard to the great Show.[1]

William Martin Murphy was equally smug. He could not hope to compete with Larkin for dramatic effect; but he did not need to, for he was a newspaper magnate. On Wednesday morning all the newspapers carried an interview, given late the previous night, in which Dublin's leading capitalist poured icy contempt on his opponent.

> I am familiar with the history of all the tramway strikes … and Mr. Larkin's so-called 'strike' today was the feeblest and most contemptible attempt that was ever made. I expected that when his strike came, if it came at all, it might last a day, but it was actually broken within half an hour after Larkin's 'orders' were issued. I must pay a tribute of admiration to the inspection and traffic staff for the work they performed in the crisis today.

'Skill and discipline' had defeated Larkin's 'malign influence' on the city. Murphy said that in his experience, tramway strikes began

> by the men refusing to take out the cars in the morning. Larkin, however, obliged us by kindly letting us know that he intended to take the illegal course of stopping the cars in the street at an appointed hour, which he thought would paralyse the traffic. But we were prepared, and it proved a much easier task to defeat him than if the men had adopted the usual method of refusing to take out their cars.

Such a strategy was not open to Larkin, because he knew that many tram crews would pass any pickets placed on the depots. Murphy explained how he had become aware

six weeks ago that Larkin was getting some of the motormen and conductors … into his meshes by inducing them to attend midnight meetings and making violent addresses attacking the Tramway Company. I did not leave all the talking to Mr. Larkin, but invited the men to meet myself soon after midnight at the Antient Concert Rooms on July 19th. After that meeting I had no doubt of that loyalty of the vast body of the traffic men which was so nobly proved today. That meeting checked Larkin's inroad on the men, and his influence amongst them has steadily waned since then.

Turning to the dispute at the *Independent*, Murphy said that he

ascertained that practically all the men and boys in the parcel department were ready to go out without notice at Larkin's command, though they never made any complaint of their conditions of employment. In this case also we declined to allow the parcel staff to wait for Mr. Larkin's threatened strike call. We temporarily suspended the parcel traffic and got rid of the Larkinites. It proved an excellent move, as it relieved us of some difficulty in dealing with the situation today. We can fill the places of Larkin's men in the parcel department any time of the week.

The only other large number of men I had to deal with were those engaged in keeping the pavement and track in repair. I found they were all in Larkin's Union ready to strike on his orders, and they did in fact go out today. I had, however, anticipated this by engaging on works which were not urgent two large gangs of men who undertook they would not join the Transport Union. They were more numerous than the road repair men who went out today, whose loss we should not feel if they never came back again. Larkin has tried to hold up our coal supply without success, and even if there was a temporary stoppage the stock we hold would last … months.

Asked if there was any danger to the power station, Murphy responded confidently:

None whatever. We believe that nearly all the men in the power house will remain at their posts; but even if they all left, the station is so equipped with automatic appliances that it could be run by young engineers in the company's service and others, of whom we have plenty of volunteers. We have taken all precautions against outrages to our plant, which alone can affect our electrical supply.

He said that only a fifth of the tramcar men were out, and these could be replaced in a matter of days. Some had already been replaced. The directors had yet to decide on their attitude to the strikers, some of whom were already anxious to return to work. He expected 'a stampede of the strikers to get their jobs back before it is too late.'

Murphy saw the strike more as an attack on the general public than on the DUTC, 'and I hope that the public will help us by assisting in giving into custody anyone interfering with the company's men or damaging their property.' He then became a little querulous, complaining that 'the labours of the police would be lightened if respectable people would not help to form crowds by themselves collecting in the streets.' Nevertheless he concluded confidently:

> I think I have broken the malign influence of Mr. Larkin and set him on the run. It is now up to the employers to keep him going.[2]

Murphy was indicating that any attempt by Larkin to use the sympathetic strike weapon against the DUTC could lead to a sympathetic lockout. There was nothing fundamentally new about this strategy. Dublin employers had tried as far back as 1907 to smash Larkin's union by banding together, but they had lacked the leadership to plan and carry through such a campaign. Their combinations had been haphazard, and the use of strike-breakers had been successfully countered by heavy picketing, attacks on the newly hired 'scabs', and damage to employers' property. Consequently, disputes in the city tended to be violent; but it was not the uncontrolled action of a mob. For instance, during the 1907 carters' dispute, when a cart was mistakenly attacked the strikers gathered up the scattered packages, rehitched the horse, and sent the shaken driver on his way 'amidst lusty cheers' after they discovered their error.[3]

As we have seen, Murphy had been involved in the only successful lockout in the city, that of the Great Southern and Western Railway in 1911. Though he did not say so in his interview with the press, it appears that he had already secured the support of other large employers for a citywide lockout of ITGWU members. On Thursday 28 August the well-informed Father Curran was able to write to the archbishop that 'the Master Builders have decided to lock out 5,000 men if there is any trouble from Larkin.'[4] In Murphy, Larkin had perhaps found his greatest convert to syndicalism, but it was a syndicalism of the bosses that Murphy espoused.

*

As usual, Larkin answered Murphy in kind. Despite the problems posed by the bankruptcy proceedings against Hunt, Larkin managed to publish a special edition of the *Irish Worker* on Wednesday 27 August. In it he apologised to the travelling public for any inconvenience the strike was causing; he then said that Murphy, by his actions, had shown 'the kind of employer the Dublin workers have to submit to—gradgrinds, scroogers, sweaters, hypocrites and tyrants of the worst type.'[5]

Larkin probably succeeded in having over 20,000 copies of the paper distributed that day. Until its suppression by wartime censors in 1914, the *Irish Worker* was the most successful socialist newspaper ever produced in Ireland. Journalism came as naturally to Larkin as oratory: indeed the *Irish*

Worker was 'Larkin's oratory congealed in print.'[6] Its unique combination of socialist polemic, hard news, gossip, humour and plain scurrility made it essential reading for anyone who claimed to have an informed opinion of goings-on in the city. The circulation varied between 10,000 and 22,000; on the eve of the tramway strike it was selling about 14,000 copies a week.[7] In contrast, the leading radical nationalist weekly paper, *Sinn Féin*, sold between 3,000 and 5,000 copies. The liberal unionist *Irish Times* sold 45,000 copies, and the *Freeman's Journal*, champion of the Irish Party, about 40,000. All were dwarfed by William Martin Murphy's *Irish Independent*, which sold 100,000 copies a day, as did his *Evening Herald*.

While its sales were only a small fraction of this, and its circulation was largely confined to Dublin, the *Irish Worker* was able to attract considerable advertising. Even the Dublin branch of the Hibernian Rifles, military section of the Ancient Order of Hibernians, placed advertisements seeking recruits, though the order's sectarian politics were a regular target of criticism in the paper's editorial columns. Patrick Belton's drapery company was the only large concern to advertise regularly in the *Irish Worker*. But Belton was a maverick. He would later become a Sinn Féin TD and then had a colourful political career as a member successively of Fianna Fáil, the Centre Party, and Fine Gael. Most of the advertising in the *Worker* came from small businesses such as butchers, tobacconists, bicycle shops—and undertakers. Fanagan's of Aungier Street offered 'coffins, hearses, coaches and every funeral requisite. Trades Union and All-Irish House.' James Larkin, a plain and fancy baker of 78 Meath Street, described himself in his advertisement as 'The Workers' Baker'. He urged customers to 'ask for Larkin's Loaf.'

Advertising revenue was worth between £10 and £12 a week, which provided the *Worker* with a net profit of about £8 10s. Without the support of its advertisers it would no more have been able to survive than Murphy's mass circulation publications. However, while Murphy's profits swelled his own coffers, the funds of the *Irish Worker* were regularly raided by Larkin to subsidise trade union activities. Nothing demonstrates the David and Goliath nature of the coming struggle better than the finances of the rival publications. The *Irish Worker* made £400 a year, Murphy's publications £15,000.

In its special edition of 27 August the *Irish Worker* accused Murphy of dismissing 'some 200 men from their employment for daring to exercise their God-given rights as freemen in combining with their fellows.' As president of the Dublin Chamber of Commerce, Murphy had supported the establishment of a conciliation board in the city to settle disputes, then, 'with deliberateness and malice,' provoked a dispute. 'We leave the case in the hands of the citizens to judge who is in the wrong and who is in the right,' the *Worker* declaimed. It called on readers not to use the trams or to buy Murphy's 'immoral literature'. The front page reminded readers in large type that 'you are not compelled to patronise shops that sell the

"Independent" and "Herald". Thiggin thu [*An dtuigeann tú*]!'

Inside, the *Worker* reported that DMP members were organising a trade union.

> The men's leave has been stopped because Wm. Martin Murphy 'anticipates trouble Horse Show week' ... The police have a right to organise and there is no power under the sun to stop them from striking against tyrannical methods to satisfy the 'Herald'.[8]

The paper reported that many policemen had to abandon arrangements for annual holiday leave 'to satisfy William Martin M., and because men on the trams are looking for a living wage. O tempora O mores.' In the great Belfast dock strike of 1907 Larkin had managed to bring out the police, but there was little evidence outside the columns of the *Irish Worker* that he would succeed in Dublin. Indeed there were disturbing signs that Dublin in 1913 would not be a repeat of Larkin's northern triumph of six years earlier.

4

A LREADY some employers were following Murphy's lead. On the same day that the tramcar workers struck, the flour-milling firm of Shackleton and Sons in Lucan, County Dublin, told employees it had become aware that many of them had joined the ITGWU. The owner, W. E. Shackleton, was something of a political eccentric. Though he came from a unionist background, he had dabbled in radical nationalist politics and had served on the Sinn Féin executive from 1907 to 1909. He was attracted by its protectionist policies rather than the radical social policies that other members espoused. He now told his employees they must choose between their jobs and 'Larkin's union'. The men refused to forswear the ITGWU; by evening the mill was closed and pickets placed. It was a foretaste of things to come. The incident at Shackleton's suggests that at least some members of the Dublin Employers' Federation needed little prompting to accept Murphy's strategy.[1]

*

For the moment the focus remained on Dublin's tramways. On Wednesday 27 August the *Evening Herald*'s headline was 'Tram strike fiasco.' It published a statement from the DUTC on its front page proclaiming that the company

> have more men to work the cars … than yesterday and are able to give a full service to Ballsbridge for the Horse Show and to Kingstown and Dalkey. On the other lines the ordinary service run in normal times is very slightly curtailed.

The *Irish Times* declared that the DUTC's offices were 'besieged' by would-be employees.[2]

However, things were far from normal. At least two trams were attacked by 'roughs' on Arran Quay, and vehicles on the Inchicore line were withdrawn to the Kingsbridge depot until stronger police escorts could be provided. A dozen drivers at Kingsbridge (Heuston Station) joined the strike, and passengers arriving at the railway station that day had to walk into the city, carrying their own luggage. In Rathmines, ITGWU pickets were placed on labourers who were repairing damage to the tramline; but these were Murphy's specially recruited men, and they remained impervious to appeals for working-class solidarity.

At Sandymount and Ringsend there was obstruction of the tracks, and stones were thrown at trams. A vehicle crossing Ringsend bridge at four o'clock was surrounded by a crowd and had its windows smashed. Three passengers had to crouch on the floor as stones flew overhead, and only the speedy response of the police saved the crewmen from the mob. Several of the ringleaders were reported to be wearing DUTC uniforms. In Thomas Street another tram was stoned. The policeman escorting it received 'a rather ugly cut on the nose' but succeeded in apprehending his attacker after a brief chase. When the culprit, a labourer from Inchicore, appeared in court on Friday he was imprisoned for a month and fined £5. The magistrate, E. G. Swifte, told him that throwing stones at a tramcar full of people was not a fair way to conduct a strike. Stones were even thrown at trams in Kingstown, and the local ITGWU branch secretary, James Byrne, was charged with intimidation and 'jostling' a tramway inspector. Byrne was the first trade union officer to be arrested during the lockout; his involvement in the dispute would ultimately cost him his life.

The most organised—and peaceful—protest on Wednesday was in the morning. Striking tram crews marched through the city centre, wearing their uniforms and sporting the ITGWU's Red Hand badge. An irate company spokesman issued a warning afterwards that the men must return the clothes or face legal action. In response to press enquiries, he confirmed that the directors were considering the position of strikers who were living in DUTC cottages. However, as the *Irish Times* pointed out,

> the number of strikers who enjoyed the benefits of the excellent dwellings erected by the company is comparatively small. Another pitiable feature of the strike is that the men who have gone out forfeit their claims upon the benevolent and pension funds established for the benefit of employees.

*

On Wednesday the ITGWU also published its rather modest claim. It wanted the pay of first-class conductors raised from 28s 6d to 30s 6d, that of second-class conductors raised from 26s 6d to 27s 6d, and that of third-class conductors from 22s to 24s. For the drivers, the union wanted the top rate of a first-class motorman to be raised from 31s a week to 33s, second-class motormen to be paid 31s instead of 29s 6d, and third-class motormen 27s 6d instead of 25s 6d. The improvements sought in working conditions were equally modest. The union wanted the maximum working day capped at nine hours, or seven hours on a Sunday. Every man should receive his eighth day off, instead of the twelfth day. Finally, employees should be entitled to a week's paid holiday a year. These were hardly revolutionary demands.

There was no response from the company; but the directors must have been gratified at receiving a resolution from over four hundred loyal employees assuring them that they would not be duped or intimidated by Mr Larkin into leaving their employment. These loyal employees also made a plea that the jobs of their misled comrades should not be taken away, or their licences to work as drivers and conductors withdrawn. 'We would … respectfully suggest that the men on strike should be afforded an opportunity of reconsidering their position, as we believe many of them were frightened into association with the present strike.' The resolution was submitted to the directors on behalf of his colleagues by T. P. Curley.

The newspapers were soon full of letters praising the 'loyal tramway men'. One writer to the *Irish Times*, signing himself 'Senex', proposed that passengers 'show their appreciation of the loyal tramway men, who refused to be his [Larkin's] slaves by not taking any change out of 6d. or 1s. when paying their fares.' A farmer from County Dublin, perhaps still mindful of the wage increase squeezed out of him by the ITGWU the previous week, suggested that a fund be set up for the 'loyal tramway men', which met with a ready response.[3]

Delighted with the coverage from his first interview with the press, Murphy gave another to an *Evening Herald* reporter. He stressed that 'my fight is not against trade unionism, but against Larkinism.' This he described as

the most pestilential 'ism' that any community could be affected with. The so-called Transport Union is not a union at all. It is merely a rabble commanded by Larkin, who is the greatest enemy of trades unionism. He calls men out on strike when it suits his game, without asking whether they like it or not, and they are so terrorised by this man's mob that they blindly obey. He then telephones to the employer and if he can get recognised he will let the employer off very cheaply and order his dupes, whom he has betrayed, back again to work.

It was not a bad summary of how many employers regarded Larkin's *modus operandi*.

Murphy followed this with a personalised attack on Larkin, which probably reflected that wider view as well.

I never set eyes on him, but I am told that he is a big man wearing a slouched hat, and with a swaggering style, throwing downstairs any smaller than himself, and giving the impression of great physical courage. I notice however that whenever there is any trouble in the wind he is not to be found where his skin would be in any danger.

Not only the DUTC but the *Irish Independent* and *Evening Herald* were flourishing, despite the strike. Murphy admitted that there had been a brief disruption to *Herald* sales, but 'the sale of the paper is larger than ever.'[4] Father Curran was to be given a franker assessment of the situation. He wrote to Dr Walsh:

The tramway company is losing heavily, as the trams don't run at night and are not patronised in the day as much as formerly. So too are the 'Herald' and 'Independent', which are not easy to get.

He added that the text of the sales legend *Progress of the Independent*, which appeared on the front page of the paper, had been altered to show the number of copies printed: previously it had shown the number sold.[5]

Meanwhile, in his *Herald* interview, Murphy was telling the public that the industrial relations situation within the Independent group was good. 'All employees of the "Independent" offices, except the unskilled labourers are in trades unions, with whom we have always the best relations and who, so far from resenting our action with regard to Larkin's bogus union have cordially supported us.' Murphy appeared well briefed on events at the Trades Council the previous Monday, for he added that

> the fellow [Larkin] had the impudence to endeavour to bring pressure on the composing staff of the 'Independent' papers, the elite of the working men of Dublin, really gentlemen in every sense of the word, whom I have had the pleasure of meeting. It was rather too much for these men to be asked to associate with scum like Larkin and his followers.

Regrettably, Dublin Trades Council, 'which used to be a respectable body,' was now 'neither respectable nor respected.' It had succumbed to Larkinism, for reasons that Murphy could not fathom. The leader of Dublin's capitalists had given, for what it was worth, his definition of a good trade unionist. An unskilled worker who consorted with Larkin was a different matter.[6]

*

Father F. E. O'Loughlin, spiritual director of the Confraternity of the Holy Family, Rathmines, had anticipated Murphy's strictures on trade unionism. He began a retreat for working men on the day the tramway strike began by reminding his spiritual charges of the injunctions of Pope Leo XIII in his encyclical *Rerum Novarum*. Employees must never 'injure the property, nor … outrage the person of the employer,' never resort to violence or engage in 'riot or disorder.' The Pope had especially warned the faithful to have nothing to do with 'men of evil principles who work upon the people with artful promises and excite foolish hopes which usually end in useless regrets, followed by absolute beggary.' Regrettably, in Ireland many workers had come under the influence of 'the Red Hand of Socialism', which used strikes to air grievances. It had benefited them nothing.

> And if, in some cases, an advance of wages was obtained, of what use was it? Because, in proportion to the advance in wages, the cost of living increased. So that now, roughly it takes £1 to provide articles for which 15s. sufficed before—surely a very poor recompense for a strike! What has been the net result of these 'strikes', so heedlessly and lightly rushed into? Homes all through the country broken up; pawnshops inundated with the belongings of the workers; the breadwinner seeking in Scotland, England and America what socialism refuses him here—work; our industries paralysed—aye, men, I will go further and I will say that

in many a graveyard in Ireland today, over many a fresh-dug grave, a headstone might be erected bearing the epitaph—'Starved by a Strike'... The storm of Socialism which has swept over and devastated Spain and France, Italy and Germany, and which at this imminent moment is passing over England—that storm must sooner or later reach our shores. God grant that when it has passed away, it will leave Ireland as she is now, the first Catholic country of Europe.[7]

In his sermon, Father O'Loughlin put the economic cart before the horse. Wage claims in Dublin were not so much pushing prices up as following them: in fact the price of some essential items had risen by as much as 15 per cent since 1906, or 50 per cent faster than in strike-torn Britain.

The *Irish Worker* regularly printed tables of statistics to hammer home the message that Irish wages were falling behind inflation and pay rates in Britain. When rent, foodstuffs and retail prices were taken together, the *Worker* claimed that the overall increase in the cost of living for Dublin workers had been 12.2 per cent between 1906 and 1912. Over the same period the wage of a skilled building worker rose by only 2 per cent and that of a building labourer by 6 per cent. The propaganda in the *Worker* carried conviction, because it reflected reality.

It was the very different labour conditions that made such big differentials possible. While the rapid expansion of British cities in the nineteenth century had enabled them to absorb migrants from the countryside and to provide alternative employment for workers in declining trades, Dublin had stagnated. Old skills, such as weaving, vanished, and the only categories of employee to expand rapidly were those of general labourer and domestic servant. This was reflected in pay rates. A craftsman in the building trade earned no more than 75 per cent of the London rate and a building labourer 55 per cent. Unskilled workers generally were particularly affected by the labour surplus. D. A. Chart's estimate of 24,000 labourers in the city was almost certainly too low. More recent research based on the 1911 census suggests that there were 45,000 unskilled workers—a seventh of the entire population and a third of the labour force. The vast majority of these workers earned between 15s and 25s a week, with 18s appearing to be the norm. The striking tram workers, with top rates of between 26s and 31s a week, were comparatively well off. If this was still 5s to 10s a week less than their counterparts in Britain, it reflected the general regional pay differentials.[8]

Only craft workers, such as printers and bricklayers, earning between 36s and £2 a week, were significantly better off than the tram crews. Even the best-paid of general labourers, those in the building trade and on the docks, could not expect to earn significantly more than 25s a week. Of course building work was seasonal, and casual dockers might earn as little as 5s a week when trade was slow, or if they were not 'well got' with the foreman or stevedore, a status usually acquired through buying the foreman drink out of a hard-earned day's pay.

Inevitably there were large numbers of workers unemployed at any given time who lived at abysmally lower social depths. When labour exchanges were established, three times as many workers signed on in Dublin as in Belfast, though Belfast had 100,000 more people.[9]

It was in 1912, almost two years after industrial unrest had begun pushing up British wage rates, that those in Dublin began to follow suit. The *Irish Worker* and Larkin were happy to claim the credit on behalf of the ITGWU; but workers organised by other unions, such as building labourers, local authority employees, brass foundry workers, and engineers, were equally successful in securing significant pay rises. The mundane reality was that, when the pay rates of Dublin fell too far behind those in Britain, emigration to Liverpool, Birmingham and beyond helped reduce the surplus, restore labour militancy, and redress the balance.

At the same time, Larkin's claim that the ITGWU's organisation drive had disproportionately boosted the wages of labourers has some basis in fact. As the *Irish Worker* had pointed out, the gap between building labourers and craftsmen, or that between other well-organised groups, such as dockers and carters, and the skilled trades generally seems to have narrowed.[10] The upward trend in wages was to continue well after 1914, when the advent of war created a labour shortage.

Twelve months before Armageddon, Dublin's employers were ready to credit Larkin's claims that he was responsible for spiralling wage costs and increasing industrial unrest. As so often in the past, when the smug world of the 'well to do' was disturbed by the starving masses, the hungry were identified as the problem rather than as one of its more distressing symptoms.

*

On Wednesday afternoon, when the Lord Lieutenant, John Campbell Gordon, seventh Earl of Aberdeen, attended the Royal Horse Show in Ballsbridge, the masses were ignored. There were no signs of unrest as Lord Aberdeen's party arrived with an escort from the 5th Royal Irish Lancers. His distinguished guests included Lord Rosebery, the former Liberal prime minister, and the Yuvaraja of Mysore. Lord Aberdeen talked about the glorious weather, the large and distinguished attendance, and the importance of improving the education system. Two subjects he scrupulously avoided were the Ulster crisis and the strike.[11]

The strike, at least, would not go away. That evening there was another mass meeting in Beresford Place. As the tram service had stopped at seven o'clock, demonstrators had no choice but to walk from home or work-place, but the crowd was even larger than the previous night. Despite Lord Aberdeen's studied avoidance of the issue at the Horse Show that afternoon, the Irish executive in Dublin Castle was concerned that the ugly but sporadic violence already manifesting itself could spread. Earlier in the day Superintendent Quinn of the DMP had called to Liberty Hall and had met Larkin and P. T. Daly, one of the ITGWU's full-time organisers, to tell them that the proposed demonstration in Sackville Street at the weekend was being proclaimed and would be stopped by force if necessary.[12] Larkin now told the crowd that the government, 'at the dictation of Mr. William M. Murphy, suppressed a perfectly constitutional procession.' He asked why Carson's meetings were not proclaimed; the workers of Dublin had more of a right to assert themselves than Carson had to establish a provisional government for Ulster. Larkin called for a volunteer army of trade unionists and 'men from the fields.' Before him he saw 'twenty thousand of the best men in the world.' He announced to cheers that the planned demonstration would go ahead on Sunday, in spite of Lord Aberdeen and his executive. The work that day would be 'men's work,' and he advised 'all women, children and boys to keep away.'

But Larkin's main task that night was to boost the confidence of the strikers. He told the crowd that more tramway men were joining the strike each day and that there was plenty of strike money to support them. He then turned on the 'scab' printers' unions, which had denied members at the *Independent* the right to come out in sympathy with the ITGWU men there. He appealed to the crowd to stop Murphy's newspapers being printed—but did not specify how this might be done.

The other main speaker was an ITGWU stalwart and former nationalist member of Belfast City Council, Michael McKeown. He too invoked Carson's example and said that if the unionists were allowed to form Volunteers to defy home rule, workers had a right to arm in their own interests.

Determined to end the meeting on a high note, Larkin announced that the men in the power station had come out. It was untrue, but it was great street theatre and brought cheers from the crowd.[13]

*

Despite Larkin's fulminations, the strike was now widely regarded as a damp squib. Newspapers looked elsewhere for their main story; an aeroplane crash on Wednesday provided it. The attempt by an Australian flyer, Harry Hawker, to win the £5,000 *Daily Mail* round-Britain seaplane prize ended when his 100-horsepower biplane hit the water a few yards off Loughshinny pier, seventeen miles north of Dublin. He suffered minor injuries, but his unfortunate passenger broke an arm. Disappointed crowds at Kingstown, who had waited since daybreak for a view of the plane, drifted away when they heard the news. The *Daily Mail* announced that the gallant Hawker would be given a consolation prize of £1,000 in recognition of his efforts.[14]

The attention devoted to the aviator's mixed fortunes suggested that the tramcar strikers were doomed to imminent obscurity. But the newspapers had reckoned without Dublin Castle. Between seven and eight o'clock on Thursday morning, Larkin and four other leading trade unionists were arrested at their homes by DMP detectives and taken to the Bridewell. One of Larkin's fellow-prisoners was William O'Brien, vice-president of the Trades Council and president of the Tailors' Society. Before he was taken away he asked his mother to telegraph the Belfast ITGWU leader, James Connolly, and ask him to come to Dublin and take over the running of the dispute. This showed O'Brien's preference for Connolly, whom he had first met through the Irish Socialist Republican Party in Dublin in the eighteen-nineties, over the brash Liverpudlian. As O'Brien admitted in a memoir fifty-six years later, it was a somewhat presumptuous action for a young tailor—who was not even a member of the ITGWU at that time.[15]

The third prisoner was P. T. Daly, the former printer who had urged the Dublin Typographical Provident Society at Monday's Trades Council meeting to back the sacked despatch workers at the *Independent*. He was another comrade of Connolly's from ISRP days, but relations between Daly and O'Brien had become strained. Now a full-time official of the ITGWU, Daly would probably have been Larkin's preferred choice to deputise for him if he had been at liberty. He had been acting general secretary of the ITGWU in 1910, when Larkin was in prison for his fraud conviction. Like Connolly and O'Brien, he belonged to a generation of working-class activists who oscillated between radical nationalism and socialist politics. Besides being a member of the ISRP, he had been a Sinn Féin city councillor and had almost run as an independent against the sitting Irish Party MP and founder of Dublin Trades Council, J. P. Nannetti, in the second general election of 1910. Daly had also served on the Supreme Council of the Irish Republican Brotherhood. O'Brien too had been an IRB member, though briefly. He was aware that Daly had been expelled for misappropriating £300; Daly had used the money to support his family while touring America for the brotherhood in 1907. Daly was a good organiser and an able speaker, but the money incident and a fondness for drink ensured O'Brien's enduring hostility.[16]

The fourth prisoner was Councillor William Partridge, the ITGWU organiser who had tried to close the DUTC power station. Like Daly, Partridge was a craftsman. The son of an English railway engineer who had moved to Ireland, he had followed in his father's footsteps and become an engineer. Though an ITGWU official, Partridge, unlike Daly, had remained active in his own union: he was president of the Dublin District of the Amalgamated Society of Engineers, a British union. This dual role would create some tension in the weeks ahead, as would Partridge's very devout, and very public, Catholicism.

The fifth prisoner was Tom Lawlor of the Tailors' Society, like O'Brien a delegate to the Trades Council. His principal offence appears to have been that he had spoken at Larkin's meetings.

All five prisoners were brought before the Chief Divisional Magistrate of the Dublin Metropolitan Division, E. G. Swifte, who also happened to be a substantial shareholder in the DUTC.[17] They were charged with seditious libel, conspiracy to disturb the peace, and causing 'disaffection and hatred between certain classes of His Majesty's subjects, to wit the working classes of Dublin and the police forces of the Crown and the soldiers of the

Crown.' They were also charged with incitement to excite hatred and contempt of the government and, finally, incitement to murder. The prosecution's case rested primarily on Larkin's two speeches and especially his advice to workers to kill two of the bosses' 'hired assassins' for every one of their own class who was shot.

A crowd of what the *Irish Times* described as 'idlers' gathered outside the court as soon as word of the arrests was out. But it was two o'clock in the afternoon before the prisoners appeared in the dock. Opening his case, the Crown prosecutor, James Rearden KC, stressed that the prosecution should not be taken as evidence that the government was taking sides in the industrial battle then being fought out on the streets of the city. Indeed the government was

> absolutely aloof from any labour dispute that exists in this city. But in this case there had been an open and unashamed defiance of the law, and such conduct could not be overlooked.

Rearden dismissed as an 'absolute concoction' Larkin's allegations that Lord Aberdeen had undertaken to provide Murphy with soldiers and police to shoot down 'these people of Larkin's.'

Henry Hanna KC acted, as he often did that year, for the trade unionists in the dock. But Larkin conducted his own cross-examination of the police witnesses. While he did not elicit a confession that the police were in the pay of William Martin Murphy, he did establish that his enemy had called to Dublin Castle on Tuesday to discuss the security situation. He told the magistrate that the prosecution case 'should be scouted out of court.' If anyone should be in the dock it was Sir Edward Carson, and those who had made out depositions against himself. A government that was too cowardly to deal with Carson would find that they would not have it all their own way when they came to deal with him and men like him.

Far from being intimidated by the court, Larkin described the government as 'too cowardly to carry out the law.' Instead they were trying to abuse it. 'Was there any law that prevented them from meeting in Sackville Street? If there was, let the meeting be proclaimed in a lawful manner.' Larkin said he stood by everything he had said. Soldiers were hired assassins, but he never accused the police of that occupation. The government might put him in jail, but it would not stop the meeting taking place. Putting him in the dock was the very thing that would stir the people up. He concluded by calling for his own acquittal, 'for I have committed no crime.'[18]

The prosecution was not prepared for Larkin's counter-attack. Rearden wound up lamely and said that he had no objection to the defendants being admitted to bail, provided the sureties were substantial. Swifte set bail at £100 for Larkin, with two sureties of £50 each. The other accused were granted bail of £50 each, with two sureties of £25. This was promptly put up by the ITGWU. The union leaders returned in triumph to Liberty Hall, accompanied by a large crowd of supporters. Larkin immediately set about planning another mass meeting for that night.

The feeble response of the Irish executive to the crisis was due to political problems. Rearden had indirectly referred to these in his opening remarks when he made the point that the prosecutions should not be interpreted as meaning that the government was taking sides in the dispute. The fact was that the British government wanted nothing whatever to do with it. The Liberals' parliamentary majority rested on the support of both the Irish Party and Labour. Murphy and Larkin might both be mavericks, but each had significant influence within these particular power blocs.

*

While the labour leaders were in the Bridewell dock, less celebrated cases were being processed elsewhere. At Kingstown Police Court the local ITGWU branch secretary, James Byrne, was facing charges of intimidation. The case rested on evidence from a tram inspector, John Fellows, and Inspector Clifford of the DMP. Both said that Byrne had jostled Fellows as he passed and said in a threatening voice, 'You won't have it all your own way.' Byrne denied the words and denied jostling Fellows. He had simply walked past Fellows on the footpath. 'If my coat struck against him, it was as much as it did,' Byrne said. He was remanded in custody for a week. James Corcoran, a labourer of no fixed address, appeared in the same court for stoning a tram. He was given a month's hard labour for malicious damage and vagrancy.

In the Southern Police Court in Dublin a young labourer arrested stoning a tram in Thomas Street was given a month's imprisonment and told he would have to serve another month if he could not provide a £5 surety for his future good behaviour.[19] There were many similar cases, but the threat of prosecution seemed to have little effect. Attacks on trams spread to the upper middle-class suburb of Dalkey, and a group of DUTC workers at Clontarf joined the strike. The company announced that it had recruited sixty new men, 'some of whom have been waiting a year or more to be taken on.' It hoped that, with the expected tapering off of demand on the Ballsbridge line as the Horse Show wound down, more trams would be available elsewhere by the weekend.

As dusk settled over the city, thousands of workers returned once more to Beresford Place to join the continuing carnival of protest and to imbibe the rhetoric of class warfare. Speaking from a window in Liberty Hall, P. T. Daly declared that he recognised no British law in Ireland. Somewhat paradoxically, he added that if British workers were allowed to hold meetings in Britain, the same rules should apply in Dublin. The ITGWU's Belfast organiser, James Connolly, told the crowd that when Orangemen marched through Belfast, the tram services were suspended; in Dublin, however, the streets 'seem to belong to the financial brigade ... Sir Edward Carson is at least a courageous man, but the present government is the most cowardly that ever held the reins of office.' Connolly invited trade unionists to emulate the Orangemen and go to Sackville Street on Sunday 'to see if there was going to be a meeting. There was nothing illegal about that.'

Larkin told a delighted audience that he had never attended an illegal meeting in his life. Nor did he use inflammatory language; he always told the truth, and if people objected to hearing it that was not his fault. The people were the law and had the right to use the streets. Again invoking the ubiquitous unionist leader, he said that what was good enough for Carson and the Orangemen was good enough for Larkin and the labourers.[20]

*

The anger of Larkin's supporters at their leader's arrest was exceeded only by that of Dublin's employers at his release. The *Irish Times* editorial next morning declared that the public had a right to be surprised at the government's willingness to admit Larkin and his co-accused to bail, given the seriousness of the charges and Larkin's continued avowed intention of holding a meeting 'which he has invited his followers to attend with arms in their hands.' Larkin had declared he would be in Sackville Street on Sunday 'dead or alive,' and the government 'has now made itself directly and personally responsible for the maintenance of … peace.' The *Times* had been relatively restrained in its reporting of industrial disputes, but it had no doubt about who was responsible for

> the deplorable situation in Dublin … The essential fact is this—that a single organisation is now exercising an abominable tyranny over the working classes of the city. Its object is to control the relations of masters and men in every branch of local industry. When recognition is refused a strike follows. The whole trade of Dublin is dislocated in order that a single firm may be brought to its knees. The organisation has no mercy on the sufferings of the poor; it never spares a thought for the welfare or reputation of Dublin. The present tramway strike is a characteristic example of its policy and methods. With the object of forcing itself on men who hate it, this body did not hesitate to try to 'hold up' the business and pleasure of Dublin in the most vital week of the year. This thing is not merely a nuisance; it has become a danger and a degradation. [Citizens had] yielded to intimidation far too quickly and easily. We learnt yesterday that, in some districts of the city, small shopkeepers have refused to sell food and other necessaries to the wives and children of loyal tramway men. These mean-spirited creatures ought to be thoroughly ashamed of themselves. But they would doubtless plead that they are only following the example of richer and more important persons.
>
> We know of cases where large employers of labour have allowed themselves to be terrorised without any protest … So long as this atmosphere of weakness and timidity exists the strike bullies will have their way … The plague will only be rooted out by the combined

action—bold and determined action—of the whole body of employers in the city.[21]

The leader-writer praised the example set by the DUTC and Shackleton's mill. If other employers followed suit 'the strike threat would soon be at an end in Dublin.' The editorial predicted that there would be a 'short, though, perhaps severe' struggle but that 'in a fortnight employers would be their own masters again and their workers would cease to be frightened slaves.' The *Irish Times* was showing a strangely prescient knowledge of what was about to unfold, though it would take much longer than two weeks for the employers' plan to succeed.

The same day, William Martin Murphy wrote a letter to his own newspaper, the *Evening Herald*, denying any complicity in Larkin's arrest.

> Had I been consulted, I would have recommended that he should not have been offered any sort of cheap martyrdom. In my opinion his speech after the strike fiasco was simply an invitation to the Government to arrest him in order to get him out of his difficulty. Larkin knows that when he is no longer able to provide his dupes with strike and lockout pay, the inside of a jail, where, as a first class misdemeanant, he can enjoy his big cigars at leisure, while his victims are starving, will be his safest refuge.[22]

To reinforce its proprietor's message, next day the *Saturday Herald* published on its front page a cartoon contrasting Larkin, sitting in his office smoking a large cigar under a sign reading *Strike or No Strike: Salary £2 10s. 0d. a week*, with ITGWU members queuing up outside for strike pay of 5s a week. Scattered on the floor of Larkin's office were documents referring to Hunt's bad debt of £227 and the £18 10s a week profit that the bankruptcy court had been told accrued to Larkin from his editorship of a 'Labour paper'. Understandably, the *Herald* was not going to name the *Irish Worker* and provide it with free publicity. Murphy's newspapers were to repeatedly stress Larkin's comparatively large salary during the lockout. In fact it was the same salary he had received when he joined the NUDL in 1905, and was £1 a week less than his wage as a foreman on Liverpool docks.[23]

Meanwhile the *Evening Herald* had prematurely proclaimed the 'utter collapse of the tram strike,' thanks to the 'determined and manly act of a city Employer.' The 'manly employer' was V. S. Freeman of Harry Street, who had sacked eight farriers after each one had successively refused to shoe an *Independent* horse. The paper also gave emphasis to a salutary sentence of two months' imprisonment imposed on a middle-aged labourer for smashing a tram window and threatening a DUTC inspector with an axe earlier that day. Again Swifte was the magistrate. He also sentenced a woman who came to court with a four-month-old baby in her arms to three weeks' imprisonment for throwing a loaf at a tram in Ringsend. She said she tossed the loaf to her son, when it accidentally struck the tram. A plea for leniency by her solicitor, on the grounds that she had a young family and a sick unemployed husband to support, failed to impress Swifte: he said he had to put a stop to these outrages. Later the same day he proclaimed Larkin's proposed meeting in Sackville Street on Sunday.[24]

*

The employers were not waiting for government intervention. On Friday afternoon the executive committee of the Dublin Employers' Federation met in the offices of the Dublin Chamber of Commerce in Commercial Buildings, Dame Street, to consider the situation. The city's coal merchants met separately. Neither body would confirm rumours that it was considering a lockout.

That evening, Swifte's proclamation was the centre of attention at the meeting in Beresford Place. Connolly waved it before the crowd and asked where 'Sackville Street' was.

> Perhaps it is in Jerusalem or Timbuctoo, but there is no such street in Dublin. There is an O'Connell Street, and there we will come on Sunday, in a very peaceful way, to see if the government has sold themselves body and soul to the capitalists.

Larkin went one better and burnt the proclamation. He then told the crowd that he wanted no-one at Sunday's meeting

> but men who are resolved to stand. If lives are lost the government and Mr. Murphy will have to take responsibility.

He also called for a show of hands—readily given—of those willing to go on rent strike if a lockout were called. He repeated his injunction that the workers should kill two for every one of their own shot down. He also warned the government, and particularly Lloyd George, who was planning to visit Dublin, that they 'would not be dealing with suffragettes' if trouble broke out. The reference was unfortunate, as Larkin supported female suffrage; and most women campaigning for it hated the term 'suffragette', generally used by the press to characterise them as violent and somewhat deranged members of their sex.

But Larkin was never renowned for his sensitivity, and he now annoyed Murphy and his fellow-directors of the DUTC even more by urging his members to board the trams on Saturday and travel as far as they could without paying the fare. The one place they should not go next day, he suggested pointedly, was the soccer match in Shelbourne Park: the visiting team, Bohemians, included 'scabs'.[25]

As the meeting ended, a large crowd hung around Beresford Place to enjoy the warm summer night. Some taunted the watching police, who responded with a baton charge that sent the crowd scurrying over Butt Bridge. Francis Sheehy-Skeffington, the well-known Dublin journalist, socialist, pacifist, and supporter of women's suffrage, was injured in the scuffle. When he threatened to issue proceedings against the police next day, he received a prompt apology. It was the first of many that would be received by middle-class Dubliners caught up in the riots of the next few days. Workers who complained in similar circumstances usually ended up in the dock.

*

In London there were indications that the British labour movement was becoming concerned at developments in Dublin. On Friday the secretary of the British Socialist Party, Albert Inkpin, sent a telegram to the Chief Secretary for Ireland, Augustine Birrell, protesting at the way the government was 'taking the side of the employers ... by the unjust prosecution of James Larkin and others, particularly when Carson and his Confederates are permitted to advise armed revolt in Ulster.' The Socialist Party was relatively small but influential, and Inkpin, a future founding member of the Communist Party of Great Britain, expressed a growing perception within the wider labour movement of what was going on in Dublin. He described the demands of the tramway workers as 'perfectly reasonable'.[26]

Some members of the government would have agreed with him, including Lloyd George. Some would even have accepted that Carson's stance was unreasonable, including Lloyd George. The problem was that British government policy was based on the assumption that the rule of reason would ultimately prevail in both these crises. Unfortunately, the Irish were not alone in their unreasonableness. The House of Lords, the Tories, the British workers and, most of all, the suffragists seemed unwilling to listen to reason any more. Larkin might not have been so dismissive of these women if, like Lloyd George, he had had to confront them at close quarters in Parliament Square, at the Epsom races, or in London's most select drawing-rooms. While loyalists were shooting up Derry there had been an arson attack by suffragists on Lord Derby's estate, where King George V was a guest, in protest at the Prisoners (Temporary Discharge for Health) Act (1913)—the 'Cat and Mouse Act'—which allowed the government to release militant suffragists who embarked on hunger strikes and then re-arrest them later. Instead of averting confrontations, the act multiplied them. The founder of the suffrage movement, Emmeline Pankhurst, had just been released after her tenth hunger strike; her youngest daughter, Sylvia, whose socialist credentials were every bit as good as Larkin's, had barely survived her latest incarceration. Still wan from the ordeal, she told a London crowd that in future women must make themselves a match for the police 'by learning ju-jitsu and drilling.' They should arm themselves with sticks when coming to demonstrations.[27]

Two days after Sylvia Pankhurst's appeal for women to take up the martial arts, Carson called on all Ulster men to join his Volunteers. Perhaps he was inspired by her example, or perhaps it was something in the air. 'Even old men can help to guard their property, their hearths and their homes, and thus release the younger and more active for whatever work may be necessary,' he told a crowd in Belfast. 'Victory comes to those who are organised and united.'[28] It could have been the slogan of the ITGWU in the summer of 1913—or indeed the employers.

Certainly Larkin's lieutenant, James Connolly, would have liked it. A short, dapper figure, Connolly looked more like a shopkeeper than a revolutionary. Yet he was the most fearless and redoubtable street agitator that Dublin had ever known. A decade earlier he had led massive and riotous demonstrations through the city in opposition to the Boer War. He was a natural warrior. 'Nobody has dared one-half what he has dared in the assertion of his principles,' an elder statesman of the British socialist movement said of him. He was scrupulously honest in all things, and, perhaps for that reason, men did not warm to him. His only dishonest act was to desert from the British army shortly before his seven-year enlistment was due to expire. He did it for fear of being separated from his betrothed, Lillie Reynolds, a domestic servant he met while serving in Dublin. Like Larkin's wife, Elizabeth Brown, she was a Protestant.[29] Connolly's military experience left him with an abiding hatred of the British army; it seemed to be based on a loathing for the institution rather than the way of life, as he retained a keen interest in all things military. Though it would be more than two years before Connolly joined with militant nationalists such as Patrick Pearse to launch the Easter Rising, the two men already spoke the language of the warrior rather than the politician.

In 1913 the links between the ITGWU and militant nationalism were fragile but real. Larkin was sending his eldest son to Pearse's school, St Enda's, and Connolly would do the same when he moved from Belfast to Dublin the following year. When rumours of a tram strike first surfaced, Larkin had assured the public that there would be no stoppages before St Enda's sports day was concluded, and he urged members to use the trams to attend.

Larkin would not have thought much of Pearse's romantic rhetoric, but the similarity of texts and images between Pearse's writings and Connolly's was already striking. In June 1913 Pearse wrote in the school magazine, *An Macaomh*, that staff and pupils should keep before them

> the image of Fionn during his battles—careless and laughing with that gesture of the head, that gallant smiling gesture, which has been an eternal gesture in Irish history; it was most memorably made by Emmet when he mounted the scaffold in Thomas Street, smiling … I know that Ireland will not be happy again until she recollects that old proud gesture of hers, and that laughing gesture of a young man that is going into battle or climbing to a gibbet.[30]

In the *Irish Worker* of 30 August 1913, the day before the proclaimed meeting in Sackville Street was due to take place, Connolly gave his own military perspective on events.

> The employers propose to make general war. Shall we shrink from it; cower before their onset? A thousand times no! Shall we crawl back into

our slums, abuse our hearts, bow our knees, and crawl once more to lick the hand that would smite us? Shall we, who have been carving out for our children a brighter future, a cleaner city, a freer life, consent to betray them instead into the grasp of the bloodsuckers from whom we have dreamt of escaping? No, no, and yet again, no! Let them declare their lockout; it will only hasten the day when the working class will lock out the capitalist class for good and all.[31]

Connolly's imagery may have been more immediate and mundane than that of Pearse, but they shared a willingness to let conflict be the arbiter of the future.

*

However utopian their dreams proved to be, they were infinitely more dynamic than those of John Redmond, who was leading the constitutional nationalists on an increasingly tortuous parliamentary path towards home rule. At a time when everyone else seemed committed to the path of unreason, the British government took comfort in the thought that the traditionally troublesome home rulers were as reasonable as could be. This was doubly fortunate because of the Liberals' dependence in the House of Commons on the eighty-four Irish Party votes. The *sine qua non* of that support was home rule for Ireland. But Redmond was no Parnell, and Herbert Henry Asquith was no Gladstone. Indeed Asquith had no great personal commitment to home rule at all, but he did have grave misgivings over the shape of things to come in Ulster. So had Arthur Balfour, the urbane leader of the Tories, who resigned in despair at the apparent enthusiasm of his own party for civil war. His successor, Andrew Bonar Law, a Scottish businessman but the son of an Ulster Presbyterian, had pledged unconditional support to Carson. The Liberal ministers were understandably nervous when they saw Bonar Law attending mass rallies and publicly endorsing Carson's outrageous paramilitary adventure. Redmond, in turn, was dismayed by senior ministers such as the Chancellor of the Exchequer, Lloyd George, and the First Lord of the Admiralty, Winston Churchill, who made bellicose speeches against the unionists and then tried privately to secure his agreement to the exclusion of Ulster, at least temporarily, from home rule.

Redmond resisted that pressure but shied away from imitating Carson—returning to Ireland and beating the tribal drum. The reasons were partly political and partly a matter of temperament. For unionists such as Carson, home rule spelt political extinction, while for nationalists such as Redmond it represented the dawn of a new age. A man facing a death sentence is apt to react more violently than one who is told that part of his inheritance has been deferred. Carson's temperament also lent itself to the dramatic, to extremes. Redmond was a fine speaker and a selfless patriot, but he lacked iron in the soul.

Redmond was also a diplomat. That was why he was the agreed leader of the Irish Party. His past history as a loyal lieutenant of the dead Chief made him acceptable to the Parnellites, while he had never said or done anything to seriously offend the anti-Parnellite majority. In any case the latter could not agree on a leader among themselves. The divisions within their ranks had left John Dillon as the leader of a rump faction. Among his enemies, Timothy Healy was now an outcast, and William Martin Murphy little better. But both were feared, Healy for his forensic skill as a debater, Murphy for his well-known malevolence and his power as a newspaper magnate.

At first Murphy had welcomed Redmond's selection as leader of the reunited party in 1900, but by 1913 relations between the two men were severely strained. While Murphy was preparing to confront Larkin in August he discovered that a bill he was sponsoring to allow the DUTC power station in Ringsend to supply electricity to Kingstown was being blocked in London by Redmondites. Seven years earlier the same group had foiled Murphy's plans to win the franchise to provide electricity to the city of Dublin. The dominant feeling in the Irish Party was that larger Irish boroughs, despite their administrative shortcomings, should run their own electricity utilities, as did most of the British municipalities—not to mention Belfast. Murphy found his only Irish allies among the unionist MPs, who were delighted at the prospect of the principal nationalist borough being denied ownership of such a symbol of modernity and progress as electrical power. Subliminally it underlined the argument that their Catholic compatriots were not ready for self-government. Murphy dismally told Tim Harrington, a former Lord Mayor of Dublin and the first editor of the *Irish Independent*, that he owed his opponents within the nationalist camp 'nothing but ill-will.' However, he took the opportunity to remind his editor that 'the Healys have always been my friends and ... should at least get the fullest consideration in the matter of reporting.'[32]

In the circumstances it was to be expected that the Irish Party's mouthpiece, the *Freeman's Journal*, would take a somewhat more detached view of the impending industrial struggle than Murphy's own publications. Like the *Irish Times*, which reflected the views of liberal unionists, the *Freeman* warned readers of the dangers of Larkinism but still strove to be accurate and fair in its news coverage.

Redmond kept well above the fray. He rarely visited Dublin and spent most of the summer of 1913 at his home in Aghavannagh, County Wicklow. Dublin, with its socialists, suffragists, Sinn Féiners, Irish-revivalists, and members of the resurgent IRB, was becoming alien ground to constitutional nationalists of the old school. Redmond, who was descended from the comfortable Catholic gentry of County Wexford, had little time for the political intensity of the capital.

Murphy, with his constant attempts to use political influence to promote his own commercial interests, repelled Redmond as well. As a landlord, Redmond was more concerned to maintain access to British markets than to erect protective barriers to suit the clique of businessmen around

Murphy. In 1912 Redmond had actually asked Birrell to amend the Home Rule Bill so that the new Irish parliament would have the power to reduce duties as well as increase them.

On the other hand, Redmond was as worried as Murphy about the financial implications of Lloyd George's new schemes for unemployment benefit and old age pensions. The extension of the free school dinners scheme to Ireland was one of the main social reforms the Irish Party successfully blocked. The Catholic middle class, who formed the backbone of Irish Party support, objected to the increases the dinners would mean on the rates.

Of course Redmond had no objections to social reform in Britain, where the radical wing of the Liberals and the Labour Party were the staunchest supporters of home rule. He also welcomed some socially progressive measures in Ireland, such as the Irish Land Act (1903), as well as modest plans for devolution proposed by the Liberal administration in 1907. But he had had to retreat on devolution in the face of criticism from the more militant members of the home rule movement, who spurned the notion of 'half a loaf'. The business lobby and the Catholic clergy were particularly active in rejecting devolution as inadequate. Businessmen wanted nothing to do with devolution because it offered them no protection from British competition; the clergy feared that the proposed structures would dilute their own power in the area of education.

The clergy were ably assisted by a new organisation, the Ancient Order of Hibernians, which developed as a response to Protestant triumphalism in the North. Like the Orange Order, it used high religious ideals and colourful paraphernalia from a historically dubious past to disguise a murderously atavistic form of communal hatred. However, it was not purely reactionary. It reflected a new assertiveness and self-confidence among middle-class Catholics throughout Ireland. The foundation of the Catholic Association in Dublin, dedicated to overthrowing the traditional predominance of Protestants in business and the professions, was another manifestation of that mood. Such movements drew their inspiration from the martyrology of penal times and the strongest Catholic variants of Irish nationalism.

Ironically, the introduction of social insurance by the Liberals in 1911 gave the AOH a tremendous organisational boost. The National Insurance Act aimed at providing social security for workers and the lower middle class. 'Almost any body of people—from a great life assurance company or a trade union to a friendly society or even a local tennis club—could become an approved society ... so long as it operated the state insurance section of its affairs on a non-profit basis.'[33] As an incentive there was an administration commission of 11d per member per quarter. By 1914 the AOH had 170,000 members in its insurance section, one out of every five insured people in the country. Some Catholic church leaders were apprehensive of the power of the AOH, including the Primate, Cardinal

Michael Logue. Ironically, the absence of sharp sectarian friction outside Ulster ensured that it never established elsewhere the influence it enjoyed within that benighted province. Nevertheless this amalgam of benefit society, sectarian secret organisation and political voting machine made it a force to be reckoned with, even in Dublin, where its national secretary, Councillor John D. Nugent, aspired to a parliamentary seat.

Inevitably its founder and leader, the former Belfast barman 'Wee Joe' Devlin, used the AOH to outvote, shout down and generally intimidate opponents within the nationalist movement. Some of the movement's most distinguished former leaders were silenced or driven into the wilderness. One of them was the irascibly eccentric William O'Brien, who managed to combine a radical stance on some social issues with a conciliatory attitude towards unionists. The AOH now stood ready to reinforce all the most conservative and divisive elements within the home rule movement.

Redmond was no bigot and he knew that Ulster unionists had to be conciliated to make home rule work; however, he was incapable of confronting his own party machine in Ulster. His dilemma in 1913 was that, while he led a national political movement that could regularly elect eighty or more MPs to the British House of Commons, that movement's ability to mobilise the terrified unionist population into armed opposition to home rule far outweighed its own capacity to mobilise nationalists to achieve their long-coveted goal. Rejuvenation of such a ramshackle, disunited coalition as the home rule movement would have been difficult for anyone; it was quite beyond Redmond and his lieutenants, whose youthful energy had been spent a quarter of a century earlier in the service of Parnell. They could still launch into the odd bout of patriotic rhetoric about the right of the Irish people to assert their freedom in arms, but it was an assertion that always carried heavy qualifications.[34]

Carson and his Volunteers provided much more credible role models for a new generation of revolutionaries, such as Pearse and Connolly. Pearse may have drawn his inspiration from Cú Chulainn and ancient Ireland, Connolly from the revolutionary socialism of Karl Marx, but it was the practical example set by Carson that proved the most potent and subversive influence on both.

*

On Saturday 30 August, Connolly was given plenty of time to reflect on such matters, for at 3 p.m. he was arrested by the DMP at Liberty Hall, along with William Partridge. Both men were brought before Swifte and charged with incitement to cause a breach of the peace at the meeting in Beresford Place the night before. Partridge agreed to be bound over and was released on bail; Connolly refused to give any such assurance, or to seek bail. He told the bemused magistrate, 'I do not recognise the English government in Ireland at all. I do not even recognise the King, except when I am compelled to do so.' Swifte told Connolly that he was talking treason and sentenced him to three months' imprisonment.

Meanwhile Larkin, who had been forewarned of the police raid, had gone into hiding.[35]

5

THE police suspected that Larkin had sought refuge with Constance Markievicz at Surrey House in Rathmines. Despite its grand name, this was a typical early twentieth-century semi-detached residence in Leinster Road. Constance Gore-Booth, daughter of a prominent Anglo-Irish family in County Sligo, had married a Russo-Polish aristocrat, Count Casimir Dunin-Markievicz, whom she had met fourteen years earlier in Paris, where they had both been studying art. Each had a small private income from their family to support their eccentric life-style, while social connections in Dublin ensured additional income from portrait work. But by 1913 both their careers and their marriage had wilted. Artists by profession and rebels by temperament, they had gone their separate ways. Con, as she was called by her friends—'Madame' or 'the Countess' to Dublin's working class—'flung herself into politics,' while Cassie became a man about town, theatrical producer, and journalist. His most lasting contribution to Irish society was to help found the United Arts Club.

A daughter, Maeve, had long since been left with Constance's mother to be reared. Through all the troubled times that lay ahead, Cassie and Constance managed to remain friends—perhaps because they spent so little time together. In the summer of 1913, after making his annual visit to the family estate near Kiev, Cassie travelled south to work as a journalist covering the Second Balkan War.

Following her abandonment of polite society, Constance's political pilgrimage was a very deliberate one that embraced nearly all the radical social and political movements of her day. But it could never be said that she 'belonged' to any of them. Her first stop was Sinn Féin, and she served on its executive. The Gaelic League attracted her briefly, but she despaired of ever learning Irish; and while Inghinidhe na hÉireann attracted her by its militancy, it was too small to provide an adequate outlet for her energies. The suffragists, the co-operative movement, even her beloved Fianna Éireann failed to absorb her constant search for excitement and commitment. As a result of her frenetic political odyssey, Surrey House was known far and wide as 'Scurry House', and her efforts to involve Cassie in her adventures no doubt contributed to his decision to go in search of his own—and also to earn some badly needed cash as a war correspondent.

The one cause that Con did not join was the land movement. Perhaps it was because she was a landlord's daughter. However, she did set up a 'co-operative' at Belcamp Park, near Raheny, then one of Dublin's outlying villages. This was used to provide what would now be called 'work experience' for young Fianna boys and give them a badly needed taste of fresh air and good food. The experiment had, regrettably, collapsed, and she had lost £250 in the process.[1] But it was during this unique venture into a form of rural radicalism that she first met Larkin. Many years later she recalled a 'scorching hot day' in October 1910 when she decided to cycle into Dublin for the meeting in Beresford Place organised to welcome Larkin home from prison. She was given a place of honour on the platform.

> Sitting there, listening to Larkin, I realised that I was in the presence of something that I had never come across before, some great primaeval force rather than a man. A tornado, a storm-driven wave. [He was] a man without the trickeries and finickiness of modern civilisation, a Titan who might have been moulded by Michelangelo or Rodin.

Recalling the event ten years later, Markievicz said: 'From that day I looked upon Larkin as a friend, and was out to do any little thing that I could do to help him in his work, but it was only much later that I got a chance to do so.'[2]

She spoke at numerous meetings with him, including the launch of the Women Workers' Union in 1911. It was natural, therefore, that the police would suspect in 1913 that she was harbouring the fugitive, but Cassie inadvertently frustrated their plans. By coincidence, he returned home from the Balkans that Saturday and threw a massive impromptu party for his artistic and theatrical friends. This made a raid by DMP detectives impossible.[3]

*

Besides, the police had more pressing problems. These started around 3 p.m. in the working-class district of Ringsend, little more than a mile from Surrey House. To quote the *Irish Times*, 'the usually peaceful and industrious inhabitants ... took leave of their senses ... and engaged in a wild attack on anybody and everybody who did not agree with them as to the doings of the Larkin gang.'[4] The trouble began outside the new grounds of Shelbourne Football Club. About six thousand spectators had come to watch a match with Bohemians, the team Larkin had accused of using 'scabs'. A picket of about a hundred tramway men stood outside the gate and were jeered by some of the football crowd. The pickets retaliated in kind and were joined by growing numbers of sympathetic locals. 'The members of the Bohemian team, who pluckily drove to the scene of the match on outside cars through a hostile crowd of roughs, were assailed with coarse epithets,' the *Times* reported. The protesters tried to rush the gates. Foiled, they turned their attention to the tramcars that were still bringing people to the match. Stones were thrown and a conductor injured before a driver produced a revolver and the crowd reluctantly let the vehicle through. With typical thoroughness, Murphy had had licences for firearms issued by justices of the peace to DUTC employees. But attacks continued on every tram that ran the gauntlet of Ringsend bridge. A section of the crowd, which now numbered between five and six hundred, decided to march on the nearby DUTC power station. At 4:30 p.m. College Street DMP station received a phone call from an anxious sergeant at the plant appealing for help. Inspector Bannon commandeered a passing tram, put his ten men on board, and headed for Ringsend. By the time he arrived the crowd had quietened and he began shepherding them back towards the centre of Ringsend. He did not get far.

In Bridge Street the crowd coagulated into a mob, with three trams firmly locked in its grip. Bannon and his men were greeted by the challenge 'Come on, and get killed.' It was, noted an *Irish Times* reporter, 'an anxious moment for the inspector.' But his men,

> a fine 'hefty' lot … with sinews like steel were … straining at the leash. Quick came the word of command. 'Draw batons and charge.'
>
> The intervening space was covered in a flash, and the R.I.C. men were romping and revelling in a ding-dong fight with the crowd, who made a mistake in thinking they could swallow up the policemen. The crowd very soon began to get sick, and were easing away, when Inspector Chase and his mounted troop came up at the gallop and scattered people in all directions.

Despite being taken by surprise, the rioters fought back; one desperate individual managed to draw the inspector's sword from its scabbard. 'The sword somehow became jammed between the legs of the officer's plunging horse, and the animal fell, bringing down its rider.' But the crowd was 'well on the run' by now, with people taking refuge in any open doorway. Two pubs were invaded, and rioters pelted the police with bottles and glasses. Further police reinforcements were needed before the pubs could be closed and the crowd subdued. The police suffered four casualties, one of them Inspector Bannon, who was hit by a glass. Sixteen civilians were arrested, including the man who grabbed Chase's sword; he later received five months' imprisonment for his heroics. Over fifty civilians received hospital treatment for wounds, along with two RIC men.

An ominous feature of the rioting was that it was no mere passing crowd of football hooligans who caused the trouble: once fighting broke out, local residents joined in with zest and threw missiles from upstairs windows at the enemy. While the *Irish Times* report reads like something out of the *Boy's Own Paper*, the casualty figures tell a different story. Trouble flared briefly in the area again between 7 and 8 p.m., but by then the focal point of the riots had moved north of the river.

Shortly after fighting broke out in Ringsend, trams running along Great Brunswick Street (Pearse Street), the main thoroughfare linking Ringsend with the city centre, came under fire.[5] A network of small streets and courts ran off it, teeming with working-class families. Archbishop Walsh's secretary, Father Curran, happened to witness the scene.

At every street corner along Brunswick Street there were large groups of people, chiefly women and children of the degraded class, obviously labouring under great excitement. As the tram passed each group they lost all control of themselves and behaved like frenzied lunatics. They shouted coarse language and threats at the tramwaymen, and with violent gestures indicated the fate that awaited the 'scabs', if the 'scabs' fell among them.

The violence was renewed, and increased from time to time, as policemen arrested men and escorted their prisoners along the street. Not only men, but women with hair all dishevelled, and even young girls of 15 or 16, rushed and surged around the police. The women, indeed, almost eclipsed the men with their wild cries, shaking their fists in the very faces of the constables, hitting them on the back and pulling them and their prisoners about. One obsessed creature seized an empty coal bag and belaboured the constable to the utmost of her power.

I saw five or six arrests, and within ten minutes matters went from bad to worse. Cries gave way to more or less violent assault, and assault to attempted rescue.

In the last case I witnessed ... two policemen who made a double arrest were subjected to a very severe mauling ... The mob did not seem to contain more than one striker, and he was more demonstrative than violent. It was composed of the roughest element of the city—people who in my opinion had no concern with the labour trouble.

The restraint shown by the police 'was the only redeeming feature of what was for a Dublin citizen a really humiliating and disgusting spectacle.'[6]

The street was cleared for a time, but trams continued to be stoned, despite heavy police escorts. Local women collected heaps of stones from Clarence Street, where road repairs were being carried out, and brought them to the men and boys on the main thoroughfare 'in apronfuls' for ammunition.[7]

But the real flash-point came shortly before the DUTC's self-imposed curfew was due at 7 p.m. A crowd of 250 blocked the road in front of an *Independent* van that was being escorted by two policemen. In that era of robust industrial relations it was normal practice to stop strike-breaking vehicles, unhitch the horses, and destroy—or distribute—the contents. If the Liffey was convenient, the wagon could end up on the tide. Two policemen were not going to end a tradition, and when they tried, one of them was knocked down and kicked for his trouble. By the time reinforcements arrived from College Street station two men were unhitching the horse and another two had commandeered the wagon. Batons were drawn, stones were thrown, and the fighting spread into adjoining streets, accompanied by the 'shrieks of women, and the cries of little boys and girls in danger from the opposing forces.'[8] A girl, a woman and an old man were among those seriously injured. When it was over, ambulances arrived to carry away the wounded. Great Brunswick Street resembled a battlefield.

The 'battle of the evening', to quote the *Irish Times*, was to take place on the other side of the Liffey, around the Custom House and the surrounding streets. It flared up as the fighting off Brunswick Street degenerated into desultory stone-throwing.

By 8 p.m. a large crowd had gathered outside Liberty Hall. There was no Larkin to address them, and P. T. Daly had taken over as 'organising secretary'. He tried ineffectually to persuade his audience to go home. O'Brien and Daly then locked themselves resignedly inside Liberty Hall to seek refuge from the storm that was about to burst. They were joined by a mixture of staff, shop stewards and terrified passers-by, including about fifty women and girls 'going from faint to faint.'

Not all the inmates were innocent bystanders. An ITGWU official and Labour member of the corporation, Councillor Michael Brohoon, warned Inspector Campbell of the DMP that the building contained a veritable arsenal of weapons. Moments later a detective seized a man outside who was in the act of throwing a stone, and a volcano of missiles erupted from the crowd. Campbell's small force was attacked with bricks, bottles, and broken pieces of sewer piping. Some of the most dangerous missiles, including lumps of cement and bricks, were thrown from the top of Liberty Hall and from the railway bridge that overlooks Beresford Place on the opposite side.

The situation was critical. Campbell and his men had been on duty at Liberty Hall since 3 p.m., when they had helped arrest Connolly and Partridge. At 7:30 p.m. Campbell had sent half his small force of twenty-two constables to Store Street station for refreshment, and he now had to send one of the remaining eleven men for reinforcements. These arrived almost immediately, under Inspector Willoughby. A scratch force of about fifty was assembled, and they baton-charged the crowd. A few of the policemen, under the command of Sergeant Maurice Woulfe, the enormous 'end man' of the DMP tug-of-war team, tried to force an entry into Liberty Hall; but they had to abandon the attempt in order to help colleagues clear Eden Quay, where the rioters fled before the familiar and feared figure of Woulfe.

Harry Nicholls, an engineer with Dublin Corporation electricity department who had gone to Beresford Place to hear the speeches, was 'knocked by a staggering blow between the eyes.' When he tried to take the number of the constable who struck him he was hit with another baton and his pipe smashed. Nicholls was a member of the Church of Ireland but, like his co-religionist Seán O'Casey, took an interest in all things radical. Years later he credited his conversion to republicanism to the batons wielded by constables 33B and 188B that night.[9]

As the police made a second sortie down Eden Quay, a 33-year-old labourer, James Nolan, was knocked to the ground and fatally injured.

Nolan came from the North Strand and, according to the DMP, had been struck by a glass as he emerged from a pub. According to other eyewitnesses it was the police who killed Nolan. Somewhat the worse for drink, they said he had been fleeing towards O'Connell Bridge when a group of three DMP and two RIC men caught up with him. According to Patrick Gilligan, an ITGWU shop steward, one of the DMP constables knocked Nolan to the ground with his baton. Gilligan later told the coroner's court that at the time, the quay was perfectly quiet.

> I saw the blow given to him on the head and heard the sound. Nolan tried to get up … He struggled to his knees and he was struck by several policemen.

Nolan fell to the ground again and lay still. He died in Jervis Street Hospital on Sunday morning.

Patrick Carton, a former tramway worker, said he remonstrated with Inspector Campbell after seeing the attack on Nolan. According to Carton, the inspector replied that there was nothing he could do, 'and that the police were not to be stoned for nothing.'

The fighting now spread across the river. The police cleared Butt Bridge at least twice. Leading the baton charges once again was the formidable figure of Sergeant Woulfe. As usually happens in sustained rioting, the crowd fell back before the batons, only to regroup and resume stoning from a safe distance. The police took advantage of breaks in the hostilities to remove their helmets and enjoy a smoke. RIC members complained loudly to their DMP colleagues that this was not what they had signed up for.

When the police caught up with their tormentors they took their revenge, and even such a pillar of the establishment as the *Irish Times* felt obliged to report that constables found it 'hard to avoid coming into collision with persons who have not actually taken part in rioting.' Among these were large numbers of people trying to reach the cross-channel steamships on the North Wall. Many were English tourists, no doubt terrified at the turn that the last day of their holidays had taken.

Having cleared Butt Bridge, the police chased their tormentors down George's Quay as far east as Moss Street. They also cleared Burgh Quay to the west. The *Irish Times* reported that 'very many of the mob were intoxicated, and were thus full of a false courage.' But they may not have been the only ones. Each of the main police stations in the city had a 'wet canteen', which sold draught stout.[10] Most policemen had been on duty all day, and it would have been a miracle if many of them had not consumed a significant amount of drink on their much-needed breaks.

Certainly the behaviour of the policemen that Lennox Robinson saw suggested they were either drunk, near breaking-point, or both. A middle-class resident of Lower Baggot Street, he managed to dart across Butt Bridge during a break in the rioting. The bridge was deserted, apart from two men leaning against the parapet. He then saw two policemen come over the bridge from the direction of Beresford Place and, without speaking to these men … one of them took one of the men and threw him violently into the middle of the road, so that he fell down. The other policeman struck the other man on the shoulder, or side of the head, with his baton.

A larger contingent of police followed and formed up to charge the crowd on Burgh Quay, pursuing it as far as the Tivoli Theatre. Robinson said the charge was unprovoked, and he followed in its wake to find 'a man lying on the ground with a crowd of people crying out that he was dead.' A cab took the body away, and Robinson resumed his trip to the Abbey Theatre. The man he saw was almost certainly fifty-year-old John Byrne, a labourer like Nolan.

According to another witness, Robert Monteith, the police who cleared Burgh Quay were drunk. Monteith was a civil servant who was sympathetic to the ITGWU and, like Harry Nicholls, interested in radical ideas. He later claimed that he saw Byrne walking quietly along the quay as a mixed group of DMP and RIC passed.

One of the constabulary walked from the centre of the road onto the sidewalk and without the slightest provocation felled the man with a blow from his staff. The horrible crunching sound of the blow was clearly audible fifty yards away. The drunken scoundrel was ably seconded by two of the metropolitan police who, as the man attempted to rise, beat him about the head until his skull was smashed in several places. Then they rejoined their patrol leaving the man in his blood. For saying 'You damn cowards' I was instantly struck across the jaw and shoulder and knocked to the ground, where I had the good sense to lie quietly until the patrol had passed on.[11]

*

While the quays and Beresford Place had now been cleared, there were still large crowds in Abbey Street jeering the police. Further crowds hung on their northern flank at the bottom of Gardiner Street. The area north of Abbey Street and east of O'Connell Street was probably the poorest and certainly the most notorious quarter of the city. Its best-known local industry, prostitution, was based around Montgomery Street, and prostitutes were reported to be among the principal tormentors of the police that night.

Dublin had a higher incidence of prostitution than any other city in Ireland or in Britain. Like so many social problems in the city, it was caused by chronic unemployment, aggravated in this instance by the presence of a sizable military garrison. Because of its prevalence there was little or no resentment of the women in the streets where they lived, much to the despair of respectable citizens, and the churches.[12] The DMP estimated that 1,677 women were earning a living as prostitutes at the turn of the century—2 per cent of the city's female population. And yet this was a dramatic reduction on ten years before, when over four thousand women in the city were prostitutes.

The trend was continuing erratically downwards. It was aided by slum clearance, including the demolition of seven of the most notorious Montgomery Street 'kips' in 1905 and a sustained campaign by groups such as the Society of St Vincent de Paul for the closing of brothels and the rescue of 'fallen women'. But in 1912 there had been a resurgence of the problem, for reasons now unclear. The closure of so many brothels may of course have forced more women to street-walk; and a public scare throughout Ireland and Britain over the evils of the 'white slave traffic' may also have made the police more vigilant. Whatever the cause, there were 1,067 arrests for prostitution in the year before the lockout, or 35 per cent more than the average for the preceding decade. It was an arrest figure to match those of twenty years earlier.

Prostitution took a terrible toll on the health as well as the morals and morale of the community. Sexually transmitted disease was a serious health problem, especially among children, who accounted for 69 per cent of all recorded deaths from syphilis and gonorrhoea. Many physicians were reluctant to list these as a cause of child death, and some experts claim that if the true incidence of sexually transmitted disease had been recorded it would have ranked as a significant factor in infant and child mortality rates, alongside bronchitis, gastro-enteritis, diarrhoea, and pneumonia. It was as much a disease of poverty as any of the others.[13]

The familiarity of these women with the police, and their hostility towards them, is not difficult to understand, living as they did in such conditions and under the constant threat of prosecution. Ironically, the year of the lockout saw a 35 per cent fall in the number of arrests for prostitution, or a return to the norm for the previous decade. Again the reasons are unclear, but no doubt the disturbed state of the city, which kept the police busy with other problems, was a factor.[14]

It was probably inevitable that prostitutes comprised a particularly vocal element among the crowd in Abbey Street. Apart from anything else, a significant part of their regular weekend clientele, the British garrison, was confined to barracks because of the tense situation. The Saturday night crowds that normally thronged Sackville Street and the pubs and shebeens off it now gathered to watch the impending battle. A less willing part of the audience comprised horrified theatre-goers such as Robinson. Instead of emerging into the carefree bustle of a summer's evening, visitors to the Abbey found themselves in the middle of a social war.

By now the DMP Commissioner, Sir John Ross, had also arrived on the scene. He ordered Abbey Street cleared immediately. Batons drawn, the DMP and RIC men charged into a shower of missiles. The fighting flared along Marlborough Street and spilled down North Earl Street into Sackville Street, to the consternation of guests at Murphy's Imperial Hotel. Among the horrified spectators was Handel Booth, businessman, financier, and

Liberal MP for Pontefract, who had come to Dublin with his wife for the Horse Show.

A heavy concentration of police quickly squeezed the mob back into the side streets, but there were casualties. Among them was Robert Monteith's fourteen-year-old daughter, Florence, 'clubbed by a policeman, in Earl Street, and brought home with her long golden hair clotted in blood. She was on a shopping tour and was not taking part in any demonstration,' Monteith wrote later.[15]

Another casualty was Larkin's tormentor, Councillor William Richardson. He later told the Dublin Disturbances Commission: 'I was attacked in practically every street in the north side of the city.' Finally escaping homewards towards Ballybough, he was recognised by a mob on the North Strand. 'A determined attack was made on me and only the use of a stick, which I carried and the presentation of a toy pistol, which the crowd took to be real, enabled me to escape.'

The police kept the crowds moving in Sackville Street to prevent any renewed disturbances, but a steady flood of injured civilians making its way surreptitiously towards Jervis Street Hospital served as a reminder of the nearby fighting. In the twenty-four hours from 8 p.m. on Saturday, the hospital treated over three hundred casualties of the riots.

With the mob denied access to Sackville Street, fighting intensified in Marlborough Street and Talbot Street and along the side streets and laneways leading back towards Gardiner Street and the North Strand. 'A remarkable feature of the encounter', reported the *Irish Times*, was that 'the male rioters, who were mostly of the lowest class, were aided in attacking the police by women from the slum area to the north of Abbey Street, who had come out armed with bottles and stones.' Clinkers, or hard cinders, were also showered on the police. Head Constable McGrath of the RIC told the authorities afterwards that the rioting was the worst he had experienced in thirty-one years and far worse than situations in Belfast, where he had seen the military called out to fire on the mob. But Dublin was not Belfast; the police therefore had to face the music, and they suffered thirty-four casualties in the process, thirty of whom were seriously enough injured to be given extended sick leave.[16]

At last the mob, chanting 'Down with the bloody police,' broke, and the largest remnant of four or five hundred people was pursued into Corporation Street and Foley Street (formerly Montgomery Street). There the fugitives sought shelter in Corporation Buildings, the largest complex of local authority housing in the city. It had 458 flats and housed almost two thousand people. Most of the inhabitants had been rehoused from local tenements, including some of the prostitutes from brothels demolished to make way for the flats. That night rioters seeking refuge from the police mingled with residents taking the air in the traditional Dublin way on the balconies and stairways. When the police entered the street they were quickly forced to retreat before a fusillade in which bottles and stones were augmented by pokers, chamber pots, and other domestic utensils, including the new weapon, clinkers.

The worst fighting of the night still lay ahead. After dispersing 'at least three disorderly mobs' in Upper Gloucester Street (Seán MacDermott Street) and Cumberland Street, Inspector Purcell of the DMP led a mixed force of DMP and RIC men back to Store Street station by way of Corporation Street. This was a regular short-cut, and the earlier attacks that night did not deter him. As Purcell's men marched four abreast down the street, 'a shower of bottles, stones, bricks, jam pots and everything came on us, as if they were waiting until the full body of police came on,' Constable Frith of the DMP recalled later. 'There were women on the top balcony, some of them without shawls, and they looked as if they lived in the buildings, and I saw men in their shirt sleeves.' Some of the attackers cried 'Come on, ye whores—we dare ye!'

The main gates of the flats were locked, but a few policemen managed to open the postern gate, only to be driven back down the narrow stairways by the hail of missiles. On the way out they smashed windows in the caretaker's office and two adjoining flats. The assistant caretaker, Thomas McDonnell, later described how an RIC man 'brandished his baton over his head and screeched as he passed by the windows.' The police finally withdrew at 1:20 a.m., having sustained seventeen serious casualties, half their total losses that night in the north inner city.[17]

Counsel for the two police forces at the subsequent Dublin Disturbances Commission, J. B. Powell, was to reserve his strongest condemnation of the riots for this incident. 'A more inhuman or uncivilised condition of affairs never existed in any city claiming the name of civilisation than that brutal and cowardly attack that was made on the police from Corporation Buildings that night,' he told the commissioners.[18] Of course one of Powell's objectives was to mitigate the behaviour of the police—for retribution would befall the residents of Corporation Buildings before the weekend was over.

Apart from theatre-goers and guests at some of the city's main hotels, most members of respectable society remained oblivious to the day's events. The Phoenix Park Races 'closed a week of brilliant functions,' according to the 'lady correspondent' of the *Irish Times*. Advance autumn fashions were on display, with 'black satin gowns, novel tailor mades with pretty sashes and small velour and felt hats' well to the fore. The local aristocracies of trade and blood rubbed shoulders with the English Beauforts and Churchills. Among them were Viscountess Powerscourt, Viscountess Gormanston, Lady Goulding, Lady Arnott and the Misses Arnott, Mrs Gaisford St Lawrence, and Mrs Dick Maunsell. The majority later motored over to the nearby polo ground in the Phoenix Park, where Lord Aberdeen was presiding at the closing stages of the Open Tournament Cup.

Aberdeen was well aware of the crisis brewing. At 7 p.m. he received a deputation of anxious city councillors who wanted the ban on Larkin's Sunday meeting lifted. He told them that sworn, but unspecified, information had been received that the meeting constituted a public threat. More to the point was his admission that he had no power to rescind the proclamation. Though his was the name at the bottom of the document, the decision was that of the Irish executive. The presence at the meeting of Sir James Brown Dougherty, the Permanent Under-Secretary, underlined the political realities.

After the next day's debacle the political judgment of those who banned the Sackville Street rally would be called into question. Leader-writers would continue to denounce Larkinism; but gradually a different view of the riots would emerge. They would be seen as a spontaneous outpouring of anger by the city's poorest and most oppressed communities. Some of the more perceptive readers would note James Connolly's remarks to the police court on Saturday morning, that 'the labouring classes should be allowed to meet in the street, just as Carson is allowed to meet in Belfast and Redmond in Dublin … We demand the same right for ourselves as other classes.' Any attempt to suppress Sunday's meeting 'would be fraught with disaster.' If 'the restraining hand' of the labour movement's leadership was removed, 'riot and disorder can be anticipated.'[19]

6

TWO men anxious to restore an element of normality to the situation were Michael Brohoon, the Labour councillor for North Dock ward, and William O'Brien, vice-president of Dublin Trades Council. O'Brien was already tired of Larkin's theatrical way of conducting the dispute. Barricaded in Liberty Hall while the fighting surged through the surrounding streets, he and Brohoon became embroiled in an argument with one of Larkin's most devoted full-time officials, P. T. Daly, the president of the ITGWU, Thomas Foran, and Larkin's brother, Peter, about the next day's meeting.

Foran had received a message from Larkin, still in hiding at Surrey House, asking him to acquire a hearse and coffin in which to smuggle Larkin into Sackville Street the next day. 'There's no undertaker in Dublin who would give equipment for such a purpose,' O'Brien said impatiently. The meeting must be abandoned. Peter Larkin objected vehemently to O'Brien's suggestion, but he held no position in the ITGWU or in the Trades Council. O'Brien phoned the Trades Council office in Capel Street and managed to talk to the president, Thomas McPartlin, and several other members who had gathered there.

The invocation of the Trades Council's authority was not unusual in the circumstances. Traditionally it arbitrated in disputes where more than one union was involved; and Larkin's disputes at Eason's, the *Irish Independent* and the DUTC were already beginning to embroil other unions. O'Brien's fellow-officers on the Trades Council agreed that they had to act. O'Brien suggested that a statement be issued to the press calling off the meeting in Sackville Street and that instead the Trades Council call a rally elsewhere in the city. He offered to take responsibility for the decision if there were problems later with Larkin.

Brohoon went out in search of a police officer to inform him of the Trades Council's decision. He returned at about 10:30 p.m. with Inspector Willoughby, who had been in the thick of the evening's fighting. Willoughby was respected by the union leaders as a fair-minded officer who kept his men in line. O'Brien and Brohoon asked him what the attitude of the authorities would be to a meeting in Beresford Place or Croydon Park next day.

Willoughby set off for Store Street station to find out. He phoned the Assistant Commissioner of the DMP, William Harrel, at Dublin Castle, where Harrel was monitoring the situation. Harrel said that the proclamation covered Sackville Street and the vicinity, including Beresford Place, but he had no objections to a meeting in Croydon Park. Willoughby returned with this news, and O'Brien agreed to transfer the meeting to the park. He dictated a statement over the phone to the *Sunday Freeman*. After condemning the police for 'brutally batoning defenceless people in all parts of the city,' the statement said that arrangements for the day were being changed 'in the interests of peace.' All transport workers 'and friends' were asked to assemble in Beresford Place at noon for a march to Croydon Park.

At 2:50 a.m. the newspaper received another statement, this time delivered by bicycle. 'I, James Larkin, intend to hold the meeting at all costs, no matter what the opinion of other Labour men may be, and if any person has notified you to the contrary he, or she did so without my authority.' It is not clear whether Larkin had been warned of O'Brien's statement or had read it in the first edition of the *Freeman*. His own statement appeared in a late edition of that paper and in a 'stop press' of the *Evening Telegraph* published that morning.[1] The conflicting statements can only have added to the general confusion to which Dubliners, and trade unionists in particular, were now reduced.

*

On Sunday 31 August the city awoke to another summer's day, and no doubt many policemen shared the view of Archbishop Walsh's secretary, Father Curran, that a little bad weather might be a good thing. All the Sunday papers published horrific stories of the previous night's events, and anyone who doubted them was invited by the *Evening Telegraph* to examine the scene for themselves. 'Evidence of the fierceness of the encounters with the police were to be seen along Eden Quay in the pools of blood and smears of dry blood on the roads and footpaths.'[2]

The *Sunday Independent* claimed, inaccurately, that the rioting occurred because members of the ITGWU were receiving no strike pay. 'The strikers became desperate, and their temper and disappointment manifested itself in a series of wild attacks on the police.' While these 'poor dupes' were being batoned right and left 'Larkin kept carefully out of harm's way, skulking in some obscure hole or corner, both from the police warrant and the fight into which he had beguiled his followers.' Placed squarely in the centre of the riot reports on the front page was a notice from the DUTC stating that 'three additional cars are running today and the service on the system is working satisfactorily.' Regrettably, it said, cars were still not running after dark.

Another sign of the times was a front-page article in the *Sunday Independent* warning pawnbrokers to look out for fake diamonds. Pawnbrokers would have their acumen tested to the limit in the weeks ahead by the ingenuity of Dublin's slum-dwellers, though few of them would be attempting to pass off fake diamonds.

The Commissioner of the DMP, Sir John Ross, had more pressing concerns than fraudsters that morning. He was at his desk in Dublin Castle to discuss the day's arrangements with Assistant Commissioner Harrel for ensuring that the proclaimed meeting in Sackville Street did not take place.[3] Neither man was popular with the force. Ross, a staunch unionist from County Down and brother-in-law of Viscount Massereene, a leading figure in the resistance to home rule, was a former Coldstream Guards officer who took up the position of Commissioner after retiring from the British army in 1900. A member of the Kildare Street Club and the Royal St George Yacht Club, he personified the Tory establishment in Ireland that home rulers hoped to sweep away. He was, predictably, totally opposed to the transfer of policing to the proposed home rule parliament and made no secret of his opposition to Birrell's policy of trying to govern Ireland 'according to Irish ideas.'

On his appointment as Commissioner, Ross had abolished the competitive examination system that had allowed Catholics in the DMP to compete on equal terms with Protestants for promotion to senior positions. The new interview panel was in effect controlled by Harrel, whose family background was also northern unionist; Harrel's father had been successively DMP Chief Commissioner and Under-Secretary for Ireland.

Inevitably, the new promotional procedures caused significant disaffection in a force of which 80 per cent were Catholics. The disaffection was serious enough for one officer, Inspector White, to write privately to Archbishop Walsh expressing the concerns of his co-religionists. He told the archbishop that in the previous four years only three Catholic inspectors had been promoted to the rank of superintendent; in the same period all four Protestant applicants had been successful. White had no written proof of discrimination, but he told the archbishop that under the old examination system the majority of promotions had gone to Catholics. Ross and Harrel were under the influence 'of a certain Biblical Society having its "home" in D'Olier Street,' White said.[4] This was a reference to the Protestant Defence Association of the Church of Ireland, run by a retired army officer, Captain Robert Wade Thompson, who was also secretary of the Reformed Priests Protection Society and one of Dublin's high sheriffs. Surprisingly, White made no reference to the Freemasons. Protestant members of the force were widely believed to be masons and to use this to manipulate promotions, while Catholics were expressly forbidden to belong to secret societies.

There was nothing Dr Walsh or other leaders of the nationalist community could do for White. To assuage the fears of unionists such as Ross, policing was to remain a reserved function of Dublin Castle after Home Rule was introduced.

*

Over the previous week, Harrel, who was responsible for the day-to-day operations of the DMP, had been in regular contact with the senior British army officer in Dublin, General T. Capper, and his staff. Capper had placed both cavalry and infantry units on stand-by. However, the Commissioner told Harrel that the military 'should not be called upon to intervene until all police resources were exhausted.' To make sure the police could contain the situation, 313 RIC men from as far away as Connacht and Munster had been drafted into Dublin by now, and all holiday leave had been cancelled for the DMP's 1,173 members. A further sixty DMP pensioners and five RIC pensioners had been sworn in for station duties, so that extra DMP men would be available for street patrols.[5]

On Sunday, Harrel allocated 5 superintendents, 9 inspectors, 23 sergeants and 274 constables to Sackville Street. These included 70 members of the RIC. Another ten men under a DMP sergeant were despatched to Beresford Place, with orders to monitor the proposed march to Croydon Park. Harrel briefed the superintendents at the Castle early on Sunday morning and told them to have their men in position in Sackville Street by 11:30 a.m. All the officers had been on duty the previous night, as had most of the rank and file. Harrel knew his men were tired, but he had no choice. The demands the dispute was making on the police were of epic proportions. Since the tram strike began five days earlier, 618 policemen, over a third of those available, had been required daily to give round-the-clock protection to the DUTC's trams, its depots, power station and warehouses.

This was only the beginning. Once the dispute was stepped up the police would have to supply an average of 92 escorts a day for carts and drays, as well as protection for sensitive locations such as the offices of the *Irish Independent*. Before the lockout was over, twenty thousand escorts would be provided. It was probably as well for the officers attending Harrel's briefing in the castle that morning that the future was a closed book.[6]

Whether the effect of the dispute so far on the temper of the police was discussed is not clear. But every superintendent was aware of the constant abuse and occasional missiles issuing regularly and anonymously from hostile crowds that his men were subjected to. The families of DMP men were also being boycotted in many instances, and constables—whose pay ran from 21s to 30s a week—cannot have felt much sympathy for striking tramway men on similar, or even slightly higher, wages.[7]

Harrel had no hard intelligence on Larkin's intentions to give to his subordinates. They had to assume that he would try to redeem his pledge to address the crowd in Sackville Street that day, 'dead or alive.' The Assistant Commissioner's *modus operandi* for crowd control was simple: he divided the street into roughly equal sections, with a superintendent responsible for each one. The superintendents had complete autonomy in deciding how to handle the situation in their own sector.

*

William O'Brien had contacted as many trade union activists as possible that morning and asked them to spread the word that there would be a march from Liberty Hall to Croydon Park.[8] Meanwhile a convoy of fifty wagonettes arrived at the hall. It was shortly before 10 a.m., and the vehicles collected the families of ITGWU members due to go on a Sunday outing to the Glen of the Downs in County Wicklow. The excursion had been organised by Larkin's sister, Delia, general secretary of the Irish Women Workers' Union. It is unlikely that she approved of O'Brien's strategy, and before setting off for County Wicklow her wagon train proceeded up and down Sackville Street. The excursionists sang 'A Nation Once Again' and jeered the police, who were beginning to appear on duty.

Once the cavalcade departed, Sackville Street resumed its normal relaxed Sunday morning air. Church-goers crisscrossed the broad thoroughfare on their way to and from services at the many large Catholic and Protestant churches in the area. In the afternoon they would normally give way to strolling crowds; but from about 12:30 p.m. the numbers in the street 'grew enormously,' according to Superintendent Dunne of the DMP. These included groups of men wearing the Red Hand badge as well as 'respectable people … that came from curiosity.'

Among the 'respectable people' converging on Sackville Street that morning was Thomas MacDonagh, assistant professor of English at University College, Dublin. A future signatory of the 1916 proclamation, MacDonagh was better known at the time as a writer and poet than as a political activist. He had recently married Muriel Gifford, one of four daughters of a Dublin solicitor who had abandoned the family's traditional unionism to become ardent nationalists. MacDonagh's curiosity that morning was probably prompted by the role one of his sisters-in-law, Nellie Gifford, was playing in Larkin's planned appearance on the street. Certainly MacDonagh's timing was almost perfect for the main event of the day.

Earlier, Nellie had gone to Surrey House, where the Abbey actor Helena Moloney and Casimir Markievicz were busy transforming Larkin into a respectable elderly gentleman, complete with Cassie's frock-coat and a false beard. Nellie had booked a room on the first floor of the Imperial Hotel in the name of a deaf uncle, 'Mr Donnelly'. Donnelly's deafness obviated the need for him to speak in his distinctive Liverpool accent. The hotel's location, just below Nelson's Pillar and almost opposite the GPO, was ideal; the fact that it was owned by William Martin Murphy gave added zest to the adventure. The 'Donnellys' arrived at 12:45 p.m., and neither the porter nor other hotel staff paid much attention to the fact that Mr Donnelly's portmanteau and Miss Donnelly's trunk were both initialled with a prominent M.

Meanwhile, a few hundred yards away at Beresford Place, William O'Brien had managed to assemble an estimated ten thousand trade unionists for the march to Croydon Park. The demonstration moved off peacefully at 1 p.m., with the small police detachment bringing up the rear. It was the largest demonstration of trade union solidarity so far for the tramway workers and was conducted 'in a manner that would reflect credit on the workers of Dublin,' the *Freeman's Journal* reported approvingly. The only incident occurred when a group broke away from the main body and attacked a tram at Fairview. Its members were checked by the conductor, who drew a revolver and fired over their heads. The company had wisely decided to suspend services on the route to Croydon Park for the duration of the march. Ominously, when the crowd reached the venue, many of the men cut branches from the trees to arm themselves for the return journey.

O'Brien was keen to emphasise the need for discipline and restraint. Trade unionists should not be downhearted over the police tactics of the night before, he said, because 'extreme measures only showed that the workers were winning.' The president of the Trades Council, Thomas McPartlin, announced that the British labour leader Keir Hardie would be coming to Dublin to address them, and he appealed for strike funds.

Only the guest speaker, William Thompson, vice-president of Belfast Trades Council, struck a militant note. He had always been an advocate of peaceful methods in the conduct of industrial disputes, but the events of the previous night had

> very much altered my views. Owing to the way in which the people were batoned in the streets of Dublin, I now recognise that disciplined forces are required in connection with trade unions—disciplined and armed forces to meet disciplined and armed forces on somewhat equal terms.

He added to cheers that

> the example set ... by Sir Edward Carson and his followers is to be disciplined and practised in arms before entering into their fight; and ... that will have to happen in the case of the workers if they are to win their fight and maintain their place in the times that are ahead of them.[9]

If Thompson's audience needed any further convincing, the police were about to provide them with a lesson in Sackville Street.

*

On their arrival at the Imperial Hotel, Mr Donnelly and his niece were appalled to find that the balcony window of the first-floor suite they had especially requested was blocked by 'a huge window box of flowers.'[10] Shortly afterwards, at 1:20 p.m., the British Liberal MP Handel Booth was assuring his wife that, despite the crowds milling outside, there would be 'no riot, no meeting, no anything,' when a tall man in a false beard rushed past their table and stepped onto the balcony beyond. Larkin's voice was too well known to be mistaken. Even as he shouted, 'I am here today in accordance with my promise,' it was drowned out with cries of 'It's Larkin! It's Larkin!' from the crowd below. He declared that he would stay until he was arrested, but then seemed to think better of it and fled through the dining-room towards the bar and the hotel's rear exit.

Superintendent Dunne had been hunting for Larkin all night. He was now in charge of the police contingent outside the Ballast Office, on the corner of Westmorland Street and Aston Quay. Ignoring Harrel's instructions to maintain order on his own patch, he sent his men racing over O'Connell Bridge as soon as he heard the commotion outside the Imperial Hotel. He then rushed into Hamilton and Long's pharmacy in Sackville Street to phone Harrel; but Harrel had already left his office in the Castle with Ross to walk the half mile to Sackville Street and review the situation at first hand. Both men were ignorant of the dramatic turn events had taken and were now out of contact with their subordinates. Meanwhile Dunne asked the duty officer at the Castle for mounted police reinforcements and for a copy of the arrest warrant for Larkin to be sent to Store Street station.

At the same moment Superintendent Murphy, in charge of a section of police opposite the Imperial Hotel, ran across Sackville Street to the hotel's entrance. The crowd surged forward, and Superintendent Kiernan, in charge of the policemen immediately outside the hotel, ordered a group of constables down from the northern side of the building to block the hotel entrance, before he also entered the hotel in pursuit of Larkin. By then Murphy had run up the main stairs and was told by a guest in the dining-room that Larkin had fled towards the bar. The two men met outside the plate room. Murphy asked Larkin to come quietly; Larkin told him, 'I have succeeded in doing what I said I would do. I have spoken to the people.' As they descended the stairs together to the main hall they met Superintendent Kiernan, Inspector McKeag, and a group of ten policemen, all of whom had entered the building looking for Larkin. The labour leader suddenly realised he had lost his hat, or rather Casimir Markievicz's hat, and there was a brief delay as the police searched unsuccessfully for it.

Outside, the small police guard left at the hotel entrance by Superintendent Kiernan was growing nervous. Constance Markievicz, her husband and another of MacDonagh's sisters-in-law, Sydney Gifford, had arrived in a brake to see the excitement. Markievicz called for three cheers for Larkin, and there were angry shouts as policemen forced the brake into a side street—all of which brought still more people pressing towards the Imperial Hotel to see what was going on. According to Sergeant Richard Butler, in charge of the six policemen left guarding the door, in the few minutes that elapsed between Larkin's speech and his re-emergence from the Imperial Hotel under arrest the crowd outside had grown from three hundred to three thousand. This probably says more about the sergeant's state of mind than about the size of the crowd or the magnitude of the threat it posed. When a large window in Clery's department store (also owned by William Martin Murphy) was smashed a few feet away, Butler told his men to drive the crowd back. 'I did not order them to draw batons,' he told the Dublin Disturbances Commission later, 'but they drew their batons themselves, when they saw the crowd rushing up, hissing, brandishing sticks and rushing over to the hotel door.' He described the crowd as 'men apparently of the labouring or trader classes.' As they fled 'they were knocked down by striking against one another.'

The crowd scattered panic-stricken in all directions. Many tried to run into the dead end of Prince's Street, opposite the hotel, which had narrow laneways leading off into Abbey Street and Henry Street, but it was blocked by a force of twenty-four constables and three sergeants posted across the entrance under Inspector Andrew Lawlor. Their main task was to protect the offices of the *Nation* and *Freeman's Journal*, as well as the rear of the *Independent's* premises, which backed onto the street. Like other officers, Lawlor had joined the hunt for Larkin as soon as the latter appeared on the balcony of the hotel. He left Sergeant Richardson of the DMP in charge with an instruction that 'the respectable part of the people are to be allowed to pass through,' but 'the rough class' are to be 'forced back.'

One of the respectable citizens was Harry Bristowe, manager of the Northern Bank in Upper Sackville Street. He and his wife were returning from church service and making their way up the relatively clear west side of Sackville Street towards the Metropole Hotel when the crowd suddenly recoiled from the police batons outside the Imperial. The couple were nearly knocked over, but an RIC man attached to Richardson's group pulled them out of the crush. The Bristowes found themselves among a small beleaguered group who sheltered behind the police line while people were being batoned a few feet away. 'They got a fair tap,' Bristowe recalled later, referring to the trapped crowd. 'A couple of them fell … but picked themselves up.'

Guests in the Imperial Hotel had a better view of events. William Croft, a man in the lubricating oil business who was a permanent resident of the hotel, had seen Larkin address the crowd from the dining-room. He recalled later that many of the people outside 'did not seem to appreciate the seriousness of the whole thing.' He added that 'the majority of the baton work was just by the corner of Prince's Street.' Here a section of the crowd was trapped between the advancing tide of police from the Imperial Hotel and Sergeant Richardson's line.[11]

Handel Booth described it as 'an ordinary Sunday crowd. They were … bewildered and did not know which way to turn.' Lapsing into the political hyperbole to which he was prone, he lamented that 'the noble street was in the hands of the most brutal constabulary ever let loose on a peaceful assembly.' The police behaved

> like men possessed. Some drove the crowd into side streets to meet other batches of the government's minions wildly striking with truncheons at every one within reach … The few roughs got away first; most respectable persons left their hats and crawled away with bleeding heads. Kicking victims when prostrate was a settled part of the police programme. Three such cases occurred in a direct line with our window.[12]

As the police finally emerged from the Imperial Hotel with their prisoner, Constance Markievicz rushed up and shook Larkin's hand, saying, 'Goodbye, good luck.' She later wrote:

> As I turned away an Inspector on Larkin's right hit me on the nose and mouth with his clenched fist. I reeled against another policeman, who pulled me about, tearing all the buttons off my blouse, and tearing it out all around my waist. He then threw me back into the middle of the street, where all the police had begun to run, several of them kicking and hitting me as they passed.[13]

The officers in charge of Larkin—Superintendents Murphy, Kiernan, and Dunne—seem to have mistaken the people recoiling from the police batons at Prince's Street for a mob trying to rescue Larkin. They simultaneously discovered that the route they had intended taking along Abbey Street to Store Street station was now blocked by another hostile crowd, probably drawn to the fighting from the north city slums, where the police had fared so badly the night before. Superintendent Murphy ordered the arrest party to make its way over O'Connell Bridge to College Street station and ordered every other policeman in earshot to drive the crowd back.[14]

Constance Markievicz reported that she

> saw a woman trying to get out of the way. She was struck from behind by a policeman with his baton. As she fell her hat slipped over her face and I saw her hair was grey ... I saw a barefooted boy with papers hunted and hit about the shoulders as he ran away.

Markievicz was struck across the face with a baton before some men pulled her out of the crowd into a house in Sackville Place. She said that one of the policemen who struck her 'smelt very strongly of stout, and ... they all seemed very excited.'[15]

Thomas MacDonagh had by now sought refuge in the *Freeman's Journal* offices, having abandoned his bicycle in Prince's Street. From the window he later told the Disturbances Commission that

> I saw the police batoning the people and striking them on the head ... I saw sometimes three policemen attack a single individual. I saw them attack an old woman with a shawl over her head and baton her brutally. I saw them attack a small man who had lost his hat ... I heard the continual rapping of batons on people's heads.

Constance Markievicz and Thomas MacDonagh were hardly disinterested witnesses. But William Francis O'Donnell was precisely the sort of respectable businessman who would look to the police for protection in normal circumstances. He was a partner in the outfitting firm of Frewen and Ryan in Sackville Street, and on Sunday 31 August he had travelled there on one of William Martin Murphy's trams to collect his post.

He bought a copy of the *Sunday Freeman* from a news stand in North Earl Street and, after collecting his post, set off up the west side of Sackville Street for lunch with some priests in the Catholic Club. He paid little attention to the crowds or the cheering until he was 'driven by a stampede to Prince's Street … I found myself wedged closely in Prince's Street, and I should say I was about a yard from the Metropole side entrance.' However, the pressure from the crowd was too great for him to reach the safety of the Metropole. 'We were like herrings in a box,' he recalled. After trying unsuccessfully to help a woman he saw trampled by the crowd, O'Donnell tried to save himself.

> I looked around and I would not like to see a cinematograph of the scene with my greatest enemy in it … I was surrounded by a forest of batons … I looked out for a friendly face from C Division [Store Street]. I could not see a face I recognised. If I had seen some of the C Division, some would perhaps have known me and I would have escaped; but they were all strangers … I put my hands up. I was anything but militant. A constable made a dive for me, and I said—'Oh! for Christ's sake have you no mercy?' or 'In the name of Christ are you going to kill me?' It is not a time one would choose tea-table words. He made a dive, I swerved, and I partly got into the arms of another policeman. The next thing happened was—I got a bash on the head … I was partly thrown on the ground and I got a stroke on the back, and went down a second time.

By now O'Donnell had raced the police gauntlet as far as the GPO. He was then struck with batons a third time, on the back and on the leg, before struggling clear, all the time begging for mercy. His clothes, from his vest to his coat and trousers, were saturated in blood, as the Dublin Disturbances Commission was to see when he produced them in evidence five months later. O'Donnell walked to Jervis Street Hospital for treatment after being turned away from an ambulance in Sackville Street because it was already full of more seriously injured civilians.

Another horrified middle-class witness of the baton charges was Thomas Patton, a barrister. He testified at the commission to

> police using their batons all the time. They used them with great force, and, almost invariably, on the heads of people. I saw two policemen single out an individual, rush after him and baton him. I saw one man standing at the corner of Prince's Street—at the Post Office side—he was a small man … There were … I think three policemen around him. He could not move in any direction and, time after time, they struck him across the head with their batons. I should say that the demeanour of the crowd, before these charges took place, seemed to me to be quite respectable. I did not see any disturbance, or riot, or any attempt at disturbance or riot.[16]

O'Donnell was to receive a formal apology from Inspector Willoughby of the DMP for his treatment, but it was a courtesy extended to few. The playwright Seán O'Casey was among those caught in the terrified crush in Sackville Street that day, and in his autobiography he retells how he watched one wounded Larkinite 'pushed, shoved and kicked by constables ... to jail.'[17] O'Casey himself was saved from a severe beating only by the intervention of Inspector Willoughby of the DMP, a fellow-member of the Church of Ireland who knew his mother.

*

Somewhere between four hundred and six hundred civilians had been injured in Sackville Street in the course of a few minutes. Only forty people were arrested. All those taken prisoner had addresses in an area bounded by Corporation Street, Gloucester Street, Foley Street, and Buckingham Street, where the rioting had been fiercest the previous night. In contrast, those treated at Jervis Street Hospital immediately after the riot show a much wider range of addresses, with only about a quarter living in the immediate vicinity. This suggests that the crowd in Sackville Street was far from homogeneous; but it also suggests that the police knew whom they were arresting, as opposed to whom they were batoning.[18]

The most celebrated arrest was of course Larkin's. While mayhem broke out behind, he was escorted by Superintendent Murphy, Superintendent Kiernan and thirty other policemen across the Liffey to College Street station. A crowd gathered outside, and the station was surrounded by fifty policemen with drawn batons, but there were no serious incidents. Larkin was accommodated first in an inspector's office and then in the sergeants' mess room, where he declined the offer of a meal.

He was in good spirits. After the stress of recent days he had done what he had promised his followers he would do: address them in Sackville Street. At about 3 p.m. he was conveyed to more appropriate accommodation, a cell in the Bridewell. He was taken there in a covered taxi, so that the crowds would not recognise him. He was still wearing Casimir Markievicz's morning-suit, and the police had finally retrieved the missing silk hat in the hall of the Imperial Hotel, so that Larkin made the journey across the city in the full regalia of a bourgeois.[19]

*

As so often with crowd events, much had happened in the space of a few minutes. Commissioner Ross and Assistant Commissioner Harrel had arrived in Sackville Street as the baton charges began. They took shelter in Butler's pharmacy as the panic-stricken tide of humanity bore past. Harrel used the proprietor's phone to call belatedly for reinforcements of mounted police. However, by the time the officers emerged from the shop the street was clear of all but the police and the injured, who now littered the wide thoroughfare. The baton charges had lasted less than five minutes. From the time Larkin appeared on the hotel balcony to the last arrests no more than fifteen minutes had elapsed. By the time Father Curran arrived on the scene from the archbishop's palace a mile away not a trace of the disturbance was to be seen. There were great numbers of police engaged in moving people from the Pillar beyond the tram offices, but no excitement.[20]

It is difficult to imagine what the outcome of the Sackville Street disturbances would have been if O'Brien and the other Trades Council leaders had not lured thousands of trade unionists away to Croydon Park. Certainly the crowd would have been larger and more militant. Whether it would have been big enough and militant enough to deter the police, or beat them off the streets, we will never know. If the police had been worsted, the army would have been on hand to restore order, but at what cost? What is certain is that O'Brien and his colleagues, for all their revolutionary rhetoric, had a very different attitude to the conduct of class warfare from Larkin, or indeed O'Brien's own hero, James Connolly. If either man had been free to organise the day's events their course would have been very different, and almost certainly bloodier.

As it was, the events in Sackville Street had shown incredible incompetence by the police. Casimir Markievicz quickly dubbed 31 August 'Bloody Sunday', comparing the police riot to the shooting of over a hundred Russian workers during a peaceful protest outside the Winter Palace in St Petersburg on 22 January 1905.

*

As on that much bloodier occasion, the question must be asked, was there any need for violence? Almost all witnesses of the 'police riot' agreed that the crowd was peaceable and composed mainly of curious onlookers, church-goers and Sunday strollers going about their lawful business.

From their own evidence to the Dublin Disturbances Commission, it is clear that many police officers were preoccupied in trying to forestall trouble by finding and arresting Larkin. The publicity that would arise from arresting such a celebrated malcontent may also have affected their priorities. It was Sergeant Butler who initiated the first baton charge to clear the entrance of the Imperial Hotel, while his own superiors, Superintendent Kiernan and Inspector McKeag, were inside hunting Larkin. It was Sergeant Richardson who had charge of the constables in Prince's Street, where the worst incidents occurred. Superintendent Murphy, who was in charge of that sector, was the officer who first found and arrested Larkin in the hotel. Richardson's own immediate superior, Inspector Lawlor, had followed Murphy into the hotel. In effect, the fateful decision to baton the crowd devolved on these two sergeants.

Afterwards much of the obloquy for what happened fell on the RIC, who were unfamiliar with the city, its people, and its ways. There is no evidence to support this assessment. Assistant Commissioner Harrel told the Dublin Disturbances Commission that no more than seventy of the police on duty in Sackville Street were members of the RIC and that all of them were under the orders of DMP officers. About half the police at Prince's Street may have been RIC men, but they were under the orders of Sergeant

Richardson of the DMP. Harrel also told the commission that no more than seventy policemen actively participated in the baton charges, and these were all men appointed to the central sector of Sackville Street, around the Imperial Hotel. The truth is that the DMP behaved as badly as their country cousins. Like most myths, the tale of RIC brutality survived because it was a convenient one that shifted at least some of the blame from the DMP.

Even the employers' apologist, Arnold Wright, could do little to justify the behaviour of the police.

> Harassed and fatigued, with minds still fresh with the vivid impressions of the previous night's savage onslaughts of the mob, it is not wonderful that some of them temporarily lost their tempers. Their conduct, of course, was inexcusable if judged by the strict principles of duty; but they were, after all, only men ...[21]

That outburst of temper transformed the situation. Public opinion was outraged. The impact of the strikes, the riots and the dislocation they caused could no longer be confined to the city's back streets and ghettoes. Seán O'Casey wrote:

> The dust and mire in which the people lived and died were being sprinkled everywhere. It drifted onto the crimson or blue gold braided tunics of the officer; on to the sleek morning coat and glossy top hat of the merchant and professional man; on to the sober black gown and grey curled wig of the barrister and judge; on to the rich rochet of immaculate surplice and cocky biretta; on to the burnished silk and lacquer-like satin frocks and delicate petticoats of dame and damsel. Those who loved where lilacs bloomed in the doorway, where the dangling beauty of laburnum draped itself over the walls, where many a lovely, youthful rose crinkled into age, and died at last in peace, where three parts of the year was a floral honeymoon—here the dust and mire came too, and quiet minds knew ease no longer.[22]

A few people remained immune, including, curiously enough, some Catholic clergymen. Perhaps exposure to the poverty and violence of the slums in small, controlled doses over the years had inoculated them against the horror it evoked in others. Father Healy, a priest from Dalkey, wrote to Dr Walsh in France that Dublin was enduring 'a veritable reign of terror ... Our only hope of salvation lies in a policeman's baton.' He blamed the government for its supineness and eagerness 'to keep the peace at any cost.'[23] His attitude may have been hardened by the series of attacks during the previous week on the Dalkey trams.

*

Batons had to be supplemented by bayonets as news of the events in Sackville Street spread across the city. By 5 p.m. rioting had broken out in the Liberties, Inchicore, Clanbrassil Street, Aungier Street, the north quays between Chancery Street and North Queen Street, and the south quays around Moss Street. Fighting also resumed in the north city, which had seen the worst of Saturday night's fighting. The outbreak of hostilities coincided with the return of thousands of trade unionists to the city from William O'Brien's meeting in Croydon Park.

The trouble began on the North Strand at about 2:30 p.m. Two RIC men lodging in a house in Strandville Avenue sauntered out onto the North Strand just as 'a vast crowd' poured down from Fairview. News of the events in O'Connell Street had already reached the marchers. As soon as they saw the two constables, men broke ranks and pursued them over Newcomen Bridge towards the Five Lamps. The RIC men were cornered and beaten with sticks until Robert Gregory, who worked as a tailor in Capel Street, ran out into the Strand and, with commendable courage, pulled them into his home at number 162. The house was besieged and several windows smashed before a rescue party arrived for the RIC men.[24]

A few stone-throws away, rioting resumed in the Gloucester Diamond, Gardiner Street, and North Earl Street. Dockers swarmed up from the North Wall area to join in. Assistant Commissioner Harrel requested cavalry from Marlborough Barracks (McKee Barracks) to clear the streets, but mounted DMP and other police managed to restore order even as the cavalrymen trotted down O'Connell Street and formed up at the Pillar. By 4:30 p.m. most of the rioters had been dispersed, and a group of police under Sergeant Haugh of the DMP escorted the last group of five bloodied prisoners from Gloucester Diamond to Store Street station. As the tattered group passed Corporation Buildings, women on the balconies called the police murderers and told them not to ill-treat the men. A big RIC man raised his baton in response and said, 'By the living Jesus, we'll be back here again.'

Shortly afterwards, Haugh returned with about ten constables and entered the buildings by the main gate. Simultaneously, Sergeant Woulfe entered by the postern gate with another group of ten constables. According to Haugh, the reason for the invasion was information that a police messenger had been attacked near the building an hour earlier. Woulfe said there had been a report that a new riot was in progress. Either way, it was a markedly suspicious group that gathered, some of the policemen in civilian clothes. They succeeded in taking the enemy by surprise as they swept onto the balconies of the north block, smashing windows and doors. Five arrests were made; but that was not the main object, which was to terrorise the inhabitants. As Haugh admitted to the Dublin Disturbances Commission five months later, the only options for the police were 'to clear the place and arrest the rioters, or else abandon that part of the city.' The proximity of the flats to Store Street, together with its poverty-bred problems, generated regular confrontations with the police. Sergeant Woulfe was a regular visitor and boasted of arresting no less than twelve husbands in the flats the previous Christmas for wife-beating.

There were 216 families in the north block—over a thousand people, the majority of them children. Residents of the larger south block, which ran parallel to it on the opposite side of the courtyard, watched events with a mixture of horror and anger. William Behan, a retired Irish Lights pensioner, saw the police come in.

> They charged up along to the front entrance on the opposite side to us, and up the stairs with their batons drawn. I went in when I saw the batons. I knew something wrong was going to happen then … They were more like madmen than Christians.

Having smashed the windows, the policemen broke in the doors and then re-emerged from the flats to throw clothes and furniture into the courtyard below. A few men tried to resist the police invasion, but most residents fled or locked themselves in the tiny toilets while they listened to the sound of their homes being smashed. But many did not escape so lightly. John McDonagh, who was paralysed, was assaulted as he lay in his bed. When his wife intervened she too was beaten. McDonagh was removed to hospital 'in a dangerous condition,' and subsequently died. Mary Lennon saw her daughter dragged by the hair from a toilet before both women were badly beaten. Frances May was spared a beating, but the sewing-machine she was buying on hire purchase was smashed with a hammer. In the flat below the police broke the windows, scattering glass over a child in bed, and then wrecked the family altar.

The sight of religious pictures and altars seemed particularly to infuriate the police. Most of the altars consisted of little more than a few candles and chalk statues. These were mainly in the slightly more prosperous and 'respectable' homes. Ironically, it was these tenants, who had managed to save enough to buy a proper bed or a few delph cups and saucers, who suffered most from police vandalism. As Ignatius Rice, the corporation's solicitor at the Disturbances Commission, put it later,

> damage to the household goods of these people is a very much more grievous thing than damage to property belonging to persons in better positions … They find it hard to make ends meet. Their little sticks of furniture they gathered together with infinite toil … [and] can only be repaired after long and difficult struggle later on.

Rice was anxious to lay the blame for what had happened on the police, because the corporation was claiming compensation. It would subsequently present Ross with an extensive bill for repairs to the buildings, including £12 10s for 1,000 feet of glass, 17s 4d for two hundredweight of putty, and £6 4s 2d for glaziers' wages.

Even the corporation rent office was attacked. When the caretaker appealed to Woulfe to stop his men, the sergeant replied, 'I don't give a damn, we're driven to it.' In fact the residents of the south block had by then set up quite a barrage of missiles across the square. Sergeant Woulfe, who had detached most of his men to escort prisoners back to Store Street, became separated from the rest. He made his way the few yards to Talbot Street, only to be stoned by a crowd of forty or fifty. Several men got behind him and knocked him down; he was then beaten with a golf club. Dazed and badly cut about the head, he was dragged by someone into a pharmacist's shop. The crowd was so angry that it stoned the car of Dr Dallas Pratt, the DMP doctor, when he arrived to take Woulfe to Jervis Street Hospital.

At his office in the Lower Castle Yard, Assistant Commissioner Harrel only gradually became aware of the scale of the rioting. The first sign of trouble was the arrival of injured policemen from the nearby Cornmarket, who reported that crowds were stoning the trams. A crowd of 400, armed with bottles, bricks, and stones, had come out of Francis Street and was blocking the line. One policeman who had been badly injured escorting a tram had been rescued by a priest in St Audoën's; the mob stoned the presbytery until the reinforcements sent by Harrel scattered them. Fourteen policemen were injured in the area, some of them seriously. Harrel commandeered a motor car in Dame Street to begin ferrying some of the most seriously injured policemen to hospital.

*

The next area where trouble erupted was Aungier Street. Again tramway crews and their police escorts were the main target. One conductor was kicked to the ground, robbed of his fare pouch with £3 in it, and saved from worse only by the intervention of 'two ladies', who reprimanded the crowd. The disturbances were concentrated around the ITGWU hall, where an impromptu protest meeting was taking place over the earlier baton charges in Sackville Street. It took a mounted DMP patrol to clear the tram tracks.

At Inchicore the situation was even worse. Thirty-four of the forty-three tramway men at the DUTC depot had joined the strike, the largest number in any part of the city. They now had the premises blockaded, with the support of a large crowd of local people. Only a sergeant and two constables were on duty. The sergeant, Kincaid, arrested a striking tram driver who was inciting the crowd to burn the depot down. The three policemen then tried to take their prisoner back to Kilmainham station. They managed to get as far as the Emmet Hall, but as luck would have it, local Labour councillors had organised a meeting at the premises to protest against police brutality, and this had converted itself into a mass picket to block the tram tracks. Two trams were caught in the protest, and when Kincaid arrived on the scene with his prisoner, the arrest party was attacked. Kincaid was beaten unconscious and spent the next month in hospital. His two constables fled; one found refuge in Richmond Barracks (Keogh Barracks), and the other, though badly beaten, managed to escape the mob by running through a house. With no reinforcements available, Harrel contacted General Capper, who agreed to turn out the West Kent Regiment, which was based at Richmond Barracks.

Once the military restored order, the police returned to Inchicore in force. They entered the Emmet Hall and badly beat two Labour councillors. One was the ITGWU organiser William Partridge; the other was Richard O'Carroll, secretary of the Brick and Stonelayers' Society and leader of the Labour group on Dublin City Council, who had earlier addressed the rally in Croydon Park. Supported by soldiers, the police now raided homes in Emmet Road and its side streets, repeating on a smaller scale the havoc wrought at Corporation Buildings earlier in the day. Among the casualties was another Labour councillor for Inchicore, Thomas O'Hanlon. It was after midnight before peace finally returned to the city.

*

One of the most striking features of the rioting was the ability of often very small numbers of police to contain and disperse large crowds. Patrols as small as ten or twelve policemen frequently dealt with crowds of three or four hundred. This suggests that, contrary to the claims of Murphy's newspapers, there was little or no organisation behind most of the demonstrations. Another surprising feature of the riots is that they did not result in more deaths. Even the testimony of hostile commentators, such as Father Curran, suggests that much of the violence was verbal and that members of the middle class, such as himself, were more alarmed at the violent pretensions of the crowd than by the action it took.

Nevertheless, Dublin had seen nothing like it for more than a generation. Blood had been shed on a considerable scale, most of it that of the strikers and their supporters. A total of 325 people were treated at Jervis Street Hospital in the twenty-four hours up to 8 p.m. on Sunday 31 August and another 108 at other city hospitals. Over a hundred more would be treated by hospitals as the result of further riots around Redmond's Hill and Capel Street on Monday night. Certainly many more casualties were dealt with by GPs and local dispensaries, not to mention those who, out of poverty or fear, relied on relatives and friends to care for them.

Apart from the thirty policemen injured sufficiently to go on the sick list after the fighting in the north city on the Saturday night, it is difficult to establish how many police were injured over the weekend. However, Commissioner Ross did provide the Dublin Disturbances Commission with detailed police casualty figures for the period from 27 August to 17 November, and it can be assumed that the bulk of these occurred between the outbreak of rioting at Ringsend on Saturday afternoon and the riots at Redmond's Hill and Capel Street on 1 September. The DMP suffered 174 casualties and the RIC 81, a total of 255. Of the DMP casualties, 122 men continued on duty without medical treatment, 12 received treatment while remaining on duty, and 40 went on sick report. The RIC breakdown showed that 69 men remained on duty without medical treatment, 3 received treatment while remaining on duty, and 9 went on sick report. However, two DMP men were injured twice, in two separate riots; one RIC man was injured in three riots; and six RIC men were injured twice in

separate riots. This brings the number of policemen injured t
and 73 RIC.

If the DMP returns are taken for 1913 as a whole they sh
constables were ill as a result of being hurt on duty, out of a total strung
of 1,173. While this is high, it is not very much worse than 1912—also a
year of protracted labour troubles—when 865 constables were absent from
duty under the same heading. In contrast, only 431 men were out under
this heading in 1914, when the main threat to public order came from the
Irish Volunteers. As in Belfast, the creation of paramilitary formations
under middle-class leadership appears to have reduced the danger of
disorder, at least in the short run.

There was one police fatality arising from the lockout. This was Sergeant
Morris of the DMP's mounted police force, who was seriously injured
during rioting in Townsend Street on 21 September. He returned to duty a
month later but was frequently out sick; he contracted pneumonia while
giving evidence to the Dublin Disturbances Commission in January 1914,
and died on 1 February. It is an attenuated martyrdom, but so were some
of those claimed on the other side.

Perhaps the most serious casualty of the weekend's events was the
reputation of the DMP. Ignatius Rice summed up the feelings of many
middle-class citizens when he said that

in normal times, under normal conditions, the police force of Dublin is
an efficient force and a satisfactory force—a credit to itself and to the
citizens. But in the days in question … their temper and their self-
restraint broke down under the strain, and … in consequence of that
fierce excitement, they lost all respect they would otherwise have—all
the respect due to property and person and life and limb.[25]

While it was the police baton charges in O'Connell Street that attracted
condemnation from the wider public, in working-class areas of Dublin it
was the attacks on Corporation Buildings and the houses in Inchicore that
excited the greatest anger. The police, never popular in working-class
districts, were now openly avowed class enemies. That feeling would find
an outlet in the Irish Citizen Army.

7

THE reaction of the *Irish Independent* to the weekend's events was predictable. On Monday 1 September it declared that

a deliberate attempt is being made to establish a reign of ruffianism in the city. Out of the reeking slums the jail birds and most abandoned creatures of both sexes have poured to vent their hatred upon their natural enemies, the police. Strikers there are amongst them. But the legions of the work-shy have not, we may be sure, emerged from their hiding place to put up a fight for any claims of labour, legitimate or the reverse. They are out for devilry and loot.[1]

The *Irish Times* described the weekend as

an orgy of lawlessness and cowardly crime. In the worst streets of the city women assisted men in assaults on the police.

While it accepted that the innocent had suffered from police action as well as the guilty, the *Times* agreed with the *Independent* that

there is a 'hooligan' and criminal element in every large city. Prolonged incitements to disorder and deliberate appeals to class hatred are bound, sooner or later, to have such results as those which we now deplore.

Nevertheless it felt that

in one sense these deplorable riots are a good omen. They indicate that the strike tyranny under which Dublin has groaned for so many months is coming to the end of its tether. So long as the labour agitators were able to terrorise honest workmen into craven submission, and to bully a rather timid set of employers, the organisers were, as we say in Ireland, 'on the pig's back.' Every successful strike, no matter how it disorganised industry, was claimed as another victory for 'the cause of Ireland.' The most complicated of all economic problems was going to be solved by the simple process of holding a bludgeon over the head of capital. Capital, at long last, has got tired of this ruinous performance. The fine stand made by the Dublin United Tramways Company has put heart into the whole city.

The *Times* predicted that other employers would follow the DUTC's example.

> The industry of the city is about to revise in very drastic fashion the half-hearted and apathetic policy which has cost it so much. We do not say that labour has no real grievances in Dublin, or that employers would not be wise to reconsider their attitude to its fair demands. We do say that events of the last few days have shown that the strike organisers are men who will lead the workers of Dublin to nothing but poverty and disaster ... We believe that the present tyranny has received its death blow, and that its dupes will soon return to the normal sanity of the Irish working man.

Only the *Freeman's Journal* seemed to accept that the responsibility for the weekend's events could not be laid primarily on the shoulders of the city's hooligan element, or its socialist tyrants. Its stance reflected the outrage of city councillors—the great majority of them home-rule nationalists—at the behaviour of the police, as well as the antipathy felt by Redmondites generally towards Murphy and all his works—particularly the *Freeman's* rival, the *Independent*. The *Freeman* gave prominence to an announcement by the Lord Mayor, Lorcan Sherlock, at that day's meeting of the city council that he intended proposing a public inquiry into the conduct of the police.

The *Freeman's Journal* was also the only paper to publish a letter by the militant pacifist and argumentative but gifted journalist Francis Sheehy-Skeffington defending the strikers. Sheehy-Skeffington contrasted the 'columns of abuse' in the city's press with the 'widespread public sympathy' for the strikers. The fundamental issue, he argued, was trade union recognition. Employers were prepared to tolerate only the old type of craft union that confined itself

> to one branch of industry, and, where possible, to the employees of a particular firm. It must conduct its negotiations with the employer in a kid-glove fashion and allow itself to be easily diverted from its ostensible purpose of protecting the worker by all sorts of irrelevant considerations—by cant about 'Irish industries,' about 'the prestige of the city,' about 'the glories of Horse Show Week,' and so forth. It must never, or hardly ever, declare a strike—certainly not without giving the employer long enough notice to enable him to beat it; and never, never a sympathetic strike.
>
> Now this attitude, in the present stage of the evolution of industry is equivalent to a ban on Trade Unionism altogether. For the old fashioned trade union has served its purpose, and its days of usefulness are over. By combining individual workmen it enabled them to contend on something like equal terms with the individual employer. But as soon as the employers themselves began to combine, the isolated Trade Union began to lose its power. Federations of employers—open or secret—to

keep up prices and keep down wages, are now the rule. In a contest with these ever extending federations, the isolated Trade Union is as powerless as was of old the individual workman against the individual employer. The only resource left to the worker, if he is to contend on even approximately equal terms with the owners of capital, is to federate his Unions—to leave no isolated union to be drowned singly, but to draw them all closer and ever closer together into a National, and ultimately International, Federation of Workers …

Now these are precisely the lines on which the Irish Transport Union is working. It assists in organising other Unions, keeps in touch with them, and helps them in their industrial struggles. It insists on the solidarity of the working class and the duty of all the Unions to help one union in difficulties by the sympathetic strike, and the strike without notice. It endeavours in some degree to redress the balance of advantage which the old fashioned strike always left to the capitalist, with his much greater power of waiting and calling up reserves when he has due notice. It ignores absolutely all the shams and pretences by which working class organisation in Ireland has been so long hampered, in short, it is the most effective fighting force now at the disposal of the Irish working class.

That is why Irish capitalism, backed by the Irish Executive, is determined to crush the Irish Transport Union. And that is why Trade Unionists of perspicacity are determined that it shall not be crushed.

Sheehy-Skeffington overestimated the commitment the British authorities in Dublin Castle had to Irish capitalism. Indeed many employers, and newspapers such as the *Irish Times*, were critical of the slowness with which the executive had moved. But otherwise Sheehy-Skeffington's letter provided a shrewd synopsis of what the struggle that had tumbled onto the streets of Dublin was all about. His preachy tone did not make his missive any more palatable to employers. The son of a County Cavan school inspector, Sheehy-Skeffington was typical of the new intellectual elite emerging to challenge old assumptions. He had cut his journalistic teeth on the *Freeman's Journal*, where he was always on the side of the underdog. When he had been commissioned to write half a column on rats, the editor told him afterwards:

> I really do not know what I can do with you. You have written about rats as if they were an oppressed nationality.[2]

He now wrote regularly on Irish affairs for the *Manchester Guardian* and the *Daily Herald* as well as editing the suffragist weekly *Irish Citizen*.

But Sheehy-Skeffington was above all a moralist. He advocated socialism, as he advocated female suffrage, because he believed it to be not just more equitable but right. He was a quixotic figure in the best sense of the word. His eccentric costume of tweed knickerbockers, the rash of red beard and an earnestness that prevented him from distinguishing between the sublime and the ridiculous left him open to easy ridicule in a society that was only beginning to emerge from the era of strict nineteenth-century conformity. The *Leader*, a Catholic nationalist weekly, dubbed him 'Skeffy'; James Joyce described him as a 'hairy Jaysus'. Another contemporary, Con Curran, described him as a man of many opinions—and every one 'a principle for which he was ready to die.'[3] These principles were often enunciated in an irritatingly high-pitched voice, which Sheehy-Skeffington used during the coming months to heckle Redmondite, Liberal and Unionist alike.

Sheehy-Skeffington's wife, Hanna, a daughter of the nationalist MP David Sheehy, was a leading figure in the Irish Women's Franchise League. If the sympathy of intelligent and sensitive people such as the Sheehy-Skeffingtons was with the workers, others would follow.

*

The events of the next few days would bear out the validity of Sheehy- Skeffington's analysis. That very morning one of Dublin's largest employers, Jacob's, locked out nearly a thousand employees at its biscuit factory in Bishop Street. Though the workers had been unionised since 1911, a notice had been put up on Saturday prohibiting the wearing of the ITGWU's Red Hand badge. The same day three workers were dismissed for refusing to handle flour from Shackleton's, the Lucan milling firm in dispute with the ITGWU. When hundreds of women workers failed to report for work on Monday morning, and some of those who did refused to remove their union badge, the company declared a lockout. George Jacob told the *Irish Times* that the factory would not be reopening 'until the company has sufficient applications from workers pledged not to belong to the Irish Transport Workers' Union.'

Relations with the union had been bad for some time. The secretary of the ITGWU branch, Gibson, was a former employee who had been sacked for being in a pub when rostered for work. He now held court in the nearby union office at 77 Aungier Street.[4] Jacob, a Quaker and teetotaller, told the *Irish Times*:

> We have no objection to our workers belonging to a trade union conducted on ordinary lines, but we must in future refuse to give employment to any member of the Irish Transport Union, an organisation which has been conducted with so much tyranny and injustice. The vast majority of our women and girls, as well a large number of men, came into work as usual, and it is a source of much regret that their employment will be temporarily interfered with.

Some Jacob's workers, such as the fitters, were in craft unions critical of Larkin, or in no union at all, but these too were told that no work was available until enough ITGWU members had renounced socialist tyranny. Not surprisingly, a large and hostile crowd gathered outside the factory in Bishop Street, and a protective police cordon had to be deployed.[5]

Later the same day the DUTC locked out 250 engineering workers at its Inchicore works, after the bodymakers refused to repair trams damaged in the weekend's riots. Murphy denounced such behaviour as 'intolerable'. The men's action had been anticipated, he said, 'and it will be rather a convenience ... than otherwise to close down the works for a month or so, in the present condition of labour affairs.'

At Wookey's linen mills in Leixlip, thirty-six men walked out after the owner, Frederick Wookey, told them to resign from the ITGWU. There had been no dispute: Wookey had simply bumped into an employee in the village on Sunday and noticed that he was wearing a Red Hand badge. The man was thirty years at the mills and said he wore the badge only on his days off; nevertheless Wookey gave him a week's notice when he refused to leave the union. On Monday morning Wookey told twelve women employees, who were not in any union, that he had no work for them until they could persuade the men to abandon the ITGWU.

*

The iron logic of the new class warfare showed itself most clearly at Tedcastle, McCormick and Company, one of the main coal merchants and shippers in Dublin port. It paid off a hundred men who refused to deliver coal until colleagues sacked the previous week were reinstated. They had been sacked because they refused to deliver coal to a farmer in Coolock who had refused to recognise the ITGWU.

Firms such as Tedcastle's, Jacob's and Wookey's were merely anticipating a plan of campaign already drawn up and agreed with Murphy. The executive of the Dublin Employers' Federation had met the previous Friday to prepare for a city-wide lockout, and a general meeting of members had been called for Wednesday 3 September to unveil the new strategy. The federation was still very much an adjunct of the Dublin Chamber of Commerce. When Murphy attended a quarterly meeting of the chamber on Monday evening he was greeted with applause. A vote of thanks was proposed

> for the prompt and energetic manner in which he has dealt with the labour dispute ... Mr. Murphy is entitled to the best thanks of the Chamber and of the mercantile community, and has also acted in the best interests of the unfortunate men who have taken part in the strike.

Edward Andrews JP, an honorary treasurer of the newly formed Loyal Tramway Men's Fund, said that

> it is a sad thing for the interests of the city that the Labour Party have come under the control of one man, and have given themselves up to that exhibition of hooliganism which has taken place during the past few days ... When their better nature prevails the men themselves will feel that they have made a mistake.

In time they would realise that Murphy 'had saved them from something much worse,' and the citizenry of Dublin would be grateful to 'the man who had thrown himself into the breach.'

Not surprisingly, Murphy concurred with the Andrews analysis. The issue involved in the tramways

> is not one of wages, of treatment, or dissatisfaction … The sole issue is whether Mr. Larkin is going to rule the trade of Dublin, and whether people could carry on their own business, or call their souls their own, without consulting Mr. Larkin.

While employers had had to seek police protection during the past week, Murphy wondered whether Larkin himself might not need it soon. 'That would be the safest position for him when his victims found themselves on the streets without lockout pay,' Murphy declared, to shouts of 'Hear, hear.'

In an effort to bolster the confidence of the many employers who had been cowed in the past by the ITGWU's tactic of the sympathetic strike, Murphy told them that his lockout tactic was

> much easier than it appears. I often tell working men that when they make demands and threaten strikes, the prospect and the anticipation of them are much more of a terror to the employer than when an actual strike takes place. When that occurs the employer has got his back to the wall, and the workman has fired his last cartridge. The employer will generally manage to get his three meals a day, but the workman has no resources in ninety-nine cases out of a hundred. The difficulty of teaching the men is extraordinary.

Murphy said that he did not suggest for a moment

> that the condition of the men in the city is anything like what it ought to be. Some … employers breed Larkinism by neglect of their men and then support Larkin by not having the pluck to stand up against him.[6]

The other important business of the meeting, the campaign to stop the Cunard liners *Lusitania* and *Mauretania* from bypassing Queenstown (Cóbh) on their North Atlantic run, hardly attracted any debate. A motion was passed and sent to the Lord Lieutenant, the Prime Minister, Sir Edward Carson, John Redmond and other luminaries appealing to them to ensure that Cunard honoured its contract to transport the mails, as well as Irish passengers and goods, direct to New York. The chamber reminded the British government that this was one of the conditions on which a £2.6 million subsidy had been provided by the exchequer towards the construction of company vessels.[7]

*

Nearer home, the forty-sixth annual conference of the Trades Union Congress was opening in Manchester. Many delegates must have read newspaper reports that morning recounting in gory detail the weekend's events in Dublin. When they reached the Milton Hall they were greeted by a telegram from Tom McPartlin, president of Dublin Trades Council, appealing for help.

The British press was far more critical of the role the police had played in Dublin than their Irish counterparts. Newspapers such as the *Daily Herald, Sketch* and *Mirror* were particularly strident. The *Mirror* carried a vivid description of events in O'Connell Street from Peter Larkin, brother of Jim. The *Herald* headline read: 'Rioting in Dublin: Crown Cossacks bludgeon strikers, women and children alike: Irish bosses write in blood.' Its Dublin correspondent, Francis Sheehy-Skeffington, reported that

> Ireland's British rulers and her home grown exploiters are acting together with a fierce and vicious energy in the desperate effort to crush the Irish Transport Workers. Both stand for capitalism at their worst … Their policy is one of savage repression.

This was the context in which delegates were asked to hear a delegation from the Dublin strikers the following day. A telegram appealing 'for strong and united action on the part of fellow-workers in Great Britain' was greeted with cheers. The Belfastman Bob Smillie, who was now a leader of the Scottish miners, called for the 'Irish massacre' to be discussed before the midday adjournment. The president of the TUC, W. J. Davies, a leader of the Brassworkers, assured delegates that the subject would be raised at the earliest opportunity; but as the afternoon session dragged on there was no sign of the Dublin dispute being debated. The truth was that moderates such as Davies did not want to become involved in an Irish strike led by an argumentative schismatic like Larkin. They had barely kept control of the whirlwind of strikes in Britain over the past three years, in which sixty million working days had been lost. Besides, their own war coffers were empty.

Even militants such as Smillie were rethinking their past support for the sympathetic strike. Whatever advocates of syndicalism might say, Board of Trade statistics showed that sympathetic strikes were the least effective form of industrial action. The most recent figures suggested that, while trade unions were completely successful in 31 per cent of sectional disputes and partially successful in another 48 per cent, only 5 per cent of sympathetic strikes ended in victory for the workers. During the same period there had been a dramatic increase in the use of conciliation schemes by unions and employers. It was clear that growing numbers of union leaders saw conciliation as an alternative road forward.[8]

But blood had been spilt in Dublin, and most trade unionists responded instinctively to comrades in trouble. When Smillie rose again at 4 p.m. to demand a debate on Dublin, he was widely cheered.

Davies and the TUC leadership were well prepared by now for dealing with the issue. It was Larkin's former mentor and antagonist, James Sexton of the NUDL, who rose to reply, and he had a motion already drafted. This was loud in its condemnation of the government and of the hapless Lord

Aberdeen for prohibiting Sunday's meeting but silent on future courses of action. All it called for was 'a very rigid inquiry into the conduct of the police.'

Sexton was reluctant to rush to the defence of the NUDL's prodigal son, and his opening remarks were heckled. 'I have not come here to say a word against any man, but the black of Larkin and Connolly, if they are black, is whiteness itself compared with the whiteness of Sir Edward Carson and those members of the House of Lords who are backing him up.' He went on to ask what right the British government had to ban a public meeting called by trade unionists in Dublin while Carson and his supporters drilled in open defiance of the law.

> We wish to be constitutional and to obey the law; but there is a limit even to our endurance. We want the law applied impartially to dukes as well as trade unionists.

The Glassworkers seconded the motion. Their delegate managed to invoke that uniquely Welsh blend of socialist and Nonconformist morality when he lamented that capitalism was the same the world over. 'How long, O Lord, how long are trade movements going to look on while the souls of our brothers and sisters are sent shuddering to Hell to satisfy the capitalists!' If the congress meant its resolution condemning events in Dublin seriously, let them declare war. If the north-east corner of Ireland could arm itself in protest at laws not yet on the statute book, what was to stop workers organising to lift the people 'out of the economic slough of despond'? He proposed to loud cheers that the TUC adjourn to Dublin.

Ben Tillet, the legendary London dockers' leader, said that 'murder and massacre have been committed in the streets of Dublin.' This was a bloody government, and trade unionists had to realise that future disputes would be violent ones. 'The man who has pluck enough to strike must claim the right to use firearms ... even if it involved civil war.'

Welsh and Scottish miners' delegates called for a general strike, and the session ended in disorder as Davies failed to bring his excited brethren to order. It was theatre of course, but dangerous theatre, made all the more so by the Irish dimension, an unknown element for many British union leaders. One thing that was agreed before chaos took over was that a TUC delegation would be despatched to Dublin to assess the facts and to offer whatever assistance it could.[9]

*

While delegates debated in Manchester, Larkin was back in court before the Chief Magistrate, Swifte. He was still wearing the morning coat, striped trousers and patent leather boots in which he had been arrested; only the false beard was missing.

The case against Larkin appeared overwhelming. On Thursday he had given Swifte an undertaking that, pending an investigation of the sedition charges he was already facing, he would not take part in any illegal meeting or use seditious language. Since then he had addressed a rally at Liberty

Hall, burnt the proclamation proscribing any assembly in Sackville Street, issued a press statement urging workers to defy the government, and made his brief but highly publicised speech from the balcony of the Imperial Hotel. Connolly was already serving three months in Mountjoy for merely refusing to give an undertaking to keep the peace similar to the one that Larkin had so spectacularly violated.

Rearden, the Crown prosecutor, took particular exception to Larkin's speech on Friday night. The accused had said that he recognised no law, and that any man who was hungry while bread was within his reach was an idiot. 'That was language of a very dangerous and inflammatory character.' Breaking into premises to steal bread seemed more subversive to him than incitement to murder policemen.

Once again Larkin had one of Dublin's best barristers, Henry Hanna KC, to plead his case, and he contested every inch of the Crown's evidence. The case had to be adjourned to Wednesday. Larkin was refused bail.

This raised a serious problem. Besides being general secretary of the union, Larkin was in charge of its sickness benefit fund. It was typical of his innovative approach to trade unionism that he was one of the first union leaders to use the provisions of Lloyd George's National Insurance Act to set up a friendly society. This meant that the ITGWU could collect social insurance contributions and distribute sickness benefit to members. The legislation decreed that all workers earning too little to be liable for income tax—the threshold was £160 a year—had to join an approved scheme. Men contributed 4d a week and women 3d. There were also contributions from employers and the government. Taken together, these ensured that a male worker who fell ill received 10s a week benefit for thirteen weeks; women workers were entitled to 7s 6d. Both were entitled to a reduced rate of 5s for a further thirteen weeks.

Providentially for the ITGWU, the scheme had come into force on 15 January 1913. Larkin had used the columns of the *Irish Worker* of 8 February to proclaim its merits:

> Remember, the Irish Transport and General Workers' Union Approved Society, under the National Insurance rules, requires no medical certificates, except in cases of malingering. All genuine cases accepted on their merits; no delay in settling claims. Maternity claims settled in 12 hours after application. Transfer now to the Workers' Insurance Society. Branches throughout the country. We paid the first maternity claim in Ireland; no deductions, no delay; not a profit making society, but a genuine Insurance Society. No highly paid officials, no titled ladies and gentlemen managing this society; working men and working women control and manage this society in the interests and for the benefit of the working classes.

The advertisement concluded with verses inspired by Tennyson's 'Charge of the Light Brigade' that drew a picture of a happy future for participants in the scheme:

Homeward those sick ones went
With money to pay the rent
Which Lloyd George had kindly lent,
Happy sick hundred!
And tho' they are badly crushed,
Into the pub they rushed,
Later with faces flushed,
Homeward they went.

As the advertisement makes clear, the society was much more than an organisational tool or fund-raiser for the union: it was part of the great design for using the One Big Union to construct the socialist future within the belly of capitalism. But if Larkin was in prison, he could not administer the fund.

Swifte suggested that Larkin ask for power of attorney, but Larkin said he would need authority from his executive, which could hardly be convened in jail. He gave his word 'not to give speeches and to be here' on Wednesday if he was granted bail. Swifte, understandably, said no; but he promised that facilities would be made available for Larkin's members to be paid.[10] The administrators of justice in Ireland might be as 'bloody' as depicted in the radical British press, but they were not inconsiderate.

*

That afternoon Dublin City Council held its monthly meeting, and, inevitably, the events of the weekend overtook the routine agenda. The priority of the Lord Mayor, Lorcan Sherlock, was to secure a united approach to the crisis by calling for a public inquiry into the conduct of the police. He hoped by doing so to allow members to vent their conflicting opinions without further inflaming the situation, or jeopardising his own role as an industrial peacemaker. He was to be disappointed on both counts.

In the absence of a home rule parliament, Dublin Corporation was considered by many nationalists to be the premier representative body in the country, even though Belfast was larger and far richer than the old capital. For much of the nineteenth century a gentleman's agreement had seen the mayoralty in Dublin alternate between Conservative and Liberal councillors, but this did not survive the eruption of the home rule movement onto the political scene. Once the home-rulers came to dominate the city council, Unionist councillors were excluded from the mayoralty. By the early years of the twentieth century the United Irish League was the dominant home rule faction, largely representative of the Catholic lower middle class. Publicans were the largest vocational group on the council, a natural development given the central role that pubs traditionally played in social and political life, not to mention the importance of bye-laws in regulating the licensed trade. The threat posed by the temperance movement (which included trade unionists such as Larkin) also ensured that publicans would continue to take a keen interest in municipal politics.

On the eve of the lockout, publicans, small merchants, shopkeepers and builders accounted for 70 per cent of the membership of the city council. Almost all of them were members of the UIL, which never held less than 55 of the 80 seats and sometimes accounted for as many as 65. The handful of more radical nationalist councillors in Sinn Féin also came from a decidedly petit-bourgeois background; the most prominent, William Cosgrave, was a grocer.[11]

Though the UIL enjoyed a reputation for jobbery and incompetence, the reforming elements on the city council associated with Sinn Féin and Labour had enjoyed limited electoral success. Labour first emerged as an electoral force following the extension of the franchise to most adult residents of the city under the Local Government (Ireland) Act (1898). But the Labour Electoral Association, which sponsored the new councillors, still held to the cautious, consensual politics of the Trades Council, whose priorities included the need to protect Irish firms, and jobs, from foreign competition. This made the Trades Council's politics indistinguishable in many respects from those of Sinn Féin or the UIL. On some issues, such as the war in South Africa, the nationalists were more radical than the Trades Council with their support for the Boers; the Trades Council refused to take a position on the war, partly out of concern for the sensitivities of unionist workmen in its ranks. In the circumstances it is not surprising that the Labour Electoral Association required Labour councillors to vote together only on 'labour' issues.

This posed an immediate dilemma. The evening before the newly elected Labour councillors were due to attend their first city council meeting, in January 1899, five of its councillors were persuaded by Nannetti to support the Parnellite candidate for Lord Mayor: he successfully argued that this was a 'political' rather than a 'labour' issue. The Labour men quickly lost their way thereafter in the maze of municipal politics, and their blunders frequently made them a butt of the nationalist press, especially Arthur Griffith's *Sinn Féin*.

Another element limiting their impact was the fact that meetings of the city council were held during working hours, and Labour councillors often found it hard to attend. William Partridge, first elected for Kilmainham in 1905, was given time off by the Great Southern and Western Railway because he was campaigning for corporation houses to accommodate railway workers in the area; once he took up more radical causes this concession was withdrawn, and he resigned rather than miss meetings.

From 1912 the Labour Electoral Association, like Dublin Trades Council, had been reformed by advocates of the 'new unionism', so that it sponsored only socialist candidates. But there remained a rump of old 'Labour' men, such as John Kelly and William Richardson, who almost invariably voted with the nationalists. As a result, the Labour group had only ten de facto councillors.

There were, of course, other reasons for Labour's lack of progress. Under the 1898 act only 38,000 Dubliners, men and women, had a vote out of a population of 250,000. While this was a huge improvement on the previous franchise, when the vote was confined to a middle-class electorate of only 8,000, the working class was grossly under-represented. In principle the act gave the vote to most householders who satisfied a one-year residence requirement, as well as to lodgers paying more than 4s a week rent; but many working-class families lived in cheaper accommodation and moved frequently as their economic fortunes varied. Changes in the electoral boundaries aggravated the problem, and tenants of landlords who had not paid their rates were automatically disqualified from voting. Some significant low-income groups, such as the city's 12,000 domestic servants, were not entitled to vote at all.[12]

Still, Labour had managed to displace the Unionists as the second-largest party on the council by 1913, when the Unionists had seven councillors, Sinn Féin four, and independents four, two of whom described themselves as independent nationalists. One of these was the council's first woman member, the portrait artist Sarah Harrison, whose brother Henry had been a Parnellite MP.

Lorcan Sherlock had briefly been a member of Sinn Féin, but it was not the natural home of a shopkeeper with strong clerical connections and high political ambitions. Archbishop Walsh was a constituent, and Sherlock was such a regular visitor to the archbishop's palace in Drumcondra to receive direction on important events of the day that his enemies called him the 'Lay Pope'. Naturally he was no friend of Larkinism, but he saw the call for an inquiry into the weekend's events as a safe option. He had a theoretical majority for whatever motion he wanted to push through that Monday afternoon; and the city's colonial status also came to his aid. Ordinarily, in a clash between striking slum-dwellers and the police, a party of shopkeepers could be expected to support the police: indeed Sexton and other delegates in their speeches to the TUC conference in Manchester that day assumed it was the nationalist-dominated council that had unleashed the DMP and RIC on the strikers. But Dublin was not Manchester. It had no Watch Committee: in fact councillors had no control whatever over the police force. Despite its name, the DMP was under the direct control of the Irish executive, just like the RIC. That Dublin's ratepayers had to contribute about 20 per cent of the cost of the force only added insult to injury.

Normally the great majority of councillors were happy to avail of any opportunity to debate and pass judgment on the city's police force and, by extension, its British masters. But the events of the weekend had frightened as well as outraged many councillors. Sherlock's innocuous call for a public inquiry was at first welcomed, but divisions opened up when another nationalist member, Dr James McWalter, proposed an addendum that 'the peace of Dublin could be best served by the withdrawal of the police and military from the streets of Dublin.' McWalter was a member of the Dublin Catholic Association, as well as a UIL stalwart. He was quite progressive on social issues but attracted Sinn Féin enmity by opposing the introduction of compulsory Irish. He was also the alderman for the North City ward and had spent most of Sunday treating casualties of the baton charges. He told the council that people 'were incensed against the police, and a scene took place in O'Connell Street yesterday which was probably unparalleled in the annals of Dublin.' His own surgery, around the corner in North Earl Street, 'was crowded with absolutely harmless, inoffensive citizens returning from devotions, who had all been batoned.' He knew that at least four hundred people had been treated in the city's hospitals and not more than thirty of these were policemen. The corporation was being asked to pay an extra £6,000 that year towards the upkeep of the police, and the least the councillors could do was help injured citizens obtain justice from their assailants.

Sherlock was somewhat nervous at the idea of the police evacuating the city, or the council actively prosecuting constables. He didn't want 'to get anything illegal into a motion and upset the whole thing.' However, the Labour councillor Thomas O'Hanlon was for retribution. He lived in Emmet Road in Inchicore. Like McWalter, he had witnessed the police excesses on his own doorstep: indeed he described himself as 'one of the wounded soldiers in this fight.' He said that Dublin Castle was responsible for 'throwing on the streets of Dublin on Sunday a lot of drunken constabulary and DMP men.' Some people had urged citizens to keep indoors to avoid trouble. He was indoors when a 'drunken Constabulary mob entered a house and bludgeoned and batoned half a dozen men that happened to take refuge there.' He claimed that Richard O'Carroll and himself had done more than all the police and military to maintain peace in Inchicore. 'Some irresponsible youths may, no doubt, aggravate the police, but that was no reason why in Inchicore now we should have scores of men wounded, and why the military should be brought out with their fixed bayonets.' This was not a matter between Murphy and Larkin, he said, but between capital and labour. The Irish MPs should step into the breach with the corporation 'to save the lives of citizens.' If they failed to do so, the workers would have 'to defend themselves against all assailants.'

The nationalist councillor Joseph Coghlan Briscoe was a businessman. He had little sympathy for Larkinism, but as secretary of the Town Tenants' Association, an organisation sponsored by the UIL, he was well aware of the dangers the social unrest posed to the Irish Party's hegemony. Like McWalter too he represented an area heavily affected by the rioting, Mountjoy ward. In fact he had not only witnessed the baton charges but had done so in the presence of the Liberal MP Handel Booth. Briscoe told his fellow-councillors that he and Booth had seen members of the RIC 'wantonly beating, not only men, but women and children.' It was 'conduct like this that murdered James Nolan … and filled the hospitals all over the city.' If Lord Aberdeen and his advisers continued 'this foolish policy' the city council must petition the King for the Lord Lieutenant's recall. Under cover of a government 'ukase' banning a public meeting, the police in his own ward

> wholly illegally entered houses and smashed every stick of furniture in some rooms. Are the police in Dublin to be [let] loose at night and baton people in their own homes? If such went on the citizens of Dublin will have to arm in their own defence, and Dublin Castle would not survive long.

In contrast, the Labour renegade William Richardson demanded action against the 'terrorism' that had forced him to seek refuge in the Bridewell from the mob. Unable to overcome his obsession with Larkin, he blamed the Irish executive for the weekend's events, because through weakness it had 'allowed people at Beresford Place to incite to murder.' The authorities were fully entitled to take action 'against the lowest dregs of the population.'

Another Labour councillor, William Partridge, angrily accused Richardson of 'acting a part in which no self-respecting Irishman would find any satisfaction,' by trying to impeach a trade union. The Tramways Company and William Martin Murphy had declared war on the ITGWU simply and solely because the workers had elected of their own free will to join it. Partridge also criticised press coverage of the tramway dispute. Reports were inaccurate and misleading and were creating 'the wrong spirit' for a peaceful resolution of the conflict.

Councillor Partridge was not, of course, a disinterested observer. Though district president of the Amalgamated Society of Engineers, he had been working as manager of the Emmet Hall in Inchicore for the ITGWU for the past year. Larkin's success in building a union for the unskilled, when so many had failed before, rested in large part on his ability to recruit a core of able, dedicated organisers such as Partridge, Connolly, and Daly, who often doubled as administrators of the Irish Transport Provident Society. The capitation fee of 3s 8d a year for each of the 15,000 members of the society brought in almost £300 to Liberty Hall, equivalent to a quarter of the union's expenditure on administration and salaries. Indeed half Larkin's own salary was refunded by the society to the ITGWU for his administrative duties. When he expressed concern in the police court earlier that day about being unable to pay sickness benefit to union members, he could have added union employees to the list of those who would be out of pocket.

How far Partridge was aware of Larkin's financial unorthodoxies is not clear. But, unlike Richardson, no-one ever questioned his personal honesty. He managed to reconcile strong socialist views with a devout Catholicism and a humane feeling for his fellows with a vituperative tongue that could rival Larkin's. He had been sacked from the Inchicore engineering works for having the temerity to write to Sir William Goulding, chairman of the Great Southern and Western Railway, to complain about the way Catholics were passed over for promotion. Subsequent appeals by Partridge against his dismissal to Catholic shareholders in the company, including the Bishop of Limerick and William Martin Murphy, fell on deaf ears. His antagonism towards Murphy had therefore a personal dimension, and Partridge took relish in boasting that he had stopped the first tram on 26 August.[13]

Like Thomas O'Hanlon, Partridge had also taken a leading role in organising the ITGWU meeting outside the Emmet Hall the previous evening. 'The police immediately attacked the crowd attending the meeting,' he said. 'The people rushed into the hall and a panic ensued, some of the children leaping through windows.' He had been batoned himself. 'The whole responsibility for everything that has occurred rests entirely on the shoulders of William Martin Murphy.'

The nationalist councillor John Nugent of Sandymount had not been in the city centre on Sunday. He accepted that the Lord Mayor's call for an inquiry was a reasonable one, but he objected to McWalter's addendum. 'Would any sane man suggest that all the police should be withdrawn from the streets of Dublin, and that all property of the citizens should be left at the disposal of every vagabond?'

'The only vagabonds are the police,' shouted another councillor; but Nugent refused to be drawn. He was not sure who was responsible

> for all this riot and disorder. No man's character or life is safe from the intimidation which has prevailed in the city. At the same time, if police officers have gone outside their duty or right, I agree that they should be arraigned after a public inquiry.

Nugent, a native of Keady, County Armagh, was one of the city's leading insurance brokers and national secretary of the Ancient Order of Hibernians. The two roles were now intimately linked, thanks to the National Insurance Act. The AOH insurance network was so large that even the ITGWU, for all its abuse of the 'Hibs', lodged its provident society funds with the Hibernian. Like Sherlock, Nugent had ambitions beyond City Hall, and he was better placed to realise them. Besides being a successful businessman able to finance his own election campaigns, his leading role in the AOH had secured him a place on the UIL's national steering committee, at which he was one of the most regular attenders. He made no attempt to pose as a friend of the workers: his appeal was to the rising Catholic middle class, and in 1915 that vote secured him the parliamentary seat for College Green on the death of Nannetti.[14] His speech showed that the Hibernians found themselves in the same quandary as other nationalists: while Nugent was virulently anti-Larkinite, he was reluctant to be seen as a defender of a British-controlled police force.

Another nationalist, Alderman William Coffey, a butcher from Arran Quay, had no such qualms. He asked McWalter if he was not ashamed of himself for suggesting that the police be withdrawn from the city. This break in nationalist ranks encouraged one of the Unionists, William Ireland, to say he was sorry the Lord Mayor had proposed an inquiry at all.

Ireland, a wine and tea merchant from Rathgar, was also a shareholder in the DUTC and a director of the Duke Shipping Company.

> It is not Mr. Murphy or the Tramway Company who are responsible for what has taken place. Recent events have been due to two causes, first the Transport Union, led by Mr. Larkin, and, secondly, the inactivity of the Government in not preserving the peace and good order in the city. Every employer and workman has a right to protect himself, but when there is a state of terrorism in the city it is the duty of the Government to interfere and take sides.

He believed the police had 'done the best they could' in performing 'a difficult and delicate duty.' Murphy had a right to protect the interests of DUTC shareholders and the public. 'Would anyone say it was a right thing to smash the glass of tramcars?'

But a Sinn Féin alderman, Thomas Kelly, representing the Mansion House ward, would have none of it. Like other councillors who had witnessed the weekend's events, he had no doubt where the primary responsibility lay for the disorder. He was

> shocked at the way in which … defenceless women and children [were] treated. The DMP men were rushing about, despite the calls of their officers, who asked them for God's sake to control themselves. Wherever they saw a civilian they hit him.

When Larkin appeared at the Imperial Hotel on Sunday there was 'no disorder or provocation … and yet the police came along and dashed even women and children against the pavement, and kicked them on the pavement in a shameful way.' When he and another gentleman tried to protect an old woman with a prayer book, a constable told them: 'If you don't get yourselves to hell out of that I will let you see whether you will save her or not.' If the authorities could not preserve the peace it would be up to Dublin's citizens 'to put these men into their places.'

However, the nationalist councillor William Delaney, a butcher living in Dollymount, shared the views of his fellow-merchants. There was 'a class of man who came out on such occasions and took advantage of the disturbance.' Some of the worst streets should be sealed off at certain times and 'something like a passport' used to control entry and exit to them. He suggested that 'respectable trade unionists' be enrolled as special constables to separate the hooligan from 'the legitimate agitator.' Another nationalist, John Cogan, representing the Royal Exchange ward, suggested as a compromise that the DMP should be left to deal with the situation and that the RIC withdraw from the city. Restraint was needed on both sides, and the attack on St Audoën's because a priest had given refuge to two policemen was work of 'the lowest ruffianism.'

One of the victims of police aggression the previous day, the bricklayers' leader Richard O'Carroll, said he objected as a Catholic to Cogan bringing the clergy into the dispute. He had no sympathy with hooligans, because they damaged the cause. The police had been withdrawn from the streets of Belfast in the interests of peace, and the same thing could be done in Dublin. Another Labour councillor, Tom Lawlor, who was a member of the Trades Council and lived in Bride Street, where some of the worst rioting took place, said bluntly that 'the police attacked the people without any cause.' They had been 'going into the public houses round O'Connell Street drinking all day ... There would have been no breach of the peace if the police were kept off the streets.'

The leading Sinn Féin representative on the council, William Cosgrave, made one of the most innocuous speeches. The future 1916 insurgent and head of a Free State government that was to execute seventy-seven republican prisoners during the Civil War said that the sanctity of human life in Dublin must be preserved. Whether it was the Lord Lieutenant or the Chief Secretary for Ireland, 'no man had a right to take the life that God gave.' That was the issue on which they should all be united.

Though many of the nationalist councillors had spoken against McWalter's addendum, it was almost passed. It secured 21 votes, compared with 26 for the Lord Mayor's original motion. The majority rejecting the addendum consisted of twenty nationalist councillors, including the MP for Dublin South, William Cotton; the four Unionist councillors present; and two independents, Councillors Thornton and Bradshaw, who represented the middle-class suburbs of Glasnevin and Clontarf, respectively. The nationalist councillors involved included all those from the wealthier elements of the business community and councillors who lived outside the districts directly affected by the riots.

The twenty-one councillors who voted for McWalter's addendum included nine nationalists, six Labour members, the four Sinn Féin members, and two independent nationalists. All the nationalist councillors who witnessed the weekend's rioting voted for the addendum, as did John Cogan, despite his concern that the 'lowest ruffianism of Dublin' was exploiting the situation. Cogan was a Poor Law guardian, which suggests that an informed social conscience may have been at work when he was casting his vote. Even nationalist councillors who had not witnessed the weekend's events but who represented areas where rioting occurred voted for McWalter's addendum. This group included Sherlock. By voting for the addendum he ended any prospect of continuing to be accepted by the employers as an 'honest broker' in future peace initiatives.

Sinn Féin's stance reflected its close ties with organised labour, as well as its strategy of trying to outflank the more moderate nationalists of the UIL. Several leading Labour activists, including William Partridge and Richard O'Carroll, were former members of Sinn Féin.

After the defeat of McWalter's addendum, the original motion was carried without a formal vote. A motion was then put by the Sinn Féin alderman Thomas Kelly that a peace committee be set up to arbitrate between the Tramways Company and the ITGWU. This was passed easily, the only opposition coming from Labour councillors. Thomas O'Hanlon said:

> Leave the employers to the men. Get the streets of Dublin cleared of the constabulary and we will deal with the employers.

It sounded ominous for Alderman Kelly's peace initiative; but O'Hanlon's reservations did not prevent his Labour colleague William Partridge agreeing to serve as an employee representative on any conciliation body, if the city council's peace initiative proved successful.[15]

One wonders if quite so many nationalist councillors would have voted for McWalter's addendum to have the police and military withdrawn from the streets if they had exercised any real discretion in the matter. The same day the Irish executive drafted another 155 RIC men into Dublin from Ulster.[16]

*

The tribulations of the police were not yet over. The inquest on James Nolan began that Monday in the City Coroner's Court, with Henry Hanna KC, who had defended Larkin in the morning, acting for the dead man's family. Nolan was an ITGWU member, and the union paid the family's legal costs. The court heard that Nolan was unconscious on arrival at Jervis Street Hospital on Saturday night and did not regain consciousness before his death on Sunday morning. He had serious injuries, including a fracture of the skull and brain compression. Hanna said he would produce witnesses to testify that Nolan, who was 'apparently under the influence of drink,' took no part in the rioting and had been batoned on the ground by members of the DMP and RIC. The DMP officer in charge at the scene, Inspector Campbell, proved evasive in the dock, compared with civilian witnesses. One witness identified by number the DMP constable who struck Nolan to the ground. The case was adjourned until Friday.[17]

It was probably inevitable that the weekend's rioting would resume on Monday afternoon. The disturbances began outside Jacob's biscuit factory; by lunchtime, workers locked out that morning had been joined by those due on for the afternoon shift. Many of the one thousand workers, which included over three hundred women, lived in surrounding tenements and remained on the street awaiting developments. At 2:30 p.m. youths began stoning the small police patrol on duty. When reinforcements arrived the rioters regrouped at Redmond's Hill a short distance away. Some of the men acquired pickaxes and began to tear up the tramlines. Cobblestones were torn free and thrown before the police charged, 'using their batons freely,' according to the *Irish Times*. The crowd retreated about half way up Cuffe Street before resuming a fierce fusillade of stones and bottles. When missiles began descending on the police from the upper storeys of tenements, they were forced to retreat. They regrouped and charged again, with much the same result.

This pattern continued into the night, and the rioting spread to Aungier Street, Camden Street, and Mercer Street. The windows of many shops and pubs were smashed, and business were premises looted. It was midnight before the rioting on the south side petered out. About ninety people were treated at the Meath, Mercer's and Adelaide Hospitals.

At 9:30 p.m. trouble flared north of the river, around Capel Street and Mary Street. The ubiquitous Councillor William Richardson found himself trapped in a laneway by the mob; he boasted later that he held his foes at bay single-handedly with a stick until rescued by the police. The worst incident occurred when four RIC men were attacked by a mob as they returned to their lodgings at the Royal Hibernian Hotel in Capel Street. The *Irish Times* commented that

> the determined spirit shown by some of the rioters was remarkable. At the corner of Strand Street a rough-looking man stood grasping what appeared to be a heavy leather belt, with pieces of metal at the end, which he intended to use. Around him was a group of boys, whom he exhorted not to run from the police, but to face them when they charged … The police eventually succeeded in driving from the street the rioters, who were mostly mere boys, and in arresting two of them. By 11 o'clock it was fairly quiet.

An unnamed American visitor who witnessed the fighting told an *Evening Herald* reporter: 'I have seen rowdy crowds in my time, but with the possible exception of a couple of South American towns … I never saw such a choice collection of hooligans as are trying to hold up your city.' He said that when the Carnegie steel workers rioted in Homestead, Pennsylvania, he had been out with the state militia.

> There were several people killed and a couple of hundred wounded by the rifle fire … but there have already been hundreds of casualties in Dublin, and nobody can say the trouble is over yet. We think that the prompt use of the militia or military is the most merciful course in the end.

This apocryphal American's memory was playing tricks on him, for the only people killed in the Homestead steel dispute were shot in gun battles between Pinkerton agents working for the company and striking workers. Yet he probably reflected accurately enough the views of the owner of the *Evening Herald.* A similar mentality lay behind the decision of the DUTC and other employers to issue revolvers to employees.

Fortunately, Monday's disturbances were far less extensive than those at the weekend. Renewed calls for calm and discipline by William O'Brien and other members of the Trades Council's strike committee were being heeded. No doubt nervous and physical exhaustion, not to mention the necessity of returning to work for those who still had jobs to go to, contributed their calming effects on the populace.

*

Normality is always hard to eradicate, and throughout that terrible weekend it was business as usual for most people. Not a Mass was cancelled nor a theatre closed—though a number of pubs in the rioting communities had been forced to shut by the police. A further sobering factor was the courts. For the police, the one consolation Monday offered was the host of rioters in the dock. According to the *Irish Times*, few of those charged were strikers or members of trade unions—and very few were sporting the Red Hand badge. However, many of the accused were sporting bandages, and the Bridewell that morning resembled a casualty station. In the Southern Police Court one of the most serious cases, reported the *Irish Times*, involved three men arrested in a house in Moss Street during Saturday night's rioting.

> The prisoners presented a very sad appearance. They were all in their shirts and trousers and all their heads were bandaged. One of the defendants had his nose smashed, and his head swathed in wrappings.

The sergeant in charge of the arresting party could not say how the men received their injuries. The men were remanded in custody. Drury, the police magistrate, said that arrangements could be made to provide them with fresh clothes, if they had any.

The crowd outside the Bridewell was large and angry, but a strong police cordon ensured that sympathisers with the prisoners were not allowed into court. During the afternoon sessions the police were quick to inform the magistrates that rioting had resumed around Jacob's factory, thus adding to the siege atmosphere in which the cases were being heard.

Among the first cases in the Northern Police Court were those of William Ryan and Thomas Carrick, both charged with involvement in the attack on Sergeant Woulfe in Talbot Street on Sunday. They had been arrested in Jervis Street Hospital by Woulfe himself. All three were being treated for injuries. Woulfe, who was heavily bandaged, gave evidence against the equally bandaged accused, both of whom denied vehemently that they had attacked Woulfe. Ryan turned out to be a former policeman, who said he sustained his injuries assisting the police; and Carrick was so far out of sympathy with the disturbances that he said he had been working normally at Eason's in defiance of the pickets. Both cases were adjourned because of the conflicting evidence.

It is an understatement to say that the magistrates had a difficult time. A typical case in the Northern Police Court before the magistrate, Mr Hunt, that gives a flavour of the proceedings—and the fighting that gave rise to them—involved two brothers, Patrick and William O'Leary. They were arrested at their home in Marlborough Place. The police claimed that Patrick O'Leary had been throwing missiles from a window three storeys up and had knocked down several constables. According to the *Irish Times*, Constable 31C told the court that William O'Leary refused to let him into the house, and when he forced an entrance the brothers attacked him with a frying-pan and a fire shovel. Sergeant 14C also complained of being attacked with the same weapons.

> Mr. Boyle, who appeared for the prisoners, asked Constable 31C if it were he who used the baton on the men that caused the severe wounds on their heads.
>
> The witness said he did not use his baton. He had not time; he was knocked down.
>
> 'You were up in private rooms batoning them for what you were worth?'
>
> 'I did not baton them.'
>
> 'Did the other men use their batons?'
>
> 'I could not say.'
>
> Mr. Boyle—'Were you so drunk that you did not know whether they were using their batons or not?'
>
> Mr. Hunt—'It is not right to say that.'
>
> The witness denied being drunk. Other police engaged in the case came forward to protest, and a heated scene ensued.

The court descended into chaos, and the case had to be adjourned.

In most instances the convictions came thick and fast. Two labourers arrested for stone-throwing in Talbot Street were sentenced to a month each. The police denied the men's claims that they had been batoned on their way to Store Street station and suggested that their injuries were sustained when missiles thrown at the police escort struck the prisoners.

Mary Ashbourne from Foley Street was fined £2 and given the option of a month's imprisonment for throwing a bottle at the police. A neighbour, Thomas McEvoy, was sentenced to two months' hard labour for throwing a bottle. A vanman Christopher Clifford, who the police said acted 'like a drum major' for the rioters in Abbey Street, received a month's imprisonment. A man up from the country who was arrested in Beresford Place during the rioting 'gave the excuse that he was drunk and did not know what happened.' He was offered the choice of a £2 fine or a month's imprisonment.

*

How many of the innocent were sent down with the guilty is impossible to say. The DMP returns for 1913 certainly show the impact of industrial strife. In the forty years to 1914 there was a steady drop in the number of criminal offences reported for Dublin. The same general pattern applies to 1913, when 132 fewer indictable offences were reported than in 1912 and 6,622 fewer non-indictable offences. But in categories likely to be affected by the labour troubles the pattern is reversed. In 1913 157 indictable offences of riot were reported, and one of unlawful assembly (Bloody Sunday). No offences were reported under either heading in 1912, and only nineteen people faced indictable charges for rioting in 1914.

The number of indictable offences for intimidation and molestation in 1913 was 114, and a further 167 non-indictable cases of intimidation were reported, a total of 281. In 1912 and 1914 no indictable offences of intimidation were reported. In 1912 only 21 non-indictable cases of intimidation were reported, while the figure for 1914 was 16.

There were also considerably more assaults on constables in 1913 than in the other two years: some 338 were reported in 1913, compared with 250 in 1912 and 185 in 1914.

According to the first historian of the lockout, Arnold Wright, 656 people were arrested in connection with offences arising from the 1913 riots. Of these, 416 received prison sentences, of whom 184 had previous convictions. However, Wright's aim was to discredit Larkinism, and a detailed analysis of the DMP returns shows his figures to be suspect.

Only 181 men and two women were specifically charged with indictable rioting offences. The two women were charged with one riot offence each. The ratio of offenders to charges suggests that the great majority of those convicted were involved in a single offence, though they could of course have had previous convictions unrelated to the dispute. Another 288 men and 50 women were charged with assaulting a constable—about 140 more cases than in an average year—and there were about 60 extra common assaults on policemen. Even assuming that all the extra assault cases in 1913 related to the riots, this would still only provide about 400 arrests that could be attributed to them. If the 163 people charged with intimidation are added to the total, it is still more than 100 short of the figure claimed by Wright.

The intimidation cases can be broken down into indictable and non-indictable offences. There were 58 men and 15 women arrested in connection with the 114 indictable cases; 30 women and 137 men were arrested in connection with the 167 non-indictable cases. These figures suggest that there were a number of 'persistent' offenders, who were presumably trade union activists rather than criminals. By definition, the majority of intimidation cases must have taken place away from riot situations; most of them probably related to incidents on picket lines, though widespread incidents of intimidation were reported against newsagents and newspaper vendors selling *Independent* titles.

Many of the women convicted were too young to be hardened criminals. The annual report of the Mountjoy visiting committee for 1913 states that women 'sent to this prison for offences committed during the unfortunate labour troubles in the city ... included a number of young girls who were classed as juvenile adults and kept apart from the other prisoners.'[18]

Some of the DMP figures suggest that the lockout may even have helped reduce the level of crime in the city. For example, the incidence of drunkenness fell significantly in 1913. The previous year 2,345 offences of drunkenness were reported and another 1,174 cases of drunkenness with aggravation. In 1913 there were only 1,811 cases of drunkenness and 946 of drunkenness with aggravation. There was a slight increase in the figures for 1914, with 1,845 cases of drunkenness and 923 of aggravated drunkenness reported. The other intriguing figure under this heading concerns women. While men formed the bulk of offenders in other years, women accounted for almost half the cases of aggravated drunkenness in 1913. Part of the explanation for these aberrations must be the lockout.

During the second half of 1913 and much of early 1914 there were perhaps 15,000 families dependent for survival on meagre strike pay, when it was available, and on food consignments from Britain. A teetotaller like Larkin would not be dispensing drink at Liberty Hall. At least twice as many people were dependent on charity. In short, cash for alcohol would have been abnormally scarce in the second half of the year.

The extent to which the concern of Councillor Cogan and others about 'ruffianism' was well founded remains unclear. There was a small amount of looting during the riots, particularly around Redmond's Hill on Monday, and the *Evening Herald* published several photographs of damage caused to trams and shops during the first week of the strike. But the DMP report for 1913 records only 396 malicious damage offences, just four more than in 1912.[19] In reply to questions in the House of Commons, the Chief Secretary for Ireland, Augustine Birrell, gave the following details of the destruction wrought throughout the strike: 272 tramcars damaged, windows in 279 houses broken, and 50 drays and other vehicles overturned with damage to the goods they were carrying.

The total cost of damage directly attributable to the lockout was £3,819, spread over five months. This compares with the £2.5 million worth of claims that followed the 1916 Rising, which lasted only a week. Estimates for loss of business during the lockout are a different matter: figures, none of them verifiable, vary from £100,000 to £350,000 a week. This works out at between £2.3 million and £8.05 million.[20]

8

9/2/13.

UESDAY saw no reduction in the tempo of the dispute. Strikers and their sympathisers continued to pour through the courts, among them the Labour councillor for Trinity ward, William Hopkins. An ITGWU organiser, Hopkins was not charged with rioting but with assaulting an RIC man within the precincts of the police court. The two men had had an argument, which ended in Hopkins jabbing Constable Kearney in the ribs. The magistrate said he disliked having to imprison 'a man in a public position,' but Hopkins had behaved outrageously. He was remanded in custody.[1]

The ITGWU now had four senior members in prison: its general secretary, Jim Larkin; its Belfast organiser, James Connolly; the Dún Laoghaire branch secretary, James Byrne; and now Hopkins. The leadership of the strike devolved in theory on the ITGWU executive committee, but in fact its day-to-day administration fell to John O'Neill, secretary of the No. 1 Branch, and its strategic direction shifted to Dublin Trades Council.

As we have seen, the committee of the Trades Council had met on Monday night and issued a statement calling for an end to the rioting. It also decided to follow up McPartlin's telegram to the TUC with a formal deputation to Manchester.[2] In the circumstances it was hardly surprising that there was not an ITGWU member among them. The president of the Trades Council, Tom McPartlin, was a carpenter, Tom Lawlor was a tailor, and William Partridge was an engineer, though he could claim to be a representative of the ITGWU. They took the ship for Liverpool from the North Wall that night, leaving a city still in turmoil.

When they were given the floor next morning in Manchester, Partridge, as the most accomplished speaker, made the main address. He told the TUC delegates that the people of Dublin 'are not only struggling for the cause of trade unionism but are defending their very lives.' A new spirit had been created in Dublin, which was uniting craft workers with general workers. In response, the employers had proposed a conciliation board, 'but in the meantime they have declared war on a trade union.' The defeat of the ITGWU would mean 'the destruction of trade unionism not only in Dublin, but throughout Ireland.' Murphy had selected Larkin's union for destruction because Larkin was a socialist, and socialism was not popular in the country. 'The police have become maniacs through drink … going into the streets, wielding their batons over their heads and shouting "Blood for Ireland".' Partridge could not resist a little baton-wielding himself and produced one captured during the rioting at Inchicore. As he flourished it before his audience, he appealed for a TUC deputation to come to Dublin and see the situation at first hand.[3]

The congress decided to send a deputation immediately, led by three senior trade unionists and MPs. These were the leader of the Gasworkers' and General Labourers' Union, Jack Jones, the vice-president of the South Wales Miners' Federation, William Brace, and the founder of the Navvies' Union, John Ward. Jones was a champion of the new unionism; Brace and Ward were Liberal MPs and represented the more conservative elements within the union establishment. Probably the most conservative was Ward, a former soldier and a hero of the war in Sudan thirty years earlier. (The Commissioner of the DMP, Sir John Ross, had served in the same campaign.) The delegation's brief was to show solidarity with the Dublin trade unions in their struggle for free speech and freedom of association. As elder statesmen of the movement they could be relied on not to commit the TUC leadership to any rash, syndicalist adventures.

The delegation was supplemented by three other senior trade unionists: Harry Gosling, president of the National Transport Workers' Federation; James Seddon, chairman of the Parliamentary Committee of the TUC; and John Hill, leader of the Boilermakers. For Gosling and Seddon, Dublin would become a second home during the next few months.[4]

*

The *Evening Herald* scoffed at the notion of the 'English Trade Congress' investigating the Dublin riots. 'In the opinion of those best qualified to judge, that is about all they will do,' it predicted. The paper gave more credence to a report that Dublin employers were about 'to decide on the best concerted means of smashing anarchy once and for all in the city.'

The Coal Merchants' Association had the honour of becoming the first employers' group to announce a formal lockout 'of the whole of the members of the Transport Workers' Union.' The effect of this action was to throw about 1,500 workers on the street. The association's members had

> no objection to their employees being members of any Union acting in a lawful and responsible manner, but, as the Irish Transport Union will not allow their members to deliver coal to certain firms, the merchants are compelled to give notice that they will no longer employ men belonging to this union, and who will not make deliveries in accordance with any orders given by their employers.
>
> The services of any man who is not prepared to agree to these conditions, and to sign an undertaking to withdraw from the Transport Union, will be dispensed with forthwith.

The association placed the blame for its actions firmly on the 'very meddlesome and vexatious character' of the ITGWU. Union officials had refused to allow deliveries 'to be made to any person or firms having any dispute with them—or, in other words, they compel a boycott.'[5]

*

There was more bad news for the ITGWU. Sympathetic strike action promised by Partridge in the Great Southern and Western Railway failed to materialise. After being beaten by Goulding and Murphy in 1911, the railwaymen were not prepared to take them on again.

Writing to Archbishop Walsh that day, a breathless Father Curran tried to keep him abreast of the rapidly accelerating pace of events.

The disorder ... has grown very seriously since Saturday. It is no longer a question of a tram strike. It is simply the scum of the slums versus the police.

Unfortunately the mob have the sympathy of the working classes and nobody helps the police. I think it is a scandal that the military have not been utilised. It would free the hands of the police immensely if the soldiers were stationed on the principal thoroughfares.

It is really surprising to see how much support Larkin commands among the artisans. Even the printers who refused to come out on strike at his command are very largely friendly to him ... The workmen have gone mad over Larkin and will do almost anything for him—even respectable carpenters and bricklayers.

I hear all kinds of detailed and definite accounts of meetings of various classes of employers. All seem determined to seize the opportunity and put an end to the employment of Transport Union men. Everything points to a general lockout in shipping, coaling, building, milling and other trades.

The rioting of the mob beggars description. The women, girls and street arabs are the worst. The worst of it is that each new lockout will establish a new centre and a fresh outbreak of violence. Jacob's district was the latest and, in consequence, our trams now run by Harcourt Street and the Green, instead of by Camden, George's and Dame Street.

The trams are running regularly, but a great many have had their glass smashed. The D.U.T.C. receipts for Horse Show week only went down by a fifth and the net increase of receipts to date for the year is very big. Certainly as far as the trams are concerned the strike is a decided failure.

The 'Freeman' and Corporation are making a great fracas about the baton charge on Sunday. I suppose the statements made are true. I am told there was undoubtedly some batoning of fallen men, but with the exception of the O'Connell Street charge, any person who got batoned richly deserved it.

The proceedings of the city council 'were in keeping with its worst traditions,' wrote Curran: 'kow-towing to the mob for its vote and the worst offender was McWalter.' After berating the members a little more, Curran regretfully informed the archbishop that it was necessary to replaster parts of the palace. The cost would be £178.[6]

*

As he acknowledged himself, Father Curran was out of sympathy with much of middle-class opinion. The majority of the letters in that day's *Irish Times*, all from readers with eminently respectable addresses, were sharply critical of the behaviour of the police over the weekend. Even the four MPs for the Dublin city divisions had found their voice at last and had written to the Lord Lieutenant to demand 'an immediate inquiry into the general conduct of the police.' While expressing no views 'upon the points at issue,' they wrote that, 'having regard to the representations made to us by constituents, we feel convinced that such an inquiry is a necessity.' The letter was signed by William Field (St Patrick's division), Joseph P. Nannetti (College Green division), Patrick J. Brady (St Stephen's Green division), and William Abraham (Dublin Harbour division).[7]

The MPs' letter encapsulated the dilemma confronting constitutional nationalists in the city. It was too feeble and qualified a protest to convince trade unionists that the MPs had the workers' interests at heart; by the same token, its pusillanimity could only outrage wealthier and more conservative nationalists, including that former stalwart of the Irish Party, William Martin Murphy. It was confirmation, for those who needed it, that most of the city's parliamentary representatives were well past their prime. Later in the lockout another Irish Party member and confidant of Redmond, Stephen Gwynn, was to provide Archbishop Walsh with an able synopsis of the crisis afflicting constitutional nationalism. He expressed concern that a lack of leadership was allowing anti-clerical and socialist ideas to spread—to the advantage of

> the radical section of the workers. All of these dangers are furthered by the fact that [there is] no law, no Government in Ireland possessing moral authority as representing the people: that nationalist members are afraid to move at this juncture for fear of creating disunion as to the main question [home rule] and that the representation of the city itself is in weak hands. Nannetti is moribund, Abraham devoid of local connection, Field too eccentric and Brady new to the work.

Of the two MPs who did not sign the letter to Lord Aberdeen, John Clancy (North County Dublin) and William Cotton (South County Dublin), Gwynn wrote: 'Clancy is very good, but very strongly conservative: Cotton no use politically and committed to the employers.'[8]

*

Men such as Field and Nannetti had been significant figures in their day. Field had won the St Patrick's division from William Martin Murphy in 1892, when he ran as a Parnellite. Though a Dublin butcher by trade, he had been a rural radical in his youth, helping to found the Knights of the Plough in Athy, one of several proto-unions set up in the eighteen-nineties. He had also represented rural workers briefly at the Irish Congress of Trade Unions, without himself being a member of any affiliated union. He had successfully opposed a motion at the 1895 conference of the Irish TUC to nationalise farms, on the grounds that 'socialism was all right if they had to deal with angels and not with human nature.' An early and respected treasurer of the GAA, he had tried to keep the association apolitical. He was popular in Dublin and had been re-elected unopposed in 1910. Successful in business, he had risen to become president of the Irish Cattle Traders' and Stockowners' Association and vice-president of the National Federation of Meat Traders of England, Scotland, Wales and the Isle of Man. He was therefore a central figure in the cattle trade, Ireland's principal export business. A self-taught man, he became a governor of the Royal Veterinary College of Ireland and secretary of the Dublin Victuallers' Association. He was also a prolific writer, wrote plays, and produced pamphlets on issues as varied as agriculture, transport, and the financial implications of home rule. His interest in financial matters made him an advocate of bimetallism, an enthusiasm he shared with such unlikely fellows as the former Tory prime minister Arthur Balfour and Archbishop Walsh.

Field's career personified the social changes wrought by the Land War. From being a fomentor of agrarian unrest he had become one of the country's leading agricultural businessmen. His enthusiasm for new ideas and penchant for bohemian clothes could not hide the transformation. A younger contemporary described him as 'a venerable figure with a wide brimmed hat and picturesque appearance reminiscent of Buffalo Bill.' It was no wonder he struck a new generation of Dubliners as an amiable, colourful but increasingly irrelevant figure. However, past services to labour, continued commitment to the memory of Parnell and tenuous links with the IRB meant that he was still the most politically credible of the city's MPs with workers and radical nationalists in 1913.[9]

Nannetti's credentials were almost as impressive as Field's. He had been the moving spirit behind the founding of Dublin Trades Council. However, his resistance to the new unionism had seriously eroded his influence among Dublin workers. After the lockout, Connolly would refer to him dismissively as a 'skunk' because of his inactivity; but this inactivity was as much due to the fact that Nannetti was terminally ill as to his alienation from the rapidly changing labour scene.

By 1913 Nannetti, who had first been elected to represent the College Green division in 1900, had been incapacitated by a series of strokes, but he remained Redmond's principal adviser on labour and trade union issues. The primary effect of his influence at this stage, unfortunately, was probably to further insulate Redmond from the changing realities of Dublin politics and life.

William Abraham was another 'labour nationalist' and former trade union activist. His chief claim to fame was the fact that he had been the MP who proposed the resignation of Parnell in committee room 15 of the House of Commons in the aftermath of the O'Shea divorce case of 1890. He was one of the few Protestant home rule MPs (a Congregationalist), and this was probably why he was asked by Parnell's opponents to accept the role of accuser. He was widely respected among the older generation of union leaders and had represented the Carpenters' and Joiners' Amalgamated Society at the 1880 conference of the (British) Trades Union Congress in Dublin.

Like Field, Abraham had made a name nationally as a Land League activist. He had first represented Munster constituencies and remained a rural politician at heart. He had shown steadiness rather than talent over the years and had been rewarded with the honorary treasurership of the Irish Parliamentary Party. Resident in London, Abraham had become one of that curious breed of absentee home rule MPs whose commitment to Ireland led to their spending most of their time at the House of Commons. By 1913 he was a rotten prop, his seat safe only for as long as the Irish Party itself was strong in Dublin. And, like Nannetti, he was in bad health and would die the following year. At seventy-three, he was the oldest of the Dublin MPs.

The fourth and youngest of the city's MPs was Patrick Brady, a solicitor. He had won the predominantly middle-class St Stephen's Green division in 1910 by only 800 votes from Lord Herbert, the Unionist candidate. He was a council member of the Incorporated Law Society and a director of the Midland and Great Western Railway. He was also a leading figure in the Society of St Vincent de Paul. He was, in short, a typical representative of a younger generation of Catholic middle-class nationalists, out of sympathy with the workers and the new mood on the streets of Dublin.

The two nationalist MPs for County Dublin were even more out of sympathy with the city's workers. John Clancy (North County Dublin), like Abraham and Field, was of the old school. Originally from Athlone, he had been a distinguished classical scholar before turning to the law. He cut his political and legal teeth in defending Land Leaguers and tenant-farmers; he edited the *Nation* between 1880 and 1885, when he was first returned for North County Dublin. In 1906 he successfully proposed the Town Tenants Bill, which extended some of the rights of tenant-farmers to urban tenants. Subsequently accepted by the Liberal government, Clancy's act was routinely invoked by the Irish Party as evidence that it was not just the party of rural Ireland. The Town Tenants' Association became an important part of the party's urban machine, but it represented small business tenants rather than the poor. Apart from comments by its secretary, Joseph Coghlan Briscoe, at city council meetings, it remained relatively mute in the face of Dublin's labour upheavals. Clancy was born in the same year as William Martin Murphy, and they had taken opposing sides in the Parnell split. Over the years Clancy had become a relic of the past, while Murphy became a leading protagonist in the battle between two new titans, Capital and Labour. Nor had Clancy Murphy's remarkable mental and physical resilience. By 1913 the UIL network in North County Dublin was growing weak and dilapidated, like its MP.[10]

The MP for South County Dublin, William Cotton, had plenty of energy but little judgment. He was a friend and business associate of Murphy, who shared his passion for yachting and sat on the board of the DUTC. He was also chairman of the Alliance Gas Company and of Findlater's grocery firm. It was hardly surprising, therefore, that he had not signed the letter to Lord Aberdeen. Neither had he spoken at the city council meeting that debated the riots, though he had attended and voted against Dr McWalter's call for the RIC and military to be withdrawn from the city. He rarely spoke in public, and when he did he was liable to blunder. Like most of his fellow-MPs, he was not long for this world and was to die in 1917.[11]

These were the six MPs who represented Dublin in the House of Commons. They were either too tired, too ill or too lacking in sympathy for the workers' cause to be moved to outrage by the behaviour of the police; they were also no doubt aware that John Dillon, the most significant figure in the Irish Party after Redmond, was deeply antipathetic to Larkin. Dillon regarded Larkin as 'a wild, international syndicalist and anarchist.'[12] Though he represented County Mayo in Parliament, he spent much of his time at his Dublin home in North Great George's Street. Little happened in the capital that escaped his notice, or his censure. His correspondence with parliamentary colleagues makes it clear that he believed Larkinism to be a far greater threat to the supremacy of the Irish Party than Carson or any agents of the Crown.[13]

Nevertheless, four of the six Dublin MPs—Field, Nannetti, Abraham, and Brady—had felt the crisis to be serious enough to risk Dillon's censure. So they wrote their rather noncommittal letter to the newspapers, only to find that most of the next day's editions had relegated it to a 'news brief'. The previous evening a fresh disaster had befallen the city: two tenement houses had collapsed in Church Street. Seven people had been killed, including two children aged four and five; another eight tenants were seriously injured.

9

CHURCH Street was an accident waiting to happen. Horrific though the number of casualties was, equally striking for the modern reader is the fact that the loss of these two houses left eleven families homeless. That it took nearly twenty-four hours to establish how many people had been living in numbers 66 and 67 before they crumbled onto the street also says much about the lack of adequate housing regulation in the city.[1]

The landlady was a widow, Margaret Ryan, who lived in a house at the rear of the doomed properties. She was visiting one of her tenants, Teresa Timmons, who ran a shop on the ground floor of number 67, when both women heard a noise from number 66. Mrs Ryan went around to the other house and found a group of women in the drawing-room on the first floor staring at a marble mantelpiece that had fallen. A series of sharp cracks 'like shots from a rifle' then shook the building, and landlady and tenants rushed for the door.[2] Some escaped, including Mrs Ryan, but fifteen of her tenants were buried in the rubble, most of them within a few feet of the door and safety. The residents of number 67 fled a minute before it too collapsed.

One of those who died was Eugene Salmon, a seventeen-year-old member of the ITGWU who had been locked out by Jacob's the previous day; he died trying to save his four-year-old sister. His mother and two other sisters escaped.

Sergeant Long of the DMP heard the rumble of the falling masonry in Arran Quay and ran to the scene. He found that the front of numbers 66 and 67 had been swept into the street, 'as if a guillotine had cleft the structure in halves.'[3] He telephoned for the Fire Brigade and worked through the night helping to clear the debris. Eight people were rescued and seven bodies recovered. An *Evening Herald* reporter described the scene.

> At five o'clock this morning the rescuers, after the appalling night's experience, proceeded grimly with their work.
>
> The piles of rotten wood, earth and stones in the centre of the space occupied by No. 66 were cleared out and the men came on the body of a woman aged about 56 years. She was so shockingly mangled that it was impossible to identify her ... About two hours before this body was

discovered, the faint moans of a dying child could be heard from under a huge pile of earth. Work was immediately begun in the place where the heart-rending sounds proceeded from, and the first body come upon was that of a woman named Mrs. Fagan. A few yards away a little boy lying in his little cot slept the sleep of death. He had been put to bed by the woman, Mrs. Fagan, who was watching over him, when the collapse came. The little fellow, who had long golden hair and was aged about five, must have been alive up to about three o'clock this morning. There was a look of fear and anguish on his tear stained face, and he had grasped the sheet convulsively in his death agony. He had however escaped mutilation, and was immediately identified as a brother of the little boy Shiels whose dead body was found in the building earlier in the night.

The older Shiels brother was sixteen and the younger five. Their mother and her two other children escaped.

The outcry was immediate. Tenement houses had collapsed before in the city—there were eleven houses in ruins in Church Street alone, not counting 66 and 67—but miraculously few people had died since two houses collapsed in Francis Street twenty years earlier, killing five people.[4] Now seven people had died in Church Street, and the number could have been much higher. Several hundred local children were at a party at the time in the Father Mathew Hall opposite, and a large congregation was attending evening Mass at the church of St Mary of the Angels, which adjoined the buildings. If the collapse had occurred a little later, the number of casualties could have run into scores.

*

Housing was an emotive issue in Dublin at the best of times, and seven deaths brought it to boiling point. In 1913 there were 25,822 families living in tenements. Four out of five of these families lived in one room, and 1,560 of them lived in cellars. Even the employers' chief apologist, Arnold Wright, accepted that nearly a third of the city's population 'live under conditions which are injurious to physique and morality.'[5]

The prevalence of slums in Dublin was in large part due to official neglect. Though there had been British legislation on slum clearance since 1851, Irish legislation was enacted only in 1875—largely at the instigation of the Dublin Sanitary Association, a voluntary body set up by socially conscious members of the middle class following a smallpox epidemic. The peculiar social geography of Dublin aggravated the situation. For a century the old city, lying between the two canals, had been decaying as a corporate organism. Slowly at first and then more rapidly, the middle class fled the increasingly unhealthy conditions for the suburban townships, where the air was cleaner and the rates much lower.

Unlike other cities in Ireland, and in Britain, Dublin found its population and its revenue falling in the nineteenth century. Property speculators and slum landlords took over whole streets, and the houses were repeatedly downvalued, or left derelict because they could not be sold and were not worth maintaining. Between 1854 and 1879 the rateable valuation of the once fashionable Henrietta Street fell from £2,280 to £1,040 and that of the unassuming Granville Street from £840 to £323. During the same period the rateable valuation of Rathmines township rose from £30,728 to £98,065 and that of Pembroke from £42,000 to almost £90,000. Despite this, actual rates paid were much lower than in the city, because the suburbs did not have the same enormous social costs. Businessmen such as William Martin Murphy, who lived in Dartry, were in fact rates exiles.

Dublin slum clearance policies were puny. Between 1904 and 1913 the corporation was able to rehouse only 4,442 people, leaving over 60,000 living in conditions that its own housing department condemned as unfit for habitation.[6] The municipal effort compared poorly with voluntary housing initiatives. Some of the largest of these had been undertaken by the more progressive and paternalistic of the employers; the Guinness and Watkins breweries, the Great Southern and Western Railway, Merchants' Warehousing and the Dublin United Tramways Company had all built accommodation for employees. But by far the most important social housing initiatives were undertaken by two voluntary bodies, the charitable trust set up by the head of the Guinness dynasty, Lord Iveagh, and the Dublin Artisans' Dwellings Company, which was sponsored by the Dublin Sanitary Association. But agencies such as the Artisans' Dwellings Company had to charge profitable rents to thrive and thus build more houses. Only 4 per cent of its housing stock was let at rents of 2s 6d a week or less; its usual tariff was about 3s for a two-roomed cottage and 6s for a four-roomed house. Almost half its housing stock cost more than 5s a week to rent. As D. A. Chart had pointed out, these rents were beyond the reach of the families most in need of decent low-cost housing; in fact the artisans' dwellings scheme often proved self-defeating, because families accepting tenancies promptly brought in lodgers to help with the rent. Nevertheless, in the years before 1907 private initiatives led to 3,936 families being rehoused, compared with 518 by the corporation. The Artisans' Dwellings Company alone rehoused 2,660.[7]

In fairness to the corporation officials it must be said that they faced serious obstacles in their slum clearance policies. Besides having to persuade the city council to approve loans that would increase the rates, the legal procedures for acquiring sites were complex and the cost of compensation high. Landlords were paid the equivalent of ten years' rent for each house, and displaced tenants received the equivalent of six months' rent.

The great majority of working-class families remained dependent on slum landlords for a ceiling over their heads. It suited both tenants and landlords to connive at overcrowding—tenants because they could not afford better, and landlords because it enabled them to squeeze extra income out of these slum properties. It was also easier to evict tenants on low rents: summary court orders were obtainable on demand from local magistrates if tenants paid rents of less than 5s a week.

What added to the political potency of the housing problem in 1913 was the fact that many councillors were themselves slum landlords: no less than seventeen members of the city council in 1913 had slum property interests.[8] In fact it would have been strange if they were not: rented property was the greatest source of unearned income for Dublin's middle class. Nor did the larger capitalists in the city spurn slums as a form of investment. When the *Irish Independent* published a series of articles in early 1913 on the rural slums of Connemara, the *Irish Worker* was quick to remind readers that William Martin Murphy owned cottages on the Dodder that regularly flooded and 'were wreaking [sic] with the germ of consumption.' The *Irish Worker* disparagingly said that more children died of preventable disease in Dublin in a week than in Connemara in a year.[9]

There was a widespread belief that political influence ensured that the corporation's sanitary officers turned a blind eye to landlords' breaches of the law. The housing inspectorate itself was compromised, as two of its members were also slum landlords. Fines were too paltry to be a deterrent, and the only alternative—closing orders—was rarely resorted to, on the grounds that these only reduced scarce housing stock.

The figures speak for themselves. Out of 22,533 dwellings inspected in the last quarter of 1913, only 26 were closed as insanitary. A further 205 prosecutions were taken under the sanitation laws, but there was not a single prosecution for overcrowding.[10] This was in a city with the highest death rate in Ireland or in Britain, at 2.31 per cent. London, with plenty of slums of its own, had a death rate of 1.43 per cent.

Church Street was one of the worst areas for overcrowding in Dublin. Of its 181 houses, 71 were let out in 396 single-room flats. These housed 1,997 people, an average of more than five people to a room.[11] And every informed citizen knew that if numbers 66 and 67 could collapse, so could many other houses in the street.

One of the first questions asked of the distraught Mrs Ryan when she recovered from the first shock of the disaster was whether her houses had been inspected recently by corporation officials. She said that they had and that she had complied promptly 'with every direction.' Less than two months before she had been served with a seven-day order to erect a beam across the ceiling of the front room of number 66 and to repair the pier between the two houses. The completed work had been passed by a dangerous buildings inspector, Michael Derham.[12]

10

WEDNESDAY 3 September 1913 was a bleak day for Dubliners. The newspapers were full of reports of the Church Street disaster of the previous night; they also published reports that the city's employers were to consider a general lockout of their workers. Thousands of those same employees were expected to turn out and pay their last respects that morning to James Nolan, the ITGWU member killed during Saturday night's riots. Trouble was expected. Meanwhile the dreary parade of rioters continued through the police courts.

The *Freeman's Journal* announced that it was opening its columns to a subscription list to help the Church Street victims. People had a right to feel safe in their own homes, the paper said, and it questioned the effectiveness of the corporation's dangerous buildings department. It accepted that the state of the housing stock in districts such as Church Street was bad. Though the houses that collapsed were four-storey buildings, they had rateable valuations as low as £12, and some houses in the street were rated at only £5.

Referring to miraculous escapes from previous building collapses, the *Freeman's Journal* suggested that the high death toll in Church Street was due to the suddenness of the collapse of number 66. Mindful of the slum property interests of so many nationalist councillors, it avoided the wider issues raised by the disaster, preferring instead to praise the heroic work of 'priests, doctors, ambulance and rescuers.'

The paper's main editorial was devoted to the letter sent by the four Dublin city MPs to the Lord Lieutenant demanding a public inquiry into the conduct of the police. It condemned the baton charges in Sackville Street, where 'scores of unoffending citizens were injured.' It endorsed 'the widely held view that ... among the large numbers of police engaged a few lost their heads and acted wildly.'

Turning to the dispute, the *Freeman* tried to distinguish between employers who had locked out workers for being members of the ITGWU and those who did so because the workers 'refuse to transact the ordinary business of the firm' by refusing to handle tainted goods. It also urged careful consideration of a letter from Ernest Aston, one of the city's leading consultant engineers. Aston was a liberal unionist with a strong social conscience, gradually becoming reconciled to the notion of home rule, provided it was accompanied by progressive social policies and proportional representation—the latter to ensure that unionist and Protestant opinion was not swamped in the new parliament.

Aston was the first person to link the Church Street disaster with the labour unrest. Indeed 'Syndicalism and slums' was the headline the *Irish Times* put on a second and expanded version of his letter that it published the next day. Aston argued that

> the growth of Syndicalism, in the form of Larkinism, I submit, cannot be accounted for by any natural tendency of the workman of Dublin. The heather of revolt against intolerable conditions of life has been dried in the one hundred thousand inhabitants of the twenty thousand single tenement rooms of Dublin. Syndicalism set the heather on fire, the conflagration extends, and even the conservative and restraining influence of the Catholic Church has failed to stay its progress. This week ... it has spread outside the slums and respectable, thoughtless Dublin is shocked by citizens wounded and bleeding in its leading thoroughfares, and by the death of Nolan ...
>
> If the smouldering furnace of discontent is to be extinguished, other methods than lockouts will have to be employed ... Only one method has ever proved successful—that of discussion and compromise.
>
> Decisions born out of panic and passion are both dangerous and useless.

Aston predicted, accurately, that the transport workers and their supporters, rather than the employers, would be the protagonists most amenable to compromise.

> Facing starvation and poverty, there is little doubt that they will welcome a cessation of hostilities, if there is any prospect of their reasonable demands receiving fair consideration. On the other hand are the employers, confident—over-confident I think—in their ability to crush syndicalist combinations. Claiming for themselves the right to federate and choose their own leaders, they also claim the right to forbid their employees the choice of a particular leader.

Aston suggested that the time was ripe for the Lord Lieutenant to appoint a special commission, with representatives from both sides, to investigate the best means of resolving industrial disputes. It would then go on to investigate 'the civic administration of Dublin and its environs' and the 'social problems which strike at the very root of the physical, moral and industrial life of the city.'[1]

*

Unfortunately, feelings on both sides were too tumultuous to allow for reasoned intervention. The effects of the sackings had still to be felt in workers' homes, and the main business of the day was burying the first martyr of the struggle, James Nolan.

Throughout the city the ITGWU had put up black-bordered placards calling on members to march behind the coffin of 'another victim in the cause of the workers.' They responded in their thousands, and the funeral procession turned into a show of strength that stretched for over a mile. In the cortege was the Lord Mayor, Lorcan Sherlock, and the leader of the British Labour Party, Keir Hardie, who was in the city to meet the leaders of the strike and to address a public meeting the next day. The chief mourners were Nolan's widow and children. Two hundred tramwaymen formed a guard of honour, marching in uniform and wearing their Red Hand badges. Behind them marched a detachment of several hundred women workers, many of them Jacob's employees, who also wore the prohibited union badge. Another ten thousand mourners made up the remainder of the procession.

At the top of O'Connell Street a bizarre incident occurred that showed how electric the atmosphere of the city had become. Cries of 'The police! The police!' near the Parnell Monument sparked off a terrified stampede of people towards Abbey Street. Men at the head of the funeral procession ran back to see what was happening. In the words of an *Irish Times* reporter, 'matters for a moment looked threatening.' But the panic proved groundless: the small number of police deployed on the streets had kept a low profile. The DUTC also behaved with restraint, and all tram services north of the Liffey were suspended from 2:30 until 5 p.m.[2] In death, James Nolan, the 33-year-old labourer from Market Garden Street, had achieved something that Jim Larkin and the entire Dublin trade union movement would fail to accomplish in five months of industrial strife: he stopped William Martin Murphy's trams from running.

*

While the funeral was taking place, Larkin, still wearing the frock coat and stand-up collar in which he had been arrested on Sunday, was appearing once more in the police court. He was charged with riot, unlawful assembly, and inciting people to steal bread and to murder 'the Constabulary and military of the Crown.' The magistrate, Drury, kept the court 'pretty well cleared,' but Handel Booth and several clergymen were among the select audience. The prosecution case rested largely on Larkin's imprudent speeches of the previous week. Its main weakness lay in the fact that the overwhelming body of evidence from Sunday suggested that it was the police who did the rioting in Sackville Street, rather than Larkin and his followers.

The case was adjourned, and Larkin was again remanded in custody. However, Drury had relented somewhat in the case of Larkin's colleague William Hopkins, and he reduced his sentence for 'jabbing' the police constable from fourteen days' imprisonment to a £1 fine.

Others arrested in connection with the weekend's rioting continued to be dealt with harshly. Thomas Byrne of Lower Dominick Street was fined £2, with the option of a month's imprisonment, for throwing stones and other missiles on Saturday night. Constable 181D told the magistrate, Mr

Hunt, that Byrne had another missile in his pocket when he was arrested. Byrne's solicitor pointed out to laughter that the 'missile' was a bottle of stout and that his client had no intention of throwing it. He also asked for time for Byrne to raise the money, 'as he had to defray the funeral expenses of his child, interred that morning.' Hunt allowed the defendant a week to pay the £2, which was the equivalent of two weeks' wages. In effect he was giving Byrne a choice between prison and the moneylenders.

Not all the incidents involved rioters. William Vernon, a water bailiff with Dublin Port and Docks Board, was accused of intimidating three tramway workers at Clontarf on Tuesday evening. Vernon knew the men and had followed them from a pub, shouting 'scabs!' and 'blacklegs!' A local priest, Father Hayden, tried unsuccessfully to persuade Vernon to go home. One of the tramway men, Patrick Moore, gave evidence of Vernon's good character. Hunt described the incident as trivial but nevertheless remanded Vernon in custody. One reason for the tough line being adopted by the police magistrates in tramway cases may have been the decision of the DUTC to retain a firm of solicitors, Gerald Byrne and Company, to keep a watching brief during the proceedings.[3]

Meanwhile Murphy was unveiling his grand strategy for defeating the ITGWU to nearly four hundred employers at the Chamber of Commerce. It was encompassed in two motions. The first stated that

> this meeting of employers, while asserting its friendly feelings to Trade Unionism, hereby declares that the position created by the Irish Transport and General Workers Union (a union in name only) is a menace to all trade organisation and has become intolerable.

The second stated that,

> in order to deal effectively with the present situation, all employers should bind themselves to adopt a common line of action by signing the agreement presented herewith.

The agreement pledged the gathering to what was in effect an employers' version of syndicalism. It required employers to

> pledge ourselves in future not to employ any persons who continue to be members of the Irish Transport and General Workers' Union, and any person refusing to carry out our lawful and reasonable instructions, or the instructions of those placed over them, will be instantly dismissed, no matter to what Union they belong.

Almost all those present signed the document before leaving the meeting.[4]

It was a remarkable achievement for Murphy. As recently as 18 August the council of the Chamber of Commerce had been prepared to form a conciliation board with the unions, and many of them, according to Wright, had been cowed by Larkin and 'the methods of the Yahoo.' Within two weeks Murphy had convinced them that they could win by turning Larkin's tactics against him. A significant consideration for many employers was the experience of conceding to the demands of the ITGWU only to face the threat of renewed action on another issue, sometimes within a matter of hours. The shipping lines were particularly annoyed at the way dockers had breached their agreements by blacking Eason's goods on the *Lady Gwendolen*. A spokesman for the industry told the *Irish Times* that the shipowners 'were agreeable to work in harmony with the Irish Transport Union, but that the latter will not carry out any agreement come to.'

In the event it was H. McGloughlin, whose ironworks had been involved in a difficult six-week dispute with the ITGWU over the sacking of a worker earlier that summer, who formally proposed the new covenant. The seconder was George Shackleton, the Lucan miller who had been the first employer to lock out his workers.[5]

Over the next few days thousands of Dublin workers were handed the following declaration to sign and return to their employers:

> I hereby undertake to carry out all instructions given to me by or on behalf of my employers, and I further agree to immediately resign my membership of the Irish Transport and General Workers' Union (if a member) and I further undertake that I will not join or in any way support this union.

It was the last clause of this pledge that in effect declared war on all workers in the city prepared to engage in secondary action to support the ITGWU. However, the majority of employers handed out a diluted and little-publicised version of the pledge for their employees to sign. This simply required them to

> carry out all orders given me by or on behalf of my employers, and to handle and deliver all goods from any source, and to work amicably with all other hands.

This document outlawed secondary picketing as effectively as the original one, but it did not contain the offensive references to the ITGWU in Murphy's 'authorised' version.[6]

On the other hand, some of the more militant employers did not give employees a chance to sign either pledge. The Coal Merchants' Association had already locked out some 1,500 men. Immediately after Wednesday's meeting of the Chamber of Commerce, the shipping companies issued a public warning to employees that they must agree to the new conditions by 6 p.m. on Friday or lose their jobs. The Dublin Carriers' Association did not even extend that courtesy to its employees: it declared that its members had decided unanimously

> that in future any employee who refuses to carry out the directions of their employers in the ordinary course of business, whether the employee at either point of loading or unloading be on strike or not, shall be at once discharged, and that the other employees be directed to deliver the goods, and in case of refusal they also to be discharged.

The members of the association pledged themselves 'to assist each other in carrying out the objects of this resolution.' Workers were warned that new conditions would be decided at a future meeting on how to fill the vacancies that arose.

In a further refinement of the employers' strategy, the Society of Motor Manufacturers and Traders announced that not only could employees not join the ITGWU but any worker canvassed to join should immediately report the matter. The services of any existing ITGWU member 'will be dispensed with unless they sever their connection with it.'[7]

*

That evening the Trades Council held a mass meeting in Beresford Place. The main speaker was Keir Hardie. Elected to the House of Commons in 1892 as the first Labour Party MP, he had built the party in close alliance with the trade union movement. Aware of the nervousness of some British trade union leaders about involvement in any strike led by Larkin, he steered a cautious but not unsympathetic course towards the Dublin workers now and throughout the lockout. He told the crowd that he was not there to offer advice but to condemn the collusion of the employers and the authorities in suppressing 'fighting trade unionism, the only kind of trade unionism worth its standing room.'

It was the massive deployment of police against the ITGWU and 'Bloody Sunday' that had struck a nerve in Hardie, as it had with many of the TUC delegates earlier in the week. He could draw on a wealth of personal experience that stretched back over almost fifty years of disputes in which employers had used police, soldiers and even gunboats to break strikes. But he went no further back than the railway strike of 1911.

> Three days before the strike was declared, the employers sent a deputation to Mr. Asquith to see if he would guarantee sufficient protection for their railways; they would undertake, with the aid of blackleg labour, to keep the lines moving and break the strike. The day before the strike was declared thousands of troops—86,000 in all—were turned out and turned over to the control of the railway companies, whilst the railways were being worked by blackleg labour. Mr. Murphy went to the authorities and undertook, if they would lend him troops, to rid the city of Larkinism, and the authorities agreed.

If anyone was to be 'brought to book' for the disturbances in Dublin it was the officials who had violated the fundamental right of workers under the British constitution to organise and meet freely, 'even in Ireland.' Murphy had made it clear that

> he was not afraid of trade unionism of the right kind. It was Larkinism he was afraid of. That was about the biggest compliment he ever had paid to him [Larkin].

What Hardie said next was aimed as much at the TUC leadership as at the employers.

> Those who know Jim like Jim. They don't like some of his faults, [but] this is not the occasion to think of his faults, but the virtues of the man and what he stands for.

Hardie warned the government that the British labour movement fully supported Larkin in defying the prohibition on Sunday's meeting. Any attempt to suppress trade union meetings was 'a question for every trade unionist under the British flag.' He urged the crowd to meet again 'on the prohibited ground' (of Sackville Street), but in the same breath he turned oracular and counselled that this 'is not a moment for precipitous action.'

Hardie then pledged support of a more tangible sort. Turning to Murphy's claim to have planned well for the lockout, intending to starve the workers into submission if necessary, he said to laughter: 'Most of you have served too long an apprenticeship to starvation to be very much afraid of that.' He assured the crowd that

> there will be no starvation. I know that the section of the movement with which I am most prominently identified in these past years—the Socialist side of the Labour Movement—will stand by you solidly and firmly.

He warned the audience against those who described socialism as 'the worst enemy of the working classes.' Hardie himself was 'a firm believer in the Christian religion,' and they 'could never have God's Kingdom upon earth until socialism had settled the working class question.'

The president of Dublin Trades Council, Tom McPartlin, assured the crowd that workers were winning the battle for public opinion at home and abroad. Certainly the ripple effect, as details of police behaviour emerged, was antagonising many respectable citizens. Earlier that day members of Dublin city's housing committee visited Corporation Buildings to inspect the damage and to talk to residents. Councillors and officials were horrified at the scale of the damage. Four months later one of the committee, the independent nationalist councillor Sarah Harrison, could still be brought to tears at the public inquiry into the disturbances when she had to recall the injuries of women she saw that day. Some officials seemed more appalled at the damage to the buildings and contents than to the tenants. On the day of the visit one senior bureaucrat told the *Freeman's Journal* that 'in some cases the police did not leave the people a cup to drink out of.'[8]

*

There was further damaging criticism for the police from Pembroke Urban Council. Its chairman, C. P. O'Neill, presented the *Freeman's Journal* with a list of complaints received about attacks on elderly citizens in Ringsend on Saturday. It included 'Laurence Keenan, up to 90 years of age, after being at confession, attacked almost at his own door by several policemen, struck on the head with a baton, rendered unconscious, brought to and at present in hospital, and he is now in a very precarious condition, not being expected to survive.' Details were also given of attacks on two octogenarians. John Carey was beaten by policemen in Thorncastle Street; bruised on the body and head, he was detained overnight in hospital. 'Michael Nolan, over 80 years, knocked down and kicked by police; carried home and in a bad way.' Another victim was 'Richard Weldrick, over 60 years, off Combridge Place, attack on the head with a baton while at his own yard (where he was carrying on boat building); brought to hospital and had seven stitches in his head.' O'Neill said that 'if these charges can be proved they will show excesses on the part of certain policemen—whether constabulary or Dublin Metropolitan Police.' The demand for a public inquiry into police conduct was rapidly becoming irrefutable.[9]

11

KEIR Hardie's arrival in Dublin for the funeral of James Nolan was fortuitous. Larkin had telegraphed before his arrest, asking Hardie to come and lend his moral support to the Dublin struggle. O'Brien had repeated the request and had met Hardie off the Scottish boat on Tuesday morning. O'Brien briefed him on the situation. Afterwards Hardie asked, 'What part do you play in all this—are you a speaker or a writer?' O'Brien explained that he was more involved in the background organisation of the movement. 'Well, I think it is as well,' Hardie replied. 'There are too many talkers in the movement and too few workers.'[1]

Hardie used his brief time in Dublin productively. Besides attending the Nolan funeral and speaking at the Beresford Place meeting on Wednesday evening, he had attended an emergency meeting of Dublin Trades Council on Tuesday night. While some of his British colleagues had problems with Irish labour's syndicalist and separatist tendencies, Hardie seems to have been consistently supportive of home rule and all the implications this had for the development of an autonomous labour movement in Ireland.[2] And, unlike many British union leaders, he was as supportive of Larkin's stance behind the closed doors of the Trades Council's offices in Capel Street as he was on a public platform. He saw his main task as instilling confidence in the young strike committee, and he told them they were right to send a delegation to the TUC in Manchester. An emergency motion was passed condemning the lockout of ITGWU members as 'an attack on trade unionism generally,' and it was decided to write to 'all English and other societies who have members in Ireland to at once consider the advisability of joining us in resisting this attack.' At local level, the delegates endorsed a proposal from the leader of the Bricklayers' Union, Councillor Richard O'Carroll, for a levy of 1s a week on craft workers and 6d on unskilled workers, to help those locked out.[3]

Impressed by the urgency of the situation, Hardie said he would visit Belfast Trades Council to seek support for the Dublin strikers before returning home. Next day he visited Larkin and Connolly in prison. He knew both men well, especially Connolly, whom he had first met when the latter was an apprentice agitator in the Scotland of the eighteen-nineties.[4]

The TUC delegation showed little of Hardie's dynamism. They refused to address the Wednesday evening meeting in Beresford Place, because one of their number, the Liberal MP John Brace, had not yet arrived. O'Brien said to Hardie: 'This man William Brace seems to be very important. They won't do anything until he shows up. What do you think about him? What is he like?' 'Well,' Hardie replied, speaking very deliberately, 'William Brace is a man with a very large moustache.' Still mystified, O'Brien asked how he should handle Brace. 'Flatter him, my boy, flatter him!'[5]

There was no flattery for Hardie in the *Evening Herald*. As he caught the Belfast train he might well have pondered 'An open letter' from Councillor William Richardson on the front page.

> I noticed that before you were six hours in Dublin you were in a position to pronounce an opinion on everything that had taken place. I am not surprised at this, for it is a failing with 90 per cent of your fellow countrymen, no matter what they call themselves—Liberal, Labour or Unionist. Of course, we poor Irishmen have long resigned ourselves to the inevitable, and are ready to willingly concede that any 'Britisher' who lands at the North Wall knows more 30 minutes after about Ireland than we do ourselves!

If Hardie was the home-ruler he professed to be, Richardson asked,

> Why not leave us to settle this matter in Dublin ourselves? ... Why should the workingmen of Dublin hearken to the voices of yourself and your colleagues?

Mindful perhaps of his own Murphyite creation, the Irish National Workers' Union, Richardson claimed that 'every trade union in Dublin which refused to bow the knee to Larkin has been denounced as a 'scab' organisation.' Larkin had thrown trade unionism back 'by a quarter of a century' with his 'rowdyism and terrorism ... Go back Keir Hardie to your own country; leave decent public opinion and a little newly awakened courage to deal with this public pest and social danger.'[6]

The *Irish Times*, which certainly saw itself as a pillar of 'decent public opinion,' next morning expressed its support for those in Dublin willing to resist the 'syndicalists' running the ITGWU. However, it also agreed

> with our correspondent, Mr. Aston, that the condition of the Dublin slums is responsible not only for disease and crime, but for much of our industrial unrest ... In such places there can be no happiness or content ... The workers, whose only escape from these wretched homes lies in the public house, would not be human beings if they did not turn a ready ear to anybody who promises to improve their lot.

New measures were needed to solve the housing problem. 'But reform, even this terribly urgent reform, must wait upon a return to normal conditions of social life.'

The *Times* fully supported the lockout tactic.

> Within a few days 5,000 men will be out of employment. A great part of

the city's business will be at a standstill. The trade of the port will be paralysed. But the employers have behind them the support of every citizen who values the welfare and prosperity of Dublin. They are fighting for the very life of the city, for the right not merely to do their business in their own way, but to do it at all. Whatever loss the present struggle may inflict on Dublin, it will be nothing in comparison with the ruin which would follow submission to the demands of the strike organisers.

The paper had 'sincere sympathy with those who suggest truce and conciliation,' but it added: 'We cannot see how any truce is possible so long as the employers are asked to negotiate with the Transport Workers' Union.'

*

Thursday saw the first breathing-space in the hectic run of events since the tram strike began. While Dublin coldly took stock of the prospect of a mass lockout, Lord Aberdeen and the Under-Secretary for Ireland, Sir James Dougherty, met the TUC delegation. The British delegates, who were, in the words of the navvies' leader John Ward, trying to get 'the hang' of the situation in Dublin, also met the Trades Council and the Lord Mayor, Lorcan Sherlock.

The *Irish Times* described it as 'a quiet day in the city.' As far as labour was concerned, this meant that all along the south quays the coal trade was at a standstill, and Tedcastle McCormick's three steamers were tied up. On the North Wall, work continued normally as the evening deadline approached for the dockers to forswear their allegiance to the ITGWU. Only at the Port and Docks Board did trouble occur: forty men were sacked for refusing to unload reels of newsprint bound for the *Irish Independent*. Four public representatives on the board tried unsuccessfully to stop the sackings: the nationalist MP William Field, the labour councillor William Partridge, and the nationalist councillors Alfie Byrne and Thomas O'Beirne—a publican and temperance hotelier, respectively. At a specially convened board meeting Partridge accused the employers, who made up the majority, of pretending to promote a conciliation system for Dublin while secretly planning to lock the workers out. To loud protests, he added that there were men sitting round the board-room table 'whose hands are dyed with the blood of their fellow-citizens.'

The nationalists were more moderate in their protests. Field argued that 'strikes and lockouts are not for the benefit of the community.' They should all wait to see if the dispute could be resolved. 'For a body like this Board to declare a lockout is not paving the way to peace.' The majority felt otherwise and endorsed the manager's decision to let the men go.[7]

The city council's conciliation committee was finding its own 'way to peace' difficult. Having been rebuffed by the employers, its members proceeded to Mountjoy Prison to meet Larkin. They had no problem being admitted, but left again when they found that prison rules required that any discussion with Larkin take place in the presence of a warder. The only progress reported was that Sherlock had received a letter from Sir James Dougherty agreeing that an official inquiry into the events of the weekend should take place—but only after order was fully restored. Meanwhile the Irish executive drafted another three hundred RIC men into the city.[8]

On this 'quiet day' the Irish district committee of the National Sailors' and Firemen's Union met in Liberty Hall and called on the union executive in Britain to support any of its members who might be locked out for refusing to handle tainted goods. The union had worked closely with the ITGWU in Dublin port, and it rented offices in Liberty Hall. This was the first indication that the dispute could spread across the channel. Employers were warned that the union locally 'will be quite prepared to face any emergency which a lockout in Dublin may entail.'

In Belfast, Hardie secured the support of the Trades Council for the locked-out workers, but the Dublin newspapers preferred to emphasise the decision by ITGWU members in the cross-channel Belfast docks to set up their own union and escape the 'tyranny' of Larkin. The dockers were reported to be deeply upset at an 'ungodly speech' Connolly had made in Dublin. In fact the Belfast Transport Workers' Union had been set up three months earlier with the encouragement of local employers and was more in tune with the theology of the Orange Order than that of the Vatican.[9]

*

That night in Beresford Place, crowds gathered for yet another meeting in solidarity with the locked-out workers and their imprisoned leader. The TUC delegates may have excused themselves on the grounds that they did not wish to compromise their role as intermediaries before meeting the employers the next day; but that was not how their absence was perceived. When William Partridge addressed the meeting he warned against attempts to settle the dispute 'behind the back' of Larkin. To cheers he announced:

> At any conference of the kind which would be held, Jim Larkin must be present. This is the mandate which he got from the workers and the fighters in this struggle; and no power on earth can move him or them from that view.

The strike leaders did not know whether Larkin would be free to join them at the planned meeting in O'Connell Street on Sunday, 'but whether he is there or not, it is his principles and policy which will be propounded, and to these we will stick in a determined and steadfast fashion (more cheers).'[10]

It was obvious from Partridge's speech that relations between Dublin Trades Council and its British visitors were already strained. The first meeting between the two groups at the Trades Council hall in Capel Street that morning had been cordial enough. 'They spoke a good deal about the right of public meeting,' William O'Brien recalled many years later. The TUC leaders then announced that they had arranged to see Sir James Dougherty at Dublin Castle.

When they came back they were very changed men. Apparently they had got a very bad opinion of us from the Castle authorities. They seemed inclined to drop the public meeting. I saw, or thought I saw what they were after and I remarked to P. T. Daly: 'What about the advertisements, Pat?' He picked up at once and he said: 'Oh, they are on the hoardings by this.' I could see then they shook their heads; it was too far gone to draw back![11]

The mutual antipathy was understandable. The TUC delegation was led by men who had grown old fighting for the basic right to organise. They knew all about the harsh reality of strikes and were used to settling them within the restricted norms of traditional industrial relations. The Irishmen they were dealing with were young, comparatively inexperienced, uncompromising, and clearly bitten by the syndicalist bug. All the TUC men except Gosling were on the conservative wing of the movement, and indeed their arrival had been warmly welcomed by the *Irish Times*. It described the two Liberal MPs Brace and Ward as 'men whom the House of Commons esteems for their candour, common sense and long experience of affairs.' It contrasted their prudence, and reluctance to comment on the rights and wrongs of the dispute, with the behaviour of Hardie, who had thrown himself 'into the arms of the strike organisers.' Even Gosling provided little comfort for the Dubliners. His own union had been at the centre of the London docks strike in 1911 and had barely survived the ordeal financially. He had little appetite for sympathetic action on behalf of Dublin.

Unlike the city council's conciliation committee, the TUC leaders appear to have had no difficulty meeting Larkin privately in Mountjoy. Larkin provided little solace, refusing to discuss the situation while he was in prison. He told them he would stand over anything agreed by O'Brien and Daly.[12]

*

If the British trade unionists found their Irish colleagues difficult, the Irish employers proved impossible. A request from the TUC delegation to meet William Martin Murphy had been relayed to him by Dublin Castle on Thursday afternoon.[13] Murphy met them at the Shelbourne Hotel next day with some of the other main employers involved in the lockout, including George Jacob, T. C. McCormick for the coal merchants, John McGloughlin for the master builders, J. Wallis for the carriers, and Charles Eason. Though the meeting lasted seven hours, no progress was made. The employers had two preconditions to negotiations: they wanted a guarantee that any agreements reached would be honoured; and they wanted the Larkinites excluded from the talks.

Gosling led the discussion for the British visitors. He said they lacked the authority to give commitments on behalf of local unions, 'declined to discountenance the sympathetic strike,' and suggested that it was in everyone's interest to bring all Irish union representatives into the talks.[14] The employers refused to budge and only reluctantly agreed to meet the TUC delegation again on Monday. They felt, rightly, that the British delegates could not deliver the Larkinite beast, in a suitably tamed condition, into their hands at this early stage in the dispute.[15]

The TUC delegation did, however, find one Irishman who was accommodating, in the literal sense. Lorcan Sherlock invited them to be his guests at the Mansion House.

*

While the TUC delegation got the hang of things, the dispute spread to the North Wall. Over a hundred workers at the London and North-Western Railway Company walked off the job in support of dockers who refused to load cases of Jacob's biscuits on the LNWR steamer *Snowdon*. Their decision took courage. During the 1911 rail strike the same men had been out for three weeks in sympathy with British workers and had only been taken back after promising to handle all goods in future.

Most of the shipping companies seemed willing to wait until the 6 p.m. deadline on Friday before taking action against workers refusing to handle tainted goods. That was certainly the attitude of the City of Dublin Steam Packet Company, the oldest operator in the port. It had the much-coveted mail contract, and this made it vulnerable to industrial strife. It had been the focal point of the costly union recognition battle with the ITGWU in May and clearly did not relish another. When the company's porters refused to load the weekly consignment of mattresses from Frederick Wookey's plant in Leixlip—because of his decision to lock out ITGWU employees—the company decided to apologise to Wookey for the inconvenience, but left his cargo standing on the quay. That evening the North Wall and the southern line of quays were eerily quiet, except for the clatter of mounted DMP patrols.

The great public event of the day was the funeral of the Church Street victims, which completely overshadowed the inquest into their deaths. The City Coroner's Court heard that remedial work had been ordered by Derham, the dangerous buildings inspector, only a month before the houses collapsed. This was reportedly carried out by 15 August, and Derham passed it, though he admitted in court that he could not see if a new supporting beam was adequate, as it had been boxed in by the time he called. He denied rumours that the landlady was related to any of the officials in his department; no-one thought to ask if any of the inspectors were themselves slum landlords. The hearing was adjourned to allow more evidence on the causes of the collapse to be gathered.

It was all irrelevant to the dead. A dismal convoy of four hearses, bearing the coffins of the seven victims, passed through the city's main streets. There were grand speeches, but the spectacle cast further gloom on the citizens.

Various special funds for the victims had already been set up. The largest donation, £52 10s, came from the members of the DMP; they sent it to the *Irish Times* fund. The paper's owner, the department store magnate Sir John Arnott, donated £10, and Viscount Powerscourt £3. By the time of the funeral the *Times* had received over £100. The *Freeman's Journal* received a similar amount, with the largest contribution of £19 contributed by small traders in the Dublin Corporation market. The sums contributed to the relief of the Church Street victims far exceeded the £155 subscribed so far to the joint *Irish Times* and *Irish Independent* fund for the Loyal Tramway Men.

Curiously, *Irish Times* readers were far more generous to the Tramway Men than those of the *Independent*, contributing £134 8s of the total, which probably reflects the greater prosperity, as well as the more conservative leanings, of *Times* readers. Indeed, the list of Tramway Fund subscribers published in the *Times* reads like a directory of the city's social elite, with a high proportion of JPs, professional people and members of the peerage contributing. In contrast, contributors to the Church Street fund spanned the social spectrum. The motivation was clear from the pseudonyms some donors used, such as 'With sympathy', 'Pity', 'A mite', 'An old slum dweller', and, of course, 'Virtute non Verbis [by virtue not by words]'. There was, however, a much higher proportion of anonymous contributors to the Loyal Tramway Men, and these tended to use more combative or even overtly political pseudonyms, such as 'Anti-Larkinite', 'No Larking,' and 'An Admirer of Pluck.' Sir William Goulding, with magisterial equity, gave two guineas to each fund.[16]

*

The DMP donation to the Church Street fund may have provided the force with some much-needed good publicity, but their activities on the previous weekend continued to come under unfavourable scrutiny. On Thursday morning the newspapers reported that another rioter injured on Saturday night had died. This was John Byrne, who had been released from Jervis Street Hospital only to succumb at his home in Lower Gloucester Place. He too had been a member of the ITGWU. He left a wife, two sons, and a daughter.

As luck would have it, the inquest on James Nolan resumed the same day. No-one was in any doubt of the political significance of the deaths. Before going to meet the Dublin employers, the TUC delegates attended the opening stages of the proceedings. There was further telling civilian evidence against the police. Almost every detail was contested by Inspector Campbell and his men, but the damning claim that Nolan was left lying unattended on the quayside for twenty minutes waiting for an ambulance could not be denied.

The jury took only thirty-five minutes to find that Nolan had died from a baton blow, but 'the evidence was so conflicting that they were unable to say by whom the blow was inflicted.'[17] It was still a damaging verdict for the police, given that they had, in the time-honoured way, selected the coroner's jury.

Police magistrates had less difficulty apportioning guilt. When James Byrne, the ITGWU's branch secretary in Kingstown, appeared that morning in the local police court he was acquitted of intimidating DUTC employees on the first day of the strike but fined £1 for 'jostling' a tram inspector. However, the most publicised court case of the day involved the irrepressible Councillor William Richardson. He was charged with assaulting a quay labourer, John Boylan, at Summer Hill the previous night. Boylan, who appeared in court with cuts to his nose and head, was a drum major in the ITGWU Band. He claimed that Richardson had made an unprovoked attack on him, beating him unconscious with a stick and threatening with a revolver local people who tried to intervene.

Richardson said that Boylan was part of a mob that had been hounding him for days. He carried the stick and a toy revolver for protection. Unlike Boylan, he experienced difficulty in finding witnesses to corroborate his version of events. The magistrate, Mr Hunt, adjourned the case to allow him more time to prepare his defence. Richardson was also in the civil courts that day, prosecuting his claim for libel damages against the *Irish Worker* and Larkin. As Larkin was in prison, this case too was adjourned.[18]

*

That night there was an attenuated crowd in Beresford Place, where Richardson's regular antagonist on the city council, William Partridge, was the only speaker. The TUC men still resolutely refused to speak before the planned protest in defence of free speech in Sackville Street. Partridge, who had visited Mountjoy that day, said that Larkin had called for a rent strike until the industrial dispute was over. For the benefit of the TUC delegation as much as the employers, he repeated his warning that there could be no settlement conference without 'James Larkin having a dominant voice in the matter; and, if necessary, they will have to go to Mountjoy Prison to have that conference.' Partridge blamed the Lord Lieutenant for the crisis. The Irish people had always given a cordial welcome to Lord and Lady Aberdeen, but now that he was locking up trade unionists and putting uniformed police on the streets 'to murder people,' he had better resign.

Lord Aberdeen no doubt felt he was being treated a little cavalierly. The real power in the executive lay with the Chief Secretary for Ireland, Augustine Birrell, and the Under-Secretary, Sir James Brown Dougherty. John Campbell Gordon, seventh Earl of Aberdeen, was a constitutional ornament with even fewer discretionary powers than the monarch he represented. A well-intentioned but often ineffectual figure, he was despised by some of his own senior civil servants. Arthur Hamilton Norway, secretary of the Irish Post Office, described Aberdeen as

a kindly, well meaning man, but dull and by no means strong enough to deal with the difficult situation which was even then growing ... I recall no observation of any value which he ever made to me on the condition of the country, or any other matter.[19]

In fact Aberdeen was far more familiar with the problems of Ireland than were Norway and most of Dublin Castle's other supercilious mandarins, not to mention Birrell, the lackadaisical Chief Secretary. A Gladstonian Liberal, Aberdeen had first served as Lord Lieutenant in the eighteen-eighties and was a party grandee of some standing. In the eighteen-nineties he had been Governor-General of Canada. The innate sympathy of Aberdeen and his wife, Ishbel, with the Irish people was probably as significant a barrier to good relations with senior civil servants in Dublin Castle—who were almost invariably appointed from the British civil service—as any personality differences. Aberdeen was fully committed to home rule and 'the strong conviction held by Mr. Birrell, and adopted as a principle of action by the ministry, that Ireland should be governed by Irish ideas.'[20] In 1910 he had released Larkin from prison, and he had repeatedly tried, usually unsuccessfully, to mediate in major industrial disputes. He had made a point of inviting Larkin to the Park and let it be known that he was sympathetic to some of Larkin's aims, if not his methods.

Like his wife, Lord Aberdeen was deeply concerned about social issues, and the couple sponsored a host of worthy causes. Lady Aberdeen had taken particular interest in promoting public health. Her initiatives included the founding of the Women's National Health Association and the establishment of sanatoriums for TB victims. They looked an incongruous pair: she was large and matronly, he slight and dapper; but ordinary Dubliners knew that their concern was genuine, and Ishbel was paid the supreme back-handed compliment of a ditty in her honour:

Sez Lady Aberdeen,
I'm next below your queen,
Who lives across the sea
and loves you dearly.
I love yez just as well
And among yez I will dwell
For the paltry sum of twenty thousand yearly.[21]

Lord Aberdeen now worked strenuously behind the scenes to avert further confrontation on the streets. He met the TUC delegation and urged them to abandon the rally planned for Sackville Street. He explained that, despite his grand title, it was up to the government to lift the proscription on meetings in Sackville Street, and that it had no intention of doing so.[22] When he failed to move them, he enlisted the aid of the DMP Commissioner, Sir John Ross, and the Under-Secretary, Sir James Dougherty, to make his case.

Dougherty was a former professor of logic at Magee Presbyterian Theological College in Derry. He belonged to the once glorious but now sadly diminished northern radical liberal tradition. He had been made Under-Secretary in 1905, after unsuccessfully contesting the Derry constituency for the Liberals. It was not unusual for Under-Secretaries to be appointed over the head of career civil servants on a party political basis, but Dougherty was the first home-ruler to be given the post. As one of his subordinates recorded, the Liberals saw him as reliable and capable of creating the desired

> atmosphere appropriate to the coming Home Rule Bill. His core was diplomacy rather than strength, though twinges of gout made his temper at times somewhat acid.[23]

Dougherty used his diplomatic gifts on the TUC delegates, but they proved no more susceptible than the unionists to threats and blandishments. The fact was that the resources of the Irish executive, both political and punitive, were extremely limited. Home rule might be imminent, but a century of union had seen control of most services centralised in London. The ineffectual figures of Dougherty and Aberdeen symbolised the impotence of Dublin Castle. In despair they appealed to Birrell; only he, they explained to the TUC leaders, could lift the ban.

The Chief Secretary rarely visited Dublin. He suffered severely from seasickness, disliked the draughty offices allocated to him in Dublin Castle, and was reluctant to leave his invalid wife alone in London. Perhaps most important of all, Birrell did not like the job of Chief Secretary and had taken it only to gain a place at the Cabinet table.

A large, burly figure whose disarmingly light and witty manner hid a sharp intellect, Birrell was the complete antithesis of the earnest, diminutive Aberdeen. He had once been considered a potential Prime Minister, but he refused to take life seriously enough and to develop the gravitas expected of a senior politician. His superficially relaxed approach to politics infuriated opponents of all political hues. His undisguised preference for the Abbey Theatre over the Chief Secretary's lodge in the Phoenix Park had earned him the soubriquet 'Playboy of the Western World'. He did not mind at all; indeed he far preferred the west of Ireland and its people to the capital—and especially to the denizens of the Viceregal palace. There an odd mixture of Anglo-Irish gentry, socially ambitious Catholics and liberal do-gooder friends of the Aberdeens proliferated.

However, Birrell's prolonged absences meant that he often had little feel for what was happening. This isolation was aggravated by the fact that Dougherty had to rely on military telegraph to contact his political master. Norway had decreed against a telephone, on the grounds that it was not secure; during the crisis Birrell was receiving 'cypher telegrams almost every day.'[24]

Fortunately he could learn most of the essential facts from the newspapers. Within a week of 'Bloody Sunday' he had decided to hold an inquiry into the behaviour of the police and was contemplating another into the housing situation. But before either could be undertaken he decided that a Board of Trade inquiry must be held into the lockout. Resolving the industrial crisis was the first step towards restoring normality to the streets of Dublin.

He was well aware of trade union feeling on the issue. In the six days following 'Bloody Sunday' his office received 272 resolutions from trades councils, unions, Socialist Party branches and other bodies condemning the actions of the police. He had also received personal representations from Labour Party MPs and his own constituents in Bristol.[25] After hearing from Aberdeen and Dougherty that the TUC delegation was adamant about holding their rally in Sackville Street, Birrell told Asquith that he intended allowing it to go ahead. However, he decided against travelling to Dublin himself, as his wife was feeling 'very far from well.'[26]

12

ON Friday, Dublin's middle class were shocked to hear that William Martin Murphy had been given police protection. For the first ten days of the strike he had 'gone about his business in Dublin without the slightest molestation or insult,' though several effigies of him had been hung from lamp-posts and burnt in working-class areas. It was another indication of the demise of social deference and the ascent of the 'yahoo' in the city.[1]

Murphy had long been a hate figure in the columns of the *Irish Worker*. On Saturday 6 September it published a cartoon on its front page showing Murphy perched as a vulture at the entrance to his home, Dartry Hall, cackling over the corpse of a worker. The caption read, with apologies to Byron: *The Demon of Death spread his wings on the blast | And spat on the face of the poor as he passed.* Partridge was editing the paper in the enforced absence of Larkin and Connolly. The 'Chief' was imprisoned, he wrote, invoking the memory of Parnell. The gutter press that Murphy had created to assail Parnell 'with all the vituperation and insult that one could possibly conceive' had been turned on Larkin. 'William Martin Murphy and the permanent officials of the Irish Government are responsible for the murder of poor Nolan and for the outrages perpetrated by hired ruffians in uniform with a lust for blood.' Beside these Partridge arraigned the other enemies of the cause. It was a long list, which included the secretary of the AOH, 'John D. Nugent, ex-bailiff and Insurance agent ... process server, rent warner and hog ranger'; the journalist John S. Kelly, 'scab hypocrite and sky pilot; Richardson the unspeakable, the trader upon skulls and bones and decomposed tissues,' as well as the generally 'dissolute and debauched, who form the lazy rich, and the overfed, and the brutal ruffians who comprise the Metropolitan and Irish (?) Constabulary.' Murphy was of course 'the mainspring' of this combination.

Nor did Partridge spare John Redmond and the Irish Party. In contrast to his role in Land League days, Redmond's new battle cry was 'to toast the King of England, the Aberdeens, including Ishbel, Moriarty [the Irish Attorney-General], Swifte [the senior Police Court magistrate] ... and all the parasites who fatten under Dublin Castle patronage.' The 'manly spirit of the race' now resided in the workers. 'At the next election for Parliament the workers will ask of Clancy, Cotton, Nannetti, Field, Brady and

Abraham … why have they remained inactive in the present crisis, and will doubtless relegate them to their original obscurity.'

*

Not surprisingly, J. F. Moriarty, a nominee of the Irish Party for the post of Attorney-General and later Chief Justice, endorsed a police recommendation that Partridge should have his bail revoked for the material in the *Irish Worker*, as well as for his speech the previous night calling for a rent strike. Birrell told Moriarty to let the matter drop.[2] He was putting his trust in conciliation rather than repression.

Birrell was rarely this optimistic. He once said that the two greatest obstacles to home rule were money and religion. 'It was a very odd thing about money and religion, that the people who got the most excited about money were the people who had the most of it—and the people who got the most excited about religion were the people who had none of it.'[3]

Birrell could well have had Murphy and the *Irish Catholic* in mind; like Murphy's other publications, the *Irish Catholic* transmitted a deeply conservative gospel in a modern guise. It sought to love Dublin's poor but found it hard to hide the revulsion that the object of its charity evoked at close quarters. Salacious prudery was often the result. In February 1913 it published an article on 'Dublin's social state,' based on a sermon at Westland Row church by a Father Larkin, who ran a large boys' sodality in Dominick Street. Father Larkin ascribed 'the extraordinary poverty of the poor of Dublin' to the want of employment. 'I am quite aware that there are numbers of men and women in Dublin, men particularly, who would not work if they got a day's pay, but there are thousands of decent, honourable men who would earn for their families but are not able to get employment.' He lamented

> the want of sympathy that there is among Catholics in Ireland. Touch one Protestant—I think the principle is a good one—and you touch all the Protestants in Ireland. You walk on Catholics and nobody will say a word.
>
> The second thing is the fearfully low wages paid to our people in Dublin. It follows that if there are 40 men ready for every little employment, of course the employers may give what they please.

He spoke of 'men of 19' trying to support their mothers and sisters on 6s a week.

Drink was 'the third great cause of poverty in Dublin,' and the fourth was bad housing. These four curses left working-class families easy prey to proselytisers and immorality. Father Larkin dwelt particularly on the risks of overcrowding and drink on children. 'If you only knew the fearful amount of immorality that exists!' he wrote. 'I am perfectly certain that there is a great deal of gross immorality amongst the children of Dublin— one bad boy or girl amongst these children may corrupt a whole score.'

The *Irish Catholic* had no time for Larkin's solutions to these problems, and it watched his progress with a baleful eye. In its issue of 30 August

1913 it condemned the tram strike as 'probably one of the most ill-conceived and foolish strikes in this or any other country.' It urged Catholic trade unionists to 'keep true to their Christian principles' and never allow 'the interests and rights of labour to fall into the hands of unscrupulous leaders who are swayed by socialistic and anarchistic principles.'

To promote Catholic activism within the labour movement the paper regularly published information from the Board of Trade on wage rates and social entitlements. It also published summaries of Catholic social doctrine, including extracts from Pope Leo XIII's encyclical *Rerum Novarum*.

On 6 September it had a sterner gospel to preach. It accepted that on the previous Sunday

> a few members of the police forces employed in the suppression of the riots committed unwarranted acts of violence against wholly innocent people. On the whole however, the behaviour of the Metropolitan Police and their allies of the R.I.C. was admirable in every way.

Turning then to 'Dublin's Peril,' it said that 'most self-respecting and educated men and women' were 'heartily ashamed' of recent events on the streets of the capital.

> Into these thoroughfares there have poured nightly all the foul reserves of the slums, human beings whom life in the most darksome depths of a great city has deprived of most of the characteristics of civilisation. In the majority of instances they are beings whose career is generally a prolonged debauch, seldom broken by the call of labour. Even when sheer necessity compels toil, it is undertaken unwillingly and merely to obtain the means to enable another spell of besotted idleness. They are essentially birds of the night, and foul birds at that.
>
> These bad, sad specimens of the human race have no interest in the cause of labour, for they scarcely understand what the word means or the nobility it implies. Their one thought is to work destruction and havoc in that existing order of society which they hate, because they cannot comprehend why it should limit their depredations or punish their excesses ... The unfortunate creatures ... are not in any way connected with artisans or labourers of our metropolis; the aristocracy of toil regard them with a pitiful contempt, desiring neither their championship nor friendship ... They have no trade claim to urge, no right of labour to maintain. They are not on strike, nor have they been locked out.

The paper expressed sympathy for

> the employees of the Tramways Company who have struck at the bidding of a vituperative socialist who is now a prisoner of the Crown, and the still larger body of persons who have either gone on strike or

been locked out because they preferred to obey the occult decrees of the Transport Union rather than the direction of their legitimate employers. For all these we think every fair minded and tolerant observer will have an infinite pity.

These workers now knew that

by the folly and malice of their so-called leader they have been placed in deplorable straits, without funds, without respect and without character, and all this to gratify the whims of an adventurer who has been battening on their credulity.

As Catholic Journalists, against whom the taunt cannot be levelled that we represent Capital or capitalist interests—we implore them, even now—to break loose from the Socialist and consequently demoniacal influences which are dragging them into perdition and ruin.

The opinions of the *Irish Catholic* probably carried as little weight with most Dublin workers as the *Irish Worker* carried with members of the Dublin Chamber of Commerce. But the paper did play on the prejudices of many middle-class Dubliners, whose fear of the strike leaders was always liable to outweigh any feelings of sympathy for the strikers. It may well, therefore, have helped reduce donations for the relief of distress among the victims of the lockout.

*

Arthur Griffith's *Sinn Féin* was another journal that had very definite views on the lockout. As an advanced nationalist, Griffith was opposed in principle to the influence of British trade unions, or international socialist ideologies, in the Irish labour movement. Despite its name and aspirations, the ITGWU was regarded by Griffith as 'foreign', because of its origins as a breakaway from the NUDL. There was also a deep personal antipathy between 'Little Arthur' and 'Big Jim', which dated from Larkin's arrival in the city.[4]

Griffith had a strong tendency to personalise his politics. If he hated Larkin, he had a warm regard for his principal lieutenant, James Connolly, who had a similar temperament to the Sinn Féin leader and shared many of his intellectual interests. Nevertheless the personality of Larkin and the union's politics militated against Griffith lending it his support. There was also the fact that it represented the unskilled. Griffith was a printer by trade and a lifelong member of the Dublin Typographical Provident Society and had the craft worker's traditional antipathy for general unions.

However, he knew that simplistic denunciations of the ITGWU would only alienate Dublin workers. Sinn Féin had already enjoyed some success in winning electoral support from the working class. Its councillors were generally seen as champions of labour interests on the city council, and several leading trade unionists, such as Partridge, Daly, and O'Carroll, had been party members in the past. Some, like Michael O'Lehane, secretary of the Drapers' Assistants' Association—the richest and one of the best-organised unions in the country—still were.

In its edition of Saturday 6 September, *Sinn Féin* declared that the common people

> were the backbone of all national movements in the past, from 98 to Parnell's days ... One must not blame them, whose condition is worse than serfs, for striving for the elementary right to live according to some decent standard of existence. If we cannot secure it for them, we at least need not alienate them, and throw them back into the arms of England.

Griffith, writing as 'Lasairfhíona', declared:

> It seems to me that if we do not evolve a national policy designed to give the working classes—almost a term of reproach, if not contempt in these days—justice and fair play, as far as we can secure them for them in their own country, we must be prepared to see the people throw in their lot with the English Labour Party, who at least give them smooth words and specious promises ... The labour problems of Ireland are not to be solved, but to be aggravated, by swallowing English quack remedies ... It is the right of every Irishman willing to work to be secured a fair living in his own country. That he can never secure while his country is exploited and governed in the interest of England, and so long as any section of Irishmen can be led to think that earthquake pills are a cure for all ills, and that there is no colourable difference between the green flag of Irish Nationalism and the red banner of English Socialism, so long will such a section of Irishmen be catspaws of England.

Sinn Féin also criticised the ineffectiveness of Dublin corporation in tackling the slum problem. But it placed the main blame with the Chief Secretary and chairman of the Local Government Board in Ireland, Augustine Birrell. Far more than any slum landlord, city councillor, or local government official, Birrell was 'criminally responsible for what has happened' in Church Street. The paper accurately predicted that the charge would not excite Birrell's apprehension. 'Following his usual custom when there is any trouble in Dublin, he is at present in a remote region playing golf, and he will continue to play it until the atmosphere is cool enough for him to return and make epigrams by the sweat of his brow.' Meanwhile,

> the vile and destructive methods of demagogues posing as labour leaders in Dublin will not divert the minds of honest and intelligent men from the fact that the poorest section of the population of Dublin has suffered and is suffering from an abominable grievance ... They are obliged to pay exorbitant rents for wretched accommodation in which even their lives are not safe.

Griffith made the telling point that

> the average Dublin working man pays actually double the rent for a one-roomed tenement in a slum that the agricultural labourer pays for a villa

residence and a considerable area of land. And there is the further fact that the majority of the skilled artisans of Dublin cannot afford as good a house as that of the agricultural labourer.

He urged the corporation to give up its practice of buying slum properties 'at enormous cost and under grave suspicion of jobbery'; instead it should build 'comfortable houses to be let at the rents now paid in the city for tenements of one or two rooms' on the lands it owned at Blanchardstown and Baldoyle. An extension of the tramway system could bring the workers to jobs in the city.

There was a touch of the futuristic in Griffith's housing and transport policies, and his imaginative approach was one of the factors that helped Sinn Féin cut the ground from under the feet of labour councillors, preoccupied as they were with the immediacy of the class struggle at one level and of strategising for the workers' republic at another. Griffith was not slow to criticise the

> several so-called labour parties in the corporation, and their united record ... represented by a 0. The one party in the Corporation that ever really attempted and really did something for the herded tenement dwellers of Dublin was the Sinn Féin party.

In all of this, Griffith managed to avoid mentioning his party's embarrassing ties in the past with one of the prime movers of the lockout, W. E. Shackleton. In the turmoil of the moment, few seemed to notice.

*

A more sympathetic, and more perceptive, view of the disturbances appeared in the *Irish Homestead*, journal of the agricultural co-operative movement. This was largely due to the happy accident of having George Russell as its editor. Poet, painter, and committed advocate of the 'co-operative commonwealth', Russell, writing under the pseudonym Æ, now began to find his true *métier* as a polemicist. He would soon be regarded by employers as a fellow-traveller of the Larkinites; at this point, however, he was still inclined to see Larkin's mouthpiece, the *Irish Worker*, as having 'a tendency to substitute rage for a policy.' That rage was only being inflated 'by the monstrous conduct of the authorities.' The action of the police 'had done more sharply to divide the classes in Ireland than anything which has happened for half a century.' Their only policy

> ... is to suppress labour and its organisation ... That is a vain hope. Larkin is not the cause of labour discontent. He is the product of it himself. Something better will have to be done than denounce labour attitudes as socialism or syndicalism. Labour is as guiltless of the charge of being socialist or syndicalist as Mr. Murphy himself.

The present unrest was 'nothing else than a passionate discontent with present conditions of wages, housing and unemployment.'[5]

*

The inquest on one victim of 'passionate discontent', John Byrne, took place on Saturday morning. The jury found that he died from a fractured skull. His widow told the coroner, Dr L. A. Byrne, that her husband came home on Saturday 30 August with his head in bandages and said he had 'got a blow of a baton from a country policeman.' This was dismissed as hearsay. After the hearing, ITGWU members took it in turns to carry their dead comrade's coffin to the Pro-Cathedral. The procession, several hundred strong, stopped for a minute's silence outside Liberty Hall.

*

The criminal courts, for a change, provided a little light relief that morning. Councillor William Richardson came up before Mr Hunt, the magistrate, once more on a charge of assaulting John Boylan, the dock labourer and drum major with the ITGWU band. Though Richardson had requested the adjournment to assemble witnesses, he produced none. In contrast, Boylan had several witnesses, the medical evidence and, most damning of all, his facial injuries to prove his case; Hunt ignored all of it and bound both men to be of good behaviour for twelve months. Richardson was outraged. He said he would not 'stultify' himself by giving such an undertaking. 'I distinctly refuse to put my hand to any statement declaring that I acted as a blackguard on the streets of Dublin.' Even the threat of imprisonment failed to move him, and Hunt, in exasperation, discharged both men with a caution.[6]

The magistrate's action was in marked contrast to the treatment that ITGWU officials such as Hopkins and Byrne had received. They had been remanded in custody on charges of 'jabbing' a policeman and 'jostling' a tram inspector, respectively. James Connolly, who was not accused of assaulting anyone, was still in prison for refusing to give similar undertakings to those Richardson found so 'stultifying'.

*

The great social event of the day was a garden party given by Lord Iveagh in the grounds of his house in St Stephen's Green on behalf of the Irish Unionist Alliance. Behind the high walls of Iveagh House the prospective Unionist candidate for South Dublin, Captain Bryan Cooper, appealed for calm in the present 'Labour crisis' in the city. When trade had returned to normal 'they could discuss the cause of the dispute, which was due to the bad conditions under which the working classes had to live.' Visiting speakers contrasted the urgency with which Dublin Castle was considering an inquiry into the conduct of the police in Dublin with its alacrity in investigating the July riots in Derry. On that occasion the RIC had allegedly stood by and allowed nationalist mobs to attack loyal subjects of the Crown with impunity.

Birrell was regarded in the same cynical light by the unionist speakers on the platform that afternoon as *Sinn Féin* had shed on him in its columns in the morning. He ignored public opinion, said the Unionist MP John Gordon, because he 'really thought that he and his colleagues knew far better than the people themselves what was the will of the people.'[7]

Elsewhere the city returned to its normal relaxed weekend air. 'The usual harmony and good humour prevailed in every quarter, the police were not obtrusively visible in any quarter,' according to the *Sunday Independent*.

Father Curran chose Saturday to write to the archbishop in France, assuring him that 'the rioting seems to have spent itself.' He confessed that it was 'wonderful that there has been no renewal of disturbances under the circumstances'—the 'circumstances' being the proposed lockout of all who failed to sign the declaration of the Dublin Employers' Federation renouncing Larkinism.

The Church Street disaster would 'give something to the Lord Mayor and Corp. to think about beside the police,' Curran suggested smugly. He asked the archbishop if he wished to subscribe to the relief fund.

> Meanwhile we are forgetting there was such a thing as a tram strike. The trams are running on the main lines as if nothing had happened.[8]

Despite his optimism, Father Curran decided to order fifty-two tins of petrol for the archbishop's car instead of the usual twenty, just in case.

*

However, the trams still observed a night curfew, and receipts for the previous week were only £2,917, compared with £6,322 for the same week in 1912. Worried coal merchants decided to increase prices, in case the situation on the docks should worsen. The price of a ten-stone bag rose from 1s 6d at the end of August to 2s in early September; by the end of another week, when the main coal importers had locked out their workers, the price was 3s. The *Irish Times* wrote that there was 'no moral justification for the increased prices now being charged by some importers.' An industry source told the paper that 50,000 tons of coal were already stockpiled in the city.[9]

*

On Sunday 7 September, Dubliners woke up in anticipation of the great trade union rally that was due to take place that afternoon. It overshadowed all other events, even the departure of 2,300 pilgrims for Lourdes with Cardinal Logue at their head. Stories that would otherwise have dominated the front pages, such as renewed suffragist outrages in England, a stepping-up of the war in the Balkans, rallies against home rule in Ulster, and the revelation that the pleasant fishing village and seaside resort of Heligoland had been transformed into a veritable 'Gibraltar of the North Sea' by the Kaiser, were relegated to the sidelines.

The *Sunday Independent*, anxious to divert attention from the rally, advised readers in its main front-page story that a 'well known employer' believed that 'important developments of a favourable character' would take place on Monday after talks with the TUC delegation resumed. 'These … are clear, level headed men who have experience in dealing with genuine disputes where many thousands of men are concerned.'

The story could have done nothing to ease the tense relations between the TUC leaders and the Dublin strike committee. Presumably that was its purpose. Far from wishing for a negotiated settlement with the TUC, Murphy wanted to use the talks to isolate the Dublin strike committee and characterise its Larkinite leadership as the main obstacle to peace. When the talks broke down, as the employers clearly expected they would, it was essential to maximise the share of blame the public would attribute to the Trades Council.[10] For the benefit of its less subtle readers, the paper published a cartoon of a blindfolded workman being led into a sea of 'unemployment, starvation and social misery' by Larkin; it then showed Larkin running off with the union funds.

Before the rally took place, the ITGWU buried John Byrne. As with the funeral of James Nolan the previous week, the union made it a demonstration of strength. The tramway strikers once more provided a mass guard of honour, and five bands attended, as did the British TUC delegation and the entire Dublin Trades Council. Byrne was buried in a plot beside Nolan's. There appears to have been no graveside oration; there would be speeches enough in the afternoon.

*

In an era when public meetings were a principal source of entertainment and diversion, as well as fulfilling their more explicit political functions, the Sackville Street rally was an extravaganza of its kind. No fewer than seven general officers of leading British trade unions were present to address the crowd, including four MPs and one former MP. It was the most distinguished panel of British labour leaders ever to address a public meeting in Dublin.

Because of the number of visiting speakers and the size of the crowd, it was decided to hold three separate but simultaneous meetings. Shortly before 1 p.m. a convoy of wagonettes left Liberty Hall for Sackville Street. When it reached the broad thoroughfare the wagonettes separated and drew up beside three of the street's best-known landmarks: the Parnell Monument, Nelson's Pillar, and the Father Mathew statue. On the blast of a bugle the first speaker at each location began to address the crowd.

However, content did not match form. If the bugle was a dramatic flourish from the Trades Council, the steadying hand of the TUC was evident in the brief speeches and moderate demands. Nor was the crowd told that the meeting had been sanctioned by the authorities on the understanding that it would end promptly at 2 p.m. The TUC leaders were men of their word, and they kept their harangues short and statesmanlike. It is unlikely that the platform performances could have matched the occasion anyway, for the most magical ingredient of all—the voice of Jim Larkin—was missing.

At all three meetings the crowd was asked to pass by acclamation a resolution asserting 'the hard won rights of free speech, combination, including picketing and the right of every worker to select his or her own trade union, without the interference of any employer.' The motion also called for 'an immediate and independent public inquiry into the conduct of the police.' When Harry Gosling proposed the motion from the base of the Parnell Monument he told the crowd that two-and-a-half million organised workers in Britain stood behind them in their demand for free speech and the right to join a union of their choice. He predicted that the following day's meeting with the employers would produce 'good results'.

The Liberal-Labour MP John Ward praised the crowd's conduct and said they had shown that 'it is possible for a great demonstration of Irishmen to take place ... without any public disturbance, provided the authorities themselves would not be present to disturb the peace.' Many felt 'it was impossible to hope for a peaceful solution to the difficulty,' but after six or seven hours' discussion with the employers they had been persuaded to attend a joint conference with representatives of the Dublin workers.

This was not strictly true, for the employers had made it clear that they would not meet the ITGWU under any circumstances. Ward preferred his own version of events and told the crowd that 'after serious difficulty and serious qualms of conscience on the part of some of your best men, we succeeded in convincing them that a conciliatory attitude was the one best likely to secure the thing we are all aiming at.' Experience in England had shown that 'the most permanent way to raise the status of their fellows ... was by orderly negotiations, and by seeing that agreements were enforced in a mutual manner. The baton is no argument.'

The secretary of the British Labour Party, Arthur Henderson MP, read a telegram of support from Ramsay MacDonald, a leading Labour MP and future Prime Minister. Henderson, who was later to play a central role in ensuring that sympathetic strikes did not spread to England in support of the Dublin workers, said that trade unionism was on trial in this dispute. Their 'great heritage of freedom, the right of combining ... is too precious, too important and too effective for the uplifting of the masses of the people ... to stand by while an attempt is being made in Dublin, Belfast or anywhere else to wrest it from our grip.'

The chairman of the TUC's parliamentary committee and leader of the National Union of Shop Assistants, James Seddon, proposed the motion from the Father Mathew statue. He was there to demonstrate that 'when labour is attacked, no matter how or where, our nationality sinks away, and we stand as brothers and will fight to the finish.' Employers must learn that 'industrial Ireland would get a greater stimulus from higher wages than any other means.' Like Ward, he promised great things from the next day's conference with the employers.

William Brace, the Liberal MP with the large moustache whom O'Brien had been warned by Keir Hardie to watch, lectured his audience on the glories of the British constitution. He demanded a full inquiry into the police, but counselled caution. 'For myself, as a constitutionalist, I prefer to wait until a report has been made, and then I will be prepared to take my stand on the floor of the House of Commons and see that justice is done to the organised workers of Dublin.'

The Co-Operative Party MP George Barnes was probably more in tune with the mood of the crowd. He said that when he attended the funeral of John Byrne that morning he had 'seen traces of battered humanity from every window of the large tenements' as they passed along. In fighting for their rights and liberties as a class, the Dublin workers were 'trying to lift the life and labour of the whole community from the miserable scramble for bread onto a higher ground.' Then, in a strange diversion, he asked:

> What is Larkinism? If Larkinism stands for breaking agreements, I am not in favour of it. If it stands for anarchic means, I am opposed to it. If it appeals to racial sentiment, I am against it.

Just as abruptly, he told his audience: 'These are matters for yourselves.' No matter what Larkin's methods might be, Barnes recognised him as 'a whole-hearted and generous-souled man who is fighting for great principles.'

The greatest press was around the Pillar, where the president of Belfast Trades Council, David Campbell, presided. A former president of the Irish Trades Union Congress who had worked closely with Connolly in Belfast, Campbell told the Dublin workers that they had the 'full sympathy' of northern trade unionists. The proposal was moved by the general secretary of the Boilermakers' Union, John Hill. He told the crowd that their blood might boil 'at what took place on Sunday week,' but they would have to be careful and seek justice 'in a businesslike way.' While he understood why some of them had resorted to 'measures which some of the deputation would not entirely endorse,' he felt confident that 'this great day will be the Magna Carta of the Dublin working man.'

The more militant Jack Jones of the Gasworkers' and General Labourers' Union attacked Dublin Castle, the Shipping Federation (the main employers' body in England), 'the employers of Dublin and their hangers-on, their lackeys and jackals,' to loud applause. They would all be 'compelled to recognise that whatever their nationality, politics, or religion, the workmen are united upon their bread and butter interests.' It had been Dublin Trades Council that had forced the employers to the negotiating table; it was to 'the credit of statesmanship and honour' that the council had agreed to further talks. If they exhausted

> the possibilities of peace we are ready for war. War declared on men in Dublin is war declared on us in England. We will spend the last dollar before surrendering what our fathers fought for. If Bloody Balfour has failed to break the political solidarity of Ireland, the local smaller men cannot accomplish it.

Flesh and blood counted for more than mortar and bricks. By their discipline the workers had shown they were fit to control the country and the police. He wanted 'no excuse for the police to play the part of butchers.' Jones had been more subtle than his colleagues, but he was equally consistent in pushing the Trades Council towards talks with the employers.

The only significant speech by a Dublin trade unionist that day came from Richard O'Carroll of the bricklayers. He said:

If the workers had been allowed on the previous Sunday to hold their meeting, Dublin would have been spared one black page which will be a lasting disgrace in its history to those who are responsible for the administration of the law in Ireland. The reason they are denied the right to meet ... is that a huge section of the workers ... are in dispute with a certain company in which the law givers of the land have a pecuniary interest ... The scales are beginning to fall from the workers' eyes.

He refused to see his wife and children 'submerged in poverty rags' because

the people who profess to make the laws for me are only making them for themselves. The workers must ... march to the [polling] booths with the same unanimity with which they came to this meeting and vote for Labour representation. This day has given birth to a better spirit of brotherhood and comradeship between the workers of Great Britain and Ireland, and Irishmen will see that they [the workers] are represented in the new House of Commons.

The final speaker at the Pillar was George Roberts MP of the Typographical Association. He steered clear of the controversies that had complicated relations between the printers and the ITGWU in Dublin. If, like his TUC colleagues, he 'preferred methods of conciliation to win their ends,' he added that 'they must be secured by forceful means if necessary.' He urged on employers that the 'wiser and saner policy would be to enter into negotiations ... grant concessions and strive to be just and right in their dealings with their workpeople.'

On that reasonable, if falsely optimistic, note the rally ended, and the thousands thronging Sackville Street departed peacefully homewards in the hope that the following day's talks would resolve the dispute.

*

In London a similar though smaller rally took place beneath Nelson's column in Trafalgar Square, addressed by the London dockers' leader Ben Tillet and by William Partridge. Tillet saw 'that sinister figure Mr Murphy, who owns Dublin and a large part of Ireland,' behind the baton charges in Dublin. He hoped that 'the Home Rule party would in future touch none of his money.' Larkin 'might be a bit wild, but there is enough oppression and robbery and murder to make every conscientious man and woman mad.'

Partridge said that the Liberal government was giving the employers a free hand in Dublin. It was when the government had harassed and locked up labour leaders, removing their restraining hand, that violence had erupted.[11]

*

On Monday the mundane task of trying to negotiate a settlement resumed at 2 p.m. in the Shelbourne Hotel. As John Ward had predicted, the employers agreed to meet members of the Trades Council face to face, provided no ITGWU representatives were present. They made no objection when P. T. Daly entered the room as part of the Trades Council delegation. Daly was a full-time official of the ITGWU, but he was introduced in his capacity as a member of the Trades Council and secretary of the Irish Trades Union Congress.

On the employers' insistence, Harry Gosling chaired the talks. The employers' stipulation that TUC representatives chair the negotiations became a regular feature of peace talks in Dublin: it was as if they wanted to emphasise that they were not opposed to unions *per se*, only disreputable Irish ones. While the TUC delegates were well aware of the tensions this role could cause between themselves and the Dublin unions, they felt they could not allow procedural problems to scuttle any opportunity to settle the dispute.

As the evening drew on, thousands of idle workers gathered outside Liberty Hall to await word from the talks. Most of them had come from the south quays, which were almost at a standstill as a result of the coal importers' lockout. Work was continuing normally at the Isle of Man, Glasgow and City of Dublin shipping companies, where managers were turning a blind eye to the blacking of tainted goods. However, the Custom House Dock was closed, and the London and North-Western Railway Company, which had laid off over a hundred men the previous Friday, shipped fifty-seven of its horses to England for use there until the Dublin dispute was settled.

Shortly after 8 p.m. the talks broke up. Ominously, the trade union leaders went to the Viceregal Lodge to see Lord Aberdeen. It was not until 10 p.m. that George Burke, secretary of the local branch of the Seamen's and Firemen's Union, arrived to address the crowds at Liberty Hall. He told them the talks were adjourned for a week. To reassure locked-out workers facing imminent hardship, he said that the promises of material support made by the TUC speakers in O'Connell Street still stood. He also announced, to cheers, that the Liverpool railway workers were to black Jacob's goods from the next day.

David Campbell of Belfast, who had been an ITUC representative at the talks, said the dispute could be resolved if the employers were willing to respect the right of their employees 'to join whatever trades union they desired … But the employers—especially William Martin Murphy— opposed the proposal and they … desire the break-up of the Transport Workers' Union.'

Campbell had not misread the mood of the employers. Though both sides had agreed to meet the following Monday, the Press Association carried a report that the talks had broken down. While the decision to break off talks was not formally taken by the employers until they met on

Friday 12 September, the Dublin Employers' Federation made no attempt to deny the report.[12]

*

With the return of the TUC delegation to England, the Dublin Trades Council strike committee was left in charge of a dispute not of its making. Larkin was still in prison awaiting trial on incitement and other charges, while Connolly was serving the three months imposed by Swifte, in default of giving bail for good behaviour.

Connolly was deeply frustrated at his enforced inactivity. When William Richardson was discharged by the police court on Saturday, even though he refused to sign a bond to be of good behaviour after his alleged assault of Boylan, Connolly decided that he had had enough; he told the authorities he was prepared to give bail on his own recognisances. His offer was refused. On Sunday he began a hunger strike. The authorities tried to keep his protest secret, but by Tuesday the news leaked out, providing Aberdeen and Birrell with another headache.[13]

One consolation was that the attention of the city council had been diverted elsewhere. For months a battle had raged in the council chamber and the press over the fate of Sir Hugh Lane's collection of paintings. The paintings had been offered by Lane to the city, provided suitable premises could be found. The donor also stipulated that the premises had to be modelled on a plan by the English architect Sir Edwin Lutyens. This affront to national pride was too much for many nationalist councillors, who wanted to know why an Irish architect was not good enough. But what really raised the hackles of the city authorities and the Dublin businessmen was the projected cost.

An initial appeal for funds to the city's wealthiest citizens was embarrassingly disappointing: it raised only £4,000. Even if the target of £17,000 was reached, a further £22,000 at least would be needed from the corporation. The independent nationalist councillor Sarah Harrison led the campaign in the city council for a subvention. While she had the support of most Labour councillors, and some nationalists, such as Dr McWalter, agreement among the council as a body on the location, cost and design of the building proved impossible. A special meeting of the council to reach a final decision had been set for 1 September, but Bloody Sunday had intervened, and the debate was deferred until the eighth.

William Martin Murphy had been associated with opposition to the project from the beginning. In a letter to the newspapers three weeks before the city council meeting he argued that Lane was not so much giving his collection to the city as selling it, the price being a gallery 'which will be of more value to him as a trader in art subjects than the pictures ever cost him.' Murphy challenged the various valuations being put on the collection by champions of the new gallery such as Councillor Harrison. He said that a Corot sold by Lane to King Edward VII had been exposed as a fake, and there might be more duds for all the city's ratepayers knew. In a memorably philistine phrase, he wrote: 'I would rather see in the city of Dublin one block of sanitary houses at low rents replacing a reeking slum than all the pictures Corot and Degas ever painted.' Of course Murphy, far from launching any such philanthropic project, had urged the Dublin Chamber of Commerce to oppose any increase in the rates to house the poor, because it 'would hardly make an impression on the evil as far as Dublin was concerned.'

The cost was certainly uppermost in the minds of members of the Chamber of Commerce summoned to a special meeting by Murphy on 12 August 1913 to discuss the gallery. They strongly backed his views. When the city council met on 8 September, the ground had been well prepared. A majority, spanning the political spectrum from Unionists to United Irish League and from Sinn Féin to some Labour members, voted down the Lutyens plan. A further attempt by Councillor Harrison to promote the project at a second meeting on 19 September was also defeated.[14]

Murphy's objections to the projected gallery were not unreasonable, and he had shrewdly exploited the rates issue, always a sensitive matter for councillors of all hues. But his campaign had also reinforced the image of Murphy in the months and days leading up to the lockout as a mean-spirited, tight-fisted capitalist. He was extremely sensitive to public perceptions of his role in the controversy, as was shown by his reaction to a poem by W. B. Yeats published in the *Irish Times* at an early stage in the controversy. The poem was dedicated 'To a friend who promises a bigger subscription than his first to the Dublin Municipal Gallery if the amount collected proves that there is a considerable "popular demand" for the pictures.' Yeats's real target was Lord Ardilaun, a member of the Guinness dynasty, who had made a small contribution to the Lutyens gallery fund; anyone reading the 'dedication' or making the most elementary inquiries at the time would have realised this. But the poem, published on 11 January 1913, stung Murphy into writing the first of several letters to the press defending his stance.[15]

It may have been Yeats's Olympian disdain of motive that most angered Murphy. Yeats took the view that the Ardilauns and indeed the Murphys of Dublin should support Lane's project on its own merits, rather than on the grounds of what 'Paudeen' or 'Biddy' wanted. But Murphy saw in the poem only the contempt of a member of the Anglo-Irish ruling caste for his own class. When he responded in the press it was from 'Paudeen's (utilitarian) point of view,' not that of the wealthy man. The clash with Yeats ensured that all Murphy's publications, including the *Irish Catholic*, subsequently campaigned against the gallery.[16]

Yeats regarded the dispute as an intellectual duel. His sense of revulsion at Ireland's emerging Catholic bourgeoisie was becoming well known. He characterised Murphy's class as one that 'thinks of divine things as a round of duties separated from life ... which showed as its first public event during the nine years of the Parnellite split how base at moments of excitement are minds without culture.'[17] Murphy's role in Parnell's downfall must have made him all the more loathsome to Yeats and reinforced Yeats's natural affinity with the aristocrat and the labourer. While it is easy to dismiss his sympathy for the workers as romantic, Dublin was small enough in 1913 for even Yeats to be acquainted with the poverty of its tenements.

Like Sarah Harrison and Dr McWalter, Yeats saw a Lutyens gallery as something that would bring beauty and intelligence into the life of the city's poor.

> The necessities of the poor got but a few lines, not so many certainly as the objections of various persons to supply Sir Hugh Lane with 'a monument at the city's expense.' And as the gallery was supported by Mr. James Larkin, the chief labour leader, and important slum workers, I assume that the purpose of the opposition was not exclusively charitable.[18]

After the outcome of the city council's deliberations became known, Yeats declared: 'I had not thought I could feel so bitterly over any public event,' and he wrote a spate of poems attacking the philistinism of the city authorities.[19] The best-known, and the one that contains the most direct attack on Murphy and his fellow-employers, is 'September 1913'.

> What need you, being come to sense,
> But fumble in a greasy till
> And add the halfpence to the pence
> And prayer to shivering prayer, until
> You have dried the marrow from the bone?
> For men were born to pray and save:
> Romantic Ireland's dead and gone,
> It's with O'Leary in the grave.[20]

*

For the moment, the Chamber of Commerce had more pressing concerns. Because of the industrial problems besetting ports, the London Chamber of Commerce and the Institute of London Underwriters had decided to introduce a 'strike clause' into bills of lading. Under this clause, customers of shipping companies would be liable to half the cost incurred if goods had to be rerouted or 'free labour' employed to deliver cargoes. When it met on Tuesday 9 September, the Dublin Chamber of Commerce, faced with the possible closure of the port of Dublin, was horrified. It appealed the decision of the two London agencies to the Board of Trade, on the grounds that it was 'unreasonable ' and 'inequitable.' It claimed—not very truthfully in the present circumstances—that its members would be penalised for events beyond their control and, more pertinently, that the extra costs could not be recovered by shippers from marine insurance policies. While the appeal was ultimately successful, the move cast another cloud on a rapidly darkening horizon.[21]

There was bad news for consumers as well that day. Fish prices were set to follow coal in an upwards spiral. The lockout had spread to the Dublin Steam Trawling Company; a dispute over pay had rapidly escalated, and what could be saved of the fleet's catch was taken on a vessel crewed by managers to Fleetwood, Lancashire, for sale there.[22]

Of far greater significance for industrial relations was the decision of the Dublin Building Trades Employers' Association 'not to employ any persons who continue to be members of the Irish Transport and General Workers' Union.' The union was 'a menace to all trade organisation, and has become intolerable,' the association said. It also decided to sack any employees who refused to carry out 'our lawful and reasonable instructions ... no matter to what union they belong.'[23]

This move was strategically important. Most of the city's building workers were either members of long-established craft unions that the employers had recognised for generations or general operatives in the United Builders' Labourers' Union. The leadership of the UBLU was moderate, and Larkin had antagonised it by attempting to poach members, as well as attacking it regularly in the columns of the *Irish Worker*. Yet the UBLU members, confronted with the ultimatum, refused to sign the employers' form. As a result, another three thousand workers were thrown on the street.[24]

The extension of the lockout to the UBLU made no sense from the point of view of conventional industrial relations, but it made eminent sense in the context of Murphy's strategy of total war. By extending the lockout so systematically, the employers could negate the Trades Council strategy of using a strike levy on members still at work to help those in dispute. Murphy may not have realised that it would also provide evidence, if more were needed, that his real aim was to smash the Dublin unions. His own newspapers discounted the likelihood of British workers contributing anything significant to the Dublin strike fund; even if they did, Murphy probably thought this would increase the influence of the TUC moderates in settling the dispute on his terms. On both counts he was mistaken.

The thinking behind this new offensive of the employers was summed up well by the *Irish Times*. It said that the city's companies had divided into 'three classes.' In the first class were those managements that 'have rejected decisively all dealings with the Union, have locked out its members and have closed down ... all or part of their establishments.' It commented with approval that these firms 'include some of the biggest employers of labour in Dublin.' In the second class was

the large and influential body of employers who at this moment are awaiting events. They have issued a general proclamation of war on the Transport Workers' Union, but they hesitate to fire the first shot in the battle.

In the third class of employers the *Times* counted those that had submitted to the tyranny of the Transport Workers' Union ... They have submitted to the fatal principle of 'tainted goods.' It is obvious that the present want of unanimity among employers must tend to encourage the strike organisers. From the lowest point of view it is exceedingly bad business. If a fight is inevitable, it ought to be short, sharp, and decisive—always the cheapest kind of fighting in the long run.

While accepting that efforts should continue to resolve the dispute, the *Irish Times* said that the refusal of the TUC leaders to accept that the ITGWU was 'a syndicalist organisation' outside the mainstream trade union movement was a stumbling-block to peace. The president of the United Irish League, T. P. O'Reilly JP, agreed. Speaking in Granard, he said that labourers 'were entitled to their privileges, but if the Socialistic tendency once got headway in Ireland it would bring ruin on the country.'[25]

On Friday 12 September, Murphy moved to end procrastination by Dublin's employers of the second and third category. At a meeting of the employers' federation in the Antient Concert Rooms, it was agreed to appoint an executive committee. This committee, headed by Murphy, would act for all employers during the dispute. Its first business would be to take all measures necessary to enforce the lockout of ITGWU members originally agreed on 3 September. 'In order to save the congress delegates a fruitless journey from England,' the new committee was instructed to write 'and inform them that the employers could not see [that] any good would be achieved by sending representatives to the adjourned sitting of the conference,' due to be held on Monday 15 September. In a statement after the meeting, the employers' executive committee said that 'premature disclosures' by Irish trade unionists at Monday's talks of the fact that any decisions reached 'would not be recognised unless they had the endorsement and signature of James Larkin' were the main reason for withdrawing from further negotiations.

The committee was willing to recognise trade unions and collective bargaining procedures when there was 'trustworthy machinery and trusty men' in control, able 'to end the system of sympathetic strikes.'

With an eye to the TUC, the committee tried to explain the peculiar difficulties employers laboured under in Dublin.

> Under ordinary conditions the Dublin Trades Council might have been looked to as a body to whom appeal could be made to enforce such agreements in the way suggested by the English Labour members. Unhappily, however, the Trades Council has been completely captured by the Syndicalist ... Dublin is now reduced to the plight in which there is no legitimate combination of trades unionists with whom 'collective bargaining' can be carried on.

The workers were 'in the toils of a stranger.'[26]

Even as the employers were establishing their new centralised executive committee, the Master Carters' Association locked out fifty carters for refusing to handle 'tainted goods'. The redundant carters had been selected from potential union militants and sent out on 'test jobs' to see how they would react.

The County Dublin Farmers' Association was not part of the employers' federation, but it also called a meeting of members in the Rotunda that day. They decided to join the lockout. With much of the harvest in, they no doubt felt confident about paying back Larkin for the extra 3s a week he had extracted from them in August. They did not have things all their own way, however: labourers rioted in Finglas, walked off the St Lawrence estate in Howth, and placed pickets everywhere.[27] The pickets were effective in several areas, and many weaker farmers felt the pinch.

An example of the rural struggle in microcosm is provided in a letter from a Dublin solicitor, William Buckley, to Birrell on 23 September, when the rural lockout was well into its second week, seeking police protection for an elderly neighbour.

Richard Grogan, a small farmer, lives on his holding of 18 acres at Artane, Co. Dublin. He has always kept a permanent farm labourer and two casual labourers. Upon the mandate of Larkin, Mr. Grogan was obliged to increase the wages of the permanent labourer by 3s. a week and to enlarge the pay of the casuals to 4s. a day, which used to be 3s. 6d.—all receiving 'perquisites' in addition, in the matter of food and refreshments.

These labourers … remain out … seeking to be paid for all the time they have remained away from work. Poor Grogan has not the means to meet this demand, and these men keep rambling over the roads which skirt Grogan's small farm in attitudes of menace. Sergeant Butler R.I.C. from Coolock gives all the personal attention in his power to Grogan, but unless you authorise some three or four additional constables from Phoenix Park [RIC depot] to Coolock, Grogan's one acre of oats and four of wheat, now matured, will be lost owing to the lawlessness of the labourers referred to and their associates, who will not permit the growing corn to be harvested.

Grogan was seventy-four and had only his daughter living with him. Buckley describes them as being 'in a helpless condition.'[28]

For small employers such as Grogan the lockout was every bit as terrible an experience as for the workers. In some respects their situation was worse, for the workers could at least disavow the ITGWU and return to work. Grogan fell into what the *Irish Times* despairingly described as the 'third class' of employers, who had no real control over their predicament. Many of them now teetered on the edge of the abyss in a crisis that threatened to throw them down into the mass of casual labourers and slum-dwellers.

*

All classes were affected by the rising prices. The early increases in the price of coal were followed by a doubling of fish prices and a trebling of prices for some fruit and vegetables. 'Prices are going up,' reported the *Irish Times*, 'not because of any scarcity in food supply, but simply because the stuff cannot be got to the markets.' The cattle trade was badly hit by the disruption at the docks, but this did not lead to any fall in meat prices at the butchers.[29]

One unexpected ray of hope for the strikers that day was Larkin's release on bail. The Irish executive strongly opposed the move. When Larkin appealed to the King's Bench division, the Crown sought sureties of £600, an astronomical sum. Mr Justice Molony set the terms at £100 from Larkin and two independent sureties of £40 each.[30]

There was further good news on the police inquiry. Birrell gave Lord Aberdeen permission to announce that there would be an investigation into the Dublin disturbances. But Aberdeen simultaneously announced the appointment of two senior British army officers, Lieutenant-Colonel Arthur Dowell and Lieutenant-Colonel William Broughton, as magistrates for Dublin city and county. They would supplement the overworked police magistrates.[31]

As if to underline the sombre mood in the city, the brilliant summer weather gave way to heavy rain on Friday. In his latest communiqué to Archbishop Walsh, Father Curran wrote that it 'is badly needed and may help to keep the Larkinites cool.'[32]

13

As soon as he was released from prison, Larkin left Dublin for England; by Sunday afternoon he was addressing a mass meeting in Alexandra Park, Manchester. The decision may seem an extraordinary one for the leader of a union involved in a fight for its very survival, but Larkin was anxious to rally support for his beleaguered forces. He was particularly concerned to give impetus to the spontaneous sympathetic action English dockers and railwaymen were already taking in Liverpool. He knew that sympathetic action in Britain and the blacking of Dublin goods was the one move to which Murphy and the Dublin Employers' Federation had no ready antidote; it also tied in with Larkin's own syndicalist philosophy.

But he must have known from the beginning that there was little chance of winning approval for such action from the leadership of the British trade union movement. We have no detailed record of his movements, but it would be strange if he did not use his extensive trade union and political contacts on Merseyside to promote the blacking of Dublin goods. If so, he succeeded beyond all reasonable expectations, for the strike spread in the coming week as far afield as Bradford and Birmingham. However, Larkin's presence in England also alerted the principal transport union leaders, including his old antagonist James Sexton of the NUDL and Jimmy Thomas of the NUR, to the need to move quickly if they were to prevent the Dublin virus from spreading.

*

Back in Dublin, a deputation waited on the Lord Lieutenant to urge the release of James Connolly. It included William O'Brien, vice-president of Dublin Trades Council; Francis Sheehy-Skeffington; and Éamonn Martin, a senior member of Constance Markievicz's nationalist boy scout movement, Fianna Éireann. All were friends of Connolly and were concerned for his health. At some point in the previous week Connolly appears to have transformed his hunger strike into a thirst strike as well. In a letter to his wife, Lillie, in Belfast, he told her not to fret, only to add in the next sentence that 'many more than I, perhaps thousands, will have to go to prison, and perhaps, the scaffold, before our freedom is won.' He clearly saw the lockout as part of a larger struggle that, even at this stage, was national as well as class in nature.

In the event, Lord Aberdeen not only agreed to the deputation's request for Connolly's release but used the Viceregal car to despatch the release order. Connolly was taken by taxi to the home of Constance Markievicz to recuperate.[1]

On Sunday afternoon four thousand people attended a rally organised by the Socialist Party of Ireland at Beresford Place to celebrate Connolly's release, but he himself was too weak to attend. The most notable feature of the gathering was the revelation by an ITGWU organiser, Walter Carpenter, that the city's chief police magistrate, E. G. Swifte, was a shareholder in the DUTC. Carpenter, English by origin and a sweep by trade, had himself served three months in prison for 'defaming the King' in 1911. He now described Swifte as a man who 'helped create this strike and in his own interests ... signed the proclamation, and in his own interests too ... sent James Connolly to gaol for three months (cries of "Shame").' The daily newspapers studiously avoided Carpenter's allegations, but they found their way to Birrell's desk via the DMP note-taker's report on the meeting.[2]

*

In Manchester, meanwhile, Larkin had been making one of his most famous speeches. He told his audience:

> The race to which I belong has never been beaten, and when the employers started out to make good their boast that they would beat Larkin they began an impossible task. I care for no man, or men. I have got a divine mission, I believe, to make men and women discontented.

He scoffed at people who said the workers of Dublin should not be aroused until home rule was won: he was 'the son of a Fenian and never felt ashamed of any man who said he was a Fenian.' But, he added, 'we have a broader gospel, a wider gospel and a clearer gospel,' which he had preached

> from Belfast to Cork ... No Murphy or Aberdeen, nor other creatures of that type can stop me carrying on the work I was born for ... Better men than I in Ireland have been cursed. I prefer to go to the Seventh Pit of Dante than go to Heaven with William Martin Murphy.
>
> Hell has no terrors for me. I have lived there. Thirty-six years of hunger and poverty have been my portion. The mother that bore me had to starve and work and my father had to fight for a living. I knew what it was to work when I was nine years old. They cannot terrify me with hell ... Better to be in Hell with Dante and Davitt than to be in Heaven with Carson and Murphy, not forgetting our good friend the Earl of Aberdeen.

Some of the TUC delegates who had gone to Dublin 'were going to sell the pass' if given the opportunity.

> I am out for revolution, or nothing. What do I care? They can only kill me and there are thousands more to come after me.[3]

It was a magnificent but unfortunate tirade; for in arrogating to himself the 'divine mission', Larkin had given a weapon to Murphy and to opponents in the trade union movement who wished to portray him as a mere rabble-rouser.

His enemies in England were already moving to counter his message. Even as he spoke, the general secretary of the National Union of Railwaymen, J. E. Williams, was sending a circular to members warning of the dangers of being sucked into sympathetic action. He pointed out that railway companies were bound by statute as 'common carriers' to accept all traffic offered. Given the nature of the business, 'if the principle of the sympathetic strike is to be followed our members must always be involved.' Though other unions never asked the NUR for advice, 'immediately a strike occurs our members have been asked either to come out in support or to refuse to handle certain traffic.' If they refused 'they have been insulted and dubbed blacklegs.' The NUR was engaged in a struggle of its own for better pay and conditions, Williams reminded the NUR members; they should not be 'frittering away their power without any real benefits to themselves.'

Another NUR leader, the Labour MP Jimmy Thomas, told a rally in Victoria Park, London: 'Our position as railwaymen is unique and I am absolutely and emphatically opposed to what is called the sympathetic strike.' But despite the injunctions of Thomas and Williams, ten thousand railwaymen in the Midlands and another three thousand in the north-west became embroiled in sympathetic action in support of Dublin workers during the coming week.[4]

As a result of the sympathetic action in England, most port traffic had come to a standstill in Dublin by Monday morning. The three main railway companies stopped taking consignments for the port.[5] The export of sheep, pigs, cattle and dairy products virtually ceased. However, a few shippers, including the City of Dublin Steam Packet Company, continued to operate an uneasy truce with their men by allowing tainted goods to be blacked by its dockers, while other goods were shipped. The city's largest employer and exporter, Guinness, managed to send 'a heavy London consignment' out of the port on a small tramp steamer, the *Hare*, owned by Lowen and Rolfe of Salford, Lancashire. It was widening its distribution network for fear that its main carrier, the British and Irish Steam Packet Company, would soon be strikebound. However, it soon discovered that diverting Dublin traffic to alternative routes would push up shipping costs to England by two-thirds.

While exporters scrabbled for new outlets, hundreds of locked-out carters and dockers were now picketing the port or hanging around Liberty Hall and the quays awaiting developments. In the city, Maguire and Patterson, the match manufacturers, had become the latest large employers to join the lockout; they laid off 90 per cent of their workers, who were mainly women and ITGWU members.

*

To everyone's surprise, the city's largest employer of women, Jacob's biscuit factory—which had been the first firm in the city to lock out its workers—decided to reopen with the help of strike-breakers. It seemed to many a Jekyll-and-Hyde transformation. The company had long been lauded as a model employer; the wages were not high, but workers enjoyed a free medical and dental scheme, subsidised canteen meals, and some modest recreational facilities. Now the plant in Bishop Street was fast becoming the centre of one of the bitterest lockout struggles.

Jacob's women workers had been to the fore in ITGWU demonstrations and had marched as a body at the funerals of Byrne and Nolan. They now took to holding marches along the tramway routes, seriously disrupting services. In the *Irish Worker* on 13 September the 'Women Workers' Column,' edited by Larkin's sister, Delia, printed the names of 'scabs' willing to work for the company.

> These scabs stated they would die if their names appeared. Jacob's and their scabs will doubtless wish they were not only dead, but dead and buried before this fight for freedom is finished.

Ironically, Delia Larkin's Irish Women Workers' Union was given a new lease of life by the dispute at Jacob's. Technically independent but in reality a section of the ITGWU, it had become almost moribund by 1913.[6]

Reports of Jacob's aggressive tactics were not alone causing the company's goods to be blacked in Dublin but were a significant factor in provoking union activists in Liverpool and beyond to boycott all Dublin exports. In a letter to the newspapers the company sought to justify its conduct by stating that its directors had given 'the greater part of their lives' to building Irish industry and developing 'pleasant relations' with employees. It accused the Irish unions of being 'extraordinarily unpatriotic.' They were blacking Irish-made flour, while happily working with foreign grain. The letter omitted to mention that the blacked Irish flour came from Shackleton's mill in Lucan.

P. T. Daly responded for the ITGWU. He accused the company of not only locking out the women but paying them such low wages that Jacob's 'was the cause of driving many of them on the streets as prostitutes.'

The other major protagonist in the dispute, the DUTC, also resumed the offensive. It announced the resumption of an evening service on some routes and said it had recruited 150 drivers and conductors. The recruits included 'many of the original strikers,' who had 'regained their common sense.' One of the city's main coal merchants, Thomas Heiton and Company, announced at its annual general meeting that it was paying only a 5 per cent dividend, because of the 'unsettled state of trade.' The directors 'considered it more important to strengthen the position of the company' to 'regain control of their business' from ITGWU 'pirates.'[7]

*

Larkin returned to Dublin on Monday to find fifteen thousand men locked out and the TUC delegation waiting to meet him. Gosling, Ward, Jones and

Seddon had decided to make the arduous trip to Dublin, despite the decision of the employers to break off talks. The TUC men visited Lord Aberdeen in the afternoon and then met Larkin and members of the Trades Council strike committee. The mood of the meeting, which lasted until 11 p.m., was grim. Richard O'Carroll left the meeting to confirm to the waiting crowd that the employers would not meet them and 'were determined to starve men out.' A number of men in his own union, the bricklayers, had been asked to sign the employers' document to boycott the ITGWU, even though the builders' association had said it would be served only on labourers. O'Carroll tried to cheer his listeners by saying, 'If James Connolly could do without food and water for seven days, why could they not live for eight months on what they can get.'[8]

When the meeting of the strike committee broke up for supper, the TUC delegates gave waiting journalists a copy of the letter they had sent to the Dublin Employers' Federation. In it the delegation said that this was

> the first occasion within our knowledge where negotiations of such a serious and far reaching character have been deliberately broken off by one side, when there has been a joint agreement ... to continue discussion ... The action of your Federation is tantamount to a ... wilful and indefensible breach of a common understanding.

The employers had lost any right they had to criticise unions for repudiating agreements.

The secretary of the employers' newly formed executive committee, Charles Coghlan, responded in a similar tone. It was the unions, not the employers, who had sought a further meeting; the federation had agreed 'with some reluctance.' If Monday's meeting had gone ahead it would only have been to convey the decision of the federation to extend the lockout.

The employers' federation was also engaged in a war of words with one of the city's shipping agents, Michael Murphy Ltd. Coghlan wrote to Murphy's stating that it had come to the federation's attention that the company was allowing employees to 'black tainted goods.' He reminded the firm of the employers' decision 'to make a stand against dictation' by the ITGWU. Joseph O'Dowd, company secretary of Michael Murphy Ltd, wrote back to say his firm was not a member of the federation 'and must, therefore, decline to furnish your committee with any explanation of the manner in which we conduct business.'[9] It was not only the unions who had to worry about 'scabs'.

*

The mood on the streets of Dublin was once more turning ugly. It was not helped by reports from the resumed coroner's inquest into the Church Street deaths. Councillor John Clancy, a nationalist and sub-sheriff of the city, told the court that the Housing Committee 'had done its duty in respect of these houses.' If anything, Church Street had been 'over-inspected.' The corporation 'should not be held up to public opprobrium for a fault which they had not committed.' The jury of middle-class ratepayers agreed, and said that the collapse of the houses and the subsequent deaths could not have been foreseen. However, it also called on the corporation to speed up its slum clearance scheme. Once the inquest was over, the *Irish Times* and *Irish Independent* quickly wound up their collections for the Church Street victims. In marked contrast, they continued to appeal for contributions to their joint fund for the Loyal Tramway Men.[10]

On Tuesday there was renewed stoning of trams and some violent scenes on picket lines throughout the city; but the attention of unions and employers alike was focusing on Britain. The TUC delegation left Dublin that morning to report to its parliamentary committee on the failure of its peace mission. Their report could critically affect the level of support the official trade union movement would give to the Dublin dispute. As we have seen, the pressure from unofficial strikes by English railwaymen was already crippling the port. The strike had spread from Liverpool to Manchester, Crewe, Bradford, and Birmingham.

Efforts to bring out the London railworkers were less successful, perhaps because the Irish element in the NUR wielded less influence there. Nevertheless 2,700 remained on strike in the north-west, and Crewe, a crucial node in the railway system, remained closed to Dublin goods. The situation was volatile. While support for the Dublin men was erratic, whenever the railway companies suspended employees for refusing to handle 'tainted' goods from Dublin, more workers threatened to come out on strike unless their comrades were reinstated. Besides, Thomas and Williams might not want a national strike, but that did not stop many militant shop stewards from calling for one regardless.

*

In the villages of north County Dublin the dispute was also spreading, and farm labourers in Finglas provided a violent coda to Tuesday's events. Patrick Daly, the seventeen-year-old son of a local midwife, was shot by police during a riot in the village. The trouble had started when strikers stoned a pub that was serving drink to 'scabs'. The local DMP sergeant and constable drew their revolvers and fired four shots to disperse the crowd. Daly was hit. The policemen went with the injured youth to the home of a local doctor, Darcy Benton. Word of the shooting spread, and an angry crowd besieged the surgery. It was not until the next morning, when a convoy of armed RIC men arrived to rescue their colleagues, that order was restored in the village. Daly was taken to the Mater Hospital, where he later recovered.

Further disturbances were reported from places as far apart as Balrothery and Blackrock. Marches, the release of livestock and damage to crops now became regular features of the dispute in the county. As the market gardens of County Dublin were the main suppliers of produce to the city, the protests further contributed to rising food prices in Dublin.[11]

The Finglas riot may have alarmed County Dublin farmers, but Birrell was preoccupied with the prospect of violence on a far greater scale in Ulster. Only a few days earlier Lord Loreburn, a former Liberal Chancellor of the Exchequer, had suggested a round-table conference to resolve the Ulster question. He had been denounced from all sides. Carson, who was due to unveil the Solemn League and Covenant on 28 September, was particularly irate. He did not want vague talk of compromise clouding an occasion on which every able-bodied unionist in the province would be asked to pledge his allegiance to a provisional government that intended resisting home rule by force.

As a preliminary to this momentous event, Carson began an inspection tour of the Ulster Volunteer Force on Wednesday 12 September, with meetings and paramilitary reviews in Newry and Kilkeel. The time for compromise was past, he declared. His colleague, F. E. Smith, told a jubilant crowd that it was pointless to argue any longer with a government

> that could only remain in existence by the support of the Nationalist vote … I am glad to see before me so large a collection of stalwart men of active and military years, because I believe it is that argument which will find an audience in the government of Great Britain, as that government is currently constituted.

While the UVF paraded in Ulster, the 5th and 6th Divisions of the British Expeditionary Force—earmarked for overseas service in the event of a European war—were on manoeuvres in County Tipperary. The *Irish Times* noted with particular approval the effectiveness of the cavalry and horse artillery in the rough terrain; however, its military correspondent conceded that mechanical transport was competing quite successfully with horse-drawn vehicles in supplying the fighting units, despite heavy rain and the poor roads around Sallypark Pass. It also confessed to concern at the possibility of a Continental war breaking out before the home rule crisis was resolved. Regarding the possibility of civil war in Ulster, it refused to believe that British statesmanship was so barren that 'some honourable means cannot be found for averting that calamity'; but if war should envelop Europe before the Ulster crisis was resolved, it urged the British government not to strip Ireland of its substantial garrison for service elsewhere.[12]

*

In Dublin, Larkin managed to mobilise five thousand strikers for manoeuvres of his own: a procession through the city centre and suburbs. It was marred by the severe stoning of a tram in Ballsbridge; passengers fled in terror as the front of the vehicle fell in. Otherwise the march passed off peacefully. Along the route women members of the union carried collection boxes for the strike fund.

There had been recurring reports in both the *Irish Times* and the *Irish Independent* that the ITGWU and other unions would not be able to provide strike pay in the event of a protracted dispute. The previous week the president of Dublin Trades Council, Tom McPartlin, twice had to announce that money would be paid and that the British unions had pledged at least £25,000. In reality, the situation was less clear-cut. The TUC had still to decide what level of support to give Dublin. A complicating factor was that the ITGWU was not affiliated to the TUC and was therefore technically not entitled to anything. The same situation obtained for a number of other unions, including some British unions, such as William Partridge's ASE.

The funds of the ITGWU were in fact relatively healthy in 1913. Income came to £8,641 5s 5d, and the union had reserves of £1,798 18s 8d. But this would not last long in a major dispute. Strike pay varied between 4s and 5s a week for men and 2s 6d for women.[13] Five shillings a week would barely pay the rent for many members, let alone meet the rapidly rising cost of food and fuel. With well over twelve thousand members who were in benefit locked out, the funds would not have lasted four weeks, even if the entire income for the year had been available that September. Like the employers, the ITGWU was hoping that the other side would crack first.

They were soon disabused. On Wednesday two model employers, the building suppliers Dockrell's and the mineral water manufacturers Bewley and Draper, locked out ITGWU members; so did members of the Furniture Warehouse and Removers' Association. In retaliation, the 1,400-strong Dublin Corporation Workers' Union decided to black Dockrell's and all building suppliers; it also refused to co-operate with any employer who enforced the lockout.[14]

The much larger United Builders' Labourers' Union took a more ambivalent stance. Its leadership had still to come to terms with the enormity of the situation. The president, W. Johnston, sent a rather tetchy letter to the newspapers pointing out that his organisation had 'no connection whatever with the Irish Transport Union, or with its 'mouthpiece ... Mr. Larkin,' who had characterised the UBL as a 'scab union'. While three thousand UBLU members had exposed Larkin's smear by refusing to sign the lockout forms and being laid off as a result, their president seemed determined to substantiate Larkin's claims by appealing to the employers for 'a round table chat' to resolve the misunderstanding that had arisen. The employers declined the invitation.[15]

*

The onset of 'economic war' was deplored by one of the city's leading Catholic theologians, Father John Condon. He told a special Wednesday morning Mass for working men at the Church of St John the Baptist in Blackrock:

> The fiercest passions have been unchained; intemperate language has run riot; misguided counsels have been followed; the Christian virtues of charity and justice have been trampled underfoot; and we have, unfortunately, already begun to reap the inevitable harvest of ruined homes, of starving children and weeping women, of horrible bloodshed and the tragedy of death.

The predominantly middle-class township of Blackrock had escaped the worst excesses of the dispute so far, but local workers had been involved in demonstrations of support for farm labourers, and some of them were DUTC employees living in company cottages. Father Condon told his congregation that he was 'painfully aware that unscrupulous men will strive to make use of what may be said from the pulpit to set up an antagonism between the working man and his church,' but he had a duty to perform. 'The working man is as dear to [the church] as is the capitalist.' The church was committed to seeking social justice, but 'the working men of Dublin are being urged to adopt a policy and methods which, if followed, will inevitably lead to social disaster, to economic ruin and to the setting up of a tyranny which will be as galling as the worst form of political despotism which has cursed our land.'

In case any of the congregation had not realised that he was placing socialism on a moral plane with the Penal Laws, Father Condon singled out Larkin's 'divine mission' speech of the previous Sunday to tackle the issue of socialism head on. Whatever Larkin may have said in Manchester, he said,

> I have to tell you, beloved brethren, that the word Socialism connotes a body of doctrine which no Catholic who values his faith can accept; and I say further, that the Catholic who, with his eyes open, gives his sympathy and support to the methods and aims of Socialism is a recreant to his creed. Is the man who uses language such as that used in Manchester on Sunday a safe leader to whom our Catholic people may confidently look for light and leading? I say distinctly and emphatically that he is not. And I say it as a priest.

Workers and employers alike should take Pope Leo XIII's encyclical *Rerum Novarum* as the touchstone of social action. If asked whether employers 'in their treatment of the working man' had 'striven to put into practice the teaching of the Pope,' Father Condon would have to say they had not done so. The president of the Dublin Chamber of Commerce had as much as admitted it. 'Yes, the working man has his grievances and I should be the last to deny it, for my sympathies are with the working man,' he said. The plight of women 'working from dawn to dark for a pitiable and miserable wage' was even worse, and their 'grievances cry aloud to God for redress.' He was at one with P. T. Daly when he went on:

> There are unfortunate women in the City of Dublin today who have been robbed of their virtue, not so much because of their own weakness or because of the unbridled passion of brutal men, as because of the unholy and undisciplined lust of gain which has caused some employers to grind the faces of the poor.

If labour had wrongs to right, 'it is not only to the interest of the working man, but it is to the interest of the whole community that these evils should be removed from our midst.'

Father Condon appealed to the 'unorganised or badly organised labour of the city and county' to

> form itself into a new Federation, whose aims will be above suspicion, whose methods will be beyond reproach and whose leaders will be men of credit ... Surely we are not so bankrupt in mind and in men and in morals that we have to import them from the other side of St. George's Channel.[16]

The sermon was widely publicised and was the first of several appeals to unskilled workers to form breakaway unions. But—with one important localised exception in Kingstown—these appeals proved futile. The problem from the church's point of view was that Larkin had too strong a grip. As Father Curran put it in yet another letter to Archbishop Walsh, the workers looked on Larkin

> as the Repealers looked on O'Connell or the farmers of the Land League days on Parnell. They talk of the 'Liberator,' 'Emancipation,' 'martyrs' and repeat absurd high sounding phrases they don't understand.[17]

With his better grasp of the realities, Father Curran had little time for the likes of Condon. He told Dr Walsh that the appeals for church intervention were a waste of time. 'The priests are unanimous that the people won't listen to reason at present.'[18] Starvation was needed to shatter the illusion workers had that socialism or Larkinism could empower them to win a better life for themselves.

14

MARCHES through the city by locked-out workers became a regular feature of Dublin life over the next few days. Learning from the attack on trams at Ballsbridge, the DUTC suspended services along routes taken by the marchers. Father Michael Curran wrote to tell Archbishop Walsh that 'the processions grow in size and danger … already you can see hunger written on their faces.' While the priest feared trouble, things remained relatively calm as both sides awaited the outcome of events in Britain, where the railway union leaders were desperately trying to contain the unofficial strikes.

Father Curran was irritated by the 'cock-sure confidence' of the strikers, and he told the archbishop that

> the general public are dead against the men, if you except Dr. McWalter, the Lord Mayor and others pandering for the votes of the workingmen. The Irish Party—even William Field—are discreet and silent.

Everything was going up in price, but Father Curran was able to reassure Dr Walsh that 'we are well supplied as regards coal and can stand a siege till summer in that respect.' His one concern was that riots might resume at the weekend.[1]

*

Among the bundle of correspondence that Father Curran forwarded to the archbishop was a letter from James Joseph Hughes, a former seminarian and a trade union activist and socialist—a rare combination in the Dublin of eighty years ago. Hughes, the son of a baker, had been a bright child, and the Dominicans had sent him to Coublevie in France to pursue a religious vocation. He returned in 1902, after the anti-clerical Radical government began closing down Catholic church establishments. Deciding that he lacked a vocation for the priesthood, he eventually found work as a clerk with Carton Brothers Ltd, egg and poultry merchants. While his education had been unusually cosmopolitan, Hughes shared many of the enthusiasms of the younger members of the lower middle class. He was an active member of the Gaelic League and the GAA and a founding member of the Catholic Association. This body campaigned vigorously against the widespread religious discrimination that still excluded Catholics from senior positions in the civil service, police, business, and higher professions. Though Protestants made up only 17 per cent of the population of Dublin in 1911, they comprised 68 per cent of its engineers, 65 per cent of justices of the peace, 58 per cent of bank staffs, 56 per cent of pharmacists, 50 per cent of doctors and lawyers, and 49 per cent of accountants.[2]

Hughes was also deeply interested in social issues. He read widely, including the *Irish Worker* and the works of James Connolly, of whom he became an ardent admirer. He was prompted to write to Dr Walsh by Father Condon's sermon, which he saw as well-intentioned but damaging to the Catholic Church. Like Curran, Hughes told Dr Walsh that 'any union founded at present, or in the immediate future, to replace the Irish Transport Workers' Union would utterly fail to gain recognition by the Trades Council, which is solid behind Mr. Larkin's union and would be branded as a "scab" union ... by trade unionists generally.'

However, in his analysis thereafter he parted company with the archbishop's conservative secretary. He argued that Father Condon's approach posed grave dangers both for the Catholic Church and for its working-class members. Those seeking to set up a new union not only aimed to divide

> the forces of Labour in the presence of the formidable array of enemies at present marshalled, nominally to smash 'Larkinism,' but incidentally and mainly to crush the principle of combination. In such an event, the Church would find itself allied with ten real enemies of its vital principles—to understate the case—to one reputed enemy on the side of trade unionism.

Hughes accepted that such a policy would have the wholehearted support of the moneyed classes and

> especially the Freemasons (the real power behind the Employers' Federation), the Tea and Wine Merchants, the slum owners and social vampires generally, employers who pay the lowest wages they can get labour at, the corrupt commercial Press, characters like W. Richardson, T.C.—a penniless tool of ward bosses ... and others more dangerous still who are exploiting religion for personal ends.

Apart from seeing a Freemason plot behind the lockout, the Hughes analysis was shrewd and was similar to the one that the progressively minded Galway MP Stephen Gwynn would shortly present to the archbishop. Hughes urged the church not to 'throw its enormous power in with all the elements of social disintegration and against the penniless masses.' The unity of the workers and their loyalty to the ITGWU was 'a fair presage of the resentment with which the Church's adoption of inaccurate information of such proposals as Fr. Condon's would be regarded by the masses of the people.' He cited the increased circulation of English newspapers in Dublin—because of the 'venal and unprincipled' coverage of the dispute by the 'commercial press of Dublin'—as evidence to support his views and to emphasise further the dangers for the church in joining the employers' lobby.

Hughes assured Dr Walsh that, 'so far from being a menace to the religion or morals of the diocese,' the ITGWU was

> a fruitful source of moral health and character building to the most forlorn of God's creatures in our slum-rotted city. The actual atmosphere of Liberty Hall is one of manly idealism, pursued with a vigour and an honest cameraderie that are refreshing to the souls of Irish-born slaves.[3]

This radically different perspective on the dispute gave Dr Walsh food for thought as he watched events from France. Given his long practical experience of industrial relations in Dublin and his intimate knowledge of some of the protagonists, especially William Martin Murphy, he probably took the opinions of Hughes at least as seriously as those of his equally partisan secretary.[4]

*

At home, the Catholic Church found itself momentarily caught up in the disturbances with a rash of school strikes. The Pro-Cathedral national school for boys in Rutland Street and the boys' national schools in Great Denmark Street and North Queen Street were the most seriously affected. The pupils, many of whom must have been the sons of locked-out workers, demanded a half-day every week and refused to use schoolbooks published or sold by firms involved in the lockout. The pupils demonstrating outside the school in Rutland Street on Thursday raised three cheers for Larkin and smashed several windows before being dispersed by the police. There were also disturbances outside the schools in North Queen Street and Great Denmark Street, while schoolchildren in Inchicore paraded through the area that afternoon in support of the ITGWU. The diocesan authorities considered closing the schools,[5] but the protests proved short-lived. There was little support for this particular form of sympathetic action among trade unionists, and anxious parents—often the same people—ordered the 'strikers' back to school.

The final contribution of the national school mitchers to the lockout came on Thursday evening, when a large number gave an impromptu concert for the crowd outside Liberty Hall with improvised instruments, dances, speeches, and songs. The Irish Women's Franchise League had decided to start holding meetings in Beresford Place to spread its message to the strikers. However, they had to abandon their first meeting that night, as they could not compete with the combination of ribald hecklers and truant schoolboys.[6]

*

On Friday there was another unusual development in the dispute. Alexander Hull, a well-known builder who ran the Pembroke Works in Ringsend, explained why he was not joining the lockout.

> I hold neither socialistic opinions nor approve of syndicalistic methods. I agree that the position created by the Irish Transport and General

Workers' Union is a menace to all trade organisation, but I cannot agree that the proposals of the Employers' Association for dealing with this difficult problem are either just or wise, or likely to prove effective towards a permanent settlement of the question at issue. If I condemn a sympathetic strike as evil, I cannot condone a sympathetic lockout as a legitimate means to combat it. Two wrongs never made a right.

Up to this time Hull had not asked his men to sign the Employers' Federation document, 'because under such circumstances I should refuse to do so myself.' He felt he would be forced to close in a few days 'for want of material,' but he believed his first duty was 'to stand fast by what I conceive to be principle, and let the consequences take care of themselves.'

Earlier, James Shanks, a member of the council of the Dublin Chamber of Commerce who had been deeply involved in the Lord Mayor's conciliation initiative in July, had written to the newspapers to express the hope that this scheme might still be revived 'under ... better auspices.' Shanks belonged to one of the oldest manufacturing firms in the city and spoke for many moderates within the Chamber of Commerce.[7] Very few employers followed Hull's lead, or the more subdued protest of Shanks; and the latter never publicly broke ranks with the president of the Chamber of Commerce. Nevertheless, these were timely reminders for Murphy that not all employers were happy with his strategy.

*

Father Curran had been right to worry about the mood in the city. On Sunday 21 September renewed rioting broke out in Townsend Street. It was 'the most determined and disgraceful riot of the whole series,' according to one commentator.[8] Again Larkin was absent from the city when it occurred, having travelled to England once more to rally industrial support for Dublin in defiance of the leadership of the TUC. Despite the clerical view of Larkin as the Anti-Christ, it always seemed to be when his powerful but restraining hand was absent that labour troubles spilt violently onto the streets of the city.

It was probably not wholly coincidental that on this occasion the trouble erupted after Connolly, recovered from his hunger strike, returned from Belfast to take charge in Larkin's absence. Connolly seemed to revel in conflict. From the time of the demonstrations against the Anglo-Boer War at the turn of the century to Easter 1916, he never showed aversion to violent confrontation with the enemies of his class or his country.

The build-up of pressure on the workers in the days preceding the riot had been remorseless. A further twenty employers, including timber importers and wine and spirit merchants, had served notice on workers to leave the ITGWU. More dockers had been laid off at the North Wall for refusing to handle 'tainted' goods, and the same fate befell thirty porters and vanmen at Arnott's department store on Saturday.

The gradual extension of the dispute along the docks had not so much stopped trade at the port as thrown it into chaos. The men of the 5th and

6th Divisions of the British army returning to England after the manoeuvres in Munster had to load their own equipment on Saturday; but the disembarkation of the thousand pilgrims returning from Lourdes had passed off without a hitch on Friday, nor were the special trains to take the returned pilgrims to their various destinations delayed. No doubt other factors affected the different treatment accorded to soldiers and pilgrims. Despite being greeted by a downpour of rain and signs of widespread industrial disruption, the pilgrims were all reported to be in good spirits. They sang 'Ave Maria' as the *Cambria* docked, and 21-year-old Grace Maloney from Killaloe, who had suffered from tuberculosis of the knee for eleven years, posed for the cameras after being miraculously cured at the French spa. She had left her crutches at the shrine.

The blissful state of the pilgrims may also have stemmed from relief at returning home. Father Curran told Dr Walsh:

> The invalid department had several hitches and was not well organised. It appears there were regular hand-to-hand fights with the Belgian pilgrims, who monopolised baths, churches, grottos etc.[9]

*

It was little less than miraculous, in the light of persistent press reports to the contrary, that the ITGWU issued strike pay to its members on Saturday morning. A payment of 10s was made to those with over thirteen weeks' membership of the union and 5s to the rest. Father Curran wrote maliciously to Dr Walsh that the 'Insurance Branch of the Transport Union is in a bad way,' as its funds were being applied 'to other purposes.' He also said there was anger among some farm labourers around Balrothery and Lusk, who had received nothing, either because they were non-members or because they had not been in the union long enough to qualify for strike pay. Union officers were chased out of the area, according to the jubilant Father Curran.[10]

The fact that the ITGWU was paying many of its members at the higher unemployment benefit rate, rather than at the lower strike pay rate, meant that the union entertained serious hopes of being reimbursed from the national insurance scheme. It felt it could reasonably argue that men locked out were unemployed rather than in dispute.

The employers had other weapons in their arsenal. By the weekend the DUTC had served a further thirty eviction notices on strikers living in company cottages, and the Merchants' Carting Company had done likewise to over seventy of its locked-out employees living in company houses in Merchants' Road, East Wall. The workers' mood was further soured by reports in the Sunday newspapers that the executive of the National Union of Railwaymen had agreed a formula for returning to work under which workers who resumed their duties by Monday would not incur penalties for the strikes of the previous week. The only condition was that they must handle all goods. A mass meeting of railwaymen in Liverpool accepted the terms late on Saturday night; it was expected that similar meetings planned for Sunday in Bradford, Sheffield, Crewe and Birmingham would do likewise. The one crumb of comfort was that resolutions were passed at some of the meetings calling for the NUR to give financial support to the Dublin strikers. However, there was no escaping the conclusion that Dublin's recognition battle would have to be won on the home front after all.[11]

*

Undeterred by what he regarded as the betrayal of the NUR leadership, Larkin spoke in Glasgow and Birkenhead that weekend. On Saturday he received a standing ovation at an Independent Labour Party meeting in Glasgow, and the crowd broke into 'The Red Flag' before he could utter a word. The one sour note was provided by AOH hecklers. Even an attack on Carson could not assuage them.

Larkin contrasted his own behaviour with that of Carson, a Privy Councillor who had hired a general to lead a private army. 'If I had done that, they would have taken me out and shot me,' Larkin said. His only crime was to fight for his class. He asked his audience 'to dip your hands deep into your pockets, and send … the necessary ammunition for those brave boys right in the heart of the firing line, fighting the greatest fight in western Europe on the industrial field.'[12]

By the time he reached Birkenhead on Sunday night, Larkin must have been well aware that the rail strike was over. He told the crowd: 'The men will not give in, even if the people of England harden their hearts and refuse them sustenance.' He said that Liverpool dockers had 'a union strong enough to smash any union of employers into smithereens.'[12] But he made no overt call for sympathetic action on the Merseyside docks, though brief unofficial action had taken place at the beginning of the week in support of Dublin, and a bitter union recognition dispute was brewing at the Manchester Ship Canal Docks.

In Ireland there had been mayhem that day. Sunday started quietly enough. There was a small march early in the afternoon to Croydon Park in Fairview; then, from 5 p.m. onwards, thousands of workers gathered for a march through the city centre. They were entertained with national airs and the 'Marseillaise' by trade union bands, including that of the NUR. At 5:50 p.m. Connolly and the other strike leaders decided to set off. There were about seven thousand marchers.

'Almost from the start … those taking part assumed a menacing attitude,' the note-taker of G Division, Detective-Sergeant Richard Revelle, reported. Revelle was the most assiduous of his breed. (His occupation would almost cost him his life six years later, when he was shot by the IRA for taking notes at Sinn Féin meetings.) The *Irish Times* reporter noted: 'There was a certain thrill in the crowd … that was not a good omen.' Revelle also reported that the large contingent from the Irish Women Workers' Union 'were no less vehement than their male comrades.' Some of the marchers had been on strike for nearly a month now, and hunger rarely makes for a good temper.

The marchers found themselves channelled between heavy police lines as they made their way up Eden Quay, with the bands to the fore. A double line of police prevented the march from entering Sackville Street, but at this point the musicians acted as a buffer between the thick blue line and some of the angrier demonstrators who wanted to break through into the main thoroughfare.

As is the wont of demonstrators deflected from their planned route, their course now became uncontrolled and unpredictable. The crowd streamed over O'Connell Bridge and up Westmorland Street towards Grafton Street, then as now Dublin's most fashionable shopping centre. Caught behind the head of the demonstration, the police, including mounted troopers, raced past the marchers along Westmorland Street to block the exit into the top of Grafton Street. Meanwhile a number of trams trapped in Westmorland Street were left to the fury of what was now a mob. They were showered with missiles and their destination boards ripped off. Denied access to Grafton Street, the crowd swung into Nassau Street, where the organisers appear to have restored some semblance of order. The demonstrators were organised in formation and told to march in step. Attacks on the trams were halted.

They proceeded down Westland Row and Lombard Street in a more or less orderly fashion. However, when the head of the procession turned into the tenements of Townsend Street, the police, fearful of a trap, tried to stop the main body from following. Their fears proved well founded, for instantly a hail of missiles poured down on them. Within a few minutes thirty-six policemen were injured, including three mounted policemen, one of whom was knocked off his horse, while another had part of his ear torn off. One of the mounted policemen injured was Sergeant Michael Morris, who never fully regained his health and died on 1 February 1914. Other police casualties included a constable with a broken nose, another stabbed with a knife, and Inspector Bannon 'hit with a jam pot and stunned.' The officer in charge, Chief Superintendent Dunne, stated that he 'had never seen such an assemblage of the disorderly class' in his forty years with the force.[13]

As usual, the mob did not have it all its own way. While the police were reluctant to pursue the enemy into the tenements, they cut off rioters in Westland Row and chased them into the railway station. In a grim game of cat and mouse they took revenge on all those they could catch.

ITGWU members returning from Croydon Park that afternoon also battled with police on the North Strand, but the disturbance passed largely unnoticed because of the larger mayhem south of the river.

That evening an angry but comparatively small crowd gathered again at Liberty Hall to complete the day's proceedings. Tom McPartlin chaired the meeting, at which nearly all the leaders of the Trades Council strike committee spoke. Anxious to forge unity between the ITGWU and the United Building Labourers' Union, McPartlin said that there had been doubt that 'some so-called unskilled workers' would stand by their comrades. But the previous Monday the building labourers had

> refused to sign the paper presented to them by the employers ... They
> thought the unskilled workers had no funds, but they made the greatest
> mistake of their lives ... The employers were now out begging for funds
> and the reason for that was clear, because the small employers were
> getting shaky.

What McPartlin said was true. The Employers' Federation had issued a
circular to companies in the wake of the 'lockout' meeting of 3 September,
asking for donations to a contingency fund. The response had, apparently,
been poor.

Connolly, still weak from his hunger strike, said he had met so many
ITGWU members in Mountjoy that he would have started a branch if he
had been incarcerated for much longer. He told the crowd that some
strikers

> had been clubbed, some ... starved and some dead, and ... before their
> freedom would be realised there will be many more of them starving,
> many more in prison and many more clubbed. Whether they were
> starved, or clubbed, or imprisoned the fight for freedom will go on until
> it is established in this country.

Like McPartlin, he predicted that the smaller employers would not be able
to hold out. But

> there is one sinister amongst them who is using the employers as a cat's
> paw to drag chestnuts out of the fire and do their dirty work ... While
> they are marching to bankruptcy William Martin Murphy's trams are
> running all the time and making money.

Connolly said he had gone without food for seven days and nights, and
there were others prepared to do the same. Employers were foolish to
starve men back to work when 'men could sign and work for a week and
go idle for a fortnight.'

P. T. Daly, who had just returned from addressing a meeting in London,
held out hope that the railwaymen would keep up their support, despite
'unauthenticated' press reports that they were returning to work. The
Transport Union had gone through 'tough times ... before and men had
remained out for three weeks without a penny piece.' The TUC's
Parliamentary Committee would be meeting on Tuesday to consider the
Dublin situation. He had already been assured that funds would be
forthcoming. 'Next week we will be in a position to carry on this fight, no
matter how long the employers call the tune.' He attacked nationalist
politicians who 'pretend friendship for the workers' but 'give nothing at all
of friendship to us.' There were 'two thousand agricultural labourers
locked out in the County Dublin by the very men for whom the workers'
fathers went to jail in the eighties and nineties, by the very men who say
they are home-rulers.'

Daly urged the crowd to go home quietly and to keep their meetings respectable. 'I never knew a respectable man coming out for a walk but would bring a walking-stick with him. Good night.'

*

The strike leader's reference to walking-sticks was underlined in the copy of Revelle's notes sent to Birrell, accompanied by a suggestion that it could provide grounds for a prosecution.

In the same batch of police reports to arrive on the Chief Secretary's desk that Monday was one from Ulster, where F. E. Smith was continuing to review Ulster Volunteers. The police report absolved Smith of saying anything inflammatory: he had referred to arms only once, when he said that he knew what fate home rule would meet when the Ulster Volunteers 'had 100,000 men armed with rifles.'[14] Birrell could be forgiven for complaining to Asquith that 'real political discernment is not a quality of the police anywhere.' But there was enough information from Ulster to 'make plain what I do not think either of us ever doubted, that we are heading for a shindy of large proportions, if nothing else.'[15]

Yet Dublin must be the priority for the moment. Besides the sympathetic strikes and resolutions being passed in support of the lockout at mass meetings throughout Britain, Birrell had another reason for intervening. Unlike the Ulster crisis, that in Dublin appeared capable of resolution, given a little good will on both sides. When Lord Aberdeen demanded action, the Chief Secretary therefore headed for Dublin on what he termed his 'gloomy visit'. Aberdeen left him to it and took a much-needed rest on the family estate at Haddon.[16]

*

Once he reached Dublin, Birrell's natural optimism asserted itself, and his political antennae convinced him that the climate for compromise was improving. The *Irish Times*, which a few days earlier had criticised employers who were shunning a 'short, sharp battle' with Larkinism, was beginning to see things in a different light. While its leading article on Tuesday 23 September acknowledged that the collapse of the British rail strike meant the Dublin workers were isolated in their 'hopeless fidelity' to the sympathetic strike and that the employers 'are bound to win,' it also called on the latter 'not to be carried away by the excitement of battle.' The men could be starved back to work, but the *Times* felt that 'neither the employers nor the workers can afford the settlement of starvation.' It thought it might take three weeks to achieve victory through starvation; that would mean

> terrible suffering, immense financial loss, and a serious addition to the rates through police taxes and overflowing workhouses. A long period of destitution will mean such an increase of debility and disease as may endanger the health of the whole city.
>
> But the settlement of starvation will have results even greater than these and far more enduring.

Hitherto, relations between upper, middle and working classes had been 'as satisfactory as an imperfect civilisation permitted,' even though the 'social conscience of Dublin has been rather obtuse.' If workers were starved back it would shatter 'a certain bond of civic affection.' Employers would be

> restless and suspicious ... and uncertain about the future. It will leave the workers beaten and broken, nursing the memory of ruined homes, filled with an unconquerable resentment against ... men who have been too strong for them.

Such an environment would 'furnish a breeding ground for all sorts of wild agitation' and 'turn tolerance into hatred and envy.'

The *Times* was probably reflecting the views of the great majority of its readers, who were neither large-scale capitalists like Murphy nor wild-eyed agitators but stolid middle-class citizens. Many of the latter saw themselves as helpless victims in the conflict. Their views were summarised in a letter from J. Justin Dempsey of Bessborough Terrace, Dublin, who wrote:

> The increasing rise in the cost of living is not due, as some of our politicians would have us believe, to a surfeit of social legislation, but to the epidemic of labour unrest which has spread over these islands. The Middle Class pays more for what it buys, but its income remains the same. There is nobody on whom it can shift its burden ... It is time the Middle Class was up and doing.[17]

Dempsey was a prophet before his time, but his letter—and there were more like it—was an indication that middle-class families saw themselves under threat as much from the impersonal forces of capital as from those of 'syndicalism'. It was an early expression of the 'little-man' syndrome that in the nineteen-thirties helped give rise to fascism.

Many of these readers probably agreed with the *Irish Times* when it asked a little petulantly 'what the heads of the Roman Catholic Church, our four members of Parliament and leading representatives of our great middle class who are not employers of labour' were doing to resolve the dispute. 'Is anybody trying to help Dublin?' it asked in exasperation. The answer was that just about the only two agencies the newspaper had not appealed to, the British trade union movement and the British government—in the much-maligned form of Augustine Birrell—were doing their utmost to 'help Dublin.' That the *Irish Times* saw no salvation from across the water says much about the degree of political disorientation of southern unionism in 1913.

The *Freeman's Journal* also believed the time was opportune for talks. Like the *Irish Times*, it welcomed the end of the British rail strike. Reason had prevailed in Britain, while both sides in Dublin continued talking of a 'fight to the finish.' The *Freeman* too counselled employers against starving men back to work and forcing them to accept terms that would not be kept. The Employers' Federation had been unwise to dismiss the efforts by the Lord Mayor to initiate conciliation talks as 'mischievous': 'the best friend of Dublin is the man who raises his voice in favour of persuading both parties to the struggle of the necessity for ending it.'

In the letters pages of both the *Freeman's Journal* and the *Irish Times* there were increasing calls for compromise. A leading businessman, Edward Lee, owner of a string of drapery stores in Dublin, Kingstown, and Bray, gave one of the most succinct variations on a now common refrain.

> The workers must give up the baneful doctrine of 'tainted goods' and the consequent 'sympathetic strike,' which has rightly been condemned by the more responsible English trade unions, and must also give effective guarantees for the keeping of any agreements entered into. The employers should withdraw the pledge requiring their employees to cease to belong to the Transport Workers' Union. To my way of thinking, such a pledge is an unfair interference with the personal liberty of the worker, although I am sure the employers did not intend it as such.[18]

Lee was the only leading figure in Dublin's business community, apart from Shanks, to break ranks publicly with Murphy.

*

As if on cue, the British trade unions provided Birrell with his opening. On Monday 22 September, Larkin had travelled from Merseyside to London for a meeting of the National Transport Workers' Federation. Despite its imposing title, this represented only a minority of transport workers, and the most powerful group of all, the railwaymen, had their own unions. As we have seen, relations between the ITGWU and the British federation were poor. Sexton led one of the main affiliated unions, and he remained unreconciled to Larkin. The ITGWU had never sought affiliation to the NTWF and, by the same token, had never been refused membership. In the present circumstances ambiguity was a virtue for Larkin and British transport union leaders alike. Both were keen to exploit it.

The leaders of the NTWF made it clear to Larkin that when they met the Parliamentary Committee of the TUC next day they would be seeking financial support for the Dublin workers rather than industrial action. The TUC would, of course, also be receiving a report from its own delegation to Dublin, the chief negotiator of which had been Harry Gosling, president of the Transport Workers' Federation. Larkin appears to have bowed to the inevitable and agreed to support the NTWF line. He could not afford to add the federation and the TUC to his list of enemies.

In the event, the Parliamentary Committee's deliberations pleased none of the warring Irish parties. Next evening it published the report of Gosling and his colleagues, which praised the 'good work' of the ITGWU in raising wages and bringing hope to 'thousands of lower paid workers in Ireland.' However, it also found that the union's general secretary had adopted 'a very aggressive policy,' involving the use of the sympathetic strike, to achieve these ends. This had now been met by an 'equally aggressive policy of a sympathetic lockout' by the employers. The report added that

Mr. William Martin Murphy, the chairman of the Dublin Tramways Company, determined to oppose Mr. Larkin in his efforts. He also determined to oppose him and the union in all other sections of industry where the union had members, and to this end he created the Employers' Federation, who have now issued a form for all their members to sign.

Murphy had used his newspapers to attack Larkin 'as a mean thief.' Larkin had used the ITGWU's own publication, the *Irish Worker*, to respond

with more vehemence than courtesy and at the time of our arrival in Dublin the dispute had degenerated into a personal quarrel between Mr. Murphy and Mr. Larkin, and this was going on with thousands of working men out of employment, the city … under a semi-military regime and the whole population suffering serious inconvenience and loss.[19]

Like Father Condon in his Blackrock sermon of the previous week, the TUC delegates were trying to isolate Larkin and Murphy as the intractable elements in a dispute that needed to be resolved in the interests of the wider community. At the same time, mindful of the interests of its own constituency, the TUC delegation condemned the 'arbitrary imprisonment' of trade union leaders, the 'serious wounding of hundreds of peaceful citizens and death of two of our comrades' by the police, and the determination of the Dublin Employers' Federation 'to crush out trade unionism in Dublin.' It concluded on the rather smug note that the TUC had vindicated trade unionists' right to free speech and freedom of association by the mass rally in Dublin on 7 September.

Of more immediate value to the Dublin strikers, the Parliamentary Committee coupled the publication of the delegation's findings with an announcement that £5,000 would be pledged to secure a shipload of provisions to be sent to Dublin 'at once' to help starving workers and their families. It also launched an appeal for financial contributions from all affiliated unions.

As so often happens in industrial disputes, the most significant development of the day passed almost unnoticed by the press. After the TUC meeting ended, the Transport Workers' Federation met once more. Larkin attended and presumably agreed to the statement that was issued afterwards over the names of Gosling, Larkin's old protagonist James Sexton, and the secretary of the federation, Robert Williams. In this the federation offered to co-operate 'with any authorised body assisting the Irish Transport Workers' Union' in terminating the dispute. It added in a sharply worded rider that,

in order to ensure the success of any movement demanding the full recognition of the rights of collective bargaining it is essential in our opinion that neither provincialism, sectionalism, nor mere race prejudice must stand in the way of the greater and real union of the working classes.

So convinced are we that these essential conditions are imperative that we regard as futile any hope of helping the transport workers of Dublin on any other basis of action than the assurance of the representatives of the I.T.G.W.U. and the representatives of the Dublin Trades Council complying with the aforesaid conditions.[20]

The National Transport Workers' Federation was in effect asking the British government to use the Board of Trade to mediate in the dispute; in return, it was offering to go surety for its wayward son. While Larkin is often, and rightly, portrayed as an extremely wilful and egotistical leader, his willingness to be publicly chastised by the TUC and to accept the dictates of old enemies such as Sexton shows that he was also capable of quelling that fiery temperament when he felt it necessary in the wider interests of the movement.

Murphy was stung into a sharp rebuttal of the TUC analysis of events, and particularly the claim that he had set up the Dublin Employers' Federation as part of a personal vendetta against Larkin. But Birrell must have felt reasonably confident that Murphy would be carried on the tide of compromise, just as Larkin had been. If the mood reflected in the newspapers was not enough to convince the Chief Secretary, there were other straws in the wind. North County Dublin Rural District Council rejected a motion of support for the farmers in locking out their labourers; and the South Dublin Board of Guardians discussed the need for a 'truce'. Otherwise the workhouse in James's Street would fill up, 'and the Guardians would not be able to keep all who came to it.'

*

The courts, inadvertently, continued to provide a stream of evidence of the appalling conditions that bred industrial unrest. The case of the O'Leary brothers, William and Pat, which had broken up in disorder when they had first appeared in court three weeks earlier, evoked particular sympathy. When the case resumed it was not so much the details of the arrests but the circumstances in which they took place that attracted attention. The principal tenant of the one-roomed tenement in Marlborough Place, where the police burst in to arrest the two men, was William O'Leary. O'Leary and his wife, Fanny, told the court that they had six children aged between one and thirteen living in the room, as well as William's brother Pat and his child, who 'might die at any moment as its lungs are bleeding.'

The case provoked the *Irish Times* into publishing an editorial on 19 September entitled 'O'Leary's room,' which described the situation revealed in the police courts as 'an appalling indictment of the civilisation of Dublin.' It asked:

Is it economy to house the workers … in surroundings which make a clear mind, a strong arm, a cheerful heart—the essentials for good work—utterly unthinkable? … The poor child who is dying in the

O'Learys' room is not merely a grave threat to its six little cousins, pent within the same four walls. It is a menace to the well cared and well-fed children of every comfortable citizen of Dublin.

The methods of the 'strike agitators' might be 'insane and ruinous, but they draw their support from material which we have all helped to prepare for them.'

There were other unwelcome by-products of the dispute, such as the spiralling cost of coal. William Partridge put down an emergency motion at the city council calling for the corporation's coal stores at the Pigeon House power station to be used to provide fuel to the public at cost price. He received support from nationalists such as Dr McWalter and Alfie Byrne, as well as Lorcan O'Toole of Sinn Féin and Labour councillors.

On Monday 22 September a nationalist councillor, David Quaid, a solicitor, used the opportunity of a meeting of the Improvements Sub-Committee of the council to call on the Lord Mayor 'to establish a fund to be distributed entirely for the benefit of the wives and children' of workers 'affected by this unfortunate dispute.' A Unionist councillor, David Crozier, said the situation was 'becoming desperate.' He had 'nothing to do with either side in the dispute, nor do I want to, but if the starving little ones of our slums are neglected it will be a bad job for Dublin.'[21] Crozier was being a little disingenuous: he was the second-largest slum landlord on the city council.

Sherlock did not respond too enthusiastically. He was 'finding it exceedingly difficult at the present moment to get even a few shillings' for the fund set up to help the families of Byrne and Nolan, the two men killed in August. 'Between the general poverty on the one hand and the position of the merchants and the traders on the other,' he was afraid 'it was next to impossible to get money for anything.' Nevertheless, by the following Thursday public pressure had led to the mayor's wife setting up a 'Women and Children' fund in the Mansion House.

*

In contrast, the *Irish Times* and *Irish Independent* had no qualms in continuing to promote the Loyal Tramway Men fund. By late September donations had reached £976 18s 8d. Much of it had come from donors with such edifying titles as 'A Lover of Duty' and 'Be Just and Fear Not'. The amounts contributed were also significantly higher than those received by the *Freeman's Journal* and *Evening Telegraph*, which were continuing to collect money for the Church Street victims. A typical day in late September shows twenty *Irish Times* readers subscribing £23 5s to the Loyal Tramway Men, while thirty-three donations to the Church Street fund at the *Freeman* came to £14 14s 6d. The average size of the donations to the *Freeman* is enhanced by the inclusion of two street collections and another from members of the Dublin Municipal Officers' Association, one of Ireland's first white-collar unions. Most of the individual contributors to the *Freeman's* Church Street fund donated between 1s and 10s. The *Times* list for the Loyal Tramway Men was headed that day by Baroness Grey with a £3 donation; the other donations were nearly all between £1 and £2. It is hardly surprising that Dublin's wealthier citizens preferred to support Loyal Tramway Men than the families of the dead strikers; but the parsimony shown to the Church Street victims suggests that whatever *Irish Times* editorials might preach, many of its readers believed the poor were responsible for their own misfortunes.[22]

*

Sherlock's reluctance to undertake an appeal for the women and children of the strikers may partly have been because he was still preoccupied with his peace initiative. Undeterred by his initial rebuff by the employers, he prepared detailed proposals for an industrial truce along the lines indicated by Edward Lee and others. He also decided to try to relaunch the joint conciliation scheme he had proposed in July. The peace formula provided for the withdrawal of the employers' form demanding that workers forswear the ITGWU; it also called for the reinstatement of all men locked out or on strike. In return, the ITGWU was to give an 'absolute undertaking' that it would not use the sympathetic strike against any employer willing to refer disputes to the new conciliation board. This would consist of six nominees of the Dublin Employers' Federation and six nominees of the ITGWU and Dublin Trades Council. Sherlock suggested that it be chaired by Sir George Askwith, head of the Mediation Department at the Board of Trade in London.[23]

The Lord Mayor had no difficulty persuading the Trades Council to consider his proposals. The collapse of the sympathetic rail strike in Britain had had a sobering effect. While Partridge continued to make fighting speeches, the most determined of all the Dublin strike leaders, James Connolly, was ready to sound a moderate note. He had already welcomed Lee's letter in the press. However, he believed the approach was flawed, because Lee

> appears to wish both sides to give way at the outset on the very points that are alleged by both sides to be in dispute—viz., the attitude of the employers to the Irish Transport Workers' Union and the attitude of the Union towards the sympathetic strike. This is hardly practicable.

Nevertheless, the union was 'quite willing to let things remain as they are—both sides in a state of armed neutrality, as it were towards each other—and to discuss these points and any others that may be brought up.' He described talk about 'a fight to the finish' as 'more or less oratory on both sides ... no fight is ever really fought out to a finish.' The pugnacious Connolly could not resist adding, however, that 'of course, if the employers persist in fighting this way, we are perfectly ready to do so; but our general position is that we are willing—anxious, in fact—to have a Conciliation Board.' Any employer who did not wish to be represented on the board could leave the Employers' Federation, and the union would 'fight the matter out' with them.

Connolly predicted, somewhat optimistically, that a conciliation board would eliminate the need for sympathetic strikes,

> because all employers would be under the moral necessity of submitting strikes to this tribunal, and also under the constraint of the conscience and interests of its own class. Of course, there would always be cases where there would be no possibility of avoiding a strike, but such cases would be rare.

It was an amazingly conciliatory vision of industrial relations from a man who was a convinced Marxist and revolutionary. With his usual knack for getting to the heart of an issue, Connolly told the *Freeman's Journal*: 'It is the bad employer, and the employer who hates trade unionism that is really the crux of the whole position.'[24] It was just such an employer, William Martin Murphy, who was dictating the employers' strategy. Indeed the previous week Murphy had tried, unsuccessfully, to embroil the Guinness brewery in the lockout.[25]

The Trades Council indicated that it was willing to accept Sherlock's proposals as early as Monday 21 September, when it held the first of two meetings to discuss the situation. As its representatives on the conciliation board it nominated the president, Tom McPartlin of the carpenters, the vice-president, William O'Brien of the tailors, Richard O'Carroll of the bricklayers, James Nolan of the bookbinders, and of course Larkin. It was perhaps inevitable that Larkin should be nominated: his absence would have represented a climb-down by the strike committee before the talks even opened; and he had by far the largest number of workers affected by the dispute. The employers nominated no-one but agreed to discuss the issue again on Wednesday. At a second meeting of the Trades Council on Tuesday night, McPartlin told his colleagues frankly that the other side were obviously engaged in 'a starving-out process.' He praised the building labourers for refusing to renounce the ITGWU, despite their past differences with Larkin. 'I never saw such loyalty displayed,' he told the UBLU delegates.

P. T. Daly, who was leading the ITGWU delegation to the Trades Council in Larkin's absence, also praised the UBLU for their support, 'notwithstanding differences which existed.' Craft union delegates from the carpenters and bricklayers said they were already levying members for the strike fund and would come out if need be.

But there were also discordant voices. Lennon of the mineral water operatives, whose members had been locked out by Bewley and Draper Ltd, said they should accept the reality that there was friction between different trades. Nathaniel Rimmer of the Amalgamated Society of Railway Servants took the cue from Lennon to criticise Partridge and the ASE for trying to involve Irish railway workers in the lockout. His own union was still recovering from the 1911 strike, he said. He proposed a motion saying that industrial action was a matter for individual unions and that the

Trades Council had no role in advising affiliates on what they should do. In a revealing response, McPartlin confessed that he regarded a general strike as 'hopeless' with regard to forcing the employers to the negotiating table; but, like most of the executive, he saw Rimmer's proposal as an attempt to distance the Trades Council from the ITGWU, as well as an attempt to dilute the influence of the Trades Council generally. Its adoption would therefore not only concede a psychological victory to the employers but leave the trade union movement in Dublin sharply divided.

Rimmer resisted attempts to make him withdraw the motion, and it was defeated comfortably, by 29 votes to 8. The council then closed ranks to unanimously pass an executive motion declaring that 'all organised workers of Dublin should refuse to work with any workers who have signed the employers' agreement, or those employed to replace men dismissed for refusing to sign.'[26]

*

When the employers finally met next day, they adhered to their position of refusing to nominate anyone to Sherlock's proposed conciliation board. Sherlock also found that he was able to win the endorsement of only three of Dublin's six MPs for his proposals: Field, Brady, and Clancy. Abraham was absent, as usual, in London, and Nannetti excused himself on the grounds that he was too ill to become involved. Cotton's refusal to endorse the proposals was a more serious setback. As he was chairman of the Alliance Gas Company and a director of the DUTC, his silence sent a clear signal that business leaders remained firm in their support of Murphy's hard-line policy.

*

However, Birrell chose to take heart from reports in the *Irish Times* and *Freeman's Journal* that several unnamed members of the Employers' Federation contacted by the newspapers—'whose authority to speak with the full knowledge of the feeling of … fellow employers cannot be questioned'—felt that a conference could be held with the Transport Workers' Federation. However, this was on the assumption that the NTWF's proposals were 'reasonable'.

There was further encouragement from Sir Horace Plunkett. He was a liberal unionist convert to home rule, founder of the agricultural co-operative movement, and a promoter of all things modern and 'reasonable'. He felt the Lord Mayor's proposals were worthy of very serious consideration, though he undermined his endorsement considerably by admitting that he had not had time to read them in detail.[27]

Even the weather favoured compromise. The end of over eight weeks of sunshine welcomed by Father Curran the previous week had turned Dublin into a wet, grey, misty town. One journalist has left a vividly dismal picture.

> The berths were practically deserted, and but for a few lighters of Messrs. Guinness and the occasional passage across the river of a ferry boat, the swollen waters of the Liffey presented a dreary sight. In the

main thoroughfares of the city business was practically at a standstill. Few people ventured out in the rain, and traders suffered in consequence. The tramcars and private vehicles had the roadways almost to themselves. In the back streets, particularly the poorer districts, the scene was dismal in the extreme, and one wondered what would happen if the dispute were to last another week.[28]

*

There was further demoralising news for the strikers when the Coal Merchants' Association found a revolutionary solution to their delivery problems. They pooled resources and acquired a motor lorry, which began supplying customers directly from the huge coal reserve stockpiled at the strike-bound Custom House Dock. Priority was given to companies whose production had been hardest hit by fuel shortages. By Tuesday 23 September the association had decided to acquire more lorries, despite heavy police escorts being required to beat off attacks by 'roughs' as they passed through, or near, working-class areas. The association found motorised transport a very worthwhile investment indeed. One lorry could deliver forty tons a day: ten carts would be required to move the same load. The association announced that when the present dispute ended it would not require many of the men again. The one problem was that 'the demand for police for other duties is ... restricting the firms in their deliveries.'[29]

As early as Tuesday 23 September, the Commissioner of the DMP, Sir John Ross, reported to Birrell that he no longer had enough men to continue providing protection to employers and maintain normal policing duties in the city. Many of the RIC reinforcements had had to be redeployed in County Dublin to deal with the agricultural labourers, while more had returned to their own divisions.

There was also the problem of rising tension in Ulster. On Thursday 25 September the 'Central Authority of the Ulster Provisional Government' assembled in Belfast to plan resistance throughout the province to home rule. The Marquis of Londonderry presided, as Carson was indisposed. This did not prevent a retired senior British officer, Lieutenant-General Sir George Richardson, being appointed commander-in-chief of the Ulster Volunteers and a £1 million indemnity fund being launched for those injured in the coming confrontation. By the end of the day £250,000 had been pledged, including £10,000 apiece from Carson and Lord Londonderry; by the end of the next day £500,000 was pledged. Compared with this war chest, the Transport Federation's pledge of £5,000 worth of foodstuffs to Dublin was small change indeed.[30]

Birrell's immediate concern remained the need to maintain order in Dublin. The urgency of the situation had been brought home to him when his own administrative director, Laurence Dowdall, said that coal supplies at Dublin Castle were running dangerously low because of the strike. When Ross formally requested military aid at the end of the week, to protect tramway depots and power stations, Birrell acceded. He wrote to

Asquith, explaining that the police were overworked and that he had no choice but to relieve them of some duties.[31] However, he assured him that soldiers would not be made available to deliver coal, except to public institutions.

The army began its strike duties on Thursday 25 September and continued them for three months, until Christmas Eve. During that time military convoys provided twenty deliveries to institutions including the Royal Hospital, Mountjoy Prison, Dundrum Asylum, the Ordnance Survey, the Dublin Museum of Science and Art, and of course Dublin Castle.[32]

*

The use of soldiers in strikes was a practice that made the British government understandably nervous. It had meant trouble in England and had led to miners being shot in Wales. For an administration heavily dependent on the votes of Labour MPs for its majority in the House of Commons, this was bad. Deploying them in a labour dispute in Ireland, where the government's other main pillar of parliamentary support was based, placed it in double jeopardy. It was no comfort that for every Labour MP who might fulminate against the use of soldiers in Dublin there would be an Irish Party MP who would criticise the government if it failed to stand up to Larkinism.

Only that week one of the elder statesmen of the Irish Party, the veteran Land Leaguer David Sheehy, denounced Larkinism at a UIL meeting in his South Meath constituency. Sheehy was no backwoodsman. He lived in Dublin and was father-in-law of both Francis Sheehy-Skeffington and Tom Kettle. However, Sheehy had recently come under attack from some of his farmer constituents because he had not ensured a better share-out of the local Leonard estate by the Land Commission. What better way was there to make up lost ground than by attacking the tyranny of Larkin over the Dublin worker? Sheehy told his audience that even now, when starvation was at the door, the poor of Dublin believed Larkin when he promised 'bread and coal from across the water.' Sheehy did not know how long the trouble in Dublin would last, but he appealed to the people of County Meath to 'keep clear of it.' The labourers of Meath, he knew, would not associate with any body outside their own labour organisation. It was 'in the interest of Ireland, and especially in the interests of the poor workers that they should not be misled by that man Larkin.' He predicted that 'when the veil was torn from his face … the people of Dublin and the workers of Dublin, would see what a hideous monster they had been following.'[33]

Sheehy's parliamentary colleague in County Laois, Patrick Meehan, warned that the conflict in Dublin could have a 'far-reaching effect on agriculture and rural enterprise.' Meehan belonged to a younger generation of parliamentary nationalists. He had inherited his seat—and with it a tradition of rural radicalism—from his father. Now he had the difficult task of balancing the continuing concerns of the rural 'have-nots' with the new majority of 'haves'. These comprised the emerging class of farmers who a generation of land agitation had transformed from tenants into proprietors. Larkin's 'divine mission' speech gave Meehan the weapon he needed. Public opinion was sympathetic to the genuine grievances of workers, he said in a letter to the *Freeman's Journal*;

> but public opinion is against Larkin, his method and doctrine, and that is why many have, against their sympathies, silently looked on the present labour struggle, and rightly so, because the Irish people cannot tolerate a man who blasphemously arrogates to himself a Divine Mission, his predilection for Hell, under certain conditions, publicly gives utterance to doctrines at variance with the Divine law and denounces the clergy as paid hirelings … In the dolorous days of famine and oppression … when the iron heel of landlordism crushed his soul and hope was dead in his breast, the toiler turned to his priest for succour and sympathy, and found him a benefactor and friend.

Meehan warned Larkin that 'neither the misrepresentations and jibes of himself or his foul brood of anti-clerical allies can loosen the bonds of sympathy and mutual reliance existing between priests and people.'

Meehan described himself as 'a convinced believer in the principles of trade unionism' but denounced Larkin as 'an adventurer who is exploiting the Irish workman for a livelihood and declared war on all honest trade unionists because they dared to expose his fallacious economics and protect their fellow workers from the disastrous consequences of his campaign.' Sensibly, Meehan suggested that the best antidote to Larkinism and the 'syndicalist doctrines of continental anarchists' was the establishment of industrial arbitration courts. In the meantime he accepted that destitution was now so severe in Dublin that a central relief committee should be set up. Money could be channelled through the clergy, of all denominations, to make sure it reached the 'proper quarters'.[34]

Mulholloran Rural District Council in County Longford offered another glimpse of nationalist feeling that week. Members complained about the effect of the dispute on farmers. 'The railway companies and other big firms may suffer for the present, but they will make the public pay for it,' one member said. There was sympathy for the working man, but 'Larkin is an Atheist and revolutionist, and his policy will bring ruin to this country.' The council unanimously condemned Larkinism and Larkin for doing the work of the 'enemies of this country.'

Nationalist perspectives on the dispute within Dublin were more diverse. While most of the city's MPs abdicated their responsibilities for fear of offending both sides, and councillors were divided on their approach to the issues, a new voice was making itself heard. In a series of articles for the *Freeman's Journal*, David Sheehy's son-in-law Tom Kettle was attempting to provide an even-handed analysis of the issues on behalf of what might be described as the progressive wing of the Irish Party. Industrial conflict was an integral part of modern economic life, the first professor of national economics at University College, Dublin, told his readers. Like Meehan, he favoured arbitration and proposed the establishment of an industrial peace committee of concerned citizens to prepare the way, because feelings had become so embittered. Indeed what made the current Dublin labour dispute both different from and more dangerous than other disputes in Kettle's opinion was 'the passion with which each of the clashing parties has dedicated itself to the gospel of violence.'

Larkin was once more singled out as the 'notable disturber of the peace and black magician' in the conflict, but Kettle insisted that employers too must accept responsibility for 'the damage ... this mad struggle' was wreaking on the city.

> We are paying already in interrupted business, and enhanced prices. When the winter comes, and the 'wounded soldiers' pitilessly locked-out in the one event, desperately encumbered with debt in any event— are tramping the streets, it is we who in private charity, public subscription, in the increased cost of poor houses, hospitals and jails shall have to pay for this sin of waste.

In a city where the financial burden of having to part-finance a police force over which it had no control was a long-standing grievance, Kettle made a telling point when he added that 'we are paying now, if I may give one example, some £1,400 a week for extra police to keep the ring.' Dubliners 'who controlled neither millions nor mobs' were 'caught between the upper and the nether millstones.'[35]

There was widespread relief when Birrell finally announced on Wednesday 24 September that he had decided to call on the services of Sir George Askwith and the Board of Trade to resolve the dispute. The Lord Mayor belatedly unveiled his own proposals the same evening, to no avail. Charles Coghlan told Sherlock bluntly in a letter released simultaneously to the press that the terms 'do not form a basis suitable for negotiation.'

It was perhaps an indication of how far the lockout had polarised feelings in the city that there was no Irish representation on Askwith's inquiry team. It would consist of just three members: Askwith, Sir Thomas Ratcliffe Ellis, and J. R. Clynes. Ellis was secretary of the mine-owners' association in Britain and the employers' representative on the coal and railway conciliation boards; Clynes was chairman of the Gas Workers' and General Labourers' Union, a Labour MP, and a TUC nominee to both the government's Industrial Council and the Royal Commission on the Civil Service. A self-educated Lancashire mill-hand who had left school at ten, he was typical of the Labour leaders of his generation. No doubt his union's general secretary, Jack Jones, had briefed him on his own dealings with the Irish protagonists earlier that month.[36]

The Trades Council welcomed Birrell's initiative, though it would have preferred the Lord Mayor's approach. Connolly told a meeting in Beresford

Place that the workers were prepared to be reasonable, even while they prepared for war. By Saturday, he promised the crowd, there would be food for sixty thousand in the city, 'bearing with it the good will of the working classes of England.' He also issued a warning to employers not to step up the dispute while the Askwith Inquiry sat. If the rumours were true that some shipping firms were planning to import 'scabs' to work the docks, 'the streets will run red with the blood of working men.' Any talks entered into in the meantime would be broken off immediately, and it would be 'war to the death.'[37]

The problem was that such a prospect held less dread for the employers' leaders than it did for the strike leaders or the British government. It was now up to Askwith to restore peace.

15

S IR George Askwith was something of a national hero in England. He
had been knighted for his role in settling a rash of strikes since 1910,
involving miners, dockers, cotton-mill hands, firemen, seamen, and
railway workers. 'Mr Askwith, so equable, so tactful, and so just, seems to
have embodied, in a special manner, the spirit of Compromise, which is a
very English spirit,' wrote one historian of the period.[1] He came to Dublin
at the peak of his career, when, wrote another, 'it seemed that he had but
to appear upon a scene of trouble for the mists of difficulty to dissolve,
leaving an atmosphere of peace and sweet reasonableness.'[2] He knew little
of the strange industrial menagerie he was about to enter, though Birrell
had done his best to inform Askwith and his officials at the Board of Trade
of how things lay.

Birrell had also briefed the prime minister. He told him that he believed
the dispute was not over collective bargaining or union recognition but
'Larkin and his methods which everybody, in all ranks outside the
anarchical party, agree are impossible.' The employers had made things
worse, driving workers into Larkin's ranks by trying to force them to
forswear the ITGWU.

> The whole atmosphere is … charged with gunpowder and the hooligans
> in the city are ripe for mischief. From the Redmond point of view this
> state of affairs is very awkward. The 'Irish Times,' very kindly, is always
> rubbing in the impotency of the four members [of Parliament] for the
> city, and of the Catholic Church, and quotes what Larkin is fond of
> saying that 'Home Rule does not put a loaf of bread in anybody's pocket.'

Birrell did not disagree and was intrigued, as well as alarmed, by the
situation that had emerged. 'Larkin's position is a very peculiar one,' he
explained to Asquith. 'All the powers that are supposed to be of importance
are against him; the party, the whole Catholic Church, and the great body
of Dublin citizens, to say nothing of the Government, and yet somehow or
another he has support and is a great character and figure.'

The Chief Secretary showed more perception in putting the Dublin
conflict in its national context.

The dispute has lifted the curtain upon depths below Nationalism and the Home Rule movement, and were there to be an election in Dublin tomorrow, it is quite likely that two of the four gentlemen I have just referred to would lose their seats. I should not be surprised if Carson holds out some sort of hand to Larkin as a brother rebel against nationalist tyranny!

Birrell took seriously Connolly's threat of renewed rioting if the employers brought strike-breakers into the port.[3]

Large employers such as Murphy and Jacob did not want Askwith interfering, but they could hardly refuse to co-operate with the tribunal. As the *Irish Times* had pointed out, with both sides unable to negotiate face to face, the inquiry provided the best means of establishing a basis for direct talks.

*

From the beginning, Askwith's task was made more difficult by the unions welcoming his intervention as a victory. This gave the strike leaders new heart. In the *Irish Worker*, Connolly denounced the government, press, police and nationalists as 'the pilot fish of the wealthy and strong.' The Irish Party came in for particularly sharp treatment. It had remained silent 'when honest men and women, and even little children, have been bludgeoned to death.' He advocated a new method of bringing class warfare home to the enemy: with increasing numbers of ITGWU members facing eviction for non-payment of rent, Connolly mischievously suggested that the union buy a house in an area 'at present the absolute preserve of our enemies.' This would provide healthy accommodation for half a dozen workers' families and in the process drive down property values, thus making it possible to buy more houses.[4]

The *Irish Worker* published a letter from Larkin promising 'ammunition for the heroes and heroines fighting labour's battle.' He told readers that during his latest visit to Britain he had arranged for a thousand tons of coal to be despatched to Dublin. That very day 'Labour's man-of-war, the S.S. *Hare*, will break the boom of starvation, loaded with £5,000 worth of food.' The 'workers of Dublin have astonished the world again,' he wrote. 'Remember, you of the disinherited class, that the future is with you.'

*

Saturday had long been billed as the occasion on which the Ulster unionists would hold a demonstration of strength in the Agricultural Society's show grounds at Balmoral. Over fifty thousand people turned up to watch twelve thousand Ulster Volunteers pass in review. Carson, with an escort of forty-eight motorcyclists, arrived at the enclosure to join his general staff of retired British army officers and Tory politicians playing at soldiers. He told the crowd:

All governments must in the ultimate resort depend on the force that is behind them. And it is because I see this splendid, overwhelming force here today that I have no doubt that if we are driven to it we can successfully persist in … setting up a provisional government.

John Redmond responded with a feeble speech in Cahersiveen, saying that the unionists were mistaken if they thought he had 'grown too old fighting for home rule' to have any fight left. The commitment of the nationalist movement to constitutional means was not born of apathy

> but of most absolute confidence in the justice and certain triumph of our cause. And I say our opponents' attitude of truculence, of bluster, of lawlessness and of recklessness is born of despair.[5]

But the Dublin dailies, and much of the British press, concentrated their attention on the very different events taking place on the banks of the Liffey. Whatever the tardiness of the British labour movement in providing industrial support for the Dublin workers, no-one could fault the efforts of the National Transport Workers' Federation and the Co-Operative Wholesale Society in supplying the immediate material needs of the strikers.[6] Between the TUC's decision to provide £5,000 worth of aid on Tuesday and the following Friday evening, sixty thousand packages of food were assembled at the Co-Op's warehouse in Balloon Street, Manchester. Crates of jam, tea, butter, margarine and groceries were made up into 'family boxes', each one designed to feed five people. Over half the consignment was made up of potatoes.

Harry Gosling, James Seddon and the secretary of the TUC's Parliamentary Committee, Charles Bowerman, travelled to Salford, Lancashire, to supervise the loading, only to find the Pomona Docks strike-bound. Ironically, the dispute was over union recognition. Gosling ended up in the unusual position for a dockers' leader of asking the men to break their own strike and load the *Hare*, which had just arrived from Dublin with a consignment of Guinness stout. A deal was struck: the ship would be released with its return consignment of empty Guinness casks, provided it also took the food for the city's strikers. By 5 p.m. on Friday the *Hare* had left Salford on its historic voyage.

In Dublin the ITGWU had acquired the use of the City of Dublin Steam Packet Company's old Manchester shed on the South Wall to distribute the goods. Seddon had ordered 12,500 loaves from co-operative bakeries in Dublin and Belfast to be delivered directly to the shed, and by 7 p.m. on Friday the bread mountain had grown to 'an enormous size', according to the *Irish Times*. Larkin sent word that the ship might arrive as early as 5:30 or 6 a.m. on Saturday. In the event, thick fog delayed the crossing, but this did not prevent crowds waiting all morning in drizzling rain for a first sighting. The only diversion was when a man, an unemployed casual labourer sleeping rough on the quays, fell into the river. The *Irish Times* reported:

> A watchman heard a despairing cry—that was all. And when a boatman rowed around a short time after, only a well worn cap, floating near the

quay, showed that this unknown loiterer had gone to his account. It was not a very unusual thing along the riverside.

Probably of more interest to the hungry onlookers was the sight of ITGWU stewards, wearing their distinctive Red Hand badge, erecting rough barriers outside the shed. They used idle gangways that would be strong enough to resist a crowd but low enough to pass food across easily. They washed away the worst of the mud, and scattered sawdust. A group of women, 'evidently the poorest of the poor,' posed for press photographers to while away the hours. A nearby crane was smothered by 'ragged urchins' peering into the mist.

Eventually the rain stopped, the fog cleared, and at 12:45 p.m. a Port and Docks Board official with a telescope announced to a cheer that the ship now crossing the bar was the *Hare*. It was easily distinguished as it entered the port by being dressed with signal flags from stem to stern as well as flying the flag of the National Transport Workers' Federation.

Seddon and Gosling, who had sailed with the consignment, addressed the crowd on the quay. Seddon told them that

> should this dispute, unfortunately, be continued, rest assured that this first ship will not be the last. We recognise, as trade unionists, that your fight is our fight and we are going to stand by you until it is won.

Gosling reminded them that it was only three weeks since they held out the hand of friendship in Sackville Street. If the workers of Dublin stuck together, the English workers would stick with them.

The police kept a discreet watch on proceedings and left it to the shop stewards, armed with sticks, to keep order. Meanwhile ITGWU dockers 'worked like Trojans' to unload the cargo. But it was not until 1:40 p.m. that the first boxes were brought ashore, and it was 4:15 before distribution could begin. This was carried out by members of the Drapers' Assistants' Association, who had given up their half-day to help.

Only workers with food tickets from their union received provisions. Despite the long wait there was no disorder. After some confusion people formed up in two long queues and waited patiently for their parcels. Each parcel contained ten pounds of potatoes and another ten pounds of bread, butter, sugar, tea, jam, and fish. There were packets of biscuits for the children. The *Irish Times* correspondent wrote:

> Many were the degrees of poverty represented by this striking procession. Here were seen the wan dweller in some noisome tenement wrapped in a shawl and huddling a baby to her breast; the carter's wife, who had a bonnet as well as a shawl; a decently attired housewife with gloves and ribbons, evidently ill at ease on such an errand ... boys and girls of all sizes and ages, from children whose heads did not show above the barriers to striplings who must find work—all were reduced to a common level by dire necessity that knows no law. Little was said as the procession went through the store. Each person had quite enough to do

to grasp … loaf and box and bag. Most of the noise in the building came from the men who were still discharging the *Hare* and supplying the drapers' assistants with the rations to keep the procession moving … For hours the scene was much the same.

One aspect struck this reporter as particularly sad.

The poorest woman dislikes to carry a loaf uncovered; to do so is to proclaim her poverty to the world. But here were respectably attired women who were thus humiliated before a curious crowd of onlookers; for many had not thought of bringing baskets to carry the provisions …

When at a distance from the centre of distribution a number of the humblest recipients stopped to examine the contents of their grocery boxes. One tattered woman appeared to be dividing her tea with a friend who was not so lucky as herself. Indeed those of the poor who were about, but were unentitled to have a portion of the food, must have been envious. Not far from the door of the shed sat a pallid woman and her daughter, utterly forlorn, looking wonderingly upon the bustle around.

It took until 8 p.m. to unload the *Hare* and until 9 p.m. to finish distribution at the South Wall. More workers' families were supplied from carts that took consignments of food for distribution in Kingstown, Clondalkin, Swords, Lucan, and other parts of County Dublin. By the end of the day nine thousand workers and their dependants had received provisions.

*

Next morning's *Sunday Independent* gave a very different account of the proceedings. It decried the 'pitiable spectacle' of 'mothers with babies in their arms' pushing their way 'through the serried ranks of dock labourers, who had gathered early with the evident intention of being first in the field for English charity.' Many of the women were

respectably attired and were weeping bitterly. They manifestly felt the humiliation of being obliged to drag themselves and their little ones several miles down the South Wall to beg for English food.

The stance taken by the *Sunday Independent* raised an obvious question that the paper declined to pose, let alone answer: where was Irish charity?

On Saturday, while £5,000 worth of 'English charity' was dispensed on the quays, the Lord Mayor's wife told an inaugural meeting of the Dublin Children's Distress Fund that it should consider 'the best means of carrying out the real objects of subscribers viz., providing food for women and children.'[7] So far £106 had been collected, and arrangements had been made with various religious bodies to provide meals on their premises. In fact most of these agencies had already been providing meals for some time, but the stimulant had been sectarian competition between proselytisers and counter-proselytisers, rather than any planned response to communal deprivation.[8]

On Monday the Ladies' School Dinners Committee, a secular agency that had grown out of the radical nationalist-feminist group Inghinidhe na hÉireann, announced that it had received nothing from the fund of the Ladies' Relief Committee. Its secretary, Helen Laird, said that they had barely been able to cope with demand in years when 'industrial conditions were normal,' let alone in the present crisis. The fact was that 'semi-starvation is a chronic condition in the poorer districts of the city,' she wrote in an appeal for funds. She described the work of the committee, which provided meals for 450 children in the Liberties during term time. At a cost of 4d per child it provided a daily ration of either stew, pea soup and potatoes, or rice and jam. But it could not survive beyond the present week for lack of funds.

> Necessity has become greater ... for even when the wage earner is still at work, prices have gone up. The workingmen of Dublin are severely criticised for the injury a strike causes the commercial prosperity of their city. Can we expect these starving children, the future generation of workers, to grow up with a respect for commercial prosperity? How can we hope to avoid future strikes if the children are neglected?

Unfortunately, that was not a question with which the employers concerned themselves. Indeed they urged people to read an article written for the *Morning Post* by a leading British Labour MP, Philip Snowden, who described strikes as ineffective. He went on to elaborate in the *Labour Leader* that it would be more merciful to let privation hasten their end than to drag them out with misguided charity.[9]

But it was the voyage of the *Hare* that would be remembered, not Snowden's lectures. The small tramp steamer was an unlikely 'Labour man o' war'. Up to a couple of days beforehand it had been engaged in activities bordering on strike-breaking in Dublin; but from the moment it steamed into Dublin port on 27 September 1913 it entered the mythology of the labour movement and became a symbol of international brotherhood that Murphy's shabby publications could not besmirch.

This was the first of many voyages by the *Hare*, and other vessels commissioned by the TUC, to Dublin. Besides bringing food to the strikers, and inspiring the trade union movement by the example of international solidarity, it had the practical effect of forcing down what Seddon described as the 'famine prices' being charged by many Dublin shopkeepers.[10]

*

British trade union support did not come without conditions. Seddon and Gosling had not travelled over with the *Hare* just to make speeches but to lead the trade union delegation at Askwith's inquiry. They no doubt hoped to control Larkin's role in the proceedings, which began in Dublin Castle at 11 a.m. on Monday.

The inquiry did not progress very far the first day.[11] The employers, led by George Jacob and William Martin Murphy, wanted more time to prepare their case. They also wanted the inquiry to sit in public. Murphy said that public hearings were necessary because the employers' case had not received a fair hearing in the past; private negotiations with the unions had failed to achieve a settlement, and the pressure of public opinion would 'help towards some sort of settlement.' Gosling protested that a public inquiry might take weeks, while day after day the workers were starving. The public Murphy was so anxious to inform 'did not care a rap' for the strikers.

To add to its perplexities, the inquiry received a request for formal representation from the United Builders' Labourers' Union. The union's solicitor, James Brady, a well-known figure in radical nationalist circles, said that his clients were innocent victims of the lockout. However, when the tribunal resumed next morning Brady withdrew. 'I have been, if I may say so, "locked out",' he complained to laughter. The UBLU had been prevailed upon overnight to allow the National Transport Workers' Federation and Dublin Trades Council to speak for it. Askwith then told the two sides he intended holding the proceedings in public, and called on the employers to state their case.

Timothy Healy headed the powerful legal team assembled by Murphy and the Employers' Federation; it also included Henry Hanna KC, who had been defending Larkin in his sedition case. Healy's appearance for Murphy was expected. They shared a vision of Ireland in which the Catholic middle class would come into their own as the political, cultural and moral guardians of the people. Mavericks and outcasts they might have become within the nationalist movement, but both possessed sufficient capital—in Healy's case political and intellectual—to survive outside the herd. One of Healy's many uncomplimentary sobriquets was 'Thersites' (an ugly, foul-mouthed character in Homer's *Iliad*), and it was used to describe with some accuracy his performance at the inquiry.

Healy's Thersitic skills were in ample evidence when he opened the case for the employers. Within the past five years Dublin had been subjected to 'more strikes than during its entire existence as a capital,' he told the tribunal.

> The action taken in the name of trade unionism … was sufficient to make every honest trade unionist throughout the three kingdoms ashamed of the abuse of the name.
>
> Wherever a man was dismissed, whether for assault or for drunkenness, or for any other cause, that man was immediately seized upon by this so-called trade union and turned into an active organiser against those who had unfortunately to get rid of his services.

The majority of strikes 'had been brought about on what was called the "sympathetic" principle.' It had enabled Larkin to achieve an extraordinary series of victories over Dublin employers, until they 'had worn out their marrow-bones in kneeling at the shrine of Larkin.'

The *Irish Worker* was the weapon used for intimidating those who refused to join the ITGWU or join a strike picket. Their names and addresses were published, and they were called 'tools, sweaters, pimps, whitewashers, detectives, etc.' English unions, which would not tolerate such methods themselves and had ordered back to work members who participated in sympathetic strikes, 'were keeping the Irish workers out, and paying them strike wages.' Larkin was preparing to use the same tactics against the Tramways Company that had worked so well elsewhere, but Murphy had anticipated him.

> Nearly all the others met Mr Larkin, dealt with Mr Larkin and yielded to him. Mr Murphy never dealt with Mr Larkin; he would not meet him. In fact, Larkin knew that Mr Murphy was of that stamp that he would not see him, and he never even applied to see him. There was one man in the city who would not deal with Larkin and with whom Larkin could not deal.

Healy now struck at the Achilles heel of the ITGWU case. Only a minority of its members had struck. 'Would any colliery in England— leaving out the question of a sympathetic strike—be "struck" when the majority of the men were opposed to a strike?' he asked the Englishmen on the tribunal. 'And if the minority of the men struck, would they have a right, according to the common sense of the country, to describe the majority who remained in as "scabs", to have their houses boycotted, and to be publicly stoned in the streets?' Murphy himself had been 'assailed in prose and in verse' for his stance.

> He was called a low toady, a renegade, an untruthful politician, a false friend, a sweating employer and a whited sepulchre. (Laughter.) It is only in Ireland that one man could fulfil all those conditions. (Loud laughter.)

Despite this, 'Mr Murphy had made his arrangements for dealing with this strike, and accordingly he put a body of men remaining faithful on the cars.'

To show Larkin's 'cruelty' in bringing out the tram workers at less than twenty-four hours' notice, Healy pointed out that

> every one of them, when taking employment, signed a bond, themselves in £15 and two sureties in £10, that they would not leave the service without giving a fortnight's notice. These are now forfeit. Many of the men have cottages from the company, and are still living in them.
>
> Someone foolishly said that the freedom of the world was not worth a single drop of blood. I do not hold that, but if they put on one side any gain Mr Larkin may have won, and on the other the enormous loss which he has caused to business, the sufferings he has caused the poor, the benefit that he has done to any man or body of men in the city is but a drop in the ocean to the mischief, misery, tumult and ruin of which he is the author.
>
> The result is that the harried employers met on the third of September, to the number of four hundred, like men in a besieged city,

to see how they could get over this cloud of wrath mounting over the metropolis. Many of them had yielded to Larkin; all of them are friendly to trade unions. [Nevertheless] these employers met and unanimously resolved that they would have nothing more to do with anybody in Mr Larkin's union, and that it was a libel to call it a trade union. This union is Larkin. That is greatly to his credit as an organiser, but employers have reluctantly come to the conclusion that no bargain made with him will be kept.

Healy informed the tribunal of the state that employers in the city and county were reduced to.

If they went out into the country for ten miles they would not get a single labouring man in employment. The very harvest was rotting, and the farmers were going about with revolvers, and all in the name of 'the divine mission to create discontent.' (Loud laughter, in which Mr. Larkin joined.) … Surely it could not be the case that every employer, every farmer, every trader, with sixpence stake in the country, that they were all wrong and Larkin only right; that everything was wrong until five years ago, when the divine missioner landed amongst us. (Laughter.)

Serjeant Sullivan, representing the farmers, made a somewhat contradictory speech. He said that a problem in the county was the lack of union organisation. Some of his clients had locked out employees because they had sought more than had been agreed with the ITGWU, while others had locked out their labourers because it was not clear what the men wanted.

We do not want a truce. There must be peace or war. We are not going to place Mr Larkin in a position from which he can come down upon us when the next crop is to be sown or reaped. Mr Larkin's object is, by coercion and agitation, to abolish employers altogether.

*

During the next few days a succession of employers were called by Healy to give evidence of the ITGWU's bad faith over the years. Several of them were cross-examined by Larkin, who almost imperceptibly took over the presentation of the union's case from Gosling. It was perhaps inevitable, for only he had the detailed knowledge to contradict their assertions. He had a particularly sharp exchange with George Jacob; when Jacob refused to disclose rates of pay and working conditions, Larkin accused him of 'damnable slavery'.

With the shipping companies Larkin had more success. When employers' representatives complained that there had been 'no trouble on the quays of Dublin' for twenty years 'until Mr Larkin came,' he made them admit that one result of 'constant strife' was that pay rates had been increased by between 3s and 6s a week since 1908.

Of course with Healy representing the employers, Larkin did not have a free run. When an exasperated Jacob said in response to Larkin's heavy cross-examination that 'it is an anarchist society my company is up against,' Larkin replied, 'You don't pretend to carry on your business as a philanthropist!' Healy riposted: 'Does Mr Larkin?'

Perhaps more worrying for the employers was the evidence that Larkin's supremacy was also being reasserted outside the inquiry rooms in Dublin Castle. On the second day of the hearing the town clerk of Dublin, Henry Campbell, appealed to Askwith to intervene in a new dispute at the corporation's electric lighting works. ITGWU members at the Pigeon House were refusing to unload coal from a Scottish vessel because it was also supplying the DUTC. When Askwith explained that the dispute was outside the remit of the tribunal, it was suggested that Harry Gosling might look into it. Gosling said he had no mandate to intervene either. 'If I poked my nose too far into the matter, the other people might chop it off.' He did not specify who the 'other people' might be, but it was clear that the ability of the National Transport Workers' Federation to control Larkin and his lieutenants was limited in the extreme.

The dispute was referred back to the president of the ITGWU, Thomas Foran, and the coal remained undischarged, thus threatening supplies to some seven thousand customers, commercial and residential, who were wealthy enough to avail of the miracle of electricity.[12]

Meanwhile the city's wealthier citizens were bombarding the corporation with claims for damages caused by the rioting of the previous month. No less than fifty-eight applications for criminal damages under the Local Government (Ireland) Act (1898) had been submitted by 2 October. The largest claim was from Clery and Company, which was seeking £23 16s 5d for replacement of the large window whose smashing signalled the start of the baton charge in Sackville Street on 'Bloody Sunday'. Some of the smaller traders had no insurance and told the Recorder, who was awarding claims, that they did not intend seeking insurance, or replacing damaged windows, until the present troubles had passed.[13]

*

While the Askwith Inquiry examined the causes of conflict, and the courts deliberated on damages, there was little the shopkeepers or other citizens could do but wait. For the strikers, Liberty Hall continued to be a focal point of hope, help, and speculation. Inside, Larkin's officials had to deal with the minutiae of the dispute. Connolly took a leading role in organising food supplies, and in this he had the assistance of two redoubtable women, Constance Markievicz and Delia Larkin. The Irish Women Workers' Union had 1,100 members locked out. 'Tall and commanding in appearance, like her brother,' Delia Larkin also had a similar temperament, 'implacable to opponents, but with a friendly warmth to the people she trusted.' She now took the lead in organising a kitchen and canteens to serve food to the strikers and their families. Union members helped her.

As it happened, the building lent itself superbly to the task. Liberty Hall had begun its eventful life in the eighteen-thirties as the Northumberland Coffee Rooms. It later progressed to a fully fledged hotel, before becoming the headquarters of class warfare in Ireland. As a result it had old kitchens, large storage areas and former dining-rooms ready for reconversion to their former tasks. Each day of the lockout Liberty Hall opened its doors from early morning until late at night to feed three thousand hungry men, women, and children. From an early stage a special dining area was set up for mothers. This was after Constance Markievicz found that many women trade unionists were taking home their soup and sandwiches to feed their families; Markievicz insisted that they eat as well.[14]

Seán O'Casey was roped into a committee to collect funds for his beleaguered union and spent most days in and around the hall. He later recalled the fascination and admiration with which many witnessed the ITGWU's efforts to feed its own. George Russell, editor of the *Irish Homestead*,

> looking like a teddy bear … would thunder slowly and heavily in … spluttering and sparkling all around him. Yeats, though he never entered, passed by, and looked up at the windows, in a trailing toga of silver and purple, a mystic rose in his hair, and a lady's glove in his girdle. Orpen would hop in, dressed in rusty red and bottle green to sketch the tired and hungry faces surrounding the pale, hardy, handsome face of their leader, Jim. And Countess Markievicz, running around everywhere, would be scintillating in the suit of a harlequin, lozenged with purple, old gold and virgin green.

O'Casey hated Markievicz even more than he hated her Liberty Hall ally, James Connolly. In all the time he had spent bustling 'through a crowd of ragged women, and ragged children, bootless as well as ragged, carrying jugs, saucepans, and even kettles to collect their ration of stew, cooked … in the damp and dreary basement,' O'Casey claimed he never once saw Markievicz 'doing anything anyone could call a spot of work.' Only when a reporter strayed in would she be 'in a spotless bib and tucker, standing in the steam, a gigantic ladle in her hand, busy as a beebeesee,' appearing 'in the heat and burden of the day' to pose for a picture.[15] And yet that she was there at all, and that men like William Orpen and George Russell should visit the kitchens, spoke volumes for the sympathy and attention the struggle was now attracting.

16

IF the city sank into a slough of misery while it awaited the outcome of the Askwith Inquiry, the county fairly bubbled with unrest. With a thousand farm labourers locked out and pockets of urban unrest in places as far apart as Lucan and Balrothery, it was hardly surprising that farmers and businessmen went about armed.

The local courts played a major role in the dispute. These, of course, were dominated by landowners and employers. Colthurst Vesey, a major shareholder and director of the DUTC, presided in Lucan; another member of the Lucan court was Frederick Wookey, the man who dismissed employees for wearing the Red Hand badge before the Employers' Federation had even agreed to a lockout. These men dealt every week with cases of intimidation, disorderly behaviour and eviction orders brought against members of the ITGWU at the behest of the magistrates' neighbours and friends. Solicitors representing the ITGWU made occasional ineffectual protests at the situation, as the following typical exchange at Swords Petty Sessions illustrates. It was an application for the repossession of a farm worker's cottage in Ballymun. The union's solicitor, Blood Smyth, said he had been instructed

> that some of the magistrates are much interested, owing to the extent of the trouble. I don't say that they would be prejudiced personally, but I would ask any of these magistrates not to adjudicate.
> *Chairman:* The fact does not admit of any legal disability.
> *Smyth:* Certainly. I am quite pleased with the bench personally, but my instructions are as I say.

The chairman, a resident magistrate called Shannon, told Smyth: 'The magistrates are determined to sit.' And that was the end of the matter. The eviction order was granted.

The rural situation was further aggravated by bad weather, which made the matter of finding shelter for evicted labourers and their families all the more urgent. It also meant that corn still unharvested might rot in the fields. When a brief spell of fine weather came in early October, farmers used the opportunity to save the crop and remove it to the haggards.

Mr Dodd, who had sat on the bench in Swords awarding eviction

The trams were the lifeblood of Dublin's transport system. These vehicles are carrying crowds to the Phoenix Park during the visit of King George V in 1911. (RTE)

Poverty and prosperity. Grafton Street, Dublin, decked out for the royal visit of 1911. Note the barefoot newsboys on the left. (National Library of Ireland)

The bare necessities. A tenement bedroom in Waterford Street, one of the areas most affected by the rioting.

Sir William Orpen's portrait of William Martin Murphy now hangs in the Dublin Chamber of Commerce.

James Larkin, drawn by Sir William Orpen, now hangs in Liberty Hall.

EVENING HERALD

6.30 WHITE

TELEGRAMS: "HERALD," DUBLIN. EDITORIAL TELEPHONE: 704.

CERTIFIED NET SALES EXCEED THOSE OF ANY OTHER DUBLIN EVENING PAPER.

VOL. 22. NO. 205.   DUBLIN, TUESDAY, AUGUST 26, 1913.   PRICE ONE HALFPENNY.

ATTEMPT TO CAUSE A TRAM STRIKE IN DUBLIN

Some of the Men Leave Work and Wear Red Hand Badge

THEIR EXAMPLE NOT FOLLOWED BY VAST BODY OF MEN

No Dislocation of Traffic and Cars Running as Usual

DUBLIN UNITED TRAMWAYS COMPANY (1896), LTD.

OFFICIAL STATEMENT.

Shortly before 10 o'clock this morning some of the Company's cars were deserted by the men in charge of them, and left standing in the streets. These cars were promptly cleared off, and the traffic was continued with a slightly reduced service.

The Company regrets the inconvenience to the public, which will be of short duration.

The cars will not, however, be run after dark this evening.

26th August, 1913.

RED HAND MEN IGNORED

OUR HORSE SHOW VISITORS

AN EXCELLENT SERVICE.

SPLENDID DISCIPLINE.

NORTH SIDE SERVICE.

HOW LARKIN'S ORDER WAS OBEYED

PLEASING FEATURES.

AN AMUSING SCENE.

TRAMS WORKING AS USUAL

SNAPSHOT SHOWING TRAMS WORKING AS USUAL THIS EVENING. —"Herald" Photo.

ALONG THE COAST.

THE ONLY DANGER.

INTIMIDATION.

LATEST NEWS

TRAMWAY TROUBLE IN DUBLIN.

SOLDIERS IN READINESS.

TRAMWAY TROUBLE.

NUMBER OF MEN OUT.

LATEST CRICKET.

SEVEN STRIKERS CHARGED

With Causing Obstruction

BY LEAVING CARS IN STREET

Man Given a Chance to go on

IT WAS ONLY OLD IRISH.

DID NOT PROFESS TO KNOW MUCH

VARIED FROM 8,000 TO 12,000.

FIRST CHARGE AGAINST THE DEFENDANT

HE CANNOT GIVE WHAT HE HASN'T GOT.

THEY WON'T PAY THEIR DEBTS

WHAT IS LARKIN GETTING PER WEEK?

For Fomenting Strikes in Dublin

EXTRAORDINARY FINANCIAL REVELATIONS

His 'Bad Debt' of £227 to a City Printer

WHAT THE TRANSPORT UNION BRANCHES

Proceedings that Every Striker Should Read

WAS ONLY ONE OPPOSITION TO THE OFFER.

MR. JAMES LARKIN EXAMIN

Caption

The front page of the *Evening Herald* on the first day of the tram strike. The 6.30 p.m. 'white' edition concentrates on the failure of the strike to stop services, and personal attacks on Jim Larkin. However, it also announces that trams will not run after dark. (National Library of Ireland)

The Lord Lieutenant, the Earl of Aberdeen, arriving in state at the Royal Dublin Horse Show, 27 August 1913.

Lord and Lady Aberdeen. Often lampooned by strike leaders and radical nationalists as liberal 'do-gooders', they were nevertheless popular for their social initiatives on public health and housing. (*Illustrated London News*, 6 September 1913. National Library of Ireland)

Hostesses for Horse Show week. They suffered no inconvenience from the tram strike.

Sir Charles Cameron, chief medical officer for Dublin. His reputation was damaged by revelations of bad housing during the lockout.

Lord Iveagh, head of the Guinness dynasty, kept out of the lockout but secretly financed other Dublin employers.

(*Freeman's Journal*, 26 August 1913. National Library of Ireland)

JUST A CONTRAST

This *Saturday Herald* cartoon of 30 August 1913 contrasts Larkin's salary of £2 10s (£2.50) a week with paltry strike pay. At first the ITGWU paid 10s (50p) to male members and 7s 6d (37½p) to female members; later both rates were reduced to 5s. Larkin often went without his salary during the lockout. (National Library of Ireland)

A photograph taken in O'Connell Street a few minutes before the baton charge on 'Bloody Sunday'. Attempts to submit such photographs in evidence to the Dublin Disturbances Commission were unsuccessful. (*Freeman's Journal*, 2 September 1913. National Library of Ireland)

Photograph taken from the same vantage point as the previous. Note the cluster of people trapped against the police cordon in Prince's Street at top left-hand corner. This is where some of the worst casualties were sustained.

O'Connell Street after the charge: mounted police take control. (*Freeman's Journal*, 1 September 1913. National Library of Ireland)

The Daily Mirror

THE MORNING JOURNAL WITH THE SECOND LARGEST NET SALE.

No. 3,076.   Registered at the G.P.O. as a Newspaper.   TUESDAY, SEPTEMBER 2, 1913   One Halfpenny.

MR. JAMES LARKIN, DISGUISED IN FALSE BEARD AND FROCK COAT, ARRESTED BY POLICE IN CONNECTION WITH DUBLIN STRIKE RIOTS.

Prohibited by the authorities from holding a meeting on Sunday of the Irish Transport Workers' Union, of which he is secretary, Mr. James Larkin vowed to appear in Sackville-street, Dublin, despite the fact that the police held a warrant for his arrest. By adopting the disguise in which he is seen above he was able to carry out his threat. On Sunday morning an apparently old and feeble bearded man took a room at the Imperial Hotel in Sackville-street. Shortly afterwards this venerable gentleman stepped on to the balcony and, announcing, "I am Larkin," began to address the crowds in the street below. Police instantly entered the hotel and arrested him. The picture shows him leaving the hotel in custody. The smaller picture is of Mr. Larkin without disguise.—(*Daily Mirror* photographs.)

British tabloid sales rose in Dublin during the lockout. The *Daily Mirror's* treatment of Larkin's arrest was typical. The emphasis remained firmly on Larkin and social issues. (*Daily Mirror*, 2 September 1913. National Library of Ireland)

Murphy's newspapers remained unrepentant after 'Bloody Sunday', as this cartoon in the following week's *Saturday Herald* shows. (6 September 1913. National Library of Ireland)

TIME TO DO THIS

DUBLIN

CITY EMPLOYERS

LARKINISM

VICIOUS STRIKES

GORDON BREWSTER

A CARTOON THAT SPEAKS FOR ITSELF

DARTRY HALL

The *Irish Worker* of 6 September 1913, depicting Murphy in the aftermath of 'Bloody Sunday'.

The mass rally called by the British TUC in O'Connell Street in protest at events on 'Bloody Sunday' passed off peacefully on 7 September.

Police on stand-by during the British TUC rally.

(*Illustrated London News*, 13 September 1913. National Library of Ireland)

The ITGWU head office draped in black. The banner over the door reads *In memory of our murdered brother James Nolan.*

Mounted police on duty at Nelson's Pillar in O'Connell Street, the focal point of the tramway system.

The British Labour Party leader, Keir Hardie, during his brief visit to Dublin in September 1913. He was more sympathetic towards the young Irish strike leaders than most of his colleagues.

(*Freeman's Journal*, 3 September 1913. National Library of Ireland)

The funeral of James Nolan, one of the 'Bloody Sunday' victims, was made a show of strength by the ITGWU. (*Freeman's Journal*, 4 September 1913. National Library of Ireland)

Collapsed tenements in Church Street. Among the dead were two children, aged four and five. Public outrage forced the British authorities to hold a public inquiry, despite the powerful landlords' lobby. (*Evening Herald*, 3 September 1913. National Library of Ireland)

British trade union leaders are unable to hide their concern as they pose for photographers on a jaunting-car. Privately they were horrified at the entrenched positions of the employers and the Dublin Trades Council. (*Left to right*) William Brace of the South Wales Miners, James Seddon of the Boilermakers, and Harry Gosling of the Transport Federation. (*Evening Herald*, 8 September 1913. National Library of Ireland)

The first annual pilgrimage to Lourdes made a profit of £14,000, of which £2,000 was donated to the relief of distress in Dublin. It was by far the largest donation of any religious body. (*Sunday Independent*, 21 September 1913. National Library of Ireland)

BLINDFOLDED TO EVERYTHING

Stalemate. This *Sunday Independent* cartoon of 21 September 1913 shows its exasperation at the failure of Dublin workers to succumb to the lockout strategy and attributes it to their blind faith in 'syndicalism'. (National Library of Ireland)

Aid from England. Boys and girls collecting provisions. Altogether nearly £100,000 was raised by the British TUC for the Dublin strikers and their families.

Members of the Drapers' Assistants' Association helping to pack supplies in Dublin. Nationally, the union was less enthusiastic about supporting locked-out workers.

(*Freeman's Journal*, 3 October 1913. National Library of Ireland)

decrees a few days earlier, sent his motor car around the Cloghran district to assemble his neighbours and draw in the corn. 'The workers included several Justices of the Peace, and other gentlemen unused to bearing the heat and burden of the day,' the *Freeman's Journal* reported, 'but they gave a marvellously good account of themselves, and actually taught lessons in sustained effort to groups of strikers who picketed the place during the progress of operations.' A large force of police stood guard while the work progressed.

ITGWU members tried to organise a march through Swords the following day to publicise their plight. It coincided with the monthly fair, and a local band was to lead the procession. Trouble began when the Swords Branch of the United Irish League, which owned the band room, tried to prevent the musicians entering to obtain their instruments. The police arrived on the scene and designated the ITGWU men an unlawful assembly. The musicians were told they could not leave the hall with their instruments; and the strikers had to settle for an impromptu indoor concert rather than a march.

On Friday there was more bad news for the labourers. After giving evidence to the Askwith Inquiry that morning, farmers' representatives announced that they would 'fight out the dispute in their own way,' by threshing without union labour. Faced with the prospect of a hungry winter, and denied legitimate expression of their grievances, it was perhaps inevitable that some labourers resorted to the practices of an earlier era by destroying crops and by arson attacks on buildings. The two worst incidents occurred at Hazelhatch, where over £600 worth of crops were burnt, as well as a pub that belonged to a local landowner, valued at £400.

But the tough stance of the farmers and magistrates had its effect. By the weekend the main task of the police in Swords appeared to be keeping the peace between men who were holding out in support of the ITGWU and those who had decided to return to work and were celebrating in local public houses with 'subs' from the farmers.[1]

*

Timothy Healy's presentation of the employers' case may have been the first highlight of the Askwith Inquiry (indeed the employers thought so highly of it that it was subsequently published as a pamphlet), but it was soon overshadowed by the second. This was the cross-examination of William Martin Murphy by Jim Larkin. On Friday the long-awaited duel took place, and the hearing was packed.

The gallery had had an appetiser the previous day, when Murphy had spent the afternoon being led through his evidence by Healy. Unlike other witnesses, he insisted on standing, because, he said, it enabled him to speak more clearly.

Towards the end of the hearing, Healy asked his client if he had been responsible for the arrest of Larkin. 'I had nothing directly to do with it,' Murphy replied.

Healy then produced a copy of the *Irish Worker* published after 'Bloody Sunday', the edition with a cartoon of Murphy on the front page, perched like a vulture at the entrance of his home at Dartry, crowing over a dead worker. In response to Healy, Murphy said the newspaper was an incitement to murder him.

Askwith asked Murphy if he had ever met Larkin personally over any of these matters. Murphy replied:

> I never saw him until I saw him here in this room. This is the first time I have seen him.
>
> *Larkin:* It is now 5 o'clock and my colleagues wish to have a consultation. I have some questions to ask Mr Murphy, and as I don't wish to murder him, he might sit down.
>
> *Murphy:* Mr Larkin is quite right. I don't see why we should work after 5 o'clock. (Laughter.)

When the duel began in earnest next morning, Larkin complained that

> there is discrimination in the admission of people to the court. Respectable working men are prevented by the police from entering the building.

Askwith said that 'not another person could be put in' on Thursday, and the press had been 'seriously inconvenienced.' Healy told the tribunal it had taken him ten minutes to get in on Thursday. 'We must adjourn to Liberty Hall,' he added to laughter. Larkin suggested to more laughter that they use instead Carlisle Buildings (head office of the *Irish Independent*). 'There is much more room now, as they are not doing so much.'

For those fortunate enough to obtain admittance, there could not have been a sharper contrast than that between the principals. A quarter of a century later one onlooker still had

> a vivid recollection of the dark inchoate face of Larkin and of his tall ungainly figure, craning forward as he bellowed forth his arraignment; and opposite him the calm handsome face of Murphy ... speaking just above his breath and glancing occasionally at his angry foe: near him rose from time to time the robust form of his counsel, Thersites Healy, releasing effortlessly his biting speech.[2]

*

Murphy had always stressed that he was a friend of respectable trade unions and that his quarrel was with the ITGWU. Larkin now concentrated his efforts on showing that his opponent had been involved in regular disputes with unions. Referring to the bitter conflict at the GSWR in 1911, he asked:

> Did you take credit for smashing up trade unionism in the last railway strike?
>
> *Murphy:* I did not say anything of the kind.

Larkin: Did you say that one of the parties to the trades dispute succeeded in beating the workers?

Murphy: I pointed out that a strike with all the forces of the Amalgamated Society of Railway Servants against the Great Southern and Western Railway was beaten in nineteen days, and I quoted that as a warning to the men in a strike against the Tramway Company.

However, when Larkin attacked Murphy's record as owner of the *Nation* and the *Independent*, Murphy was able to point out that he allowed them both to become union shops.

Larkin: You felt all along, in the last two-and-a-half years, that I intended to cause disruption with your work and industry?

Murphy: I thought so.

Larkin: You complained bitterly that I had been attacking you in the *Irish Worker.*

Murphy: I did not complain.

Larkin: Did you say I suggested you should be murdered?

Murphy: I stated facts … I stated that the paper was an incitement to murder, and so it was.

Larkin: Do I look like a person who would incite to murder?

Murphy: I don't know what you look like. Your paper did suggest it, certainly.

Larkin: Did you go to the Castle and ask for police protection?

Murphy: I did not.

Larkin: You did not go to the Castle at all?

Murphy: I have been to the Castle to ask protection for the property and people I am concerned with.

If Murphy betrayed no personal animus to Larkin over the attacks on him in the *Irish Worker*, Larkin certainly resented the articles in Murphy's newspapers aimed at himself. When he asked about the reports that alleged he was earning £18 a week in profit from the *Worker*, Murphy denied any knowledge of the articles. Larkin asked Murphy if he read his own newspapers. 'Yes,' Murphy replied coolly, 'but not each portion of them— not the sporting columns. (Laughter.)'

Turning to the Tramways Company, Larkin succeeded in exposing some of the worst conditions of the drivers and conductors, as well as the company's preference for 'countrymen' over Dubliners.

Now you think that these men are always fairly treated, and there is no complaint amongst them?

Murphy: I don't think so. Everybody has some complaint to make. I have a good deal to complain about myself. (Laughter.)

Larkin tried to prove that the Tramways Company was a 'system of terrorism carried on by an organised mob of officials and spies' against the employees. The aim was to drive the workers hard and prevent them joining a union. However, cross-examination of Murphy on the only incident Larkin could produce to illustrate his claim was ruled out, because it was the subject of legal proceedings.

Larkin then asked Murphy about the dismissal of six tramway men on 6 July, a few hours before Murphy summoned his tramway employees to a meeting in the Antient Concert Rooms to warn them against being seduced by a few 'hotheads' into joining the ITGWU. Murphy retorted:

> No-one prevented them belonging to whatever union they liked, but I would not allow any man to be terrorised or threatened if he did not choose to belong to a particular union. I gave notice that any man against whom it had been proved that he had threatened or intimidated any other man should be dismissed. In consequence of that six men were dismissed on July the nineteenth.
>
> *Larkin:* Are you still of the opinion that a man is entitled to join any union he likes?
>
> *Murphy:* He is not entitled to intimidate any other man. A man might join any union he likes.
>
> *Larkin:* You don't agree with your fellow-conspirators in that view?
>
> *Murphy:* If he joins the Transport Union and is guilty of intimidation, I am not obliged to keep him if I don't like.

Larkin then asked whether Murphy had ever seen himself or any official of the ITGWU go 'about your premises and interfere with your men?'

> *Murphy:* I have no report. With regard to yourself, personally, you are generally in a safe place.
>
> *Larkin:* Yes, you generally see that I am put there. (Laughter.)

On the issue of intimidation, Larkin also had the last word.

> Will you tell us what you call 'intimidation'? Is it intimidation to say to a man, 'Will you belong to this union or that union?'?
>
> *Murphy:* That is not intimidation.
>
> *Larkin:* 'If you join a certain union you will be deprived of your livelihood and your children will starve'—is that intimidation?
>
> *Murphy:* I don't think so.

Larkin also challenged the employers' characterisation of himself as a troublemaker. 'Did you ever know me to call out any man, or section of men, on strike?' he asked Murphy to loud laughter. 'I do, of course,' said Murphy, taking the bait. But when Larkin asked him to name the strikes, Murphy found himself naming a couple of lockouts. 'This is the sort of information the respectable employers of Dublin are getting,' Larkin replied dismissively. 'These men were put out because they threatened to combine.' He also asked Murphy if it did not follow

> that there must be two parties to a strike—the exploiters and the exploited—the wage slave and the owner of the wage slave. There must be the man who is making money out of other men's bodies, and the

other people who are getting their bodies crippled.

Askwith interrupted at this point in Larkin's polemic and asked him 'to get on to the next question. Of course there must be employer and employee.'

Larkin deftly took the chairman's point. 'The strike-mongers must be Mr Murphy and myself,' he said. 'There must be two parties to a strike. There must be employer and employee. There could be no lockout except there were two parties.' But then he added: 'In the lockout only one of the parties operate—the employer.'

Larkin went on to challenge Murphy's role in defeating efforts by the Trades Council and the Chamber of Commerce to set up conciliation machinery earlier in the year. Murphy conceded that there had been some support for a conciliation system. 'But the vast majority of employers, when this convulsion took place, felt that a Conciliation Board was only a pill to cure an earthquake,' he said, taking his lead from the article by 'Lasairfhíona' in *Sinn Féin*.

Larkin then attacked Murphy's record as an employer abroad. He accused him of refusing to pay compensation to British employees who fell ill with tropical diseases while building railways in Africa. Murphy answered that the men were well rewarded by 'four or five times the wages they would get at home.'

Healy intervened whenever he could to defend his client; but towards the end of the session he intervened once too often. Larkin said coolly that if Murphy was not objecting to his line of questioning, he did not see why Mr Healy should. 'We are not getting £100 a day for attending here.'

> *Healy:* I am obliged to Mr Larkin for that suggestion. (Laughter.) My solicitor will attend to it. (Laughter.)
> *Larkin:* I once wanted Mr Healy's assistance and he wanted £100 a day.[3]

*

Though it had been the employers who asked for the inquiry's hearings to be held in public, by the close of Friday's session it was clear that the union side had gained most from the arrangement. The other employers who had given evidence were less formidable than Murphy, and all those arguing the employers' case—Murphy and Healy included—were far less familiar with the thinking of the tribunal members than Larkin, who shared with Askwith, Clynes and even Ellis a common industrial relations culture and experience.

Healy had fulminated against syndicalism and the immorality of British unions subsidising anarchy in Ireland, but Larkin had concentrated his fire on the central issues of low pay, appalling working conditions, and union recognition. Pay and working conditions were much better in Britain, and Larkin knew that this part of the evidence must damn the employers in the eyes of the tribunal, especially as none of them would have a particular interest in giving competitive advantage to Irish industries by allowing them to abuse industrial relations procedures that were the norm across the Irish Sea.

When Larkin had finished cross-examining Murphy, the trade union nominee on the tribunal, J. R. Clynes, asked Larkin if he had wanted a conciliation board. 'I have been advocating it for twenty years,' Larkin replied, rather disingenuously. He then took the opportunity to remind the tribunal that employers as well as trade unions had agreed to it in principle before the lockout began.

Clynes then turned to Murphy and asked him if describing the ITGWU as a disreputable organisation 'was not likely to provoke trouble?' Murphy replied bluntly that that depended on how many workers had joined the union.

Clynes went back to the mass meeting Murphy held with the tramway men on 19 July 1913; he asked if the threat not to employ any man who went on strike was not intimidation. Murphy replied:

> You can draw any conclusion you like. I was trying to do what Mr Larkin does when he is addressing men in a room. I was trying to influence them not to go on strike.
>
> *Clynes:* Did you point out that the shareholders would still have three meals a day? What impression did you mean to leave on the minds of the men by that?
>
> *Murphy:* The impression was that a section of them would have to go without sufficient food if they went on strike, and that they were not on equal conditions with the employers and shareholders, who did not rely solely upon the Tramway Company. I wanted to point out that it was an unequal contest that they were entering upon.
>
> *Clynes:* Did you declare that the Tramway Company was willing to spend £100,000 in dealing with the men and opposing a strike?
>
> *Murphy:* In resisting a strike.
>
> *Clynes:* Had any demands been made collectively which would have cost the company anything like the same amount if they were conceded?
>
> *Murphy:* I could not tell you. I do not think it would cost anything like that sum.
>
> *Clynes:* Don't you think that the net effect of a speech of that sort was to lead to trouble?
>
> *Murphy:* I do not think so at all. I knew the men were being intimidated to join Mr Larkin's union, and I wanted to check the tendency in that direction, because I knew it would lead to a strike. If I had not made the speech, the tramcars would not be running today. They would be in the sheds today, or in the hands of Mr Larkin. I make no apology for the action I took to enable the people of Dublin to travel in the trams today. (Applause.)

Murphy's speech may have won acclaim from his supporters at the tribunal, but he had made it clear, in his usual crisp fashion, what he thought of the ITGWU and the rights of his employees.

The employers must have been heartened by another event on Friday, which suggested that the tide might be turning in their favour. The dispute at the corporation's power station was over. After spreading as far as the stores in Hawkins Street, it had folded in upon itself. Officials told the workers to accept the 'tainted coal' or be sacked. They were all casual labourers, and, with little prospect of alternative employment during the lockout, they agreed to discharge the 500-ton consignment.

*

On Saturday morning the second food ship arrived. This was the *Fraternity*, which, as its name suggested, belonged to the Co-Operative Wholesale Society. It berthed at Sir John Rogerson's Quay, within sight of Liberty Hall. Larkin, Gosling and the other strike leaders were at the tribunal, and only a small crowd waited at the quayside; ITGWU members had been told in advance that huge numbers of spectators would delay the unloading. 'The moment the steamer was near enough to the wall,' the *Irish Times* reported, 'the men scrambled on board with a professional alacrity ready to tackle once more work of a kind with which they are familiar.' On board were between 15,000 and 20,000 bags of potatoes, 10,000 packets of assorted vegetables, half a ton of bacon ribs, and 15,000 to 20,000 parcels of other provisions.

Seddon supervised the unloading and said that another shipment would come at the end of the following week. The details of low wage rates and long working hours in Dublin revealed by the Askwith Inquiry had sent a shudder of indignation through the British labour movement. The future Prime Minister, Ramsay MacDonald, told a rally in Leicester that the Dublin employers 'had sown the wind and must now reap the whirlwind.' Another future leader of the party, George Lansbury, told the International Syndicalist Congress in London that

> the spirit of fraternity … is binding the Dublin workers and the British workers into one solid army against wagedom. Best of good luck to Jim Larkin and the brave and devoted men and women in Ireland.

The London dockers' leader Ben Tillet told the same meeting that 'all the richest men in the country are syndicalists.' Sir Edward Carson was 'a legal, political, economic and racial syndicalist.' When they had the courage to follow his example they might frighten the government into conceding the workers' demands.

Syndicalism of the national and religious varieties was already rife in Ireland. On Saturday there was a rally of UIL and AOH members in Dundalk to support home rule, while throughout Ulster that weekend there was a veritable blight of military camps—many of them accommodated in the grounds of some of the noblest residences in the province—to oppose the same object. But the proceedings at Dublin Castle continued to dominate the headlines.

The main event of the day was the conclusion of the trade union leaders' case. Harry Gosling spoke first, then Robert Williams, secretary of the National Transport Workers' Federation, and Tom McPartlin, president of Dublin Trades Council. But it was Larkin everyone had come to hear, and he was magnificent.[3]

He spoke, as always, without notes, and showed why he was considered such a great orator in an age of oratory. He began slowly, the human engine of his intellect warming slowly to the task before him. After some preliminary remarks he said:

> The first point I want to make is that the employers in this city, and throughout Ireland generally, have put forward a claim that they have a right to deal with their own; that they have a right to use and exploit individuals as they please ... They take to themselves that they have all the rights that are given to men ... but they deny the right of the men to claim that they also have a substantial claim on the share of the produce ...
>
> They say further that they want no third-party interference. They want to deal with their working men individually. They say they are men of such paramount intelligence and so able in their organising ability as captains of industry, who can always carry on their business in their own way, that they deny the right of the men and women who work for them to combine and try to assist one another in improving their conditions of life.

In fact the employers had shown 'their incapacity ... and had proved that industry in Ireland was carried on in a chaotic manner.' The employers and their 'able counsel' had proved Larkin's own case for him. 'There are rights on both sides, but these men opposite assume to themselves certain privileges, and they deny to the working man, who makes their wealth and keeps them in affluence, his rights.' In a rough adaptation from *The Merchant of Venice*, Larkin said:

> 'He who holds the means whereby I live holds my life and controls me.' It means that the men who hold the means of life control our lives, and, because we working men have tried to get some measure of justice, some measure of betterment, they deny the right of the human being to associate with his fellow. Why, the very law of nature is mutual co-operation.

What was the state of affairs in industrial Ireland under these men? Citing figures produced earlier that year by the city's chief medical officer, Dr Charles Cameron, Larkin said there were

> 21,000 families, four-and-a-half persons to a family, living in single rooms. The gentlemen opposite ... would have to accept the responsibility. Of course they must. They said they control the means of life; then the responsibility rests on them. Twenty-one thousand people

multiplied by five, over 100,000 people huddled together in the putrid slums of Dublin, five in a room in cubic space less than 1,000 feet, though the law lays it down that every human being should have 300 cubic feet.

Why, in Mountjoy Prison there is better accommodation. They give 800 cubic feet of space to each man. I have had the honour of being there a few times (laughter), and, by the way, it is the criminals who are outside, men who carry on a system of brutality and despotism— Christian gentlemen, so called; and these are the men who deny the right of the working men to combine for the protection of their own interests. Men and women are being brutally murdered by the capitalist system. Such things are happening in Dublin, the greatest church-going city ... in the world.

We are determined that this shall no longer go on; we are determined the system shall stop; we are determined that Christ will not be crucified in Dublin by these men.

Turning to his own controversial role in events, Larkin said that the main argument used against him was that he came from Liverpool.

Well, if that is so, it is time that someone came from some place in order to teach those whom I address their responsibilities. What about the gentlemen on the other side: are they to be asked to produce their birth certificates? Can they all speak as men who represent the Irish race? These men have no feeling of respect for the Dublin workman, or for his development. The only purpose they have is to grind out wealth from the poor men, their wives and children.

Larkin's own aim was 'human and universal,'

and I am not going to be limited in my views by any geographical limits. My claim is a human claim ... Let people who desire to know the truth go to the factories and see the maimed girls, the weak and sickly, whose eyes are being put out and their bodies scarred and their souls seared; and when they are no longer able to be useful enough to gain their £1 a week, or whatever wage they earned, are thrown onto the human scrap heap. These things exist in their midst, yet the people who cause these conditions ... describe workers as loafers.

True, Mr Murphy has said that the Dublin workman is a decent man; but he would deny him the right to work in his own city on terms of decency, on the streets or on the quays.

Murphy wanted to bring 'poor, ignorant serfs from the country into a congested city to make them an instrument to bring down wages.' Of the employers as a whole, Larkin said: 'The souls of these men are steeped in the grime of profit-making.' This dispute had at least aroused the social conscience of the city. Larkin was 'in this struggle to elevate the class I belong to ... and in doing it I believe I am going to elevate those opposite who oppose me.' He called on the employers to work with the unions

> all together in a co-operative way ... Mr Murphy has very strong views
> on the subject of the rights of property, and he is one of the strongest ...
> capitalists in this country, in western Europe, or in America. But the day
> of the capitalist, as endorsed by Mr Murphy, is passing, and the workers
> are getting on a higher plane. Mr Murphy said he has beliefs in the rights
> of men to combine and belong to a trade union.

He gave Murphy 'the credit of being one of the ablest exponents of the
capitalist system,' but it was clear from the evidence he gave the tribunal
that he did not know the details of his own business.

  Though he denied it, Murphy's life had been 'one continuous struggle
against the working classes.' In a great many cases 'he had come out on top,
because he had never been faced by a man who was able to deal with him.'
Now he faced a social conscience as well,

> according to which the working classes could combine to alter the
> conditions of labour ... Mr Murphy might try to realise during the later
> hours of his life, before he passes hence, that those who gave him
> affluence and wealth deserve something to encourage them from the
> lower plane on which they exist to the higher plane on which they
> might live.

Referring to home rule, Larkin said that the workers were home-rulers
because it would give 'an opportunity for the people to govern the country
in the interests of the country ... not for a few individuals who are
concerned with ... building up their bank balances.' He was concerned
with 'something greater, something better, and something holier: a mutual
relation between those carrying on industry in Ireland. These men, the
employers, with their limited intelligence, cannot see that.'

Lawyers and politicians were also chastised.

> If we had fewer Healys and more Shaws, Ireland would be a much better
> country. (Laughter.) Lawyers and politicians have misled the workers
> and are the cause of all the trouble in Ireland.

He reminded the tribunal that he had sought a conciliation system and
simply wanted to 'socially ostracise' employers not prepared to pay decent
wages.

> When I came to Dublin the workers ... were treated brutally. Their
> wages were paid in public houses, and a man would not get employment
> from a stevedore on the quay unless he was prepared to spend his wages
> in a public house ... I have helped to close more public houses in Dublin
> since I came to the city than were ever closed before.
>   I have given men stimulation and have put heart and hope into the
> poor. I have brought men who were regular jailbirds and drunken
> wastrels to realise their position: and though we are told that the Dublin

workers are drunkards and loafers, I can say that the world has never produced a finer or better type of man. ('Hear, hear.') If the employers try to drive these men over the precipice and force them by starvation and other barbarous methods to recognise their agreement, the time will come when they will break the bonds and when they will give back blow for blow. The workers cannot be beaten.

After a further attack on politicians ranging from Carson to Redmond— and taking in Healy on the way, because, 'for all his eloquence, he will not preach … unless he gets a fee'—Larkin concluded by saying:

> We are out to break down racial and sectarian barriers. My suggestion to the employers is that if they want peace we are prepared to meet them, but if they want war, then war they will have.

*

McPartlin was not given to oratory, and his presentation was no better than usual. But the text, read by the cold light of day in Monday's newspaper columns, made a cogent argument for the unions—probably because it had been written by Connolly.[4]

McPartlin told the tribunal that the unions in the city had 'banded together to elevate our class.' Employers complained that there had been more strikes in Dublin during the past five years than ever before; but industrial unrest in the city had arisen out of a poverty bred out of decades of quiescence.

> Practically every responsible man in Dublin admits that the social conditions are a disgrace … scarcely to be equalled outside Bombay or Constantinople.
>
> Now that the Irish Transport Union and its officials have set out to arouse the people; now that fierce, and it may be sometimes reckless, fighting has inspired the suffering masses with a belief in their own ability to achieve some kind of emancipation; now, in short, that the luxury, comfort and even security of the propertied classes are menaced, we see a quickening of a faint sense of social conscience in Dublin. But, until aroused by the shock of industrial war, the propertied classes of Dublin have well deserved their unenviable notoriety for, like the typical Irish landlords of the past, enforcing their rights with a rod of iron and renouncing their duties with a front of brass.
>
> They tell us that they recognise trade unions. For answer, we say that when they did so it was wherever the necessity of a long apprenticeship made it difficult to replace a worker if he went on strike.

Where the unskilled were concerned, the employers had waged 'fierce and relentless war'. The shipping companies were particularly vindictive. Tedcastle McCormick had twice crushed attempts to organise their workers, and the workhouse, the insane asylum and the emigrant ship received the ruined lives of those who made the efforts.

They complain that the Transport Union cannot be trusted to keep its agreements. The majority of shipping firms in Dublin today at present working, refusing to join in this mad enterprise engineered by Mr Murphy, work with full confidence in the good faith of the Transport Union. They complain of the sympathetic strike; but the members of the United Builders' Labourers' Trades Union—a union recruited from the same class of labourers as the Transport Union—have been subjected to a sympathetic lockout because of their refusal to pledge themselves not to help the latter body if they so desired at any time in the future. A more unreasonable pledge was never asked for … To such an extent has the madness of the employers led them.

We on our side say that we are proud of the spirit of solidarity exhibited in Dublin; we are proud of the way organised labour in these islands has rallied to help us … We are proud of the skilled workers who have thrown in their lot with the unskilled in resisting the enforcement of an ubiquitous agreement. We are doubly proud of the men who are prepared to risk their livelihood in order to help the girls and women who … are battling for decent human treatment. We cannot, will not counsel trade unionists to abandon their brothers and sisters.

Like Larkin, McPartlin offered the olive branch of a conciliation board to allow the 'investigation and, if possible, settlement of all disputes.' If employers showed any inclination to settle, 'we will meet them half way.'

He then submitted proposals that were, in essence, those of the Lord Mayor. The unions wanted all workers in the dispute reinstated and the withdrawal by employers of the ban on membership or co-operation with the ITGWU. In return, the ITGWU was prepared to give 'an absolute undertaking' along with other unions to submit disputes 'to a permanent Joint Trade Board.' All companies that agreed to use the new disputes procedure would be 'exempted from any form of sympathetic strike.'

Employers and unions should also agree 'that no strike or lockout shall be entered upon until the matter in dispute has been referred to the Joint Trade Board and its decision thereon received.' If the Employers' Federation was willing to sign such an agreement, so would the ITGWU, Dublin Trades Council, the National Transport Workers' Federation, and the Parliamentary Committee of the TUC.

McPartlin then submitted his proposal to the tribunal. It carried his own signature as president of Dublin Trades Council and that of William O'Brien as vice-president. Larkin had also signed, along with his two principal deputies, Connolly and Daly. The other signatories were Richard O'Carroll of the bricklayers and Nathaniel Rimmer of the Amalgamated Society of Railway Servants.

*

McPartlin had cleared the way for the British delegates to ask for a reasonable response from the employers. Havelock Wilson of the National Sailors' and Firemen's Union was reason personified. Eyebrows must have been raised all round when he said that more than one of his colleagues had praised Mr Healy for his 'very moderate statement indeed' of the employers' case. He could understand their concerns over the sympathetic strike. This was not a complex question of wages and hours: 'reasonable men ought to be able to settle it within four hours.' What was needed was a conciliation board made up of such men.

Gosling, who now had experience of dealing with the Dublin employers, took a harder line. When he met them before, he had been 'treated with every courtesy.' But he had also been left in no doubt that the employers believed that the only way 'to deal with trouble in the city was to destroy trades unionism.' He wanted to put it to them that 'if that was going to be the course they would adopt, there was nothing for the English trade unionists to do but stand by their Irish friends.' He knew from the response in England that 'if this is going to be a fight to the finish, we are going to be in it as long as it lasts. (Applause.)'

The Dublin workers had had 'a most difficult task' in fighting for their rights,

> and I don't think that any weapon but the sympathetic strike would have done any good. That is the conclusion I came to, and I don't generally approve of the sympathetic strike. We were deliberately told that the Transport Workers' Union should not be allowed to exist. I say the Transport Workers' Union shall exist here as long as trades unionism exists in England.

Now he too offered the olive branch. 'The more complete the organisation was on the side of the workers and employers,' the fewer strikes they should have. Both sides should therefore encourage, 'in every way they could, complete organisation.' He knew 'the employers' difficulty was that they were still afraid of the sympathetic strike.'

Healy asked Gosling if guarantees he had signed were always carried out. Gosling answered:

> I don't pretend that everything I signed we were able to carry through, and I don't want any employer or the public to believe that because we are going to have a settlement of this trouble that there is going to be no more trouble; but I believe there is a chance of gradually settling it down. I have not always been able to carry out my obligations, but no-one who knows me will say I have not tried.

In a further effort to win over the employers, Gosling produced a copy of a new rule of his own Transport Workers' Federation, which restricted sympathetic strikes. Members could not even take action in support of other members of their own union without the endorsement of the district committee and the national executive of the federation. These rules had been framed in the light of experience, he told Healy, including the great dock strike of 1911.

> We are trying to improve bit by bit. What I want to say is: don't expect too much from us. We will do our best. If you are not prepared to do that, we have no other guarantee. I believe if this matter could now be handed over to Sir George Askwith to put into a little shape—and if there is a desire for a settlement—we should be able to settle.

The secretary of the National Transport Workers' Federation, Robert Williams, may have felt that Gosling had ended on too conciliatory a note, for he told the employers that his members

> will not stand by and see the workers ground into pulp by the cumulative forces of the machinery of the whole capitalist class. In the Welsh ports, where Dublin receives their coal, all the men are well organised, and if they get the word they will go out.

If Murphy had strong convictions, so had the worker, and these convictions were 'becoming increasingly strong.'

Healy was immediately on his feet to say that the threats of the last speaker 'were not calculated in any degree to bring matters to a settlement.' They could well understand 'the abuse of Mr Larkin, but we will not yield to the threats just made.'

Askwith adjourned the proceedings for ten minutes to allow tempers to settle. Gosling then made one last, carefully pitched statement to the opposition.

> What we want to make clear is that we have to fight it, or settle it. If the fight is to go on, we must, in honour to our friends here, stick to it. But we want to settle it … We want to settle it honourably. We don't want to settle it by starving women and children.

Gosling had made a mistake in thinking he could appeal to the employers through the hearts of Murphy or Healy. When the tribunal tried to adjourn for the evening, Healy produced a bombshell.

He began by saying that he wished to refute a number of claims made against his clients that had not been covered under cross-examination, but he soon showed his real purpose. After complimenting McPartlin on his 'moderate' speech, Healy said that he had also put forward a proposal that had to be addressed.

> Mr McPartlin puts forward as condition number 1 that all workers in the dispute shall be reinstated. I am obliged to say that any person who has since come into the employment of the employers, and who is found suitable, cannot be dismissed.

The union leaders immediately sought the right to hold a side conference to discuss the implications of Healy's statement. When they returned, Gosling made it clear to the tribunal that if Mr Healy's statement meant the victimisation of the men it would be quite impossible to go on. If he would withdraw it and allow the matter to be considered by the conference—

Healy: What I say is this: the masters have taken men into their employment within the last four or five weeks, men who have proved themselves to be suitable and honest men. We don't intend to dismiss these men. You understand, my friends, the use of the word 'victimisation' … We will not victimise these men.

Gosling: We will not have our men victimised either.

Pressed on the issue by Askwith, who made it clear that the tribunal had yet to consider its own attitude to the settlement terms proposed by McPartlin, Healy refused to move from the stance on 'victimisation' he had taken on behalf of the employers. 'On that point I say emphatically we will not yield.' Askwith concluded the proceedings by telling Healy, a little crustily, that 'whatever attitude is taken up at this stage by either side, it did not affect the functions of the court.'

*

If Healy had hoped to warn the inquiry off including the reinstatement of all strikers as a condition of the peace settlement, he had made a serious miscalculation. However, it is more likely that he was preparing the ground for rejecting the tribunal's findings. Healy was experienced enough to see the way things were going, and he saw that the inquiry was not lending itself to the employers' primary objective, the destruction of the ITGWU and its leader.

At this stage in the dispute, comparatively few employers had recruited strike-breakers, and therefore it was not a significant issue for them. One company, of course, had made a policy of instantly filling vacancies with 'loyal' employees: that was the DUTC. Its chairman was on record as saying that those tramway men who had gone on strike and stayed on strike would not be taken back.

If anyone was in doubt that Healy was acting other than to protect Murphy's position, they had only to read the front page of Saturday's *Evening Herald.* It announced that the 'talks' at the tribunal had 'collapsed.' The next day's *Sunday Independent* drew back a little from such a stark prognosis, but its front page spoke of a crisis in the talks and was dominated by a large cartoon entitled 'Things that strike one.' The cartoon consisted of four panels. The first was entitled 'Exposed' and showed a sheep beset by the 'Wolf of anarchy'. The next caption was entitled 'The enemy at work' and showed a figure wearing the distinctive type of broad-brimmed soft hat favoured by Jim Larkin digging a grave for 'Christian principles'. The third panel showed the same Larkinesque figure standing, whip in hand, with his foot on the neck of a worker and musing, 'If I could get the other on the employer.' The final panel, entitled 'The marching order', showed a respectable, bowler-hatted 'ordinary man' giving a departing 'syndicalist' a kick in the behind.

The main news story was entitled 'Strike inquiry sensation.' It stressed the refusal of the employers 'to dismiss those men who had remained loyal during the trouble, or had since been engaged.' (It conveniently ignored the fact that the unions had not sought the dismissal of strike-breakers.) It also carried the headline 'Breakdown' over the section of the report in which Healy had informed the court that the employers would not give a commitment to reinstate strikers. The coverage of Saturday's hearing dwelt on what the newspaper characterised as the socialist, syndicalist and anti-clerical sections of Larkin's speech and gave very little coverage to other contributions—excepting Healy's interjections.

Gosling saw the *Herald* before he caught the boat on Saturday night. He told a *Freeman's Journal* reporter that the story suggesting the talks had collapsed 'is not justified by the facts.' He also rejected reports in the *Herald*, repeated by the *Sunday Independent*, that the English delegates would not bother returning to the tribunal on Monday. 'We shall attend on Monday, ready to go on, as if Mr Healy's subsequent comment [about victimisation] and statement had never been made. It was certainly not made as part of the official proceedings of the inquiry.' Gosling accepted that reinstatement was a difficult issue but one that 'crops up on the settlement of almost every labour dispute, and is not found insurmountable.' These were not matters that could easily be dealt with in a public arena, where

> the exchange of a few words can lead to ... apprehension ... These are delicate matters and they should be handled freely and confidentially.

Asked if there were any ground for hope of a settlement, he said:

> I am quite certain that Dublin cannot get back into a peaceful state until this thing is settled across the table by both parties. It cannot be fought out for ever in the brutal way in which it is now being fought.

Adding his voice to the chorus of peace that night, Connolly said that the union was

> only interested in seeking the reinstatement of strikers, not pursuing the fate of 'scabs' ... It would be in the best interests of a clear understanding to attend on Monday, and await developments.

*

Sunday passed peacefully, no doubt in part because of the heavy rainfall that deluged Dublin. In spite of the inclement weather, a large crowd turned out for a Trades Council demonstration through the city and a public meeting in the Phoenix Park. At least seventeen unions carried their banners through the rain-drenched streets, and twelve bands entertained the marchers. However, the rain grew so heavy that only a few hundred people survived as far as the meeting. 'Tim Healy must have arranged for the weather,' Larkin told the faithful few who remained to hear the speeches.

Those people are out to beat the working class. They can't beat the working classes. For a time we may sit quiet, but then, like an army refreshed, and with new ammunition, we will come up and fight again—and fight to win. (Cheers.)

Seddon also spoke. He generously praised Larkin's performance at the tribunal and said to cheers that 'if there was a proper order of society … Larkin would be Lord Chancellor.' He also promised there would be another food ship the following week, 'and if the dispute is not settled, I will go back and bring a fourth ship. (Cheers.)' If they persevered with the struggle it would lead to 'happier homes, brighter lives, and a more contented people.' He told the soaking crowd to go home and get their dinner.

If you haven't got a dinner at home, you can go to Liberty Hall, where you will get soup, ribs, beans, and other things. Indeed we will give our opponents 'beans' before long. (Loud cheers.)

*

Not all British trade union leaders were as supportive of Larkin as Gosling and Seddon. That weekend Larkin's old adversary, James Sexton of the National Union of Dock Labourers, addressed a meeting in Galway—ostensibly in support of the Dublin workers. While he said that the employers of Dublin 'had no right to dictate to a trade union,' he spent much of his time denouncing the evils of syndicalism. 'We want a clearer, a more thoughtful, a more reasonable policy than mere pulling down.'

That sounding-board of 'reasonable' business opinion, the *Irish Times*, awaited the outcome of the Askwith Inquiry with some trepidation. In its Monday edition it called on 'every responsible citizen' to refrain from saying anything that 'might in any way embarrass the negotiations,' only to ignore its own advice for the perverse reason that this would be 'a critical day' for the inquiry.

There were two points, it said, that the inquiry must address. First of all, 'the sympathetic strike must go, and reasonable guarantees must be given by the men's representatives against any attempt to reintroduce that illegitimate industrial weapon.' The second issue was reinstatement. This was, apparently, a much more complex issue—opaque even. 'This is a question which, while it is very difficult, gives room for concession on both sides.' What those concessions should be was not explained, but the *Times* was sure that it was an issue 'perfectly capable of settlement by moderate and tactful men.'

*

A letter from Archbishop Walsh, who had at last returned from his long convalescence in France, was published in all the papers that day and may have given pause for thought to the protagonists. It urged both sides to continue working with the Board of Trade inquiry; and, knowingly or not, Dr Walsh endorsed Gosling's suggestion that the meetings would be more effective if held in private.

Some of the archbishop's comments could be interpreted as critical of Healy's role in the proceedings and, by implication, of Murphy. He suggested that the private discussions should take place between 'accredited representatives of both sides to the dispute, with such assistance as the members of the Commission and, if desired, some legal advisors, can give them.' From his own experience of mediation in strikes, he said that 'nothing could more effectually block the work of those engaged in an effort to bring such a dispute to an end, than a discussion in public of terms of settlement.' He admitted that he was not familiar with the issues, because of his long absence, but 'it seems ... pretty obvious that there have been faults on both sides, and surely it is in the interest of both to come to a real settlement.'[5]

In the event, his intervention had come too late to make any difference. Askwith already had his report written, and there was an air of inevitability about what followed.

At 10 o'clock the tribunal resumed before a packed chamber, and Askwith read out the findings. His report recounted the history of disputes in the city since 1908, including the circumstances that led to the founding of the ITGWU in 1909. The tribunal found that the workers had significant grievances, especially over pay, but it condemned the way in which the sympathetic strike had been used to seek their redress. 'In actual practice the ramifications of this method of industrial warfare have been shown to involve loss and suffering to large numbers of both employers and workpeople who not only have no voice in the original dispute, but have no means of influencing those concerned in the original cause of difference.'

Under the influence of this 'ever widening method of conducting disputes,' the tribunal found that

> the distinction between strike and lockout became obscured, attacks on one side being met with reprisals on the other in such rapid succession as completely to confuse the real issues. No community could exist if resort to the sympathetic strike became the general policy of Trade Unionism.

It was a phrase the employers would latch onto in justifying their future actions.

> Possibly it was with the hope that it might result in a termination of this method of industrial warfare that a large number of firms in the city agreed to require people to sign [the employers' document]. Whatever may have been the intention of the employers, this document imposes on the signatories conditions which are contrary to individual liberty, and which no workman, or body of workmen, could reasonably be expected to accept. We understand that many of the workmen asked to sign this, or similar documents were in no way connected with the

Transport Workers' Union, and we think it was unfortunate that they should have been brought into the dispute.

It will be obvious that the effort to secure signatures to such a document would be likely to create a maximum of ill feeling.

Given the determination of thousands of the city's workers 'to organise themselves' under the ITGWU, even if the employers succeeded in their objectives, 'the industries of Dublin will not, we think, be free from further serious troubles.'

Askwith then unveiled the tribunal's own proposals for resolving the dispute. There were no panaceas; the tribunal gave no definitive rulings on the three issues that most exercised the protagonists: the sympathetic strike, the lockout, and 'victimisation'. Instead Askwith proposed fairly standard procedures for resolving these and other differences. Firstly, conciliation committees should be set up for each industrial sector, or each individual enterprise if this was required in particular cases. These committees would deal with all questions of 'wages, hours of labour, or conditions of service, other than matters of management or discipline.' The workers covered by a particular conciliation committee could elect their representatives by ballot. The employers could use their own selection process. The system allowed for shop-floor representatives, as well as trade union officials, to be elected onto the committees, and Askwith recommended that such representatives be given time off, 'without prejudice to their employment,' to attend meetings of the conciliation committee.

Secondly, each side should appoint its own secretary to the committee. A secretary could 'take part in discussions and act as advocate, but shall have no vote unless he is a member of the committee.' The Workpeople's Secretary should be chosen by a majority of the workers' representatives on the conciliation committee, 'from any source they please.' The Employers' Secretary could also be appointed by the employers 'from any source they please.' Each side within the committee would determine the conditions of office of their own secretary. The tribunal appears to have been trying to ensure that the principals on the conciliation committees were local representatives of shop-floor workers and their employers, probably to ensure that neither Larkin nor Murphy dominated the process. By fragmenting the dispute, the Askwith tribunal would also be undermining the potential for further trouble from sympathetic strikes, or lockouts.

Thirdly, the tribunal proposed that where a dispute arose it should be dealt with initially by the firm's foreman, or some other immediate supervisor. If the problem was not resolved within seven days, the workers could refer it to their representatives on the conciliation committee.

The committee members, 'accompanied, if they so desire, by the Secretary of the workpeople's side of the Committee, shall be granted an interview with the management for the discussion of the dispute.' If agreement was not reached within a further seven days, the Workpeople's

Secretary could contact the Employers' Secretary and request a meeting of the full Conciliation Committee within fourteen days. The committee would then meet under a mutually agreed independent chairman. Where agreement on a chairman was not possible, the Board of Trade could appoint someone. The chairman would endeavour to achieve a negotiated agreement, but where this proved impossible he could recommend 'such terms of settlement as he thinks fair and reasonable.' If the two parties to the dispute were agreeable, he could give a binding decision.

Pending the outcome of these procedures, the Askwith tribunal recommended that 'no strike or lockout shall be entered into.' If any trade union or employer breached the procedures they should receive 'no assistance, financial or otherwise,' from the relevant trade union or employers' body.

The tribunal did not favour 'compulsory arbitration', and 'we do not suggest that the ultimate right to strike or to lock out should be abandoned. What we do suggest is that, before the method of strike or lockout is adopted, there should be opportunity for impartial discussion and independent enquiry.'

It accepted that personality clashes had arisen in Dublin but argued that, given the crisis now facing the city and the interdependence of all the parties, these should not be allowed to block discussion of the tribunal's proposals. It proved a vain injunction.

Recognising how deep the divisions now were between the two sides, the tribunal proposed that any complaint about one side or the other breaching existing agreements could be referred to the chairman of the relevant conciliation committee for final adjudication. The final sanction that could be imposed for breach of an agreement was the same as where a union or employer breached the conciliation procedures: ostracisation by their relevant trade union or employers' body.[6]

*

When he had finished reading out the proposals of the tribunal, Askwith asked both sides to examine them in detail before responding. At 4 p.m. the principal parties reassembled and met in closed session for thirty minutes. Afterwards Gosling issued a statement that the trade unions were willing to accept the findings of the inquiry 'as a basis for negotiation'; but it was clear that the employers were deeply unhappy.

Though the executive committee of the Employers' Federation refrained from comment, it published Healy's closing address to the tribunal, which explained their position clearly enough. In it Healy criticised Askwith and his colleagues for allowing Larkin to abandon the normal rules of evidence, and for indulging him by allowing a long speech that contained 'fresh imputations against the employers.' The tribunal's error had been compounded, Healy said, because he had not been given an opportunity to cross-examine Larkin on his allegations, in order to 'sift' the truth. In the circumstances, their counsel informed the tribunal that the executive committee felt it 'unwise' to enter discussions on the peace proposals until it had consulted 'the general body of employers.'

He told them that the 'elaborate machinery' they proposed would be submitted to

> careful scrutiny, but in our view it offers no effective solution of the existing trouble. The employers are much more concerned to put an end to present difficulties than to consider difficulties relating to future unrest. Accordingly, we feel that the failure of the report to touch on the question of guarantees for preventing further outbreaks affords proof that the Court has found itself unable to devise a remedy for the difficulty which led to the breakdown of the recent negotiations with members of the English Trades Union Congress. This, we need hardly say, is to us a matter of deep regret.

Reluctant to enter negotiations in the first place, the employers were glad of the opportunity to break them off. Healy had every right to criticise the procedures adopted by the tribunal from a legal viewpoint: from the beginning he had approached the inquiry in an adversarial manner, bent on successfully prosecuting his case. The unions were equally anxious to condemn the opposition for past misdemeanours; but their main concern, and that of the tribunal, had been to find a way out of the impasse. Ironically, the union leaders who preached syndicalism and social revolution wanted compromise; it was the employers' leaders—who insisted that they were in favour of moderation and were anything but anti-union—who wanted total victory. One apologist for the employers said patronisingly that the members of the tribunal

> are very well suited to a state of affairs in which parties are reasonable and there is a wholesome sense of responsibility on the labour side, but they were quite out of place in Dublin, owing to the abnormal methods adopted by the labour leaders and the pernicious principles upon which their organisation is based.[7]

17

WHATEVER the strategic wisdom of the employers' decision not to embrace Askwith's peace proposals, they paid a high price in public support. 'For a brief space the Dublin merchant was the best-abused man in the three Kingdoms,' wrote Wright.

The abuse began that night in Beresford Place, where the union negotiators told a mass meeting about the day's happenings. The very fact that a government inquiry, from which the workers feared the worst, had produced a report vindicating their right to organise—if not to engage in sympathetic strikes—strengthened their sense of grievance against the employers. 'Every line of the report justifies our acts,' Connolly told the meeting. 'If the employers put our backs to the wall and say it is going to be war, then let it be war. (Cheers.)'

Connolly never used words lightly, and he assured the crowd he was not using the term 'war' in any lurid sense. 'When one body of the community tried to deprive another body of their living and starve them into submission, it was as much a state of war as any war carried on amidst the firing of guns and the rattle of musketry.'

Always mindful of the influence of the Catholic Church—of which he frequently reminded people he was a practising member—Connolly pointed out that not only the TUC but the Archbishop of Dublin, Dr Walsh, had suggested that the inquiry be held in private. The employers rejected this approach through their counsel, Healy.

> If the employers wanted a man to bring about a settlement, they could not have got a worse advocate … Mr Healy, during thirty years, has been mixed up in every quarrel in Irish public life, and he made every quarrel worse.

Larkin described the inquiry as

> a victory for the men. (Cheers.) The employers are beaten to a frazzle … and the workers got a verdict in their favour, though two members of the court were men of the capitalist class. (Cheers.) When the inquiry was over the employers felt they had got a slap in the teeth, and acted vindictively.

Larkin asked the crowd: 'Are the workers going to be slaves?' ('No, no.') 'Are you prepared to sign away your liberty?' ('No, no.') 'Are you going to continue the fight?' and he called for a show of hands. A forest of arms shot up.

Seddon spoke for the TUC representatives. 'In England and Scotland the workers are watching every move ... with an interest just as intense as if it were their own.' He was returning to Manchester to organise a consignment of coal. 'But I hope to be back again for the next conference, and still more for the celebration of the victory which I feel assured will be yours.'

*

Earlier that evening, at a special meeting with the Trades Council, Seddon and Gosling had given assurances every bit as firm as those offered publicly in Beresford Place. Seddon told the strike leaders that 'the Court of Inquiry and its findings have put the employers on the defensive.'

Some of the British unions were already following up the initial TUC consignment of food with pledges of further support. At the weekend, the Miners' Federation of Great Britain had voted at its annual conference to contribute £1,000 a week 'as long as the strike continued,' and the Co-Operative Baking Society of Glasgow decided to donate nine hundred loaves a week to the Dublin workers. By Monday the TUC had announced that its Dublin Relief Fund totalled £8,711, including the initial miners' contribution.

The only dissenting note at the Trades Council meeting on Monday was struck by the Dublin printers. One of their delegates complained at yet another attack in the *Irish Worker.* John Simmons, himself a printer and secretary of the Trades Council since its foundation, said his society had been affiliated to the council for twenty-five years and did not deserve such treatment. Other delegates maintained a tactful silence; they were reluctant to be drawn into the long-running feud between the ITGWU and the printing crafts.

Of more moment was the problem of locked-out workers being denied the dole. As far as the Trades Council was concerned, the men were not on strike but locked out and therefore unemployed through no fault of their own. It was agreed to seek a meeting with the manager of the local unemployment exchange, who happened to be another old antagonist of Larkin in the trades council and ITUC, E. L. Richardson—and yet another printer. Failing satisfaction from Richardson, the council agreed that the cases should be appealed to an Insurance Board referee in Britain. If need be, the assistance of the TUC's legal counsel would be obtained.[1]

*

The condemnations of the employers in Beresford Place that night were to be expected, but that by the *Times* of London the next morning was not. Its verdict on the Askwith proceedings was that the employers were the authors of their own misfortunes, and it felt they had nothing to lose by entering further negotiations.

Conciliation Boards will eventually be formed in any case—they are inevitable. And it is impossible to destroy the Transport Workers' Union ... The day of suppression has gone by; all experience proves that it defeats its own object. If the Dublin employers do not know that, then it is time they learnt the lesson; and here is another—Mr. Larkin is their own creation.

The inquiry found that wages have been extensively and substantially raised in consequence of Mr. Larkin's agitation, which means that employers have refused to give terms they could well afford until they were compelled. This conduct is playing into the hands of the agitator. It gives substance to the charge that employers care for nothing but money. This is the chief secret of Mr. Larkin's influence and the Dublin employers have themselves to thank for it.[2]

The *Irish Times* continued to support the employers. It deeply regretted the failure of Askwith's inquiry but argued that the employers had taken the 'only possible course' open to them when 'reasonable guarantees' were not forthcoming from the English trade unions. It placed the primary blame for the breakdown in discussions on the English trade unions for refusing to 'stand up to Mr. Larkin, dissociate themselves honestly from his ruinous policy, put some sort of substantial pressure on him, and give tangible guarantees—if need be, financial guarantees—for the future conduct of trade unionism in Dublin.'

How these contradictory courses were to be pursued was not spelt out, but the *Irish Times* was in a contrary mood that day, for it also published what was to become a famous indictment of the employers from George Russell. The paper described Russell's letter in a leader as 'exaggerated and unfair ... and irrelevant,' and then displayed it prominently on its news pages.[3]

Like the attendance of so many celebrities at the Liberty Hall food kitchens, Russell's letter showed that the workers were garnering support beyond their traditional spheres of influence. Nor could Russell be dismissed as either a 'syndicalist' or a dilettante. Poet, painter and theosophist he may have been, but from 1905 he had been editor of the *Irish Homestead*, the journal of the Irish Agricultural Organisation Society. Like the founder of the IAOS, Sir Horace Plunkett, Russell had a sharp practical bent to his nature. He too was a strange Janus, his gaze fixed simultaneously on the mundane and the heavenly. At the *Homestead* he showed a strong grasp of the realities of rural life and agricultural economics, while urging farmers to aspire to a co-operative commonwealth. 'Irishmen should aspire to "carve an Attica out of Ireland," to develop in rural Irish parishes an intensity of life such as had existed in the city states of ancient Greece or mediaeval Italy,' he wrote. He also believed that the problem of creating an organic unity to Irish life must come from within.[4]

Russell had first questioned the good faith of the employers in the *Irish*

Homestead after Bloody Sunday. In his letter to the *Irish Times*, published over his nom-de-plume 'Æ', Russell moved significantly closer to the workers' position; and the indictment of the employers was so superbly phrased that it has been in circulation ever since. Indeed his letter to the *Irish Times* has been remembered long after Russell's artistic work has fallen into neglect.

I address this warning to you, the aristocracy of industry in this city, because, like all aristocracies, you tend to grow blind in long authority, and to be unaware that you and your class and its every action are being considered and judged day by day by those who have power to shake or overturn the whole social order, and whose restlessness in poverty today is making our industrial civilisation stir like a quaking bog. You do not seem to realise that your assumption that you are answerable to yourselves alone for your actions in the industries you control is one that becomes less and less tolerable in a world so crowded with necessitous life.

He compared them to the rapidly dwindling ascendancy class—the anathema of all sound Irish nationalists, including Murphy and Healy.

Some of you have helped Irish farmers to upset a landed aristocracy in this island, an aristocracy richer and more powerful in its sphere than you are in yours, with its roots deep in history. They, too, as a class, though not all of them, were scornful or neglectful of the workers in the industry by which they profited; and to many who knew them in their pride of place and thought them all-powerful they are already becoming a memory, the good disappearing with the bad.

If they had done their duty by those from whose labours came their wealth they might have continued unquestioned in power and 'prestige' for centuries to come. The relation of landlord and tenant is not an ideal one, but any relations in a social order will endure if there is fused into them some of that spirit of human sympathy that qualifies life for immortality. Despotisms endure while they are benevolent, and aristocracies while 'noblesse oblige' is not a phrase to be referred to with a cynical smile. Even an oligarchy might be permanent if the spirit of human kindness, which harmonises all things otherwise incompatible, is present.

You do not seem to read history so as to learn its lessons. That you are an uncultivated class was obvious from recent utterances of some of you upon art. That you are incompetent men in the sphere in which you arrogate imperial power is certain, because for many years, long before the present uprising of labour, your enterprises have been dwindling in the regard of investors, and this while you have carried them on in the cheapest labour market on these islands, with a labour reserve always hungry and ready to accept any pittance. You are bad citizens, for we rarely, if ever, hear of the wealthy among you endowing your city with munificent gifts which it is the pride of princes in other merchant cities to offer, and Irishmen not of your city who offer to supply the wants left by your lack of generosity are met with derision and abuse.

Those who have economic power have civic power also, yet you have not used the power that was yours to right what was wrong in the evil administration of this city. You have allowed the poor to be herded together so that one thinks of certain places in Dublin as a pestilence.

You were within the rights society allows you when you locked out your men and insisted on the fixing of some principle to adjust your future relations with labour when the policy of labour made it impossible for some of you to carry on your enterprises. Labour desired the fixing of some such principle as much as you did. But, having once decided on such a step, knowing how many thousands of men, women, and children, nearly one third of the population of this city, would be affected, you should not have let one day to have passed without unremitting endeavours to find a solution to the problem.

What did you do! The representatives of labour unions in Great Britain met you, and you made of them a preposterous and impossible demand, and because they would not accede to it you closed the Conference: you refused to meet them further: you assumed that no other guarantees than those you asked were possible, and you determined in cold anger, to starve out one-third of the population of this city, to break the manhood of the men by the sight of the suffering of their wives and hunger of their children. We read in the dark ages of the rack and the thumbscrew. But these iniquities were hidden and concealed from the knowledge of men in dungeons and torture chambers ... It remained for the twentieth century and the capital city of Ireland to see an oligarchy of 400 masters deciding openly upon starving 100,000 people, and refusing to consider any solution except that fixed by their pride. You, masters, asked men to do that which the masters of labour in any other city in these islands had dared not do. You insolently demanded of those men who were members of a trade union that they should resign from that union; and from those who were not members you insisted on a vow that they would never join it.

Your insolence and ignorance of the rights conceded to workers universally in the modern world were incredible, and as great as your inhumanity. If you had between you collectively a portion of human soul as large as a threepenny bit, you would have sat night and day with the representatives of labour, trying this or that solution of the trouble, mindful of the women and children, who at least were innocent of wrong against you. But no! You reminded labour you could always have your three square meals a day while it went hungry. You went into conference again with representatives of the state, because, dull as you are, you knew public opinion would not stand your holding out. You chose as your spokesman the bitterest tongue that ever wagged in this island, and then, when an award was made by men who have an experience in industrial matters a thousand times transcending yours, who have settled disputes in industries so great that the sum of your petty enterprises would not equal them, you withdraw again, and will not agree to accept their solution, and fall back again on your devilish policy of starvation. Cry aloud to Heaven for new souls! The souls you have got, cast upon the screen of publicity, appear like horrid and writhing creatures enlarged from the insect world ...

You may succeed in your policy and ensure your damnation by your victory. Then men whose manhood you have broken will loathe you, and will always be brooding and scheming to strike a fresh blow. The children will be taught to curse you. The infant being moulded in the womb will have breathed into its starved body the vitality of hate. It is not they—it is you blind Samsons pulling down the pillars of the social order. You are sounding the death-knell of autocracy in industry. The fate of you, the aristocracy of industry, will be the fate of the aristocracy of land if you do not show that you have some humanity still among you. Humanity abhors, above all things, a vacuum in itself, and your class will be cut off from humanity as the surgeon cuts the cancer and alien growth from the body. Be warned ere it is too late.[5]

Russell's prediction of the demise of Dublin's capitalists proved premature; but everyone recognised Murphy and Healy from his caricatures, and the powerful image of an oligarchy of four hundred masters starving the city into submission would linger down the generations.

*

Other voices were also joining the chorus of indignation. The previous week's *Irish Worker* had published a letter from Tom Clarke, the veteran Fenian dynamiter and felon, sometime tobacconist and newsagent, and constant revolutionary. It contained one of the strongest public condemnations so far of police behaviour on Bloody Sunday.

Clarke, who had travelled widely and had spent fifteen years in English prisons, said that 'the ruffianism of the criminal classes of London's underworld' and 'Bowery hooligans' in New York could not match the 'downright inhuman savagery that was witnessed recently in the streets and some of the homes of our city.' Dublin, 'with its people the most easy going and peaceful of any city I know, is staggered by what has happened.' There was 'an avalanche of evidence' against the police.

The old Fenian had been one of the pivotal figures in reviving the Irish Republican Brotherhood. He had done so by the simple expedient of involving its members in the public movements of the day, rather than in pub conspiracies. Clarke helped launch *Irish Freedom*, a monthly journal that gave a voice to advanced, militant nationalism. The paper had rarely commented on things as mundane as labour disputes, though the first edition had published an article on 'Sweating in Ireland,' and a very favourable review of Connolly's seminal book *Labour in Irish History*. An attempt by Seán O'Casey to develop stronger links between the IRB and *Irish Freedom* on the one hand and Jim Larkin and the *Irish Worker* on the other came to nought, despite Clarke's support for the initiative. Ironically, P. T. Daly in his IRB days had been among the opponents of Clarke's new departure.[6]

The war waged on the ITGWU by William Martin Murphy and the DMP was something the IRB could not ignore. From October 1913 to May 1914 an increasing amount of space in *Irish Freedom* was devoted to the evils of capitalism. In the October edition the crimes of the 'Irish Cossacks' in O'Connell Street were excoriated; and the future head of the Provisional Government of 1916, Patrick Pearse, wrote one of his finest polemics in his regular column 'From a Hermitage.'

Pearse compared the attitude of Dublin employers to 'Poor Marie-Antoinette', who

> did not quite grasp the situation in France. In the end the situation grasped her and hurried her to the guillotine. There are only two ways of righting wrongs: reform and revolution. Reform is possible when those who inflict the wrong can be got to see things from the point of view of those who suffer wrong ... I would like to put some of our well-fed citizens in the shoes of our hungry citizens.

Very rich men 'who know all about everything, from art galleries to the domestic economy of the tenement room,' claimed that £1 a week was enough 'to sustain a Dublin family in honest hunger.' Pearse suggested that they try the experiment themselves and

> hand over their surplus income ... to some benevolent object. I am quite certain they will enjoy their poverty and hunger. They will go about with beaming faces ... they will drink their black tea with gusto and masticate their dry bread scientifically (Lady Aberdeen will tell them the proper number of bites) ... When their children cry for more food they will smile; when their landlord calls for rent they will embrace him; when their house falls upon them they will thank God; when policemen smash in their skulls they will kiss the chastening baton. They will do all these things—perhaps; in the alternative they may see there is something to be said for the hungry man's hazy idea that there is something wrong somewhere.
>
> If I were as hungry at this moment as many equally good men of Ireland undoubtedly are, it is probable that I should not be here wielding this pen: possibly I should be in the streets wielding a paving stone.

Pearse also condemned the housing situation, with rooms in which

> over a dozen persons live, eat and sleep. High rents are paid for these rooms, rents which in cities like Birmingham would command neat four roomed cottages and gardens.

As a teacher, he estimated that up to half the children attending primary schools were ill-nourished. 'Inspectors of the National Board will tell you that there is no use visiting primary schools in Ireland after one or two in the afternoon: the children are too weak and drowsy with hunger to be capable of answering intelligently.'

But Pearse made it clear that he was no socialist, or syndicalist. 'Poverty, starvation, social unrest, crime are incidental to the civilisation of such states as England and America, where immense masses of people are herded into great Christless cities and bodies and souls of men are exploited in the interests of wealth.' Such a 'Christless' milieu did not exist in Ireland; yet it had

> dire and desperate poverty … Before God, I believe that the root of the matter lies in foreign domination. A free Ireland would not, could not, have hunger in her fertile vales and squalor in her cities. Ireland has resources to feed five times her population: a free Ireland would make those resources available.

The clear implication of Pearse's argument was that 'any ruthless capitalist', as he characterised Murphy and his associates, could not be a good Irishman. Such men might even be tools of the foreign domination that was the source of Ireland's problems. Ireland must

> govern herself as no external power—nay, not even a government of angels and archangels—could govern her. For freedom is the condition of sane life, and in slavery, if we have not death, we have the more evil thing which the poet has named Death-in-Life. The most awful wars are the wars that take place in dead or quasi-dead bodies, when the fearsome things that death breeds go forth to prey upon one another and upon the body that is their parent.[7]

Again the resonance with Connolly's speeches and writings of the time is striking. If the emphasis in Connolly's analysis was on the economic basis of the foreign domination that sapped the nation's health, the practical conclusions for future political action were almost identical. Pearse showed an intuitive sympathy with the strikers, as if he sensed a coalescing of strategic revolutionary interests between proto-communists and proto-republicans. Others would come to the same conclusion by slower, more mundane and rational routes.

*

No movement claimed to be more rational than the women's suffrage movement. The *Irish Citizen*, founded in 1912 by Francis Sheehy-Skeffington and James Cousins, was the main voice of feminists in Ireland. When Cousins emigrated to India, Sheehy-Skeffington's wife, Hanna, took over the task of joint editor. She was a daughter of David Sheehy, the Irish Party MP who had so recently been denouncing the evils of Larkinism in south Meath. She had inherited all her father's militancy: she had led a successful campaign by younger women to gain membership of the United

Irish League in 1907 but had left when the UIL ghettoised them in its Young Ireland Branch. The league had earlier tried to persuade Hanna and her friends to set up a 'Ladies' Branch', and it resolutely refused to give women members a vote at party conventions. This was in line with the party's policy of opposing female suffrage in the House of Commons, and in the proposed home rule parliament.

Hanna Sheehy-Skeffington soon drifted from the UIL into more radical activities. In 1911 she helped found the Irish Women's Suffrage Federation, which brought together most of the existing feminist organisations. By 1913 she was already a veteran of the suffrage campaign. Among her exploits the previous year had been a window-breaking assault on Dublin Castle, for which she received a two-month prison sentence from Swifte. When her father tried to reason with her, she reminded him that he had been imprisoned six times during various agrarian and home rule agitations; she cited Tone, Emmet and Davitt as her precedents, and boasted that 'in certain emergencies' women 'are more dangerous to despotism than men.'[8]

Both Sheehy-Skeffingtons were ardent allies of the labour movement, but the *Irish Citizen* was not a socialist journal. Its readership was predominantly middle-class; many readers bought it by subscription, and it was heavily dependent on advertising from drapers, jewellers, furriers and other businesses interested in appealing to women with significant disposable incomes, including, of course, the 'new woman'.[9] The *Citizen's* slogan—'For men and women equally, the rights of citizenship; from men and women equally, the duties of citizenship!'—had a decidedly middle-class, though militant, ring.

There was another reason why the Sheehy-Skeffingtons had to be cautious in promoting the cause of labour in their columns. After Francis resigned as registrar of UCD—in protest at the unequal treatment of women students—Hanna had been the main breadwinner. But as a result of her imprisonment in 1912 she had been sacked from her post as a teacher in Rathmines College of Commerce. With her income of £80 a year gone, they were dependent on journalism. Francis may have been making as little as £40 a year at this time from his freelance writing.[10]

The *Irish Citizen* took no sides in the home rule controversy, for the women's suffrage movement spanned the political divides, and it was in a spirit of social concern that it addressed itself to the problems affecting working women. In the process it could be as critical of trade unionists as of employers. As late as 16 August 1913, while Dublin simmered, the *Citizen* was criticising Labour MPs in the House of Commons for their contributions to the debate on the provisions for maternity benefit in the National Insurance Act. Philip Snowden and other Labour speakers were described as 'especially remarkable for their anti-woman concern.' The MPs in question had argued that the law should not be changed, because working-class husbands would feel insulted if maternity benefit was paid directly to their wives.[11]

But the appalling conditions of women workers inevitably drew the *Citizen* towards what the Sheehy-Skeffingtons saw as a natural ally in the trade union movement. On the eve of the lockout it turned its attention to sweated labour in the linen and allied trades of the north of Ireland. Citing a government report, it said that four thousand women outworkers were drawing threads in handkerchiefs for 1s 5d per dozen, and 'the worker has to work very hard to do 1 dozen in an hour.' Women making medium-sized chemises were earning only a halfpenny an hour. Compared with them, the fourteen-year-old 'beginners' in Jacob's biscuit factory were in a workers' nirvana on 4s a week.[12]

Nevertheless, the *Citizen* refrained from systematic coverage of labour disputes. The issue for Horse Show Week carried a report from Somerville and Ross, the popular authors of *Some Experiences of an Irish RM*, but no references to the threatened tram strike. It was only after Bloody Sunday that the Sheehy-Skeffingtons felt confident enough to change tack. In an article entitled 'Suffragists and the strike,' Francis argued that 'although the IRISH CITIZEN, as a purely Suffragist organ, takes no sides in the struggle between organised labour and organised capitalism now going on in Dublin, yet the situation has many points of particular interest for Suffragists.'

The man who had been writing furious reports for the radical press in Britain on the police brutality of Bloody Sunday chose very different grounds for appealing to middle-class feminists. In a clear if inaccurate reference to the Jacob's lockout, he wrote: 'A conflict which suddenly throws out of employment over six hundred girls cannot fail to be of deep concern to all who are interested in women's conditions of work.' He cleverly compared the way the press covered labour disputes and the suffrage movement. 'The uniformity with which the papers, of all shades of politics, join in condemning the men, is in itself enough to give pause to suffragists, accustomed to a similar suspicious unanimity in their own case; and the flagrant partisanship of the Executive, whose forces are placed unreservedly at the disposal of one side in the dispute, awakens similar misgivings.'

He also brought into play 'the personalities of the Labour leaders involved.' These had

> a special interest for suffragists. Almost every one of them has in some way or other helped the Suffrage cause, or shown his adhesion to it. Mr. Larkin was the initiator of the vigorous resolution passed by the Irish Trades Congress, last Whitsuntide, in condemnation of the Government's attack upon freedom of speech and freedom of the press, and calling for the resignation of 'that incapable irresponsible, McKenna' [the Home Secretary responsible for enforcing the 'Cat and Mouse Act'].

Larkin had also supported 'suffragist resolutions at the Dublin Trades Council, and his paper, the IRISH WORKER, has repeatedly attacked the

Government for its coercive policy towards the suffragists.'

Larkin was 'an old personal and political friend' of the leading women's suffrage champion in the ranks of Labour MPs in the House of Commons, George Lansbury. Sheehy-Skeffington reminded readers of the protection offered by members of the ITGWU to women hecklers 'from the Hooliganism of the Ancient Order of Hibernians—the body that is now organising strike-breakers—during the Dublin Home Rule rallies of 1912.' As for Connolly, he was described as 'the soundest and most thorough-going feminist among all the Irish labour men.' William O'Brien was 'a useful though unobtrusive friend,' and Councillor Tom Lawlor had made 'a trenchant denunciation of the Cat and Mouse Act.' Sheehy-Skeffington also reminded readers that

> when the petition against the Cat and Mouse Act was proffered to members of the Dublin Corporation, no man wearing the Red Hand badge of the Transport Union refused to sign it—a unanimity which could not be asserted of any other party in the Corporation.
>
> In view of the unmeasured condemnation to which these men have been subjected by the entire press, we think it right to remind our readers of these facts. The clearly exposed brutality of the police also deserves special notice; what prospect of fair treatment at the hands of such men have the women who are most under their power! Whatever be the immediate outcome of the labour dispute, there cannot be the smallest doubt that in the long run Mr. Larkin must win, because he has behind him 20,000 of the workingmen of Dublin—VOTERS EVERY MAN. It will be interesting to note the attitude of Mr. Redmond's Party towards Mr. Larkin (whom they hate) when they realise that his organisation can control three of the four Dublin City constituencies.

In his 'Comment' column, Sheehy-Skeffington also attacked Redmond and his followers for 'shamelessly' betraying pledges over the vote for Irish women. He also took 'Carsonite insolence' to task for failing to give any indication whether women would be given a vote in the proposed 'Provisional Government' for Ulster; and he attacked the British Government for refusing to extend to Ireland new legislation admitting women to the legal profession.[13]

There was a universalism to his condemnations characteristic of the age. It was a widespread mood, which goes some way towards explaining the feeling of helplessness that frequently overcame the Asquith administration. The agendas of the government's enemies were so vast and unreasonable that even ministers of the calibre of Lloyd George and Churchill felt daunted.

If the Sheehy-Skeffingtons feared they had gone too far in their support for the strikers, the *Citizen's* correspondence suggests they need not have worried. Within a few days Mary Lawless wrote to congratulate the paper on its 'courageous reference ... to the present industrial situation in

Dublin.' A daughter of Lord Cloncurry, she was one of those aristocratic women as much imbued with the militancy of the age as were the unionist peers drilling tenants to 'man the last ditch' in the North.

> Owing to the wide influence of the corrupt press in this country, the majority of progressive Irishwomen has so far failed to realise the close connection there is between their own struggle for emancipation, and that of the organised workers, so that anyone who draws attention to that connection is performing a useful task in the cause of freedom. I think one of the most hopeful signs of the times, in England, is the way the suffrage and labour movements are coming to realise that they are both struggling for the right to live against a common enemy—modern capitalism, with its ruthless exploitation of the helpless—and the sooner we come to the same realisation here in Ireland, the sooner will both parties be in a position to claim, for themselves and for each other, that economic freedom which should be the birthright of every human being.
>
> In standing up for sweated women, and trying to see both sides of industrial disputes, the IRISH CITIZEN is proving itself worthy of its title.[14]

The lockout continued to dominate the columns of the *Irish Citizen* during the following weeks. Another champion of the workers was Louie Bennett. The daughter of a prosperous Anglo-Irish business family, she had been educated abroad, and it was only in early middle age that, like Constance Markievicz, she embarked on a new career as a social radical. She joined the Women's Social and Political Union, founded by Emmeline Pankhurst. Unlike Markievicz, Bennett's instincts were always social rather than national in orientation; nevertheless she seriously questioned the wisdom of the WSPU's decision to oppose home rule because the Ulster Unionist Council had declared itself in favour of female suffrage—a position from which it subsequently retreated. She had helped found the *Irish Citizen*, and in the issue of 20 September she made a case for supporting Labour that was at once convincing and naïve.

> The question of women's suffrage is closely interwoven with the Labour question. Had the woman's point of view been allowed to influence legislation in the past decade or so, much of the bitterness which characterises the struggle of the working classes against capitalism would have been averted.

Like Pearse, she blamed a combination of bad housing, high rents and low wages for much of the trouble.

> The cost of living has steadily risen and the lives of the poor become more and more intolerable. Is it any wonder that a spirit of fierce and sometimes unreasoning revolt has arisen amongst the people who live as our poor in Dublin live?
>
> So bitter a spirit would never have arisen had women been allowed to

influence legislation ... For women of all classes are keenly alive to the value of good homes and healthy children in a community, and would make it their first aim to secure such. In advocating such reforms they would not so often be hampered as men are by business or financial interests: they would be free in most cases to obey their first and best instincts without sacrifice.

Larkinism and the sympathetic strike would not have found acceptance amongst a class who had felt that those in power realised their hardships and were endeavouring to mitigate them. Only a purely masculine Government would remain passive when aware of the nature of those hardships. The Dublin Labour troubles are a fresh example of the need for the feminine point of view in politics.[15]

The readers of the *Irish Citizen* were also reflecting the wider concerns of the middle class about where the lockout might lead. One correspondent suggested that

a Committee of citizens should be formed to watch and protect the interests of the public. We have the employers organised on one side and the employed on another; but the public is a third party, and almost equally as interested a party in this trouble, and yet for the most part they are ignorant of the issues at stake, and are taking, generally speaking, but little part in the development of the struggle.

Such a committee's functions would be

to collect reliable information with a view to publishing it, and, if possible, suggesting some method of arbitration. To enquire into the food and coal supply. To protect children from unnecessary suffering ... The one short-sighted and impossible attitude seems to be for the public to stand aside.[16]

*

The plight of the children struck a chord throughout the community. As editor of the *Irish Citizen*, Francis Sheehy-Skeffington expressed the hope that 'some women of leisure will interest themselves in this project, and that it will not be left to those already overburdened with public work.'[17]

If Helen Laird's appeal for funds to pay for school dinners was not sufficient reminder of the crisis, a report on reformatories and industrial schools showed that Dublin was accounting for 37 per cent of all committals to these institutions. Belfast, with a population a third larger, contributed only 21 per cent of inmates. Eighty-two per cent of the girls and 63 per cent of the boys in these institutions were there as a result of 'offences due to hunger.'[18]

However, an attempt by Labour councillors on Monday 6 October to seek the extension of the British school meals legislation to Dublin was referred back to the Town Clerk by the nationalist majority. Labour councillors had no satisfaction either in their efforts to prevent Councillor

William Richardson being appointed to a newly formed Dublin Children's Distress Fund. Thanks to Irish Party support, Richardson prevailed over the labour candidate, Michael Brohoon of the ITGWU.

There was another acrimonious debate at the city council's Housing Committee. Nationalist councillors wanted tenants in a new scheme at Inchicore to pay rents of 5s a week; Sarah Harrison said the council should be providing homes for the neediest families at rents of 2s 6d, or 3s 6d a week at most. The AOH secretary, John Nugent, countered that most of the tenants in Inchicore would be railway employees, well able to pay 5s a week. Many councillors—nationalist, unionist and even Sinn Féin in affiliation—objected in principle to rent subsidies. Schemes that did not pay for themselves would mean higher rates, just as certainly as providing free school dinners for the children of the poor. It was left to the Lord Mayor's wife, Marie Sherlock, and women like Louie Bennett to see what they could raise with the new fund for 'women and children who are hungry through the present industrial dispute existing in Dublin.'[19]

*

One leading nationalist who broke ranks with his more parsimonious colleagues was Tom Kettle. On Tuesday 7 October he organised a meeting at the Mansion House to call a 'truce' in Dublin's industrial war. The son of one of the founders of the Land League, Kettle, at thirty-three, was still the great young hope of parliamentary nationalism. Elected MP for East Tyrone in 1906 at the tender age of twenty-six, he had given up his seat after becoming the first professor of national economics at UCD because he refused to 'double-job'. It was an unusual decision in an era when most of his parliamentary colleagues, including Timothy Healy and Sir Edward Carson, saw no conflict between representing constituents in the House of Commons and pursuing careers in business, at the bar, or in academia. It says something for the importance Kettle attached to his new project of formulating 'an economic idea fitted to express the self-realisation of a nation' that he wished to pursue it full time; and it may also say something about the dreary and futile existence that was the lot of most nationalist MPs that he was happy to relinquish his seat.[20]

Despite his withdrawal from parliamentary politics, Kettle's admirers regarded him as a potential prime minister of an autonomous Ireland within the Empire. He had shone at university—outshone indeed contemporaries and friends such as Francis Sheehy-Skeffington and James Joyce. He had the best feminist credentials of any prominent home-ruler; he had shared a platform in Dublin with Emmeline Pankhurst in 1912, but he had damaged his reputation with the suffragists the same year by reneging on a promise to support a resolution within the UIL that called for the Home Rule Bill to extend the vote to Irish women. This lack of resolution soured relations for a time with the Sheehy-Skeffingtons, who were that most difficult breed of relations: in-laws with a cause. (Tom Kettle was married to Hanna's older sister, Mary.)

It was clear from Kettle's series of articles in the *Freeman's Journal* in September that he saw strikes and lockouts as among the natural growing-pains of a modern economy. His concern was that employers and unions had allowed local class animosities to overshadow national needs. In the last of the three articles he had called for an Industrial Peace Committee that might bring the two sides to their senses. Subsequently he launched such an initiative himself but deferred the inaugural meeting to see if the Askwith Inquiry would succeed. When it failed, he moved quickly to revive the committee. Its composition paid tribute to his wide network of friends and associates.

The platform in the Mansion House that Tuesday evening was a broad one, but it included only two members of the business community. One was E. A. Aston, widely regarded as an eccentric champion of lost causes; the other was Edward Lee. Lee not only owned a chain of drapery stores but was a director of the Dublin Distillers' Company. He remained the only significant figure within the Dublin Chamber of Commerce to distance himself publicly from William Martin Murphy's strategy. However, with no other leading businessman publicly following his lead, he appeared an increasingly isolated dissident.

The other speakers included two Catholic priests; a Protestant clergyman; the poet and writer Pádraic Colum; the painter William Orpen; the surgeon, raconteur and writer Oliver St John Gogarty; a lecturer in English at UCD, Thomas MacDonagh; and another friend, the poet Joseph Plunkett. If there was anything wrong with Kettle's platform it was that it was too literary in composition, theatrical even.

Kettle chaired the meeting and said it had been called because a dispute involving perhaps 27,000 people was

> injuring day by day the lives of the rest of the population of Dublin, say 340,000. But I don't place our right to interfere upon the mere fact that we are suffering material injury. When the time comes when it is ruled and decided that anybody, even if he has the misfortune to be a professor in a university, is precluded from his rights of citizenship, then it will be a sad day for Dublin ... And we, who love Dublin, have we no right to interfere in a crisis that might mean the ruin of Dublin?

Putting on his economist's cap, Kettle estimated that the dispute was costing 'the trade of Dublin £12,000 a day, or £500 an hour,' not to mention the 'moral deterioration' it was causing in employer and worker alike. You could 'search the British Empire and ... not find a man, in ordinary times, more loyal to his craft and his employer' than the Dublin working man, Kettle said to cheers—many of them from the large contingent in the hall wearing Red Hand badges. But

> create a state of war, take your good workman and set him wandering the pavements and, in one week, he is not quite the man he was. In a fortnight he is still less the man he was, and keep him wandering the

streets on strike for three months, and the good workman you will find becoming a really dangerous and spoiled enemy of society. Hunger and desperation are not very good mothers, or foster-mothers, of industrial prosperity.

Kettle then turned Murphy's well-worn saw against its author.

The employer, of course, does not wander the street. In the words of the famous dictum, he has his three meals a day no matter what happens; but does anyone think that it is a good thing for the employer to be for any considerable time at war with the men who have helped create his business? Does anyone think that hatred and uncharitableness are foundations on which one can build a great city? The further trouble went, the worse it became. We cannot live an eternity in a state of war. A truce should come some time, and the Peace Committee asks its fellow-citizens to say that the time has come for an immediate truce.

Everyone had been told that

the employers of the city have found the ablest leader that ever in their history they found. ('Hear, hear.') They were told that upon the other hand, the workers of the city have found the ablest and most heroic leader they have ever had (Continuous cheers from a section of the audience.) ... Was it not a paradox that the very first time that capital found a great leader in Dublin and that labour had found a great leader in Dublin, capital and labour found it impossible to come to terms? It made one desire that they were back to second-class people on both sides. ('Hear, hear.') If this really great labour leader, and this really great employer in Dublin cared one farthing for the general prosperity of Dublin, then it was time to ... call off the dogs of war.

Kettle himself called for a renewed look at the Askwith proposals. They were not particularly original and could only succeed in an 'atmosphere of peace and good will'; but the same stricture applied to any alternative scheme.

It was as fine a speech as emerged from the troubles of 1913. It was full of honesty, good sense, humour, and above all charity—values that were to count for very little in the months ahead.

There is a tragic prescience to Kettle's concluding remarks on the long-term consequences of the strike and subsequent upheavals for Ireland—and not least for his own breed of politics.

At present, moderates are a minority. Extremism is the fashion, but at the end of every war, industrial or international, there came a moment when it was necessary for men who lived valiantly in the light of their own consciences to speak out and demand peace. Then, gradually, the dawn would break and the people who were against them stole their ideas. The Dublin Peace Committee will hold together until Dublin employers and workmen had stolen its ideas, and then it will be glad to dissolve.

The meeting passed a resolution calling for 'a truce to be declared between the employers and workers, as it appears that only by a truce can a settlement be reached, and the trade of the city saved from ruin, and its inhabitants from starvation.' The tone of most of the speakers that night, however, suggested that the Industrial Peace Committee was neutral in favour of the workers. Sarah Harrison, in her contribution, strayed so far towards the workers' corner that Kettle had to call her to order and remind her that the speakers had agreed to adopt 'a non-partisan attitude'.[21]

What the emergence of the Industrial Peace Committee signified remained to be seen. This modern, urban middle-class view of the world was still in its infancy. Many people looked to a more traditional mediator, Archbishop Walsh, for direction, now that he had finally returned from abroad.

Part 2

Saving the Children

18

O N Thursday 9 October the Catholic Archbishop of Dublin, Dr William Walsh, sent £100 to the Lord Mayor's wife for her Dublin Children's Distress Fund. This was double the largest donation to the Church Street fund; that had come from Lord Iveagh, head of the Guinness dynasty and the city's greatest philanthropist, who had spent £50,000 housing the poor. He gave nothing to the new fund.

A Unionist MP for Dublin in the days before an extended franchise and a rising Catholic middle class made unionism an endangered political species in the capital, Lord Iveagh adopted a stance of Olympian indifference to the lockout, as did his company. Of all the city's major enterprises, Guinness's brewery alone suffered little disruption to its activities as a result of the lockout.

There were two reasons. Firstly, fewer than 500 of its 2,400 employees were members of the ITGWU, which made 'sympathetic' industrial action impracticable. Secondly, the company deftly avoided Murphy's efforts to drag it into the war being waged outside its precincts. Even Larkin knew that it would be folly to take on the most powerful, popular and benevolent employer in the city without a compelling cause. Not all ITGWU members in the company, who tended to be concentrated among the general labourers and boat crews, realised this. In mid-September and again in late October some of the crewmen refused to handle 'tainted' goods being shipped through the port. On the second occasion the company made an example of one crew and dismissed all the members, including the boat captain. Larkin subsequently threatened to call a boycott of Guinness's products, but he never implemented his threat. Though a teetotaller himself and a vehement denunciator of the evils of drink, he knew that such a tactic would never work when it involved the most popular beverage in the country. The union did, for a time, black goods consigned to the brewery, but this was a largely symbolic gesture, as Guinness employees collected all the supplies for the brewery in James's Street.

Similarly, the company resisted attempts by William Martin Murphy and the Dublin Employers' Federation to embroil it in the lockout. The Guinness board did not meet a delegation of the federation until 16 September. It politely declined Murphy's invitation to add 'the moral support of the great company of Guinness' to the employers' ranks; instead, as a gesture of good will, a donation of twice the largest subscription to the federation's contingency fund was offered. As the largest donation so far had been £50 from Murphy himself, Guinness's contributed £100.[1]

The company's strategy was well summed up by Ernest Guinness in a letter to his father, Lord Iveagh. Ernest, who was vice-chairman of the board and the last member of the family to play an active part in the management of the company, said he intended steering a firm but non-provocative course with the ITGWU. 'It would not do for us to accuse any of our men [of] being so foolish as to belong to Larkin, but that if we have any trouble … the men who gave the trouble should be got rid of at once, and never taken back again, as that I believe will do more than anything to prevent more of our men joining Larkin.'

Guinness estimated the number of ITGWU members at between 200 and 450 and saw his policy as the best means of neutralising the union's growing influence. 'I think we owe it to the other employers of labour in Dublin to make a firm stand now, while they are all in line, and what I propose is nothing like so drastic as the line other employers are taking.' He did not think such a policy

> will cause any trouble at all, but even if all our boatmen left us I believe I could replace them in a couple of weeks.
>
> If I prove to be wrong, and all our Draymen [and] Motor drivers do go out in sympathy with the boatmen, I should feel that we are much better able to fight it out now, cost what it may, than later on when Larkin has matured his plans, and we are possibly under Home Rule.[2]

In October, therefore, Lord Iveagh and the Guinness board did not wish to do anything that might be misconstrued, such as contributing to the distress fund. Dr Walsh was well aware of the inferences that might be drawn from his own donation; he told Marie Sherlock that he was sending the money because any

> widespread industrial conflict such as is now in progress … cannot but bring with it … widespread distress. It would discredit us all if the children, helpless victims as they are of the conflict, were to be allowed to suffer.

However, he could not have been surprised when the strike leaders—as early as the next evening at a meeting in Beresford Place—seized on the donation as an implicit endorsement of their cause. He let the claim pass unchallenged.[3]

At this stage, despite the highly partisan accounts of the dispute sent to him in France by Father Michael Curran, Dr Walsh's sympathies appear to have lain mainly with the workers. It was an ironic beginning to his intervention in the dispute; within a fortnight he would be virulently denouncing Liberty Hall for putting the souls of these same starving children in jeopardy.

But then the canny prelate, whom one admirer described as having 'the cunning of the serpent recommended by Our Lord,'[4] proved no wiser and no more prescient than Sir George Askwith in trying to resolve a dispute that had already overflowed the normal confines of industrial strife.

*

Dr Walsh deserves a kinder place in our memory. He was one of the architects of land reform and of higher education in Ireland. He was born into nationalist politics. His father, a Dublin watchmaker, enrolled him in the Repeal Movement when he was nine months old, and he met Daniel O'Connell as a child. Gifted with a brilliant intellect, his interests ran to fields as varied as scientific research, tenant law, bimetallism, and the legality of bequests to pay for Masses for the dead. He loved gadgets and, being a poor horseman, eagerly embraced the bicycle and the motor car. By the eighteen-eighties he was, with Archbishop Croke of Cashel, the acknowledged leader of the nationalist clergy. Dr Croke, fiery patron of the GAA, was so reckless in his attacks on the British government that he incurred the public censure of Rome; Dr Walsh was more prudent, but he was still too strong a nationalist to be awarded the red hat. The pair were known as

> the Castor and Pollux of the National movement led by Parnell. Such a leader, supported by two such priests resembled Moses with his arms upheld by Aaron and Hur during battle. No wonder that Ireland won all through the Eighties till 1890 brought the Parnellite split.[5]

When Parnell was attacked as an adulterer, Dr Croke threw a bust of him out of his palace; but it was Dr Walsh who was the first member of the Catholic hierarchy to call publicly for his resignation. He did so reluctantly, but unequivocally.[6] Once the gauntlet was taken up by Parnell and his supporters, it fell to Dr Walsh to ensure they were defeated. He had some redoubtable accomplices in organising the anti-Parnellites, including William Martin Murphy and Timothy Healy. Given the prickly personalities of both men, it was inevitable that their paths subsequently diverged from that of the archbishop. However, Walsh recognised the value of Healy in particular to the nationalist cause and tried to maintain a working relationship with both of them.

At the time of Parnell's fall, no less a figure than Lord Salisbury, leader of the Conservative Party, paid a subversive tribute to the role Croke and Walsh had played in events. The two prelates, he said,

> have turned the whole [home rule] organisation that seemed to embarrass and baffle the British government ... clear away from that man Parnell ... What will be the state of the loyal minority in Ireland, supposing you hand them over to such an ecclesiastical government?[7]

It was an unfair characterisation of Dr Walsh, who appears to have had little time for the Catholic Association, the AOH, or other movements mobilising to replace the old Protestant ascendancy with a new Catholic one. 'He realised that without his Protestant brethren there was no united Ireland,' wrote one contemporary.[8] If so, he cannot have been blind to the increasingly sectarian hue that the nationalist movement was assuming.

In the politically barren years after the Parnell split, Dr Walsh was able to pay more attention to the spiritual and physical needs of his flock. A small, shy person, he was nevertheless well known in Dublin's north city from his frequent walks and cycle rides. The favoured route for his daily constitutional took him from the newly built palace in Drumcondra to the Custom House, via Gardiner Street. It was a route that led him by gradations from the comfortable abodes of the middle class to the worst of the tenement slums and back.[9]

By 1913, however, he was no longer able to take much exercise. Two years earlier he had suffered a mental and physical collapse following his difficult and protracted negotiations with the British government on the Irish Universities Bill.[10] The effort he put into education, at the cost of his own health, shows the importance he placed on the intellectual and, by extension, the spiritual advancement of his people.

It was for health reasons that he spent so much of the summer of 1913 holidaying in France, where he pursued his favourite hobby of photography.[11] On his return it was inevitable that efforts would be made to use him as a peacemaker. He had arbitrated in numerous disputes over the previous twenty-eight years and had good connections among employers and the trade union movement. His conciliation technique was similar to that adopted by the state when the Labour Court was set up over thirty years later: he would bring the opposing parties to the palace, sit them in different rooms, and engage in shuttle diplomacy until they were ready for direct negotiations.

The value of his services was widely recognised by unions and employers. In 1890 he was made a freeman of Cork for his role in settling a crippling rail and dock strike. On that occasion, as on many others, he had worked with Michael Davitt, the leading social reformer and ideologue of the left within the home rule movement. Davitt's death in 1906 placed a scarcely sustainable burden on the aging archbishop as a mediator in the troubled world of industrial relations.[12] Inevitably, his connections among the craft union leaders were stronger than with the younger generation of trade union activists who advocated the 'new unionism'; but, as his later support for Sinn Féin showed, he was not opposed to new movements or new ideas—provided they did not threaten the spiritual well-being of his flock.

On Thursday 9 October, the same day on which he sent his donation of £100 to Marie Sherlock's fund, Dr Walsh received a letter from Lord Aberdeen, who told him that he had written (by cypher) to the Under-

Secretary, Sir James Dougherty, asking him to suggest to Sir George Askwith that he 'spontaneously offer to reopen the proceedings of the enquiry.' Lord Aberdeen felt that the employers had a legitimate grievance over the way Askwith had handled the proceedings; at the same time he did not feel that the employers' refusal 'even to consider the question of reinstatement should … be regarded as final.' He accepted that Askwith's speedy return to England posed problems with regard to reopening the inquiry, and therefore he was grateful for Dr Walsh's announcement that he was available to help in the process of conciliation. 'Your Grace would, I think, have every advantage as a mediator.'[13]

Dr Walsh responded coolly. He had no intention of intervening prematurely, or without the consent of both sides. He had nothing good to say about Askwith's intervention, and he agreed with Lord Aberdeen that the tribunal's failure to allow Healy an opportunity to cross-examine Larkin was a mistake. But he also felt that Larkin 'has an exceedingly strong case.' The response of the employers to Askwith's report

> has strengthened the position of the workers and cannot fail to bring them abundant help from England. I must say that on the merits of the case generally my sympathies are altogether with them and I trust that the outcome of the present case will be a radical change for the better in the position of the employed in Dublin.

However, he told Lord Aberdeen that his offer to mediate was just that. 'I am prepared to intervene when I have reason to think that my intervention will be welcomed, but not otherwise.'[14] Despite his long sojourn abroad, Dr Walsh, unlike the Lord Lieutenant, realised that the employers were still too bruised by their experience at the Askwith Inquiry to rush into renewed negotiations.

*

Even the employers' battle-hardened champion, Timothy Healy, felt sore at the Askwith tribunal. When his brother, Maurice, ribbed him about his role in scuttling Askwith's peace initiative and the criticism it was attracting back home in Cork, Healy told him it was Larkin who was to blame. Healy claimed that an arrangement had been brokered with the TUC delegation to the effect that nothing would be said in public after he had opened the case for the employers. Both sides would then adjourn to reach a private accommodation. Instead, Larkin had launched into his attack on the employers, proving that he was

> not only false to his promise but abused the employers personally and falsely. This is what led to the fact that no settlement was made. Had Larkin kept faith, then instead of men in Cork abusing me, as you state, they would have been throwing their hats at the settlement I had made secure.[15]

Self-serving as Healy's explanation is, it shows that he shared the ambivalence of many Irish Party MPs towards events in Dublin. However, his public stance remained that, whatever the human cost, Murphy's strategy was a necessary evil. The strike could be settled only 'by the surrender of the men.' Not surprisingly, Healy was disparaging of Larkin's allies in the nationalist ranks. 'Despite the fool-patriots of the day, he [Murphy] defeated Larkin's hold-up of Dublin, and brigaded its merchants in self-defence.'

Healy's correspondence with his brother, a solicitor and former Irish Party MP for Cork, illustrates vividly how the lockout was inflaming tensions within the home rule movement. His anger was fuelled by the fact that Larkin was not only a threat to the hegemony of constitutional nationalism in the capital but was becoming a stick with which rival factions within the nationalist movement would beat each other. In one letter to his brother Healy wrote: 'I told Murphy he was fighting Redmond's battle, and he was well aware of it.'[16]

If Redmond had to be defended, Healy saw no reason why the protection should extend to the AOH. The order's growth in Dublin, and with it the influence of its president, Joe Devlin, rankled. 'Personally,' he wrote to Maurice, 'I should prefer Larkin to Devlin, and I told Murphy so.'[17] A further cause of animosity was the fact that Devlin was a protégé of John Dillon, the man who had ousted Healy from the leadership of the anti-Parnellites in the eighteen-nineties and then led them back into a reunified Irish Party in 1900. Redmond was the nominal leader of the party, but Healy perceived Dillon as the *éminence grise* of the reunited movement.

Maurice Healy had further bad news for his brother. He wrote to say that another long-standing enemy, the Cork MP William O'Brien, was using the Dublin labour troubles to settle old scores at home. Like Healy, O'Brien had been an anti-Parnellite, and he too had been cast into the political wilderness by the reunification of the Irish Party. But there the similarities ended. O'Brien was more radical than Healy on social issues, had an organised electoral machine (the 'Mollies'), and was infinitely more conciliatory in his approach to the unionists. O'Brien found Healy's brand of nationalism as abhorrent as that of Dillon or Devlin. Healy can hardly have been surprised when Maurice told him that O'Brien was using his newspaper, the *Cork Free Press*, to characterise him as a champion of the employers. The paper also attacked Redmond for playing golf while Dublin simmered, placing him on the same moral plane as Birrell, the fun-loving Chief Secretary.

O'Brien was of course no lover of Larkinism either. The *Cork Free Press* had earlier condemned the Redmondites for associating with the 'socialists, secularists and land nationalisers' of the British Labour and Liberal Parties; it is little wonder that Healy wrote back in despair to his brother that 'it is deplorable that his [Larkin's] overthrow will mean a victory for the Mollies, and that we should be fighting their corner!'[18]

Dillon, far nearer the centre of power within the nationalist movement than either Healy or O'Brien and not directly involved in the Larkinite controversy, should have taken a more detached view of the lockout.

'Honest John', as he was called by his followers—'the melancholy humbug' to his detractors—was practically an institution of nationalist Ireland. His father, John Blake Dillon, had been a prominent member of O'Connell's repeal movement and a founder of Young Ireland. John Dillon was a veteran of the Land War, during which several bouts of imprisonment had permanently impaired his health. In 1911 and 1912 he was involved in two traffic accidents, which had forced him into a largely passive role during the early phases of the third home rule crisis.[19] Though much of this time was spent at his Dublin home, and he had seen the power of Larkinism at first hand, he was strangely out of touch with Dublin politics. He represented County Mayo in the House of Commons and was still caught up in the agrarian politics of his youth and middle age. He had spent the weekend of 'Bloody Sunday' in County Sligo unveiling a monument to two Land War martyrs and denouncing the twin evils of landlordism and unionism.[20]

Even after 'Bloody Sunday' Dillon declined to comment publicly on the Dublin labour troubles. This provoked an angry response from at least one old comrade, Richard McGhee, the MP for Mid-Tyrone. A poultry merchant, McGhee appeared an odd champion for socialism, but he had been a close friend of Davitt and had been an active member of the Irish Party's 'labour' wing. As a young Irish immigrant in Glasgow he had helped found Sexton's NUDL and had served as its first general president.[21] After 'Bloody Sunday' he had written to Dillon saying,

> I had expected to see a letter from you in the 'Freeman' today denouncing the murderous attack upon peaceful citizens on Sunday last. It will be a serious mistake for our entire Irish Party to remain silent as if we approved of the devilish work.[22]

He told Dillon: 'The trade unions of Britain are stirred to the deepest indignation' by the behaviour of the police. 'I know nothing that will cause more injury than for those unions to think that we the Nationalist Party are indifferent to the conflicts between William Martin Murphy and his victims.' McGhee, who was also a former Fenian, expressed the hope that 'working men will begin to see the real necessity of arming themselves with revolvers for self-protection, for it is every day growing clearer that the real offence of such men as Larkin is that they have simply increased the wages of the sweated working man.'[23]

On 16 September, McGhee travelled to Dublin to meet Havelock Wilson and the other TUC delegates 'for the purpose of devising means to meet the syndicalism of Murphy and his men.' He told Dillon that two days earlier representatives of the Dublin employers

> were in our office in London whining to get us to leave them alone on the British end ... But they were plainly told that their organised [drive] on what they are pleased to call Larkinism was regarded by us as an attack upon trade unionism.[24]

Only McGhee's end of the correspondence with Dillon appears to have survived, but it is clear from his letters that the Lurgan man received little satisfaction from 'Honest John'. Indeed he appears to have struck a raw nerve, and he responded in kind. At one point McGhee wrote angrily:

> I am not in the least convinced that my obligations to the Irish Party were a better guide than my conscience when it conflicts with the safety of that cause. I never for a single moment suggested that you, or any member of the party were to follow Larkin, or be 'dragged by his tail,' but that was not in the least necessary to enable you to make an open protest against the unlawful butchery of innocent people walking through the streets of Dublin.[25]

Dillon and the Irish Party leadership were in a quandary. The constitutional nationalists were always prone to wrangling on issues as varied as the Irish language, the composition of public bodies, and land reform. As we have seen from Healy's correspondence, issues and personalities were often inextricably linked. Such disputes were inevitable in a broadly based coalition, but usually they manifested themselves only at local level. The lockout was proving divisive nationally at the very moment when unity was essential in pursuit of home rule. It was also causing complications with the party's Labour and Liberal allies in London. Redmond, who spent most of the summer of 1913 at his County Wicklow retreat in Aghavannagh, seemed to have been blissfully unaware of the situation in the capital; but Dillon had only to look out his window in number 2 North Great George's Street to see the mayhem. He wrote to one of his closest friends, T. P. O'Connor, in early October:

> Dublin is hell! And I don't see a way out. Murphy is a desperate character, Larkin as bad. It would be a blessing to Ireland if they exterminated each other.[26]

*

Even the political antics of the irrepressible First Lord of the Admiralty, Winston Churchill, could not distract Dillon from the threat posed by Larkin and 'international syndicalism'. On Wednesday 8 October, while Askwith was packing his bags in Dublin, Churchill chose the occasion of the annual visit to his constituents to fire a political torpedo at the good ship Home Rule and all who sailed in her. He suggested that the demand of Carson and his Ulster unionists to be excluded from the Home Rule Bill

> could not be ignored or brushed aside by any Government dependent on the present House of Commons, and I say to Ulstermen that there is no demand which they can make which will not be met and matched, and more than matched by their Irish fellow countrymen and by the Liberal Party in Great Britain.[27]

Five days before Churchill went to Dundee, Dillon had received a warning from his friend T. P. O'Connor, the Irish Party MP for Liverpool, that Churchill was likely to state 'his real views' in Dundee. O'Connor, who had excellent contacts among the Liberals, told Dillon that 'Winston is thoroughly unsound on Ulster.' He urged him to see Asquith and forestall Churchill; however, Dillon repeatedly refused to intervene, or to encourage Redmond to do so. He told O'Connor that Churchill would simply isolate himself. O'Connor believed that if Dillon or Redmond remained silent it would sow doubt in the government about the strength of Irish Party objections to partition.[28] In the event, O'Connor's analysis proved the more prescient.

One reason why Dillon's usual shrewdness deserted him was his preoccupation with the disturbances in Dublin. While Churchill was addressing his Dundee audience, Jacob's vans were being attacked on their way to the railway stations, and serious rioting broke out in Swords, seven miles north of the city.[29] About a hundred labourers gathered at the Dublin end of the village and dispersed livestock being driven to the Dublin market by non-union drovers. It was dark by the time the police arrived, and the fighting became dispersed and confused. One constable was seriously injured, and the farm labourers attacked the RIC barracks in a futile attempt to rescue two comrades arrested in the scuffles.

Dillon, oppressed by these developments on his doorstep, also felt that a rally planned by the UIL for Limerick on Sunday would be the most fitting place to contradict Churchill and remind the British government of its obligations. He restricted himself therefore to a few comments in the official organ of the home rule movement, the *Freeman's Journal*, on Saturday. He said that Churchill's comments could only have the effect of 'pouring oil on a dying fire' and inflaming 'Orange Ulster afresh.' It was 'perfectly absurd to suggest that that is a part of Ireland which can be dealt with separately. It would be intolerable and quite unacceptable.' The accompanying leading article in the *Freeman* suggested that the Dundee speech would promote 'the policy of intimidation, and [be] a fresh encouragement to the organisers of intimidation in the Northern province.' It drew some comfort from the fact that Churchill indicated that only the four Ulster counties with clear Protestant majorities could expect to be excluded from the provisions of the Home Rule Bill.

Such an offer was forcefully rejected by the organs of unionist opinion, such as the *Belfast Evening Telegraph* and *Irish Times*. If anything, the latter was more opposed to partition—and the subsequent abandonment of southern unionists—than its nationalist opponents. Like the Conservative Party, the *Irish Times* urged a general election on the home rule issue, in the hope that the British electorate would not abandon its loyal British citizens across the water.[30]

On Sunday, Redmond, Dillon, Devlin and other Irish Party leaders used the Limerick rally to reiterate their opposition to anything short of home rule for the whole of Ireland. Also on the platform were the mayors of Cork, Limerick, Waterford and Clonmel and twenty-eight Catholic clergymen. The Bishop of Limerick, Dr O'Dwyer, sent his apologies, as did Willie Redmond, John Redmond's brother and fellow-MP. Willie Redmond's telegram said that the new home rule parliament would 'make every safeguard for minorities.' John Redmond told the crowd that the 'two nations theory' being advocated by some defenders of Ulster unionism was 'an abomination and a blasphemy,' an unfortunately ecclesiastical turn of phrase.[31]

*

Dillon subsequently wrote to O'Connor that the crowd in Limerick was even larger than that which answered Daniel O'Connell's summons in Munster during the Repeal agitation of the eighteen-forties. O'Connor wrote back that he was 'delighted' with the speeches, but he struck a raw nerve when he mentioned the lockout.

> The growing unrest of our organisation in England with regard to the strike in Dublin has at last taken shape. The Gaelic League has called a meeting for this day week, and has invited representatives of our own organisation.
>
> Several of our branches will certainly be represented there. Fortunately the committee are inclined to raise subscriptions only for the Lord Mayor's fund and not to intervene directly in the struggle itself. I myself have been inclined for the past fortnight to take some action; but of course I will never do anything without the assent of my colleagues, and my ignorance of the actual conditions makes me hesitate. I think however, subject to what my friends advise, I ought to go to the meeting; and I dare say they would be very glad to have me preside over it. But I want to hear what you and Devlin say.[32]

Dillon wrote back to O'Connor next day, saying he had discussed the proposal with Redmond, who had agreed with him that

> it would be better for you NOT to attend the meeting called by the Gaelic League. 1) The Gaelic League in London is by no means friendly to us. 2) If you attend you would be unable to secure that no resolutions in speeches of questionable characters would be made. How could you be sure that attacks might not be made on the party for not having taken action. If individual members of the UIL attend and subscribe, that cannot be helped. As regards the situation in Dublin, nothing could be more mixed and mischievous. Larkin is a malignant enemy and an impossible man. He seems to be a wild, international syndicalist and anarchist and for a long time he has been doing his best to burst up the party and the nationalist movement.
>
> The employers have been led into a false position by Murphy. It is a devilish situation and I feel convinced that any attempt on our part to interfere in any way will do NOTHING BUT HARM. One overwhelming objection, in my mind, to you attending this meeting called by the Gaelic League, is that your action will immediately be commented on in

Beresford Place by P. T. Daly, Larkin and Co.—and construed with the BRUTAL attitude of Mr. Redmond and Mr. Dillon who, altho' on the spot etc., etc.

Last week Dr. Walsh sent £100 to the Lady Mayoress' fund, and the following night in Beresford Place P. T. Daly announced that there could no longer be any doubt as to the archbishop's attitude, as he had subscribed £100 to the strike fund.

Here Dillon was stretching the truth. Daly had certainly cited the archbishop's donation to Marie Sherlock's fund as evidence of support for the strikers' cause, but he never said the money was going to the strikers.

The English labour leaders have, it seems to me, acted in a most weak, and contemptible manner. They all hate Larkin and condemn his methods, and he does not conceal his contempt for them, but openly denounces them as humbugs and traitors. Yet they are financing Larkinism in Dublin and thereby prolonging this wretched strike and threatening Dublin with absolute ruin—and sowing an abominable crop of bitterness and hate, which it will take years to get rid of.

If those men had put their feet down on the sympathetic strike, and tied up Larkin, when they came over, they could easily have compelled the employers to give excellent terms and settled the whole business before it had gone too far for an acceptable settlement. These gentlemen will have to record bitterly one day [that] they allowed Larkin to boss them.[33]

Dillon assured O'Connor that any danger arising from Churchill's speech had now passed. In another letter that week he said that the three main causes for political anxiety were—in descending order of priority— Larkin and the lockout situation; the renewal of internecine warfare between the Irish Party and O'Brien's 'Mollies' in Cork; and the forthcoming by-elections in Britain.[34]

Dillon's correspondence shows the disorienting effect the lockout was having on the Irish Party leadership at a crucial point in the home rule crisis. Dillon would continue to underestimate the depth of opposition to home rule in Ulster and the level of irresolution in the Liberal government for some months to come, partly because of the distractions of the labour crisis in Dublin.[35] Not surprisingly, his reaction to the failure of the Askwith intervention was to blame the British trade unions.

*

Of course Dillon could afford to be a lot franker with T. P. O'Connor than with the world at large. O'Connor was one of his oldest and closest friends. Like McGhee, he had emigrated as a young man to England, where he carved out a highly successful career in journalism for himself. In 1880 he was elected Parnellite MP for Galway, and in 1885 he successfully contested the Scotland division of Liverpool, becoming the only Irish Party MP to represent an English constituency, which he continued to do until his death in 1929—long after Dillon and most of his other contemporaries in the home rule movement had passed on to greener pastures.

O'Connor was extremely sensitive to labour issues. He was dependent not just on the Liverpool-Irish vote but on the wider working class to hold his seat. In his early days he had been a social radical, and when he founded the *Star* in 1888 he used it not just to promote support for home rule in Britain but to champion domestic reform. 'The charwoman that lives in St. Giles, the seamstress that is sweated in Whitechapel, the labourer that stands begging for work outside the dockyard gate in St. George's-in-the-East—these are the persons by whose condition we shall judge the policy of the present political parties,' he wrote in the first issue. The *Star* counted George Bernard Shaw among its luminaries, and a campaign in support of the dockers led to a lifelong friendship between O'Connor and Larkin's Merseyside nemesis, James Sexton.[36] At its peak the paper had a circulation of 140,000, though some of its more salacious stories made it unpopular with the Catholic clergy. By 1913 O'Connor was in journalistic semi-retirement, earning a comfortable living as a columnist.

Inevitably O'Connor's social views led him into conflict with some of his more conservative Irish Party colleagues, but they did not prevent him taking the anti-Parnellite side in the split.[37] He owed much of his success as a journalist and a politician to his ability to be at once gregarious and discreet; it is a tribute to his political judgment that he could count both John Dillon and David Lloyd George among his friends. If Redmond was the leader of the home rule movement, Dillon its directing political genius, and Devlin its principal organisational man—as well as leader of the northern nationalists and the AOH—then O'Connor was the vital link between the Irish Party and the leaders of both the Liberal and the Labour movements in Britain.

While he would not break ranks with the Irish Party over the lockout, and accepted that Larkin was 'a rather wild leader,' O'Connor told Dillon that 'all my sympathies are with the workers.' Nevertheless he agreed not to attend the London meeting and promised 'to do nothing more than send a subscription for the women and children to be added to the Lord Mayor's fund.'

O'Connor's political instincts were sounder than Dillon's on both the home rule crisis and the lockout, because life's lottery had given him a greater knowledge and understanding of British politics and the labour movement. Dillon, firmly based in Ireland, remained a rural radical of the eighteen-eighties, wedded to faith and fatherland. That political legacy was becoming a handicap in the uncharted waters of the lockout and the home rule crisis. His dismissive response to the military theatricals of the Ulster unionists, and what he saw as Churchill's attempts to pander to Unionist friends, was rational enough. If it was a misreading of the situation based on wishful thinking, Dillon was at least in good—and rational—company.

His reaction to Larkin and the lockout was more profound. There was a revulsion at all Larkin stood for that was involuntary in its intensity. 'Dillon's hostility to Larkin … ran deeper, perhaps, than he was prepared to admit even to himself,' writes his premier biographer. 'He belonged, as did most parliamentarians, to the men of property and in any class war, real or incipient … there was no doubt on which side he would be found.' Dillon hated Larkin for the same reason he hated the IRB and Carson: they were prepared to lead 'simple people' into hopeless confrontations that must lead either to defeat or to the end of civilised political discourse—at least as Dillon understood the term.[38]

*

Not only O'Connor but Healy—another man much exposed to the complexities of modern life—had a better sense than Dillon of what was afoot in Dublin. In the wake of the Askwith tribunal he told Maurice that Murphy had been wrong to think he was simply fighting an industrial battle.

> I think he is up against a theory, which however erroneous will render Larkin immune from unpopularity in his defeat. The nationalists of yore cared nothing for defeat. Dublin has ceased to be the capital for Redmondism.[39]

One of history's little ironies is that the meeting O'Connor had been invited to attend, and which led to such a vituperative outpouring of rage from Dillon, proved innocuous. There were no revolutionary speeches, and it was decided to do nothing more subversive than plan a series of events to raise money for Marie Sherlock's relief fund. This was to be done under the auspices of a new organisation, the United Irish Societies. Its patron was the eminently respectable Lord Ashbourne.[40]

There is something bordering on paranoia in the response of Dillon and other home rulers to the labour crisis in Dublin. It was akin to their equally vehement rejection of the female suffrage movement. Every rival call on the public's attention, be it from syndicalists or from suffragists, was perceived as treason and an attempt to divert the Irish nation from the holy grail of home rule that they had sought for over forty years.

For many thinking people in Ireland and Britain not blinded by the home rule obsession, the most pressing issue arising from the lockout was how best to provide relief for the families of Dublin's workers. It seemed both a laudable and a non-contentious object; that belief was to prove a profoundly mistaken one. It was perhaps appropriate that it was Dora Montefiore who opened this Pandora's box. She was a socialist feminist and a member of a wealthy liberal dynasty in Britain who had been involved in similar projects before. Her proposal was that, rather than leave the children to starve in Dublin, they should be brought to England to be cared for until the dispute ended.

She launched her appeal at a meeting in the Memorial Hall, London, less than twenty-four hours after Marie Sherlock received the archbishop's £100 donation to help those same starving children. Her philanthropic gesture would arouse all the darkest fears of Larkinism that lurked in the souls of middle-class Catholics; it also gave Larkin's enemies a more effective weapon with which to beat him than any that had so far come to hand.

19

THE feminist movement of the early nineteen-hundreds was new, modern, uninhibited, and not a little naïve. In other words, it was the complete antithesis of the Catholic Church. Dora Montefiore was only one of a glittering platform of speakers in London on Friday 10 October, which included Charles Lapworth, editor of the *Daily Herald*, Ben Tillet of the Dock, Wharf, Riverside and General Workers' Union, and Frances Greville, the 'Red' Countess of Warwick and a former lover of King Edward VII. The guest of honour was Jim Larkin.

The politics of none of the speakers would have commended them to nationalist Ireland, and the morals of Frances Greville would have been anathema. Nevertheless the hall was filled to capacity, and the audience included thousands of Irish immigrants. In a rare burst of national ecumenism, an AOH fife and drum band preceded Larkin on his triumphal progress to the platform. It was the first time he had addressed a mass meeting in London, and the crowd welcomed him with a chorus of 'For he's a jolly good fellow'; this was followed by an encore, at the request of the London dockers' leader Ben Tillet, to the words 'For he's a jolly good rebel.' Larkin was in the ascendant, and everyone knew it. Even the Dublin newspapers gave extra space to his speech in Monday's editions, as he spoke too late for a full account to appear on Saturday.

He began on a sour note. He could not resist the opportunity to lacerate the British trade union leadership for stamping out unofficial strikes by dockers and railwaymen in support of Dublin. The union officials had been

> about as useful as mummies in a museum. The weapon that is wanted is the sympathetic strike used in a sympathetic manner. There are hypocrites who tell us we must not have sympathetic strikes, because they caused inconvenience to the public. The officials of the Railwaymen's Union plead that there are agreements and contracts. To hell with contracts! The men are far in advance of their leaders. They will tell their leaders to get in front or get out.

He had been told by an unnamed union leader to be careful, 'because although the rank and file are with me the union leaders control the money.'[1]

It was a rash speech, even by Larkin's standards; his declaration of 'To hell with contracts' would haunt him like his previous claim to have a 'divine mission' to spread discontent. Besides berating the railway union leaders, he took the National Transport Workers' Federation to task for its handling of the 1912 dock strike in London. Implicitly he was criticising Ben Tillet, who refrained from responding in kind. He must have found it difficult: not only had he led the chorus that greeted Larkin but two days previously his own hard-pressed section of the federation had voted to give £25 a week to the Dublin strike. In a letter already despatched to Liberty Hall he had informed Larkin, rather apologetically, that his union could not afford more in the wake of the 1912 strike.[2]

And yet what gripped the audience, as usual, was Larkin's description of the Dublin conflict. Dora Montefiore was as deeply moved as anyone in the hall. She later wrote in her memoirs:

> As I listened to his appalling story, it flashed across my mind that here was a great opportunity for organised workers in England to prove their solidarity with the locked-out men in Dublin, by taking into their homes some of the Dublin children who were suffering so severely from the effects of industrial strife. When Larkin finished speaking I wrote out a slip of paper and passed it across to him, asking ... if a plan like this, which had already been successfully carried out by Belgian comrades, and in the Lawrence strike, in the United States, could be arranged, would it have his backing. He wrote a few words in the affirmative, and I then passed along a line to Lady Warwick, asking if she would act as Treasurer to the Fund, which she agreed to do. With the consent of Mr. Lapworth ... I wrote the next day to that paper, setting forth the idea, and in less than two days I had upwards of 110 homes offered by workers in England and Scotland to the 'Dublin kiddies'.[3]

Larkin's acceptance of the offer was probably instinctive; and the heady atmosphere in the Memorial Hall that night did not lend itself to reflection. But Dora Montefiore's proposal was not as spontaneous as she suggests in her autobiography. She had already proposed in the British press that 'when the next shipload of food is sent by the trade unions, cannot it return laden with little Irish lads and lassies, who will find in England mothers' hearts and hands to care for and cherish them, until the Irish workers have won the battle.' Anticipating Lapworth's endorsement, Montefiore, who was a member of the Daily Herald League, said she was prepared 'to put all other engagements aside to go over with a batch of Herald Leaguers to Dublin in order to help in the organisation of such a scheme.'

She could have expected a positive response from Frances Greville, who had prepared a similar scheme for the families of London dockers during the 1912 strike; but Lapworth's support was essential. The mass-circulation *Daily Herald* could publicise this 'best and most practical answer' to the problem of the starving children as no other agency could. Over the coming days the paper was inundated with offers of help, and further offers came through the sponsorship of *Votes for Women*, the main journal of the British suffrage movement. The co-operative movement also responded with characteristic generosity, promising to furnish the children with jumpers and boots to guard against the coming winter.[4]

Montefiore continued: 'When 300 responsible homes had been offered (the foster parents in many cases ... being Catholics) I started for Dublin on the evening of October 17th with two friends, Mrs. Elbridge Rand and Miss Grace Neal.'[5] Grace Neal had helped organise the Domestic Workers' Union in London four years previously and was a well-known figure in the labour and suffrage movement. Lucille Rand was a very different proposition. She was the recently married daughter of Henry Gage, a leading American lawyer who had served as a member of the US Senate and was a former Governor of California. The family was devoutly Catholic, and Lucille Gage had been married by the Papal Nuncio in Portugal when her father had been ambassador there. In short, her social and religious credentials were impeccable.

While Dora Montefiore's scheme never received formal endorsement from either the Daily Herald League or the TUC, it was clear that her initiative gave an unexpected opportunity to working-class women, many of them housewives, to help their counterparts in Dublin in a way not anticipated by the male-dominated trade union movement.

Despite the publicity given to Montefiore's scheme in Britain, Catholic Ireland seemed strangely ignorant of the imminent peril it faced. The church militant may have been biding its time—because the response, when it came, was swift, highly organised, and devastating. Or perhaps there was simply so much happening that no-one at first noticed the advent of the British missionaries and their new gospel of humanity.

*

While Larkin was speaking in London, the police were battling in Bray with locked-out workers. Trouble began when dockers refused to unload a consignment of coal for Heiton and Company. They had been handling cargoes diverted to the small County Wicklow port by other Dublin coal merchants earlier in the week, but the ITGWU managed to extend the sympathetic strike to Bray on Thursday; by Friday all the main coal merchants in the town had locked out their workers in retaliation. When farmers tried to bring in coal supplies on their own carts, the vehicles were upended, and rioting became widespread by nightfall. At a public meeting in the Town Hall the local ITGWU branch secretary, John Dunne, appealed for members to 'keep from the drink and remain solid to beat the employers.' A colleague, intoxicated perhaps on ideology rather than on alcohol, assured the crowd that 'Larkinism will in the end beat down clericalism.'

The struggle was being seen increasingly as an ideological one. At the miners' conference in Scarborough, Yorkshire, delegates from as far apart as the Northumbrian and south Wales coalfields supported a proposal to approach all transport unions with the aim of co-ordinating a general strike. A Northumbrian delegate seconding the motion said he favoured 'syndicalism, anarchism or even nihilism, if by those means we can combat Murphyism.' The motion was passed with only one dissenting voice.[6]

If Swords remained quiet over the weekend it was partly because of the strong police presence. In Dublin there was an attack on a Brooks Thomas van in Grafton Street; a riot broke out in Townsend Street when police rescued two 'scabs' from their assailants; and attacks on trams were reported from places as far apart as Sutton and the Phoenix Park. The renewed spate of attacks on trams may have resulted from eviction orders being issued in the police courts against thirty-two striking DUTC workers and their families; the workers were given seven days to vacate their homes. Proceedings against two other tramway employees had been withdrawn by the company, as they had agreed to return to work. There were worrying signs for the ITGWU that the tramway strike would collapse under the threat of evictions.

*

There was some succour for the strikers. At 7:30 a.m. on Saturday the third food ship, the *New Pioneer*, arrived at Sir John Rogerson's Quay with another 30,000 pounds of foodstuffs. There were also rumours that the Dublin Employers' Federation might accept new settlement proposals being drafted by Tom Kettle's Industrial Peace Committee.

A new twist to the conflict was the emergence of posses of strikers to hunt down 'scabs'. In Luke Street two strike-breakers fled their homes during a search of tenements by ITGWU members, and a crowd of three hundred rioted in Denzille Street after police rescued a strike-breaker who had been working for Wallace's, a Ringsend coal merchant. Scab-hunting became widespread, and in the emotionally charged atmosphere the innocent often suffered along with the guilty.

Most such incidents went undetected, but when the perpetrators were caught the pendulum of justice swung the other way with a vengeance. A typical case involved a building labourer, John Fagan, his wife, Elizabeth, and an alleged strike-breaker, John Byrne, in Mary Street. Byrne worked at the Dublin Japan Works. There was no dispute at the works, but two labourers there who were members of the ITGWU walked out in sympathy with the lockout. Byrne was verbally abused by the Fagans, and John Fagan was arrested by two DMP men as he was about to strike the alleged scab with a jug. In the Northern Police Court, Fagan was sentenced to two months' imprisonment and his wife, Elizabeth, to one month.

Walking off the job in sympathy with locked-out colleagues was also becoming a frequent occurrence. One of the best-known cases involved Dockrell's, where there was a mass walk-out on Monday 20 October. The company had withdrawn a requirement that employees sign the Employers' Federation form, after having its goods blacked by Dublin Corporation workers. When the chairman of the board, Sir Maurice Dockrell, asked the workers for their grievances, he was told they had none. They said they had been ordered out by Liberty Hall; but the uncharacteristic silence of that establishment suggests that the action was spontaneous. New workers were recruited, and deliveries continued under police escort. Dockrell switched from being a relatively benign employer to one of the ITGWU's most vehement opponents. He even issued revolvers to strike-breakers.

The newspapers saw these wildcat tactics by workers as acts of desperation and predicted an imminent end to the dispute. In the county it looked as if farm labourers would be laid off indefinitely, as most of the harvest was now in through a combination of farmers working their land jointly and the use of 'free labourers'. Some of the strikers, fearful of eviction and a hungry winter, tried to negotiate a return to work, only to find their former employers disinclined to take them back.

The situation in the DUTC was even worse. On Monday the company announced that 'large numbers of former employees who went on strike during Horse Show Week' had applied on Saturday for reinstatement. Clearly the threat of evictions was a potent factor for these workers too. 'Men with a good record were taken back,' the company said. However, they found their wages cut by 3s or 4s a week. In some instances they were relegated to 'spare work', that is, casual status. The threat of having their licences withdrawn by the DMP was another potent factor in persuading many drivers to return.[7] The tramway men were not a significant group in numbers locked out, but the virtual collapse of the strike that had ignited the dispute was an important psychological victory for the employers.

At the weekend the DUTC felt confident enough to announce it would resume a full service within a matter of days. It said that late trams were already running on the Dalkey, Terenure, Howth and other lines. However, on Saturday night a police escort on the Howth tram had to drive off a group of attackers. One of the assailants, Laurence Rooney of South Burrow, Sutton, was caught in the pursuit; when he was searched at Howth station a Red Hand badge was found in his pocket. 'By that badge we stand or fall,' he told District Inspector Carey. He was subsequently sentenced to a month's imprisonment and was told by the magistrate that only his previous good character had saved him from a second month in jail.[8] Such incidents did not augur well for the Industrial Peace Committee's initiative.

*

A delegation from the Industrial Peace Committee, including its chairman, Tom Kettle, the draper Edward Lee, and the irrepressible E. A. Aston, met Dublin Trades Council on Monday night. The committee's joint honorary secretaries also attended; these were the poet and future member of the IRB's Military Council Joseph Plunkett, and Thomas Dillon, a nephew of John Dillon and another literary friend of Kettle's. The Trades Council delegation was led by William O'Brien, with James Connolly representing the ITGWU in Larkin's absence.

The union leaders agreed in principle to the Peace Committee's proposal that a 'truce' be declared and that a mutually acceptable mediator be appointed to 'discuss final terms.' The Trades Council accepted the proposals on the understanding that the 'final terms' were not binding.[9] It was now up to the employers to respond.

In the event they did not even await a visit from the Peace Committee. Instead the secretary of the Dublin Employers' Federation, Charles Coghlan, made a pre-emptive strike by issuing a formal response to the Askwith Inquiry's findings; he said the federation had been unable to state its position sooner because of the necessity of consulting all its members. He repeated the complaints made earlier about the procedures adopted by the tribunal, which had prevented the employers' counsel, Healy, from refuting 'a long series of charges, many of which were obviously untrue, interspersed with attacks on Messrs. Jacob and other respected firms in the city, calculated to seriously injure the businesses of those firms.'

The employers rejected the tribunal's finding that the requirement that employees of affiliated firms not be members of the ITGWU was contrary to individual liberty. Coghlan pointed out that the inquiry team itself had decided that no community could exist where the practice of sympathetic strikes was the general policy of trade unionism.

The employers were prepared to accept conciliation procedures in principle but denied their practicality in a situation where the sympathetic strike had become widespread,

> due to the domination of the legitimate trade unions by the Irish Transport Union. Relieved of this tyrannical control ... the amicable relations heretofore existing would be restored.

Inevitably, the employers seized on Larkin's outburst in London on Friday night to hammer home this point. While they had no wish to interfere 'in the internal management of trade unions,' they had no option in the light of statements made by Larkin since the conclusion of the Askwith Inquiry, 'including the declaration in London "To h— with contracts,"' but to refuse recognition to his union until

> (a) the union be reorganised on proper lines
>
> (b) with new officials who have met with the approval of the British Joint Labour Board.
>
> When this has been done the Executive Committee will recommend the employers to withdraw the ban on the Irish Transport Union and re-employ their workers as far as vacancies and conditions permit, but until then they regret that existing circumstances compel them to continue to insist on the undertaking referred to being signed.

The statement concluded with a call for legislation 'to ensure labour agreements are kept.'[10]

The invocation of the Joint Labour Board, which was composed of representatives of the TUC, the Parliamentary Labour Party, and the co-operative movement, was an obvious attempt to reject the claim that the

Dublin Employers' Federation was anti-union, as well as seeking to exploit the tensions between Larkin and the British union leaders. The Dublin employers were clearly impressed enough by the moderation of the TUC to see its continued involvement as the best means of wearing down Larkin.

The TUC might be as anxious as any employer to end Larkin's syndicalist crusade, but it could not be seen to abandon the Dublin workers, to whom £17,000 had now been pledged by trade unions, co-operative societies and individuals throughout Britain.[11] At this stage in the dispute the Dublin employers' statement was seen by trade unionists everywhere as more evidence of intransigence by the followers of 'Murphyism'.

Despite the stance taken by the Employers' Federation, there was still an expectation of some sort of breakthrough in the dispute, and there were relatively few incidents during the week; 'awaiting developments' was the journalistic cliché the *Freeman's Journal* assigned to the situation. Besides, there was plenty of other bad news to report. The Cunard passenger liner *Volturno* had caught fire in mid-Atlantic on Monday, with 650 passengers and crew on board. With memories of the *Titanic* disaster of the previous year fresh in the public mind, there was huge press interest as another Cunard liner, the *Carmania*, steamed seventy-eight miles in four hours to effect a rescue. 'But for the invention of Signor Marconi we should be mourning today a holocaust of the seas,' the *Daily Telegraph* wrote in its Tuesday edition. As it was, twenty-seven lives were lost after one of the *Volturno*'s lifeboats was holed by a davitt as it was being launched.

Closer to home, over nine hundred Welsh miners were trapped by an explosion in a Universal Colliery mine at Senghennyd, near Cardiff, on Tuesday. On Wednesday there was yet another railway accident in north-west England, this time at St James' Station, Liverpool; eight people were killed and twenty-eight injured. In Senghennyd more than 500 miners had been brought out of the pit by Wednesday morning, but there were 40 known dead and 386 still unaccounted for.

In Dublin, merchants were predicting that the protracted industrial dispute would have a dreadful effect on the Christmas trade. 'If the strikes were settled tomorrow their effects will be felt all through the winter,' the owner of one large shop told the *Irish Times* on Wednesday. At the Mansion House, Lorcan Sherlock received a letter from the Lord Mayor of London seeking funds for the bereaved families of Senghennyd, where the death toll had risen to 429. There was no point looking for donations to the Dublin distress fund there.

*

If Dublin was relatively calm, Larkin was continuing to whip up working-class emotions in Britain. He told a meeting in Birmingham that English workers had no idea of the conditions of the Dublin workers. 'In England … there is a sense of fair play.' In contrast, there never was an organised system of blood-sucking in any other country such as we have in Ireland. Ireland wants home rule to get rid of the gang that is fattening upon the workers' vitals.

That veteran Irish Party campaigner T. P. O'Connor drew the same conclusion, from somewhat different premises, when he addressed a Liberal Association meeting at Peterborough. He did not allow Dillon's injunctions to cramp his style unduly. 'The conditions which led up to the strike in Dublin are a disgrace to the Empire,' he said. He nevertheless managed to inject a backhanded compliment to Larkin by immediately adding:

> And considering those conditions, it is perfectly evident that it does not require any man of any exceptional ability to raise a revolt against those conditions. Why is there not an assembly in Dublin whose whole function and business should be to deal with this local problem in Dublin and other local problems in Ireland? We cannot deal with it in the House of Commons, as the House of Commons is too busy.[12]

What view a Dublin parliament should take of the dispute was something O'Connor did not go into. There Larkin had the edge on his Irish Party opponents, and he berated Redmond as much as Carson: they were 'both simply the mouthpieces of the capitalist class.'

Yet the argument that an Irish parliament would be better able to deal with the lockout than a House of Commons that was 'too busy' with other matters made sense. It was a view echoed by speakers at the annual conference of the Association of Municipal Authorities in Dublin that week. Lorcan Sherlock, who hosted and presided at the conference, complained that 'during the past twelve months the Imperial Parliament has been fully occupied with what it considers to be great public issues.' As a result, 'the everyday life of the country cannot receive the attention … [its] importance under ordinary circumstances would demand.' A home rule parliament would resolve this problem.

In the wake of the Church Street disaster, housing conditions inevitably dominated the agenda, and Lady Aberdeen read a paper to the delegates on 'The effect of Better Housing for the Working Classes in Exterminating Tuberculosis and Other Preventable Disease.' However, Sherlock's remarks had struck a deeper chord. While Lady Aberdeen was thanked for her speech, there were complaints that the Lord Lieutenant himself had not attended, nor the Chief Secretary.[13] Birrell sent his regrets, but not his reasons for staying away. If he could have done so he would only have reinforced the argument that Larkin, O'Connor and Sherlock were each making in their different ways. For he had been exceptionally busy in recent days with the home rule crisis. At the beginning of the month he had been to Balmoral trying to assure King George V that civil war was not imminent. He later told Asquith, somewhat irritably, that the king was 'confused by the succession of Liberal Ministers briefing him on

Government and their own views.'[14] It was as near as he would come to saying that Churchill and Lloyd George should keep their noses out of his department.

Birrell had also spent some time trying to reassure the Belfast shipping magnate Lord Pirrie and his wife that they were not about to be assassinated in their beds by Carson's Ulster Volunteers. Pirrie occupied a unique position among Ulster's ruling class by remaining a Liberal and, therefore, supporting home rule. Margaret Pirrie expressed her fears to anyone who would listen; in one letter to the Chief Secretary that summer she had written of

> the feelings of bitterness, resentment, and malice of the people of Belfast towards those who, like Pirrie and others, hold Liberal views, and people have threatened that should Home Rule pass, our works will be levelled to the ground and that we, and those connected with it, will be amongst the first fired at. This may be bluff, but it is not pleasant.

It was when Pirrie threatened to lay off his entire work force if Carson seized power that Birrell decided that a meeting with the shipyard owner and his excitable wife could be put off no longer. He saw them on his return from Balmoral and told Lord Pirrie: 'I don't know that the lockout of THOUSANDS of fighting men would confer peace on the city.' He later told Asquith that Lady Londonderry and other unionist friends of Lady Pirrie were deliberately exploiting her fear in order to undermine her husband's support for home rule. Nevertheless he conceded that the Pirries needed cossetting. 'After all he pays £20,000 a week in wages in Belfast.'[15] In fact something like a quarter of Belfast's population in 1913 was dependent on Pirrie, directly or indirectly, for a livelihood. Much of this came of course from the government's naval rearmament programme, and there was an element of the dog biting the hand that fed it about the unionist militancy of the shipworkers.

*

No sooner were the Pirries placated than Birrell had to meet Redmond in Dublin to assure him that Churchill's speeches in Dundee did not represent British government thinking. Redmond told him that the nationalists 'would do anything for a United Irish Parliament and Executive, to meet the forebodings of the Protestants of Ulster.' They could even have an administrative Council for Ulster, 'but without legislative powers.' When Birrell wrote to Asquith he said he had assuaged Redmond's fears with a promise that Asquith would shortly make the government's position clear in a public speech. Though Redmond was preoccupied with Devlin's concerns about the Ulster business, Birrell complimented himself that Redmond 'looked very well and cheerful' by the time he left.

As the Chief Secretary sat down to write his report on the meeting with Redmond he received an untimely reminder that unionists were not confined to Ulster. The Lord Lieutenant of County Sligo called to his office to demand soldiers to protect the Protestant community. I asked what risk they ran. He replied quite sharply, if the Catholics were handled roughly in Belfast there would be reprisals in Sligo.

Birrell assured him that if Catholics were attacked in Belfast the military would be sent in,

with so stern a hand as would ensure protection to ALL law abiding citizens. Thereupon he became angry and wanted to know how people who flew the Union Jack could be treated as rebels! Fortunately he had to catch the five o'clock train to Sligo. It is an odd country.[16]

It was about to become odder, thanks to Dora Montefiore.

20

O N Thursday 23 October, James Connolly organised a march of eight thousand ITGWU members in protest at the employers' outright rejection of the Industrial Peace Committee's initiative. 'A more quiet and orderly procession never passed through the streets of Dublin,' the *Irish Times* reported with some relief. It also commented on the low turn-out, when up to 25,000 workers were now reputedly locked out or on strike; but only 12,500 of these were ITGWU members,[1] and, as the meeting was called at short notice, the numbers indicated that the drift back to work by tramway men, some farm labourers and others had not significantly weakened the members' resolve.

The marchers carried banners with such slogans as *It is impossible to destroy the Transport Workers' Union* and *No surrender.* Women, who headed the parade, carried banners declaring *Our men shall not give in* and *Women workers locked out by the sweating employers of Dublin.* In a retort to the employers' conditions for settling the dispute, one banner declared: *We are willing to recognise the Employers' Federation provided it is completely reorganised with a new set of officials.* But pride of place went to an enlarged photograph of Larkin, in a gilt-edged frame, borne on a lorry; and many of the individual marchers carried handwritten placards with the simple message *God bless our Jem.*

The union leaders made the customary speeches at the procession's end outside Liberty Hall, and Connolly called for a minute's silence for the dead Welsh miners. He also engaged in what for him was an uncharacteristically theatrical gesture at the conclusion of his speech. If people wanted to know what the workers were fighting for, 'Here it is,' he said. A three-year-old child was handed up to him, and he displayed it at arm's length to the applauding crowd. It may have been coincidence, but he did so only hours before Dora Montefiore and her helpers boarded the night mail for Dublin.

The City of Dublin Steam Packet Company, which had the government mail contract, was one of the few cross-channel lines still operating. It continued its uneasy truce with the ITGWU by avoiding the handling of 'tainted goods', and there were plenty of untainted items to fill the hold, including Guinness stout. Deep-sea freighters were also largely unaffected by the dispute, but 'smokeless funnels, diminished vehicular traffic and vessels riding at anchor awaiting hands to discharge their cargoes' were now the dominant characteristic of the port of Dublin.

Everyone knew it was only a matter of time before the shipping companies brought in 'free labour', as had happened in Connolly's old stamping-ground at Leith, the port for Edinburgh, two months earlier. In the meantime Shackleton, the Lucan miller who had introduced the lockout tactic in August, announced that he was resuming normal business with 'new staff'. This provoked nightly processions in the village, culminating in a riot on Sunday, when police cleared the streets with batons.[2]

On Monday the dispute in the port was stepped up when two hundred unskilled workers struck rather than unload 'tainted' coal for the power station operated by the Port and Docks Board. Members of the Amalgamated Society of Engineers, William Partridge's union, also threatened to down tools in the power station, but the union leadership in England instructed them to work normally. It was a blow to the ITGWU, as the board needed the engineers to operate the power station, whereas it could always hire 'free labour' to replace the general operatives.

There was some excitement later that day when the DMP raided Liberty Hall and seized files of photographs collected by the ITGWU of members who had returned to work. However, these events were quickly overshadowed by the activities of Dora Montefiore and her helpers from England.

*

Since their arrival on Saturday morning, the women had gone about their business at Liberty Hall with great efficiency, if little discretion. They outlined their Dublin plans to send children to England at a mass meeting in Liberty Hall on Sunday evening of women whose husbands and sons were out of work, or who were in dispute themselves. On Monday night they addressed a second meeting, where Montefiore said the cheering stopped only 'to boo Murphy.' It was 'choked with Celtic emotion, but the main fact stood out that the Dublin mothers were prepared to trust the English mothers and that the work of organisation for moving the kiddies out of Dublin for their great holiday adventure in England is to go on.'[3]

Grace Neal drew up a register of mothers

> anxious to take advantage of our offer. The passage leading to our room was blocked from morning till evening with women and children ... We rejected many who were not wives of strikers, or of locked-out men.[4]

On Monday the first group of six children, accompanied by their mother, caught the midday mail boat for London, en route to the home of Emmeline Pethwick Lawrence, joint founder with Emmeline Pankhurst of the Women's Social and Political Union. At 6:30 p.m. the late edition of the *Evening Herald* published an exclusive report on this 'amazing' development in the dispute. By next morning all the papers published a letter from Archbishop Walsh denouncing it as 'the most mischievous development of our labour trouble in Dublin.'

To understand the vehemence of the reaction to the scheme by this traditional friend of labour, and by the Catholic Church in general, it is necessary to look briefly at the history of proselytism in the city.

The war for souls in Dublin had been raging since Famine times. While it was waged on a number of fronts, the strategic cockpit of the struggle was education. At a time when Catholics and Protestants sincerely believed that converts lost to the other side faced eternal damnation, there was little room for Christian charity in this struggle. Inevitably, the home rule crisis aggravated traditional sectarian animosities and religious susceptibilities.

Proselytism took on a particularly intense form in Dublin, where the large Protestant community had significant human as well as financial resources with which to keep Catholicism at bay. The growing Catholic middle class had responded with the Catholic Association, and also the more militant Catholic Defence Association, to challenge Protestant hegemony in the higher professions and in the arena of business. One of the prime movers in both bodies was David Patrick Moran, editor of the *Leader*, Dublin's principal current affairs review. He was a gifted journalist who had learnt his trade in England from T. P. O'Connor on the *Star*; however, little of O'Connor's social radicalism appears to have rubbed off on him.

Disillusioned with politics by the Parnell split, Moran saw the cultural and economic rejuvenation of the country as the most viable route to salvation for the Irish people. Figures as diverse as W. B. Yeats, Sir Horace Plunkett, Tom Kettle and Arthur Griffith had arrived at a similar conclusion, but none of them had equated the Irish nation with the Catholic Church, and then reduced both to their middle-class essence. In retrospect, Moran can be seen as a bigot who fanned the flame of sectarian hatred in the city; and he did so with a humour, wit and acuteness of observation that was far more effective than the hysteria of the *Irish Catholic*. He also proclaimed his beliefs with an honesty and clarity of vision that shamed the constitutional politicians, whose speeches were full of mawkish sentimentality and ambiguity.

It was a winning editorial formula, and within a few months of its launch in 1900 the *Leader* was established on a commercially sound basis. Catholic businesses advertised heavily in it, none more so than those religious orders that ran fee-paying schools and colleges to train the sons and daughters of the country's aspiring elite. What might be termed the ancillary sector of the clerical industry also advertised heavily in it: firms such as West and Son, manufacturers of church plate; the publishers M. H. Gill and Son, who published such edifying works as the *Letters of Mary Aikenhead*; Todd's of Limerick, leading 'clerical and general tailors'; and Lalor's, which made 'Green Cross' altar candles from 'Irish-bleached' beeswax—not that Moran refused advertising from Protestant firms, such as Pim's or Eason's, though he drew the line at British manufacturers.

During 1913 the *Leader* published a series of articles based on the census returns since 1861, which charted the progress of Catholics up the socio-economic ladder on a county-by-county basis. Dublin presented a particularly edifying picture. Sectarian head-counts had become an increasingly popular journalistic pastime during the home rule crisis, especially after the proposal that Ulster counties with a Protestant majority should be excluded temporarily from its provisions. By an unfortunate coincidence, the week before Dora Montefiore arrived, the *Leader* concluded a series of five articles of the head-counting variety featuring the proselytising activities of the Irish Church Mission. The author bore the highly appropriate nom-de-guerre of 'Vigilans'.

The Irish Church Mission had been set up to proselytise the rural poor—the consequence being the notorious 'soupers' of Famine days—but by the eighteen-sixties it had begun operations in Dublin. It sought out quarters such as the Liberties, a 'stronghold of Papal darkness and intolerance,' where it built the Coombe Ragged Schools. These establishments stood 'in strange contrast with the filthy mansions around them, a beacon in the darkness and a protest against the system which perpetuated it.'[5] Naturally, Catholics saw things somewhat differently. Selecting the children of the poor particularly enraged Catholic opinion. The St Brigid's Order of nuns declared in 1862:

> It is the poor and helpless and the innocent that are attacked by the enemies of their faith. It is base. It is cowardly. They go, or send their agents to the poor widow who has pawned her last article of dress and while the hunger cry of her infant is rending her heart they say, 'We will take your children, and educate them and raise them in the world.'[6]

Fifty years later, 'Vigilans' would conclude his series in the *Leader* by stating that the Irish Church Mission had been 'an abject and ignominious failure in every part of Ireland outside the city of Dublin.' Unfortunately, the organisation had early realised that 'there would be much greater chance of success among the slum population of the city, degraded by pauperism and drunkenness, than in smaller towns and country districts.' Out of 105 teachers and Bible readers employed by the Irish Church Mission, he estimated that 64 were based in Dublin.[7]

Vigilans's figures probably came from Dr Walsh, the Society of St Vincent de Paul, or Moran's confidant in the Jesuits, Father Thomas Finlay. The Society of St Vincent de Paul had provided Dr Walsh with a confidential report in July 1913 giving details of the activities of the Irish Church Mission and other proselytising groups in the capital.[8] The information had been culled partly from the published annual reports of the Church Mission schools, but much had come from a surveillance operation on the institutions, which appeared to include the infiltration of some of the

Protestant food centres catering for adults. The report said there were thirteen schools and nine other proselytising institutions in the city, between them catering for 1,468 children, over 500 men, and over 100 women.

The secretary of the society's anti-proselytising committee was T. J. Fallon. His committee had been

> instrumental in taking from proselytising day schools ... between 240 and 250 children. All of these, as well as 19 rescued from institutions ... have been transferred to Catholic schools and in the overwhelming majority of cases dealt with the work gives every promise of permanency. We have found the parents most amenable to our appeals and in many cases it was surprising to see the obvious delight exhibited by them at the prospect of being able to resume the full practice of the Catholic faith.
>
> Although it is difficult to say with certainty that there was one common motive to all these cases, we are able to assert that the wily manner in which the proselytisers dangle their wretched bait before the eyes of poor slum-dwellers makes it almost impossible for the necessitous poor to remain in ignorance of the fact that candidates for apostasy need never starve. In many cases we satisfied ourselves that appeals had been made IN VAIN to Catholic charitable organisations before the evil step was taken.

In his report, Fallon states that in many instances the families involved had stopped practising their religion before associating with the proselytisers; some had not received the sacraments for eight years. 'To remove the possibility of reproach against the St. Vincent de Paul Society for failure to help those who alternatively must seek non-Catholic help, a new Conference [branch] has been founded in a district hitherto held unworthy of visitation (the Mabbot and Purdon Street areas).' This was the notorious Montgomery Street area, popularly known as Monto; Mabbot Street was the former name of Corporation Street. The Dublin Council of the society had decided it would finance this project 'till we can show the charitable public the claim we have on them.'

The details of some of the families 'rescued' from apostasy make sorrowful, if inadvertently humorous, reading. Many of the children in the north city went to Rath Row School, just across the river, off Townsend Street. Forty-nine children were observed by the Society of St Vincent de Paul leaving the school at 2:30 p.m. on 31 March.

> Half an hour before the children left the school eleven mothers entered for the purpose ... of hearing the scriptures and doing sewing. It would appear from what we hear that the women get 3d. each for this attendance, as two of the mothers who were shadowed entered the first public house they met. Most of the women had parcels of food with them when leaving and the children had pieces of bread.

At the Christian Union Buildings in Lower Abbey Street, 420 men, 90 women and 50 children were observed entering at 8 a.m. on Sunday 6 April for a free breakfast. There were Scripture readings and a sermon from a lay preacher while they ate. The society's spy reported that

> one of the breakfasters—evidently a Catholic—remarked to another, 'We will burn for this yet, but God bless them for giving us our breakfast when our own won't.'

At the Mill Street Mission off the Coombe, 'hundreds of Catholic Men, Women and Children' were reported attending Sunday hymn and prayer services. 'For this they get a quarter loaf of bread each.' The mother of one family 'rescued' from Rath Row told the society that she had received 3s in cash, 1s worth of groceries and a bag of coal in return for entering her boys on the school register. The mother of another boy attending the Birds' Nest (a residential school at Mounttown, County Dublin) said she was given 10s. Both mothers reported frequent follow-up home visits by the schools.

The Society of St Vincent de Paul also made visitations to the homes of the apostasising families. These provide a revealing glimpse of conditions in the Dublin tenements in the months leading up to the lockout. In Gloucester Street the society visitor reported on the case of an eleven-year-old girl who had been attending the Church Mission ragged school in Lurgan Street for six months, whose father was

> a delicate man—labourer—out of work. Wife—a Catholic—but was brought up in Birds' Nest. Brought father, mother and child to Confession in Gardiner Street today—father had not been there for four years—mother for three years, and C. [the daughter] for 12 months. Furniture of their room was on the landing as they were evicted for arrears of rent. Got them reinstated. Paid 8s. rent for them. Gave them … 2s. and order on Grocer for 3s. and bought dress for C. for 3s. C. is going to North William Street Convent School today. Her younger sister, Bridget, aged 8, was never at school but will go to North William Street when clothes are procured for her.

A few doors away the society visitor found a widow with nine children. 'Would have found it difficult to have got into the mother's confidence—but hearing her Southern accent spoke to her in Irish.' Three of the children, aged seven, nine, and eleven, were attending Lurgan Street.

> An elder sister thirteen-and-a-half years had been attending Lurgan Street School. She now picks cinders on the Sloblands at Fairview.

Several families in Corporation Buildings were also sending children to Church Mission schools. While most of them were willing to send their children to Catholic schools when material help was offered, this was not always so. The visitor reported that one couple had

> four children going for a long time to Rath Row. Mother resisted all appeals to remove children. Father would be willing to do so.

In some cases it was the children who resisted the move. A society visitor to the Summer Hill tenements reported an eleven-year-old boy who had been transferred from Rath Row to North William Street School, but

> this boy was so perverted that he would not repeat the words of the Hail Mary for us. He knew the Protestant version of the Our Father off by heart.

Another boy, aged six,

> was rescued from the Birds' Nest, Kingstown, where he was for a month. He frequently said to his mother since his return home, 'We must never pray to the Virgin Mary—We must never say the Hail Mary.' We got the lad a new suit of clothes to replace the uniform he had on him.

In the Liberties the visitors found a three-year-old girl who could 'rattle off scripture texts' after her two older brothers went to the Coombe ragged school. Her mother attended sewing classes there.

Sometimes the issue of sending the children to Protestant schools became a bitterly divisive one between the parents. In Chapter Place, off Kevin Street, a mother went to the local nuns after the father placed a six-year-old daughter in the Birds' Nest.

> Sister Ursula provided money for the mother and clothes for the little girl, and after great trouble the girl was rescued. D. is now undergoing six months imprisonment for assaulting his wife because she refused a Protestant minister the care of the child in presence of her husband.

Where the visitors were unsuccessful in their efforts they tended to attribute the cause to the parents. 'Bad Mother' was the reason given for one boy returning to a ragged school. In another case the visitor reported:

> Impossible to keep Children to Catholic Schools. The father had an organ [i.e. barrel organ]. Lately found mother drunk in the streets and ladies got children sent to Industrial schools.

But in some instances it was the children who were felt to be at fault. One child in Mercer Street who was continually returning to a Protestant school was found to be 'hopelessly demoralised from bribes and feasts.' Another girl in Mercer Street 'could not be got out of Protestant Schools, nor to the Sacraments, but was caught stealing and committed.' However, the visitor triumphantly reported the rescue of three children in the same street. They were 'my First fruits—got me all the others by telling me the names and addresses.'

Rescue from the proselytisers rarely meant a better life for the child. In Chancery Street, when the Society of St Vincent de Paul investigated the placing of five children in a Protestant industrial school, the visitor

> found mother dying in a cellar of cancer. Got her to St. Vincent's Hospital where she died and promised her to save children from the worthless father.

This the society did by placing four of the children in Catholic industrial schools. The youngest child, a baby, was removed from the Protestant institution, and it 'died with us, nine months old.' Three children in Townsend Street 'in great danger' from apostasy were transferred to an industrial school in Kinsale after the 'Mother burned to death. Father threw a lighted lamp at her. Father deserted children.'

But there were happy endings too. The father of six children attending the Coombe ragged school was found a job in Jacob's biscuit factory by the Society of St Vincent de Paul. The Jacobs, who were Quakers, turned out to be more ecumenical than the educationalists, and the children were all transferred to Gardiner Street Catholic school.[9]

The Irish Church Mission was not a passive observer of the Society of St Vincent de Paul's activities. At its annual meeting in Dublin on 15 April 1913 Rev. Michael Goff of the Dublin Mission told members that 'it had been found necessary to organise a band of pickets' to prevent children being 'interfered with on their way to school' by unnamed individuals. 'These children come to school of their own free will and of the will of their parents, but for some weeks past they had been hunted and harassed on the public thoroughfare.'[10] Disingenuousness was an attribute of both sides in the war for souls in the slums of Dublin.

For its part, the Society of St Vincent de Paul committee, appalled at the scale of the problem it faced, approached several priests and nuns for help in tracking down and 'rescuing' apostates. The Jesuits in Gardiner Street and regular clergy in several city parishes agreed, as did the Sisters of Charity and a nun in the Holy Faith convent school in Strand Street. But in the report sent to Dr Walsh, Fallon pointed out that a fundamental problem was the disparity of resources between the two sides. 'We feel our little income has been providentially multiplied, so that it may with truth be said that in this fight for souls a Catholic shilling will undo the work of a Protestant sovereign.' Fallon argued that with a little more generosity Catholics could be 'free from the humiliating reproach of inactivity while the souls of our little ones are being purchased for Protestant pence.'

The figures in his report tell a different story. In cash the society had received only £100 for this work, of which £50 came from one parish priest and most of the remainder from the Jesuits. The society's own conferences based at St Francis Xavier's (the Jesuit parish) and the Pro-Cathedral (Dr Walsh's parish church) had also provided credit for £30 worth of provisions to be drawn on merchants in the north city. The cash donations had gone on a wide range of items, including school clothes, paying off rent arrears, free Sunday breakfasts, and the purchase of prayer books, Rosary beads, and religious pictures. But by July the money was gone, and the society's anti-proselytising committee was £50 in debt. In contrast, the Birds' Nest school alone had an income of £4,403 in the previous year, and the total income of the ragged schools in Dublin that year was about £14,500.[11] Middle-class Catholics may have felt for the souls of their poor co-religionists, but most of them were not prepared to enter a Dutch auction with the Irish Church Mission and bid for them.

Fallon appears to have been particularly concerned to maintain the provision of four hundred free Sunday breakfasts a week through the society's headquarters in Ozanam House, Mountjoy Square, and school breakfasts for three hundred children every weekday in local schools. Without it these Catholics would be going to the nearby Christian Union, which was feeding over six hundred men, women and children, or the Mill Street mission off the Coombe, where hundreds more received free meals. The society also began providing Sunday breakfasts in the Liberties to combat the Church Mission's activities there.[12]

*

It was into this protracted, low-intensity conflict that Dora Montefiore and her helpers now wandered, gloriously ignorant of the sectarian minefields all around them. Dr Walsh was unequivocal in his condemnation of her visitation.

> I have read with nothing short of consternation … that a movement is on foot, and has already made some progress, to induce the wives of working men who are now unemployed, by reason of the present deplorable industrial lockout in Dublin, to hand over their children to be cared for in England by persons of whom, of course, they have no knowledge whatsoever.
>
> The Dublin women now subjected to this cruel temptation to part with their helpless offsprings are, in the majority of cases Catholics. Have they abandoned their faith? Surely not … I can only put it to them that they can be no longer held worthy of the name of Catholic mothers if they so far forget that duty as to send away their children to be cared for in a strange land, without security of any kind that those to whom the poor children are to be handed over are Catholics, or, indeed, are persons of any faith whatsoever.

But Dr Walsh tried to turn this latest development in the lockout to good purpose. 'I am much mistaken if this recent and most mischievous development … fails to appeal to all who are involved in the conflict … to strive with all earnestness to bring the conflict to an end.'

In an effort to encourage new talks, he said that the employers were 'to some extent justified in hesitating to enter into an agreement' without a guarantee that it would be kept. 'For my part, I should like to see guarantees given at both sides.' He also pointed out that Harry Gosling, 'one of the leading representatives of labour,' had offered 'ample guarantees' if the parties could come together. 'May I venture to ask why, in the face of this explicit statement, the parties should not come together, and see whether something cannot be done to put an end to a conflict that is plainly disastrous to the interests of both?'

Unfortunately, the more positive elements in the archbishop's letter were largely ignored, while the denunciation of the 'kiddies scheme' was taken as a licence for holy war by many Catholics. Montefiore, who responded promptly to the archbishop's letter in Tuesday morning's papers, did not help matters with her unfortunate turn of phrase, which echoed accursed Famine days. 'The English workers feel that the Irish workers are in the soup today and that they themselves may be in the soup tomorrow.' She assured readers that satisfactory references must be forthcoming before offers of help would be accepted. 'The children will be provided with a pleasant holiday while the troubles here last. Lady Warwick is the treasurer of the fund we are collecting.' The reference to the involvement of the 'Red Countess' would not have reassured many Irish parents of the political or moral propriety of the scheme.

Perhaps most damaging of all were her remarks to a *Freeman's Journal* correspondent. She compared Dublin unfavourably with cities in America, South Africa, and Australia.

> It is not a superficial knowledge I have of the workers. I think the condition of the children here is so deplorable. Looking out of my hotel window I saw three little nippers about four or five years of age—you know how they are dressed, or undressed—turning over the garbage, putting bits of coal and stuff they found into a sack and 'wolfing' any bits of bread and meat that they got mixed up in the refuse. This is an incredible state of things. It is a disgrace to any civilised country.

The *Evening Herald* was quick to seek the views of clergymen on Montefiore's 'amazing proposal'. Most Catholic clergy said they had nothing to add to Dr Walsh's comments, but one unnamed priest was quoted as saying he was

> quite sure that ... Catholic parents will not part with their children. They will not let them be in danger of losing the Faith, even losing Christianity and becoming Atheists.

Another anonymous priest said that,

> whilst better housing conditions are essential and sweating an abomination, a policy of merely material advancement will never succeed, for the simple reason ... It is a direct ANTITHESIS OF CHRISTIANITY.

The only favourable comment came from the mother of one of the batch of six children who had travelled to Mrs Pethwick Lawrence's cottage in Surrey on Monday. Mrs Cottle, who lived in George's Quay, said that her daughter Catherine

> took her scapular with her and will be all right. Mrs Geraghty will take care of them as long as they remain in England'[13]

Mrs Geraghty was a neighbour who had travelled with the children. The party included her own daughter, Mary. However, press reports suggested that most mothers were not so sanguine.

By Wednesday morning, when fifty children assembled at Tara Street baths to be washed and 'clothed with English charity garments' before their trip, many of the mothers were reported to be unhappy. In contrast, the fathers seemed determined enough to push on with the experiment. A large crowd soon gathered, and no less than five priests from St Andrew's in Westland Row arrived to try to dissuade the parents from letting the children travel. They were led by Father Landers, who read passages of Dr Walsh's letter aloud and then harangued the crowd on the dangers the children would face in 'the homes of Atheists and Socialists.' He and a colleague, Father Fleming, claimed to be speaking 'on the directions of Dr Walsh.'[14]

Lucille Rand was supervising a group of women hired to 'cleanse' the children, and when Dora Montefiore arrived she found her colleague 'being personally annoyed and technically assaulted by the priests, who were shouting and ordering the children about in a passageway leading to the girls' baths.'[15] She recalled later that some of the women were 'answering back' to the priests, but the *Evening Herald* declared the women 'unanimous against sending their children away.' Even some of the men uttered 'murmurs of dissent.'

By the time the party reached Westland Row station, en route for the ferry at Kingstown, the proceedings resembled a macabre carnival. The station was besieged by crowds who cheered the 'many priests' as they arrived.[16] 'Mrs Rand and I were the only two calm persons in that yelling, wailing, hysterical multitude,' Montefiore claimed. Some children separated from their parents in the crush were taken into custody by the priests, while the rest of the party retreated to Liberty Hall 'through a crowd that threw mud at us ... and raised cries of "Throw them in the Liffey".' Only at Liberty Hall were 'kindly hands stretched out to us on all sides.'

Larkin was among those who welcomed the fugitives, having arrived back from his speaking tour in England that morning. There was the usual throng in Beresford Place, and he immediately addressed the crowd from a window of Liberty Hall. Imitating Connolly, he showed them one of the youngsters destined for England; but his usual power over the crowd had deserted him. The *Evening Herald* reported with some relish:

> The meeting in Beresford Place was one of the most remarkable in one respect ever held there ... It was small and ... sullen. There was not a solitary attempt at cheering and Larkin's harangue was listened to in chilly silence.

Once again Dora Montefiore and a much-depleted group of sixteen children, with a few parents, renewed their efforts to catch a train from Westland Row to Kingstown. Luck seemed to be with them for a while. The redoubtable Father Landers and his ferocious flock had been diverted to the North Wall by a false rumour that the children were to be 'exported' from there. However, the priest and his followers managed to catch up with

Montefiore's party as it was about to board the train. The little group was 'pushed back and forth' on the platform. A priest grabbed Montefiore by her shoulder, and another 'flung the door back against me, hurting me considerably, and making me feel very faint.'[17] Railway officials held up the train, already behind schedule,

> at the command of the priests … Just as it was starting two priests, who had no tickets, pushed two women into the carriage where I was and then got in themselves.

The priests were Father Thomas McNevin and Father Thomas Ryan, two colleagues of Father Landers from Westland Row.

> The journey down to Kingstown takes about twenty minutes and during that time the two women were kneeling in hysterics on the floor of the carriage, calling on the saints to forgive them, while the priests started a systematic bullying of the four boys … They pulled off the labels and the rosettes we had put on the boys' jerseys, and told me, as I sat passive and contemptuous in the corner, that they did not want any of our English charity for their children. The same gross scenes of intimidation … were repeated at the boat.[18]

Ten children refused to leave the train. Montefiore accompanied Lucille Rand and a helper, Mrs Ward, as far as the gangway of the *Scotia* with 'the remnant of the children.'[19] Father McNevin and Father Ryan (still presumably without tickets) pursued the tiny group aboard.

> Fr. McNevin made a speech to the passengers. He declared that the boys were being taken away by trickery, fraud and corruption to proselytisers, without the permission of their parents. He charged Mrs. Rand and those for whom she was acting with kidnapping some of the children and he said he would see to it that Catholic children were not stolen from their parents and brought to a strange country where there was no guarantee as to what religion, if any, the children would be brought up in.

He was still speaking when a DMP detective arrived to search for a boy reported missing. Several priests had now joined Father McNevin on board, including Father Landers, who had motored all the way from Dublin. Yet despite their threats, the priests left the ship empty-handed as it was about to depart. So did Lucille Rand, who left the children in Mrs Ward's care. At the last minute the youngsters

> fled the ship, followed by Mrs. Ward. Three seconds later the *Scotia* was off. Loud cheers were raised from the boat and the pier, someone crying 'This is the end of Larkin's career.'

On disembarking, the two women were charged with kidnapping.[20] The complaint had originated with Josephine Plunkett, whose son Joseph was a member of the Industrial Peace Committee. Her own views were much closer to those of her husband, George, a papal count whose old-fashioned 'whiggish' brand of nationalism had allowed him to vie with Sir James Dougherty for the position of Under-Secretary for Ireland. He was now director of the Dublin Science and Art Museum (later the National Museum). Countess Plunkett had visited Liberty Hall earlier in the day to protest at the kiddies scheme and had been unceremoniously thrown out. She descended on Westland Row presbytery, where she obtained details from the priests of some of the children 'rescued' from Dora Montefiore. She then lodged a formal complaint of kidnapping with the DMP. Father Ryan, one of the priests at Westland Row, obtained depositions from two of the parents, travelled once more to Kingstown, and handed them to the police just in time for Lucille Rand to be arrested on the pier. While she languished in Kingstown police station, 'frenzied scenes of wild delight' were witnessed in the seaport.

> An enormous crowd of townspeople, who had assembled outside the police station, cheered lustily when the children were conveyed to the railway station en route to their homes. Prominent amongst the people were many clergymen ... Loud and continuous cheering greeted the priests, and as the lads, borne shoulder high by strong men, were carried to the Royal Marine Road, the excitement of the people knew no bounds ... The homecoming of some conquering hero could not have equalled it and in the intense joy of their childish hearts, the boys who were to have been deported, joined in the cheering, and with excited glee waved their caps above their heads.

Similar scenes greeted the children and their clerical escorts when they arrived back at Westland Row station. The crowd roared repeatedly, 'God bless our priests.'

It was late that evening before Lucille Rand was bailed by the ITGWU solicitor and allowed to return to the Edinburgh Hotel, where she was staying with Montefiore. Luckless parents of the 'kidnapped' children, tracked down by a relentless press that night, were understandably evasive about their reasons for letting their little ones go. Most said they thought the children had gone to school, or were only on an outing to the baths. Margaret Duffy of Upper Gloucester Street was probably the most honest. She had agreed to send her seven-year-old son away because she thought the child would be better off. She regretted it now. 'I thought all of the children were going to be sent away,' she said.

One group of eighteen children did make it. They boarded the City of Dublin packet *Carlow* at the North Wall at 7 p.m. under the care of Grace Neal. A small group of priests arrived on the scene from north city parishes and boarded the ship. They used similar tactics to those of their confrères in Kingstown, but ITGWU members were present in force, and when one of the priests, Dr William Doherty of the Pro-Cathedral parish, tried to address the crowd, he was drowned out by the ship's whistle and choruses of 'God save Jem Larkin,' to the air of 'God save Ireland.' As the ship pulled away from the quay, the 'kidnapped' children joined in the singing.[21]

Something approaching religious hysteria seemed to have seized hold of Dublin that day. One reporter was among those on the receiving end. Emerging from the home of one family that had sent a child to Tara Street baths, he was mistaken for a member of the Salvation Army and had to flee. ITGWU members seemed cowed by the ferocity of the priest-led crowds. One reason for this uncharacteristically supine attitude may have been that many ITGWU activists were in prison. Severe sentences, sometimes as much as six months with hard labour, had been imposed in the police courts; the jury trials of another hundred members facing more serious charges were due to begin shortly. That prospect, together with the effects of two months on the picket lines, would have dampened the ardour of any group of workers; but many ITGWU members must also have been confused and disoriented by the strength of the clerical reaction to the kiddies scheme.

One of Larkin's most loyal supporters in the trade union movement, William Partridge, took the unusual step of writing to the newspapers as early as Tuesday to express his personal reservations about the scheme. 'The natural affections of the Irish parents and children present, to my mind, insurmountable obstacles to the generous offers made by our kind friends across the channel.' He suggested that a more practical alternative would be

> that our Irish Catholics wake up even now and do something for these innocent victims. We are not far from Christmas and a little stranger in our home might exert beneficial influence. I have two children of my own, and am prepared to try and provide for two more on the little available.

He added obsequiously: 'I trust I may not be taken in any way as being disrespectful to his Grace the Archbishop.'

Partridge's letter, displayed prominently in Wednesday's *Freeman*, was in stark contrast to Dora Montefiore's approach. The very name she gave to the project, the 'Dublin kiddies scheme', offended many nationalists, who felt it smacked of uncomprehending British condescension.

There were also legitimate concerns over the speed with which the scheme was being implemented. There was nothing, beyond Montefiore's personal assurances, to show that the host homes had been properly vetted. There were also signs that the system used for vetting the children themselves was inadequate. No doctor was involved in the procedures, and one child 'rescued' from Tara Street ended up in hospital, having been found to have the measles. Such a blunder might have been glossed over if public opinion had been more sympathetic to the scheme, but it was adroitly exploited by the priests to whip up further hysteria.

The controversy also deflected attention from more embarrassing events for the authorities. Earlier that day the inquest had taken place into the death of James Carey, the 68-year-old fisherman who died as a result of head injuries sustained during the rioting at Ringsend on 30 August. His daughter Mary gave strong evidence of him being batoned by the police. The jury, hand-picked by the police, ignored the evidence and returned a verdict exonerating the constables of all blame.[22]

At Beresford Place that night Larkin was unrepentant about the kiddies scheme. He said the clergy well knew that the last thing the ladies connected with the scheme wanted to do was interfere with the faith of the children. Some clergymen were 'a disgrace to their cloth' for what they had done that day. 'The religion which cannot stand a fortnight's holiday in England does not have much bottom or very much support behind it.' Many of these clergymen had shares in the Tramways Company and other firms, but while these 'soul-destroying agencies were at work in Dublin for many years there was no protest made against them.'

Larkin saved some of his most scathing comments for Countess Plunkett and her friend Mrs Bridget Dudley Edwardes. She had earlier announced that she was organising accommodation in Dublin to take 150 children, rather than see them sent to England.

> Women of the type of Lady Plunkett and Mrs Edwardes and their class never knew until now that there were slums and poverty in Dublin. They have their cat shows and hang about on the skirts of the so-called nobility, and they look at the workers with scorn. Why don't Lady Plunkett and the clergy look after the proselytising homes in Abbey Street and other places? ... If they look up the list of persons who are supporting the proselytising homes they will see the names of Dublin employers.

Another speaker attacked the clergy in even sharper vein. An organising secretary of the Associated Society of Locomotive Engineers and Firemen called Drummond had come over from Scotland to lend his moral support to the Dublin strikers. 'Your church is against you and on the side of the rich,' he told the crowd. 'Their politics is their pocket.' He was fiercely heckled, and Tom Lawlor, who spoke next, did his best to undo the damage.

> In my opinion, if Mr Drummond had the intimate knowledge of Dublin I have, he would not make that statement. The priests' politics in this city are not their pockets. (Cheers.)

However, Lawlor still defended the kiddies scheme.

> The man or woman who would be satisfied to send their children to England, Scotland and Wales ... would not be worthy of the name of mother or father (cheers), provided that in their own homes they are able to keep these children from suffering the pangs of hunger. But the man who would keep his children ... while there is a door of refuge open would be unworthy of the name father.

To reassure the crowd of his own nationalist credentials, Lawlor told then he was 'a home-ruler out and out.' (Cheers.) Home rule would 'clear the decks for the workers,' he said. But Drummond's words came back to haunt the strike committee over the next few days, and the Mullingar branch of ASLEF publicly dissociated itself from his comments and asked the union to recall him.[23]

*

The ITGWU and its leader were looking increasingly isolated. That day Tom Kettle's father, Andrew, had brought in farm labourers from surrounding counties to replace his striking workmen. A large police escort accompanied the 'free labourers' to his lands at St Margaret's, County Dublin, and the newspapers reported that other employers were expected to follow Kettle's example. 'It is time to take some active measure to save the remainder of the crops and prepare for next season,' Kettle told the *Irish Times*. 'The people on strike seem to be bewitched or hag-ridden in their adoration of Larkin.' Andrew Kettle had been a leading figure in the Land League, who had defied landlords and police in his day. His decision showed the gap that now existed between the rural radicals of the eighteen-eighties and the urban radicals of 1913.

Kettle's view of Larkin was shared by increasing numbers of union leaders in Britain. In his speeches at London, Birmingham, and Liverpool, Larkin had returned to his favourite theme, the failure of the TUC to back sympathetic action in support of Dublin. While most of them continued to maintain a diplomatic silence, the president of the National Union of Stewards, Cooks, Butchers, and Bakers, Joseph Cotter, said that Larkin had 'gone out of his way to attack men like James Seddon, the president of the Trade Union Congress, and Harry Gosling … men who have done magnificent work for the trade unionists of Great Britain and Ireland.' He declared that 'Larkin must go … The almost unanimous feeling in England is that Larkin is a good organiser but a bad negotiator.' Cotter suggested that it was time for Harry Gosling to ask Sir George Askwith to use his good offices once more to end the dispute.[24]

It was not, of course, Joseph Cotter's remarks that had driven Larkin back to Dublin but the fact that he was due to stand trial next day—along with other leading Dublin trade unionists—on charges of sedition and inciting workers to riot and loot in the city. There was a serious prospect that the workers, already in dire straits, would soon be leaderless as well.

21

'THE Liverpool trade unionist who described Mr James Larkin as a good organiser but a bad leader will find ample corroboration of his estimate in the position in which the workers' cause has been placed by the latest move in the Dublin struggle,' the *Freeman's Journal* told its readers on Thursday morning.

> Judging it solely from the workers' point of view, this project of deporting Irish Catholic children to English homes is the capital mistake in tactics not distinguished by foresight. It has, as anybody knowing the people of Dublin could have foretold, aroused intense indignation even in quarters where sympathy was felt with the men in dispute.

Larkin's attacks on women 'distinguished amongst the actively charitable ladies of Dublin … will appear simply malevolent as well as ridiculous.' The *Freeman* welcomed Dr Walsh's intervention and his call for renewed talks between the unions and employers. It also chided the 'British Unionist Press' for its praise of Dora Montefiore's experiment; it hoped that unionist employers in Dublin would take note of the lack of support they were receiving from such pillars of the British establishment as the *Times* of London.

The same could not be said of the *Irish Times*. Its liberal-unionist readers might take a more detached view of the battle between Catholic clergymen and trade unionists for the souls of the Dublin 'kiddies', but it seemed to accept unquestioningly the assumptions of Dr Walsh and his clergy on this issue. Its reports of Wednesday's events rivalled those of the *Evening Herald* in its use of pejorative terms such as 'Deportation of strikers' children' and 'Exporting of boys and girls' to describe the efforts of Montefiore and her friends. Unlike the *Freeman*, it did not get around to editorialising on the problem until Friday's edition, but it was no less hostile.

> Apart from its religious aspect, the deportation scheme was foolish to the point of lunacy, and well deserves the failure which has been its fate. It does not appear that Mr. Larkin was the only begetter of this notion. It seems to have originated with certain English and American ladies of that philanthropic class which regards the world as its parish.

However well-intentioned these women were, they had acted with 'unpardonable impertinence to the city of Dublin.'

While the paper deplored the fact that Dubliners could not find room for 'one tenth' of the moral energy generated by the kiddies scheme to deal with 'the material miseries which surround us on all sides,' it felt that

> the deportation business may have one good result. Mr. Larkin has controlled the situation because the bulk of his followers remained loyal to him and because the English trade unions continue to supply him with food and money. But the English unions are beginning to find him impossible, and the events of the past two days must have shaken, if not the loyalty of his followers, at any rate their confidence in his intelligence and judgement. Mr. Larkin is no longer quite so formidable an obstacle to settlement as he was a fortnight ago.

He had made 'a serious—perhaps, a fatal—mistake … His prestige is badly hurt, and for a democratic leader prestige is everything.'

In truth, Thursday had gone no better for the kiddies scheme than Wednesday. It began with the successful departure of three children, accompanied by their father and uncle, on the midday sailing from Kingstown. Both men, members of the ITGWU, were impervious to the pleadings of priests who were 'in attendance at the departure of almost every train to Kingstown,' and, in the absence of any large crowd, the group suffered no other hindrance. However, the *Evening Herald* reported the incident on its front page, along with information that arrangements had been made 'to send 50 children from Dublin to Scotland tonight.' It gave details of the sailings that evening from the North Wall. 'Several priests will attend to make a strong protest against this action, and it is hoped that every Catholic in Dublin will attend in order to lend their moral support to their clergy in the firm and Christian attitude they have taken up.' The paper also published on its front page an anonymous letter from 'A Lover of Children', who said that 'measures should be taken … to stop the delivering of children up to persons pretending to be lawful and natural parents of said children, in order to bring them away for the purpose of having them clothed, fed and housed.'

Probably a more effective deterrent was the practice that most Dublin newspapers had now adopted of publishing the name and address of parents who had consented to their children joining Montefiore's scheme. All the papers published a letter from Father T. J. Ring, rector of St Mary and Michael's Church in London's East End, known as the 'friend of the London Catholic docker'. He told readers that during the great dock strike of 1912 his relief committee had received

> several tempting offers of 'happy homes' for Catholic children. In no case were these offers accepted, and in no instance did we find a Catholic mother willing to part with her little ones. I hope Dublin mothers are of the same mind.

A priest in Holyhead telegraphed the Dublin newspapers offering his congratulations to Father Thomas McNevin and Father Thomas Ryan in rescuing 'kidnapped and other children, labelled like cattle,' from the ferry.[1] Colleagues at Liverpool, including Canon William Pinnington, secretary of the Catholic Children's Aid Committee, met the *Carlow* on its arrival.

Also waiting on the quay was Fred Bower, a stonemason, veteran trade union activist and syndicalist. 'The time was five o'clock in the morning,' he recalled vividly over twenty years later.

> Detective Inspector McCoy came up to me. We knew each other. 'Hello,' he said. 'What brings you down so early?' 'The same business as what brings you, I expect, Inspector,' I replied. 'I hope there will be no trouble.' 'There won't be any, if I can help it,' he promised. The gangway was let down, and I went aboard to meet Miss Neale who had charge of the bairns, pinched and ill-clad, most of them barefooted. I set off to board the ferry-boat which was to take us over the Mersey to a beautiful house in Cheshire ... when a priest stopped me. 'Where are you going with the children?' he asked. I told him. 'Have you their parents' permission?' 'Not on me,' I replied, 'but it has been given.' 'Then I must give you in charge,' he said, and called a policeman.
>
> I explained to the officer. The detective inspector could vouch that I was known to him. Eventually we were corralled into a customs shed around a fire, and the children were regaled with cakes and hot tea. Another priest, a canon began asking the scared mites what church they went to, had they attended Mass, and so on. The priests soon had the children crying. I said, 'If you please, you might leave the children alone, they were quite comfortable before you interfered.' Other things were said, but Miss Neale soothed the youngsters, and we waited.
>
> In about a couple of hours, Inspector McCoy came back to report the police had got in touch with the Lord Mayor of Dublin. 'He had the written consent of all the parents in his hands,' he said. So we were allowed to pass on. 'Now,' I said to the two priests, 'they are in my charge and you will have to stop annoying them, or else I shall call a policeman.' 'But may we go with you?' one said. 'I cannot stop you,' I replied, 'the ferry-boat doesn't belong to me.' A press photographer had come aboard and asked me would I mind posing the children. 'Not at all,' I replied. 'It may evoke sympathy with the plight of the parents, amongst the unthinking general public.' I stood at the end of the line and just as the camera was going to click the priest stood in the centre, and bless me, if the picture didn't appear with me cut off, and an article stating 'our picture shows some of the strikers' children being taken to a palatial foster-home in the charge of Father Walsh of Liverpool.'[2]

Canon Pinnington was undaunted by his failure to rescue the children. Later the same day he wrote to Father James Flavin, administrator of the Pro-Cathedral in Dublin and one of the clerics most prominent in stopping the 'export of children'.

As soon as they are placed out I will communicate with the Priest of the district and ask him to see them. In the meantime, if any of the parents can be persuaded to revoke their consent—and will furnish me with a properly attached statement to this effect, I will do my best to obtain custody of the children and return them to Dublin.[3]

Across the water, Father Flavin and other Dublin priests were able to adopt a strategy based on direct action. All afternoon 'priests from all parts of the city were on the "qui vive",' the *Freeman's Journal* reported, as well as 'many ladies associated with philanthropic and social work in the city.' Well before six o'clock a large crowd, led by seventeen priests and composed largely of members of the AOH and confraternities throughout the city, marched down the quays to the cross-channel steamers berthed at the North Wall. As the procession passed Liberty Hall there were clashes with a small number of ITGWU members, but a strong police escort quickly cleared a path. Among the marchers were the national secretary of the AOH, John Dillon Nugent, and two fellow-members of Dublin City Council, the publican Alfie Byrne and Patrick Mahon, a jobbing printer and the probable supplier of the leaflet that marchers distributed to passers-by. This read:

FATHERS AND MOTHERS OF CATHOLIC DUBLIN—Are you content to abandon your children to strangers, with no guarantee to have them placed in Catholic or Irish homes? You may never see them again! Kidnappers and soupers are at their deadly work. There is no excuse for exiling your children. Provision has been made in Dublin for all cases of distress amongst them. No city has ever been so disgraced!

The crowd searched every ferry on the dock between the first departure at 6:30 p.m. and that of the night sailing at 9:20 p.m. The eagerness with which large numbers of women 'watched every child travelling by the boat or being brought to the gangway, showed the earnestness with which they were imbued,' reported the *Freeman's Journal*; while AOH members held up approaching vehicles to make sure there were no 'kidnappers' or 'soupers' inside. At Kingstown a smaller group of priests and their supporters kept guard, but again there was no-one desperate or foolish enough to run the gauntlet.

*

One reluctant visitor to Kingstown that day was Lucille Rand. She appeared in the local police court on a charge of taking an eleven-year-old boy, George Burke, from his father, Terence Burke. She was also charged with 'receiving' the boy knowing him to have been stolen. George Burke, whom the court reporters volunteered was 'an intelligent boy', said he had been passing Liberty Hall when he was introduced to the accused by another woman collecting money for the strikers. She had given him a gansey, taken him to Tara Street Baths, and then to the boat in Kingstown by train. He ran off the ship after 'a big tall girl told me to take the priests' advice.' The boy said he thought he was going on holiday, and his mother knew nothing of the scheme. Terence Burke said he was a cattle-drover and thought his son had gone to school that day. The first he knew of the abduction was when a policeman from the Bridewell arrived at his home in North Anne Street on Wednesday evening, accompanied by a priest. He told them he knew nothing of George's trip, and was then driven by the priest to Kingstown.

Father McNevin and two DMP men gave evidence of what had happened at the ferry. Dora Montefiore testified that Lucille Rand was 'a lady of the highest respectability.' This cut little ice with Mahony, the police magistrate. When Rand's solicitor, T. J. Campbell, protested at the magistrate's decision to send his client for trial, Mahony replied that the only alternative was to deal with the case summarily. 'And that might be worse for you, Mr Campbell.' Montefiore said that if anyone should be on trial it was her, and she rejected Terence Burke's claim that he had not given his consent to his son's travelling to England. Mahony said that from his experience 'of this class of man, Mrs Montefiore might be perfectly right,' but there was nothing more he could do for her. In fairness to Terence Burke, it should be said that the *Freeman's Journal* that morning had published several interviews with named children who said they had gone to Tara Street baths under the impression that it was the start of a day's outing. This may have been done simply to allay the children's fears, but it also suggests that in her haste, Montefiore had not adequately briefed or monitored her more enthusiastic helpers.

On Thursday evening, as the two women recovered from their ordeal, they received a visit at the Edinburgh Hotel from the DMP. Montefiore was taken to the Bridewell and charged with the same offences as Rand. Once more the ITGWU supplied a solicitor, and David Hewston and William Sinclair, the men who bailed out Lucille Rand, arrived as sureties for Montefiore. The *Freeman's Journal* told its readers that the men's addresses were unknown but that they 'were believed to be of the Jewish persuasion.' Among the welcoming committee for Montefiore on her release was Constance Markievicz.[4]

*

That was not the end of the day's bad news for the promoters of the kiddies scheme. The Parliamentary Committee of the TUC announced that it was not connected in any way with plans to 'transport' children to England. It attributed the scheme to 'an attempt on the part of certain notoriety hunters to exploit the dispute for their own ends.'

Fortunately, the controversy did not affect financial support from British workers for Dublin. The Dublin Relief Fund set up by the *Daily Citizen*, the official paper of the TUC, collected £30,921. In contrast, the Loyal Tramway Men's Fund sponsored by the *Irish Times* and *Irish Independent* totalled a mere £1,283 18s 8d and was about to be wound up.

However, the decision of the TUC to use the opportunity of the kiddies controversy to distance itself publicly from Larkin shows how deep tensions now were within the trade union movement. On Wednesday, when the Parliamentary Committee met to review the situation, Harry Gosling referred angrily 'to the scandalous manner in which Mr Larkin ... boomed by the capitalist press, was vilifying the Trade Union leaders of this country.' While others felt similarly, it was agreed 'in the interests of the men on strike and locked out in Dublin, not to take any definite action for the time being.'[5]

Whatever Larkin thought of the TUC's comments, that night in Beresford Place he directed his anger at the AOH. 'If Nugent and his order had any love of Dublin they would not have allowed Dublin to be under the disgrace it has been for the past twenty-five years—low wages, insanitary conditions and vile tenements.' Dora Montefiore

> has come here with her money and her strength. She has tried to send some of the poorest children of Dublin away for a holiday. Why should they not have a holiday? (Applause.) Countess Plunkett's children have holidays, and why not the slum children!

He said that his sister, Delia, had been told the previous day by Mrs Dudley Edwardes 'that she would take four poor children, but she added of course, she could not put them with her own boys.'[6] Larkin was not allowing the forthcoming trial to blunt his tongue.

*

On Friday morning a large crowd of supporters cheered Larkin and the other strike leaders as they arrived at Green Street. The throng was prevented from approaching the courthouse by a heavy police guard, including mounted DMP men. The accused had been arraigned before the Commission for the City and County of Dublin, presided over by a senior judge, Mr Justice Madden. He was accompanied on the bench by the sheriff and sub-sheriff for the city, both nationalists, and by their counterparts for the county, both unionists. Their task was to oversee the proceedings of the Dublin Grand Jury, which would have to decide if the men should go to trial.

Altogether there were fifty-two cases to be considered, of which thirty-three related to what Mr Justice Madden described as the 'violence and wrong-doing with which economic disturbances have too often been accompanied.' Twenty-two of the cases arose from the riots of late August and early September, 'when it really seemed for a time as if the forces of disorder were being let loose in the city.' Turning to the cases involving intimidation, he said that any attempt to compel a person not to work for an employer violated 'one of the elementary privileges of a free citizen.'

Henry Hanna was back in his familiar role as senior counsel for the trade unionists. He protested not so much at Madden's address as at the composition of the grand jury to which it was made and that of the petty jury, which would actually hear the case. (Juries in those days were composed exclusively of male owners of property.) Hanna told the court that the recent activities of the AOH, speeches by leading members of the

UIL such as David Sheehy and statements by 'influential members of the Catholic Church' would make it impossible for his clients to receive a fair trial. There were cheers from the gallery, and Mr Justice Madden threatened to clear the court. He told Hanna he was 'satisfied that the trial of the question of fact could be committed to the jurors of the city of Dublin with every confidence that they would do justice impartially.' He also rejected an application that the thirty-three cases arising out of the riots be deferred— Hanna had argued that simultaneous hearings of the riot cases could prejudice the trial of the trade union leaders.[7] Larkin was sent to trial the following Monday.

22

O VER the next few days the newspapers were full of the latest developments in the Dublin kiddies saga. Several of the priests leading the campaign against the scheme were photographed. An extremely well-dressed George Burke posed for pictures between Father McNevin and Father Fleming, another priest involved in the 'rescue' at Kingstown. Father Landers appeared in a *Freeman's Journal* photo-montage wedged between two larger images: on his left is a picture of the DMP mounted police keeping back the crowd at the start of Larkin's trial in Green Street; on his right is Sandymount Castle, a 'fine old mansion,' which Countess Plunkett had acquired to house 150 children 'suffering through [the] present labour trouble.' Directly beneath Father Landers is a portrait of Mrs K. M. Shewell of Galway, who had just been elected honorary secretary of the All-Ireland Donkey Protection Society. It was as ill-assorted a collage as ever appeared in a newspaper, but it faithfully reflected the confusion of the moment.

In the midst of the circus that had now developed around the kiddies scheme, efforts were still being made to deal with the more fundamental problem of the lockout. On Friday, Archbishop Walsh again proposed talks, suggesting that Sir Anthony McDonnell, a former distinguished colonial administrator and Under-Secretary for Ireland, or Sir A. M. Porter, a retired Master of the Rolls, be invited to chair a peace conference. He suggested that the British Labour Board, in line with Harry Gosling's suggestion, could arrange guarantees that any agreement reached would be honoured by the ITGWU.

That evening the president of the TUC, James Seddon, arrived in Dublin to help with the archbishop's initiative. He gave a guarded welcome to the proposal, though he avoided giving any commitments to accepting the negotiating structures proposed. In an obvious reference to the kiddies controversy and in an effort to conciliate the archbishop, he added that he was 'deeply sorry that other circumstances have arisen to complicate an already awkward and serious position.' He hoped that 'good sense will prevail' and that the archbishop's suggestions would lead to 'a speedy and happy consummation of this most unhappy dispute.' Dr Walsh's initiative was also endorsed by Tom Kettle's Industrial Peace Committee, which had called a meeting in the Mansion House for the following Monday to exert public pressure on employers and unions to re-enter talks.[1]

*

Meanwhile the protagonists went about their war with gusto. The ITGWU had managed by now to tie up fifteen large ships in the port, mainly grain vessels. Some had been there almost two months, and the cargoes were rotting. Even shipping companies that had so far managed to avoid the dispute could feel the upper and nether grindstones crunching closer. Dockrell's took the City of Dublin Steam Packet Company to the High Court that Friday for refusing to return boxes of glass. 'Apparently this company has handed themselves over body and soul to the Transport Union,' Dockrell's barrister told the police magistrate. The shipping company argued lamely that its employees objected to the heavy police escort that accompanied the men Dockrell's sent for the glass. Dockrell's counsel asked if his clients were being 'asked to allow their employees to be attacked and possibly murdered, and the goods thrown into the Liffey.' The court gave an order for the delivery of the goods, or their value, to Dockrell's. The plaintiff company was also awarded costs.

Dora Montefiore appeared in the same court on a charge of feloniously taking away George Burke (whose age was now given as fourteen) with intent to deprive the boy's father of his custody and care. She protested that she had been arrested without a warrant. 'When so arrested last evening I refused to make any replies. I told the police they had my body and they must be satisfied with that. (Laughter.)' The magistrate said he would look into the arrest and remanded her on her own bail of £100 until the following Wednesday. Despite the huge amount involved, the prosecuting officer, Superintendent Flynn, objected. 'Are you afraid she'll go away before Wednesday?' asked the magistrate. 'No,' replied Superintendent Flynn. The magistrate responded: 'I suppose you would not be sorry if she did. (Laughter.)'

Most defendants were dealt with more summarily. In the Southern Police Court that day workers sentenced for offences arising from the industrial troubles included four fourteen-year-old boys. Each was sentenced to two weeks' imprisonment for tripping up another boy and threatening him after he decided to return to work at Jacob's biscuit factory.[2]

The sentenced boy workers received only a passing mention; public attention was still centred on the battle for the souls of the children involved in Dora Montefiore's scheme. On the advice of Larkin and his sister, Montefiore agreed that the next batch of children should be despatched to Belfast and efforts made to ensure they went to Catholic homes. Grace Neal, just returned from Liverpool, accompanied Montefiore, Delia Larkin and several mothers to Amiens Street station that evening to put seventeen children on the six o'clock train. Word of the plan inevitably seeped through to the enemy, who were vigilantly patrolling the

North Wall in Dublin and Carlisle Pier in Kingstown.

No doubt many in the crowd gathered at Amiens Street station had seen that day's *Evening Herald*. It published on its front page a telegram from Father James Leech of Liverpool, the priest appointed by the Liverpool Catholic Children's Aid Committee to visit the children who had arrived there on Thursday morning.

> Had the priests and people of Dublin known the atmosphere—anything but Catholic—to which the children have been taken, and in which I was forced to leave them, because their parents had tied the hands of the priests here, their opposition would have been more strenuous. I blush as a priest and a Dublin man to think of what I saw yesterday morning, that Irish parents could forget their sacred trust as parents of these children have done.

The scene that greeted Montefiore on her arrival at the station was one of which she later wrote:

> I had not thought possible in any part of the United Kingdom. At one end of the platform, in front of the compartment into which the parents were attempting to get their children, there was a compact, shouting, gesticulating, fighting crowd of Hibernians. In the centre of this crowd was the little party of children and parents, scattered among them were priests, who were talking, uttering threats against the parents, and forbidding them to send their children to Protestant homes.

Some of the women argued back, and an American journalist covering the scene saw one of the women slap a priest across the face. Montefiore's group admitted defeat when a detachment of police arrived.

> I watched the reinforcement of twenty spike-helmeted destroyers of law and order march on to the platform, make a ring round the little group of parents and children, and then, when they had successfully played the priests' game, and prevented the children leaving for Belfast, the train was whistled and left the station, leaving the now infuriated parents to take their children back to the slum homes which capitalist conditions in Dublin provide for the workers and their children.[3]

The Dublin newspapers reported events somewhat differently, emphasising the religious fervour of the crowd and its catchcries, *Why sell your children!* and *This is not trade unionism, it is socialism*. The names of priests active the previous day, such as Father McNevin, Father Landers, and Father James Flavin, featured prominently, as well as John Nugent and the AOH, whose members were augmented by the National Foresters, another Catholic insurance-cum-nationalist-cum-social-cum-secret society, which shared an overlapping membership with political groups ranging from the UIL to the IRB.

After successfully preventing the small group of women and children from embarking for Belfast, the AOH organised a march to the Father

Mathew statue in O'Connell Street. 'It was one of the most magnificent demonstrations of Catholic devotion and loyalty to the clergy ever witnessed in the city and could not fail to create a profound impression as it marched through the city, loudly cheered by thousands of enthusiastic spectators,' the *Freeman's Journal* reported. Nugent and Father James Fottrell led the marchers. Before they set out, Nugent told them they had done

> noble work … this evening. We are patient in this country, almost I may say to a fault. We are patient with wrong; we are patient with poverty; we are patient with the violation of our rights; but there is one thing that we are not patient with, for patience then would be a crime, not a virtue—we have no patience with them who would deprive the little ones of their faith. (Loud cheers.)

Father Fottrell thanked the crowd in the name of

> the illustrious prelate who has given in time a word of warning to stop the little ones from being robbed from us. (Loud cheers.) His Grace's words came in time and it is a splendid sign of the manhood and the faith of our people that they have so readily taken up his words and carried out his instructions. (Cheers.) May this union between priests and people never be destroyed. (Cheers.)

He directed them to march six abreast down the quays to O'Connell Street 'singing those hymns that remind us of our early instruction.'[4]

There were no speeches at Liberty Hall that night, but there were scuffles between strikers and anti-proselytisers when another procession of priests and AOH members passed Beresford Place at 9:45 p.m. on their way back from the long vigil on the North Wall. Afterwards a small crowd assembled outside Liberty Hall. According to the *Freeman's Journal*,

> they cheered for Larkin, sang 'God Save Larkin,' shouted 'To H— with the A.O.H.' and 'Down with Nugent,' then lapsed into music hall and ragtime melodies, led by the voice of a woman, who appeared, judging from the laughter around her, [to be] improvising topical lines.

The lights in Liberty Hall dimmed just after ten o'clock, and most of the crowd dispersed. A group of young workers, women as well as men, continued the singsong for a while and then set off on an impromptu march through the city.[5] The *Irish Times* put the marchers at no more than four hundred. They wended their way as far as the AOH offices in Rutland Square (Parnell Square), roaring 'Put out the scabs' and 'Down with Nugent,' before someone threw a stone that smashed the fanlight over the door. As the marchers returned to O'Connell Street they were scattered by a police baton charge.

*

On Saturday the *Irish Times*, which had so far given uncritical coverage to the activities of the Catholic clergy and their militant allies in the AOH, began to revise its opinion. Its main leader said that while Larkin's plans to 'deport' children remained 'a foolish scheme that deserved to fail … a word of warning seems necessary—namely, that, when Mr. Larkin and his friends observe the law, they are entitled to ordinary rights of citizenship.' It appeared to the *Times* that

> some persons have taken the law very improperly into their own hands … Intimidation by a transport worker in the cause of trade unionism is not a whit more objectionable than intimidation by a member of the Ancient Order of Hibernians in the cause of religion.

The voice of southern unionism still shrank from reprimanding Catholic clergy directly.[6]

The same day the *Times* published a special report on street begging. A reporter toured the slums with an inspector from the National Society for the Prevention of Cruelty to Children, who told the journalist that the police had their hands so full with the troubles that those trying to enforce the provisions of the Children Act and the Street Trading Act 'are without help.' There were 'hundreds of … poor mites … driven out to beg by drunken and idle parents; but in the present crisis I am forced to believe that the majority of begging children are out on their own.'[7]

23

ONE last attempt was made on Saturday afternoon to take some of the strikers' children out of the city. Given the atmosphere that now existed, it required extraordinary physical and moral hardihood to even contemplate such a forlorn hope. Earlier that day the *Evening Herald* published 'remarkable revelations' about the Dublin children in Liverpool, announcing to readers that all had been placed in non-Catholic homes, where their faith was in imminent danger.

A report had been commissioned from an investigative journalist in Liverpool who, the *Herald* assured its readers, was 'absolutely unbiased.' He had tracked down eighteen children. The largest group, five boys and seven girls, were staying at Kelmscott, a large house owned by a Mrs Helah Criddle standing in its own grounds in the middle-class suburb of Wallasey. He found the children playing in the gardens and the surrounding fields. 'Most of these mites—their ages range from four to thirteen—have never seen "the country" before and they were making the most of the unexpected holiday and the equally unexpected luxury.' They had been reclothed and were well fed, though on a strict vegetarian diet. Most of the other children were living in comfortable if less luxurious surroundings in the Liverpool suburbs, including three boys at Fred Bower's own house.

Father Leech was quoted in the report, and he admitted the children were well cared for materially. But he was concerned 'for the little travellers' spiritual welfare.' The problem was that members of all the host families were active in local labour and trade union circles; Father Leech described them as 'Socialists of the most extreme kind.' Their efforts to co-operate with him in sending the children to Catholic schools and to Mass on Sundays had not allayed his suspicions.

> As to proselytising, all I can say is that if their faith is not in danger, I do not know what proselytism is … A 'Birds' Nest' could not be worse.

The *Herald* also published a telegram from Canon Pinnington. In a box of bold type on the front page headed 'Their faith is in great danger,' he said that two girls are already placed in a non-Catholic home for destitute children in Liverpool. Others are boarded out with non-Catholics and extreme Socialists. The children are being exploited for party purposes.

In fact the two children in the home for destitute children had nothing to do with the Montefiore scheme: they had been put there by their parents, who had arrived in Liverpool penniless after being evicted from their home in Foley Street.[1]

It was Francis Sheehy-Skeffington, that man of moral steel and quixotic gallantry, who escorted a small group to Kingsbridge station shortly before 4 p.m. It consisted of the young suffragist veteran Mary Lawless, a seven-year-old boy, and a father with three small children in tow. The plan was to put the children on the four o'clock train for Hazelhatch. Mary Lawless had made arrangements for the children to stay with a Catholic family on the nearby estate of her father, Lord Cloncurry. Perhaps the group hoped for safety in small numbers; but Sheehy-Skeffington was too distinctive a figure to pass unnoticed. The suspicions of the crowd were no doubt heightened by the fact that the ultimate destination of the train was Rosslare Harbour.

Sheehy-Skeffington was, in the words of the *Sunday Independent*, 'rather badly handled.'[2] According to his own account he was knocked to the ground and 'bruised about the head and body.' One man punched him in the face several times, and there were shouts of 'Kill him!' The assault must have been serious, because the police not only rescued him but charged two of his assailants on the spot.[3] Meanwhile the seven-year-old had been seized by members of the mob; the other three children 'ran outside, screaming and shouting,' while their father was 'hustled by the crowd.'[4] It may have been because of Mary Lawless's involvement in the fracas that the police took the unusual step of charging the organisers of the protest, John Nugent and two priests, Father Flood and Father Clarke, with assault, riot, and kidnapping.

The charges were later withdrawn. Characteristically, Sheehy-Skeffington refused to testify against his assailants after charges were withdrawn against the more prominent accused. 'If ... more astute persons ... cannot be put in the dock, I don't want to press for punishment against these men,' he told the court.[5]

A kidnap mania now seized the city. Just before the 6:55 p.m. train for Rosslare left Kingsbridge, a taxi drove up and a boy got out, accompanied by 'a well dressed man and young lady.' They were immediately surrounded by the crowd, who refused to let them board the train. The man gave his name and address and explained that the woman was his daughter and the boy his grandson; he was taking them to his farm in County Kilkenny. But the crowd refused to release the group until the man agreed to a policeman and a priest returning with him in the taxi to the Dublin address he had given the crowd to check his bona fides.

In Meath Street the secretary of the Philanthropic Reform Society, Miss

Isherwood, had to seek refuge in the presbytery of the Catholic Church after being mistaken for 'one of the women engaged in ... the deportation of children.' On the North Wall another well-dressed woman was prevented from boarding the 7:45 p.m. ferry with her child. Even after she opened her luggage and produced her marriage certificate she failed to convince the mob that she was not a 'proselytiser'; it took police intervention to secure her release and the return of her child.

Far from protecting passengers, the ferry companies that night gave the priests 'every facility in seeing that no children were being smuggled away.' As the last ship sailed there was 'a great outburst of cheering,' and several Jesuits spoke to the crowd. Father Fottrell was once more to the fore in addressing what the *Irish Times* described as the 'vigilance party'. He reminded them all that they were there as Catholics and took no sides in the current industrial dispute; it was only when their religion was touched that the church intervened, and in such situations 'the priests would always be to the fore.' Father Potter reminded them that they were a religious gathering, but immediately added that 'if there be opposition from some quarters I would ask you to act as Catholic men and true Irishmen.' Father Fottrell then organised the crowd into ranks and marched them back to the city singing 'Faith of Our Fathers,' 'Hail, Glorious St Patrick,' and 'Ave Maria.'[6]

The clergy and AOH now controlled the movement of children in and out of Dublin more effectively than the ITGWU controlled the traffic of goods. The rough justice dispensed by the priest-led crowds smacked far more of the type of 'French Revolutionary' behaviour so decried by Father Curran during August's riots than anything the ITGWU had attempted.

*

With Dora Montefiore and Lucille Rand facing charges in the police courts, Larkin and his fellow union leaders consigned for trial in the same week, and many trade unionists in Ireland and Britain dissociating themselves from recent developments, an early collapse of the strike appears to have been expected by the employers. Indeed Dr Walsh's success in aborting the Dublin kiddies scheme appears to have helped undo the other arm of his strategy—the achievement of a negotiated peace.

While Sheehy-Skeffington was being assaulted at Kingsbridge, secret talks had been taking place between Murphy and Seddon, who had come to Dublin as part of a TUC delegation that also included the TUC secretary, Charles Bowerman—who was helping Seddon administer the British relief fund for the strikers—the secretary of the National Transport Workers' Federation, Robert Williams, and its president, Harry Gosling. Seddon, however, had arrived ahead of his colleagues and had met Dr Walsh privately. The archbishop had been briefed on the situation by several employers, including Frederick Wookey and J. and C. McGloughlin, a leading manufacturer of ecclesiastical metalware. As a result of these briefings he probably warned Seddon that there would be serious resistance to a negotiated settlement.[7]

It was the Sunday edition of the *Freeman's Journal* that broke the story of the secret talks and, in the process, seriously damaged their slim prospects of success. Nevertheless Dr Walsh persevered. He left early from a beginning-of-term luncheon at University College to attend 'business of the most pressing character.'[8] His aim appears to have been to have a settlement formula agreed before the meeting of the Dublin Industrial Peace Committee at the Mansion House on Monday night. Lorcan Sherlock was to preside at the meeting, and it would be a triumphant vindication of the political status quo in the city if a holy trinity of the Catholic Church, the nationalist Lord Mayor and the moderate elements within industry could end the dispute.

The six Irish Party MPs for Dublin had also been persuaded to come out of political hibernation and appeal for peace. The difficulty in their agreeing to a joint initiative may be gauged from the language of the letter they sent to the newspapers on Saturday.

> Though we repudiate any responsibility in the matter at all, and though we refuse emphatically to take sides, still, as the Parliamentary representatives of the areas affected by the present labour troubles in Dublin City and County, we desire to say that the action of his Grace the Archbishop of Dublin, in endeavouring to find an end to those troubles, commends itself in our judgement as the first proposal calculated to lead to a settlement, and that we earnestly hope that it may be accepted by representatives of both parties. Yours faithfully, J. J. Clancy, W. Field, J. P. Nannetti, Patrick J. Brady, W. Abraham and W. F. Cotton.[9]

*

There was another reason why Dr Walsh might have felt hopeful that a settlement might be near. Seddon had probably told him of the decision of the Parliamentary Committee of the TUC at its meeting on 5 October not to send any cash, as opposed to provisions, to Dublin Trades Council. The TUC clearly intended using its financial muscle to make the Dublin men amenable to talks.

All the unions affected by the lockout were in dire straits, but none in direr straits than the ITGWU. Its bill for strike pay was £2,909 a week, but it had only £706 left in the bank. At the same meeting at which Gosling had given vent to his feelings about Larkin, the Parliamentary Committee had received an appeal from the ITGWU for 'a loan of £1,000 to tide them over the present deadlock.' Bowerman had been instructed to reply that the TUC fund could be used only to supply food, clothing, and fuel.[10] Once they arrived in Dublin, the TUC men no doubt made it clear to Larkin that his attacks on the British trade union establishment were not helping his cause.

If so, it did nothing to cramp his style, or that of the other strike leaders. The ITGWU held a march to the Phoenix Park on Sunday afternoon, and all the members of Dublin Trades Council facing trial during the coming assizes spoke at the meeting that followed. They freely admitted that the unions were in grave financial difficulties but said that their members would not be starved back to work. With one exception they defended the Dublin kiddies scheme, on the grounds that it was not aimed at undermining the church. William Partridge went so far as to say that he had sought an interview with Dr Walsh to explain face to face the intentions of the scheme's organisers.

The speaker who would make no concessions to the archbishop was, of course, Larkin. Unrepentant, he attacked the Hibernians, the British union leaders, and the clergy; he attacked the archbishop in all but name. Nugent he despatched quickly with the telling remark that his actions over the past few days 'have done more to jeopardise the cause of home rule than all the Carsons in Ireland.' As for the church, he declared:

> The priest who says I dared to allow a child to be proselytised is a liar in his heart. The religion that won't stand a month's holiday is not, by God, the religion I hold. I have starved and hungered through every town in England but it never weakened my faith.

While workers were being arrested 'for calling a scab a scab,' parents who took their children to a railway station were being brutally assaulted while the police stood by. Turning to the controversy with the TUC, Larkin said he had been blamed

> for saying things across the water … I have found it necessary to criticise the actions of certain men, and I did it in a friendly way, helpful to them as well as to myself.

In a veiled reference to the financial pressure the TUC was trying to exert on the ITGWU, he added cryptically that 'no English trades union could buy me for £30,000.' He and some of his fellow-speakers were going on trial before a packed jury shortly, but if he went to jail 'for years and years, I have done the work I was born for.'

Robert Williams, secretary of the National Transport Workers' Federation and the British union leader most sympathetic to the strikers, also spoke. He was anxious to maintain unity. He attacked the *Freeman's Journal* for alleging that Seddon had been holding secret meetings with employers behind the backs of the strike committee.

> It is an abominable and pernicious untruth. We are not here to give guarantees. We are here to demand guarantees from Murphy and his gang, and that they should withdraw their abominable document. (Applause.) There is a suggestion that you are divided among yourselves. ('No, no.') We want you to be loyal. Present a united front. Victory is within your reach. The employers are running to try to meet a man like Seddon, and because our friends, in their desire to settle the whole dispute, meet some of them, the press are watching them. The employers have given away a private conference and 'blown the gaff,' and the press has been ferreting out information to which it is not entitled.

How this convoluted explanation of the secret negotiations was received by the crowd is lost to posterity, but they cheered when Williams said that Gosling and Seddon were bringing £2,000 in cash for the strikers. They might not have cheered so lustily if they had known what had really been decided at the Parliamentary Committee, and that Williams was in effect trying to force his colleagues' hands.[11]

As expected, the employers rejected the overtures of the TUC leaders that weekend, and Dr Walsh's efforts were once more wasted. Charles Coghlan, secretary of the employers' executive committee, told the archbishop that the ITGWU's record of violating agreements, engaging in sympathetic strikes and 'tyrannical action' generally made it 'impossible' to deal with the union. He reiterated the claim of the Employers' Federation that it was not out to break trade unionism but that it was 'determined to fight against ... the methods of the Irish Transport Union.'[12]

As that shrewd observer of the scene Stephen Gwynn, Irish Party MP for Galway, put it in a letter to the archbishop a couple of days later, 'those idiot women have developed a situation which gives victory to the employers.' He felt that such a victory 'means infinite trouble in the future,' and would be

> inevitably, even if not reasonably, regarded by the Radical section amongst the workers as a win by 'clericalism'. It is the seed of a dangerous growth.[13]

*

The attention of most nationalists that weekend was concentrated on Scotland, where Asquith had promised to deliver the long-promised antidote to Churchill's mischievous Dundee speech. Speaking in his own neighbouring constituency of East Fife, he said the British government would not be intimidated by the threats of force coming out of Ulster. Nevertheless, he hoped for a settlement by consent, as it was 'of supreme importance to the future of Ireland that her new system of Government should not start with the apparent triumph of one section and the humiliation of another.' As for Lord Loreburn's suggestion of a formal conference,

> there is no need for the machinery of a conference. If there is a general disposition for an interchange of views and suggestions, free and without prejudice to consider the question ... both I and my colleagues are perfectly ready to take part in it.[14]

Redmond was 'quite satisfied with Asquith's speech' and seemed blind to its ambiguities.[15]

The *Sunday Independent* and *Freeman's Journal* gave an ecstatic welcome to Asquith's 'great speech'. The *Sunday Independent* also found space on the front page for a speech T. P. O'Connor gave in support of the Liberal candidate at the forthcoming by-election in Reading, in which he challenged the unionists to produce a single instance where 'the Catholic majority in the South represented religious bigotry and persecution.' O'Connor was obviously out of touch with events in Dublin—as was Birrell. The Chief Secretary had spent the week 'on a little tour of Ulster.' Sir James Dougherty had introduced him to a host of 'thin lipped, bitter, black, teeth neglected Presbyterians, with queer old churches—and services without a squeak of music or a hymn.' While he admired Belfast City Hall, he told Asquith: 'Personally, my instinct tells me these people are WRONG.'

In the same letter he referred in passing to 'the kidnapping of the Dublin children' as

> an outrage. In the first place, there are no starving children in Dublin. In the second place, if there were, the place swarms with homes. It was a new advertising device of a few silly women, but it broke the strike.

It was a damning indictment of his own ignorance of the realities; and if further evidence were needed of how detached he had become from life in the capital, he provided it with his casual aside to the Prime Minister that 'Larkin has gone to prison for seven months.'[16]

24

ON Monday 27 October, Larkin finally stood trial. Huge crowds of workers filled the streets surrounding Green Street courthouse that morning; once again a strong police presence, including a squad of twenty mounted DMP men, kept them well back. Those seeking entry were 'closely scanned,' according to the *Evening Herald*, which also noted that clergymen were 'prominent amongst those who followed the proceedings.'

At one point it looked as if the trial would not take place. Larkin was delayed by the crowds, and then a lengthy legal battle took place over the empanelling of a jury. Henry Hanna KC objected to several employers being selected; in truth, some employers were not keen to serve, including Hugh Wallace, one of the city's leading coal merchants. Another was John Byrne, a small employer whose men were out because of the lockout, who probably summed up the view of other reluctant jurors when he told the court he would 'do what is fair, but would just as lief be off the jury.'

Some jurors, on the other hand, were keen to serve. Thomas Ladd of Varian and Company, the brush manufacturers, did not feel that past clashes with Larkin disqualified him, nor did Thomas Nicholls of A. C. Taylor and Company, shippers and carriers, whose men were now locked out.

Employers were not the only jurors hostile to Larkin. John Kavanagh, a farrier by trade, at first denied having called Larkin a thief and unfit to represent trade unionists in Dublin but admitted under cross-examination that he had done so in the Unionist-sponsored working men's club in Wellington Quay and elsewhere. 'I said that men were taken out of work who should not be taken out, and I say it still,' he said doggedly.[1]

It was an indication of the seriousness with which the Irish executive took the case, and the urgent need to put Larkin away, that he was tried separately from the other strike leaders and that the prosecution team was led by the Attorney-General, J. F. Moriarty. He opened his case by stating that Larkin was not on trial for being a strike leader but because he was 'a wicked and dangerous criminal.' He had preached sedition and incited citizens to riot, to pillage, and to rob.

> The city is in a sad way, and no doubt a great number of timid people are very greatly afraid of the outcome of all this business, but … the best

panacea for troubles such as are prevailing at present … has been found by experience to be the firm and impartial administration of the criminal law.

He predicted that if Larkin was not convicted

then anarchy must prevail. There would be an end to the bonds of society, and for a short time Mr Larkin or somebody in his position will be at the head of affairs, and then that will be followed by military despotism. That has been the history of the past. It is to stop that kind of thing that this prosecution is taken.

He recalled the meetings in Beresford Place in late August when Larkin announced that a 'monster demonstration' would take place in Sackville Street on Sunday 31 August. He told how the meeting had been proclaimed, and that Larkin had burnt the proclamation banning it.

The main evidence against Larkin was his own words, and Moriarty cited at length from his speeches of 26 and 29 August.

One can't help thinking that there is a great deal of the Ancient Pistol about Mr Larkin, but … it would never do not to treat him as a person responsible for his language, having regard to the tremendous influence he exercises over so many people in the city … I understand that Mr Larkin is too proud a man to take back one word of what he said. The King is no King to him. He recognises no law but his own law. He proclaims through windows, from chimney pots and elsewhere his doctrines, which are subversive of all law and order and good government.

The ubiquitous police note-taker, Detective-Sergeant Richard Revelle, was then called to give evidence from his shorthand notes, which he took 'unobserved under his top coat' in the 'middle of the crowd.' He accepted under cross-examination from Hanna that the meeting was orderly, apart from Larkin's burning of the proclamation.

Hanna's main defence was that his client could not expect a fair trial in the present climate. Given that Larkin was condemned out of his own mouth, his counsel had little option but to attack the legitimacy of the legal process itself.

Larkin is a man opposed to the jurors in almost every way … The jurors represent to a certain extent capitalism, and the man who has to be tried by them is … the enemy of their interests. But still the Crown said, 'Try him,' and the unworthy appeal was made to the jury that it would probably settle this strike if Larkin was got out of the way.

In the five years since Larkin came to Dublin he had 'reached down his hand to the people who were in the very mire of poverty and degradation.' The workers were 'entitled to a leader,' and as 'the tribune of the poor,' Larkin 'is not bound on every occasion to use honeyed words.' He had at least 'always counselled temperance and sobriety amongst his followers,' and even the police admitted that his meetings were orderly and well behaved.

Summing up, Mr Justice Madden said that Detective-Sergeant Revelle's notes had not been disputed. While trade unions and strikes were perfectly legal, 'a certain class of words spoken in furtherance of a strike are illegal … Taking the speech as a whole, it was an appeal to angry passions likely to cause violence and breaches of the peace.'

It took the jury only thirty minutes to return with a verdict of guilty of uttering seditious language. In a speech from the dock, Larkin said he was never afraid to accept his responsibilities.

> I have led a clean life. I have always stood up for my class. The government … has brought the prosecution for a purpose, and it will recoil on themselves.

Unfortunately, he concluded his address by drifting into the personal recriminations that so often spoiled the effect of his speeches. Mr Justice Madden, clearly annoyed, sentenced him to seven months' imprisonment. 'We'll keep the flag flying, Jim. Don't fret,' William O'Brien shouted from the body of the court.[2]

*

William Martin Murphy had no doubt of it. He believed that Larkinism had nearly run its course but that the halo of martyrdom would undo much of the damage inflicted by the Dublin kiddies fiasco.[3] The lockout was indeed about to enter a new, even grimmer phase without the lightening touch of the great labour impresario. The man who only two days earlier had assembled five hundred members of the ITGWU at Liberty Hall for a cinema newsreel and told them 'to wave their caps and … give life to the picture'[4] was in Mountjoy prison.

Not surprisingly, the *Daily Herald* correspondent reported on Monday that

> to walk in Dublin streets is almost enough to make one despair. Women and children with hollow cheeks and hollow eyes, barefooted, ragged, and splashed with mud, accost one every few yards, and trot alongside until one is shamed into turning out a coin. The place is swarming with police. Jaunting cars dash along with loads of laughing RIC men, and laden lorries must have two or three police passengers added to their loads. Capital, the Law, and now the priests, are against the industrial rebels, and yet they refuse to go back to wage slavery. It is magnificent.[5]

That night a crowd of about two thousand gathered outside Liberty Hall, despite heavy rain, to hear the speeches. The main burden fell on William Partridge, the union's finest public speaker after Larkin. For once his normal religious inhibitions deserted him and he attacked the priests 'who now appear to be in league with the employers.' He told the crowd that 'a fictitious agitation has been got up,' and some of the priests 'who acted as corner-boys, and seemed to forget their sacred calling, would be better employed in assisting the starving children than in leading mobs with sticks to attack the members of the Transport Workers' Union and otherwise aiding the employers.' The best way to keep faith with their imprisoned leader was to continue the fight to an honourable and honest settlement.

> We are not downhearted. We know we have right and justice on our side. We know that our Saviour was vilified and cast into jail … We are satisfied that those who wrong us will one day hang their heads in shame.

The now nightly procession of priests and Hibernians formed a bizarrely appropriate backdrop to Partridge's words as they marched past stridently singing 'Faith of Our Fathers.' But their numbers were small, possibly because 'kidnapped' children were becoming an increasingly scarce commodity. The strong police escort kept the two groups apart.[6]

The meeting of the Dublin Industrial Peace Committee in the Mansion House that night was similarly subdued. Instead of being able to preside over a major peace initiative, Lorcan Sherlock could only appeal to the combatants to take up the suggestion of a peace agreement proposed by Dr Walsh. 'The trade, the commerce of the city, is receiving every day a more deadly blow—a blow that is striking at both employers and workers—and our whole industries are endangered, as well as the peace of the general community.'

The Church of Ireland Archbishop of Dublin, Dr Joseph Ferguson Peacocke, was on the platform to say that he 'most heartily agreed' with Dr Walsh's proposal of a peace conference. In a further demonstration of consensus by the religious of the city, the Dean of St Patrick's, Rev. C. Ovenden, proposed the motion calling for 'a private and unconditional' conference, where the two sides could avail of Dr Walsh's good offices. For himself, he said that 'living in the slums—and delighting in the slums—it breaks my heart at what I have seen.'

Pierce O'Mahony, an extensive Catholic landlord, former Parnellite MP and maverick constitutional nationalist who preferred to be known as 'the O'Mahony', seconded the motion. He reminded his audience of Sir George Askwith's warning that 'even if a victory were ultimately won by the employers it would not lead to permanent peace in this city.' O'Mahony had 'two very firm convictions' about the present crisis. The first was 'that no man living could cause a strike like the present one—there must be some real grievances at the back of it. (Applause.)' His other conviction was that

> organised labour is always more moderate than disorganised labour. (Applause.) … What industries require more than anything else is a self-respecting working class living under reasonable conditions. (Applause.)

At this stage supporters of the strikers in the audience grew so boisterous that it looked as if they might turn on the police note-takers, whose evidence had helped convict Larkin earlier in the day. When the Lord Mayor asked the policemen to leave, they did so with alacrity.

Father Aloysius, president of the Workmen's Temperance Committee, then addressed the meeting. He was widely respected in the trade union movement, not least because he never used his work among the poor for political purposes. The man who, less than three years later, would hear the confession of James Connolly on the eve of his execution expressed his sorrow at a dispute that had 'rent the capital of Ireland in twain.' He felt that 'in the storm of excited passion we cannot expect men to listen to calm reason.' Why previous initiatives had failed he could not say, but 'feelings ... have changed to some extent, and a conference might succeed today that failed yesterday. (Hear, hear.)' It was hardly a great speech, but the very presence of a Catholic priest on the platform was an important development.

Even more surprising was the appearance of William Field, the longest-sitting MP for the city and, though sixty-four years of age, still by far the gamest. His long service did not save him from a heckling, but he talked his way through it with aplomb, and without being any more contentious or partisan than Father Aloysius. 'Money has been lost, employment has been lost, bitter feelings engendered, and nobody is the better for it,' he said. As a 'non-combatant' and 'man of peace' he hoped that public pressure on both parties would make peace prevail. It was no wonder that the next morning's *Irish Times* published a letter from 'Onlooker' asking that

> the Nationalist members for Dublin ... give us some hint of their policy on ... strikes and lockouts ... They are sitting on the very centre of the fence. Even for the sympathetic strike, condemned not only by Sir George Askwith, but by some of the best known trade union leaders in England, they have not a word of disapproval. If a Bill were brought into the Irish Parliament to declare this kind of strike illegal, can anyone predict how they would vote?

It was left to others to abandon the 'very centre' of the fence that night. The Warden of Trinity Hall, Miss Cunningham, said she felt nervous speaking about children and the strike after the controversy of recent days. Nevertheless she felt they had to achieve industrial peace for the sake of the children. 'If children are to be brought up in an atmosphere of hatred, it would be worse than bringing them up ... starving.'

W. B. Yeats could never be accused of sitting on any fences; he leaped right over this one. He said he knew it was his duty to be impartial, but

> I cannot imagine a more difficult task. No man who walked through the slums of Dublin, and saw the tumbling rabbit warrens of misery, could easily be impartial ... The dispute has done untold damage not only to

the financial but also to the moral interests of Dublin. Every one of us has a right to speak here, even those who have no part in the dispute, like myself, and whose selfish interests are suffering. I am one of the directors of a theatre, which is suffering every week as a result of the dispute. (Laughter.) Those who went into the conference would have to think of those outside, who are not combatants.

I do not complain of the fanaticism of Dublin. I do not think that we can have strong religious feeling anywhere without fanaticism; but I have not words sufficient to express my contempt for the press of Dublin. (Applause.)

Sherlock told Yeats to 'stick to the resolution.' The poet replied that when he came to the meeting he wondered

whether the Lord Mayor was a tall man or a short man. If he is a tall man I shall be able to say all I want, because his head will not be sufficiently near his heart to get enough blood to think quickly. (Laughter.) I see …that the Lord Mayor is a short man, and I knew I would be stopped. (Laughter.) All I will say is this: some day we will have to reckon with those who have fomented fanaticism in Dublin to break up the organisation of the workers. (Applause.)

Rev. Denham Osbourne came next, and he managed to refocus the meeting on the business in hand. A leading shipping firm had told him that goods worth a million pounds had been left lying on the docks and that £30,000 worth might have rotted already. Equally pressing was the plight of the unemployed. Even workers 'outside the fighting line' wanted housing and wages for the thousands of unskilled workers that would make life bearable for them and their families.

Once more Edward Lee was on a peace committee platform. He avoided apportioning blame for the dispute but said that once it was out of the way he was convinced that the question of the slums should be tackled. 'Men of capital ought to be ashamed to have it go out to the ends of the earth that so many families are living each in one room. (Hear, hear.)'

It was left to Tom Kettle, the architect of the Industrial Peace Committee, to close the meeting, and he used the opportunity to attack Yeats. Perhaps it was the failure of Dr Walsh's initiative that made him uncharacteristically petulant.

I am not going to talk platform religion. If there is anything worse than cheap platform religion it is cheap platform irreligion. (Applause.)

When Yeats tried to protest that he had attacked no man's religion, he was ruled out of order. Sherlock then had to contend with heckling from suffragists and their labour supporters in the hall, who demanded to know why no women had been nominated to the Industrial Peace Committee. Sherlock quickly put the motion supporting Dr Walsh's initiative and declared it passed, amid the uproar.[7]

Despite the acrimony over Yeats's contribution to the debate, the meeting at the Mansion House showed that there was another, liberal Ireland emerging. However, despite the ambitions of Tom Kettle, it had none of the raw power that the main protagonists displayed on the streets.

*

The deliberations of the Industrial Peace Committee had little impact on events over the next few days. On Tuesday the hopes of Dublin employers were raised by reports of 'an important change' in the attitude of the TUC to the dispute, which came from the usually reliable Labour Press Agency. Once more the secretary of the NTWF, Robert Williams, who was still in Dublin, denounced the newspaper reports.[8] He told the *Irish Times* that 'the most effective safeguard against the sympathetic strike is the granting and maintenance of decent wages and reasonable conditions of employment.' He described the attitude of employers as

> similar to that of the British employers during the middle of the last century ... Employers must make up their minds that trade unionism in Ireland is going to stay ... and all this talk of ... syndicalism, socialism or any other ism is a puerile attempt to throw dust in the eyes of the public.

It was whistling in the dark. With Larkin imprisoned, the employers began to move more onto the offensive. Firms such as Dixon and Company, which owned the Erne Soap and Candle Works and which had been closed by aggressive picketing earlier in the dispute, announced that they had 'gradually employed a completely new staff of men and boys, who are rapidly learning their work, and the soap works are now running at full speed.' However, the company admitted that its foreign trade continued to suffer because of the situation at the docks.

The previous week the *Irish Times* had published a letter from 'A Small Employer' pointing out

> the urgent necessity of the importation of ... strike breakers. It is simply amazing that Dublin shipping companies should stop all their sailings for such a lengthened time; and the policy—to say the least—is decidedly weak.[9]

Even the larger coal merchants, who were beginning to recruit new employees, knew that without ships to bring the coal in, this was only a short-term expedient, and they began to look more seriously at the possibility of using strike-breakers. They were no doubt heartened by reports from the Free Labour Congress in London that week. On Monday its new president, W. Collier, said that 'sympathetic strikes, mob law, cowardly assaults by pickets, reckless blockading of business and wanton disregard of the rights of free labour will bring about a revolution in trade unionism such as will put an end to the labour agitators for ever.'[10]

On Wednesday morning the first large group of 'free labourers' arrived at the North Wall on the London and North-Western ship from Holyhead to work for T. and C. Martin, the leading timber merchants in the city. They were supplied by a Free Labour Congress affiliate, the Independent Labour Association of Manchester.[11]

*

Opponents of Larkin and all his works could also draw comfort from the latest reports in the *Evening Herald*, as it continued its campaign to stop the 'export' of children to Britain. On Tuesday its front page featured another telegram from Father Leech with the 'startling revelation' that only sixteen of the nineteen children staying in Lancashire were known to have attended Mass the previous Sunday. 'I ask the parents in the name of God to take back their children at once,' he wrote.

Next day the newspaper triumphantly announced 'Child-exporting at an end: Splendid victory of Catholics of Dublin: Mrs. Rand and Mrs. Montefiore to leave.' That morning in the Northern Police Court, T. J. Campbell, instructed by the ITGWU's solicitors, said he was 'authorised to say that the work of these ladies is at an end in Dublin.' On the basis of these assurances, the Attorney-General agreed to let the charges be held over.

Even now opponents of the scheme were far from satisfied. Father Thomas Ryan from Westland Row appealed to the court not to let the women go until they guaranteed to return the children already in England. The magistrate told the priest he had no jurisdiction to make such an order.

Defeated but unbowed, Dora Montefiore would resume the war of words from England. Lucille Rand appears to have suffered a breakdown after her ordeal, which horrified her society friends in both London and America. One of them wrote a strong letter to Dr Walsh expressing her outrage at the way his priests had behaved; the State Department in Washington instructed the US ambassador, Walter Page, a committed Anglophile, to raise Rand's treatment with the British government.[12] Such protests made little impact on an increasingly self-confident breed of Catholic nationalist.

25

FAR from being abashed by the bad publicity that vigilante activity had attracted to their cause, the AOH militants were boasting that soon they would be setting up a union of their own to replace the discredited ITGWU. The *Irish Times* struck a more sober attitude in its editorial of Tuesday 28 October, the day after Larkin's conviction.

> It would be very unwise … to exult at Mr. Larkin's discomfiture, or base overweening hopes on the removal of his personality from the arena. We must allow to the transport workers of Dublin the same instincts of pride and loyalty which we claim for ourselves. The best way to enlarge Mr. Larkin's halo at this time would be to make capital out of his imprisonment.

The employers had a right to be 'up in arms' at the methods of Larkin and his union, which had 'deeply wounded the city's trade and commerce,' but this was

> not a time for contemplating, much less talking about, victory or defeat.
> We are all sick and tired of the labour troubles; we are all out of pocket by them; we are all ashamed of the exposure which this strike has made of the misery and poverty of our slums. The moment has come for an effort to end the whole wretched business, and to break down the barrier which now divides Dublin into hostile camps.

The *Times* proclaimed that 'peace is in the air … but everybody is in a fog' about how to achieve it. But it added to the confusion. It welcomed the intervention of the British labour leaders and their offer of pledges of good behaviour for the ITGWU, only to berate them for continuing to send food and money to the strikers. It welcomed Dr Walsh's suggestion that the employers and unions agree the appointment of 'some prominent Irishman' to chair a new round of talks (a clear signal that Sir George Askwith was no longer considered suitable) but dismissed the Industrial Peace Committee's efforts to promote a similar project.

In a clear reference to the clash between Kettle and Yeats the previous night at the Mansion House, it said: 'It is a pity that these friends of concord should have built a temple to discord in the shape of a sharp altercation between a professor and a poet.' Yet it accepted that the citizens of Dublin are getting rather tired of waiting for the critical overture. They will not greatly care from which side it comes, so long as it comes soon.

It added that citizens were particularly impatient at the 'silence of the dead' maintained by the six Irish Party MPs for the city and county. P. J. Brady, the solicitor, railway company director and St Vincent de Paul activist who represented St Stephen's Green ward, was singled out for special mention.

Messrs. Jacob pay wages to the sons and daughters of many hundreds of Mr. P. J. Brady's constituents, but Mr. Brady was dumb. In the astonishing letter which we published yesterday the six members repudiate 'any responsibility in the matter at all.' They have, on the contrary, a terrible and disgraceful responsibility.

The following day's *Freeman's Journal* maintained an understandable silence over the inactivity of the Irish Party MPs, but its editorial echoed the sentiments of its rival in every other respect. There was a feeling that, with Larkin out of the way, a settlement could be made.

*

Within hours of Larkin's conviction, the executive committee of the Employers' Federation issued a statement reiterating the need to end the 'tyrannical action of the Irish Transport Union,' the 'violation of agreements,' and 'sympathetic strikes.' Scenting victory, its secretary, Charles Coghlan, said that his members were 'prepared to consider any proposal that will have the effect of permanently removing these objectionable conditions.'[1]

The secretary of the NTWF, Robert Williams, who had remained in Dublin to monitor the situation, tried to calm things. He said the Dublin unions were anxious for peace but that rumours of British union leaders moving to settle the dispute 'from the other side of the channel' were 'calculated to prolong rather than to shorten the dispute.'

The reality was somewhat different. When the TUC's Parliamentary Committee met on Tuesday 28 October it followed Seddon's advice and authorised only the disbursement of the £2,000 Williams had promised at the Phoenix Park meeting to those Dublin unions affiliated to the TUC. This automatically excluded the ITGWU.[2] Next morning, Seddon, Gosling and Bowerman caught the boat train from London on yet another peace mission; they arrived at the Gresham Hotel the same evening. By then Larkin's successor as leader of the ITGWU, James Connolly, had seized the initiative. His first act was to announce on Tuesday that the kiddies scheme was at an end. He told the press that he disagreed 'to a certain extent' with the scheme, because of the hostility it had aroused in Dublin. Besides, the 10s it cost to send a child to England would keep the same youngster fed at home for three weeks.[3]

On Wednesday night, in Beresford Place, he went much further. First he appealed to the crowd, 'as James Larkin's representative ... to be as loyal to me as you have been to ... Larkin.' There was a more measured timbre from the platform now. With discipline and solidarity, and acting on the instructions of their leader, they were bound to carry their flag to victory. They would have

> no peace, or no settlement, except on terms laid down by those who belonged to the Transport Workers' Union. That is our motto, and by it we will stand or fall. (Cheers.) Everything will depend on ourselves for an honourable settlement; nobody can betray or sell us but ourselves; no-one can make terms for us but ourselves; and I am confidently sure that our friends who have crossed over tonight from England will not go back on these terms.
>
> If the trades union leaders from across the water are prepared to accept peace at any price, and threaten to withdraw their food ships and support from the workers of Dublin, if they do not accept our settlement, then I would say to those delegates, 'Take back your food ships, for the workers of Dublin will not surrender their position for all the ships on the sea.' (Cheers.)

But he was not finished there. He had a warning for the Liberal government, which had imprisoned Larkin and 'ranged themselves on the side of the capitalists in this fight.' If they did not release Larkin,

> men will be sent out from Dublin into the constituencies at every by-election to oppose the candidates of the Liberal government. That will imperil home rule, we might be told; but we have waited long enough for home rule, and the only home rule we are prepared to accept will be one which is satisfactory to the whole people ... including those of the working classes, who are the only ... sincere home-rulers in this country. (Cheers.)

The employers had flouted Dr Walsh and the Industrial Peace Committee; they had imported fifty scab labourers into the city, and were planning to bring more. The duty of the workers now was to 'be out early in the morning to picket ... and ... picket in battalions.' If necessary, 'the streets of Dublin will run with blood, and we will see how far the employers are prepared to go with this work. (Cheers.)'

Williams also spoke, and he matched Connolly for militancy, though it was a militancy riddled with skilfully crafted qualifications. 'I am a socialist,' he assured the crowd, and 'there can be no peace between the employing and the employed class; it might be a temporary truce, but the fight will have to go on until we establish the principles of socialism amongst ourselves.' Amid the rhetoric of war he was still trying to plant the seeds of a settlement. He promised them food and he promised them cash, waving a telegram he had received from Ben Tillet.

Williams, a Cardiff coal-trimmer by trade, showed his Nonconformist distaste for Catholicism in his attack on the opponents of the kiddies scheme. 'People might talk of religion, but ... with certain classes who are

opposed ... to the workers ... their religion is in their pocket. (Cheers.)'[4]
A few days later he gave freer rein to his views on the Catholic Church as
editor of the NTWF's *Weekly Record*.

> The Black International cares a great deal about the way by which the
> children of the workers ascend to Heaven, but it does not care a jot how
> soon Murphy sends them there ... The whole business stands as one of
> the most disgraceful examples of religious bigotry, and ignorance, and
> venom, that has ever disgraced the Black International in all its long
> history of effort to keep the poor oppressed and ignorant.[5]

*

Connolly's threat to run spoiling campaigns in Britain was a shrewd move.
There were no fewer than four by-elections pending; the first one, in
Reading, was only ten days away. Gooch, the Liberal candidate, had been
strongly endorsed by John Redmond and T. P. O'Connor as a 'true friend of
... Home Rule for Ireland';[6] but he was expected to face a strong challenge
from Labour, which would be drawing support from suffragists as well as
trade unionists disillusioned with the government's handling of the
industrial crisis of 1910–12. The very night that Connolly issued his
challenge in Dublin, Sydney Buxton, president of the Board of Trade, was
forced to abandon a meeting in Poplar town hall because of the hostility of
his audience when he appealed for quiet. 'We will not give you free speech
while Larkin is in prison,' 'What about the women you are murdering?' and
'Why don't you arrest Carson?' were among the verbal epizoons to rise,
amid fisticuffs, from the body of the meeting.[7]

Perhaps it was an inkling of the need to keep its growing list of enemies
to a minimum that led the Irish executive to seek an adjournment of the
trial due on Wednesday of Larkin, Daly, Lawlor, Partridge and O'Brien for
seditious speeches at the meeting of 26 August. Besides, the court was now
processing a huge number of cases arising from the riots and the troubles
that had followed that meeting: altogether 158 convictions were handed
down for indictable offences involving rioting and another 114 for cases of
intimidation and molestation. To judge by newspaper reports of the
hearings, six months was the standard sentence.[8] Connolly might call for
workers to picket 'in battalions,' but the reality was that it was the police,
supported in many instances by army escorts, whose battalions now
controlled the streets.

As long as the strike held, this did not matter. It was a remarkable
testimony to the leadership of the Dublin unions—and to the tenacity of
the strikers—that the great majority of workers had remained out for two
months. However, this strategy could be undone if the employers once
decided to resort in a serious way to the use of 'free labour'. Already T. and
C. Martin had brought in fifty 'free labourers' from Manchester, and other
Dublin employers had been secretly making arrangements with the
Shipping Federation to bring in more.[9]

Meanwhile the TUC leaders took some hope of reaching a settlement on 30 October from the news that Dublin employers were estimated to have lost at least £750,000 as a result of the strike. They spent most of their first working day in Dublin at Liberty Hall; they also visited the food stores on the quays to watch the latest consignment of food being distributed; later they met separately Dr Walsh and some of the employers. However, no progress was reported; and the basic weakness of the British negotiators' position was underlined by the speech Gosling felt compelled to make at a meeting of strikers in Liberty Hall that night. He assured them that

> no settlement will be made without the consent of the men's leaders. The strike ... might go on until Christmas, or for the next three months, but the supplies from England will be maintained in the meantime.[10]

No doubt he also had in mind the need to assuage militants in Britain. Dockers in Liverpool were threatening to renew sympathetic strike action against Irish firms that imported strike-breakers, and more than three hundred branches of the National Union of Railwaymen, representing 80,000 members, had passed a vote of no confidence in their leaders for tolerating 'blacklegging' and 'tainted traffic'. What was more, Connolly was due to address a meeting in London on Saturday, and Gosling did not want to give any more ammunition to the TUC's critics.

26

THE plight of the children remained a central concern of all. In his speech at Liberty Hall, Harry Gosling felt the need to reassure people that the British unions fully understood the concerns about the 'deported' children. British workers admired the desire of their Irish colleagues to keep the children at home, he said; the TUC would 'send more supplies than ever, so that nothing could interfere with their faith.'[1]

Privately, the kiddies scheme was seen in Britain as further confirmation of Larkin's poor judgment. His old mentor and antagonist James Sexton arrived at the meeting of the NTWF executive in London in 'a state of boiling fury,' not just at Larkin but at Robert Williams for the latter's 'anti-clerical excess' in the *Weekly Record*. As a former Fenian who had been converted to home rule by T. P. O'Connor, Sexton epitomised the Irish Catholic working class in Lancashire. He believed that religious and national loyalties had been as important in securing support for the Dublin workers among groups such as the Liverpool dockers and Birmingham railway workers as class solidarity, or an opportunity to let off steam over their own industrial grievances. Even the *Daily Herald*, hardly an apostle of Catholicism, noted that solidarity with the Dublin workers had been strongest 'in those districts … bound by religious and political ties to the Irish transport workers.'[2] In the next issue of the *Weekly Record*, that of Saturday 1 November, Williams significantly modified his stance and conceded that 'Archbishop Walsh may have meant well in the action he took.' However, he reserved the right to distinguish between what Connolly had defined as religion and 'ecclesiastical politics, or organised clerical capitalism.'[3]

Of course, the labour movement was not the only section of society divided on the issue of the kiddies. These starving, poorly clad, unshod casualties of the struggle were now being recast as weapons in several ideological armouries. The lockout had introduced new complexities to Irish politics that confused traditional Catholic versus Protestant and nationalist versus unionist divides. The land struggle, which had dominated nationalist politics for generations, offered no terms of reference for the new dilemma.

A former Unionist candidate in the parliamentary elections, Major G. B. O'Connor, used the kiddies issue to condemn 'the cowardly repudiation of responsibility' for the state of the city by the six Irish Party MPs. Dublin 'resembles a Russian city engaged in a Jew-baiting pogrom,' he wrote in a letter published by the *Irish Times* on Wednesday 29 October. While citizens' rights were being 'flouted and ignored,' the Irish Party MPs 'take refuge behind the apron of the Roman Catholic Archbishop of Dublin.' He called on the MPs to 'cast off the fetters forged by a clever demagogue' on the city's working class, and pointed out that the methods being used to stop 'well meaning, but misguided ladies' were 'illegal and brutal.'

If O'Connor's views were as predictable as they were partisan, those of the professor of Romance languages at Trinity College, T. D. Rudmose-Brown, were probably more representative of much liberal-unionist opinion in the city. In a letter to the *Irish Times* published on Tuesday 28 October, he wrote:

> The 'deportation' of children may be indiscreet and tactless. But the proceedings of priests, police and Hibernians at Amiens Street Station ... were altogether illegal ... I happened, by the merest chance, to be on the platform at Amiens Street shortly before six o'clock on Friday evening, waiting for my train, the 6.15 [to Clontarf] ... I can honestly say that it appeared to me that unjustifiable obstruction was being practised. The children were obviously accompanied by their parents. Parents have the right to send their children away to friends in Belfast, Scotland, or England, if they so desire. The liberty of the subject must be guarded from all illegal interference.
>
> I made careful inquiries afterwards. My wife has for some time, from motives of simple humanity, been helping at 'Liberty Hall' with the feeding of the women and children suffering from the lockout and strike ... She happened to be present when the consent of the fathers was obtained for the 'deportation' of the children in question, and was able to assure me that she saw them sign their names on the necessary documents ... Mr. Larkin has, in this case at any rate, scrupulously observed the law, and is entitled to protection from illegal interference. It is perfectly scandalous that Miss Larkin and Miss Neale should be threatened with arrest, as they were at Amiens Street station, merely for insisting on their legal rights as free citizens.
>
> All this seems to provide an interesting foretaste of the joys of unfettered Rome Rule to which we are hastening.

As a member of a threatened minority himself, an admittedly unconventional academic such as Rudmose-Brown could discover a new-found sympathy that bordered on solidarity with the poor, and even with syndicalist trade union leaders. But some members of the emerging Catholic urban middle class were equally outraged by the 'vigilance parties' that had been roaming the streets, railway stations, and quays. Isabella Richardson was a feminist and a nationalist, a member of the same circle as Tom Kettle, Mary Lawless, and the Sheehy-Skeffingtons, who had been a leading figure in both the Irish Women's Franchise League and the Young Ireland branch of the UIL. On the day after it published Rudmose-Brown's letter, the *Irish Times* carried one from Isabella Richardson, who described Dublin as the 'most amazing' place 'in the so-called civilised world.'

> Here you may find jumbled together in one seething cauldron the old and the new, modernism and mediaevalism, sodden poverty and arrogant wealth and newborn Socialism. 'Labour! I'd sweep them off the streets with grape-shot!' said an elderly lady to me last week ... 'Catherine will be all right, she has her scapular,' says the poor mother, thinking that her little girl may well be spared from the poverty stricken home to spend a few weeks with kindly working folk in England, and little dreaming that even a scapular could not save her from the attack of the Ancient Order of Hibernians! I have seen these 'Irish homes', from which it is such a disgrace to a mother if she sends her child for a brief holiday. I have seen these single-room tenements, which are the shame of our city, and I have seen the places where kind-hearted women labour that poor, little, dirty tatterdermalions may at least have a bit in their mouth. But the hunger and rags, the dirt and the over-crowding were such very familiar facts that it scarcely occurred to anyone here to notice them much until Mrs. Montefiore came over to offer a helping hand from the other side of St. George's Channel—and then the hullabaloo began! Positively, to listen to the language that was used, one might have thought that a scheme was on foot to 'deport' the children to Timbuctoo and compel them to embrace the Mohammedan faith. Irish mothers were 'unnatural' if they allowed their children to go to England, although Irish mothers who send their boys to Stoneyhurst or Marlborough have never been denounced either by priest or people, as far as I can remember. But it is the poor, no doubt, who have to be kept in subjection, and as long as you are anti-Larkin it does not matter if you call people 'kidnappers,' who have the written consent of the parents, or 'proselytisers' who place Catholic children under Catholic priests. Well, now, the hunt is up, and if you are an old gentleman, and want to take your grandchild down to the country for a few days, you had better apply for police protection, if you do not want to be surrounded by a howling mob. And what is it that animates that mob? A deep desire for the eternal welfare of the children? Meanwhile, let their wretched bodies be hustled and chivied as much as possible.

But most nationalists took a different view. One letter-writer using the popular pen-name 'Irishman' asked if

> the Catholic workingmen of Ireland no longer trust their priests, or do they prefer that they and their wives and children should be the playthings of English and Continental Socialists? Is this to be the reward to the Church which from its foundation has been the helper of the poor and oppressed?

He suggested that workers found a trade union 'on honest lines, where they would not be under the tyranny of a glib-tongued Socialist—a trade union in which they would have the guidance of their spiritual advisors.' As for the children, if they needed

> a temporary home of refuge, are there no convents to shelter them? Surely Catholic parents would prefer entrusting their infants to these good ladies, the Irish nuns, who have sacrificed position and wealth in the service of the poor, rather than unknown visitors from an alien land?

One of the problems was that the Catholic Church just could not cope with the social crisis that now gripped the city. An opponent of the kiddies scheme who knew this better than most was Maud Gonne. To Yeats she was a 'goddess', to militant socialists and nationalists an icon, but to hundreds of schoolchildren this debutante turned actor, feminist and revolutionary was the woman who had brought them a square meal every day. She had been the guiding force behind the Ladies' School Dinner Committee, set up three years previously by Inghinidhe na hÉireann, a small but militantly feminist and nationalist grouping. Announcing the scheme in the organisation's newspaper, *Bean na hÉireann*, she had explained that the objective was not primarily charitable but to force Dublin Corporation to accept its social responsibilities to these children. Her friend Helen Hayes wrote in the *Irish Citizen*: 'She gathered a small band of workers round her, including some members of the Irish Women's Suffrage League, and with the sum of £20 and the consent of Canon Cavanagh, the manager of St. Audoën's School, began distributing dinners daily to about 200 children attending the school.' The experiment was such a success that

> the next winter the Committee undertook to give dinners in another very poor school in John's Lane. There dinners have been given every school day, summer and winter, since they were started, in spite of the slenderness of the banking account opened by the Treasurer ... It was like the widow's cruse of oil, never quite empty, though there never seemed to be more than enough for the next week.

At the end of 1912 Maud Gonne came close to achieving her larger objective. After she had organised a highly successful meeting in the Mansion House, the City Council passed a resolution to strike a special rate to feed the children. However, the law agent advised councillors that they were acting beyond their powers: it would take a new act of Parliament to introduce school dinners in Dublin. That was something the Irish Party had no stomach for, and the project was dropped. Maud Gonne and her collaborators had to continue relying on voluntary support. In October 1913 Helen Hayes reported that

> over 600 are receiving meals daily at the schools, and arrangements are being made to commence work in another school. The dinners consist

of Irish stew, about a pint for each child, and smaller portions for the babies, for there are some only just over three years old, varied by pea soup, which is in great demand, and on Friday boiled rice and jam is served.[4]

Maud Gonne was in France for much of 1913 nursing her sick son, Seán; she was afraid to bring the child to Ireland for fear that her estranged husband, Major John MacBride, would seize him. But a letter from her appeared in the *Irish Times* on 23 October in which she strongly supported Dr Walsh's position on the Dublin kiddies scheme.

> While recognising the kindness which prompts English workers to offer homes to 350 Irish children during the lockout, most Irish people must realise it is a terribly dangerous thing to send children across the sea to unknown homes, and after the letter of His Grace the Archbishop of Dublin, I feel sure few, if any, Irish mothers will consent to part with their children.
>
> The fact remains, and is a disgrace to us all, that there are always starving children in Dublin.

Anyone who took the trouble to read the city's health reports, she wrote, would quickly convince themselves of 'the terrible waste of child-life caused by starvation.' Their deaths were 'in great part due to want of food. The lockout has greatly increased the numbers of starving children.'

She also pointed out a serious flaw in the kiddies scheme. 'The danger of actual starvation is less, probably, among the children of men belonging to trade unions, who are getting strike pay and some food than among the children of casual labourers who belong to no unions, but are out of work because of the general standstill in business.'[5]

The ITGWU had, at most, half the general labourers enrolled in its ranks in 1913, and food parcels were given out only on the production of tickets issued to members in benefit. At a special meeting of the ITGWU strike committee on 15 October it had been decided to co-opt a number of representatives from among casual workers to issue food tickets, as even some ITGWU members who were casual labourers appeared to be experiencing difficulty in obtaining food and fuel.[6] Maud Gonne's argument that it would be more useful to direct limited resources into the schools had therefore a strong basis in fact.

During a brief visit to Dublin to investigate the situation that autumn she found that

> in schools where dinners are being served daily the attendance has increased during the lockout. At St. Audoën's and John's Lane schools teachers say they never remember having so many children in the school … In schools where no dinners are being given the attendance has gone down very much … I asked one of the mothers of children attending a school near the quays why had her children given up going to school.

She answered, 'They are out looking for a bit of food.' And one cannot blame them. It is foolish to ask a starving child to work.

A convert to Catholicism, Maud Gonne expressed concern that hundreds of these children were now attending the Christian Union buildings and Salvation Army for meals. Without openly criticising these agencies, she wrote that it was 'the plain duty of Irish people to see that Irish children do not die of starvation, and the easiest and surest way of doing this is to provide food, dinners and, where possible, breakfasts in national schools in the city.' At a cost of 5d for a pint of stew, which would provide a child with dinner for six days, and 3d to cover a breakfast of cocoa and bread over the same period, she did not see the cost as excessive. Unfortunately, many councillors did not agree.[7]

The distress of the poor was too emotive for nationalist and unionist councillors to come out openly—as they had done in the case of the art gallery—and oppose school dinners on the grounds that they would increase the rates. In fairness to them it must be said that the issue also challenged deeply held beliefs about the 'deserving' and not-so-deserving poor. The independent nationalist councillor for the South City ward, Sarah Harrison, expressed these concerns well in a letter to the newspapers. She had supported the Hugh Lane gallery project but nevertheless baulked at the idea of free school dinners. Dr Walsh was her guiding light.

> His Grace protests strongly—and I am glad to see it—against the habit of looking on the clergy and nuns as 'the relieving officers of the city' and reminds us that 'the common duty of charity to the poor' is 'as much the duty of the laity as it is theirs.' I think it is high time that we all, rich and poor alike, realised that fact.
>
> Those in constant need come to look upon such assistance from the Church not in the proof of kindly sympathy, as they would if it came through a private individual, but as theirs by right, and thus they lose the best part of the gift.

She argued that this tendency would be vastly augmented if state agencies played a significant role in providing relief. It would increase the 'danger of indiscriminate assistance,' which

> at the present juncture is very great, and the deadly legacy it will leave [is] hard to realise by the inexperienced; it will need just and firm handling to prevent that demoralisation feared by His Grace. He advises that the giving of meals be kept as far as possible away from schoolrooms, that the children who do not need them, especially those on the border line, should not be confused with those who do.

She suggested that, if need be, meals should be provided in schools of the poorer districts, but with 'the less needy parents' paying 1d or 1½d towards the cost.

I know there is a strong objection on the part of many to the institution of school dinners by law, and the argument that free school dinners would really be a subsidy in relief of low wages—as parents should be able to earn enough to feed their children—is a view that has much to commend it, but is the health of the workers of the future to be sacrificed pending the attainment of a desirable state of affairs?

She suggested that subscriptions to provide meals could be raised by the Society of St Vincent de Paul. This would relieve the burden on the clergy and nuns; and once the crisis was over the free meals could gradually be 'reduced to A MINIMUM.'[8]

T. P. Gill, Secretary of the Department of Agriculture and Technical Instruction, saw the issue of helping the strikers' families in simpler and starker terms. A keen supporter of native business and the recently formed Industrial Development Association, he described the lockout as 'something not unakin to national insanity.' He expressed the widespread view that it was in the interests of British trade unionists to promote a struggle that undermined Irish industry; his only surprise was that British employers were not subsidising the dispute as well.[9]

*

Dr Walsh's order of priorities in the present crisis was broader and more complex than that of a civil servant. They were—in descending order—religious, social, and economic. When he addressed a meeting of the Society of St Vincent de Paul at its head office in Upper Sackville Street on Monday 27 October he reiterated his basic opposition to any scheme that placed 'our Catholic children ... in homes, and under the guardianship of persons for whose fitness ... there is no guarantee.' He pointed out that it would make better financial sense to keep the children at home—an argument against the kiddies scheme that, as we have seen, Connolly was quick to adopt.

We need not go even to Lancashire. Ample accommodation could be found in Dublin if it were needed. (Applause.) I have had from convent after convent most generous offers of help in this matter if, and whenever, such help is needed.

He then turned to the 'falsehoods' being circulated against the Catholic Church. Within the past few days people in England and Scotland had written to him asking 'why I do not get the priests and nuns of Dublin to provide the school children with, at all events, some sort of meal each day.' It was then that Dr Walsh made the remark taken up by Councillor Harrison. 'Why, one would think that the clergy and the nuns are the relieving officers of the city.' The clergy had been 'exemplary' in their social duties, but they knew better than anyone that the result of indiscriminately distributing food and clothing to children would 'infallibly be the demoralisation of hundreds of poor parents who, if left to take care of their children themselves, would be able and willing to make the effort.'

He went on to criticise the working men who had listened 'in cowardly silence' to attacks on the clergy from public platforms when their own children had been fed and clothed by the church. 'They had not the manliness to utter a word of protest.' He told the society that three of his city parishes were providing 2,450 breakfasts daily to children attending Catholic schools, more than double the normal number. In four other parishes 2,045 children had been clothed. 'I need not point out how much more the numbers of children thus provided for could have been increased, if the money expended so foolishly, to say the least of it, in sending children away from their homes, had been devoted to strengthening the hands of those who are working, as they have for years been working, for the assistance of the poor.'

The archbishop contrasted the generosity of middle-class women who contributed to such funds with the behaviour of mothers

> so degraded as to send their children out into the streets to beg for them. They know that the sight of poor ill-clad children makes a powerful appeal to the hearts of our charitable people. Our people then, must harden their hearts against this.

People should contribute generously instead to the Dublin Children's Distress Fund organised by the Lord Mayor's wife, Marie Sherlock. He reminded his audience that the British trade unions were also contributing generously to the families of the strikers. 'There can be no excuse then for begging in the streets.'

It was then that Dr Walsh made one of his most revealing statements and one that expressed the most fundamental objection that many defenders of the status quo had to the kiddies scheme.

> The fantastic policy, as I have called it, of spending money in taking the children away for what I heard is called a holiday, can do no real good. It can have but one permanent result, and that, surely, the very reverse of a beneficent one. It will but make them discontented with the poor homes to which they will sooner or later return, that is to say, those of them who will return at all. (Applause.) That surely is a result by no means to be viewed with anything but abhorrence by anyone sincerely anxious for the welfare and happiness of the poor.

The archbishop knew his city, he knew its tenements and the schools where the tenement children were taught. Seventy years of experience had taught him that the burden of poverty on the city was so immense that it could not be lifted by the church, by the state, or by society in general. Nothing better illustrated his profound sense of pessimism, his defeatism even, in confronting the material social challenge posed by the slums than his remarks that day; yet he was simply voicing the deeply held views of his church and of his class. 'It passes my powers of comprehension to understand what practical end the periodic jeremiads ... in the press and elsewhere are directed to' on the city's housing crisis. Some commercial men had done what they could to tackle the problem 'by putting money into the work. I may say that I have myself put money into the work. But ... it is all insignificant in face of the gigantic need that has to be met.'

It was perhaps inevitable that he would add, 'At all events, it is enough to say that the problem of housing of the poor in Dublin has nothing whatever to do with the actual present problem ... of helping the poor children.' If the archbishop doubted the ability of society's leaders to eliminate poverty, he dismissed outright the belief of Larkin and his fellow-socialists that the poor could save themselves by some form of social revolution. He believed that happiness was possible in this urban hell only for those willing to accept their lot; 'holidays' in England would make the attainment of that spiritual goal far more difficult.

At least Dr Walsh differed from many of those who had answered the call of the vigilance groups, because he accepted that victory over Dora Montefiore and her scheme imposed a heavy moral responsibility on the victors. Having outlined what the church had achieved by way of meals and clothing, he told the society that 'the work before us is that of getting all the help we can for the continuance and extension of the work that is already being done.' Nor did he share the qualms of city councillors about using the schools as a conduit to feed the children. While he had bewailed the dangers of 'indiscriminate' charity, he said that in the present crisis school meals were not only the most direct way of reaching those most in need but achieved the equally useful objective of removing the spectacle of hundreds of child beggars from the streets.[10]

*

The archbishop showed his usual shrewd touch with his remarks on street begging. If anything might loosen the purse-strings of Dublin's middle class it was the conjuring up of a plague of child beggars. The inspector of the National Society for the Prevention of Cruelty to Children interviewed in the *Irish Times* the previous Saturday had said there were always

> hundreds of cases ... in which the poor mites are driven out to beg by drunken and idle parents; but in the present crisis I am forced to believe that the majority of begging children are out on their own ... A shocking state of things—yes, that they are dropping out of school, making friends with the 'dregs of society'; stopping in common lodging houses, even when they have respectable and comfortable enough homes ... I never knew a worse state of things—children seem to be losing all sense of discipline and self-restraint.

The police were too busy combating the strike to keep an eye on this growing army of beggars, and some of the 'starving' children posing for press photographs and newsreels had parents who were working. One boy that he knew

> is now shown on the cinematograph in London as a victim of starvation. His father, who is earning 25s. a week, has been out night after night

looking for him since the strike began![11]

The inspector's view is borne out by the available statistical returns for the year. Those of the Dublin Children's (Street Trading) Court show an unseasonal increase in the number of licences issued at the end of 1913, which was attributed to 'the effects of the present industrial unrest in the city.' But the total number of registered child traders at the end of 1913 was actually lower than in 1912 and was in line with the long-term downward trend in the numbers of children hawking.[12]

The annual reports of the NSPCC suggest that children were actually better off during the lockout than in normal times. In 1913 there were fewer complaints of cruelty to children than in either 1912 or 1914: in 1912 there were 1,538 complaints to the society, involving 4,411 children, while in 1914 there were 1,503 complaints, involving 4,273 children; but in 1913 there were only 1,441 complaints, involving 3,993 children. The number of adults charged with cruelty to children shows a similar pattern. In its report for 1913 the NSPCC felt it necessary to comment on the significant drop in the number of cases.

> Such a fact may naturally evoke comment when the disturbances and distress prevailing in the city for several months of the year are recalled … During the strike, though money was scarcer, the children, owing to various agencies, received a sufficiency of food more regularly than usual, the effect being that complaints of neglect to provide support were considerably reduced in number.[13]

It does not say which agencies gave the most effective help. Significantly, this was an issue that the newspapers, churches and nationalist establishment did their best to obscure; presumably none of them wished to draw attention to the fact that it was the much-maligned English trade unions that had come to the rescue.

*

There were some Irish philanthropists. The first and most generous response came from a woman who was a favourite target for Larkin's jibes, Josephine Plunkett. As early as Wednesday 22 October, when news of the planned 'deportations' first broke, she wrote to the papers announcing that she was

> prepared to take charge of any Dublin children whose parents are unable to take proper care of them during the continuance of the strike or lockout. I will house the children comfortably at Sandymount, where they can be visited by their parents.

Priests at St Andrew's in Westland Row, soon to distinguish themselves in the battle against the 'kidnappers', had agreed to act as an information centre for the scheme. This was presumably agreed on the grounds that most of the children seeking accommodation in Sandymount would be from the south city and docks area. Over the next couple of weeks the papers would publish reports of the work of renovating the house to accommodate the children, along with photographs of the happy inmates.

Countess Plunkett had discussed her proposal with Dr Walsh before the public announcement but had apparently suggested a modest scheme for just six children. He was so alarmed at reading a report in the *Evening Telegraph* on 23 October to the effect that she was appealing for public subscriptions to accommodate 150 children that he immediately wrote to her objecting.

> If you are prepared to do this out of your own generosity I should, of course, be slow to interfere with the project. But apparently the idea is to have it done by the pubic, and this being so, I am bound to say that in my opinion the idea is an exceedingly ill-advised one.

It was advisable to remove children from their homes only when circumstances were

> altogether exceptional—as, for instance, in the case of an evicted family … But the withdrawal of 150 children from their parents would be wholly unjustifiable … What I am aiming at is the providing of food, and, as far as needed, of clothing for the children,—simply an extension of the work that has long been an established part of our church.[14]

Countess Plunkett apologised for her precipitate action and said that her offer to accommodate 150 children at Sandymount Castle was given 'very reluctantly' in answer to a question from a journalist about 'how many COULD the castle accommodate.' However, she went on to give the archbishop an account of her experiences over the past few days, which suggested that the circumstances he considered 'altogether exceptional' were becoming an everyday occurrence in the city.

She began with his own instance of evictions and told him that her impulsive gesture to make Sandymount available for children arose from three families facing eviction who had sought help at Westland Row presbytery. One woman evicted from her home in Luke Street had

> consented to allow her children to 'Go for a holiday,'; then refused when she heard the clergy did not wish her to do so; went for them at Tara Street baths and asked for their own clothes; they were refused, so she took the children, almost naked, back.

Countess Plunkett accepted the two girls, aged thirteen and eleven, to her house in Sandymount, along with a boy of eight. A woman who had been evicted because her husband was locked out agreed to stop her children going to England only after Countess Plunkett agreed to take her two daughters, aged eleven and seven, and had given the woman 2s for herself.

> Josephine R— summonsed for non-payment of debt—'locked out' has five children; two girls 8 and 6 years, admitted [to Sandymount Castle]; she has three other children 4, 2, and half year—given 2s. for food. A

case of a starving woman who was about to become a mother was given 1s. and was told to make arrangements with another woman to feed her and her boy of three years until she had to go to hospital ... Mr. Murray of Townsend Street Mission offers to take the unborn child if Mrs. W— will allow it to be baptised a Protestant ... A young girl Lizzie P— had consented to allow her two brothers to go away. She had nothing left but an old bed as she had been out of work for some weeks. The two boys were shivering and very hungry. They were given food and were admitted at ten o'clock last night. They have no father nor mother.

If money enough could be had to give to the poor ... very few would ask to have their children taken, once this trouble caused by the socialists passes over.

Her hostility to the socialists was no doubt partly due to her treatment at Liberty Hall—though she was at pains to tell the archbishop that she had not been thrown out of that institution, as reported in the press: she had simply gone there to 'rescue' more of the children, after her successful efforts at Tara Street baths. She found Dora Montefiore

dressing the batch of girls who left for Liverpool. The language used there against the clergy by some of the mothers ... made me feel so sick that I found it difficult to reply ... and when I objected to Mrs. Montefiore taking the children she told me to get out. J. Larkin did likewise.

She estimated that it would take £2,000 to counteract the kiddies scheme. The money could be given 'with discretion and after investigating, with care, the needs of each case.' She warned the archbishop that 'the quiet of the streets gives no indication of the depth of misery to which thousands of our decent people have been reduced.'[15]

The urge to help the poor and the call to battle evoked by the proselytising activities of Protestant missions and socialists alike were closely interwoven in Countess Plunkett's response to the crisis. But local factors were also clearly important. She was an active lay member of the Westland Row parish, one of whose priests, Father Thomas Ryan, had been involved from an early stage that year in the anti-proselytising activities of the Society of St Vincent de Paul. The leading part played by Jesuits in the campaign against the kiddies scheme on the north side of the city also reflects their strong support for the anti-proselytising activities of the society. Some Jesuits would soon be heavily involved in another initiative that would further challenge Protestant hegemony in the business community: the establishment of the Knights of St Columbanus.[16]

Inevitably, the offers of accommodation for the children and of money to the mothers reflected the methods of the Protestant enemy; so too did the concept of helping only the 'deserving' poor, deeply ingrained in most middle-class Dubliners of that era. Unfortunately, most middle-class Catholics did not take as seriously as Countess Plunkett did St Paul's injunction that charity without works is dead. Far from Dr Walsh's concern about a plague of begging children evoking a charitable response, it led to calls for stronger measures to be taken against beggars. Even the *Irish Citizen*, which saw itself as the champion of all that was best and most progressive in civil society, felt obliged to complain that

> the number of child beggars has greatly increased of late. Indeed they constitute a nuisance of the worst possible kind. Beggars are one of the greatest obstacles which confront decent working people today: because they make the well-off despise the poor. It is far better to give 2s. 6d. to the dinner fund than 1d. to 30 beggars! Prevention, rather than the satisfying of our own merciful emotions, must be our aim. Policewomen, more Probation Officers, adequate Poor Law Relief, Day Industrial Schools, efficient National Education, are needed.[17]

Many of these initiatives would have been worth while, but they did not happen. Instead, most readers of the *Irish Citizen*, like their less progressively minded middle-class sisters, left it to others to feed the poor that winter.

27

THERE was of course an initial burst of Christian enthusiasm following Archbishop Walsh's own contribution of £100 to the Dublin Children's Distress Fund. The provincial of the Society of Jesus, Father T. V. Nolan, who was also president of the Society of St Vincent de Paul, gave £25, and a number of priests and prominent lay people gave amounts ranging from £10 to £25 each. Maud Gonne contributed £5. By the end of the first week over £760 had been collected; but then the money began to dry up.

Even at this early stage it was clear that most of the contributions were coming from traditional sources: religious congregations, branches of the Society of St Vincent de Paul, and individual clergymen. The 'innocent victims' of the lockout had not struck a strong chord of sympathy among Ireland's burgeoning middle class; in fact a fifth of all contributions came from Britain. Most of these came from individual exiles, but there were also many contributions from British branches of the United Irish League.[1] These were obviously taking their lead from T. P. O'Connor and the Irish Party leaders, who were telling them to direct their collections to the Dublin Children's Distress Fund, organised by the Lord Mayor's wife, Marie Sherlock, rather than to those organised by their traditional allies in the British trade union movement.

There were also some donations from individual trade union branches in Lancashire and in Scotland. The largest of these was £4 10s from the Liverpool branch of James Sexton's NUDL.[2] The covering letter from the secretary, James Hanratty, suggests that Sexton's concern at the damage that might be caused by Larkin's attacks on the clergy—and Robert Williams's anti-clerical flourishes in the NTWF's *Weekly Record*—was not unfounded. 'I hope the day will never come that the Socialists … have anything to do with the children of Dublin or … any other part of Ireland,' Hanratty told the archbishop. 'If Your Grace should call to the Holy Faith Convent, Glasnevin, my sister, Sr. Mary Loyola will be delighted to know we have done a little for the Children from a Catholic Point of View.'

Perhaps the most dynamic group of exiles was the newly formed United Irish Societies Association in London, about which John Dillon had expressed so much concern. The initial meeting, which was called on the initiative of the Gaelic League, was attended by representatives of the AOH, GAA, Gaelic League, Irish Association, UIL League of Great Britain, Irish Literary Society, Irish Athletic Club, London Irish Football Club, Irish League for Women's Suffrage, and United Irishwomen, as well as the Union of Four Provinces Club, which hosted the inaugural meeting at its premises in John Street. In the absence of T. P. O'Connor, Art O'Brien of the Gaelic League was elected to the chair, and Lord Ashbourne was unanimously elected president in his absence.

The gathering was overwhelmingly middle-class and respectable. It contained none of the numerous Irish immigrants active in London's trade union and socialist circles; yet it proved earnest and energetic. It decided immediately that 'it is not desirable to discuss the merits of the industrial dispute in progress, but it is a fact that there is a very large number of people in great want on account of it.' A letter was read out from the Lord Mayor of Dublin appealing for funds to provide meals through the city's schools. An AOH delegate proposed that any money raised be sent to the Dublin Children's Distress Fund, which was seconded by a UIL delegate— probably by prior arrangement.

Over the coming weeks the association sent a number of donations to Dublin, the largest of which came from a concert at the Pavilion Theatre in November. In the ecumenical list of sponsors were Roger Casement and the Earl of Clonmel. Several well-known Irish artists of the day gave their services free at the concert, but the final administration and promotional costs of £55 3s 8½d made a big inroad into the £210 13s 5d collected. After the concert a Gaelic League delegate proposed that the committee discontinue its efforts, as 'the strike trouble was almost over'; however, the association continued in existence for a number of years. It was still active in 1916, when it raised funds for the families of insurgents killed or imprisoned as a result of the Easter Rising. Art O'Brien would go on to become president of the Irish Self-Determination League in Britain and would present the Irish Treaty delegates to the British Prime Minister, David Lloyd George, in 1921. One of those delegates, Michael Collins, had represented the GAA on the society's relief committee in 1913; it was on his suggestion that the committee decided that details of its bank account be published on all appeals, to ensure that no funds went astray.

The association would probably have raised more money but for the hostility of the Catholic Church in London. The administrator for the London archdiocese, Monsignor Howleth, refused permission for collections either inside or outside churches. He said that Cardinal Bourne was unlikely to overturn that policy, 'unless asked by the Archbishop of Dublin to do so.' The society sent letters and reply-paid telegrams to Dr Walsh but failed to evoke a response. The only British prelate to show any interest in what was happening in Dublin was Peter Amigo, the Gibraltarian Bishop of Southwark. A lifelong supporter of Irish nationalism, he could be undiscriminating in his political enthusiasms, which would include support for Mussolini and the British fascists in the nineteen-twenties and thirties. He wrote to Dr Walsh offering his help and told him that he had found the six 'deportees' sent to Surrey. He subsequently wrote to Lady Ashbourne, 'near whose oratory the children are quartered.' This was the home of Emmeline Pethwick Lawrence, who had received the first contingent of Dublin 'kiddies'. When Ashbourne sent his own 'small contribution' to Dr Walsh he assured the archbishop that Mrs Pethwick Lawrence was not only taking good care of the children but had written to Lady Ashbourne 'asking details about Mass and religious instruction ... and had arranged for a priest to visit them.'[3]

*

Lord Ashbourne wrote to Dr Walsh giving him assurances about the children on 3 November; but the archbishop appears to have made no effort to allay public fears, which continued to be fed by alarmist reports in newspapers owned by William Martin Murphy, such as the *Evening Herald* and *Irish Catholic*. On Saturday 1 November the *Irish Catholic* published another account of the activities of the 'kidnappers', praising those priests who had 'publicly denounced these interlopers and their socialist allies. No better, more holy, or more necessary work could possibly be conceived.'

It also published a detailed report of Dr Walsh's address of the previous Monday to the Society of St Vincent de Paul and, perversely, misrepresented his position on school meals. Given that the Lord Mayor's wife had already announced that the distress fund would use schools as a channel for distributing aid, the *Irish Catholic* could hardly have done more to confuse its readers.

It was also disingenuous in its account of the work the church was already doing to help feed hungry children. It claimed that 25,451 were being cared for already by the religious, but the list it published included industrial schools, orphanages, the school for the blind, and ordinary national schools as far away as Arklow; it also included groups of pupils, such as the two hundred in the South Dublin Union, who were being taught by the Sisters of Mercy but fed by the ratepayers. A detailed examination of the list suggests that the true number of children being helped in areas where the lockout was having an impact was no more than 2,500; this would correspond roughly to the figure Dr Walsh had given in his speech to the Society of St Vincent de Paul on 27 October.

The total inadequacy of the help given by the Catholic Church to children in working-class areas would not be revealed for almost another year, when a Dublin Corporation report, prompted by the lockout, established that there were at least 7,259 schoolchildren in dire need of dinners. The committee that drew up the report included the managers of twenty national schools, all of them Catholic priests. Of the 7,259 children identified as seriously undernourished, 4,253 were in schools run by members of the committee; these included clergymen such as Father James Flavin and Father Hatton, who had been vociferous in their denunciation of the 'kidnappers' in October 1913 but had remained silent on the misery being experienced in their own schools.[4]

The same issue of the *Irish Catholic* that denounced the 'kidnappers' also turned its venom on two of its favourite bugbears: the 'few Ulster parishes' that were attempting 'to dictate the policy of the British Empire' in the home rule crisis, and James Larkin. The labour leader, it protested, was being treated as a 'first class misdemeanant' in prison. This meant that 'he will pass a much more comfortable time during the coming months than any of his unfortunate dupes are likely to.' The paper seemed unaware of the implicit condemnation these lines carried of living and working conditions in the city; one reason may have been that it was still intoxicated with the victory over the 'kidnappers'.

'Resurrecta est!' was the title of its leader that week. It declared that

no Catholic can have witnessed or read about the marvellous uprising which filled many of the main thoroughfares of our city with vast concourses of earnest, resolute, and vigilant men and women without being convinced that the croakers who had told us things of gloom, and spoken of a race debased and sunken in the darkness of materialism, had uttered naught but foul falsehoods. Foremost in the ... mighty throng which rushed to our quaysides and stormed our railway stations were the pastors and priests of the city. Secular and regular came to guide, to counsel, to control, but, above all, to strangle a nefarious plot and to save the souls of imperilled children, of little ones who were to have been shipped to the depths and darkness of English paganism as Cromwell shipped the children of Ireland ere now to the poisonous swamps and jungles of an older barbarism.

According to the *Irish Catholic*, 'the thing had to be stopped, and stopped at once—there was no time for lawyers' quibbles.' While the *Irish Times* had been 'profoundly impressed by the fact that "some persons, very improperly, took the law into their own hands," never was the law in better hands.' Now that the children were 'safe from the new soupers ... Money must be found to clothe, feed and shelter the children whom degraded and dissolute parents would fain surrender to Socialism or to any other Satanic influence.'

However, after producing a detailed list of subscriptions to the Dublin Children's Distress Fund in its edition of 8 November, the *Irish Catholic* published no further information on the subject, though appeals for other worthy causes, such as the China mission, continued to appear regularly. This did not prevent the paper from referring disparagingly to the efforts of the unions to raise funds in Britain. A meeting addressed by James Connolly at South Shields the previous week had reportedly raised '14s. and a few coppers'; in fact the Dublin Strike Fund organised by the TUC had provided £13,136 19s 11d in food shipments alone during October 1913. In November it despatched another £16,260 1s 5d worth of foodstuffs and £10,422 4s in cash to Dublin Trades Council.

In December 1913 the TUC excelled itself by despatching food consignments worth £20,866 5s 2d, the highest figure for any month of the lockout. This included £9,009 8s 9d worth of food shipped on 22 December to coincide with the Christmas holiday. The same month, £9,344 16s was sent in cash to the Trades Council. Even in January 1914, by which time Larkin's differences with the TUC had seriously eroded British trade union support, £11,406 6s 5d worth of food was despatched to Dublin and £5,608 16s in cash to the Trades Council. The last food consignment, worth £1,219 13s 7d, was despatched on 3 February 1914; but the cash remittances continued well into the spring of that year. There was £800 in February, £1,600 in March, and £1,200 in April, including a final instalment of £400 on 9 April. There was also a separate payment of £300 to Constance Markievicz for the Women and Children's Relief Fund; and £2,294 1s 8½d had been paid out on transport and administration costs.

Altogether, the Parliamentary Committee of the TUC received £93,518 13s 9½d from British supporters of the Dublin strikers. Of this, £31,819 18s 8½d came through the *Daily Citizen*, the TUC's newspaper. Pride of place went to the Miners' Federation, which donated £14,000 in fourteen weekly pledges of £1,000 each. Many local miners' associations in Nottinghamshire, Wales and Scotland gave additional donations ranging from £100 to £500. Other large donations came in from the Amalgamated Society of Engineers (William Partridge's union), which donated £3,854, and the Carpenters' and Joiners' Amalgamated Society, which gave £1,550. A great many unions made single donations of between £200 and £800; these included the Weavers' Association, with £769 14s 11d, the NUDL (James Sexton's union), the Mersey Quay and Railway Carters' Union, and the United Society of Boilermakers and the Iron and Steel Shipbuilders' Union, which each gave £500. James Seddon's Shop Assistants' Union gave £200. The National Union of Railwaymen gave a series of contributions, of which the largest was £250, and the National Union of Teachers made a series of large donations totalling almost £1,000.

There was also a generous response from the various political strands within the British labour movement, with the Independent Labour Party to the fore. The ILP was still the strongest element within the congregation of socialist groups that had allied itself to the trade unions with the aim of breaking the grip the Liberals still had on the working-class electorate; but its relative organisational weakness is clear from the food fund records. ILP branches contributed less than £35 to the fund, and even the newly formed Labour Party managed to raise only £513, mainly in street collections. But then, the *métier* of these groups was agitation and education rather than organisation.

Besides supplying the TUC with provisions, many co-operatives made generous donations. The Wholesale Co-Operative Society in Manchester, the main conduit for food supplies to Dublin, donated £1,000. Newcastle-upon-Tyne Co-Operative Society and Windhill Co-Operative Society gave

£250 each, while the Northern Co-Operative Company in Aberdeen gave £150. Bishop Auckland Industrial Co-Operative gave £100 worth of provisions, which was specifically designated for children.

Trades councils helped organise meetings and collections for the Dublin strikers. If their financial contribution to the fund was smaller than that of the major trade unions or the co-ops, it was still significant. London Trades Council took pride of place, with donations totalling £573 13s 10½d. Manchester and Salford Trades Council contributed £205. Often the size of the contribution was more a reflection of local militancy and a sense of solidarity with the Dublin workers than the size of the city. For instance, the third-largest contribution came from Sunderland Trades Council and Labour Representation Committee; this stronghold of the new unionism gave £196 16s 4d. Accrington Trades Council gave £175, of which £100 came from a 'Shamrock Day' collection. Nottingham Trades Council also raised £100 from a Shamrock Day collection and contributed a total of £170 12s 8d to the Dublin Food Fund. Great Harwood Trades and Labour Council gave £131 19s 6d, and North Staffordshire Trades Council donated £110. In contrast, Liverpool Trades Council raised only £103 9s 6d, though many trade unions in the city gave generously to the TUC. Other trades councils tended to make smaller contributions; the £5 from Rochdale and District Trades Council or the £11 8s 8d from Middlesbrough Trades and Labour Council were nearer the norm. But Crewe Trades and Labour Council gave £18, and the local co-operative another £50. Though a small town, it was a key railway centre, and many NUR members had come out spontaneously in defiance of their union to support the Dublin workers in the early stages of the lockout. At the other end of the scale came Birmingham Trades and Labour Council: this representative body of the working class in Britain's second-largest city donated only £2 10s.

Thousands of pounds came from local union branches, groups of workers, small societies, and individuals, rich and poor. J. Adamson at 'W. A. & Co.' took up ten collections of 8s each, almost matching the £5 sent by Lord Henry Bentinck. A Shamrock Day collection in Blackburn yielded £43 12s 7d. The Oxford University Fabian Society contributed £4 16s, and the senior class of Swinton Unitarian Sunday School 9s. One wonders what John Dillon would have made of the decision of the Rawtensall Branch of the United Irish League to send £1 1s to the fund, or how Dr Walsh would have reacted to the £3 8s 9½d donated by the congregation of St James the Less in the same town. Stokers on HMS *Duke of Edinburgh* gave 10s, and so did the Irish Association in Sheffield. Thanks to the extensive coverage of the dispute in the British press and the cinema newsreels so beloved by Larkin, the Dublin strike had struck a deep chord among British workers.

But not all the funds came from Britain. While Dublin Trades Council received £28,975 16s in cash from the TUC, another £13,338 was sent to it directly in donations. No records survive of where this money came from, but presumably some of it at least was from Irish trade unions and individuals. The records of individual Irish unions suggest that support could be generous in relation to their size. The United Corporation Workmen of Dublin Trades Union, one of the oldest and one of the smallest general unions, sent £185 10s to the Trades Council between October and December 1913—despite the fact that it had become the butt of Larkin's humour in the *Irish Worker* after refusing to merge with the Transport Union. Its donations represent £1.34 per head, or substantially more than a week's wages, from each of its 1,384 members.

In contrast, one of Ireland's most affluent unions, the Drapers' Assistants' Association, gave only £100 to the strike fund. With 4,002 members on its books, this was equivalent to less than 25p for each member. Drapers' assistants earned on average £1 10s a week, compared with £1 for corporation labourers.[5] The DAA also gave a loan of £20 to the ASE to help members who had been locked out. However, appeals for help from other unions were turned down. Efforts by the Dublin branch of the DAA to secure more contributions for the Trades Council met with delaying tactics at executive level. Shortage of funds was not a consideration: the DAA opened new premises in fashionable Grafton Street during 1913 and invested £2,500 in GSWR debentures; this was the company that had locked out its workers so effectively in 1911 and that included on its board Sir William Goulding and William Martin Murphy.[6]

The DAA is often cited as an example of the 'new unionism', which revolutionised Dublin working-class politics in the decade before the First World War. However, its attitude towards the lockout betrayed the petit-bourgeois background and aspirations of its members, many of whom were farmers' sons hoping to become managers or shop-owners in their own right. Another factor militating against support for the lockout was the fact that more than half the DAA's registered membership were not drapers at all but hairdressers. Well over two thousand hairdressers had been enrolled by the DAA in its insurance scheme, and these were not organised on trade union lines. Even the Dublin drapers appear to have been a far from homogeneous group. While James Seddon singled out members of the DAA for their help in organising the distribution of food parcels,[7] there were also complaints of drapers engaging in strike-breaking activities at some of Dublin's large department stores.

The composition of the union helps explain the ambiguous attitude of its general secretary, Michael O'Lehane, to the great political issues of the day. He was on the one hand an advocate of the new unionism and on the other a firm supporter of Sinn Féin. The *Draper's Assistant*, which he edited, was clearly uncomfortable with some of the internationalist implications of the sympathetic strike. In the October issue O'Lehane explained 'Where we stand' to members.

> Whilst entirely disagreeing with any action which would involve a number of trades ... without due and careful deliberation and without the concurrence of the Executives of the trades concerned, we do not at

all agree with those who believe that a Sympathetic Strike cannot be logically and successfully worked out.

Without referring directly to syndicalism, O'Lehane said that sympathetic action was 'a very live issue' in Britain and Ireland. This made the creation of 'an Irish Federation of Labour, controlled and governed in Ireland,' all the more important. There had of course been an Irish TUC since 1894, and O'Lehane himself had been president in 1912. However, it was still a pale replica of its older British cousin, as evidenced by its irrelevance during the lockout. O'Lehane was now clearly worried about the implications for the fledgling national trade union movement of too much British involvement in the 1913 dispute. Until an Irish trade union federation was firmly established 'there can be no such thing as a "Sympathetic Strike" in the full sense of the word, even if such were desirable.'

The conditions he put on such a federation included safeguards that 'each Society should have full control of what may be termed all domestic affairs, such as sick, unemployment, superannuation, and mortality benefits,' and that all should contribute to the funds of the federation 'in proportion to their effective membership.' He argued that the funds of the federation should be used only for strikes sanctioned by 'the Executive Committee of the Society, or Societies affected, and subject to the sanction or ratification of the National Council or Executive Committee of the entire Federation.' His proposals anticipated some aspects of the all-out picket rules adopted many years later by the Irish Congress of Trade Unions.

O'Lehane did not make clear whether he saw the infant ITUC or some new body as the vehicle for this Irish version of the new unionism. But he was unequivocal about the need for change.

It is useless to think that, with the growth of Capitalism and with the every day increasing mobility of Labour, the methods of industrial warfare must remain the same. We are, therefore, of the opinion that the time has arrived when a Conference of representatives of Irish Societies, whether branches of Amalgamated [British] Unions, Local Unions, or National Unions, should be called to put into concrete form the many suggestions which have been made ... towards the closer welding together of Labour in Ireland.

He accepted that British unions might have organisational difficulties in granting more autonomy to their Irish sections, but he believed these could be easily overcome.

At a time when we hear so much of being entrusted with the management of our own affairs, and when the representatives of labour in Great Britain are foremost in their advocacy in this respect, surely it should be possible for every branch of Amalgamated Unions in Ireland to arrive at a working agreement by which there could be a financial arrangement between them and the Amalgamated Unions. If Irish Trades Unionism is to be a force, a great national force in this country, it must be laid down as a first principle that Irish Trades Unionism must be completely autonomous in so far as its management is concerned. Having once laid down this and acted upon it, then by all means let us federate with Great Britain, and with the world over.[8]

O'Lehane's concerns about the dangers of a British take-over during the lockout were shared by socialist colleagues such as William Partridge and James Connolly. But where trade unionists such as Connolly saw in the British labour movement a class ally that needed to be educated out of its chauvinist ways, O'Lehane saw the same movement primarily as a threat. He had clearly thought at length about the issues involved, but the very thoroughness of his proposals militated against their acceptance: they were too specific and complicated to be seriously considered in the middle of a life-and-death struggle.

Besides, whatever the merit of O'Lehane's proposals, they did not offer a real alternative to the simpler 'hands across the sea' strategy of Larkin, nor did they offer an effective means of reining in Larkin's syndicalist gallop across Dublin's industrial battlefield. O'Lehane admitted as much when he concluded his article with a warning to members that they 'must absolutely refuse to perform work which belongs to others, and which they would not be asked to perform if no dispute existed.'[9]

It proved an instruction hard to enforce in some cases. Shop assistants tended to look down on manual labourers; in some drapery establishments this superiority was explicit in practices such as porters having to wait until the shop assistants finished their meals before being allowed to eat the 'scraps'. At Clery's and Arnott's the ITGWU complained that members of the DAA were doing the work of porters on strike. At Clery's, antagonism towards the ITGWU appears to have been a particular problem. The DAA members there contributed £2 10s to the archbishop's appeal at the end of October, the largest donation to the fund recorded from any group of employees in the city.[10] It is probably more than coincidence that William Martin Murphy was a director of the firm.

*

The DAA executive showed greater resolution in holding on to its funds than the Parliamentary Committee of the TUC. The latter's early injunction that only unions affiliated to the TUC could receive funds proved impossible to enforce.

The question remains, where did all the money go? The vast bulk of the funds, £35,794 14s, went to the ITGWU. It had 11,989 men and 840 women in dispute by the end of November. Another £3,371 1s 9d went to the United Builders' Labourers' Union, which had 1,192 members locked out for refusing to 'scab' on the ITGWU. The bricklayers received £1,606 9s for their 520 members affected, showing that pay differentials reigned even in a lockout. Smaller unions received amounts varying from £510 for the Amalgamated Carpenters' two hundred locked-out members to £1 2s for the Marble-Polishers' seven.

The funds were essential in sustaining the strike. The ITGWU was collecting only £35 a week in subscriptions and faced a bill for strike pay of nearly £3,000 in November. The Bricklayers were paying out £128 a week and collected only £10 that month, while the building labourers were still managing to collect over £30 a week in mid-November while paying out £212. All the unions were still experiencing difficulty obtaining money from the Board of Trade for their unemployed members, especially those locked out.

Food made up the greatest portion of the aid sent from Britain. By late November, 255,330 packets of tea had been shipped to Dublin, 255,000 bags of sugar, 255,330 packets of margarine, 597,000 loaves of bread, 251,804 bags of potatoes, 1,856 lb of biscuits, 72,639 pots of jam, 85,330 tins of fish, 12,500 boxes of cheese, and almost 885 tons of coal. As much again was on the way. Large amounts of clothing were also distributed.[11]

*

The figures from the report of the Dublin Children's Distress Fund tell a very different story. Launched in October 1913 and wound up in February 1914, it raised £6,482 3s 11d. Almost half of this, £2,996, was spent on food and just over half, £3,319, on clothing; £116 was spent on publicity, and £40 on administration. Only £2,046 4s 7d came from the Lord Mayor's public appeal. The diocesan collection, taken up on 2 November, when the activities of the 'kidnappers' would still have been fresh in the minds of congregations, netted a mere £2,435 19s 4d.

By far the biggest contribution came, quite fortuitously, from the organising committee of the First Irish National Pilgrimage to Lourdes. This body had made a profit on the venture that would have sated even William Martin Murphy's appetite. After all costs had been deducted it had an 'excess of income over expenditure' of £14,953 5s 4d. On 29 October 1913 the Bishop of Derry, Dr Charles McHugh, who was chairman of the Lourdes committee, wrote to Dr Walsh to tell him that the committee had decided to place £2,000 of the surplus at his disposal. His committee wanted the archbishop 'to accept this offering made in honour of Our Lady of Lourdes and to see that it is judiciously spent on the wants and comforts of the children of the Dublin workingmen, who owing to the existing state of things, are out of employment.'[12]

Dr McHugh was exceptional among churchmen of the day not only for the size of the donation he sent to Dr Walsh but in his refusal to use the opportunity to lecture Dublin's hard-pressed archbishop on the city's labour troubles. In contrast, Cardinal Logue wrote a four-page letter to Dr Walsh denouncing the strike leaders.

> Judging by their speeches the Larkinists and their abettors do not want a settlement. They are … using the men for the purpose of propagating

and establishing their socialist and syndicalist principles. As long as they are receiving support from England they will go on without shedding one iota of their pretensions; and when the support ceases they will leave the men to take the consequences, unfortunate victims of their own folly.

Dr Logue could only wonder that

the men, many of whom must be intelligent, do not see through the game. If they had an ounce of sense, they would go back to their work and leave the Larkinites to air their theories elsewhere. The real misery will come when the thing collapses and ... the men find themselves without employment.

The cardinal speculated that the strikers' places had already been taken by others, and the employers could not be expected 'to dismiss these men who stood by them in their need and take back the rebels.'

His attitude was not very different from John Dillon's. Though Dillon would never have used a word like 'rebels' to describe the Dublin workers, the term does convey the depth of betrayal felt by Dr Logue and many other nationalists, who now saw themselves as a new ruling class in waiting. Dr Logue said as much when he told the archbishop that

another consideration is that this unfortunate business is a greater backset [sic] to home rule than all the vapourings of Sir E. Carson. I sympathise with Your Grace in all the annoyance and anxiety this unfortunate state of things must cause you.

It is a wonder, in the light of his views, that Dr Logue still felt it possible to enclose

a trifle for the support of the children. I cannot spare much. I have three or four broken down priests on my hands, whom I must provide for.[13]

Yet an aspiring ruling class can hardly expect loyalty from the poor when it fails to look after them in their hour of need. The Catholic Church provided over 68 per cent of the total collected for the Dublin Children's Distress Fund. In the circumstances, it is hardly surprising that its clergy played the leading role in administering the funds. Marie Sherlock's committee was in fact composed of the administrators for Dr Walsh's city parishes, supplemented by the president of the Dublin Council of the Society of St Vincent de Paul, Father T. V. Nolan, and the presidents of the three conferences of the society operating in the most affected areas. The two honorary secretaries of the committee were also honorary secretaries of conferences of the Society of St Vincent de Paul. The funds were distributed through sixteen parish committees, in each of which the parish priest acted as both chairman and treasurer. Local conferences of the Society of St Vincent de Paul liaised with the parish committees in distributing the food and clothing concerned.

In its final report, the committee gives no details of how the funds were used, but it states that during November, December, January and the first half of February between nine and ten thousand children were provided with a meal every school day.

In most of the parishes the meals were also given on Saturdays and in some on Sundays. From the middle of February, the numbers gradually diminished: but in a few schools the work is being carried on to a small extent, as it has been carried on for years. The total amount expended on the provision of food was £2,996.

The committee spent more on clothing. The report states that boots and stockings were provided for 3,461 boys and 3,348 girls. Boys were also the recipients of 1,434 suits, 1,416 jerseys, 1,424 underpants, and 1,959 shirts. Girls received 2,840 dresses and 4,894 other garments.

In addition, grants of material to be made into clothing for girls were made to certain Convent Schools. The total amount expended in the provision of clothing was £3,319.[14]

The Protestant relief agencies engaged in similar work, but on a much smaller scale. The Samaritan Committee of Lady Aberdeen's Women's National Health Association delivered ninety-eight food parcels weekly in the central Dublin area, as well as small quantities of garments and coal. Lady Aberdeen also opened the Sláinte restaurant in Ormond Street, where half a pint of mutton broth was available for 1d and rice pudding with currants for ½d.[15] Inevitably these efforts attracted the usual contemptuous comments from the *Irish Worker*; but the main concern of Dublin trade unionists remained the attitude of the Catholic Church.

*

During the lockout, it was frequently alleged that the Catholic clergy discriminated against the families of strikers when food and clothing were being distributed. Given the massive aid from Britain for the unions and the bitter antagonism of many priests towards the labour movement, it would have been amazing if this had not been so.

An insight into the tensions that arose is given in the correspondence of Father Stafford, the parish priest of St John's, to Dr Walsh. Father Stafford was not unsympathetic to the labour movement. He knew John Bohan, a local Labour councillor and ITGWU activist, as well as being on good terms with some of the employers. His parish in Dolphin's Barn was largely a working-class one but by no means the worst affected by the lockout. The local ladies' committee, which was providing meals in the schools, appears to have come in for criticism from Canon Ryan, one of the Westland Row priests so active in combating the Dublin kiddies scheme. Given the different attitudes of the two clergymen, it was not surprising that by December 1913 relations between them had reached crisis point. Father Stafford decided to raise the canon's activities in his own parish directly with Dr Walsh; he told the archbishop that things had taken 'a very unfortunate turn' after the canon had told the committee that he intended reducing the number of children being fed from thirty-five 'to 12 or 14 at most.'

The canon had apparently taken to visiting families receiving relief in order to vet them. Father Stafford assured Dr Walsh that the scheme had been strictly run, with no child being supplied with food 'unless he or she is actually attending school here.' Every child had to have a 'meal order' issued by the Society of St Vincent de Paul and certified by the child's teacher. 'No food of any kind is given in the school itself, but only in the shed at the end of the playground, and never during teaching hours.' Meal orders were given only 'in such cases as they had reason to believe were genuine.' The cost was £2 5s a week, and local tradesmen were providing the foodstuffs 'very cheap.'

The ladies' committee had asked Father Stafford for direction, and he had told them to keep up the good work. As a result, the ladies

> went from house to house themselves and got the greater portion of them [the children] back. Some parents, however, refused owing they alleged to the treatment they received and in one or two instances they said they would send the children where their parents would not be so treated.

Father Stafford cited one case where Canon Ryan had called to a house and asked a man whether he belonged to Larkin's union.

> The man said unfortunately he did not, for if he did … he wouldn't trouble Canon Ryan or his school for they would have food for their children without begging it, and 5s. a week strike pay. He only had 2s. a week from a poor society since he was locked out. Canon Ryan told him he could get work if he liked, and upon 'C' asking him where, he was advised that work was to be had in the Baldoyle district … The man asked if the Canon wanted him to be murdered, and was answered that no man had been murdered there up to this.
>
> There was a scene in which, I understand, the wife took part. When the ladies came to me I went down at once, and tried to explain that there was a misunderstanding. The wife was very bitter over it. I begged them to send the children back to the school but they have both refused to do so up to this. Unfortunately there were several other houses visited and somewhat similar scenes took place, and the matter has got abroad here.

Father Stafford assured his lady helpers optimistically that 'things will come right.'[16]

*

It is easy to understand the attitude of the worker who told Canon Ryan that he wished he were a member of the Transport Union. Though the scenes at Liberty Hall struck many nationalists as degrading, at least paid-up members of the union were entitled to a meal ticket as a right. Less fortunate victims of the lockout were dependent on the grace and favour of their social superiors.

Three thousand meals a day were being provided at Liberty Hall.[17] A correspondent described the scene there not long before Canon Ryan's visitation on the 'undeserving' poor of Dolphin's Barn.

Crowds of waiting women press close to the railing—waiting, watching with the intent concentrated gaze of the hungry. Numbers of children, all ages, all sizes, whose grimy little hands clutch vessels of every known shape—waiting ... Inside Liberty Hall ... a steam laden atmosphere, an appetising smell of good food directs one to the kitchen—the headquarters of the 'Dinner Scheme'. Here, under the capable supervision of Madame Markievicz, about a score of girls are at work peeling potatoes and cutting up meat. They are all intelligent, they are all keen, they are all tidy, and they are all 'locked out'. Some half-dozen men are also busy—stoking the fire under the huge cauldron, fetching water and bringing from the store-room great stacks of bread.

And now comes the great moment. The doors are thrown open, and in stream the waiting women and children; each one presents a ticket, and is given in exchange a loaf of bread and about a quart of stew. A woman comes with no vessel in which to take away her portion—but she is not sent away hungry—some of the stew is given her on a plate, or in some dish improvised for the occasion. Others arrive from time to time who have also neglected to bring vessels, reminding one quite unreasonably and unwarrantably, but none the less forcibly, of the 'Foolish Virgins'; and soon there are rows of women and children seated round enjoying the good food. They talk together in low tones, and occasionally one hears scraps of conversation, in which the words 'Suffragettes' and 'Votes for Women' occur with almost startling frequency, for members of the Irish Women's Franchise League are at work here, and the little orange and green button does not escape observation. Here comes a wee maiden—almost four years of age—who typifies in her small person all the fundamental qualities of her sex—a sense of responsibility has graven an anxious little frown on the baby brow, and she has to be reassured on many points before parting with the precious ticket. 'Are you the right lady?' she asks. Reluctantly she yields up her little can and takes her stand near the door. 'Will she get the right can back again,' she wonders. Such a careful, diminutive little housewife—one smiles perhaps at the scene—but the pity of it—weighed down with care and responsibility at the age of four. Heralded by a storm of sobs and cries, one of Dublin's future citizens makes his appearance on the scene. Patience and diplomacy eventually elicit the two-fold origin of his grief—(1) he has lost his ticket; (2) he has likewise mislaid his mother. On being assured, however, that the loss of the ticket will not deprive him of his dinner, he permits his grief to be assuaged, and over the minor loss displays an amount of philosophy which fills the beholders with admiration.

The big cauldron is empty at last, and 200 people have been fed. Two more meals will be given before nightfall, and perhaps the last child in that patient queue will have been fed—perhaps; but the queue is long.[18]

On both sides the protagonists in the struggle to feed the children saw it, quite rightly, as a fight to mould the future.

28

A NOTHER vulnerable group was the homeless, especially migrant workers. In a city as dependent on casual labour as Dublin, large numbers of working men slept in the hostels when they could afford to do so, and slept rough when they could not. The Society of St Vincent de Paul had opened a fifty-bed night shelter in Great Strand Street in 1912, and the service had been overwhelmed by demand within a few months. A much larger purpose-built shelter with 150 beds was planned in Back Lane, off High Street, for 1913, one of a number of social initiatives to celebrate the centenary of the birth of the society's founder, Frédéric Ozanam.

One of these was the opening of Ozanam House in Mountjoy Square, which played a major role in providing Sunday meals for adults and children in the north city. The society also established a Secretariat for the Poor, to provide 'a bureau of information and of business and professional advice for the poor.' The more ambitious project for a new night shelter in Back Lane was delayed for lack of funds; only when Archbishop Walsh issued an urgent appeal in November 1913, and donated £500 himself, did serious construction work begin,[1] though too late to alleviate distress during the lockout.

As a result of its experience with the homeless at Great Strand Street, the Society of St Vincent de Paul discovered that 'even its widespread organisation left untouched those who ... dwelt in the lower deep.'[2] Casual labourers and itinerant workers were very hard hit by the lockout, if the society's returns for the shelter are anything to go by. In 1913 the number of admissions almost doubled—from 17,297 in 1912 to 33,462. The number of meals provided more than doubled, suggesting that it was feeding many homeless men it could not accommodate. There were 37,271 meals consumed at Great Strand Street in 1913, compared with 18,768 the previous year.

The members of the society who ran the night shelter appear to have been of a kindlier and certainly a less judgmental cast than their colleagues in the anti-proselytising wing of the movement. They had a strong sense of being involved in a social as well as a religious mission. The author of a report on the night shelter wrote in the society's bulletin:

The majority of men who seek food and a night's shelter are ... from one cause or another ... temporarily out of employment. Some have come from hospital after a long bout of illness and being without money have to face the streets in search of work, when they should be in a warm house with good food. There may be seen the hardy casual labourer, always living on the verge of starvation, to whom a few weeks idleness means dire privation; here is the small dealer who, through unforeseen misfortune, has lost his little capital and drifts into the shelter until he has time to get some help and start again; there will be found the artisan passing through in search of work, the tramp baker or tailor, ever restless or unwilling to settle down in the country; and, occasionally, one who has lived in a different world from that in which he now finds himself.

One has to mix with these men to see how unjust is the charge that they are tramps or ne'er do wells. It is true that many have lost their work through drink, but it is equally true that they have not lost their manhood, nor their self-respect.

Of course the religious aspect of the work was not neglected. The bulletin reports that in 1913, besides the meals, 1,032 scapulars were distributed, 2,532 Rosary beads, and 5,904 religious medals;[3] this was three times as many Rosary beads and four times as many medals as in 1912. Perhaps these spiritual artefacts were needed to combat the inroads of Larkin's materialist ideology; or perhaps it was all the society had to offer those it could not house.

The society also gave relief to 19,434 families in 1913. This, however, was a reduction of 1,525 on the number of families visited in 1912. On the other hand, the number of visits to families rose from 107,936 in 1912 to 127,560, an increase of over 18 per cent. In other words, members visited each family the society helped an average of 6.6 times in 1913, compared with 5.1 times during 1912. This suggests that the society was identifying those it felt to be most in need, or most deserving of help, during the lockout. In some of the worst-affected areas the average number of visits was as high as nine. Altogether there were 80,334 individuals in the families visited, making an average of just over four people per family.[4] If this average is used as a basis for the typical family affected by a lockout of 25,000 workers, then 100,000 individuals were suffering hardship in the city that winter as a direct result of the dispute.

However, we will probably never know the exact figure. What figures have survived refer only to the most organised groups of workers affected, those who were receiving strike benefit from the TUC fund. In November 1913 there were 15,018 workers receiving relief from this fund.[5] A significant minority of these must have been single men and women, and in some families sons and daughters may have been locked out as well as parents; this suggests that the unions were, at most, helping between 50,000 and 60,000 individuals. In contrast, the Society of St Vincent de

Paul helped almost 85,000 people, when the 4,000 who stayed at the night shelter are added to the families visited.

The scale of assistance rendered is a very different matter and, for the Society of St Vincent de Paul, much harder to estimate. No breakdown is given in the society's reports for the amount spent in Dublin as against the rest of the country, nor for the amount spent on the night shelter as against families in Dublin. Nationally, the society spent £18,754 on relief in 1913—only £658 more than in 1912. Even assuming that £10,000 was spent in Dublin, this would work out at 2s 3d per person. The real allocation for the capital was probably considerably less. The amount spent on the four thousand residents in Great Strand Street is also likely to have been disproportionately greater than that spent on families in the tenements.

In contrast, various trade union sources provided the average striker and his family with £7 2s 5d, or £1 17s 2d per individual, assuming three dependants for each striker. Many union members locked out would also have been entitled to unemployment benefit, ranging between 4s and 10s a week. However, most unions were complaining to Dublin Trades Council that they were experiencing difficulty in obtaining remittances from the Board of Trade under the National Insurance Acts. This problem persisted until the end of the lockout.[6]

Even allowing for the breakdown of the unemployment benefit system, trade unionists and their families were still far better off than those dependent on the Society of St Vincent de Paul, for another reason. Almost 40 per cent of the relief from trade union sources was paid in cash, whereas for the society, 'relief in kind is the rule, and the exception a grant in money.'[7] There was the added disadvantage that members of the society worked with the poor to satisfy an internal spiritual need as well as an external material one. There must have been many families who had to endure visitations similar to those of Canon Ryan in Dolphin's Barn. The message was clear: it paid to be in a trade union in the winter of 1913.

At the same time, the work of the Society of St Vincent de Paul should not be dismissed. In concentrating on the poor who were trying to survive outside the trade union network, it helped save many from starvation. It also has to be remembered that the society had only 3,755 members, of whom just over half were actively involved in branch work. On average, these members contributed a thirteenth of their own income to relieving distress.

Within Dublin much of the work appears to have been done by the various 'ladies' guilds' within the society, operating under the direction of the clergy. The Jesuits played a particularly prominent role in the north city, where they had a hand in the establishment of the society's only new branch that year. This was the Conference of Our Lady of Perpetual Succour, which covered 'a district hitherto held unworthy of visitation' in the heart of the brothel district. The initiative had been taken before the lockout in response to the activities of the proselytisers. Children were therefore one of its priorities, and 161 were transferred from 'souper schools' to Catholic schools in the Pro-Cathedral parish.[8] The new conference also visited 500 families in the area, and provided relief to 310 of them in December alone. 'Notwithstanding the exceptional necessity of conveying material relief to the poor in this crisis,' the conference reported, 'the work of spiritual improvement has not been neglected.' While members, particularly Jesuits, had strongly opposed the 'deporting' of children to England, they had no qualms about sending six boys 'to situations in the country with desirable families,' and helping consign nine others to industrial schools.

The lockout had its effects, however, even on the Jesuits. If members of the Society of Jesus were instrumental in founding the Knights of St Columbanus in 1915 to promote a Catholic freemasonry for the middle class, they also began producing publications on social issues during this period. The best known would be *The Social Teachings of James Connolly*, published by Father Lambert McKenna, headmaster of Belvedere College, in 1920.

Elsewhere in Dublin, practically every branch of the Society of St Vincent de Paul was drawn into relief work brought on by the conflict. The Conference of St Teresa held catechism classes 'for poor newsboys and other boy street-traders, to prepare them for the worthy reception of the Sacraments.' The Conference of Sts Michael and John set up a coal fund, which helped sixty-eight families through the winter; and the Conference of St Colman rejoiced that, as a result of its involvement in the work of the Dublin Children's Distress Fund, it had discovered a family where the father had become a 'Free Thinker'; he had since been persuaded to attend the Jesuits, and the society was 'hopeful that he will shortly return to the practices of his religion.'[9]

*

For most of Dublin's middle class, religious fervour was not an adequate motivation to help the poor. It is perhaps unfair to have expected them to match, penny for penny, the generosity of the TUC; but a fair idea of the general attitude towards the strikers may be gauged from how much was raised for other contemporary charitable causes. The Loyal Tramway Men's Fund was finally wound up at the end of October after realising £1,302 8s 11d, a not inconsiderable sum for the company's eight hundred employees—all of whom were also receiving weekly wages.[10]

Antipathy towards charity for the working class predated the lockout. In April 1912 there had been widespread hardship in Dublin as a result of the British coalminers' strike, which led to most of the city's workers being laid off through no fault of their own. It is hard to think of a more favourable climate for softening bourgeois hearts; but the subsequent appeal raised only £1,000, including a donation of £50 from William Martin Murphy. During the same month £2,000 was raised for the survivors of the *Titanic* disaster,[11] and a fund set up for the families of nine County Wexford men who drowned when the Fethard lifeboat was sunk on a rescue mission in

February 1914 raised over £1,000 within a week. It is doubtful if any of the *Titanic* passengers or the families of the Fethard crew were in more desperate need than Dublin's poor; no doubt the more dramatic nature of their loss added to the strength of the relevant appeals. Distance and the romantic hue it cast may also explain the success of the appeal for the China mission, which received £1,173 in the month following Dr Walsh's appeal for the distressed children of Dublin.[12] The £4,482 raised for distress in Dublin contrasts even less favourably with the £22,064 12s 0d raised that year for the Home Rule Fund.[13] Dublin may have been full of poor people, but few of them were deemed 'deserving' by their better-off brethren.

29

MEANNESS of spirit and meanness of pocket explain much of the bitterness that pervaded Dublin during the lockout. They also fuelled the vehemence with which Dublin employers, and the city's middle class, reacted to gestures of solidarity with the strikers. Whether these came in the form of food ships from British trade unions, peace initiatives by Tom Kettle, letters to the newspapers by George Russell, or poems by W. B. Yeats, they evoked resentful responses that sometimes reached hysterical levels.

To some extent, the parsimony of the Dublin ratepayers is understandable. Even before the troubles began they were facing a 17½ per cent increase in rates because of the corporation's spiralling wages bill and the housing crisis. On Friday 31 October they discovered that the six hundred RIC men in the city and county had cost £7,411 5s so far, which would add an extra 7½ per cent, or 1s 6d in the pound, to next year's rates. Because Dublin Castle controlled the police, the city council had no say over how long these guardians of the peace remained on their streets, or what the final policing bill for the lockout would be. In the circumstances, some ratepayers must have wondered at the failure of the DMP and RIC to provide better protection for the city's trams. The following Tuesday the city received a malicious damages bill from the DUTC for £167 10s 8d.[1]

However, one considerable saving did accrue to the ratepayers from the lockout, though they were unaware of it at the time. Thanks to the voluntary efforts of people as diverse as British trade unionists and the Society of St Vincent de Paul, the number of people seeking workhouse relief actually fell in 1913. The cost of administering the Poor Law in Dublin, at £52,000, was the heaviest charge on the municipality; in contrast, the cost of policing was only £31,000. Yet the frequently expressed fears during the lockout that the Poor Law system would be overwhelmed by 100,000 beggars proved unfounded. The number of people claiming outdoor relief from the workhouses fell by over 4 per cent during the year. Most of this reduction came after the lockout had begun. The number of workhouse admissions fell by a similar figure.

At the South Dublin Union, the city's largest workhouse, the number of admissions in September 1913 was 150 less than in 1912. Through the winter months, admissions continued to lag well behind the previous year.

In October 1913 there were only 1,801 admissions, compared with 1,938 in 1912; it was in fact the lowest rate of admissions in nine years. The gap widened still further as the lockout progressed. There were only 1,418 admissions in November 1913, compared with 1,814 in November 1912; while in December there were 1,422 admissions, compared with 1,726 in December 1912.

January was always the worst month for workhouse admissions, but in 1914 only 1,711 people were admitted to the South Dublin Union, compared with 2,004 in January 1913. Even when the TUC funds began to dry up in February, the number of admissions was still only 1,446, compared with 1,682 in February 1913. In March 1914, when all but one of the major disputes related to the lockout had ended, there were 1,396 admissions, compared with 1,724 in March 1913. By April, when the lockout had been over for more than a month, the gap in admissions closed a little: there were 1,454 in April 1914, compared with 1,648 in April 1913.[2]

Stricter criteria for admission to the workhouses no doubt played a part in reducing the total; and it could be argued that the passing of the Old Age Pensions Act and the introduction of social insurance in 1911 would see the start of a long-term decline in the numbers seeking relief, especially of older people. However, these measures had been introduced only in 1913, and it was February 1914 before most of the unemployment benefit that was due to locked-out trade union members was actually paid.[3]

*

The crudest indicator of human well-being in the city was, of course, the death rate. Two years earlier, the *Medical Press* had pointed out that Dublin's death rate was not only higher than any other city in Ireland or in Britain, or on the Continent, but higher even than Calcutta. The relevant passage has been etched in the collective memory of the labour movement, because it was later cited at length by James Connolly, in *The Reconquest of Ireland*, to indict the nationalist-dominated City Council.[4] Ironically, the occasion of the *Medical Press* report was the conferring of the freedom of the city on Dublin's chief medical officer, Sir Charles Cameron, for his success in reducing the death rate by over a quarter in the previous decade.

That trend, which was to continue, did receive a setback during the lockout. In the third quarter of the year the death rate in Dublin was 19.8 per thousand, compared with 17.4 during the same period of 1912. For the last quarter of 1913 it rose to 20.4 per thousand, compared with 20 per thousand for the same period in 1912. For the first quarter of 1914, traditionally the worst time of year and the period when the privations of the lockout would have taken their heaviest toll, the death rate rose to 25.9 per thousand, compared with 23.3 in the first quarter of 1913.

The increase in the number of deaths from infectious diseases, particularly those that affect children, was especially marked. In the third quarter of 1913 the death rate from these sources was 3.7 per thousand, compared with 2.5 during the same quarter of 1912. The biggest increase was in deaths from diarrhoea, enteritis, and dysentery; these caused 91 deaths in 1912 and 244 in 1913. The pattern was repeated for the last quarter of 1913, when the death rate from infectious diseases was 2.8 per thousand, compared with 1.5 per thousand in the last quarter of 1912. Again, deaths from diarrhoea, enteritis and dysentery accounted for most of the increase, at 149, compared with 55 during the same quarter of 1912.

In the first quarter of 1914 the increase in deaths from infectious diseases was less than for the comparable quarter of the previous year, at 2.3 per thousand, compared with 1.5 during the first quarter of 1913. On this occasion the increase was entirely accounted for by a measles epidemic. This caused 65 deaths in early 1914, compared with only 2 in the same quarter of 1914.

The causes of the sharp swings in the rate of infectious disease are unclear. The weather was warmer than usual in the summer of 1913, and the early winter was mild, which may explain the increase in gastro-enteritis. It could even be that the food ships added to the problem by introducing a new and richer diet to babies traditionally weaned on weak milky tea and to small children used to eating dry bread. What is clear is that the underlying death rate rose sharply in the first quarter of 1914, when the food ships stopped.

The health statistics also give a glimpse of the impact the lockout had on home life. These largely derive from visits made by sanitary officers to inspect newborn infants. At the start of the lockout, 75.5 per cent of fathers in families visited were working, and 6.8 per cent of mothers. During visits made in the second three months of the dispute, sanitary officers reported only 51.8 per cent of fathers working, while the number of working mothers had risen to 8.2 per cent. In the final phase of the lockout, from January to March 1914, the number of working fathers had climbed back to 70.6 per cent, while the number of working mothers had fallen to 5.2 per cent.

A breakdown of the figures for working parents into regular and casual employment also tells a story. At the start of the lockout, 36 per cent of working fathers were in casual employment; in the second three months of the dispute the number had risen to 67 per cent—a complete reversal of the situation in the previous quarter. By the end of the first quarter of 1914 the situation had returned almost to the status quo, with 38 per cent of working fathers in casual employment and 62 per cent in regular jobs.

The number of women affected was obviously much smaller, but it shows a similar trend in reverse. At the start of the lockout there were 64 mothers in regular employment and 66 in casual employment; in the quarter from October to December 1913 the number in regular employment dropped to 40, but the number in casual jobs rose to 104. By the next quarter, January to March, which marked the end of the dispute, the number of mothers in regular employment had shrunk to 39, while the number in casual employment had dropped to 61.

These figures suggest that, with the drastic fall-off in food shipments from Britain after 10 January, strikers and locked-out workers had little choice but to return to work and, if possible, find a regular job, so that their families would not starve. On the other hand, mothers who had gone out to work within days of giving birth during the height of the lockout were once more able to spend greater time in the home.

One further statistic reinforces this interpretation, and illustrates the toll the lockout had taken on the everyday lives of working-class families. Before and after the lockout, less than 3 per cent of homes were judged to be in a 'dirty state' by sanitary visitors, who were usually middle-class women; the balance were described as 'clean and in good order.' During the lockout the proportion of homes in a 'dirty state' rose to almost 11 per cent.[5]

More research is needed to establish the effect the lockout had on the well-being of Dubliners; but there is a strong *prima facie* case for suggesting that it was the poorest families, and especially the children of those families, who suffered most.

*

The popular image of the trade union militant as the most downtrodden and oppressed member of the community during the lockout is misleading. At the very bottom of the heap, without access to regular work or to the largesse of the TUC or Dublin Trades Council, were thousands of casual labourers, hawkers, the unemployed, the sick, and the indigent, who were dependent on bodies such as the Society of St Vincent de Paul and the workhouses.

Yet all the indicators suggest that the lot of most of Dublin's poor, whether trade unionists or not, was not significantly worse during the lockout than in normal times. Contrary to popular belief, the fall-off in the numbers seeking workhouse relief, the lower incidence of cruelty cases reported to the NSPCC and the sharp drop in prostitution reported by the DMP indicate that the living conditions of many poor Dubliners during the winter of 1913 were no worse than usual. Some families, particularly those of ITGWU members, may even have been warmer, better fed and better clothed than they had been for many a year.

Only an end to the food ships could force the workers off the picket lines. That was still a remote, and to many unthinkable, prospect in November 1913.

*

William Martin Murphy and the hard-liners among the employers argued, with some justification, that British aid was prolonging the agony of the conflict; but that was not how most trade unionists or many British people saw it at the time. To them, the actions of the TUC and of dozens of valiant middle-class women who provided relief work—be it as sanitary visitors, socially concerned suffragists, nuns, members of St Vincent de Paul ladies' committees, union organisers, or indeed professional revolutionaries—

provided a salutary contrast to the meagre-spirited responses of the government, the employers, and the ratepayers. The public humiliation of this parsimonious trinity was still far from over. As Murphy had predicted, the imprisonment of Larkin won him a new halo, and the indiscretions of recent weeks were forgotten.

On Saturday 1 November the *Irish Worker* published on its front page a message from the imprisoned leader. The fact that most of it was probably written by Connolly did not prevent its widespread dissemination in the British radical press.[6] The writer reminded ITGWU members:

> We have been associated together for the past seven years. Throughout that period [we] were always and ever advancing ... Attacks on us have been made in front and flank, and we have always prevailed unconquerable ... This great fight of ours is not simply a question of shorter hours or better wages. It is a great fight for human dignity, for liberty of action, liberty to live as human beings should live, exercising their God-given faculties and powers over nature; always aiming to reach out for a higher betterment and development, trying to achieve in our own time the dreams of great thinkers and poets of this nation—not as some men do, working for their individual aggrandisement.

The writer warned against attempts to 'seduce' members from their allegiance to the union.

> Without wishing to cast any reflection upon our friends across the Channel, this fight must be settled by the men here at home in our own union. Without in any way disparaging any ... section of the organised working class, we of the Irish Transport and General Workers' Union cannot only claim, but make good our claim of being the pioneers in the grand class war.

Larkin named Daly, Partridge, McKeown and Connolly as his successors. 'These and these only must we allow and authorise to act for us.' He also urged members to wear the Red Hand badge, which 'struck terror in the hearts of the Sweaters and Slum Property Owners.'

There was more to come. Inside, the *Irish Worker* published the speech that Yeats had been prevented from making by the Lord Mayor at the Mansion House the previous Monday. It was even more envenomed than Russell's famous address to the masters of Dublin, and it too received widespread distribution in Britain.

> I do not complain of Dublin's capacity for fanaticism whether in priest or layman, for you cannot have strong feeling without that capacity, but neither those who directed the police nor the editors of our newspapers can plead fanaticism.
>
> They are supposed to watch over our civil liberties, and I charge the Dublin Nationalist newspapers with deliberately arousing religious passion to break up the organisation of the working man, with appealing

to the mob law day after day, with publishing the names of workingmen and their wives for purposes of intimidation. And I charge the Unionist Press of Dublin and those who directed the police with conniving at this conspiracy.

He compared the concern that unionist newspapers, such as the *Irish Times* and *Daily Express*, showed for the defence of civil liberties in Ulster with their indifference

to that liberty here in Dublin … I want to know why the mob at North Wall and elsewhere were permitted to drag children from their parents' arms, and by what right one woman was compelled to open her box and show a marriage certificate; I want to know by what right the police have refused to accept charges against the rioters; I want to know who has ordered the abrogation of the most elementary rights of the citizen and why the authorities … have permitted the Ancient Order of Hibernians to besiege Dublin, taking possession of its railway stations like a foreign army. Prime Ministers have fallen and ministers of state have been impeached for less than this. I demand that the forthcoming Police Inquiry shall be so widened that we may get to the bottom of a conspiracy, whose like has not been seen in any English-speaking town during living memory. Intriguers have met together somewhere behind the scenes that they might turn the religion of Him who thought it hard for a rich man to enter into the Kingdom of Heaven into an oppression of the poor.

In the same issue, Maud Gonne, who had opposed Larkin and the ITGWU over the Dublin kiddies scheme, described the employers as 'criminals'.

*

This was but a foretaste of the vituperation that descended on Dublin's social elite from the platform of the Royal Albert Hall in London that night. The hall was filled to capacity, and there was an overflow crowd of twenty thousand. The principal speaker was George Bernard Shaw, who was there, he told the crowd,

as a Dublin man to apologise for the priests of Dublin. The honest truth … is that those men, although they are pious and doing a good deal of good work, are very ignorant and simple men in the affairs of the country and especially industrial affairs. If by any means these words reach them, I hope they will be obliged to me for the apology I have made for them.

There is something even more terrible than the horror of their individual action, and that is the terror of the great Church to which they belong being made the catspaw of a gentleman like Mr Murphy. (Laughter.)

As to the employers of Dublin, I am utterly ashamed of them. I do not, however, apologise for them. Why, even an Englishman could employ people at decent trade union wages occasionally, and make his business pay. (Laughter.) And there are Irishmen like Mr Murphy and the biscuit gentlemen who told them they are so destitute of business capacity that they are unable to make their business pay under the conditions in which business is made to pay in England.

Suffragists, in particular members of Sylvia Pankhurst's East End Federation of the Women's Social and Political Union, had played a prominent part in organising the meeting, and Shaw did not intend to let the audience forget it. He said he could not claim any great sympathy with Larkin in his present misfortune: he could not forget that Larkin,

in the first division in Mountjoy Prison, is a happy man compared with many people who are not men, and who are not in the first division, but are dying of torture at the present moment. (Cheers.) They demand law and order with regard to every other class ... but it has been the practice to let loose the police in connection with the working class ... telling them to do their worst to the people, and in no city ... has that principle been applied more gloriously than it has ... been in Dublin.

If you put a policeman on a footing with a mad dog it can only end in one way, and that is that all respectable citizens will have to arm themselves. (Cheers.) I suggest you should arm yourselves with something which should put a decisive stop to the proceedings of the police.

I hope that this observation of mine will be carefully reported. I should rather like to be prosecuted for sedition and to have an opportunity of explaining ... what exactly I mean by it. (Laughter.)

Connolly told the crowd that the high death rate in Dublin meant that its working class was being killed daily. 'Children are being murdered continuously by the abominable conditions under which they are compelled to live.' It was these conditions that 'had raised the banner of revolt.' He said that 'until James Larkin comes out of prison, the working classes should at every by-election vote against the Liberal jailers. (Cheers.)'

The author of the now-celebrated letter to the *Irish Times*, George Russell, also spoke. Russell hated public speaking and once told Yeats that he approached such events 'with something of the trepidation of a martyr anticipating his torture on the rack.'[7] He probably realised his speech that night would cause even more outrage at home than Shaw's.

The great generosity of English to Irish workers has obliterated the memory of many an ancient tale of wrong. I come from Dublin, where most extraordinary things have been happening. Humanity long dumb has found its voice, it has its prophet and its martyrs. We no longer know people by the old signs and the old shams. People are to us either human or sub-human. They are either on the side of those who are fighting for human conditions in labour or they are with those who are trying to degrade it and thrust it into the abyss.

Ah! but I forgot; there has sprung up a third party, who are super-human beings. They have so little concern for the body at all, that they assert it is better for children to be starved than to be moved from the Christian atmosphere of the Dublin slums. Dublin is the most Christian city in these islands. Its tottering tenements are holy. The spiritual atmosphere which pervades them is ample compensation for the diseases which are there and the food which is not there. If any poor parents think otherwise, and would send their children for a little from that earthly paradise, they will find the docks and railway stations barred by these superhuman beings and by the police, and they are pitched headlong out of the station, set upon and beaten, and their children snatched from them. A Dublin labourer has no rights in his own children. You see if these children were even for a little out of the slums, they would get discontented—so a very holy man has said.

Without naming Archbishop Walsh, Russell went on to cite his view that once getting full meals, the children

might be so inconsiderate as to ask for them all their lives. They might destroy the very interesting experiment carried on in Dublin for generations to find out how closely human beings can be packed together, on how little a human being can live, and what is the minimum wage his employer need pay him. James Larkin interrupted these interesting experiments towards the evolution of the underman, and he is in jail.

Like an escaper from a concentration camp, Russell told his audience: 'You have no idea what the slums in Dublin are like.' With 'more than twenty thousand families each living in one room,' many of them

are so horrible, so unsanitary, so overrun with vermin that … the only condition in which a man can purchase sleep is that he is drugged with drink. The Psalmist says the Lord gives sleep to his beloved, but in these Dublin dens men and women must pay the devil his price for a little of that peace of God.

He appealed to those assembled not to forsake these men.

They may have been to blame for many an action. The masters may perhaps justifiably complain of things done and undone. But if the masters have rights by the light of reason and for the moment, the men are right by the light of spirit and for eternity. This labour uprising in Ireland is the despairing effort of humanity to raise itself out of a dismal swamp of disease and poverty. James Larkin may have been an indiscreet leader. He may have committed blunders, but I believe in the sight of Heaven the crimes are all on the other side. If our Courts of Justice were courts of humanity, the masters of Dublin would be in the dock charged with criminal conspiracy, their crime that they tried to starve out one-third of the people of Dublin, to break their hearts and degrade their manhood, for the greatest crime against humanity is its own degradation.

The men have always been willing to submit their case to arbitration, but the masters refuse to meet them. They would not abide by the Askwith report. They refused to hear of prominent Irishmen acting as arbitrators. They said scornfully of the Peace Committee that it was only interfering. They say they are not fighting trades unionism, but they refuse point blank to meet the Trades Council in Dublin. They want their own way absolutely. These Shylocks of industry want their pound of flesh starved from off the bones of the workers ... You have no idea what labour in Ireland, which fights for the bare means of human support, is up against. The autocrats of industry can let loose upon them the wild beasts that kill in the name of the State. They can let loose upon them a horde of wild fanatics who will rend them in the name of God. The men have been deserted by those who were their natural leaders. For ten weeks the miserable creatures who misrepresent them in Parliament kept silent. When they were up for the first time in their lives against anything real, they scurried back like rats to their hole. These cacklers about self-government had no word to say on the politics of their own city, but after ten weeks of silence they came out with six lines of a letter signed by all the six poltroons. They disclaimed all responsibility for what was happening in the city and county they represent ... but they would agree to anything that the Archbishop might say.

Russell now shared at least some of the ambitions of Larkin for the Ireland of the future.

The landlords of industry will have disappeared from Ireland when the battle begun this year is ended. Democratic control of industry will replace the autocracy which exists today. We are working for the co-operative commonwealth, to make it the Irish polity of the future, and I ask you to stand by the men who are beginning the struggle ... I have often despaired over Dublin, which John Mitchel called a city of genteel dastards and bellowing slaves, but a man has arisen who has lifted the curtain which veiled from us the real manhood of the City of Dublin. Nearly all the manhood is found among the obscure myriads who are paid from five to twenty-five shillings per week. The men who will sacrifice anything for a principle get rarer and rarer above that limit of wealth.

I am a literary man, a lover of ideas, but I have found few people in my life who would sacrifice anything in life for a principle. Yet in Dublin, when the masters issued that humiliating document, asking men—on penalty of dismissal—to swear never to join a trade union, thousands of men who had no connection with the Irish Transport Workers—many of them personally hostile to that organisation—refused to obey. They would not sign away their freedom, their right to choose their own heroes and their own ideas. Most of these men had no strike funds to fall back on. They had wives and children depending on them. Quietly and grimly they took through hunger the path to the Heavenly City. They stand silently about the streets. God alone knows what is passing in the hearts of these men. Nobody in the press in Dublin has said a word about it. Nobody has praised them, no-one has put a crown on their brows.

Yet these men are the descendants of Oscar, Cú Chulainn, the heroes of our ancient stories. For all their tattered garments, I recognise in these obscure men a majesty of spirit. It is in the workers of the towns and in the men in the cabins in the country that the hope of Ireland lies. The poor have always helped each other, and it is they who listen eagerly to the preachers of a social order based on brotherhood and co-operation.

There were other speakers that night, including Sylvia Pankhurst and Pethwick Lawrence, whose wife was still looking after the first contingent of Dublin kiddies at their home in Surrey. But their criticism could be dismissed as predictable; and, as it happened, most of their wrath was directed at the pusillanimous Liberal government. This was something to which Irishmen of every hue could subscribe.

*

As Russell had expected, he returned

to find Dublin one prolonged howl of indignation at my Albert Hall speech. The *Freeman's Journal* leadered my iniquity on Monday, also on Tuesday, also on Wednesday, and only fainted on Thursday through a complete loss of epithets.

The *Freeman* also raised the question whether Russell should be allowed to continue editing the *Irish Homestead*, the journal of the Irish Agricultural Organisation Society. The AOH was already looking for Russell's head over his celebrated letter to the *Irish Times*.[8] However, the founder of the IAOS, Sir Horace Plunkett, thought Russell's stand 'a glorious indiscretion.' Plunkett, the unionist aristocrat who had founded the Irish co-operative movement and flirted with home rule, was an institution in his own right. The IAOS head office in Merrion Square, Dublin, had already been named after him, and he had no intention of kowtowing to Hibernians and their fellow-travellers.

On Monday 10 November the IAOS held a meeting to consider the calls for Russell's dismissal. It passed a resolution declaring that, as a co-operative body, it was 'stringently prohibited from taking part in religious or political controversies.' However, the resolution also stated that the editor of the *Irish Homestead* was not an official of the IAOS, and the society respected 'the liberty of every member of our co-operative societies to adopt and express, outside the field of co-operative work, any opinion on public questions which commends itself to him.'

The only hint of obeisance to the new Catholic-nationalist order was a recognition of 'the generous sympathy of the Roman Catholic clergy, as of the clergy of other denominations, with the struggles and hardships of the workers upon the land.' That sympathy had 'prompted the success of agricultural co-operation in Ireland.'

The resolution was published in the form of a letter to the press, over the names of the entire IAOS committee.[9] It showed that rural Ireland could, on occasion, be a good deal more liberal than Dublin. A month later, Plunkett confided in a letter to one of Russell's friends that the London speech had caused him problems; but he added that 'to attack the Dublin employers, Dublin Castle, the police, the nationalist M.P.s, the A.O.H, the R.C. Church, over the condition of the Dublin slums was a magnificent exhibition of moral courage so magnificent that I can forgive all his recklessness of consequence to my own little schemes.'[10]

Shaw's comments attracted far less anger. A cartoon in the *Sunday Independent* portrayed him as 'G.B.S., the Buffoon,' and placed him alongside 'Æ, the Pal of the Fairies,' 'W.B., the Spook,' and 'Skeffy', who brandished a *Votes for women* banner. The *Irish Times* attributed Shaw's speech to the 'sublime insolence' of a man who

> boasts that he left Ireland at the age of twenty, and has not lived here since. As a licensed buffoon and the consecrated prophet of the patently absurd, he has to support his reputation by insisting that what is obviously wrong is quite clearly right. But, to our great regret, we find such a logical thinker as Mr. George Russell in this gallery of extremists. The burden of Mr. Russell's speech appears to be that the employers of Dublin are wholly responsible for the conditions in which many of the working classes of Dublin live. Mr. Russell, in a less enthusiastic moment, will realise that this is arrant nonsense ... The people ... primarily responsible are the members of Dublin corporation, and it is notorious that the employers, as a class, have little or no say in the selection of that body. It is time Mr. George Russell imported his own principles into this discussion. If he did, he might abandon the 'accepted myth' that the employers of Dublin are brutal and callous tyrants in favour of his own 'golden heresy' of the truth.[11]

The *Leader* was even more affronted by Russell's defection. It was unforgivable that one of the most articulate exponents of Irish nationality had run off and told tales to 'the Big Brother ... Johnny Bull.' Russell's 'jibe' at Dr Walsh, for saying that the children of Dublin workers might grow discontented with their lot if allowed out of the slums for a few weeks, was 'another gem from the minor poet, acting as a Carrion Crow.' Like the *Times*, the *Leader* dismissed Shaw as 'a clever buffoon: whenever he appears on a platform he has to act the funny man or else disappoint the audience.' He had long been numbered by the *Leader* with that dangerous breed of intellectuals who posed as Irishmen only to subvert their fellow-countrymen from their true allegiance.

In the issue after its denunciation of Russell, the *Leader* published a cartoon obviously inspired by that in the *Sunday Independent*. It portrayed Russell as the 'hairy fairy', presiding over a fairy ring that was raptly contemplating Russell's 'vision of the Co-Operative Commonwealth.' Among the gathering was Yeats, 'a minor poet, abuser of employers,' and perched in a tree overhead was Sheehy-Skeffington, the 'President of the Millennium Board'.[12]

Ironically, it was the lockout that ended a nine-year estrangement between Russell, the practical nationalist, and Yeats, the mystical one. In a letter congratulating Yeats on his speech at the peace meeting in the Mansion House 'and above all ... your letter in the "Irish Worker",' Russell said, 'it falls on us to make a fight for social and intellectual freedom.'[13] The *Leader* caricatured them as arcane seers, contemplating mushrooms in the woods, only because Moran felt that ridicule was the best weapon for dealing with enemies. It put them on a par with Carson and Larkin in the *Leader's* gallery of rogues that autumn.

*

As far back as 1908 the *Leader* had warned the Irish Party that it was losing touch with the workers of the towns, and particularly Dublin. However, D. P. Moran and his paper had been as preoccupied as any parliamentary nationalist that summer with the threat posed by Carson and his Volunteers. This quickly changed in the aftermath of the 'Bloody Sunday' riots.

In an Ireland without home rule, the *Leader* accepted that 'it is hard to expect the public view to be clear on many matters involving Law and Order.' However, in an Ireland that was self-governing,

> the legitimate and established authorities ought to be supreme in secular affairs ... The organisation of all Labour in a class would not fit in with the well-ordered state, for in many ways it would tend to usurp its authority, and an Ireland under Home Rule would see that very clearly. The working world would be impossible under the organised and terrorised sympathetic strike. And after all that is what the Labour movement aims towards.[14]

Predictably, the *Leader's* attitude continued to harden as the strike dragged on. 'Labour in Ireland, we have often said, badly needed shaking up,' it was arguing by mid-September; 'though where a shaking up may be good, an earthquake is not necessarily welcome.' People should not become 'alarmist and needlessly pessimistic on a little provocation.' The Land League, which freed the tenant farmers, was 'one of the greatest movements of labour history,' and it was inevitable that the labour movement in the towns should now emerge as something more than 'an echo or a tail of Trades Unionism in England.' Nevertheless it was unreasonable for Irish workers to expect that they could enjoy the 'standards of countries with centuries of industrial history behind them, when Ireland has only just emerged from the catacombs of English-made landlordism.' Ireland was 'unique every way. We want an Irish labour policy for Ireland.'

The same edition published a cartoon of 'Éire' bringing Labour and Capital together to join her in a 'Triple Alliance'. 'Oh, children, children, do be wise | And end this strike in compromise.' Inadvertently or otherwise, the heading echoed the recent emergence of a British trade union Triple Alliance between miners, railway workers, and dockers.[15]

Employers were far from immune from criticism, and the *Leader* took them to task severely for asking their workers to sign undertakings to have nothing to do with the ITGWU. They were as guilty of sympathetic industrial action as the workers. Nationalist politicians received similar criticism.

> Did the Irish Parliamentary Party ever take leading action in an Irish labour dispute? The attempted eviction of a Cottier in Mayo might, and probably would call out their strength; but a strike or lockout?

Dublin workers were becoming Anglicised and divorced from the city's Irish Party MPs, the *Leader* lamented. 'Whilst our M.P.s clamour for Home Rule … they allow Irish labour to hitch itself onto British labour without so much as a protest.'[16]

In another issue, the *Leader* pointed out that 'one result of the unfortunate labour mix-up in Dublin is that England has got a chance of interfering very much in our Irish affairs.' It shrewdly identified recent statements from the National Transport Workers' Federation denouncing 'provincialism, sectionalism, or mere race prejudice' as a demand that the 'Irish Transport Union must … place their necks in the English halter.' Larkin might describe the relief ships bringing food from Britain as 'hands across the sea,' but, the *Leader* reminded its readers,

> 'Irish Ireland' does not stand for 'hands across the sea,' it stands for Ireland a self-contained entity … We don't want to take our labour, politics, or our Laws from England.

The British trade union leaders might say that the lockout was 'no longer a Dublin nor an Irish fight,' but 'what do these men know of Ireland or the Irish?' When Irish employers paid their workers decent wages, 'the name of Mr. Gosling, of England, and all the other economic quacks will have been forgotten here.'[17]

The advent of Dora Montefiore and her Dublin kiddies scheme dispelled any doubts the *Leader* had about which side in the lockout posed the greater threat to Irish Ireland. Moran himself went down to the North Wall to witness the defeat of the 'Montefiore gang' and the 'child deportees' by Catholic vigilance groups. 'This is a great time for England. She has it every way,' the paper told readers on 1 November, the same day that Shaw and Russell were berating their homeland in London.

> At a very small cost she is feeling very virtuous at feeding thousands of people in Dublin, and at the same time she is pushing her trade in Ireland in soap, candles, biscuits, matches and other forms of merchandise. Talk of the sweated labour of Belfast, London and Liverpool: it is nothing to the sweated strikers for England in Dublin ... The meanest employer in Ireland never asked people to work for them for the wages that England is sending over here mainly in the form of potatoes, tinned fish, jam and margarine. The solidarity of labour! One arm of Dublin industry is tied and ... poor chaps here are fighting England's battle for lumps of margarine.

The *Leader* dismissed the notion of a 'phantom ship' of free labourers invading the port, but asked, not unreasonably, why Irish trade unionists ready to cause a 'tumult' if such an invasion took place were allowing in English lorries to do their work.

> If these motor lorries were men their lives would not be safe, but being only English machines made presumably by Trade Union labour ... the men who are fighting the battle of England for doles of tinned meat and ... margarine appear to be quite satisfied with the importation of the lorries.
>
> If 'tainted' goods—Irish goods, for we don't hear of any 'tainted' English goods—were offered to one of the steamboats, we assume they would be refused else the men would go on strike. Why did not the crews of the boats that were offered ... the Montefiore goods in the shape of Dublin children insist that such goods should not be taken on board, or threaten to strike if they were carried?

To ram home Moran's point, the *Leader's* cartoon that week provided an illustration of 'untainted goods' in the form of two children being led up the gangway of a ferry.

The *Leader* also took the *Irish Times* to task for trying to make political capital out of the 'deportation of Irish children' in pursuit of 'its own anti-national and anti-Catholic purposes.' In reality, the *Leader* said, the controversy had provided the Archbishop of Dublin, Dr Walsh, with an opportunity to explain how much 'Catholics, particularly the Catholic clergy, were doing for the poor.' For good measure it provided readers who wished to know more with a list of recent publications on 'the Church and Labour and Social Questions.'

> The Catholics of Ireland must not allow themselves to be jostled out of labour politics. The unskilled men and women workers need to be organised, and, as in the days of the Land fight ... we must have priests and people working together.[18]

*

Few priests shared Moran's enthusiasm. Only a week earlier, the *Irish Worker* had reported that five priests were seeking eviction orders in the Dublin police courts against tenants. On the very day that the *Leader* was urging clergymen to involve themselves in positive social action, the *Irish Catholic* sprang to the defence of the priest as private citizen.

> Our clergy cannot build modern lodging houses for the workers, they cannot prevent men, or women either, from drinking themselves into poverty, from committing transgressions of the public law, or breaking some of the regulations of their employers, which may result in leaving them without work or wages. The priests can ... but ... counsel and shrive ... No attic in Dublin is too noisome, no cellar too dark or pestiferous for the priests of our city to ... bear the Viaticum.

It refused to enter the debate with the 'English gutter press of the Socialists,' which had denounced the Catholic clergy as 'aiders and abettors of "the capitalists".' Regrettably, 'even in Dublin there have been found people so debased and demoralised as to listen without protest or even receive it [the denunciation] with applause.'[19]

If Moran could not presume to speak for the Catholic Church on social issues, there were also dissenting views from his own among other inhabitants of Irish Ireland. Arthur Griffith's weekly, *Sinn Féin*, which had a smaller but more focused audience of advanced nationalists, had already denounced the 'vile and destructive methods of demagogues posing as labour leaders,' and now bewailed the defection of Russell. Commenting on his speech in London, *Sinn Féin* said, 'Let him recall that Dublin, not London, is the capital of the Irish nation, and that no differences or quarrels between Irishmen can ever justify recourse to the method of Diarmuid Mac Murchadha.' Russell was travelling the road of Yeats and Rolleston before him, it warned, and would end up 'in John Bull's bosom.'

The reference to Rolleston was significant, for it showed that Griffith saw nationality as first and foremost a matter of political allegiance. The son of a County Court judge, Thomas William Rolleston was a leading figure in the Irish literary revival. He had founded the *Dublin University Review* and promoted the work of young writers such as W. B. Yeats and Katharine Tynan. Rolleston had been the first secretary of the Celtic Literary Society, which is probably where he met Griffith. A falling out was inevitable, as Rolleston's politics were liberal unionist; he supported Britain in the Boer War and was to find himself increasingly at odds with cultural compatriots as time passed. When the First World War broke out in 1914 he became a censor, translator and publicist for British Intelligence, and he remained with his new employer until his death in 1920. His knowledge of Irish proved particularly valuable to the British authorities. Among the letters he censored were those of Griffith when the latter was imprisoned at Reading after the Easter Rising—though Rolleston's command of Irish was not required for that purpose, as Griffith never mastered the language.

Rolleston symbolised the plight of those Irishmen who clearly valued their country's unique culture but also wished to remain within the empire. Griffith, on the other hand, shared Moran's sense of outrage that British trade unionists were exploiting the lockout to undermine Irish business and using Dublin as 'the cockpit for deciding whether the Syndicalist method of discussing industrial disputes might be hereafter tried in England without any danger of causing English trade to go elsewhere.'

Griffith's remarks show a profound misunderstanding of the debate then raging among socialists and trade unionists about the significance of the lockout; but his knowledge of the issues and the personalities involved still went deeper than Moran's.[20] Griffith's position on the lockout was undoubtedly influenced by his deep antipathy towards Larkin. As far back as the 1908 carters' strike he had written:

> The sooner the men who were brought out on strike … by an English organiser erect themselves into an Irish labour union, as the Corporation workmen have done, and affiliate themselves directly to the Trades Council the better. English trades unionism has no interest in this country except England's interest.

At that time Larkin was still an official of the NUDL, a British union. But his decision a year later to defect from Sexton's union and set up the ITGWU did nothing to assuage Griffith. He wrote a few weeks later:

> The English Union of Dock Labourers having repudiated the Strike Organiser, that person is now seeking an opening for himself as organiser of an Irish Transport Workers' Union. We wish it well and will give all our assistance to any genuine Irish organisation of transport workers, but to assure the public that it is genuine the first essential of such a body is that those connected with it are not suspended or dismissed officials of the English Union.[21]

Griffith's refusal to accept Larkin's Irishness anticipated his rejection a decade later of Erskine Childers as a 'damned Englishman' for opposing the Treaty settlement. Like Larkin and Childers, James Connolly was born in Britain of Irish descent; but Griffith's attitude to him was very different. Connolly, Griffith told his readers, was 'the man in the leadership of the Transport Union with a head on his shoulders.'[22] The two had known each other since they campaigned together against the Boer War, and Griffith had even endorsed Connolly's unsuccessful candidature in the city council elections of 1902. Very different in their politics, they nevertheless enjoyed a relationship based on a critical mutual respect. When Connolly therefore argued for the establishment of a conciliation board to resolve the dispute in September 1913, Griffith welcomed it, especially as his own paper had been proposing such an approach for some time. The fact that Larkin had also been advocating such a measure was blithely ignored; and when the Askwith tribunal made a similar proposal in October, *Sinn Féin* riposted airily that 'Conciliation Boards or Arbitration Courts are things so good in themselves that we in Ireland are not under the necessity of learning [of them] from three of the Superior Race after they had cogitated in the Castle for a week.'

Sinn Féin went as far as New Zealand and Australia to bring its readers details of how industrial arbitration bodies operated.[23] In fact the New Zealand scheme was in serious trouble by 1913, because of growing opposition from trade unions. Like his enthusiasm for 'dual monarchy' based on the Austro-Hungarian model, it is hard to escape the view that Griffith was happy to find solutions to Ireland's problems anywhere and from anyone, except England and 'Englishmen'.

Sinn Féin did at least accept that Dublin workers had legitimate grievances in their appalling housing conditions and in the way wages had fallen behind prices. The lockout provoked Griffith's own seminal article 'Sinn Féin and the Labour Question,' which appeared in *Sinn Féin* on 25 October 1913.

> When a cry echoes in this country today that Capitalism and not England is the enemy, the reply is obvious—the Capitalism that denied its obligation to the moral law and the law of the nation ... that concept of Capitalism had its germ in no Celtic or Latin civilisation, but in the Teutonic Hansards and its modern development the world owes to England. England, with her savage doctrine of irresponsibility of Capital to aught but itself has begotten a misery on the social system which has driven men to dream that in a revival of Feudalism with the State instead of the Noble as the all-provider—wherein the subject is relieved by benevolent despotism from the exercise of his personal initiative and the discipline of personal responsibility—the Salvation of humanity is to be found.[24]

Though Connolly is not mentioned, Griffith's target appears to be a recurring theme in Connolly's writings: that the Irish path to communism could be reached, in part, by invoking communal aspects of Ireland's Celtic past.[25] Each man was, in his own way, being hopelessly romantic. If Connolly ignored the existence of slaves and endemic violence in his evocation of a now vanished Celtic commonwealth, Griffith believed that an independent Irish legislature would rid the country of the 'English' characteristics that made capitalism so objectionable.

> Not Capitalism, but the abuse of Capitalism oppresses Labour ... Not in the destruction of the Capitalist, but in his subjection to the law of the State, interpreting the conscience and the interest of the Nation, will Labour be delivered from its oppression and restored to all its rights.
>
> I affirm that the evils of the social system, as they exist in this country and in Great Britain, are wholly due to English policy and Government, and that that policy and that Government are partly responsible for those evils, as they exist in a modified form, outside the radius of the British flag.

It was a racial analysis of British imperialism, which would have found no sympathy from socialists such as Larkin, though Connolly might have been more tolerant of its shortcomings.

Griffith, of course, had no more tolerance for socialism than he had for British imperialism. He continued his incantation against the forces of modernism:

> I deny that Socialism is a remedy for the existent evils or any remedy at all. I deny that capital and Labour are in their nature antagonistic—I assert they are essential and complementary the one to the other. I deny to any member of the human race as a member of that important part of creation any natural right except the right to live, and I affirm that every other right man becomes possessed of he holds through religion and the nation.

It was not, however, the right of the nation to abrogate to itself the use of capital.

> It is the right and function of the Nation to say: 'You are a capitalist and it is your right to use your capital as you please so long as you do not use it to the injury or oppression of the poorer of your brethren and my children.'

Nor could the nation say to Labour:

> 'You are Labour. You shall sell yourself to Capital at Capital's price, or my policemen shall punish you.' It is the right and function of the Nation to say to Labour: 'You are Labour. You shall sell your services to Capital for a lawful price, and a lawful price is that which will enable you to live in decency and comfort and provide against the material ills of the world. For I am the Nation—your father and the father of Capital also, and in my house my children shall not oppress the other—it shall not be a house divided against itself.[26]

This elevation of the nation to a deity, and the insistence that only through identification with a religion, a culture and a nationality could an individual hold any rights, was the stock in trade of most nationalists throughout Europe. Griffith's denial of the right of Larkin or Childers to claim Irishness was also a denial of their right to a political existence. In Childers' case the argument was taken to its extreme conclusion of death by firing-squad. It would be unfair to equate Griffith's exclusivist version of nationalism with those of Hitler or Milošević, but it came from the same stable.

Griffith's antidote to English capitalism was protectionism. 'I believe in the protection of the capital of my country against the power of England or any other foreign capital.' After the defence of its people from military invasion, the first duty of the nation was to 'use all its strength to repel an industrial invasion which threatens its people with the loss of their means of livelihood.

The protection of labour was the third priority.

> A thousand years ago in Ireland, when Irish Law ruled Irishmen, the rights of Labour were recognised … in the civil code … And in the adaptation of the spirit of the Irish labour legislation of our ancestors to the conditions of our own time will be found a true solution. If the working men of Ireland are wise enough to realise that the true emancipation for Labour is the political instrument operated through the legislature these things it can have done.[27]

Like Russell, Griffith despaired of anything being done by Dublin's present legislators, the six Irish Party MPs whom he dubbed the 'Sleeping Beauties'. He asked whether these men 'posing as representatives of the people of Dublin' would repudiate the £400 a year they drew in parliamentary salaries in the same way that they repudiated any responsibility for what was happening in the city. Griffith contrasted their inertia with the activity of the TUC delegates to Dublin, including Labour MPs. 'A horde of English members of Parliament' had set class against class, while those

> whose position entitled them to intervene in the dispute, and whose imperative duty it was to have done so, kept silent and let things drift to the permanent destruction of a portion of the city's trade and the permanent loss of hundreds of Dublin working class men who had cast their votes for them … Two of these six farcical representatives are rich men—will Messrs. Cotton and Brady put the £400 for their present year's salary into their pockets or will they have sufficient shame left in them to hand it over either to feed the children or relieve the unfortunate ratepayers.[28]

Griffith was as depressed as Moran at the spectacle of 'food ships' bringing relief to Dublin. However, he was relatively restrained in his reaction to Dora Montefiore's Dublin kiddies scheme, estimating that 'the number of Dublin parents who would consent to send their children to be nurtured in the homes of the enemies of their race and nation do not form five per cent of the parents affected by the strike.'[29] Nevertheless it posed the question of faith and fatherland too acutely to be passed over.

In the following issue of *Sinn Féin* he allowed the argument over the relationship between a unique Irish nationality and the undiscriminating modern ideology of socialism to be taken a step further, though not by himself. On Saturday 8 November, *Sinn Féin* published a front-page article on 'Gaelicism and Socialism,' which was in effect an extended quotation from an article by Father Phelan in the *Catholic Bulletin*. Griffith, who had dubbed the *Bulletin* 'the best written Catholic publication in Ireland,' said it had excelled itself with an 'unusually fine' piece. Father Phelan argued that

> for the first time Ireland has a concrete example of how the two civilisations, Gaelicism and Socialism, mutually repel and antagonise

each other at every point. The greedy crunching of the begged crust, the low animal standards, the acceptance of foreign doctrines that have blasted every other country wherein they have found even a partial footing, the leaning on the outsider for food for both head and stomach, all this constitutes everything the Gael loathes and reprobates. To any man who wished to see the very antithesis of the dream of Gaeldom, Dublin during the strike has presented it.

However much Griffith might insist on the nation's detachment from the mundane everyday preoccupations of capital and labour, the effect of *Sinn Féin's* coverage of the lockout reinforced the prevailing view within nationalist circles, especially in Dublin, that the only sound nationalist was a Catholic nationalist. But not all *Sinn Féin's* readers or contributors shared that view, and Griffith had the courage, tolerance and foresight to provide such people with a platform. One of them was Séamus Ó hAodha, who struck at the weak link in the argument made by some Irish-Irelanders against the food ships. He pointed out that the employers had been the first to resort to 'syndicalist' methods by their 'Sympathetic Lockout'. He reminded *Sinn Féin* readers that 'many employers whose dividends or profits were helped by the voluntary taxation that we in the Irish-Ireland Movement imposed on ourselves for many years [through paying higher prices for Irish-made goods] desired their workers to renounce membership of an Irish labour organisation. It was 'no secret' that the employers had resorted to

> the dread weapon of hunger—the starvation of women and children, who after all should be regarded as non-combatants in industrial as in other war. Reluctantly I must state, a considerable section of our people considered it perfectly moral and just to stand aside while the women and children suffered starvation. A certain class in England, knowing what hunger is, interfered, and commenced sending shipments of food. If we were within three hours' sail of France or Belgium or Germany, and the workers in those countries realised that our fear of being regarded as 'taking sides' prevented us succouring our hard-hit women and children, do you not think they would realise the duty of sending food?[30]

Another contributor was Tom Clarke of the IRB. *Sinn Féin* published his letter denouncing DMP brutality on 'Bloody Sunday'. The IRB's own publication, *Irish Freedom*, continued to take a much more sympathetic stance towards the strikers than other nationalist publications. Its November issue made no reference to the activities of Montefiore and her gang of 'child kidnappers' who had so upset Moran; nor had it much time for Griffith's arbitration project. 'Advocates of industrial arbitration abound; but no heed should be paid to them,' Earnán de Blaghd told readers of *Irish Freedom* in an article on 'Labour Policy.' Advocates of arbitration consist of three classes, astute enemies of labour, foolish and timorous labourites, maudlin sentimentalists who love to cry 'Peace, peace,' when there is no peace. The end of conciliation, if labour leave its head long enough in the loop, will be compulsion. The worker will not only be obliged to sell his mental and physical energy for the greater part of the working day but to sell it at a price considered proper by the representatives of a capitalist-controlled government ... The right to strike must be maintained unimpaired.

The strike was 'a weapon of immense value,' he wrote, but it was 'no longer the be-all and end-all of labour policy.' While workers could use strikes to win pay increases, employers simply passed the cost on to the consumers, most of whom were workers. 'Even in the case of a general strike the dog will be fed on his own tail,' was how de Blaghd put it. Instead, workers should use the strike weapon to undermine the capitalist and promote co-operative rivals. 'Co-operative organisations ought, in future, to be the main item of urban labour policy.' He dismissed the failure of the co-operative movement to make greater strides in the past, because its enterprises were set up mainly by

people who were out, not for the emancipation of labour, but to save a few bee-baws for themselves. Consequently their enterprises have been run on capitalistic lines.

As befitted a member of the revolutionary elite, de Blaghd put a strong emphasis on the power of voluntarism and the ideological impulse to transform the potential of the movement, so that

Labour would use, for its own advancement and emancipation, not merely its power of striking, but its power of working and its powers of purchasing.

In Dublin, for instance, if the workers chose co-operation as their main weapon and way of progress their power could speedily be made unwithstandable and their victories would be no barren ones. At the present moment there are dozens of businesses run with wage-slaves which could almost immediately be taken over by partnerships of free labourers. Every capitalist enterprise is a citadel of the exploiters and they should all be taken over or cut out by the workers as soon as possible.

This was Russell's co-operative commonwealth with a vengeance. In a footnote, the editorial board of *Irish Freedom* confessed to readers that 'we are at a loss to understand some of the terms used, which to us seem somewhat reminiscent of certain English doctrinaires.' But the board assured them that 'with his main argument in favour of a co-operative solution of the labour question we are in thorough agreement.'

Better known as Ernest Blythe, the son of a County Antrim farmer, the writer was a Protestant recruit to cultural nationalism and, unlike

Rolleston, graduated to full-blown revolutionary nationalism and the IRB. His views in 1913 would have surprised the new citizens of the Irish Free State. Blythe was its most fiscally rigorous and unpopular Minister for Finance; in 1924 he balanced the books by cutting the old age pension from 10s to 9s a week.

Irish Freedom gave a more qualified welcome in its editorial to de Blaghd's proposals. It differed little from the *Irish Times* in telling readers that 'in all such disputes Ireland loses far more than either party ... can possibly gain.' With Griffith and Moran it believed 'that every stoppage of trade here means impoverishment of Ireland and the enrichment of England.' At the same time, it stopped well short of condemning the workers, or engaging in the razor wit that made Moran's articles so entertaining, so cruel, and ultimately so alienating to thoughtful opinion.

Employers, *Irish Freedom* warned, must realise that as workers became better educated and better organised

—and both things are happening—they will be less and less likely to tolerate the wretched conditions under which many of them live. They will more and more insistently demand a more equal distribution of wealth ... to purchase better food, better clothes, better houses, better opportunities for them and for their children. The claim must either be conceded or contested. The employers, to judge by recent happenings will not concede it until they must ... That contest will mean irreparable damage to the nation.

Unlike other nationalist publications, *Irish Freedom* seemed confident that the workers must win such a contest. If it commended de Blaghd's vision of a co-operative commonwealth, it was because

this solution, if developed wisely and equitably, would avert many disastrous conflicts, would lead to a juster and for that reason stronger social bond and more stable social order, would lead to greater national unity and consequently a greater national strength.[31]

*

It was left to Stephen Gwynn, the MP for Galway—and, with Tom Kettle, one of the modernisers within the UIL—to try to reconcile the constitutional nationalists with the lockout and the new forces at work in Dublin. In a letter published in the *Freeman's Journal* on 5 November he took the paper to task for carrying leaders 'calculated to set every young man of brains and education in Ireland against the main national movement.' He had kept silent so far 'to avoid creating dissension ... But there is a limit in everything!' Condemnations from other quarters were one thing, but the *Freeman's Journal* was the 'accredited organ of the Irish Party.' Shaw and Russell were

two Irishmen of genius ... both of them strong Home Rulers; both of them loyal lovers of Ireland. It is not many months since we were very glad to get Mr. Shaw's help at a most successful meeting in London—successful mainly because of his presence—in support of Home Rule, at which the speakers were all non-Catholics, and some, I dare say, highly unorthodox persons. Do you desire to pick a quarrel with all these people, and all whom they influence?

Russell's speech in London was

> unwise, unfair and mischievous, but it was a speech filled with burning indignation against a horrible state of things, against those who seem to tolerate it.
>
> Naturally I resent his imputations on my colleagues. Neither fairness of judgement nor charity of construction has ever been among his virtues as a controversialist, or he would have understood the extraordinary difficulty in which the Irish members of Parliament stand while such a matter, so intimately Irish, has to be dealt with by an alien Government, which we cannot afford to weaken. Heaven knows how one has wished for the open arena of an Irish assembly, in which this matter could be thrashed out, and in which people might assume their natural groupings without fear of consequences.

Gwynn's attitude was infinitely more generous and more in touch with the modern world than Dillon's. He understood the spring that motivated younger and secular-minded men and women who wanted to drag Irish life into the twentieth century. But there was no fundamental difference in practical politics between him and Dillon. Mesmerised by the parlous state of parliamentary politics, they demanded that all other issues be held in suspense until home rule was attained. Unfortunately, locked-out workers with families facing starvation could not afford to wait, and a new breed of nationalist, voicing the exclusivist concerns of an increasingly confident Catholic middle class, would not tolerate the challenge to their vision of Ireland posed by a Russell, a Shaw, or a Larkin—or even a Gwynn.

Catholic nationalists were equally impervious to Gwynn's prophetic warning that the vehemence with which they had hunted down Dora Montefiore and her collaborators would have consequences far more dangerous than any strike.

> You sow the seeds of evil ... when you denounce as enemies to Irish Catholicism and Irish nationality men of genius like Shaw and Russell, who love Ireland and love humanity ... If such men are to be banished from the pale of our Irish citizenship, or admitted only under suspicion, a good many of us will not be eager for the full franchise.

*

The issues at stake in the lockout were largely academic for many nationalist-minded middle-class intellectuals, especially if they lived outside Dublin. For the most modern—and potentially most modernising—movement in Ireland at that time, the women's movement, the lockout posed intensely practical challenges as well.

The groups campaigning for female suffrage in 1913 presented an interesting anomaly. Ideologically they were divided in their attitude to the lockout, and particularly by Montefiore's activities. But the most active elements within the movement were galvanised into unity of action by the heightened level of distress the dispute had provoked. By mid-September the *Irish Citizen* had moved from its initial coy support for the strikers to a more open stance, due mainly to the response of activists such as Mary Lawless, who had been involved in the fracas at Kingsbridge station. She had argued that there was a clear link between the struggle of workers for economic and political freedom and that of women.[32]

By the end of September more and more correspondents to the *Irish Citizen* were becoming impervious to the argument that charity would only prolong the strike agony. They urged women to participate in Marie Sherlock's distress scheme to feed the women and children left destitute by the lockout. Louie Bennett wrote:

> We all know that this distress is very great, and is daily increasing. When human beings within our reach are in extreme and immediate need, we cannot stand aside to study the causes of that need. When children are hungry, we cannot refuse to give them food because some of us may disapprove of their fathers' actions … We are not all of one opinion as to whether workers or employers are in the right in this struggle: but none of us can witness misery unmoved, and misery abounds in Dublin just now. There are those who will say that to help the strikers' families with food will only prolong the strike. Apart from the question of the morality of the employers forcing submission from the employees by starvation, this argument is otherwise unsound. The giving of a few meals to the men's families cannot really affect the issue, for these men do not want charity: it is only the failure of their own funds which can starve them into submission.[33]

The paper endorsed her appeal and expressed the hope that

> this task will not be left to active suffragists … If it is their business to lead, it is the business of other women to follow. There are hundreds of well-to-do women in Dublin who never do anything of public value, either for the suffrage or for anything else. If some of these women could be roused by the urgency of the present appeal to do something for the starving in Dublin, it would be exceedingly good for their own souls, and might lead them to a higher conception of citizenship, while relieving some of those strenuous workers who never spare themselves in any cause. We trust the suffragists who are taking the initiative in this movement will above all exert themselves to secure the co-operation of women not ordinarily interested in suffragist or public work.[34]

The Irish Women's Franchise League, probably the most active and militant suffrage group in Dublin at the time, decided to hitch itself to the Larkinite bandwagon and, from 18 September, transferred its weekly meetings from sedate Foster Place, beside the Bank of Ireland, to Beresford Place, adjoining Liberty Hall. Unlike the *Irish Times*, the *Irish Citizen* published no reference to the antics of the schoolboy 'strikers' who heckled the speakers at their new venue on that first night. Instead, it reported approvingly that

> amongst the immense crowd which gathered round the speakers, it was satisfactory to notice a number of the girls locked out in the present industrial struggle. It was an admirable opportunity for pressing home the doctrine of votes for women, and the veteran suffragette Margaret Connery, who presided, dealt at length with the social and economic grievances of working women. She pointed out how vain it was to hope for any material improvement in their condition until they possessed political rights. Countess Markievicz, who followed, and whose appearance was greeted with applause, spoke of the moral and educational value of the vote, and what a large factor it was in the mental growth and social development of the men of the community. She declared there were three great movements going on in Ireland at present—the National movement, the Women's Movement, and the Industrial movement. They were all really the same movement in essence, for they were all fighting the same fight, for the extension of human liberty.[35]

But it was the plight of the children that most concerned the majority of suffragists. 'Is it generally known that in Ireland the children may not be given meals in the schools,' one *Citizen* correspondent asked. 'In the cases where meals are given to children, it is done by a charitable institution.' Marie Sherlock and other visitors had been struck by

> the difference in the appearance of the children at the [Little] Denmark Street Schools for instance, where there is no food provision for the children, and those where meals are given at an institution in connection with the School. This question of meals for hungry school children ... deserves serious consideration from thinking women. If working men are not paid a wage sufficient to maintain a family, ought the State to pay for meals for hungry children? or to impose a minimum wage in all trades? When an Education Bill which shall extend to Ireland was introduced, how are the women of Ireland (incontestably the persons whose opinion on such a question is of real value) to make known their views on the matter? Mr. Asquith has said—'There is only one way in which we can find out what people want, and that is, by the representatives they send to Parliament.' So, on a question such as this, of vital importance to the health of the nation, women have no way of making the legislators know what they think.[36]

A week later the *Irish Citizen* felt confident enough to attack the attitude of the 'Antis'—women who opposed female suffrage—towards the lockout and the issues it raised.

> While Suffragists—militant and non-militant—have vied with each other in feeding the hungry during the Labour troubles, it is interesting to observe that the Antis confine themselves to their own comfortable homes. One would have thought that as there are only two remedies for industrial injustice—voting and striking—they would have been glad to see men preferring the latter alternative. A very heavy responsibility rests upon those who urge the uselessness of the vote! One thing is clear: meals for school children must be provided by the State; employers cannot be permitted to use the hunger of the children to compel the submission of the fathers.[37]

In a subsequent issue the *Irish Citizen* asked:

> How many of us have had sufficient experience or imagination to realise anything of the tragedies of child life in the city slums? Here are facts, whose horrors some of us have, for the first time, realised in this crisis. There are thousands of children in Dublin who are never sufficiently fed, because the unskilled workers do not receive sufficient pay to maintain even a small family in comfort; consequently the young generation of the working class are growing up deficient in physical health, and therefore morally deficient. Owing to the poverty of their parents, numbers of children, of only 11 years of age, are allowed to sell on the streets, with the frequent result that boys become worthless ragamuffins and girls sink into a life of vice. There are in Dublin numbers of derelict children without homes, without parents. For those who love children, that is surely a heart-breaking thought. In the Courts, a lamentable number of cases of criminal assault upon little girls are heard in private. These things are happening all the year round. But at the present crisis such evils are doubly ripe, because the respectable homes are disorganised, and the children, who, under ordinary circumstances, would receive a certain amount of care, are running wild and acquiring habits which will lead them onto lives of viciousness. This is testified to by Miss Gargan, the Probation Officer, who attended a committee of the Ladies' Relief Fund, specially to plead that the meals supplied from our funds should be given only to children attending schools, so that more might be induced to attend school regularly, where, for part of the day, at least, they would be kept from the streets, and habits of discipline maintained amongst them. The committee were glad to be able to assure Miss Gargan that this had been their aim in the method of distribution adopted. The women who refuse to help the children of Dublin at this time, are laying upon themselves an awful responsibility.[38]

More and more, speakers at the IWFL meetings in Beresford Place stressed the links between a working woman's lack of a vote and her social problems. Cissie Cahalane, an activist in the Drapers' Assistants' Association, told a meeting on 13 October that 'the sweating and systematic under-payment of women for all kinds of work is indirectly traceable to their voteless condition.' The *Irish Citizen* commented that the speaker

> proved the futility of the argument that women are not equal in strength for the work of men, and therefore cannot be paid an equal wage, by contrasting the laborious occupation of the charwoman or the washerwoman with that of the young man 'who sells ribbons over the counter.'[39]

The same issue had an interesting comment to make on the proceedings of the Askwith tribunal.

> Mr. Larkin, speaking on the subject of sweated wages before the Board of Trade [Askwith] Inquiry last week, said that 'there was one aspect of the question he could not go into before a mixed audience.' No doubt he meant prostitution. His reluctance to allude plainly to this scourge before a 'mixed audience' is an example of how even an avowed rebel may be the slave of an out-worn and evil masculine convention. It is precisely 'mixed audiences' that want to be instructed as to prostitution, its meaning, its causes, and its results. The evils of silence on these topics are incalculable.

To show that it practised what it preached, the *Irish Citizen* published a report entitled 'Free Speech on Sex.' It asserted that women's lack of political power left them 'a helpless prey to the sweating employer, and is therefore one of the causes of prostitution.' The writer warned that 'prostitution is the cause of venereal disease, the greatest scourge of our civilisation, and one which will finally sweep it away unless its ravages are checked.' Suffragists, 'to awaken public conscience, and to show the urgent necessity of woman's emancipation, are taking steps to enlighten women, and the public generally, on the subjects of Sweating, Prostitution and Venereal Disease, with the direct causal relation between the three.' The article alleged that an organised market existed to sell young women into prostitution, and that the vested interests involved were among the most determined opponents of women's suffrage. These had included two prominent men who had died of syphilis within the last few months; but no names were mentioned, and the article itself was unsigned.[40]

Prostitution was a political as well as a social problem in Dublin. If it offered a cruel survival strategy for many working-class women, and was a rude reminder to their middle-class sisters of women's subordinate role in society, it also enraged nationalists. Arthur Griffith regularly fulminated over the fate of Ireland's deposed capital as an extended brothel for the British army. He claimed that even the military authorities were alarmed at the incidence of sexually transmitted diseases in the city. And in 1907, during one of his first excursions to Dublin as an organiser with the NUDL, that 'English' trade unionist James Larkin had asked his audience of Dublin trade unionists, 'Why did they not put a stop to the disgraceful scenes in O'Connell Street, when fellows from the slums of London, in red uniform, were coming along with Irish girls on their arms, whom they would ruin in body and soul?'[41]

By the time of Dora Montefiore's trip to Dublin, the *Irish Citizen* felt it safe to give her a warm welcome. 'Though best known for her work in the international Socialist movement,' the *Citizen* assured readers that she was

> also a keen Suffragist, and was one of the earliest tax resisters. The siege of her house, on refusal to pay taxes, was one of the first pieces of suffragist militancy.[42]

However, the *Citizen* quickly fell silent in face of the wave of anger unleashed by the kiddies scheme. At the same time it gave generous coverage to two speeches Montefiore gave to IWFL meetings during her dramatically brief visit. It was as if the militant suffragist making the usual appeals for the vote and the 'kidnapper' of children were two different people. The *Citizen* made only one veiled reference to her 'kidnapping' adventures, when it told its readers:

> In connection with the Dublin Labour troubles, it is interesting to note that Countess Markievicz has been accepted as bail for some of those [Dora Montefiore and Lucille Rand] charged in the Police Courts. This is an advance, as the Dublin Police have hitherto always refused to accept any woman as bail—an insulting rule which apparently is now broken down.[43]

It was a small and inadvertent result of Montefiore's foray to Ireland, but no less significant for that.

*

That week, the *Irish Citizen* gave more coverage to the news that 'Ulster Unionist women are … encountering difficulties raising the suffrage issue at meetings because Rule II of the Ulster Women's Unionist Council says that no other subject than maintaining the legislative integrity of the Union may be discussed.'

The national question was also to be raised in a more traditional context by Elizabeth Somers (writing as Lasairfhíona Nic Sharaighin). She was a founder-member of Sinn Féin who was also active in the newly formed Industrial Development Association. In an article entitled 'Suffrage policy' she criticised Louie Bennett and others for diverting women from their primary task. They were apeing the English suffragists, who had

> a different set of conditions and a different political standard of values. The franchise is of the first importance to them because the Government of their country is in the hands of the voters. In Ireland, with no government of our own through which to translate our wishes, the vote is of much less importance and utility. There is no reason why

Irishwomen should follow the lines laid down by people whose policy is dictated by their own needs and not, of course, by ours. In England, a heritage from feudalism, the bad, old tradition that holds woman a chattel, whose very name and identity are merged in those of her lord and master, is still very much alive. In Ireland, though anglicisation has lowered our standard in many things, enough of the old free spirit of Gaelic civilisation remains to ensure that the right of women to full citizenship and equality of opportunity will not be seriously challenged by any section of the community, apart from professional politicians and our small but select assortment of old fogies.

These two circumstances—first, the fact that the nation has not denied, and does not deny, our claim to citizenship, but has at present no power to grant it; and, second, the comparative inefficiency of the vote as a weapon of offence or defence in a country without constitutional government, render our case a different one from that of the English suffragists. Our claim to citizenship of the Irish nation does not and cannot rest on any right conferred by an usurping government … If women in Ireland yearn for the right of citizenship of Great Britain, of the British Empire, or of the world, they are, no doubt, entitled to work for that consummation; but I do not recognise their right to call themselves IRISH women.[44]

She did not go unchallenged. Helen Baker of the Irish Women's Suffrage Society wrote to tell the *Citizen*: 'I do not agree [that] the vote is of much less importance and utility in Ireland than in England.' In exasperation at the decision of the Irish Party to defer consideration of female suffrage for at least three years after the introduction of home rule, she said that this alone was 'sufficient provocation to make all Irishwomen drop every bit of social and of church work, I think, and to become actively militant.'[45]

However, Irish women in the suffrage movement—and outside it— continued doggedly with their 'social and church work' long after the lockout ended, just as they had beforehand. Maud Gonne's attempt to embarrass Dublin Corporation into living up to its social responsibilities towards the children received a fresh impetus from the lockout. In the following year she worked closely with Hanna Sheehy-Skeffington, who produced a draft bill, in lobbying for new legislation. Stephen Gwynn was persuaded to sponsor it in the House of Commons, and it emerged as the Education (Provision of Meals) (Ireland) Act (1914). Dublin was one of the first local authorities to avail of its provisions.[46] Along with women being accepted as sureties by the courts, this was to be one of the forgotten victories of the lockout.

In many ways the debate in the suffrage movement over the relationship between women as citizens and women as workers mirrored that in Britain. In both countries the founders of the movement were middle-class, but in both also the labour movement was among their earliest and most ardent supporters. It was the sharp increase in industrial conflict in Britain after

1910, and in Dublin in 1913, that forced suffrage leaders to review their strategies. Even the redoubtable Pankhursts split on the class issue: Emmeline and her older daughter, Christabel, opted, paradoxically, for more extreme action by middle-class women to achieve the vote; they broke off links with their early labour sponsors and even with Emmeline's youngest daughter, Sylvia, who had become a socialist. By 1914 the British suffrage movement was split again by its attitude towards the First World War. Emmeline and Christabel Pankhurst would enthusiastically support the British war effort in the hope that in proving their patriotism women would be rewarded with the vote. Sylvia joined the minority of British socialist leaders, such as Keir Hardie (who was her lover), in denouncing it.

In Ireland, the competing demands of nationalism and unionism complicated the situation for suffragists. In the circumstances, such figures as the Sheehy-Skeffingtons and Louie Bennett probably took the Irish movement as far as it would go in aligning itself with the labour struggle. Unionist suffragists were too preoccupied with the home rule crisis and the debate over whether the promised Ulster provisional government would give them the vote to dwell much on class issues.[47] In Dublin, on the other hand, class warfare was a fact of life. Women such as Hanna Sheehy-Skeffington, Constance Markievicz, Mary Lawless, Helena Moloney, Muriel, Grace and Sydney Gifford, Maud Gonne, Kathleen Clarke, Margaret Connery, Cissie Cahalane, Delia Larkin and Louie Bennett were all involved in feeding the children. If, like the Pankhursts in 1914, they took different sides in the political struggles ahead, they at least brought a strong awareness of social issues to those new debates.

It is clear that the kiddies scheme and, only slightly less vividly, the arrival of the food ships forced members of the nationalist and labour movements to confront issues of class, sex, nationality and religion in unexpected ways. What was more, they had to do so in a manner that required an immediate response. For socialists such as Larkin, both phenomena were living proof of the reality of internationalist solidarity; but other labour leaders reacted more cautiously. Even Larkin found the strings attached to TUC support irksome; and the general effect of the lockout experience was to push Dublin union leaders further down the separatist road.

Of course, in looking for British support Larkin had never intended opening a Pandora's box. The food could easily have been brought in by less conspicuous means. Larkin welcomed the food ship idea because he knew that the memory of proletarian solidarity would remain to sustain the Dublin workers long after the provisions had been eaten. However, for people as diverse as Archbishop Walsh, Maud Gonne and D. P. Moran the ships raised the spectre of a new form of English colonialism, all the more insidious because it came in the guise of help. Even Sinn Féin trade unionists, such as Michael O'Lehane, had their doubts.

Today's trade unionists are more likely to agree with Connolly's assessment. He described the spontaneous generosity of British workers in 1913 as the 'highest point of moral grandeur—towards which the best in us must continually aspire.'[48] Just over seventy years later, in 1984, the memory of the food ships was invoked to raise funds in Dublin for the British miners' strike.

Part 3

War to the Knife

30

WHILE others pondered the wider implications of the dispute, those practical men of affairs, the employers, were calling a potent new weapon into play: the Shipping Federation. This was the most powerful employers' organisation in Britain. If Larkin could seek help from across the water, so could his class enemies. It was another case of William Martin Murphy taking a leaf out of Larkin's tactical manual.

The Shipping Federation had been established in 1890 to combat the National Sailors' and Firemen's Union. (This was ironic in view of the role the NSFU and its founder, Havelock Wilson, would have in forthcoming events.) The federation had a reputation for ruthlessness and had smashed strikes in many ports. In the process it had recruited a standing army of 'free labourers' and a fleet of six vessels; it supplied dockers as well as ships' crews willing to work in defiance of union pickets. The strike-breakers could live on board the federation ships if conditions ashore were unsafe.

In 1913 Britain had the world's largest merchant fleet, and the Shipping Federation represented 95 per cent of the 1,050 shipping companies with vessels weighing more than 300 tons. Most of these were the small to medium-sized firms. The forty-eight largest companies, which accounted for 21 per cent of the total tonnage of 16½ million tons, remained aloof from the federation: these were the White Star lines, the owners of the large transatlantic liners, which combated trade unionism by the simple, if expensive, expedient of paying employees well above the union rate. With the exception of Cunard, which was trying to withdraw from Ireland, none of these companies called regularly to Irish ports.[1]

The Shipping Federation was a source of fear and loathing in trade union circles. In April 1913 its general manager, Cuthbert Laws, had told a parliamentary inquiry into the industrial unrest of the two previous years that 'so far as the men are concerned, there is no influence which will operate so powerfully to secure the keeping of agreements as the knowledge that failure to observe its terms may mean loss of employment.' He assured MPs that the federation had no difficulty negotiating with trade unions, 'provided they are representative.' However, employers should be free 'to employ men irrespective of their membership, or non-membership, of a trade union.' Furthermore, such workers 'should have the assurance that the authorities responsible for the maintenance of law and order will provide them with adequate protection against violence and intimidation, whether exercised during labour disputes with the object of preventing them from working in place of men who have gone on strike, or at any other time, with the object of compelling them to join a union.'

Personal relations between the leaders of the Shipping Federation and those of the National Transport Workers' Federation were so bad that the only way that Sydney Buxton, President of the Board of Trade, could bring them together to discuss the 1912 dock strike was by inviting them all to dinner. Half way through the meal, Harry Gosling stormed out when Laws suggested that NTFW members should work alongside 'free labourers'.[2]

But twenty-three years of industrial warfare had taught members of the Shipping Federation that compromise was sometimes necessary, and at first Laws fought shy of the Dublin lockout. When Dublin employers made a tentative application for assistance in September, the Shipping Federation decided against supplying a vessel—though it had intervened in disputes at Sligo, Galway and Dublin earlier in the year.[3] It was probably the federation's involvement in the dispute at the City of Dublin Steam Packet Company at the beginning of 1913 that made it reluctant to be drawn in again; it was resigned to the fact that Larkin was 'dictator of the port.'[4] The decision to intervene in early November was therefore a complete reversal by the federation.

The reasons are not hard to find. The first request for help had come when sympathetic action in support of the Dublin workers was at its height on Merseyside and on the railways. Intervention by the Shipping Federation at that stage might have ignited the highly combustible industrial relations situation in Britain. The request had also come shortly after a particularly bitter dockers' strike at the Scottish port of Leith, which had cost the federation over £3,800. Victory had been secured only after the Admiralty sent a gunboat and a contingent of sailors to protect the federation ships and workers.[5]

By November the federation had no major disputes at British ports and was free to deploy all its resources in Dublin. Another factor was that the lockout was now into its third month, and the Dublin employers were showing a new determination to make a fight to the finish. The third factor was the imprisonment of Larkin, whose leadership had been considered the decisive element in the port battle of the previous spring.[6] And perhaps a fourth was the opportunity to pay back Gosling and the NTWF for the annoyance they had caused the federation the previous year.

The rebuff of September had been kept secret by the Dublin employers, and they were no doubt anxious that no word of their new approach to the Shipping Federation should leak out. If it did, there would be the danger of renewed intervention from various parties, ranging from Birrell and Lord Aberdeen to Archbishop Walsh, the Lord Mayor, or even the six 'sleeping beauties' who represented Dublin in the House of Commons. It must be the arrival of the first ships on the Liffey that would herald the entry of the Shipping Federation into the fray.

The matter was almost certainly discussed when the Dublin Employers' Federation met on Monday 3 November, for word quickly reached the press that something was afoot. Deniable statements were issued that evening through unofficial employers' sources that 'no further importation of free labourers' was planned.[7] Publicly, the Employers' Federation continued to hold out an olive branch to the TUC leaders; this was so convincing that the NTWF executive decided to hold its meeting in Dublin that week in the hope that new negotiations might be possible.[8]

But the signs that Dublin employers were planning to step up the dispute were there for anyone who cared to read them. The most obvious was the increasing use of 'free labour' by farmers to break the strike in north County Dublin. Following the success of Tom Kettle's father, Andrew, in bringing in a batch of strike-breakers to work his lands at St Margaret's, County Dublin, Tom's brother Charles brought twenty men from the midlands to pick his potato crop at Coolock on Monday 3 November. Another twenty strike-breakers were hired by a Kinsealy farmer, Joseph O'Neill. In this case the 'free labourers' were women from Crumlin, then a village south of the capital. They arrived by train at Portmarnock, and carts took them to O'Neill's farm. The women shouted 'Down with Larkin!' as the convoy passed under heavy police escort through Kinsealy, and the local band turned out to provide a musical accompaniment as they began picking forty acres of potatoes.[9]

Jacob's, the biscuit manufacturers, did not have to go as far as Crumlin to recruit strike-breakers. The company's obvious success in beating the strike provoked mass pickets outside its factory in Bishop Street that Monday, and 'scabs' had to run the gauntlet of jibes from women sporting the Red Hand badge as they arrived for work. By evening verbal abuse had been replaced by running battles, and two picketers, who lived in the nearby York Street tenements, were arrested before the police managed to restore order. One of them was sixteen-year-old Mary Ellen Murphy, who received a month's imprisonment for giving a strike-breaker of her own age 'a box in the face and calling her a "scab".'

The protest must have had some effect, because Jacob's, which had stopped advertising for workers to replace the strikers by mid-October, placed display advertisements in the 'situations vacant' columns of the newspapers over the following few days, looking for 'respectable girls' in its packing, wrapping and labelling departments. 'Good wages can be earned by industrious workers,' the advertisement said, but no rates were quoted.[10]

*

On Tuesday, the ITGWU buried its latest martyr in the dispute. The Kingstown branch secretary, James Byrne, had died of pneumonia in Monkstown Hospital on Saturday 1 November. He had fallen ill in Mountjoy prison while on protracted hunger and thirst strike. He had been arrested on 20 October for alleged intimidation of a labourer at the Heiton coal depot in Kingstown, where many men had returned to work the previous weekend. He had been offered bail of £10 but, following Connolly's example in August, refused to be bound over. Unfortunately, his hunger and thirst strike went unnoticed. Not only did he lack Connolly's high profile in labour and nationalist circles but his protest coincided with the hysteria over Dora Montefiore and her Dublin kiddies scheme. By the time Byrne's condition came to the attention of the authorities, it was too late. He left a wife and six children.

Father Patrick Flavin visited Byrne in prison. He let it be known to the newspapers that he was 'interesting himself … on behalf of the bereaved family'; in fact his role in the dispute was to extend far beyond what most people would regard as Christian charity, as we shall see.[11]

Connolly had no lessons to learn from Father Flavin when it came to wringing political capital out of a tragedy. And if he lacked the charisma of Larkin, he still had a strong sense of street theatre. A special train was hired to bring a thousand ITGWU members and two bands from Dublin to the funeral. Altogether an estimated three thousand people gathered outside the Byrne home in Clarence Street, and it took two hours for the procession to wend its way to Dean's Grange cemetery. At the gates Connolly mounted the roof of a cab to tell the crowd that Byrne had been

> murdered as surely as any one of the long list of those who had suffered for the sacred cause of liberty. The police vultures and master vultures were not content until they had got Byrne into prison. He had been thrown into a cold, damp, mouldy cell, but … so contemptuous was he of those who put him there, that he had refused food and drink. If their murdered comrade could send them a message it would be to go on with the fight … even if it brought them hunger, misery, eviction, and death itself.

Connolly then thanked the local businesses along the route for closing during the procession, and assured the crowd that the dead man's family would be looked after. He asked them to return home in an orderly fashion that would not besmirch the memory of the dead. They dutifully tramped back to Kingstown and the excursion train, leaving Byrne to rot in his 'cold, damp, mouldy' and unmarked grave.[12]

*

Meanwhile two developments in the city that day probably reinforced the employers in their belief that the time was ripe for intervention by the Shipping Federation. The first was an announcement by the DUTC that it was reopening its parcel service, as the majority of those ITGWU employees who had struck in August had decided to return to work. The second was a decision by Mooney and Morgan, the fertiliser manufacturers, to lay off 160 workers in Alexandra Basin, because the company's crane-drivers and carters had joined the strike. The company explained to customers that 'there is no dispute as to wages or conditions, but it is impossible for us to carry on our business if our employees mix themselves up with disputes that do not concern us.' The management had

> never objected at any time to our employees belonging to any union …
> After this experience, however, we will have to make it a condition of employment that our workmen give an undertaking not to go out on strike without due notice; and … are not compelled to disobey our reasonable orders in connection with any so-called 'sympathetic strike' in which they are not directly concerned.[13]

In their different ways, the capitulation of the tramway employees and the wildcat action of the Mooney and Morgan workers suggested that Liberty Hall was losing control of the situation in Larkin's absence. The reaction of Morgan and Mooney, who had avoided confrontation with the ITGWU thus far, must also have encouraged Murphy to believe that support was growing among more moderate employers for action that would end the chaos on the docks.

Murphy's hopes of drawing a far more important employer into the fray also rose. On Wednesday 5 November the chairman of the Dublin branch of the Shipping Federation, Samuel McCormick, led a small deputation to meet Colonel H. Renny-Tailyour and other senior managers at the Guinness head office in James's Street. McCormick was a leading coal merchant in the city, and he revealed plans to bring Shipping Federation workers into Dublin surreptitiously next day. They would be used to unload twenty-three Leyland lorries and a trailer ordered by Guinness's on 30 October, which were being brought in on the *Wearwood*, a ship requisitioned by the Shipping Federation. The delegation wanted to know if the company would accept delivery of the lorries. Renny-Tailyour said they would, but he baulked at suggestions that Guinness's should provide weighing facilities for other companies in the port, and he firmly refused to pay increased handling charges. These were almost twice those originally quoted and were claimed because of the high cost of 'free labour' dockers.[14]

Though Guinness's had not taken the bait on Wednesday, Murphy had not abandoned hope of the company joining the lockout. On Friday 7 November he sought a further meeting at James's Street, ostensibly to discuss how the unloading of the *Wearwood* was proceeding. Charles Sutton, one of the assistant managing directors, met him in the afternoon. After some preliminary small talk over the *Wearwood*, Murphy explained that the financial situation of the Dublin Employers' Federation had become grave. Its 'monetary requirements' had grown enormously since he had last visited Guinness's in September and the company had made its £100 donation; without further funds 'it will be impossible to keep together the employers' interest in Dublin.' He told Sutton that he placed sole responsibility for the crisis on 'the action of the Transport Union,' which the employers had resisted 'at considerable sacrifice to themselves.'

So far the Dublin employers had raised £4,000, including a donation of £1,000 from the Engineering Employers' Federation, a British body similar to the Shipping Federation, though much smaller. Murphy explained that £3,000 had been spent or was already committed to various purposes, including a £500 indemnity for the owners of the *Wearwood*, as compensation for loss of business should the owners discover that the vessel was blacked on its return to Britain as a result of its delivery of the lorries to Guinness's. Murphy then said that he was doubling his own subscription to the employers' fund, and so were a number of other leading businessmen. Unfortunately 'the length of the strike had seriously affected a large number of the employers ... who were unable to give any very large monetary assistance.'

Sutton reported Murphy as saying that 'they had to support certain small carriers who were in financial difficulties and also smaller coal merchants.' The Employers' Federation had thought of sending a larger and more formal delegation to Guinness's to seek help, but Murphy told Sutton that he had advised them that an informal visit by himself might be more appropriate. Sutton thanked him for calling and promised to relay the information to the board.

Guinness's maintained its aloof stance for the moment. It was not until the end of the year, when the lockout was already on the verge of collapse, that Lord Iveagh finally succumbed to Murphy's pleas and made a donation of £5,000 to the employers' fund. However, this was kept a closely guarded secret. When Fane Vernon, chairman of the Great Northern Railway, met Renny-Tailyour for a pre-Christmas drink at the Kildare Street Club and asked if the rumours were true, he denied any knowledge of the matter.[15]

*

Guinness's had an understandable reluctance to become embroiled in what threatened to be an extremely unpleasant intensification of the dispute. Both sides were gripped by a renewed bout of war fever. At the meeting with the Shipping Federation on Wednesday, Renny-Tailyour had been told by McCormick that he had written to the Admiralty requesting a 'gunboat in the river ... with a searchlight' to improve security. For more than a month, shipping companies had been complaining to Dublin Castle about the vulnerability of vessels to sabotage, and their patience was at an end. The British and Irish Steam Packet Company had gone so far as to make a formal complaint to the Under-Secretary, Sir James Dougherty, who investigated the situation and concluded that the employers' fears were exaggerated.[16] But Dougherty, who was still being kept in the dark about plans to bring in the Shipping Federation, was not looking at the security situation in the event of hundreds of strike-breakers being used to work the port.

On the same day that he met Renny-Tailyour, McCormick wrote to the Admiralty seeking assistance. He said that Dublin was gripped by a crisis involving almost all the shipping in the Port. There is no question of wages in the dispute. It is solely one of discipline. Much disorder has prevailed and many serious assaults have been committed.

He told the Admiralty that 'some steamer owners have requisitioned imported labour from the Shipping Federation,' and the first of its depot ships was due next day; 'the advent of these vessels is certain to cause great disorder and much risk to life and property.' Dougherty and the DMP Commissioner 'regard the situation as fraught with danger,' he added disingenuously. 'I would respectfully urge on the Lords of the Admiralty the necessity of stationing a Gun Boat or a Destroyer in the Liffey for protection against violence.' The following day Charles Coghlan, secretary of the Employers' Federation, advised Dougherty that a gunboat had been requested 'immediately for the protection of shipping.'

The Admiralty was quick to respond. On Friday, McCormick was told rather frostily that their lordships could not consider any request for assistance other than 'by the Chief Secretary to the Lord Lieutenant of Ireland.' McCormick was advised that his letter was being forwarded to Sir James Dougherty. It had in fact already been shown to Birrell, who had approved the text of the Admiralty response.[17] The employers of Dublin had been put in their place.

*

Doing the same with the workers would not be so easy. By Wednesday afternoon reports that the Shipping Federation was preparing its flagship, the *Ella*, at Liverpool for a voyage to Dublin were rife. Over a hundred men had been recruited already in Britain at a basic rate of £1 15s a week. In Dublin, permanent dockers earned only £1 10s, and casual dockers £1 5s.[18] Robert Williams, back in Dublin for the meeting of the NTWF executive, told an angry, broiling crowd in Beresford Place that day that they could count on unconditional support from across the water. If the English employers supported the Irish employers' efforts 'to break the Trades Unionist spirit of the people of Dublin,' they would find that 'the power of the sympathetic strike was not confined to Dublin. (Cheers.)'

> Every ounce of coal that is being used to generate power and to drive the trams of Dublin was raised by trades union miners. Every coal ship is loaded, freighted and discharged by trades union transport labour workers, and by God we will not lie down quietly and see the workers of Dublin beaten. (Cheers.) There is such a feeling of burning resentment being fostered in the minds and in the hearts of all trades unionists in connection with the employers of Dublin that we would risk the overthrow of society rather than see the workers of Dublin beaten. (Cheers.)

It was more than rhetoric. In the nine days since Larkin's arrest, more than 85,000 members of the National Union of Railwaymen had called for a national strike in support of the Dublin dispute; so too had 63,000 miners and 150,000 dockers and carters. These numbers were still small, but they were growing as fast as union activists could summon meetings. Addressing the same meeting as Williams, the leader of the Scottish Union of Dock Labourers, Joseph Houghton, said the workers of Britain would 'raise a storm of protest' to release Larkin from prison. He favoured conciliation boards only until they had built a movement capable of defeating 'any power put into the industrial field against them.'

Connolly renewed the call for British workers to vote against Liberal candidates in the forthcoming by-elections. He was still prepared to negotiate with the employers, 'but only on reasonable terms.' They would never consider themselves bound by agreements reached

> at the pistol's mouth. From night until morning I will continue to sign such agreements, until I get hold of the gun myself, and then I will tell the other man what I think … We are at the start of a great revolution … which nothing but our own ineptitude and want of energy in a good cause can withstand. (Cheers.)

While the workers listened to their leaders, the docks were almost at a standstill. An *Irish Times* journalist mused that, away from the stormy atmosphere of the meeting, 'the plenitude of sunshine … gave to the quays the character of interesting promenades.'[19]

*

The *Ella* arrived in Alexandra Basin at 7:30 a.m. on Thursday 6 November. It had 160 'free labourers' on board, and it moored well out from the wharf in anticipation of trouble. Only one entrance to the basin was open, and that was guarded by a hundred DMP and RIC men. Extra soldiers had been drafted in after hasty consultations between the commander of British forces in Ireland, General Sir Arthur Paget, and Sir James Dougherty over a cup of tea at Parkgate. Senior military officers called to the harbourmaster's office, and soldiers, including a troop of lancers, provided larger than usual escorts for coal deliveries to barracks.

By now the army was as tired of the strike as the police. Captain Vane de Vallance told his mother in England that officers were having to perform 24-hour tours of duty every four days, 'escorting coal carts and guarding the tramway depots.' Officers did not expect such socially inconvenient or distasteful peacetime duties.[20]

The heavy police and military presence appeared to have had the desired effect on the strike leaders in Liberty Hall. There were no mass meetings that day, and some ITGWU dockers worked normally, even unloading ships where goods were being removed by non-union carters. But Liberty Hall's instructions not to unload the motor vehicles and a malt consignment for Guinness's from the *Wearwood* still held good from the previous day. That afternoon the ship's captain had the vessel towed from its original berth at Sir John Rogerson's Quay to Alexandra Basin, where the 'free labourers' from the *Ella* at last began to earn their keep.

Four powerful new lorries carried the malt unmolested to the Guinness brewery in James's Street. The only serious incident involved a cartload of cement attacked in Tara Street. The bags were thrown onto the street, and the driver fired a revolver over the heads of the crowd when his helper was stabbed in the arm. Police arrived before the situation worsened. Several employers told the *Irish Times* they had issued their men with weapons for self-defence in anticipation of attacks. As many of them were justices of the peace, they had all the legal authority they needed to do so.[21]

*

The *Irish Times* published an unusual letter that day. It was written jointly by Rev. Thomas Hammond, rector of St Kevin's and secretary of the Dublin by Lamplight Institution, and Henry O'Connor, general secretary of the City of Dublin Young Men's Christian Association, protesting against the summary dismissal of G. H. Walton from the firm of Gill and Son. Gill's was the leading Catholic publishing house in the city and a supplier of religious requisites, such as chalices and vestments. Walton, a Protestant, had worked with the firm for thirty-nine years. On 28 October he was sacked and given a month's pay in lieu of notice. His offence, claimed Hammond and O'Connor, was that he had been helping distribute free breakfasts to the poor at the Christian Union in Abbey Street. They also alleged that an unnamed Catholic organisation had brought the matter to the firm's attention and in effect forced the dismissal.

The *Irish Times* published a response from the secretary of M. H. Gill and Son, Patrick Keoghane, on 8 November, which only aggravated the situation. He said that Walton had admitted 'that he was actively engaged in certain objectionable practices at the Metropolitan Christian Union Buildings.' These premises were a veritable bastion of Protestant evangelism in the city: among the organisations accommodated there were the Evangelical Alliance, Dublin Free Breakfasts for the Poor, Hibernian Band of Hope, Dublin Protestant Deaf and Dumb Association, Army Scripture Readers' and Soldiers' Friends' Society, Lord's Day Observance Society, and Open Air Mission for Ireland. The 'objectionable practice' that Walton had engaged in was, of course, proselytism, and proselytism 'in its most insidious forms,' according to Keoghane. 'Under these circumstances, my board did not conceive it consistent with their obligations as recognised Catholic publishers that a gentleman engaged in such practices should continue in their service.' Walton had been given an opportunity to resign, and had availed of it. Keoghane pointed out that the company had 'no quarrel whatever with Protestantism' and had in its employ other Protestants, 'who enjoy its full confidence and respect.' However, the directors would not tolerate those 'endeavouring to wean little children from the faith of their fathers.'

Keoghane's letter might have carried more conviction if Walton had only recently entered the proselytising fray, but he had been helping at the Christian Union for thirty-four years. The *Irish Times* made the case the subject of its first leader on Saturday 8 November and in it accused the company of treating Walton 'not merely harshly, but brutally.' It disliked proselytism, from any source. 'Proselytism and the suspicion of proselytism have done an immense amount of harm in Dublin by preventing the hearty co-operation of Protestants and Roman Catholics in works of social reform.' But even if Walton had 'by means of tea and bread and butter ... tempted little children to swallow his theological opinions,' he had at worst behaved

> foolishly and with a want of what we may call Christian delicacy ... He has committed no crime. Probably he believed, as most citizens of the Empire believe, that his spare time was his own ... In part of his free time Mr. Walton, exercising the civil and religious liberties of his citizenship did certain things of which his conscience approved. Messrs. Gill objected to these things, and so they have turned an old and faithful servant into the street. Their legal right is unquestionable, but their action can be defended on no other ground. It sets up a claim which, if many employers were to assert it, would justify the hardest things that Mr. Larkin has said against employers as a class.

It was not only employers the *Irish Times* placed in the dock but the Irish Party as well. Two weeks earlier the Church of Ireland Archbishop of Dublin, Dr Peacocke, had been criticised by P. J. Brady, the MP for the St Stephen's Green division, for daring to suggest that home rule posed a threat to the civil and religious liberties of Protestants. Brady had challenged Dr Peacocke 'to give a single instance ... in which the civil and religious liberties of Protestants had been menaced by their Catholic fellow-countrymen.' The *Irish Times* now replied. 'We present Mr. Brady with the case of Mr. G. H. Walton. We invite him to justify it if he can.' Walton was 'a test case'; if Brady 'by speech or silence endorses the conduct of Messrs. Gill ... all Mr. Redmond's and Mr. Brady's assurances on the subject, while they may be quite honest, have been, and will continue to be, worthless.'

It was a call echoed by Rev. J. O. Gage Dougherty, rector of Walton's church, St Mary's. He described his parishioner as 'a quiet, inoffensive, respectable citizen' who had led an 'exemplary life ... This is surely a case where Mr. John Redmond could step in, as he promised to do if a case of intolerance was brought under his notice in Ireland.'[22]

Redmond and Brady remained silent. Redmond could no doubt plead pressure of more important business; and Brady may not have had much choice. The organisation that had 'outed' Walton was almost certainly the Society of St Vincent de Paul, of which Brady was a prominent member. It had maintained a close surveillance of Protestant proselytising organisations in the city and had reported its findings to Dr Walsh in July. Normally such low-intensity sectarian warfare did not have such dramatic consequences; however, circumstances were anything but normal in Dublin. The coinciding of the lockout and the home rule crisis made normally tolerable sectarian tensions suddenly intolerable.

The debate that followed Walton's dismissal was similar to that in the north two years earlier during the infamous McCann divorce controversy. The McCanns had been a mixed couple in Belfast whose marriage broke up. The father, a Catholic, had subsequently emigrated and taken the children with him. Outraged unionists had accused the Catholic Church of helping him 'spirit away' the youngsters in pursuance of the papal decree *Ne Temere* of 1908, which required Catholic parents in a mixed marriage to ensure that any children were reared in the Catholic faith and which had proved deeply divisive in Ireland. The McCann incident had been revived by unionist propagandists in the home rule crisis to demonstrate that home rule would lead to Rome rule; Dublin unionists were quick to draw comparisons between the Walton dismissal and the McCann case.

Catholics and nationalists were equally quick to defend M. H. Gill and Son. They argued that the company had acted with great forbearance and tolerance towards Walton, which he had seen fit to abuse. Robert Gibson, a Protestant home-ruler and businessman in Limerick, wrote in a letter to the *Irish Times* that if he found a Catholic employee engaged in proselytising Protestant children he would also feel entitled to sack him. 'The Roman Catholic, or the Protestant, who tries to pervert little children is neither a good Catholic nor a good Protestant, and utterly unworthy of the name of Christian,' he wrote. However, his attitude was not typical of southern Protestants: they saw Walton's dismissal as a crude assault on their civil liberties and the Irish Party's silence as evidence of the supine attitude it adopted when confronted with the prerogatives of the Catholic Church.[23]

Walton's dismissal was indeed a worse example of religious intolerance than the McCann case. It had been argued, with some justification, by Irish Party MPs such as Joe Devlin that in the McCann case religion had been no more than a weapon used by warring parents in the closing stages of an unhappy marriage.[24] Why then did unionist politicians not make more of it? The probable explanation is that if they had done so they would have risked drawing attention to widespread discriminatory employment practices among Protestant employers.

The charge of attempting to proselytise children also served to isolate Walton from public sympathy, though no concrete evidence was produced that he had done anything at the Metropolitan Hall other than help feed the hungry. Where social work ended and proselytism began was of course a sensitive point in the Dublin of 1913. But, as one *Irish Times* correspondent pointed out, the city was too small a place for any seriously objectionable behaviour by Walton to have gone unnoticed by his employer for thirty-four years.

Keoghane's own condemnation of proselytism was undermined when a caller to the Gill shop in Upper Sackville Street found that it distributed material from the Society of the Holy Childhood. This organisation was appealing for funds to 'buy' the children of 'pagans' so that they could be reared as Catholics. Another publication distributed by the company was the *Annals of the Propagation of the Faith*, which reported that 'the nuns of a convent in Peking had ... bought nearly 900 Buddhist infants at five pence ha'penny a head,' and could save more souls if given the funds.[25]

Nor was the company's case helped when it emerged that eleven days after his dismissal Walton had been given a testimonial that described him as 'a most experienced man in matters connected with the book business,' regular in attendance at work, 'strictly sober and honest,' and that he left the company's employment 'with our good wishes for his future prosperity.' This was read to much laughter at a public meeting in the Metropolitan Hall on 19 November. Rev. Hammond told the audience that 'an upright man' had been victimised and had been thrust,

> friendless and forsaken in his old age to become, for aught his persecutors cared, a burden on the rates ... If every alleged case of proselytism is to be followed with relentless and material damage, then let them look for a reign of anarchy ... of ... which no parallel can be found.

There were plenty of instances of proselytism by Catholics and other 'well-meant interference. Such incidents warn us that peace can only be preserved in a community divided on religious questions by a frank recognition that a wide liberty must be permitted.' When he asked if there were any 'brethren of the reformed faith' in the audience prepared to 'serve under Roman Catholic directors or managers' who compelled them 'to submit to a censorship of their religious activities,' there were angry cries of 'Never.'

Another speaker was the rector of St Mary's, Rev. J. O. Gage Dougherty. 'Mr Walton's case does not stand alone in Ireland. There are many Protestants suffering in just the same way.' Organisations such as the Society of St Vincent de Paul did not exist 'only for the relief of the poor, but to win over heretics,' he said. The meeting passed a resolution condemning M. H. Gill for their 'intolerant attitude', and this received prominent coverage in the *Irish Times*.[26] The paper also launched a fund for Walton, which had raised over £130 by late November.[27] Though most of the contributors were presumably Protestants, one donation, for 10s, was from 'A Catholic working in a Protestant Bookshop.'

Few people can have doubted that M. H. Gill and Son sacked Walton because the company was dependent on the good will of the Catholic Church for survival. Defending Walton's right to a job could have jeopardised the employment of all its other employees.

In his post mortem on the affair, 'Vigilans', who had written the detailed reports on the activities of the Irish Church Mission in the city for the *Leader*, suggested to the *Irish Times* that Walton's employment was 'as great an anomaly as would be the employment of a Catholic in the book depot of the Irish Church Missions Society.' He took the view that when Mr. Walton was taken on 39 years ago it must have been on the distinct, though, perhaps, tacit, understanding that, though free to practise his religion ... he would not take part in any shape or form of proselytism, which is recognised by everybody to be a contrary propaganda to that out of which, through the tolerance of Messrs. Gill, the man was making his living.[28]

The truth was that Walton was not so much an anomaly as an anachronism. Another *Irish Times* letter-writer, S. A. Quam-Smith of Dalkey (who enclosed a guinea for the Walton fund with his letter), said that commentators such as 'Vigilans' were mistaken in assuming that M. H. Gill had always been in 'the business of ... religious propaganda.' When Walton joined the company it was the firm of McGlashan and Gill. The Gills had been printers to that pillar of the Protestant ascendancy, Trinity College; and, though James McGlashan had long departed the scene when Walton was appointed, the company's ethos had not been overtly Catholic. 'It is the firm that has changed, not Mr. Walton,' he concluded.[29] The Walton affair was another episode marking the eclipse of Protestant Dublin; within a few short years, similar protest meetings would be unthinkable.

31

THE trials and tribulations of G. H. Walton were of little concern to the embattled leadership of the ITGWU that weekend, preoccupied as they were with the impending threat of an invasion of 'free labourers'. The *Ella* was followed within twenty-four hours by the *Jocelyn*, and the *Paris* was scheduled to arrive shortly. By Monday it was expected that there would be six hundred federation hands in the city.[1]

In the past, the activities of the Shipping Federation in Dublin had been hampered by the lack of suitable safe accommodation for its strike-breakers. It was the misfortune of the Leith and Dublin dockers that the federation had acquired these purpose-built depot ships relatively recently, at a cost of £9,441, to counter such militant tactics. Members of the federation would later be told in its annual report for 1913 that the effectiveness of these vessels in the Scottish and Irish ports had 'amply justified the outlay incurred ... on the purchase and fitting out.' The savings on the hire of steamers to accommodate and supply the 'free labourers' at the two ports were put by the federation at over £7,000, of which £500 was accounted for by the savings in fares by men being transported by its own steamers.

At Leith the use of shipboard accommodation was considered particularly essential, because of the 'weak-kneed policy' of the local police and harbour commissioners, who allowed union militants to injure and 'frighten off' the federation men. In Dublin, security was not a serious problem, because of the very different attitude of the Irish executive to the use of police and military.[2]

On Friday, Connolly issued mobilisation orders for his own troops, in the form of a manifesto calling out mass pickets, which was distributed by hand and pasted up around the city. It stated that from now on all ITGWU casual labourers would have to sign on at Liberty Hall every day for picket duty. Permanent men would have to report 'to their respective committee men, delegates, or shop stewards.' Failure to picket could mean the loss of meal tickets; and 'any member found hanging around Liberty Hall without special reason will forfeit strike allowance.' The instructions appear to have been taken seriously, for on Saturday the *Irish Times* reported that there were fewer men 'lingering about Beresford Place ... than have generally assembled there, but it was noticeable that they had gathered in greater numbers along the quays.' Despite the crowds, particularly outside Alexandra Basin, where the *Wearwood* was discharging the Guinness shipment, there was no trouble.

At one point the Dublin secretary of the National Sailors' and Firemen's Union, George Burke, managed to board the federation ship, and he tried unsuccessfully to call the federation hands out. Only five responded, and one of them, who was unwise enough to stay in the city, was subsequently arrested and charged with deserting his ship, for which he was fined £1 and put back on board![3]

*

On Saturday the *Irish Worker* railed against the AOH and its camp-followers for preventing Dublin children from finding 'shelter and comfort' in Britain but allowing 'English blacklegs to enter Dublin without a protest.' It would probably have shocked Dr Walsh if he had known that the author of a particularly virulent piece on the front page was the former seminarian James Hughes. The paper once more honoured Murphy with a large cartoon. On this occasion he was being marooned 'On the Rocks' as the crew of the good ship *Employers' Federation* mutinied and left him stranded. It was to prove wishful thinking.[4]

However, there was good news from another quarter when the results of two British by-elections came in. The Liberals lost Reading and only retained Linlithgow by the barest majority. Partridge had been despatched to Reading to campaign against the Liberal candidate there, and Connolly had wired Labour supporters in both constituencies with a message that 'locked out Nationalist workers appeal to British workers to vote against Liberal jailers of Larkin and murderers of Byrne and Nolan.' There was a fireworks display that night on the roof of Liberty Hall after Connolly announced the results to a waiting crowd shortly before midnight.

The *Sunday Independent* described the by-election result as a 'stab at Home Rule.' It reported: 'The result was received with great cheering' in Beresford Place,

> and Mr. Connolly went on to refer to what might appear to many a strange spectacle of Dublin working men showing pleasure at a Unionist victory. It was not, however, he said a question of who got in, but who was kept out. The first blow had been struck at the treacherous Libeal Government that jailed Jim Larkin.

Among the other speakers was Hanna Sheehy-Skeffington. She publicly thanked Connolly for allowing the Irish Women's Franchise League the opportunity of 'being in at the death of the Liberals. It was on women they had commenced war and I am glad to take part in this knock-down blow to the government.' Heckled about her family connections, she replied, 'I have, God help me, relatives in the Irish Party.' Referring to her imprisonment in Tullamore for suffrage activities the previous year, she said that her father (David Sheehy), 'in his grand love for the Liberal Party voted for a Bill in favour of forcible feeding.' That measure was now being used against trade unionists as well. Another former inmate at Tullamore, Margaret Connery, told the crowd that 'workers would be fools to starve so long as there is bread in Dublin.' Having incited it to loot, she then urged the crowd to march on Mountjoy, where Larkin was imprisoned for making similar speeches, and to smash the trams.

The speeches at Liberty Hall may have indicated how far some radical feminist nationalists had travelled from allegiance to the Irish Party and its alliance with the Liberals; but not all trade unionists in the city rejoiced. James Dolan of the National Union of Bookbinders and Machine Rulers announced that he was resigning from Dublin Trades Council because of the 'coercive policy adopted ... demanding the immediate release of Larkin.'[5] The bookbinders could be dismissed as an old union with dwindling influence; nevertheless, Dublin must have presented a paradoxical sight that weekend, with socialists, feminists and unionists rejoicing at the by-election results and nationalists downcast.

*

The unionists had most reason to celebrate. Linlithgow was in some ways a greater achievement than Reading. It had been a Liberal stronghold for eighteen years, and yet a majority of 2,915 in 1910 had been cut to 521. At Reading, always a marginal constituency, the Unionist candidate had cruised in with a comfortable majority of 1,131. The Liberals had last won it in 1910 by a mere 99 votes. The candidate then had been Sir Rufus Isaacs KC, as formidable an advocate as Carson. It was his appointment as Attorney-General that had led to the by-election.

The British government and the Irish Party put the best face they could on the results, saying it would not affect the implementation of home rule. The reality was otherwise.

The Belfast nationalist leader Joe Devlin, who toured the British constituencies speaking on behalf of Liberal candidates, sent a bitter letter to Percy Illingworth, the Liberals' chief whip, blaming the irresolution of the government concerning home rule for the setbacks. It was 'positively heartbreaking to go through the length and breadth of the land and to witness the marvellous enthusiasm of the English and Scottish people in favour of self-government for Ireland and to find on the other hand their leaders indulging in exhibitions of oscillation ... without any clear or defined policy on the Irish Question.' He expressed concern that the forthcoming Keighley by-election, due to be held on Tuesday 11 November, could also be lost. 'I visited this constituency and rallied both the Irish and Labour vote, despite the intervention of a Labour candidate.'

The problem, according to Devlin, was that the Liberal candidate, Sir Stanley Buckmaster, had said that he supported the exclusion of Ulster from home rule; this had 'filled radicals and Irishmen with surprise and anticipation. It will galvanise Irish votes in Keighley and play into the hands of the Tory Party.' He asked: 'Is Sir Stanley ... speaking for himself or reflecting the mind of the government? As one of the representatives of Ulster I [have] already repeatedly declared my opposition [to exclusion] in any shape or form.' He went on to express the growing concern of the Irish Party about the links between Churchill and leading Conservatives such as F. E. Smith 'and other irreconcilables.'

Devlin was shrewd enough to realise that Churchill, a formidable combination of social reformer, aristocrat, and opportunist, personified elements in the establishment more concerned with the corrosive effect the home rule controversy was having on British politics than with its importance for Ireland. 'Ireland trusted Asquith,' he told Illingworth. 'We trust him still. We have stood faithfully by the Liberal Party in every crisis: we are prepared to do so still.'[6]

The letter's omissions are telling. Devlin was the Irish Party leader closest to the labour movement. He had spoken from the same platforms as Larkin during the great Belfast disputes of 1907; his role then as a friend of the working man ensured that Catholic workers in the city did not slip out of the political grasp of the AOH and UIL machines. It was part of a fierce rearguard action he fought to deny the 'new unionism' its increasing influence throughout Ireland. The AOH was the weapon he used, and he encouraged Hibernians to be active in their unions. 'The rights of labour and the dignity of labour can no longer be ignored,' he told an AOH convention held just after the 1911 rail strike; but he also reminded his audience that 'whatever rights labour enjoys in Ireland, it owes them to the Irish Party.'[7]

In 1913 there had been rumours that Devlin intended setting up a rival organisation to the ITGWU, and there were calls in the press for him to do so. His failure, therefore, to mention Larkin's imprisonment in his letter to Illingworth does not necessarily mean it was not an issue: it may simply be that there was no political advantage for Devlin in drawing it to Illingworth's attention. Of more significance may be Devlin's failure to mention the Larkin factor in his correspondence with John Dillon, his political mentor. Nor are there are any references to Larkin's imprisonment being an issue in the by-elections in Dillon's surviving correspondence from his other political confidant, T. P. O'Connor. O'Connor was a close observer of the British labour scene and would surely have mentioned it if he had felt it important. Of course there are none so blind as those who will not see; and the Irish Party may simply have refused to accept a painful reality.

Much of the significance subsequently attached to Larkin's imprisonment as a by-election issue in 1913 rests on one remark that the Chancellor of the Exchequer, David Lloyd George, made at the National Liberal Club on Sunday 9 November, the day after the by-election results. Asked about the outcome, he said there were various explanations, 'the most prominent of which is, probably, Jim Larkin.'[8]

There is no doubt that Lloyd George was extremely annoyed at Larkin's imprisonment, as was Sir Rufus Isaacs, the new Attorney-General. Isaacs shared Lloyd George's belief that Larkin's prosecution had been a mistake. Lloyd George had been lobbied by Liberal MPs representing working-class constituencies about the political embarrassment Larkin's imprisonment was causing them. Dr Christopher Addison, who represented Hoxton in London's East End, told him that

> the case of Larkin ... arouses the greatest possible resentment amongst many quite moderate working men ... It seems that the manner and conduct of his trial were not as fair as they might have been, and what on earth was done by arresting him I cannot imagine. I think it is quite right to let Carson & Co. have their fling and whilst we do so, no amount of argument will convince the average man that we are acting fairly, if, at the same time, we put Larkin in jail.

He felt that Larkin 'is no doubt excitable and extravagant; but the housing and wage conditions in Dublin are a disgrace to the country and I think he has done a good service in showing them up.'

Lloyd George replied immediately, even though he had a Cabinet meeting later the same day.

> You are quite right in the view you take of the Larkin business. No amount of argument could persuade the British working man that the difference in ... treatment accorded to Larkin, as compared with that meted out to Carson is anything but pure class distinction. However, before you receive this letter you will realise that there are members of the Government who take the same view.[9]

He was as good as his word, and the Cabinet meeting that day began with 'prolonged consideration' of the Larkin case. Even the diplomatic summary of proceedings prepared subsequently for King George V by Asquith could not disguise the fact that it had been an acrimonious debate.

> A large majority of the Cabinet was of opinion that the prosecution was impolitic and unnecessary and calculated to do more harm than good. Mr. Birrell defended it in view of the dangerous condition of affairs in Dublin. The Chancellor ... and the Attorney General commented severely on the manner in which the jury was 'packed' and on the tone in which the prosecution was conducted by the Irish Law Officers. After much discussion, the Cabinet came unanimously to the conclusion that, in view of the fact that Larkin was acquitted on the two most serious counts on the indictment—those of inciting to larceny and riot—the sentence of 7 months was frankly excessive and, in accordance with the practice in such matters, it was left to the Minister responsible (in this case the Chief Secretary, in connection with the Lord Lieutenant) to determine the precise amount of the reduction.[10]

The question that was causing such acrimony within the Cabinet was a much weightier one than whether Larkin should spend seven months in

Mountjoy. Birrell was the real target of the debate. He was becoming an increasingly isolated figure in the government. First and foremost, he found himself under increasing pressure from Lloyd George and Churchill to resolve the impasse with the unionists. Birrell was already depressed by his visit with Dougherty to Ulster, and he was convinced that the Ulstermen would 'fight like lions' if forced into a home rule parliament.[11] But he was equally unwilling to confront the Irish Party. His handling of the situation caused by the lockout had weakened him politically and had convinced Lloyd George at least that he was unfit for any post requiring hard work or decisiveness.

Birrell's morale was now at rock bottom. Only the previous week an initiative to tackle the Dublin housing crisis had backfired. After committing himself to an inquiry into the condition of the slums in the wake of the Church Street disaster, he had been inundated with demands and deputations from other local authorities that the inquiry should include them as well. Local politicians scented that government money was available, and they did not see why Dublin should scoop the pool.

Birrell dithered for almost two months. On 29 October, Lady Aberdeen introduced a delegation of the Women's National Health Association to the Chief Secretary at Dublin Castle, and they too pressed for a slum clearance programme, with her obvious approval. Two days later it was Lord Aberdeen's turn to escort a delegation from the Housing and Town Planning Association of Ireland to Birrell's office. Lady Aberdeen attended this time as president of the association and apologised to the beleaguered Chief Secretary for lecturing him once more on the issue by explaining that it was her duty to do so. Birrell tried to counter-attack by telling the Aberdeens brusquely that 'it does not rest with me to decide aye or nay as between a Viceregal Commission and a Departmental Committee.' The pressure was telling.

The following Tuesday he suddenly announced that he was setting up a departmental committee after all. It would be made up of three inspectors from the Local Government Board, and it would be looking only at the Dublin situation. Even Dubliners were not satisfied with this half-way house and demanded that the inquiry should at least have the status of the Viceregal commission that Birrell had hinted at the previous week. Municipal pride was at stake. As the *Irish Times* put it, 'Mr. Birrell has not only flouted public opinion; he has endangered the prospects of reform which is vital to the health and social peace of Dublin.'[12]

It was small wonder that Birrell was complaining to Asquith.

The Aberdeens are back and fussing about attending delegations which are waiting ON ME. They won't be left out of anything for a moment. It is a capital disaster their being here at this crucial time.

He admitted that his complaint was an 'agonised cry' from the heart and obviously did not feel strong enough to demand the removal of the popular couple.[13]

More serious was the threat posed by the forays of his Cabinet colleagues into the home rule crisis. It was Birrell's job to brief the King on events in Ireland, and he clearly enjoyed his visits to Balmoral, where George V spent much of the summer and early autumn of 1913. The twenty-first of September was one of Birrell's better days. He told a disappointed king that the government would not accede to the Unionist demand that an election be held before the Home Rule Bill became law, but he did broach the subject of excluding Ulster from its provisions. He felt the King had responded positively, and Birrell was granted leave to go off and shoot four stags, 'including the heaviest shot this year,' he subsequently boasted to Asquith.[14]

Within a fortnight, however, Birrell was again complaining to the Prime Minister that the King was becoming confused by the succession of Liberal ministers coming to Balmoral to present their own views on Ulster as those of the government. He was particularly critical of Churchill and the effect of his Dundee speech. Birrell had had to reassure Redmond that the government's resolve to introduce home rule for all Ireland remained unshaken. He told Asquith that he felt he had handled the situation well. He had also persuaded Redmond to consider some form of Ulster council, 'without legislative powers but with some administrative autonomy,' if Asquith repudiated the exclusion suggestion.

Asquith's Sunnybank speech and Larkin's imprisonment seem to have lifted Birrell's spirits momentarily,[15] but it must have been with a fragile ego that he re-entered the Cabinet room on 13 November to resume the adjourned discussion on Ireland.

In the meantime the Keighley result had been announced. Despite Devlin's concern that Sir Stanley Buckmaster's stance on Ulster might jeopardise the result, he was returned with an increased majority. No doubt this confirmed Lloyd George and Churchill in their view that the British electorate was in no mood to support coercion of the Ulster unionists. The result also helped prepare the ground for Lloyd George to unveil his own proposals for resolving the home rule crisis.

However, the Cabinet debate began with Birrell giving a briefing on the Ulster situation. He said that RIC estimates put the number of actively enrolled Ulster Volunteers at fifty thousand and their armaments at around five thousand rifles. However, this figure was 'purely conjectural.' Ministers then discussed various options for defusing the situation but admitted that the party's own rank and file was 'strongly and growingly opposed to any form of compromise' because of 'Ulster threats.' Birrell told colleagues that excluding Ulster from the provisions of the Home Rule Bill would be 'a bad and unworkable expedient,' because of nationalist opposition. Nevertheless the Postmaster-General, Herbert Samuel, suggested that they look again at Lord Loreburn's proposals, one of which was to give Ulster MPs in a home rule parliament the power of veto over the application of legislation to their own province. Other members felt this would only antagonise all the Irish parties further.

Lloyd George then unveiled his own project, which received a much more enthusiastic response. Supported by Churchill, he argued for the exclusion of Ulster's 'Protestant counties … for a definite term of five or six years, with a provision for … automatic inclusion at the expiration of that time.' The beauty of the scheme, he argued, was that it would be difficult for the Ulster Volunteers to resist by force something that was not going to happen for several years, while still holding out to the nationalists the ultimate prospect of a united Ireland.

The essence of the ultimate Irish settlement had been laid out for the first time in a formal political arena and been given qualified Cabinet blessing. Asquith subsequently told the King he intended discussing the proposal with Redmond when next they met.[16]

It must have been a dispiriting meeting for Birrell, who was now faced with the prospect of having to admit to Redmond and the King that government policy on Ireland was being dictated by others. When the meeting was over, Birrell sent a note to Asquith to say that he was 'just off in no very exulted frame of mind to meet the mob in Bristol.' This was his own constituency. But he had something more important to confide.

> Having regard to the discussions of the Cabinet today that pourparlers should be AT ONCE exchanged with Redmond—I feel convinced that in the real INTERESTS of peace and party—I ought at the earliest possible date—to be relieved of my present office, which all of a sudden has become extraordinarily distasteful to me.

He didn't mind 'how it is done, or what people say. I hope that you; amidst the pressure of other things, won't overlook this—which I do not think [I] can stand over until Christmas.' It was a vain hope. Asquith was too busy, and Birrell would have to stagger on for another three years, until the 1916 Rising signed his political death warrant.

When the Prime Minister received Birrell's resignation offer that afternoon, he was already preoccupied by his meeting with Redmond. This took place next day and ended inconclusively, with Redmond promising, ambiguously, 'to close no door to a settlement.'[17]

*

The significance that has been given to the 'Release Larkin' campaign as a factor in the three British by-elections of November 1913 has been exaggerated. The results were part of a trend; the Liberals continued to lose seats right up to the outbreak of the First World War. This was partly due to the usual anti-government sentiment expressed at by-elections; but other important factors were at work, to which a politician as experienced as Lloyd George would not want to draw attention. By blaming the by-election results on Larkin's imprisonment, Lloyd George did a number of things. Firstly, he undermined Birrell. Secondly, and more importantly, he sidestepped more unpalatable explanations for the government's defeats— namely that Labour was at last seducing the working-class vote away from the Liberals, and that the Unionists were winning the debate over home rule with middle-class voters.

Certainly that was the view taken by the opposition. The *Irish Times* editorial after Reading may have been triumphalist, but it contained a large grain of truth when it said of the British government that 'at the most critical moment in its career—at a time when it claims a popular mandate for a tremendous and revolutionary programme—its pretensions have been denied and its PRESTIGE shattered.' Lloyd George's Cabinet proposal to exclude Ulster temporarily from home rule, which was still secret when that editorial was published, was a tacit admission of this.

Of course Larkin's imprisonment was an embarrassment the British government could well do without; but once he was released, the Dublin lockout was never again discussed at the Cabinet table. In contrast, the London dock strike of the previous year had dominated no less than five Cabinet meetings, and senior ministers had discussed initiatives to settle it, including a visit by the King to the port. If there was ever an argument for home rule, the contrasting attitude of the British government to the two disputes provided it.[18]

32

L ARKIN was released at 7 a.m. on Thursday 13 November, less than twenty-four hours after the Cabinet decision; he had served just seventeen days of his seven-month sentence. The newspapers had been notified in advance, but Larkin refused to answer reporters' questions and went home to his family in Auburn Street.

At about 10:30 a.m. someone in the press of workers outside Liberty Hall, where news of the great 'victory' had spread, shouted, 'Here's Jim, here's Jim!' The attention of the crowd was directed to the corner of Abbey Street; and there, 'walking towards Liberty Hall was Jim Larkin, wearing his usual soft hat and dust coat.' He was lifted shoulder-high and carried into the building.[1]

Larkin reappeared to address the waiting multitude at noon. He was reported to be looking 'well and strong, but his voice did not carry as far as usual.' His first words were for 'all the men and women who are now in prison in connection with the dispute.' He said they should be released. He had obviously been briefed on the intervention of the Shipping Federation, because he went on to tell his audience:

> This is a bigger movement than some people realise. The great labour movement is not going to be stopped by a few imported blacklegs. The government has been forced to release me, and my advice is the same as always: 'Stand determined; we are going to win.' (Cheers.)

'This fight is only really starting,' Larkin promised the crowd. The government had made a mistake in arresting him, and an even bigger one in releasing him. He was going in a few hours 'to light a fiery cross in England, Scotland, and Wales. The government are going to get a lesson before they get out of this fight.' The DMP, Dublin Castle, John Dillon Nugent, the AOH and the 'scabs' were all warned that their day of reckoning was nigh.[2]

A rally was organised that evening, with another fireworks display on the roof of Liberty Hall to welcome Larkin home, but he failed to appear. He felt too unwell after his stint in Mountjoy to risk the strain of speaking again. His indisposition provided an unexpected and rare break for his wife, Elizabeth, to go out, and she took her husband's place with the marchers as they thronged through the city centre.

When she had married the handsome, hard-working foreman docker ten years earlier she can have had little inkling that his bent for socialist debates would lead to a helter-skelter existence as the wife of a roving missionary of syndicalism.[3] The Larkins were no longer able to enjoy some of the luxuries possible on a foreman docker's wages. At times even his reduced salary as a union official was not forthcoming. During protracted disputes there was little or no ready cash in the union funds. One week during the 1911 strike by ITGWU members in Wexford, Larkin split a pound with the former English sweep Walter Carpenter, one of the union organisers. 'Even Jim shrunk from offering Mrs Larkin 10s for her weekly housekeeping, and begged Carpenter to call round and leave the money with her,' one early historian of the Irish labour movement wrote. Later the general president of the ITGWU, Thomas Foran, arranged for Larkin's wages to be sent directly to his wife, 'as Jim had the habit of giving much of his money away to poor families on his way home.'[4]

Eviction for non-payment of rent was an ever-present prospect for the Larkins, and increasingly likely as the lockout dragged on. When a *Daily Sketch* reporter called to the family home to interview Elizabeth, he told readers:

> She seems to feel the strain of being a rebel's wife, although she is herself keenly enthusiastic for the cause of labour. She has three children, the eldest boy at school, but smilingly declared that they were young to be rebels yet.[5]

The victory march Elizabeth Larkin joined that night was one of the largest demonstrations of working-class power ever seen in Dublin. It set out from Beresford Place shortly after 7 p.m., and the crowd was so huge that it took two hours to return to Liberty Hall, where, in the absence of Larkin, Connolly was the main speaker.

Larkin might have made a more colourful speech, but he could not have made a more chilling one than his lieutenant. They were there, Connolly said,

> to celebrate our first great victory in the fight. We have shown in a way our opponents cannot question that we possess a greater power than the government, a power which makes governments impossible.

Perhaps it was as much the amorphous nature of the crowd that had flooded through the streets as its size that prompted his next remarks. Connolly told the workers they were 'in a state of war.'

> The next time we go out for a march I want to be accompanied by four battalions of our own men. I want them to have their own corporals and sergeants and men who will be able to 'form fours.' Why should we not drill men in Dublin as well as in Ulster?
> When you come to draw your strike pay this week I want every man who is willing to enlist as a soldier to give his name and address, and

you will be informed when and where you have to attend for training. I have been promised the assistance of competent chief officers, who will lead us anywhere. I say nothing about arms at present. When we want them, we know where we will find them. (Laughter.)

ITGWU members wanted the restoration of their rights from the employers; they wanted the release of 'every man, woman and child who is a member of the Transport Union and who is now in prison in Mountjoy. (Cheers.) ... No vessel will leave the port of Dublin until these demands are met.' There was no need to take a vote on such action, he said. He wanted them 'ready to obey the word of command, and when the fight is over we can take a vote, if we please.'

Among the other speakers was Constance Markievicz, soon to be the most colourful figure in Connolly's new Citizen Army. She described the rally as 'the proudest moment of my life, to be associated with the workers of Dublin when their great and noble leader has been released.' Connolly apologised for the absence of that 'great and noble leader,' who was 'off colour and not as well as we would like him to be.'[6]

*

About the same time, Birrell was keeping his rendezvous with the 'mob' in Bristol. If he had hoped the release of Larkin would appease their anger, he was to be disappointed. Rising to address the city's Anchor Society, he was met with a barrage of heckling about the lockout as well as the now mandatory cries of 'Votes for women.' He did not shirk the issue.

> I must ask you to bear with me in silence, if you like with disapproval, to allow me to make an observation or two on the trial, imprisonment and very happy release of Mr Larkin. (Prolonged applause.) I said a happy release. I do that because I think justice required it. (Renewed cheers.) I say 'let justice be done though the sky fall.' I dare say a number of you, I should not be surprised if it were a very large majority, shared the opinion expressed this morning by the organ of public opinion which advertises itself as 'the organ of all thinking men and women,' the *Times* newspaper, that Larkin ought not to have been tried at all. (Cheers.) That opinion is shared not only, evidently, by a large number of sound and sensible Liberals in this hall but by bishops and deans in other parts of the country. A man, therefore, would have to be very self-confident and very vain to believe that such an opinion was not one for which a great deal could be said.

Birrell made his case regardless.

> I know ... that a very great number of you think I made a very great mistake in sanctioning the trial of Mr Larkin. You think I ought to have let him alone. (Hear, hear.) I respect your opinion. I respect my own. (Cheers.) What is the main duty, the primary duty, the overwhelming duty of an executive officer? I am not speaking of great statesmen such as yourselves: I am speaking of an executive officer in a great city like

Dublin, agitated, stirred to its very depths. His duty is not the romantic duty of settling the dispute, if he could, but of bringing the employers and employees together, and imploring them to act like Christians, one to the other. That is his duty, and we have attempted it to the best of our ability, but the primary duty of an executive officer is to keep the soldiers in their barracks. (Cheers.)

There was a certain amount of poetic licence in Birrell's argument, for Dublin had been swarming with soldiers on strike duty for the past two months; but the audience understood his meaning. He had maintained order without gunning down citizens on the streets, and part of that process had entailed the arrest and trial of Larkin.

Juries are often nowadays spoken of disrespectfully. Find a substitute for them. (Cheers.) The jury which tried Mr Larkin was not biased in his favour. It would have been difficult to find a jury in Dublin, based on the jury list, who were biased in Mr Larkin's favour ... but they gave him a fair trial ... After the fullest possible consideration of the case they found him guilty of the speech and acquitted him on two counts. My honest and deliberate judgement ... required that this Mr Larkin should have the benefit of these acquittals ... having regard to the fact that he was found guilty of speech and speech alone.

[It was said that] this was all electioneering. There was not much electioneering about it. Reading, Linlithgow, and Keighley, were fought under the whole weight of whatever unpopularity the action of the Irish Executive had created in the country, and that unpopularity, I quite agree, was grave. We did not in any way seek to interfere with those elections. Nor did we release Mr Larkin till the moment came when, on my honour and conscience, I can say that I think the time he had served was fully enough on the evidence on which he was found guilty. I, as a lawyer, would be the last man in the world to go behind a jury's finding. The great thing now is not to indulge in recriminations.

This part of his speech was, at best, a disingenuous performance; but he now came to the core of his appeal.

We are approaching a graver and a greater question. In Dublin we have a strike that is working like a canker ... I am afraid, unless a better spirit can be introduced into the minds of both parties, it will leave Dublin, when it is over, as over some day soon it has got to be, poorer and more miserable than it was before.

The government had 'done what they could,' and Birrell still believed that Askwith's conciliation proposals 'even now' provided 'a basis for settlement.' The government was

working day by day and hour by hour to accomplish this great end, to secure to the working class the fullest and completest right of trades unionism, to be represented in their fullest force, to be in no way interfered with by law or tampered with by authority. They said to this class, 'Have your organisation, have your leaders, make your representations, come to your bargain and stick to it.' There is nothing Socialistic in this, and I do not believe that any Dublin employer entertained notions to the contrary. It would be a monstrous thing if an agreement could not be come to which would liberate the enormous number of men now idle.

He asked his audience

not to be led away by sentiment or emotion, but to believe that they were the best citizens who strove the hardest to produce amongst both employers and employed in Dublin the recognition on the one hand of the complete principle of trades unionism, on the other of sane and honourable dealing between man and man. (Cheers.)[7]

One wonders whether Birrell would have made such a speech if he had not thought himself on the verge of resignation. It was more passionate than his usual offerings, but it was still very much in the classical liberal style: it appealed to the intellect and to the virtues of common sense, decency, compromise, and restraint. Events would ultimately prove that Connolly's direct and brutal approach was more in keeping with the times. Of course Connolly had to deal with harsher realities than Birrell, whose bleakest prospect—exile from the Cabinet—was far removed from the destitution and hardship of the tenements.

*

Birrell's appeal fell on deaf ears. Even while Larkin spent his last few days in prison, the chances for a compromise settlement had slipped further away.

There was, at first, an air of anti-climax to the Shipping Federation's intervention. On Monday 10 November heavy rain ensured that the potential for conflict between ITGWU pickets and the imported 'free labourers' was minimal. It also transpired that the *Lady Jocelyn* had not brought the hundreds of extra 'blacklegs' expected but only supplies for those already in the city. Originally a three-masted sailing-ship, the sixty-year-old vessel was little more than a floating hulk. A shabby transport with a shabby role, it looked 'battered and worn' as it entered Alexandra Basin and berthed astern of the *Wearwood*. It had taken two days to beat its way up from Falmouth; but it had not been acquired for its sailing qualities. It would soon accommodate six hundred men in its cramped quarters.[8]

While the *Lady Jocelyn* idled at anchor, an ugly spectre of things to come, Connolly was confronted by the failure of many union members to respond to his call for mass pickets. Those who did turn out were so few that many were redirected to the city centre to register a public presence at the firms most prominently associated with the lockout, such as Eason's, the DUTC, and Jacob's. The only serious incident of the day was the stoning of a group of home-grown strike-breakers as they marched along Sheriff Street to the docks under police escort.

One reason for the ineffectiveness of the pickets may have been the ever-accelerating use of lorries by employers. Since the coal merchants had introduced the first motorised transport in late September, other employers had also begun to discover its advantages. Lorries were far less vulnerable to obstruction, or attack, than a horse and dray. The Dublin Employers' Federation had quietly introduced a subsidy scheme for companies acquiring lorries for the first time. A clear demonstration of the advantage this gave came that morning when a convoy of fourteen Guinness lorries collected grain from the *Wearwood* and then roared unmolested down the quays.

The existence of the subsidy for smaller employers was revealed in the latest edition of the British trade magazine *Motor Traction*. To coincide with the annual London Motor Show, the magazine published a report on the Dublin lockout. It included a photograph of Liberty Hall, the 'headquarters of the Irish Transport and General Workers' Union ... primarily responsible for the great success of motor transport in Ireland.' The article stated that the dispute had seriously affected traditional carriers, such as John Wallis and Son, one of the main transport firms in the city. It had two hundred horse-drawn vehicles lying idle, and many of its larger customers 'have themselves adopted motor vehicles. Asked why they did not do likewise, this company explained that they considered it would be prejudicial to a settlement.'

The magazine described the lead that the city's larger coal merchants had given in switching to motor-lorries. W. G. Nicholl, whose firm usually had eighty horse-drawn drays delivering two hundred tons of coal a day, was, 'when the writer met him ... utilising his four seated Ford touring car for the transport of coal, taking six sacks each time.' The Irish Motor Company reported that it was converting the chassis of charabancs for use as lorries to try to cope with demand. Guinness's had taken the lead in mechanising its fleet, using Straiker-Squire and Leyland lorries. Already the company had twenty vehicles in operation, and it expected to have thirty shortly. It would continue to use drays, though many of its horse men were being taught to drive lorries at the company's own driving school.

Few firms had Guinness's resources. Though prices had fallen dramatically over the previous decade, a lorry still cost four or five times as much as a horse and dray. The big advantages of the new technology were greater productivity and lower wages. The Guinness management told *Motor Traction* that a lorry could deliver 275 barrels of malt a day, compared with 30 by a horse and dray. Low interest rates also made investment in motor transport attractive. In a report on 'The Motor and the Merchant,' the *Irish Times* costed horse-drawn vehicles against mechanised; it estimated that over two years the running cost of motor vehicles, including depreciation and interest, ranged from 3½d to 9d a mile, while the horse-drawn equivalent cost 1s a mile.[9]

*

Another sign of growing intransigence from the employers' side was the dissolution of the Industrial Peace Committee. This initiative by Tom Kettle to employ the city's intellectuals and clergy as mediators between the classes had finally run its course. In a report outlining its work, the committee left no-one in any doubt where it believed the blame lay for continued strife.

> It appears to the committee that the employers feel their duty to themselves makes it impossible for them to pay any attention to the claims of the Irish workers, or to public opinion in Dublin.
>
> They are however willing to meet the English trade union representatives … presumably to justify their action to them, for they will not meet their own disemployed workers, even if urged to do so by these gentlemen. Consequently the Irish workers cannot ask their English comrades to accept an invitation insulting in its essence to both nationalities and, therefore, the English workers reject it.[10]

This was strong criticism from a body that included the Dean of St Patrick's Cathedral, the president of the Royal Irish Academy, and other social luminaries; but it had no visible effect on the employers. If anything, their resolve was strengthened by the failure of Connolly's efforts to mobilise the threatened mass pickets. In later years the aura of martyrdom transformed Connolly's memory, but the reality of 1913 was very different. The veteran Belfast trade unionist Jack Carney would recall later:

> He lacked that human warmth so characteristic of Larkin. The main defect in Connolly was his shyness. He could not tolerate company. He could not mix with the masses. After lectures or meetings he would rush away because he lacked that human warmth so characteristic of Jim and so essential in … labour organisers.[11]

Certainly union members failed to respond to Connolly that week, and it could not but have had an unsettling effect, given the critical situation. There were rumours that the United Builders' Labourers' Union was considering a ballot on a return to work. Already some ITGWU men and craft workers had gone back at Jacob's.

On Wednesday morning the *Ella* finally returned from Liverpool with three hundred more 'free labourers', and after shifting their gear to the *Lady Jocelyn* they joined their brethren in the hold of the *Wearwood*, unloading the huge Guinness shipment.[12]

Connolly retaliated at noon on Wednesday by closing the port. No strike notice was given, even to shipping lines such as the City of Dublin, which had turned a blind eye to ITGWU members blacking 'tainted goods'. So sudden was the decision that among the ships held up that day was the

TUC food ship *Hare*, whose mixed cargo included a large consignment of food for the unions.

Connolly has been strongly criticised for taking this action, which in effect made a further thousand dockers and their families a charge on the strike fund. It has also been argued that it was a 'fatal move' in forcing all the port employers into the arms of the Shipping Federation. Carney cited it as evidence that Connolly 'knew little of the practical problems'.[13] What Carney and other commentators chose to ignore was that the Shipping Federation was already in the port, as evidenced by the presence of its vessels in Alexandra Basin. What they could not know was that even the City of Dublin Steam Packet Company, and other shipping lines not yet involved in the dispute, were seeking strike indemnities from the federation as a preliminary to joining the lock-out. In the case of the City of Dublin line, the main cause of delay appears to have been that its subscription to the federation was in arrears.[14]

The only valid criticism of Connolly's move is that it left the union open to the charge of stepping up the dispute. In other words, it lost the ITGWU some of the moral high ground; but the strikers had acres of that commodity already. Besides, Connolly's move gave the workers a sense of retaining the initiative; and if mass picketing was not working, some alternative was urgently needed before demoralisation set in. As we have seen, when Larkin was released next day he publicly endorsed Connolly's action in the speech in which he also announced that he was undertaking another trip to Britain. He obviously believed there was little more that could be done in Dulbin, and he heard the syndicalist siren calling once more to spread the struggle.

Larkin's optimism as he set out for Britain was understandable. Throughout his seventeen days in prison there had been a growing trade union chorus for a general strike. Only the day before his release the ITGWU's strongest sympathiser in the leadership of the NTWF, Robert Williams, had called for a boycott of all goods bound for Dublin.[15]

33

THE closure of the port caused consternation among Dubliners and a return to the panic buying that had marked the early days of the dispute. However, businesses reacted more calmly. Cattle exporters, for instance, accustomed by now to the vagaries of port traffic, arranged for two thousand head already en route to the city to be diverted to other ports.[1]

The businessmen most concerned at the stoppage appear to have been the leaders of the Shipping Federation, who suddenly found themselves at its epicentre. As it happened, the general council of the Federation was due to meet on 14 November, the day after Dublin port closed. The decision to support the Dublin employers had been taken by the federation's general purposes committee, and one of Britain's largest shipping magnates, Sir Walter Runciman, had already written to Cuthbert Laws expressing his dissent. But Runciman was Minister of Agriculture in the Liberal government, and many other shippers felt that he was merely expressing the general disapproval of the Cabinet for any involvement by British organisations in a Dublin squabble.

Of more immediate moment were the reservations of delegates representing shipowners in the north-western ports. One of these, Mason, expressed concern when the chairman revealed that £5,000 had already been voted by the general purposes committee for the Dublin dispute. Mason said that involvement in the dispute was 'opening up a very dangerous principle.' If the federation backed the Dublin employers and insisted 'on the men coming out from membership of the Irish Transport Workers' Union as a condition of employment—they were asking a condition which was contrary to individual liberty.' He even questioned the legality of the action, and argued that the aims of the Dublin employers went beyond the federation's objectives. Another north-western delegate, Haw, said that Liverpool members were 'dead against this,' and the chairman, F. S. Watts, accepted that there was even stronger opposition from Newcastle.

However, Watts said that 'everybody else' in the federation was for intervention if it was considered critical to the outcome of the dispute. Delegates who spoke from other regions agreed, though there were questions whether they should be providing funds for small Dublin businesses that 'have nothing whatever to do with the strike,' simply because those firms now faced financial ruin. Even delegates who supported intervention expressed surprise at pay rates in Dublin; one of them described the rates as 'too absurd, and not a living wage.'[2]

Before the dispute was over, the federation would contribute £9,967 to the Dublin employers. This may pale beside the £93,673 worth of aid sent by the TUC to the unions, but it is still more than twice the amount that William Martin Murphy had managed to raise at this stage from other sources, and shows how critical the federation's intervention was to the success of his strategy.

The Dublin dispute was by far the biggest financial commitment of the Shipping Federation in 1913. In contrast, it spent £3,811 on combating the Leith strike. Only the great London dock strike of 1912 incurred greater expenditure in the years leading up to the First World War: it had cost the federation £28,810.[3]

If the ITGWU could not have held out for six months without the massive transfusion of food, clothing, fuel and cash from Britain, the same argument applied to the other side. However, because the records of the Shipping Federation were confidential, the critical role that its cash and 'free labourers' played has never been fully appreciated. There was little practical difference between Larkin's 'hands across the sea' strategy and Murphy's; it was their perceptions that were different. Larkin saw the help as a vindication of his syndicalist faith, something to shout from the rooftops. Murphy kept his own counsel. It was in his nature to keep any aces up his sleeve, and he no doubt felt a little uncomfortable, as an Irish nationalist, accepting hand-outs from Britain.

*

How much, if any, of the money went into Dublin's 'yellow press' will probably never be known. The *Liberator and Irish Trade Unionist* appeared on the streets of Dublin on 23 August 1913. Like the *Irish Worker*, it was a weekly and cost a penny; but the *Liberator* was printed on better-quality paper, and its message was anti-Larkinite. Its offices were in Parliament Street, and its editor was Bernard Doyle, a printer and publisher who had actually printed the first *Irish Worker and People's Advocate* in the eighteen-nineties, when the paper had been the organ of a more conservative Dublin Trades Council.

Doyle had also been the first printer of Larkin's revived *Irish Worker*. Like Councillor William Richardson, he appears to have fallen out fairly early on with the ITGWU leader. But, unlike Richardson, there appeared to be no passion to Doyle's anti-Larkinism. His paper was a feeble affair, and one gets the impression that the motivation was money rather than hatred— which raises the question, who was footing the bill? As a small businessman, Doyle lacked the resources to launch and sustain such an ambitious venture on his own. It is hard to believe, therefore, that the *Liberator* was anything other than a front for Murphy. Though it posed at first as a moderate alternative voice to Larkinism for Dublin trade unionists, its editorial opinions quickly became indistinguishable from those of Murphy—even down to its hostility towards the Hugh Lane gallery proposal. In any case, the *Liberator*'s preoccupation with Larkin meant that it was certainly never seen by its potential readership as anything but a propaganda sheet for the employers.[4]

Nevertheless, the *Liberator* claimed various laudatory aims, including 'better housing of the people … the development of industries on Trade Union lines … relief of unemployment,' and the eradication of 'the curse of sweating.' Its primary aim was to restore Dublin Trades Council to 'the esteem of the citizens—both employers and workers.' Regrettably, 'bogus Socialists' had 'terrorised the more respectable and intelligent delegates into handing the entire business over to their tender mercies.' Doyle took 'bogus Socialism' so seriously that he engaged in it himself, cheerfully making up quotations from authors such as Karl Marx and Belfort Max when he found that the originals were not outrageous enough to meet his needs.

The best features of the *Liberator* were undoubtedly its excellent cartoons and the doggerel. Larkin was almost invariably the subject of both. On 27 September, for instance, it published the following lines about Larkin's 'divine mission of discontent' in Britain:

To Manchester Jim started,
Came back, and went again;
And left us all parading
The city in the rain.

While he on Irish stew did dine,
On ham and eggs and chicken fine;
He made the English workers laugh,
And said a loaf—or even half—
Will do for you!

But doggerel and cartoons were not enough to keep the *Liberator* afloat. Doyle was a lazy journalist. His newspaper published little news, and what there was was often inaccurate. For example, he told readers in the issue of 6 September that Larkin was sending a son to St Enda's College in Rathfarnham 'for fear he might pick up any religion in the schools of the Christian Brothers.' The following week there was an abject apology to the college principal, Patrick Pearse, and an acknowledgment that St Enda's was 'a purely Catholic school.' The incident says as much about the attitudes of Larkin and Pearse to education and religion as it does about Doyle's talents as a journalist. The only wonder is that the newspaper survived until 22 November—just long enough to see Larkin released from prison. It passed away unmourned.[5]

*

In October, another 'yellow sheet' had appeared. The *Toiler* was a cramped little paper, with densely printed columns on cheap paper, but it survived remarkably well. Its editor, P. J. McIntyre, was a very different journalistic animal from Bernard Doyle. A renegade from the socialist movement, he worked with the zeal of the convert. His animus, like Councillor Richardson's, appeared to be hatred of Larkin, with whom he had first clashed in 1909. A former Dublin branch secretary in the Workers' Union (a British union), McIntyre had flirted with plans to bring the Irish membership into Larkin's newly established ITGWU. However, the motives of McIntyre and his associates were largely pecuniary, and when they failed to do a deal with Larkin, McIntyre decided to campaign against 'imported English strike mongers'—a practice in which Arthur Griffith's *Sinn Féin* indulged him, by publishing several of his articles.

McIntyre's falling out with Larkin also led to his expulsion from the Independent Labour Party, and he devoted much of the remaining few years of his life to denouncing the 'false doctrine' of 'Socialism, Syndicalism and Anarchism.' In 1912 he had inadvertently helped Larkin secure the expulsion of Councillor Billy Richardson from the ITGWU, by implicating him in one of his own scurrilous articles for the *Evening Telegraph.*

By 1913 McIntyre himself had been sacked from the Workers' Union for allowing his anti-Larkinite zeal to lead him into strike-breaking activities against the ITGWU. Ostracised by most trade unionists, he appears to have scratched a living from freelance journalism and running a lodging-house. In his younger days he had been involved in proselytising activities in County Wicklow, an experience that perhaps prompted him to characterise the TUC support for the Dublin dispute as 'souperism', even before D. P. Moran did so. Larkin returned the abuse in kind, using the columns of the *Irish Worker* to denounce the editor of the *Toiler* as the 'proselyte keeper of a doss house.'[6]

McIntyre's former involvement with proselytisers did not prevent the *Irish Catholic* from allowing him to use its premises to produce the *Toiler*, suggesting another possible link with Murphy.[7]

In its first issue the *Toiler* announced that 'extraordinary allegations' had reached it that James Larkin was a son of James Carey, the informer who had betrayed the Invincibles. McIntyre's evidence was Larkin's 'striking resemblance to ... members of the ... Carey family' and the fact that Larkin, like Carey, had shown himself to be 'an able organiser of the most reckless elements in the Irish Capital.'[8] McIntyre challenged his enemy to prove him wrong.

Larkin at first ignored the baiting, but the *Toiler* persisted. It even went as far as to publish photographs in December of a bearded Carey and of Larkin sporting the false beard he was wearing when arrested on Bloody Sunday, asking readers to tell the difference, and offered

> a prize of £5 to any Larkinite in Ireland, who will prove that James Larkin is not the son of James Carey. Surely the Larkinites are not following a man who cannot produce his baptismal lines?

Larkin made several ineffectual attempts to dismiss McIntyre's allegations. The problem was that he could not in fact produce a birth certificate. He always asserted that he was born in Ireland, though he sometimes varied the location between his father's townland of Lower Killeavy in County Armagh and other places. He simply may not have known for certain. In the late nineteenth century the world was on the move, and Larkin's records, like those of millions of children of peripatetic Irish emigrants, were not easy to trace. It was only in 1980 that the late C. Desmond Greaves tracked down the correct birth register for Larkin, in Toxteth, Liverpool; it also showed that he was two years older than anyone, himself included, had thought. To some extent Larkin was the victim of his own pride and stubbornness. Having once proclaimed that he had been born in Ireland, he could not admit he was wrong—particularly to the likes of McIntyre and his *Toiler*.[9]

Larkin's birthplace became yet another weapon in the debate over the legitimacy and *bona fides* of the protagonists in the lockout. Nationalists such as Griffith, Moran and Murphy constantly used Larkin's English origins against him. And Larkin, despite his own internationalism, loved Ireland dearly—particularly Dublin. In Manchester he once told a crowd that though he was an internationalist, he loved Ireland 'as I love no other land and no other people.'[10] To question his place of birth was tantamount to questioning his political legitimacy.

And it was not just Catholic nationalists who considered where a man was born to be relevant to his political credentials. When the ITGWU split over Larkin's leadership in 1924, his enemies in the union, including his former ally William O'Brien, thought it worth while producing a birth certificate that they claimed proved their opponent was born in Liverpool. It was subsequently found to belong to another Jim Larkin.[11] In 1913 the taunt that he was a 'Carey' seems to have been taken seriously only by Larkin himself. He complained in his speeches that he felt he was being 'crucified'; coming on top of all his other woes, it made the strain of the lockout 'almost unbearable.'[12]

*

However, Larkin was probably too busy in the week following his release to be bothered by McIntyre's barbs. Despite his announcement that he would be leaving 'within hours' for Britain, he had to spend Friday at Liberty Hall clearing a backlog of outstanding business. He was too busy to give press interviews or even to address that night's meeting in Beresford Place. These were tasks left to Connolly.[13]

Larkin was also preoccupied with the British situation. There were striking similarities with the state of affairs when he had been released in September. Once more the dispute was at a critical stage in Dublin, and there were signs that the intransigence of the employers had made the situation ripe for sympathetic action across the water. The Labour Party leader Keir Hardie said that 'the action of the Dublin employers has succeeded in bringing the whole thing within measurable distance of the biggest industrial conflict which the country has ever seen.' (The 'country' Keir Hardie had in mind was the United Kingdom.)

On a trip to Liverpool for supplies, the *Ella* was blacked, and it was unable to re-coal and return with its next draft of 'free labourers' to Dublin. In Wales, railwaymen were again refusing to handle 'tainted goods', and the general organiser of the NUDL, Harry Orbell, said that 'in all my experience I have never known a time when there has been manifested such a desire to help any union dispute than there is among the dockers, both in London and the provincial ports, towards their Dublin comrades.' These were strong words from an official of James Sexton's union. But Orbell added the caveat that his members would await the 'instructions of the Parliamentary Committee of the British TUC.'

The union had actually deployed officials in all the ports where it had members, 'with the express purpose of preventing any disorganised move ... It has been with the greatest trouble ... that we have so far been able to keep the men in check.' Jimmy Thomas, the NUR leader, managed to isolate the danger of any new conflagration in south Wales, and official NUR sources told the Irish newspapers that 'the bulk of the men have still unpleasant memories of the failure of their strike two years ago.' The same sources added that 'there is still some strong feeling ... amongst Dublin railway men against Larkin's union' because of the events of 1911.[14]

Everyone knew that the decisive moment would come on Tuesday 18 November, when the Parliamentary Committee met in London; everything said in the meantime was pitched by the various parties at that gathering. In case anyone should be unclear about the NUR's position, Thomas, who was also a Labour MP, told a public meeting in Swindon that 'no strike by railwaymen could take place at the instigation of any Tom, Dick or Harry, but only on the instruction of the union officials. I deprecate sectional or sympathetic strikes.'

The government let it be known that it had no intention of prosecuting Larkin or the other Dublin strike leaders further on the charges arising out of the August mass meetings, thus removing another grievance around which militants could mobilise trade union opinion. The Labour Press Agency in Britain, which had good government and union sources, even went so far as to claim that

> the Government are at last awake to the dangerous character that has developed in connection with the Dublin dispute and the possibility of developments on this side.
>
> Ministers are said to be far from satisfied with the way in which the situation has been handled by the Dublin Castle authorities and, for the future, the policy of the Government will be determined towards the dispute from Downing Street. The immediate intention is to apply to the disputants in Dublin such pressure as it is possible to apply without special legislation.

If 'informal efforts to restore peace to the distracted city fail, action of a more formal and effective character is likely to be taken.' The government sources also warned that there was mounting pressure, not just from Radical and Labour MPs but from 'public opinion', for 'any effort to coerce the employers, provided that similar coercion was applied to the men, where necessary.'

On the same day that the Labour Press Agency was briefed in London, Augustine Birrell met a trade union delegation in Bristol and assured a militant young dockers' leader called Ernest Bevin not only that there would be a public inquiry into the behaviour of the police in Dublin but that it would contain 'a representative ... of the working classes in Dublin or its neighbourhood.'[15]

*

On the same day that the Labour Press Agency report appeared, Murphy wrote a letter to the British as well as the Irish newspapers giving the most comprehensive exposition of the Dublin employers' case yet. He too was anxious to explain himself before the TUC leaders met.

He said that the letter was necessary because he received frequent 'letters, visits, and telephone messages from amiable people who have various nostrums for settling the labour unrest in Dublin, which they want me to put into operation.' He had 'no power to settle the trouble'; but that did not prevent him from going on to analyse the conflict and offering his own solution.

He began by stating that the 'deadlock in Dublin has not been so bad as it is represented.' It was 'only in the port that it has become serious but, such as it is, the people who can settle it are Mr. James Larkin and the officials of the Irish Transport Union, who produced the deadlock by terrorising the men into going out on sympathetic strike and who, by the same methods are restraining many from returning to work.' Murphy then seemed to offer an olive branch.

> There are not five per cent of the men out of employment who may not return, before their places are filled up, without any sacrifice of principle, or without giving any undertaking to do the work they are paid for doing ... Men who have returned to work say they never knew what tyranny meant till they joined the Irish Transport Union. Personally, I would rely mostly for future peace on the experience of these men and the strength of the employers' organisation.

Employers' representatives had engaged in 'hours of discussions' with the TUC and Dublin Trades Council to seek a settlement, 'but no-one now pretends that a Transport Union agreement can be relied on.'

He declared that 'there is not a man out of work in Dublin today on the question of wages or conditions of labour, although the idea had been spread abroad, especially in England, that all the trouble arises from sweated and underpaid labour.' Blithely ignoring the testimony of George Jacob, Murphy asserted that 'not a word of evidence' had been given to the

Askwith Inquiry to support that claim, and he cast himself as the principal victim of George Bernard Shaw's malign tongue at the Royal Albert Hall in London a fortnight earlier. 'The public memory is so short, and so many lies have been disseminated, that it is desirable to recall the fact that the origin of the present trouble was the attack made on the Tramway Company by Mr. Larkin, of which I am chairman.'

Here Murphy was on stronger ground. 'This attack commenced long before the actual calling out of the men and was in pursuance of a policy of "breaking Murphy's heart" publicly announced by Mr. Larkin.' Murphy admitted to

> having an objection to allowing my heart to be broken. I prepared to resist Mr. Larkin's attack, and inflicted a defeat on him from which he will never recover, even with the help of the cheap martyrdom bestowed on him by the Government.
>
> The claim, as I understand it now, of those who speak for trade unionism is that, while the union leaders are entitled to attack an employer and destroy his business whenever and however they like, an employer commits a high crime and misdemeanour if he takes any measure to defend himself ... The action of Mr. Larkin in attacking the Tramway Company was not due to the fact that the men were underpaid ... nor was it due to the slums of Dublin, which are supposed to be the root of all discontent. These men are well paid, and they live mainly outside the slum areas in the suburbs of the city, many of them in houses at cheap rents provided for them by the company, close by the car depots, where their day's work begins and ends.
>
> The sole reason for this audacious attempt ... to paralyse the tramway traffic in the busiest week in the year, was the colossal vanity and vaulting ambition of Mr. Larkin, who thought to make himself the unquestioned labour dictator of the city.
>
> I would, therefore, respectfully suggest to my friends of the Labour Party that it was unwise and unfair to make trade unionism an issue in this dispute, when the real question at stake was the personal supremacy of Mr. Larkin. While leaders of trade unionism are just now denouncing Mr. Larkin's proposal to raise the 'fiery cross' in England, is it not rather cynical that he should be enabled by the support of these same people to keep this city in a state of turmoil for months, and to do here what they will not permit him to do on their side of the channel! ...
>
> The employers of Dublin are really fighting the battle of sane trade unionism, for if by any chance Mr. Larkin achieved success here, the successful missioner could not be restrained from going on with his fiery crusade in Great Britain.

Murphy spoilt some of the effect by boasting in his conclusion that if Larkin had succeeded 'in getting a great many men out of their employment ... he has not got one of them back again.' His last point, on 'free labourers', was, however, adroitly made. Instead of trying to defend the measure, he blamed Larkin for being 'the cause of introducing a large amount of additional labour into a city where even in normal times there was not enough work to go round.'[16]

The Dublin employers also took steps to brief their counterparts in Britain on the struggle. They produced a pamphlet outlining their case, and on Monday 17 November two of Murphy's closest allies addressed a meeting of the United Kingdom Employers' Defence Union at the Whitehall Rooms in London. They were two of the city's master builders, John Good and H. McLaughlin. Good was a member of Pembroke Town Council and had clashed sharply with Larkin in the past, while McLaughlin had proposed the now infamous motion requiring workers to sign the form repudiating the ITGWU.[17]

The British organisation had been set up only a few weeks previously as an employers' response to syndicalism. It aimed to create a £50 million guarantee fund, which would be used to help employers combat the sympathetic strike. However, it proved a short-lived venture, largely because existing bodies, such as the Shipping Federation, saw it as a rival.[18] Nevertheless, during its brief existence it provided a useful platform for the Dublin employers.

McLaughlin told his audience that the only weapon forcing workers to 'leave good employers' in Dublin was 'the most appalling terrorism. It is impossible to handle ... goods without a terrorism of the lowest type, where even the women and children are attacked.' One man 'who had been fourteen years in my employment said: "I am bound to go for the sake of the wife and kids."'

He told his British counterparts they would laugh if they knew how tolerant Dublin employers were of trade unionism.

> In nearly all the trades in Dublin there is an agreement between the men and the employers that they will only employ trade unionists ... You, gentlemen, here, have free labour clauses in all your contracts.

They were no doubt even more surprised when he said:

> I believe in trade unionism; I uphold it. We have good men in Dublin in trade unionism, and some of the finest men I have met on this side of the water are the labour leaders of trade unionism.[19]

The statement suggested that McLaughlin and Good had used their visit to London to lobby trade union leaders as well as employers; and evidence of such contacts would emerge shortly.[20]

Trade unionism 'must be true to its ideals,' McLaughlin told his audience. 'The union we are against is the union of Syndicalism and terrorism, and the whole secret of the Dublin strike is written in the one word, "Terror".' He also tried to distance the employers from the slums issue. Dublin Corporation was responsible for the housing problem, he declared. Echoing the *Irish Times*, he said that the employers had 'practically no representation' on that body and 'were quite powerless to handle the question of the slums.' Councillors were elected 'by the Labour vote,' and McLaughlin, having conjured up his own unique account of how local government worked in Ireland, was then able to prove that Dublin's Labour councillors were responsible for the problem.

Good reiterated McLaughlin's main argument—that the dispute was not with trade unions but with the ITGWU. He made a particularly vigorous defence of Jacob's biscuit company, whose wages 'compared very favourably with those paid in any other factory of the same description in England.' The organisation passed a motion commending 'Dublin employers and free workers' for 'acting in the interests of freedom and of the whole community in resisting the tyranny and intimidation of the Irish Transport Union.' It pledged itself 'to do all in its power to support the employers and free workers in their fight for equality of right to work for both union and non-union men.'[21]

The stance taken by the Employers' Defence Union—of defending the individual rights of employers and 'free workers' rather than overtly opposing trade unions—was identical to that taken by the Shipping Federation. Indeed most employer bodies have used this argument ever since to counter the influence of trade unions, rather than oppose them outright. However, the blatant misrepresentation of the situation in Dublin can hardly have helped the Dublin employers with the constituencies that mattered most: the British government, the Parliamentary Committee of the TUC, or their fellow-citizens at home, all of whom knew the reality of the situation.

*

Larkin and Connolly also sought to influence the outcome of Tuesday's meeting but did so by appealing over the heads of the trade union leadership to the rank and file. However much they differed in temperament, and would ultimately differ in methods, the two men shared an instinctive distrust of the British trade union leadership. A few months later Connolly was to sum up that attitude in an article for the magazine *New Age*, in which he tried to draw out some of the lessons of the lockout.

> I believe that the development of fighting spirit is of more importance than the creation of the most theoretically perfect organisation. That, indeed, the most theoretically perfect organisation may, because of its very perfection and vastness, be of the greatest possible danger to the revolutionary movement if it tends, or is used, to repress and curb the fighting spirit of comradeship in the rank and file.

He praised the wave of strikes that had recently swept Britain, singling out 1911 as a particularly successful year—presumably because it was the period when trade union leaders had least control of their members. Without offering any attempt at an objective assessment of the effectiveness of the strikes, Connolly argued that the great wave of … solidarity caught the workers in its grasp and beat the terrified masters. Let me emphasize the point that the greatest weapon against capital was … the sporadic strike. It was its very sporadic nature its swiftness and unexpectedness that won. It was the ambush, the surprise attack of our industrial army, before which the well trained battalions of the capitalist world crumpled up in panic, against which no precautions were available.[22]

One of the results of the 1911 strike experience had been an accelerated movement by union leaders towards an amalgamated organisation for transport workers in Britain along the lines so abhorred by Connolly. The National Transport Workers' Federation was a staging-post towards what would become ten years later the Transport and General Workers' Union. Such a development, in principle, should have corresponded to the vision Connolly and Larkin shared of 'One Big Union'; but they had not liked what they had seen of the NTWF at close quarters in 1913. Connolly wrote:

The numbers now affiliated have become imposing enough to awe the casual reader and silence the cavilling objector at trade union meetings. But I humbly submit that, side by side with that employment and affiliation of organisation, there has proceeded a freezing up of the fraternal spirit of 1911. There is now, despite the amalgamations, less solidarity in the ranks of Labour than was exhibited in that year of conflict and victory. If I could venture an analysis of the reason for this falling off in solidarity, I would have to point out that the amalgamations and federations are being carried out in the main by officials absolutely destitute of revolutionary spirit.

Even Robert Williams, the person in the NTWF who had done most to help the Dublin strikers, was included by Connolly in this category.[23]

Given their opinion of the British trade union leaders, it is hardly surprising that Larkin and Connolly believed that re-creating the conditions of 1911 was the best means of securing support for their own struggle. It was playing for high stakes, as the inevitable corollary of failure was isolation and defeat; but the ITGWU men could never be accused of timidity.

While Larkin prepared for his British trip, Connolly told the crowd at Beresford Place on Friday night that he had received

a dozen messages today from various firms asking for permission to unload their goods, and saying that if it was refused they would have to dismiss their men. All the better; if it were fifty firms involved it would serve their purpose just as well.

Once more he called for volunteers for drilling. 'If we had a disciplined body of men there would be less danger that any of us might fall up against a policeman's baton.' That weekend a new poster was pasted up on the walls of the city, headed *War in Dublin*. Issued over the names of Larkin and Connolly, it declared:

> Dublin has won the first great victory in this great dispute. At 1 o'clock on Wednesday, November 12th, all hands on the cross-Channel boats 'downed tools,' and in quarter of an hour the whole port of Dublin was closed tight as a drum. In 18½ hours Larkin was at Liberty, but he left behind him in prison scores of loyal and devoted men, women and girls, jailed like him for their devotion to the cause of Labour. Larkin is not satisfied that 100,000 men, women and children should be still subject to a fate worse than jail—to a fate of slow starvation.

Dublin port would remain closed, and any goods reaching it could only do so 'under "scab" conditions,' the poster proclaimed.

> The Government have withdrawn from us all rights guaranteed by civic society. It has made outlaws of the working class of Dublin, and as such we will wage war upon that Government by withdrawing from society the aid of our labour until our rights are restored, until the employers resume proper relations with our unions, and until our brothers and sisters are at liberty ... If we are treated as outlaws ... then we shall act as outlaws.

To reinforce the sense of solidarity with those in prison, a march organised for Sunday included Mountjoy prison on its route.[24]

*

By then Connolly and Larkin were in England for a massive meeting at the Free Trade Hall in Manchester. It says something of the strain Connolly was under that before leaving Dublin he made one of his rare and intemperate attacks on the Catholic Church. It was over the issue of women prisoners.

During 1913 more than forty women were arrested on charges arising from the labour disturbances, and there were serious prison accommodation problems as a result. This was particularly acute for young women, and arrangements were made in Mountjoy to keep them apart from other prisoners. One of the youngest was Mary Ellen Murphy, the sixteen-year-old Jacob's striker from York Street serving a month for giving a box on the ear to a strike-breaker. Lack of space led to her transfer to the care of the Sisters of Our Lady of Charity, who had a reformatory in their grounds at High Park, Drumcondra, which also housed their Magdalen institution. This was the largest and best known in the city and provided suitably purgatorial accommodation for reformed prostitutes and unmarried mothers; the women in return provided the order with a source of cheap labour.

Connolly, having heard that Mary Ellen Murphy had been transferred to High Park, assumed she was in the institution. At the meeting in Beresford Place on Friday night he accused 'a Sisterhood' of placing a girl convicted of intimidation in 'an institution for fallen women.' The order responded sharply next day to say that the girl was not in the 'Magdalen Institution' but another of its homes.

So sensitive was the issue of 'fallen women' that neither Connolly nor the press referred to the order by name. But the ensuing controversy had given the Murphyite press more evidence of 'anti-clericalism' to throw at the strikers and their leaders.[25]

*

Connolly's impulsive indiscretions were small compared with what his leader would say when he raised the 'fiery cross' in Manchester. That Larkin used the primitive imagery of a charred wooden cross dipped in blood, used by Highland clans as a rallying symbol in times of war, shows how he regarded the coming fight. The meeting in the Free Trade Hall had originally been organised to demand Larkin's release, and he now turned it into the opening of a new propaganda and fund-raising campaign in Britain.

It says a lot for Larkin's reputation as a crowd-puller that when it became clear that he would be present at the Free Trade Hall, the demand for tickets soared, and they could not be had at a guinea apiece. The meeting was due to begin at 3 p.m., but from 1:30 p.m. there were long queues forming outside, 'just as if it were the "first night" of a new play,' the *Irish Times* reported. When Larkin appeared on the platform, 'the whole audience, as one man leapt to its feet, and stood cheering and shouting hurrahs.'

When order was restored and Connolly made the opening speech, it was clear that the strike leaders had determined to nail their battle colours to the mast. Connolly castigated those who had 'deliberately and callously starved to death' the population of Dublin in order 'to compel them to bend the neck.' He spoke of the slums and the low wages and 'the inhuman greed ... of the capitalist class.' But most of all he spoke of the workers who 'were now so powerful and united that even the powers of hell could not defeat them.'

Larkin rose 'very pale, and complaining that he was not in the best of health,' only to speak for over an hour with an intensity and speed that the shorthand note-takers had difficulty keeping up with. He damned the British empire, denounced the armaments race between the great powers, and demanded home rule. But it was of the Dublin struggle that the crowd wanted to hear, and of his own experience in prison.

> You don't know what I have gone through daily. Why, jail is heaven to it. Jails are nothing to the horrors of the slums, and the degradation of humanity going on in Dublin day by day.

He defended the efforts to send the children to Britain, for the Poor Law guardians of Dublin were only 'office-seekers and wire-pullers,' while 'all that is best in the intellectual life of Ireland is rallying to the workmen's side.' He came as 'the ambassador from the working classes of Ireland.' As such he complained of trade unionists who were conveying scab labourers to Dublin. If that is trades unionism, then damn trades unionism.

It is time we woke up. If you disgrace your manhood and the unions by pretending you are friendly and sending us money help and at the same time sending us 'scab' labour, I say damn you and your money; we don't want it. We want to carry out the fundamentals and ethics of trade unionism, so don't scab us.

Larkin appealed to the audience 'to go back to your unions and say that the ugly compact with the capitalist classes must be broken down at once.' They must 'not only send money to Dublin but go to your union branches and resolve to stand by the men and women of Dublin till death.' Despite, or perhaps because of, the harsh criticism of the TUC, the crowd remained enormously sympathetic and passed a resolution calling for an immediate national conference to discuss ways of increasing support for the Dublin dispute.

The *Manchester Guardian* did not know what to make of Larkin's performance.

Even the most convinced and implacable opponent, if he is honest, must admit that he is a man to be reckoned with—must admit, too, that a personal influence so extraordinary must be backed by a cause or a principle that deeply moves his fellow-countrymen. He may be … a man labouring under the stress of overmastering emotion, and therefore incoherent, violent; one who states rather than reasons, and a man of masterful and domineering temper, and therefore difficult to deal with. But if that were the whole truth about him he could not wield the immense influence he does over, not only the men he works amongst, but those he has never seen.

Like most newspapers, the *Guardian* published William Martin Murphy's letter, but the leader of the Dublin employers received little satisfaction. The *Guardian* said that Larkin could not be dismissed 'with a sneer.' Largely thanks to him, the British public now knew the conditions in which Dublin's population lived and worked. 'It is sufficient to say that nothing so appalling, so shocking even to the slackest and most easily satisfied social conscience has been discovered in our time.'[26]

*

The membership of the TUC's Parliamentary Committee were made of sterner stuff than leader-writers of the *Manchester Guardian*. Larkin could be as apocalyptic or as offensive as he liked, but they had no intention of showing their hand before the showdown with the Dublin strike leaders on Tuesday. Pressed for comment by journalists, the secretary, Charles Bowerman, gave a masterly summary of the situation. 'Events are so developing, and the situation has become so critical, that it is a question whether this is not one of those moments when the less said the better.' The Parliamentary Committee 'will make no further pronouncement until it has had the opportunity on Tuesday next of threshing out the matter with the representatives of the Dublin Trades Council and Irish Transport Workers' representatives.'[27]

34

HUNDREDS of sightseers gathered in the rain outside the TUC offices in London on Tuesday 18 November to catch a glimpse of the charismatic Dublin strike leader. But few of them had any idea what he looked like, and Larkin was able to take refuge unnoticed in a café in the Strand, not fifty yards away, waiting to be summoned to the meeting. Eventually a journalist recognised him sipping a cup of coffee. He described Larkin as 'tired and haggard.' Larkin refused to answer questions but agreed to pose for photographers. William O'Brien and Thomas McPartlin were with him, representing Dublin Trades Council. At 4 p.m. they ran the gauntlet of the crowd and entered the Aldwych Buildings to loud cheers.[1]

The Parliamentary Committee had already been sitting for an hour. It had heard a report from its chairman, James Seddon, who described the financial situation of the Dublin unions as critical. Defending the grant of £2,000 already paid out, he said that the alternative would have been to see the strike 'collapse'; in the circumstances, that collapse 'might have been imputed to the Parliamentary Committee.' He suggested that the best way forward was to persuade the Dublin delegation to meet a section of the employers, 'assuming that a section was willing to negotiate.' This might 'drive a wedge between the employing class in Dublin and force a settlement of the strike.' Seddon had 'an intimation that a section of the employers would be willing to treat with the men.'

The 'intimation' probably came from the Board of Trade, which was under government pressure to restart talks and had been in contact with McLaughlin and Good, as well as with Archbishop Walsh. Despite Larkin's fighting talk in Manchester, he had not—to the relief of the TUC leaders—called for a general strike. They now felt they had to establish what the Irish wanted before deciding their next move.

When the Dublin delegates arrived, McPartlin, as president of the Trades Council, made the opening submission. He thanked the committee for the 'unequalled help' given to Dublin. He suggested that the employers would prolong the dispute in order to defeat any government attempt to settle it. A defeat for Dublin's workers would see an extension of the employers' tactics to Britain, he warned; what was needed now was for the Parliamentary Committee to call a 'conference of the unions'.

Friend and foe. (*Right*) Robert Williams of the Transport Federation supported the Dublin workers throughout the lockout, but even he was eventually alienated by Larkin's attacks on the British TUC. (*Below*) The Seamen's Union leader, J. Havelock Wilson, was a consistent critic of Larkin and ordered his Irish members back to work. (*Freeman's Journal*, 3 October 1913. National Library of Ireland)

Tom Kettle, former Irish Party MP and professor of national economics at University College, Dublin, tried unsuccessfully to create a 'third force' in the city mobilising public opinion through his Industrial Peace Committee. (*Irish Times*)

Coal leaving Tedcastle, McCormick and Company's depot under military escort. The company played a leading role in the dispute, and its convoys were frequently attacked. (*Freeman's Journal*, 6 October 1913. National Library of Ireland)

Soldiers with fixed bayonets escort a coal cart, also driven by soldiers, past the Evening Herald offices. Such large bodies of troops overawed the ITGWU mass pickets. (*Freeman's Journal*, 10 October 1913. National Library of Ireland)

This *Sunday Independent* cartoon shows the growing concern of employers at the effects on local business that the lockout and support for Dublin workers from the TUC would have. (*Sunday Independent*, 12 October 1913. National Library of Ireland)

Lay members of St Catherine's Guild of the Little Flower help at a new food kitchen set up in Meath Street in 1913 to combat the activities of Protestant 'proselytising' food centres in the area. (*Freeman's Journal*, 13 October 1913. National Library of Ireland)

Sisters of the Holy Faith dining-hall in the Coombe. There was fierce competition between Catholic and Protestant charities to feed the hungry and win souls.

Queen Alexandra being shown around Maynooth in 1907 by its president, Dr Daniel Mannix (*left*), and former president, Dr William Walsh. As Catholic Archbishop of Dublin for over thirty-five years, Walsh reached an accommodation with successive British governments, the Irish Party, and Sinn Féin. But he found Larkin impossible to deal with in 1913, and his peace efforts were snubbed by William Martin Murphy. (National Library of Ireland)

EVENING HERALD

CERTIFIED NET SALES EXCEED THOSE OF ANY OTHER DUBLIN EVENING PAPER.

TELEGRAMS: "H.-R.D." DUBLIN.
EDITORIAL TELEPHONE: 104.

VOL. 22, NO. 253.   DUBLIN, TUESDAY, OCTOBER 21, 1913.   PRICE ONE HALFPENNY.

DUBLIN CHILDREN FOR ENGLISH HOMES

An Amazing Proposal Explained

"A PLEASANT HOLIDAY"

The Views of Clergymen and Others in Dublin

LONDON LADY'S STATEMENT ON THE SUBJECT

SHALL DUBLIN CHILDREN BE SENT TO ENGLAND?

Dublin has been aroused by the proposal that little children shall be sent to England to the care of Socialists and others. Above picture shows a group of little ones—the real sufferers in the present disastrous strike.
—*Eclipse Press Agency, Dublin.*

DUBLIN STRIKE AND ITS CONSEQUENCES

Sequel to Recent Riots at City Sessions

134 MEN OUT AT PORT AND DOCKS

A Visit to the Firm of Messrs. Jacobs and Co.

A REVELATION IN IRISH INDUSTRY

CORK BANK MANAGER'S AFFAIRS

Remarkable Replies in Public Examination

VIEWS IN DUBLIN

What Clergymen Think of Proposal

DANGER OF SOCIALISM

LONDON LADY

Explains Nature of the Scheme

"A PLEASANT HOLIDAY"

OFFERS FROM SOCIALISTS.

EXPLAINING THE SCHEME.

LATEST NEWS

134 MEN OUT TO-DAY

The Strike at the Port and Docks

OFFICIAL'S STATEMENT

MESSRS. W. & R. JACOB

Larkin's Reckless Statements

A VISIT TO THE FAMOUS FIRM

("HERALD" SPECIAL.)

"JOAN OF ARC" STATUE.

Woman Charged with Larceny of It.

THE WORD "SCAB."

A Dundrum Definition.

The front page of the late 'white' edition of the *Evening Herald*, 21 October 1913, reporting the 'amazing proposal' to send Dublin children to England. (National Library of Ireland)

Father Landers, the Westland Row parish curate, who played a leading role in opposing the Dublin 'kiddies' scheme.

Sandymount Castle, where Countess Josephine Plunkett offered to accommodate up to 150 children rather than see them 'deported' to England during the lockout.

Mounted police in a show of strength outside Green Street courthouse before Larkin's trial.
(*Freeman's Journal*, 24 October 1913. National Library of Ireland)

DEPORTING CHILDREN---DUBLIN CASES.

(1) Rev. Father Fleming and Rev. Father McNevin, with the boy George Burke, with the abduction of whom Mrs. Rand and Mrs. Montefiore are charged. (2) Thomas MacMahon and his brother James, who followed him to Kingstown...

Dora Montefiore's ambitious attempt to provide English foster-homes for Dublin children during the lockout came to grief at the hands of militant priests such as Father Fleming and Father McNevin. (*Freeman's Journal*, 25 October 1913. National Library of Ireland)

EVENING HERALD

6.30 WHITE

CERTIFIED NET SALES EXCEED THOSE OF ANY OTHER DUBLIN EVENING PAPER.

TELEGRAMS: "HERALD," DUBLIN.
EDITORIAL TELEPHONE: 104.

VOL. 22. NO. 260.　　DUBLIN, WEDNESDAY, OCTOBER 29, 1913.　　PRICE ONE HALFPENNY.

CHILD-EXPORTING AT AN END

Splendid Victory of Catholics of Dublin

MRS. RAND AND MRS. MONTEFIORE TO LEAVE

After Giving Undertaking to Send No More Away

PRIEST'S PLEA IN COURT FOR RETURN OF CHILDREN

In the Northern Police Court to-day, before Mr Mahony.

Mrs. Lucille Rand, aged 31, of 81 St George's square, London, appeared on remand on bail to answer the charge preferred by Inspector Beary and Detective Sergeant McCabe, for having on the 23rd inst. feloniously taken away from Liberty Hall, Beresford place, a boy named James Burke, aged 11 years and 5 months, with intent to deprive Terence Burke, his father, of the lawful possession of the child. Mrs. Rand was also charged with having unlawfully received the child knowing it to have been taken away from the lawful care of his father.

When the case was called,

Mr T. J. Campbell (instructed by Messrs Smyth and Son) said he appeared for the accused, and also for Mrs. Montefiore, who was also charged with a similar offence. His worship at Kingstown on Thursday was good enough to divert out the suggestion that though these ladies might have been entrusted by the very best motives, and though their work may have been one of charity, yet they might consider the wisdom of not going further with the work.

HAVING REGARD TO THE STRONG FEELING THAT HAD ARISEN

in Dublin. His clients were grieved in Dublin, and they thought that their first visit to Ireland should have ...

[remainder of columns illegible]

AN OLD AGE PENSION ROMANCE

There was a happy marriage sequel to an old age pension romance at Braintree, Essex, on Monday. The bride was Miss Susannah Clarke, aged 78, who has been an inmate of Braintree Workhouse for nearly twenty years, and the bridegroom being Walter Townsend, aged 77, who has been a widower for two years. The smiling bride and her husband photographed after the ceremony.

FREE LABOUR IMPORTED

50 Men Arrive in Dublin

AN IMPORTANT STEP

Two Hundred Dockers Resume Work

CARGOES DISCHARGED

Guinness's Getting More Motor Lorries

Two important developments occurred to-day in connection with the strike—the free labour men were brought from England, and two hundred of the labour men, after the mid-day meal, returned to work at the North Wall, and 200 of Messrs Palgrave Murphy's men who were on strike at the North Wall, and 200 ...

[remainder illegible]

BONAR LAW AND CARSON

To Speak To-Night

ULSTER QUESTION

"Home Rule Within Home Rule"

THE LORDS AND THE BILL

To-night Mr. Bonar Law and Sir Edward Carson will speak at Newcastle. They will reply to the recent overtures of Mr. Churchill, Mr. Asquith, and Sir Edward Grey regarding Ulster ...

[remainder illegible]

THREE GUINEAS

Next Sunday's Hurling Final

TIPPERARY VERSUS KILKENNY

A SIMPLE COMPETITION

On next Sunday Kilkenny meet Tipperary in the All-Ireland Hurling Final at Jones's Road, Dublin.

We offer one prize of two guineas for the first correct result received by us, and a cumulative prize of one guinea for the next received.

The conditions are simple in the extreme. All forecasts must be written on postage, and must reach our office before 12 noon on next Sunday.

The result only will be required.

Envelopes must be stamped or handed in at our offices, Castle Building or Mid and Harford, the team conductor. Tommy Moore was engaged in the courtyard of the police court. He was pouring into the dock when he was hauled out by the collar. There are others much worse than it, said ...

CAMBRIDGESHIRE

Won by an Outsider

Today at Newmarket Lord Harewood's Cantilever, b. c. by Brides of ...

LUCKY LOCAL LADY.

Mrs. Gahan, Gresham Hotel, drew Wiseman in the Baccarat (Cambridgeshire Sweep, and becomes entitled to £100. A Clondalkin gentleman will gain a larger sum by drawing Cantor.

RUGBY.

Dublin Univ. 2nd. 1 goal 1 dropped goal 1 try (12) —
King's Hospital nil.

ACCEPTANCES—DERBY CUP.

Revel, Cyllene Boy, Alegar, Wingstaff, Countside, Lacuna, Redwood, Dalmatian, Aurette, Night Hawk, Wise Man, Coloradon, Glitterer, Election, Sunma the Junior, Subterranean, Amesty, The Curragh, Pulhu, Bowman, October, Frankeleash.
Weights raised: Tita.

LIVERPOOL AUTUMN CUP.

Malden, Eleigh, Iorana, Eiveli, Scott's Sniff, Sunlate, Bachelor's Double, Harrison, Ukraine, Spontaneity, Sub Rosa, Gambado, Almerie, Sands of Time, Gambrinus, Cheveril, China Cock, Pulhu, Spear Bridge.

NEWBURY AUTUMN CUP.

Wagstaff, Fantastic, Lady Eileen, Cyllo, Aurette, Bormaso, Provreant, Borders, Equanimity, St. Medusan, Lael Stand, Sandwort, Iron Duke, Shambox, Chantraine, Entulsha, Bolted Earl, Charmeuse, St. Crispin, Vintery, Lido.

RUGBY—Result
Lansdowne II., 15 pts.; Vet. Coll., 3
—Dublin University II., 3. Church of I
2, College 3.

LATEST LONDON MONEY.

In Shipping Shares, P. and P. Steam rallied 1; Isle of Guernsey steady ¾; many, declared 1; Steam Allianc Mines dull; Do Beers declared and shortfontein declined 1-16, and Rand Mines 1-32; Rio Tinto declined ¼; on Pres sales, but Amalgamated rallied ¼.

FUSILLADE OF STONES

Recent Aungier St. Riot

TEN YOUNG MEN CHARGED

With Assaults on the Police

Further charges of riot in connection with the labour troubles in Dublin were investigated to-day at the Commission Court, Green street, before Mr Justice Madden ...

[remainder illegible]

£400 WORTH OF MEAT

Eaten By Parties at Castle

DURING THE VISIT

Of the Late King to Ireland

"ROYAL WARRANT"

Action Against a Dublin Victualler

To-day, before Mr Justice Bar Chancery Division, the case of t Warrant Holders' Association v D ...

[remainder illegible]

Other columns:

CHILD KILLED BY TRAIN

An express train dashed into a flock of sheep being driven over a level crossing at Northallerton to-day, fifteen sheep being killed.

IRISH-BRED SCOTCH SHEEP

The *Evening Herald* of 29 October 1913 announces the defeat of Dora Montefiore's scheme—and the arrival of the first 'free labourers' or strike-breakers in Dublin port. (National Library of Ireland)

The *Sunday Independent* cartoonist is noticeably optimistic, reflecting the growing confidence of the business community that Larkin's forces are spent. (*Sunday Independent*, 26 October 1913. National Library of Ireland)

LATEST DEVELOPMENTS

THE FAITH.

IRISH CHILD

SOCIA...

Saved

THESE WEEDS MUST GO.

FARM WORKER

LARKINISM

Back at work

LIMERICK

IRISH INDUSTRIAL DEVELOPMENT ASSOCIATION

IRELAND

For the Good of the Land

1913.

ROYAL HORTICULTURAL SOCIETY WINTER SHOW

Growing

On the eve of their appearance before the courts, Dublin Trades Council leaders address a rally in the Phoenix Park. (*Clockwise from top left*) Jim Larkin, William Partridge, P. T. Daly, and Tom Lawlor. (*Freeman's Journal*, 27 October 1913. National Library of Ireland)

Calls by leading intellectuals for Larkin's release from prison, coupled with their denunciation of the employers, enraged many nationalists, as this *Sunday Independent* cartoon testifies. (9 November 1913. National Library of Ireland)

Members of the Irish Women Workers' Union 'imprisoned in the cause of labour'. Note the youthfulness of the women, many of them only girls. Jim Larkin's sister, Delia, secretary of the IWWU, is seated at the centre in a white blouse. She did not go to prison. (National Library of Ireland)

Unionists claimed that the lockout showed that nationalist Ireland was unfit for home rule. In a city distracted by industrial strife, only suffragists such as Margaret Connery attempted to disrupt a rally of Southern Unionists. The Conservative leader, Andrew Bonar Law (*left*), smiles at the demand for female suffrage in Ulster. Edward Carson was less amused. (National Library of Ireland)

Schoolboys at play in Beresford Place, opposite Liberty Hall, imitating their fathers, late 1913. (RTE)

Full-page advertisements for Christmas luxury goods, such as this one from the *Irish Times* of 15 December 1913, show that the lockout had little impact on Dublin's wealthier citizens. (National Library of Ireland)

The Toiler.

Established to Advance the Interests of Labour, & Protect Industry & Commerce.

Vol 1. No 15)   Dublin, Saturday, December 27, 1913.   (One Penny.

IS JIM LARKIN CAREY'S SON ?

Photos of the Careys before the Park Murders and at the Imperial Hotel.

Above we reproduce three Photos, one of James Carey, the common Informer, another of the man called Larkin, and a third of Carey in another attitude. Number one is Jim Carey; number two, in the middle, is Jim Larkin, and the third is Carey again. We have asserted from time to time in the Toiler that Jim Larkin is a son of Jim Carey, the Informer, we were told that if Carey's photograph were published it would establish our case. Old and middle-aged people in Dublin, who knew Carey well, have often remarked the great resemblance, the remarkable resemblance there is between himself and Larkin in every detail, and certainly the photos show it, especially when Larkin has on the whiskers.

Let our readers look well at the features of both number one and number two, why it is plain that Jim Larkin has the very eyes, the very same prominent nose, and the same wide mouth as Carey had. Look carefully at the foreheads in both men, you will also note the same long face and features, and the same cast of head in both men.

Supposing Larkin was dressed in the same cut of clothes as Carey, and was as old as Carey was in 1882, it would be impossible to distinguish one man from another. In number three photo we see the swagger attitude of Carey,

the swagger lounging gait, which gait is also a peculiarity of Larkin. Notice the peculiar angle at which Carey wears his head, a marked peculiarity which Larkin also possesses, and if my readers want confirmation let them put these photos under a glass, and they will find the very lines and outlines and features of the face almost identical in both faces, that is, making allowance for the years of difference between father and son.

An old Dublin doctor who attended Carey when he was ill, and who knew the kind of flesh which surrounded Carey's bones, has been heard to declare that Larkin has the same mould of flesh. Of course there are several classes of flesh known to medical men, and medical authorities inform us that the same mould of flesh goes from father to son, and is it not strange, and very strange that Jim Larkin should resemble Jim Carey in eyes, mouth, nose, forehead, cast of head, and features generally, and have the same peculiar kind of flesh, and is it not stranger still that Larkin refuses to tell where he was born, or where he was baptised. Surely no man was ever ashamed to tell where he was born.

Is Larkin afraid that if he gave his birth place it would be looked up, and so it would be, hence Jim Carey's son is trying to lie low. But we are going

to probe this startling piece of information to the bottom. We have at considerable expense reproduced the photos of James Carey and Larkin. There must be hundreds of people in Dublin who knew Carey personally. We want them to write to us to prove that the photos we give are correct, and if they like to make an affirmation that they believe that Larkin is the son of Carey, we will publish it in our columns. We want also the opinion of the relations and friends of the men whom Carey sent to the gallows.

In conclusion, we offer a prize of £5 to any Larkinite in Ireland, who will prove that James Larkin is not the son of James Carey. Surely the Larkinites are not following a man who cannot produce his baptismal lines?

The men who follow Mr Redmond know where he was born. Mr Redmond, Mr Wm O'Brien, Sir E Carson, and Mr Wm M Murphy can produce their birth and baptismal certificates, and why is Larkin afraid to produce his ? If he is not the son of James Carey, can any Larkinite in Dublin or Wexford answer the question, why will Larkin not produce his birth certificate ? In our next issue we will tell a lot more.

The *Toiler* was the most scurrilous of the anti-Larkin newspapers. Few took its claims seriously, but they took their toll on Larkin himself. (27 December 1913. National Library of Ireland)

GENTLEMEN OF THE JEWRY

Larkin's *Irish Worker* had the largest circulation of any radical newspaper in Ireland, but, like Arthur Griffith's *Sinn Féin*, its politics could sometimes be erratic—and anti-Semitic, as this cartoon illustrates. (*Irish Worker*, 26 August 1911. National Library of Ireland)

The new National Executive of the Irish Trades Union Congress and Labour Party in 1914 shows that the influence of the lockout leadership was undiminished by defeat. James Connolly is standing on the far left with the new president of Dublin Trades Council, William O'Brien, beside him. The Bricklayers' leader, Richard O'Carroll, is standing on the far right. Thomas McPartlin, president of Dublin Trades Council during the lockout, is seated far left. Beside him is the Belfast representative David R. Campbell, who was a friend of Connolly. P. T. Daly and Jim Larkin are next, with the Sinn Féiner Michael O'Lehane of the Drapers' Assistants' Association seated far right.

Jim Larkin crosses the city for the last time: the funeral cortege approaching Glasnevin cemetery on 2 February 1947. (*Irish Times*)

Seddon then asked for 'a frank statement' on where the Dublin strike committee stood. McPartlin said they wanted to 'fight to a successful finish.'

Larkin supported McPartlin's view that the dispute had reached a crisis and that the outcome 'affected four countries.' Warming to his theme, he described the lockout as the culmination of 'a series of struggles.' He was well aware of the damage Murphy's letter might have done with members of the committee unfamiliar with the Dublin situation. 'Mr Murphy has seen that he is going to be dealt with as the other employers, namely that he will have to concede the right of combination to his employees.' Larkin could not resist personalising the dispute. Murphy had 'boasted for years that he had smashed union after union, that he had cajoled or beaten the leaders, and his last ... triumphant speech was that he had even beaten the great Railway Union, with all its powers and money.' This remark was no doubt aimed at J. E. Williams, who was the NUR representative on the Parliamentary Committee and who had been heckled by the crowd on his arrival.

Larkin claimed that Murphy had begun the dispute by locking out four hundred men and had then persuaded the rest of the employers to support him, on the grounds that victory 'would bring wages down to their former low level. To frustrate the plan of Mr Murphy, who was bringing up a reserve army of labour, the Transport Workers' Union called the other men out.' Now it was the turn of others to show their solidarity.

'We ask you, in no uncertain way, that the working class of England be called together, and be asked to give their opinion, and we will abide by whatever verdict they give.' He added rather pointedly: 'There is not a rank-and-file man of any value who is not prepared at this moment to aid us in our struggle.' He also urged the TUC to 'get trade unionists to cease working traffic to and from Dublin.'

The Parliamentary Committee skirted these issues for the moment and asked Larkin if he would meet 'any section of the employers or [the] whole of them' to try to reach a settlement. Larkin said he would, 'on the understanding, if I meet a section of the employers, that the settlement would be conditional.'

William O'Brien, there as vice-president of Dublin Trades Council, hardly spoke that day. The future arch-critic of Larkin is recorded in the minutes only as saying that 'I support Mr Larkin in his request ... to keep Dublin port closed.' The meeting adjourned without reaching any decision after a telephone call from the Board of Trade seeking a meeting next morning.[2]

*

That night Larkin addressed a rally at Bow, where he pronounced that 'the tide is flowing with Dublin.' He had appealed to the rank and file of the British trade union movement and to 'Caesar', as he called the TUC leadership; he hoped that Caesar would stand by the working class of England, Ireland, Scotland, and Wales.[3]

Philip Snowden, the leading British Labour Party ideologist of the period, saw the relationship very differently. He was regarded as an expert on economic and financial issues, apparently because he had spent two years working as a tax collector in the Orkneys. He wrote in the *Christian Commonwealth* the same day:

> Mr. Larkin and his friends must be prepared to practise more of the idea of Labour solidarity about which they talk. It is not fair for them to stand aloof from the rest of the trades union movement of the United Kingdom, and then accept its help when they are in difficulties. It is not suggested that the leaders of the Dublin men should surrender their leadership ... but it is necessary, if this dispute is to be settled honourably, that they should debate with the Trade Union Committee, who have had a far longer and more varied experience of industrial disputes than Mr. Larkin and his colleagues can claim.[4]

Next morning at the Board of Trade the TUC leaders found that Larkin's perspective on solidarity had not changed. He no doubt saw the meeting with Sir George Askwith as an ambush, an attempt by the Parliamentary Committee to push him back into talks before they had to consider the thorny issue of how British solidarity for Dublin could best be demonstrated. The TUC's three musketeers, Seddon, Bowerman, and Gosling, also attended; but the combined persuasive talents of Askwith and the TUC leaders failed to move Larkin. He refused to consider reopening talks with the employers until the Parliamentary Committee had decided its line of action.

When the committee reconvened at 2 p.m., O'Brien took the initiative. He said he and his colleagues 'have to know the mind of the Committee before we enter into any debate with the employers. There has been continual talk of peace, which has acted as a wet blanket upon our efforts.'

The response from the British trade union leaders, if any, is not recorded. Instead they asked Larkin why he had refused to meet the employers after promising the previous afternoon that he would. Larkin was equally unswerving of purpose. He said that he and his colleagues had 'only come over to England to deal with the Trades Union Congress Parliamentary Committee, and we have not yet accomplished our work.' He had told Askwith that the Dublin strike leaders were prepared to negotiate, but

> we still feel we have no right to do anything further ... until we know the mind of the Parliamentary Committee. When the Parliamentary Committee has announced their decision, we are prepared to go down and meet the employers.

Larkin made it clear that the Dublin men wanted a special meeting of the Trades Union Congress. He argued that 'a national conference would, among other things, compel the government to force the employers to come to reason, for they could threaten to withdraw the police and military protection afforded to blacklegs.' He suggested that if the TUC once called a conference, the government might apply pressure on the employers to settle before the delegates convened.

As further bait, Larkin said that all the Dublin strike leaders were seeking was 'the status quo before the strike.' Any question of wages and conditions 'should go to a Wages Board.' He defined this as different from the usual Board of Trade conciliation body: it would consist of equal numbers of trade union and employer representatives, and the chairman would be there 'merely to keep them in order.'

A. H. Gill, the cotton-spinners' MP, asked Larkin if he would be prepared to settle on the basis of a Wages Board and to abide by its findings. 'We never break agreements,' Larkin said. 'We are too honourable. The other side never carry them out.' But if there was to be an agreement, the strike leaders 'want the men on the spot to settle the dispute,' not the TUC. 'To take the matter out of their hands would mean defeat.' What he wanted was TUC pressure, 'not only on the employers but upon the Labour Party, the Irish Party and the Liberal Party to put a stop to the conflict.' The Dublin employers 'should be isolated and receive help from nobody.'

At this point several members of the committee pointed out to Larkin that if men were called out

> to stop goods going to and from Dublin, it would mean that money flowing to Dublin would be diverted in other directions. Have you thought of that possibility?

Larkin said he had, and, 'although money is a very useful thing, it has never won a strike.'

'For want of it, many have been lost,' riposted W. J. Davies, the Brassworkers' leader who had chaired the TUC conference at Manchester in September. Larkin agreed, and wound up the Dublin delegation's submission by thanking the committee for the 'courteous way' in which it had heard their case. He also thanked the unions 'and outside people' for their help.

When the delegation retired, the committee decided unanimously to convene the conference that the Dublin men were so intent on. However, it stipulated that the only people entitled to attend would be delegates from affiliated unions, and 'the whole of the Labour members of Parliament.' The date was fixed as 9 December,[5] and in the meantime, financial aid for Dublin Trades Council would continue.[6]

The decision to limit attendance to affiliated unions immediately disfranchised many Irish unions and even some British ones, such as William Partridge's ASE, which had not paid its dues that year. Later the rules would be amended to allow a delegation from Dublin to speak, but not to vote, at the conference.

*

The outcome of the meeting was described by the *Irish Times* as 'a decided rebuff for Mr. Larkin.' It showed that 'the leaders of British trade unionism have no affection for the "fiery cross" at close quarters.' It also claimed that the British union leadership realised 'there is all the difference in the world between the Irish Transport Workers' Union, as at present constituted, and legitimate trade unionism.' But it also realised that the deliberations of the Parliamentary Committee left the situation in Dublin itself 'practically unchanged. If they change it at all, they change it for the worse.'

The *Irish Times* was right. The TUC might not have accepted Larkin's high-risk strategy of a blockade of Dublin to force the issue, but it had agreed to a conference to consider future strategy and continuing financial support in the meantime for the dispute.

The Dublin Employers' Federation wisely refrained from a knee-jerk condemnation of the TUC. Instead it attacked the ITGWU for 'strangling Irish Industry' by its activities. Poverty was due 'not to low wages, but to want of employment for a surplus labouring population,' according to Charles Coghlan, secretary of the federation's executive committee. Only the promotion of industry could solve this problem He criticised the ITGWU for closing the port 'without notice or reason,' and pointed out that dockers' rates agreed the previous May were as good as those in many British ports. He omitted to mention that this was only because the union had won large increases after a bitter three-month strike at the beginning of the year.[7]

Larkin put a brave face on the outcome of the discussions when he spoke at the Royal Albert Hall a few hours later, just over two weeks since Russell and Shaw had excoriated the Dublin employers and clergy from the same platform. There were an estimated ten thousand in the audience, with as many again gathered outside. Many joined in the 'Marseillaise', played on the hall's organ. They cheered repeatedly, and there was uproar at attempts by students to disrupt the proceedings. 'It was only when at last Larkin rose, and, with stentorian voice, demanded [that] the crowd sit down that something like quietness prevailed,' one journalist wrote.

> It seemed as if Larkin had magnetised his audience. He told them not to be alarmed at the antics of the students. 'There are enough men in the hall from the docks of London to beat all the pups who ever attended a university.' (Cheers.)

Larkin launched into a rambling peroration, and even he found it hard at times to reach the furthest elements of the vast audience. 'I would sooner be doing a hard day's work with a pick or shovel than the present particular job I am trying to handle,' he said, wiping his forehead. He admitted that he had little sympathy with the TUC proposal to wait three weeks for a special conference. 'I do not pretend to be a leader,' he said, 'but if I had the power tonight that men in this country do possess in the working-class ranks, the fight in Dublin would finish in a few hours. (Cheers.)'

> Three weeks is a long time to go on, but I will undertake on behalf of the men who know how to fight in Dublin that the fight will go on until the leaders in England are ready. Let us not forget there are three

hundred men lying in jail in Dublin who are guilty of no illegal act. We have over fifty-seven mothers and daughters of these men lying there because they dared to say, 'Up Larkin.' Think of a Christian government doing that!

As usual, Larkin was exaggerating. The number of prisoners serving sentences in Mountjoy at that moment for strike-related offences was sixty men and ten women.

He went on to challenge Birrell to a debate. 'If he will come and meet me on a platform at Bristol, although he is a well-educated man and I am only an illiterate workman, I promise him that it won't be a dead kitten that he will baffle. (Laughter.)' He had not finished with the Chief Secretary yet. He called on him 'to come into Dublin, where he gets his wages, and carry out his work that he is paid for. He is a loafer, he is an idler (laughter), he is a trickster, he is a joker, and he wants shifting out of a pack. (Loud laughter.)'

Larkin demanded home rule and almost in the same breath denounced Redmond and Devlin. 'John Redmond only dances when Joe whistles. (Loud laughter.)' Asquith and Lloyd George received similar treatment. He concluded:

People of England, we have put our face to the sun, and there is no power on earth will keep us from going forward to enjoy its effulgence. We have a right, we serfs in Ireland, to stand in the rays of that sun, and, by the living God, the men who will try and stop us have got to answer to us.[8]

If Larkin tore at society's 'whited sepulchres', as he often called them, he only seemed to answer a mood of the times. British audiences seemed to respond to him even better than Irish ones, perhaps because the speeches of their own labour leaders were often so pedestrian and restrained.

The contrast between Larkin in the Royal Albert Hall and Larkin before the Parliamentary Committee is a striking one, and yet the two are recognisably the same man, with the same 'divine mission of discontent'. Like all great orators, he underwent a transformation before an audience, and the audience reciprocated, suspending its critical faculties. Larkin certainly did not sway them by the power of argument: his relationship with the masses was emotional and psychological. Where the text of speeches made by some of Larkin's great oratorical contemporaries, such as Jaurès, Trotsky, or even the cliché-ridden Lloyd George, still stand the test of time, his own sometimes appear unstructured to the point of incoherence. Yet he always hit home. Birrell's speech in Bristol the previous Thursday was far superior to Larkin's in the Royal Albert Hall, but he had been greeted by polite applause and the 'illiterate workman' with rapture. For the targets of his wrath, such as Murphy, Larkin in full flight must have seemed a terrifying and loathsome spectre; but for his adherents he was an avenging angel who could do no wrong.

The Parliamentary Committee of the TUC could not be numbered among either category. The record of the meetings on 18 and 19 November shows the pragmatic side of the man—Larkin the negotiator. He had in fact achieved much of what he wanted. The conference might be three weeks away, but in the meantime the British unions would continue with their financial support, and the danger of a general strike would put pressure on the employers and the British government to reach a settlement. Sanitised as it is, the TUC record also shows what a chasm of distrust and conflicting visions of the future divided Larkin from the British leaders. The very fact that more fundamental issues were never raised is indicative of this. Both sides shied away from a debate that could only deepen existing divisions and animosities.

Like his lieutenant, Connolly, Larkin wanted to invoke the 'fighting spirit' and 'sporadic strikes' of 1911. He was quite willing to plunge British cities into the same catastrophic conflict as Dublin, because he believed that out of the catastrophe would come victory. Men such as Seddon and Davies, however, remembered the years from 1910 to 1912 with a shudder. Significant gains might have been won for many workers, but the trade union structures had survived by the skin of their teeth. The TUC needed time for its affiliates to reorganise and replenish their resources. The spectacle of thousands of pounds a week draining away to a dispute in an Irish port, where they had no control over events, must have been a distressing one.

*

Meanwhile in Dublin, citizens went about the mundane task of survival with varying degrees of resignation, truculence, or even compromise. For instance, the ITGWU agreed to its members unloading all the cargo of the *Hare* in order to gain access to much-needed food stores for the workers. Food was uppermost in many minds with the port closed. The *Irish Times* tried to allay fears of shortages with reports of plentiful supplies of most commodities; but the Retail Purveyors' and Family Grocers' Association, which represented 320 city merchants, said that 'the scarcity of many necessaries of life' would inevitably lead to increased prices, 'pending an amicable settlement of the present trouble.' A sceptical *Irish Times* made its own inquiries and found that many members of the association were more concerned at the prospect of prices for basic commodities being driven down by 'the action of the English trades unionists in importing foodstuffs into the city.' The paper described Liberty Hall as 'a huge commissariat'; and there were complaints that some strikers were selling food parcels.

In fact, if there was a scarcity it was of luxury items, which were no longer being shipped from Britain. Early fears of petrol shortages disappeared after businesses opted for the simple expedient of having their drivers collect fuel along with supplies diverted to other ports. Similarly, exporters followed the example of the cattle men in diverting traffic to ports as far away as Wexford and Belfast. Without a rail strike, the Trades Council could handicap, but could not paralyse, Dublin trade.[9]

The city's unionists did not allow the problems in the port to distract them from the more fundamental threat of home rule. Over a thousand 'ladies of all classes and creeds' had joined the newly established Women's Unionist Club. They elected Lady Arnott as president. The club's activities were extensively covered in the *Irish Times*, which was owned by her husband, Sir John Arnott. At the inaugural meeting in the Civil Engineering Hall on 17 November, Lady Arnott told members that the present troubles of the city were but 'a prelude to the riot and strife and, perhaps, horrors unthinkable' that would follow the passing of a Home Rule Bill. On the same day, delegates to a conference of Women's Unionist Associations in Wales must have had Dublin in mind when they passed a resolution proposed by their president, the Duchess of Abercorn, that temporary accommodation should be provided in British homes for unionist women and children 'in the event of civil war.'[10]

Meanwhile a more surreptitious unionist group had been organising, the Dublin Volunteer Corps. Its commanding officer was a retired colonel, Henry Master, who was also Grand Master of the Orange Order in the city. According to a DMP report, there were four hundred members, most of them from the middle-class townships circling the city, such as Kingstown, Blackrock, Rathmines, and Pembroke, and they kept about a hundred rifles in the Fowler Memorial Hall off Rutland Square (Parnell Square).[11] Former British army NCOs drilled the various companies, whose aim was to protect Protestant families should they be 'unjustly and unlawfully attacked by their Catholic neighbours in the event of Home Rule being passed.' Some of the men were also prepared to serve as part of the UVF reserve, and their Ulster counterparts had promised additional weapons and ammunition if hostilities broke out.

Marching feet would soon be the order of the day for Dublin workers too. Connolly, who had returned to the city after the Manchester meeting, was still trying to organise a workers' army. On Tuesday evening, while Larkin was speaking in Bow, Connolly was urging ITGWU members to attend a meeting of the Civic League in the Antient Concert Rooms next day. The league was a new organisation, a direct descendant of Tom Kettle's Industrial Peace Committee, which had been made redundant by the intransigence of the employers. Kettle and a few of the more moderate elements had bowed out, but the league was still a remarkably respectable body. It arose out of the final meeting of the Peace Committee on 11 November. Having agreed the text of its final report—which placed primary responsibility for the continuation of the dispute on the employers—a majority of the committee agreed to reconstitute themselves as a Civic League. Among the proposals it considered was one from Captain James (Jack) White to establish a Citizens' Army. Rev. R. M. Gwynn of Trinity College, who hosted that night's meeting, recalled later that 'the title Army was not intended to suggest military action, but merely drill on military lines to keep unemployed men fit and self-respecting.'[12]

After the meeting, White approached Connolly, *de facto* leader of the ITGWU while Larkin was in prison, who advocated a drilling scheme at the great rally to celebrate Larkin's release the following Thursday, 13 November.

White was another of those maverick scions of the upper class who adorned radical movements of the era. His father was the late Field-Marshal Sir George White, hero of the Siege of Ladysmith in the Anglo-Boer War. White himself had served with distinction in South Africa and had been decorated for bravery. When he retired from the British army he returned to the family estate at Broughshane, near Ballymena, but he was repelled by the sectarianism of politics in his native County Antrim and drifted south, where he was to find a new, if brief, military career with the Citizen Army.

Only a figure as politically naïve as White could have failed to realise the direction in which men such as Connolly would take his project. At the very meeting in Beresford Place at which he urged ITGWU members to attend the Antient Concert Rooms, Connolly spelt out very clearly the direction in which such a Citizen Army would march. In one of those sanguinary word-pictures of the future that were fast becoming his stock in trade, he explained:

> Our rebellion is against the employing classes … and to that end we mean to fight until victory crowns our flag. In our movement we have the eyes of the world centred upon us, being the pioneer army, and with the same resolution and determination which you have so far shown, we mean to put up a bigger fight than has yet been attempted, for before we surrender or will be beaten we will pull down civilisation and go down with it ourselves.

Every man who enrolled in the ITGWU would be trained by capable officers. 'Yes, Captain White is prepared to lead you, to drill you, and to train you.' He described White as 'a heroic soldier', and the union meant 'to have a regular establishment—majors, captains, sergeants, and corporals.' It sounded as if the union was to be turned into a paramilitary organisation, for Connolly continued:

> We mean to defend our rights as citizens, and any man who means in future to become a member of the Transport Workers' Union must be prepared to enrol himself in the Citizen Army; so that we will not leave the whole of that work to the Ancient Order of Hibernians or the Orangemen who, I hear, have ordered a supply of rifles. We have not done so yet … but we want our men to be trained and drilled, so that when it comes to the pinch they will be able to handle a rifle; and when King Carson comes along here we will be able to line our own ditches. (Cheers.)[13]

A threat by Carson to march his volunteers to Cork if necessary in order to defeat home rule had brought home to many nationalists their own lack of preparedness for the looming conflict. Again there is a striking symmetry between the language of Connolly that night and that which Pearse had used in his column in *Irish Freedom* earlier in the month.

> When the Orangemen 'line the last ditch' they may make a very sorry show, but we shall make an even sorrier show, for we shall have to get Gordon Highlanders to line the ditch for us ... The rifles of the Orangeman give dignity even to their folly.

Pearse characterised the changes wrought by recent events in Ulster and in Dublin in equally original terms. 'Hitherto England has governed Ireland through the Orange Lodges; she now proposes to govern Ireland through the A.O.H.'[14] Any perceptive contemporary who read reports of Connolly's speeches in the *Irish Times* or Pearse's column 'From a Hermitage' in *Irish Freedom* would not have been surprised to hear of their ultimate joint destination. Indeed an increasing number of young Irishmen was coming to agree with them.

The shared vision of these two political militants needed time to mature, and there were of course more immediate and practical reasons why Connolly endorsed White's proposal for a citizen army that week. Essentially it came down to the failure of the ITGWU and the police to agree 'terms of engagement' on the picket lines. Pickets are both the ritual and the substance of any dispute; their effectiveness, in both capacities, does much to determine the final outcome. The week preceding Connolly's call for recruits to a citizen army had been a bad one for picketing. The mass pickets he had summoned had failed to materialise—even under the threat of the withdrawal of strike pay. Yet only with mass picketing could the union enforce its closure of the port. In their absence, 'free labourers' were pouring into the city, and the *Irish Times* was predicting that traffic in the port would soon be back to normal.

One reason for the failure of the mass pickets to materialise was the enormous police and military presence on the streets. An incident from the Jacob's picket line was typical of the problems ITGWU members were experiencing. John Hanratty—a future commandant in the Citizen Army—was told to 'Beat it quick!' when he and another striker began their vigil at the factory gate. When his companion protested that they had a right to picket, both men were set upon by the police, until a clergyman passing on a bicycle came to their rescue. The ITGWU sent the men to its solicitor to begin proceedings for assault; however, the case was dropped when the police threatened to counter-charge. The solicitor advised that, in the atmosphere of the times, the strikers were likely to receive up to nine months' imprisonment if the case went against them. Instead the union, after consulting the police, decided to issue members with armbands bearing the word *Picket*. They were also given leaflets that cited the relevant section of the Trade Disputes Act (1906) protecting their legal right to picket. Hanratty and his companion were despatched once more to Jacob's, fully equipped with armbands and leaflets, only to return to Liberty Hall shortly afterwards covered in bruises.

ITGWU sympathisers were not immune from police attention either. On 4 October the *Irish Worker* reported that a 'big cossack of a policeman had put his foot through the big drum' of St Patrick's Brass and Reed Band after it took part in an ITGWU march. Bands appeared to cause particular annoyance to the police—none more so than the ITGWU's own Fintan Lalor Band, which was established during the lockout. Its rendition of 'The Peeler and the Goat' regularly drew a violent response. After one particularly bad incident in Aungier Street, sixty hurleys were ordered by the nascent Citizen Army to protect the musicians and more especially their instruments, which had cost the union £25.[15]

Connolly addressed other concerns that night in Beresford Place. He reminded his audience that the annual commemorative march for the Manchester Martyrs—the three Fenians hanged for killing a policeman in Salford forty-six years earlier during a prison van rescue—was being held in the city on Sunday. He told the crowd that the men had 'died for a principle and an ideal which … was always sustained by the working class of Ireland—the attainment of their freedom.' He endorsed the methods of the Fenians, as well as their aims. 'It is work such as that in which we are engaged that will make that grand ideal a possibility,' he said. The 'uplifting of the working class' by the ITGWU was bringing nearer 'the day of our emancipation,' and their presence at the rally 'will make the absence of … so-called patriots all the more conspicuous.'

Connolly's stance on political violence was no different from that of most advanced nationalists of the day—including many supporters of the Irish Party. Even the opposition to violence by constitutional leaders such as Dillon was based on pragmatism, not principle.

In an effort to boost the spirit of his troops, Connolly also described a hopelessly optimistic and characteristically apocalyptic vista of heightened class solidarity emerging between Irish and English workers with 'dramatic suddenness'. He began by contrasting the way in which a Manchester mob had 'acted towards those prisoners … showing the hatred and enmity in which the name of an Irish rebel was held at that time,' with the very different scene

> witnessed in Manchester on Sunday last, when another Irish rebel appeared there, and the people of that city gave a splendid reception to James Larkin. (Cheers.) The workers in all parts of Great Britain … look upon you with admiration for the splendid struggle you are making for a grand principle. They are prepared to co-operate with their fellows in Dublin.

To cheers and cries of 'When?' Connolly replied: 'It will come, my friends, but I am not at liberty to tell you our programme … at present.'

The British trade union leaders who opposed the policy of the ITGWU were 'only fossils of the movement, or young members who are waiting the opportunity to sell the pass. (Cheers.)' It was a comment as strong, as indiscreet and as ill-timed as any Larkin could have uttered.

This thing of which I speak will come, as I say, with dramatic suddenness. Some morning the employer will put his foot on his yacht and the sailors will come out; again he will enter a railway carriage, and the drivers, firemen, and guards will leave the train; while when he calls Mary to bring him his breakfast in his bed, Mary will not come. (Cheers.)

The picture Connolly conjured up of the syndicalist strike was Biblical in its simplicity and its completeness.

All you have to do is to stand doing nothing, as you have been doing. When the wife gets up in the morning and calls John or Paddy to go to work, if John and Paddy remain in bed, and decline to go to work for twenty-four hours, they would cause more consternation than if a German army landed at Plymouth in the morning. It would give the employers a bigger fright than all the barricades the working class could throw up. So it is your duty to remain as you are. Stand up and throw your upper classes off your back.[16]

And yet if it was that simple, Connolly would not have been herding his members towards Captain White's army.

*

The meeting of the Civic League next evening was largely overshadowed by Larkin's speech in London and the deliberations of the TUC. While the platform contained many eminently respectable survivors of the Industrial Peace Committee, such as Pierce O'Mahony, Rev R. M. Gwynn, and E. A. Aston, and even sported a woman in the person of Councillor Sarah Harrison, there were also significant gaps. The most obvious were Tom Kettle and Lorcan Sherlock. Sherlock had even refused to allow the new body the use of the Mansion House for meetings. 'Veritas', a regular contributor to Moran's *Leader*, was not far off the mark when he described the new body as 'our short-lived friends, the so-called "Peace Committee", under another name.' Their 'cloak of Impartiality' was thrown off when the new body invited James Connolly and Francis Sheehy-Skeffington to address the meeting.[17]

Connolly used the opportunity to attack not only the employers but the leadership of the TUC. People accused the Dublin strikers of being

disturbers of the peace ... but ... the peace they have disturbed is the peace of slavery and degradation. Mr Murphy at least should get the credit of having told them he was fighting them, but there are others who, while they fight them, tell them they are dying with love for the working classes.

White said he wanted only to 'bring about healthy economic and social relations between all classes and interests in Dublin.' Larkin's methods had been described as destructive, but 'there is a necessity for destruction just so long as there are great evils to be destroyed.' He seemed to think that machines of destruction could be switched on and off with the ease of orders issued from a drill manual.

Larkin's sister, Delia, was more realistic and modest in her aims when she suggested from the floor that the league should prepare a list of fair employers that the public could patronise in preference to those who engaged in 'wage slavery'.

Support for the movement was impressively broad, despite the warning by 'Vigilans'. The Home Rule MP for Galway, Stephen Gwynn, and Roger Casement sent telegrams of support, and a hundred Trinity students marched in a body to the meeting, in defiance of a ban by the Provost.

Anthony Traill, Provost of Trinity College, was one of unionism's leading ideologists. He issued his prohibition after White had told a meeting of Dublin University Gael Society the previous night that he hoped the meeting in the Antient Concert Rooms would 'lay the foundations of a great national movement for the creation of that order and discipline which we so sadly lack, by raising again the standard of the Irish Volunteers.'[18] Dr Traill had shown prescience by his ban.

*

Public meetings do not win strikes. There were worrying indications that the working man, far from heeding Connolly's advice to stay in bed, was out strike-breaking. The coal importers and shipping lines appeared to be having no difficulty recruiting 'free labour' at home, as well as through the Shipping Federation in England. By Saturday 22 November there were nine hundred Shipping Federation men in the port, almost as many as the number of ITGWU dockers who had struck. The *Lady Jocelyn* was no longer able to accommodate all of them. Another federation vessel, the *Paris*, was brought into Alexandra Basin, and the federation also acquired three houses. One was in Sheriff Street, near the entrance to the basin, the other two at the opposite end of Beresford Place from Liberty Hall. It was rumoured that these houses would accommodate a hundred strike-breakers being brought up from the country. A large force of police was on duty as bunks and other furnishings were delivered.[19]

The confidence of the shipping lines was underlined by the latest recruit to the struggle, the City of Dublin Steam Packet Company. At its annual general meeting that week the chairman, Sir William Watson, was able to tell shareholders: 'We are shipping any goods that are handed to us.'[20] Some employers without ready access to federation labour were also finding it elsewhere. When Lord Talbot de Malahide's estate workers struck rather than use coal transported by 'scab' labour to his threshing works, he had no difficulty recruiting replacements from Balbriggan.

In Kingstown the redoubtable Father Patrick Flavin ensured the defeat of the ITGWU's efforts to black coal imports diverted from Dublin. After a week, the union admitted defeat and ordered its members back to work. From being a relative stronghold of the strike, Kingstown became a source of 'free labour', which was used for strike-breaking activities as far afield as Bray.

The activities of Father Flavin, the priest who had shown such an interest in the family of the late branch secretary, James Byrne, were crucial to the destruction of the union locally. He had organised a working men's Sodality of the Sacred Heart and recruited a membership of between six and seven hundred. He did not publicly attack the ITGWU, but he condemned sympathetic strikes and any activity that led to 'victimising the innocent.' Far from simply opposing trade unions, he set up a Workers' Union of his own in Kingstown, which by the end of the lockout had over three hundred members, divided into sections representing coal workers, municipal labourers, and builders' labourers. He later boasted to Dr Walsh's secretary, Father Michael Curran, that he had recruited 'seven-eighths of the coal-workers of Kingstown,' who for the previous three years had belonged to the ITGWU. The sixty-eight municipal labourers who joined were men he had persuaded to withdraw from the ITGWU in 1910. The largest section was that of the building labourers, who had all been poached from the United Builders' Labourers' Union. When his activities were subsequently investigated by Dr Walsh, Father Flavin insisted that he had been invited in by the disillusioned workers and had 'joyfully consented.' His assistance included drafting the new union's rule book, which provided, among other things, for the holding of secret strike ballots.[21]

*

It was, as usual, the smaller traders, without access to the resources of the Shipping Federation and without adequate funds of their own to take exceptional measures, who suffered most. Inevitably the high cost of 'free labour' pushed up the price of many items, particularly coal. As winter approached, the price of a 10-stone bag rose to 3s 6d, compared with 1s 4d a few months previously. Even the middle class felt the pinch; and it must have been a source of some resentment to know that British trade unions were distributing coal to their strike-bound Irish brothers free of charge. Nor were food ships stocked by co-operatives for the workers impeded by the strike. The vessels continued to be supplied by Lowen and Rolfe of Salford, owners of the *Hare*, and continued to be discharged by ITGWU labour. Like Guinness's, the company resisted pressure from the Shipping Federation, and some Dublin employers, to join the fray.[22]

Despite the best efforts of the Shipping Federation, there was little prospect of the strike ending as long as the food ships ploughed their way across the Irish Sea. All eyes turned therefore to England, where Larkin was continuing with his 'fiery cross' campaign. Murphy could take some comfort from the thought that now as ever Mr. Larkin constitutes the best missioner ... the employers could possibly have. He seldom opens his mouth without being guilty of some extravagance which goes a very long way to justify ... the determination of the Dublin employers to have nothing to say to any arrangement in which he has a part.[23]

35

JAMES Larkin, the man who had fought the Dublin employers, the Irish Party, the Shipping Federation and the Liberal government to a standstill, now took on the TUC. Having secured the agreement of the Parliamentary Committee to a special conference on 9 December, he lost no time in appealing over its head to the rank and file of the trade union movement to support their embattled comrades in Dublin.

On 23 November 1913 he published a strongly worded appeal in the *Daily Herald*. He accused the TUC of being 'apathetic ... to the Dublin struggle.' They had agreed to a special conference only to defer it for eighteen days in the hope of settling the dispute. The British trade union leaders had no vision.

> They seem to think that round table conferences, nice language, beautiful phrases, conciliation boards and agreements are the be all and end all of life ... Tell your leaders now and every day until December 9th ... they must stand for Trade Unionism, that they are not apologists for the shortcomings of the Capitalist system, that they are not there to assist the employers in helping defeat any section of workers striving to be free, or act as a brake upon the wheel of progress.[1]

The response came fast and furious. On Saturday 22 November the TUC's own *Daily Citizen* warned that Larkin

> does no service to his cause, or to the cause of labour, by sowing distrust between leaders and followers. The delay which is involved in [calling] a special Congress may be irksome to Mr. Larkin's impetuous spirit; but the longest way round is sometimes the shortest way home. The interests and the issues at stake are too big and too momentous to be jeopardised by any rash or ill-considered action. The exhortations which Mr. Larkin addresses to the workers of this country are not necessary to enlist their sympathy on behalf of the Dublin strikers; and—may we add?—the reproaches which he directs against responsible trade union leaders are not deserved. As an example of the ill effect of blind impetuosity we could not point to anything more conclusive than Mr. Larkin's manifesto.[2]

Worse was to follow. That afternoon Joseph Havelock Wilson, president of the National Sailors' and Firemen's Union, made a highly personal attack on Larkin. For the past two years the Dublin branch of the NSFU

> has been subject absolutely to the control of James Larkin. We have been continually in disputes, without reference or consultation to the governing body of our union.

He was particularly critical of Larkin's handling of the strike at the City of Dublin Steam Packet Company at the beginning of the year. Larkin, he claimed, had used the NSFU to win higher rates for his own members than those that dockers with other companies were earning.

But Wilson's immediate grievance was the decision of the ITGWU to close the port and black the work of companies such as the City of Dublin line, which had 'continued to work with union labour on the docks and in the ships until a week ago.' He pointed out that his own members were now being laid off because the employers no longer had work for them. The Dublin crisis was due to Larkin's policy of breaking agreements 'recklessly for the past eighteen months.'[3] The strike 'could be finished with honour to all parties if common sense would prevail.' He then announced that his own union would be entering into talks with the employers.

The *Sunday Independent* immediately hailed Wilson's stand. 'Larkin's Joy Ride Comes to a Sudden Full Stop,' it declared on its front page. Beside the article it printed a cartoon of Larkin trying to light a safety match marked *English Trade Union* on a matchbox with *Liberty Hall Sandpaper* on the side. William O'Brien is looking on doubtfully, advising Larkin, 'We are not going to light the fiery cross with that.'[4]

Monday's *Irish Times* also exulted.

> The English leaders now know that Mr. Larkin is 'out' not to vindicate trade unionism, but to smash capital. They know that any agreement made by him must be worthless without guarantees. They know that the declaration [of war] against the Transport Workers' Union was forced on the employers by the grim necessities of the case.

It described the situation as 'radically different', because of the changed attitudes of British trade union leaders. There now existed a basis for 'a fair and permanent settlement.'[5]

Larkin must have felt betrayed by Wilson's outburst. Not only had he wrongly accused him of closing Dublin port, but during the seamen's strike of 1911 it had been the ITGWU that had taken the lead in supporting the NSFU in Dublin. Nevertheless, he held his peace and left it to Connolly (the man who had in fact closed Dublin port) to reply in the *Daily Herald* to Wilson's charges.

Wilson has long since entered the demonology of the British labour movement for his role in the general strike of 1926—which he denounced as a 'revolutionary plot'; and his attack on Larkin in 1913 was seen in retrospect as nothing more than a particularly contemptible milestone on the road to betrayal. But in 1913 the reputation of the seamen's leader still stood high with many trade unionists. He was certainly autocratic and erratic, but so was Larkin. His life had been as hard as Larkin's. He had run away to sea at fifteen, and the Shipping Federation had been established in 1890 specifically to oppose his activities as a trade union organiser. At a time when union leaders had no immunity from tort, the federation repeatedly tried to bankrupt him.

Wilson belonged to the older school of 'Liberal-Labour' trade unionists, whom Larkin had prematurely relegated to the category of 'fossils'. He had travelled so far down the road of respectability as to serve as a Liberal MP until 1910. However, he was still regarded as one of the founders of the new unionism in Britain.[6]

What separated Wilson and many leaders of British general unions from Larkin was 1911. In that year the NSFU had snatched victory from the jaws of defeat and finally won recognition as a union from the shipping lines. That concession was based partly on the militancy of NSFU members but also on Wilson's ability to deliver those members once a deal had been struck. Jimmy Thomas, the NUR leader, was equally keen to demonstrate responsible leadership to the railway companies and consolidate his own agreement, which was up for renewal in 1914. Men such as these saw Larkin's 'reckless' alternative strategy for securing union recognition in Dublin as jeopardising years of struggle. He, on the other hand, saw them as unprincipled class collaborators who, having secured recognition, pulled up the ladder behind them.

It was not just the right wing of the British labour movement that was worried by Larkin's strategy. In the period leading up to the special TUC conference, Robert Williams was having second thoughts about his earlier call for a boycott of Dublin. In the NTWF's *Weekly Record* he wrote:

> Among the regrettable features of the Dublin dispute is the fact that … it leaves us little or no time to deal with our own domestic problems. It would be idle to pretend that, deplorable as are the conditions in the City of Dublin, our own conditions are in any way satisfactory.

It was no doubt a plea from the heart that other TUC leaders, who had regularly made the penitential boat-train journey from Euston to Westland Row, shared. Williams also pointed out that the involvement of so many British transport union leaders in talks to resolve the Dublin dispute had seriously disrupted their own timetable for amalgamating the NTWF unions into a single organisation. He added perceptively: 'We are living in a period when our Trade Union organisation is in a period of becoming rather than being.'[7]

Far from seeing the Dublin strike as the spearhead of a syndicalist revolution that would ultimately consume British capitalism, Williams was now depicting it as an impediment to the serious work of modernisation that confronted the NTWF and the TUC at large. It is no wonder that Connolly would single him out for special mention in one of his own post-mortems on the lockout. In 'Old wine in new bottles,' published by *New Age* in April 1914, he would write:

> The amalgamations and federations that are being built today are, without exception, being used [as] a shield and excuse for refusing to respond to the call of brothers and sisters in distress, for the handling of tainted goods, for the working of scab boats ... I have no doubt that Robert Williams ... is fully convinced that his articles and speeches against such strikes are and were wise; I have just as little doubt that they were the best service performed for the capitalist by any labour leader of late years.[8]

*

By late November, the break with Williams was only days away. Of course many union activists, including some full-time officials and senior lay officers of British unions, continued to support the Larkinite strategy unconditionally. Walter Halls, organising secretary of the NUR, wrote to William O'Brien on 23 November, the day after Wilson's attack on Larkin, telling him to keep up the good work but warning him that 'the Irish will have their work cut out' to win the vote on 9 December. He told O'Brien to make sure the proposer of their motion would be someone 'able to beat down any points the official crowd may make against extreme action.' He assured him that 'our men are in a state of revolt in a good many centres.' Funds would continue to flow in for 'as long as you can keep the rank and file conversant with the facts.'[9]

Unfortunately, facts were never Larkin's strongest suit as a speaker. He must have alienated many by his outbursts that winter, and embarrassed his allies. In Sheffield he called Jimmy Thomas 'a double-dyed traitor to his class' and accused Havelock Wilson of sending scabs to break the London dock strike of 1912. He repeated the charge later the same day at a meeting in the London dockers' stronghold of East Ham, a claim that obliged Robert Williams, as secretary of the NTWF, to issue a statement rejecting Larkin's claim and defending Wilson.[10] At Cardiff, Larkin told the crowd that out of 404 employers in Dublin who had signed the agreement to lock out and starve the workers, only two were Catholics; the rest were 'Orangemen, Protestants, and agnostics.' At the same meeting he castigated 'the Castle clique' of the 'Earl of Aberdeen and his good lady, who get £25,000 a year—and who have no children to keep, so far as I know.'[11]

His increasingly personalised diatribes against opponents provoked hostile reactions. 'If you put up clay idols, then I have no more pleasure in life than in knocking them down,' he told hecklers in Leicester, where he had attacked the local Labour MP and future prime minister Ramsay Macdonald.[12] And, as with the Aberdeens, much of what he said went beyond normal political invective. Macdonald and Snowden were 'serpents' who 'spit out poison'; Birrell was a man 'without bowels';[13]

Havelock Wilson and Jimmy Thomas were union leaders who had 'neither a soul to be saved nor a body to be kicked.'[14] The strain of addressing two or three meetings a day, sometimes in venues as far part as London and Hull, was clearly taking its toll.

Far from winning support for his position, Larkin's tornado of meetings throughout Britain was increasing his isolation from the mainstream labour movement. Even the London dockers' leader Ben Tillet had begun to distance himself from Larkin, though not from the strikers. The only major figure in the British labour movement who stood by Larkin was George Lansbury, who kept open house for socialists and constituents at his home in Bow Road. Lansbury had been a Liberal MP, a militant in the proto-Marxist Social Democratic Federation, and a founder of the Labour Party. He had been physically removed from the House of Commons for his opposition to the forcible feeding of suffragists, and if he was a great orator whose reputation could attract thousands, he could also recall the early days of preaching the socialist gospel from a soap-box to tiny audiences consisting of 'a dog or two and, perhaps, a stray child.'

Lansbury continued to call for 'a real and effective blockade of Dublin,' and went further than Larkin ever dared to go when he declared that 'any man who drank Guinness's stout was acting a treacherous part to the labour men and women of Dublin.' In short, his great heart and crusading commitment sometimes outweighed his judgment. His courageous pacifism would shortly cost him the leadership of the Labour Party, when he joined Keir Hardie in trying to stem the war fever that swept through the parliamentary party on the outbreak of the First World War.[15]

*

Williams moved rapidly from oblique attacks on Larkin in the NTWF *Record* to open chastisement. Exasperated by the attack on Wilson, he asked Larkin to stop criticising trade union officials. 'Why, is he not a trade union official himself?' he asked.

> Mr. Larkin, in his eagerness to prevent the officials of the British trade union movement from seizing any pretext for repudiating him, is … proffering them a distinct reason by his wanton attacks. This fight and its consequences are immeasurably bigger to us than fifty Larkins.

A few days later the NTWF executive unanimously passed a motion condemning Larkin's attack on Havelock Wilson. While it pledged continuing support for the workers 'in their fight against the unscrupulous opposition of Dublin employers,' Larkin had now been disowned by the most powerful and heretofore most sympathetic union federation in Britain.[16]

The NUR's *Railway Review* drew up its own indictment of the Dublin strike leader.

> The British Trade Union movement and the Labour party have, after considerable struggle secured Mr. Larkin's release from prison. They

have also subscribed large sums of money to prevent the Dublin workers being starved into submission, and they have made several efforts at an honourable peace. Not having succeeded, they have decided to call a special conference to consider the position. For these services they are now being subjected to a series of attacks from Mr. Larkin worse than if they had been his bitterest enemies. His manifestos and speeches are as irresponsible as his acts. He pretends to be anxious to consult the rank and file to control policy, but in no single instance has he consulted the rank and file himself, nor has he even had the courtesy to consult other trade unions before taking action in which they might be involved.

The *Railway Review* advised members, 'in such circumstances, to take no action which is not sanctioned by their Executive Committee, who are not paid officials, but members of the rank and file.' One miners' leader in the south-west felt obliged to remind his members that they should not allow 'the ungrateful remarks and fiery cross vapourings of Mr. Larkin for one moment to dampen your affection for the gallant fight ... in Dublin.'[17]

The *Daily Citizen* wrote:

We had hoped that Mr. Larkin ... would have formulated in precise terms some line of policy, would have said plainly what he expects ... of organised labour in Britain; but his Sheffield speech—wild, illogical, untrue—closes the door finally on any hope of guidance from that quarter.

It suggested to Larkin that his 'obvious duty to his members and trades unionism is to stay in Dublin and work for a just settlement.'[18]

36

E VEN the lockout could not avert the seemingly inevitable march
towards civil war. At the end of November, Dublin itself became,
momentarily, the cockpit in which the militant passions provoked by
the home rule crisis played themselves out.

Unionists had held a series of mass meetings throughout Ulster in the
summer, followed by similar gatherings throughout Britain in the autumn.
As winter set in, a mass meeting was announced for southern unionists on
28 November, to take place in the Theatre Royal, Dublin.

By coincidence, a new organisation was to be launched at the Rotunda
Rink on 25 November. This was the Irish Volunteers. A perplexed and
overstretched police force already had Captain White's Citizen Army to
worry about.

The Citizen Army began drilling in the ITGWU grounds at Croydon
Park, Fairview, on Monday 24 November, and by Thursday it had enrolled
1,200 members.[1] That day it held its first march through the city, and
nearly three thousand ITGWU members turned out. Even the *Irish Times*
had to admit that 'the processionists … presented quite a martial
appearance' as they set out from Liberty Hall for Fairview. They blocked
trams along the North Strand, but there were no violent incidents. On
arrival at Croydon Park only those men who could answer the challenge
from sentries with the correct password were allowed enter. A 'general
muster' was announced for Croydon Park on Sunday.

Some Citizen Army men had already made their unofficial first outing
on Tuesday night to the founding meeting of the Irish Volunteers. It had
not been a fraternal visit. Less than three years later, members of the
Citizen Army and the Volunteers would fight, and die, side by side in the
streets of Dublin. They were seen as common tributaries to the current of
modern militant nationalism that was emerging as a result of the home rule
crisis. Some historians, and some participants, have seen that bloody
fusion as inevitable and the workers' militia as a natural precursor of the
Volunteers. In fact there was nothing natural or inevitable about it.

In the middle of July 1913 the chairman of the Dublin board of the IRB,
Bulmer Hobson, had proposed the creation of 'an Irish Volunteer
organisation' as a response to the mobilisation of the Ulster Volunteers in

the north.[2] Plans had proceeded slowly until 1 November, when an article appeared in the Gaelic League journal, *An Claidheamh Soluis*, by Eoin MacNeill entitled 'The north began.' In it he unwittingly endorsed Hobson's idea. Referring to the reluctance of the British government to confront the Ulster Volunteers, he wrote:

> It appears that the British Army cannot now be used to prevent the enrolment, drilling, and reviewing of Volunteers in Ireland. There is nothing to prevent the other … counties from calling into existence citizen forces to hold Ireland.[3]

Hobson later described the article as 'very providential'.[4] MacNeill was that rare political commodity, a nationalist who combined in his person social respectability and political integrity. Professor of early and mediaeval history at University College, Dublin, he was also a founder of the Gaelic League. Providentially, he was a scholar sufficiently removed from the hurly-burly of Dublin political life to have avoided becoming enmeshed in the lockout controversy; he was therefore an acceptable authority figure to nationalists ranging from the most conservative constitutionalists to the most radical republicans. As Hobson and his fellow-conspirators in the IRB subsequently discovered, he was also easily hoodwinked.

Less gullible was a former editor of *An Claidheamh Soluis*, Patrick Pearse, who contributed an article in the following issue entitled 'The coming revolution,' heartily approving of MacNeill's idea. Expanding on the nascent militarism that already marked his journalism, Pearse announced:

> I am glad … that the North has 'begun.' I am glad that the Orangemen have armed, for it is a goodly thing to see arms in Irish hands. I should like to see the A.O.H. armed. I should like to see the Transport Workers armed. I should like to see any and every body of Irish citizens armed.

If George Russell wished to people his new 'Attica' with educated farmers and artisans, Pearse was willing to supply the hoplites.

> We must accustom ourselves to the thought of arms, to the sight of arms, to the use of arms. We may make mistakes in the beginning and shoot the wrong people; but bloodshed is a cleansing and a sanctifying thing, and the nation which regards it as the final horror has lost its manhood. There are many things more horrible than bloodshed; and slavery is one of them.[5]

Again, the language is remarkably similar to that used by Connolly when he addressed the first meeting of the Civic League in the Antient Concert Rooms on 20 November. People had accused the strikers of being 'disturbers of the peace,' but 'the peace they had disturbed was the peace of slavery and degradation,' Connolly had told the audience. It seems highly likely that he had read, and noted with approval, Pearse's call to arms.

Hobson recruited the unwitting MacNeill and Pearse to his plan of campaign, and by the time of the Rotunda meeting the IRB had managed to construct a committee that was broad enough to carry a wide appeal but narrow enough to be dominated by the IRB and its fellow-travellers. It was not quite broad enough to win the endorsement of the Lord Mayor, who refused the organising committee—like the Civic League before it—the use of the Mansion House. Significantly, Hobson did not see the Citizen Army as either a precursor, an ally, or a rival, merely as a potential source of drill instructors.[6]

The group of Citizen Army men who attended the Rotunda Rink on 25 November had therefore no particular sympathy or sense of affinity with the Volunteers—quite the contrary: they had gone with hostile intent, to heckle that well-known north County Dublin farmer and strike-breaker Laurence Kettle, another son of the veteran Land League leader and Parnellite Andrew Kettle and a prominent member of the United Irish League, who had agreed to act as secretary to the meeting.

A crowd of four thousand men filled the rink that night, 'drawn from all ranks of Irish nationalism,' according to the *Irish Times*. It described the bulk of the gathering as members of the Gaelic League, AOH, and Sinn Féin, as well as students of the National University.

The ITGWU men stood in a compact group along one side of the hall and listened quietly as MacNeill opened proceedings. However, as soon as he introduced Kettle and asked him to read the Volunteer manifesto, uproar broke out. Kettle appealed for a hearing with the words 'Our work tonight is national work. This is no place for the introduction of small quarrels.' The rest of what he said was lost in choruses of 'God save Larkin.' Many in the body of the hall began counter-singing with 'God Save Ireland.' A picture of Larkin was held up, detonators were thrown, and scuffles broke out at the edge of the crowd.

Most of the ITGWU men eventually left the meeting in a body, and order was restored; however, there was some heckling of the next speaker, Alderman Peter Macken, who was denounced as a 'blackleg'. Macken, a painter elected on a Labour ticket for the North Dock ward only a few months earlier, angrily denied the charge. After that, peace descended on the meeting that saw the birth of modern militant Irish nationalism.

The manifesto adopted at the meeting anticipated the arguments of democratic opponents. It stated:

From time immemorial, it has been held by every race of mankind to be the right and duty of a freeman to defend his freedom with all his resources and with his life itself. The exercise of that right distinguishes the freeman from the serf, the discharge of that duty distinguishes him from the coward.[7]

Ideologically, constitutional nationalists were powerless to challenge the new movement. The speeches of parliamentary leaders were peppered with references to Ireland's glorious military resistance to English rule in the past. They rejected the physical force tradition—often apologetically—on grounds of expediency. They could not reject the notion, implicit in the Volunteer manifesto, that the right to bear arms and to use them antedated the ballot box. For many nationalists, physical force was not only justifiable but a preferable route to freedom. The example of the Ulster Volunteers had already shown them that the gun was mightier than the vote.

The manifesto adopted in the Rotunda was an unremarkable document for the time, which was characterised by the enthusiasm with which millions of young men throughout Europe embraced the idea of military service—the right to slaughter and be slaughtered—as a badge of citizenship.[8] The Volunteers called into being at the Rotunda were part of a trans-European phenomenon that would soon sweep away the 'fiery cross vapourings' of men such as Larkin and Lansbury.

*

The more immediate effect of the formation of the Irish Volunteers was to give a new sense of urgency to the great unionist rally in the Theatre Royal. The previous day, Thursday 27 November, 150 'leading businessmen in the three Southern Provinces' issued a joint statement spelling out the commercial dangers of home rule. Support by the British government for home rule was based on financial as well as political expediency, they declared.

> This country is now in the extremely favourable position of profiting from the large and beneficent schemes of material development and social reform such as land purchase, the creation of the Department of Agriculture and Technical Instruction, the Congested Districts Board, and old age pensions ... If Home Rule had been conceded in earlier years it is now certain that the British Parliament would not, and the Irish Parliament could not, have extended such reforms to Ireland. This would have meant ... [that] in respect of old age pensions alone, Ireland would have been deprived of nearly £3 million a year of Imperial expenditure.

The unionist businessmen predicted that an Irish parliament would not be able to afford the extension of 'costly schemes of social betterment' being planned by their Liberal enemies. Its inability to do so 'will cause unrest among the Irish democracy.' Only by putting 'disproportionately heavy burdens on Irish industry could an Irish chancellor of the exchequer hope to assuage such unrest.'

The document emphasised serious flaws in the tax provisions of the legislation.

> The Home Rule Bill ... offers no conceivable prospect of reduced taxation. Assuming a prosperous Ireland, the growing tax revenue, which is one of the natural results of such prosperity, should be available, as in every independent country to finance new services or

additional expenditure on old services, or to reduce taxation. By the scheme of the Bill, any such additional revenue would not reach the Irish Exchequer at all. It would remain with the Imperial Exchequer as a set-off against the so-called deficit. It would be available to reduce British taxation, but not the Irish burden.[9]

The proposed 'deficit' arrangement was one of the most unattractive aspects of the Home Rule Bill for nationalists as well as unionists. It arose because Irish revenue had been dwindling for twenty years, while British government expenditure had doubled over the same period. In 1910, with the introduction of social insurance, Ireland finally became a net burden on the British exchequer. The deficit had grown to over £2 million by 1912 and was expected to rise further. Under the deficit arrangement, Ireland would receive a block grant of £6 million a year, while the proceeds of all Irish revenue would go to the exchequer. When the home rule government succeeded in producing a revenue surplus for three consecutive years, the arrangement could be reviewed. Southern unionists suggested that such a prospect was remote. The only way in which a home rule government could reduce the deficit was by cutting back on social insurance benefits, thus increasing class tensions within unionist and nationalist communities alike, or by increasing taxes on industry or agriculture—which would be divisive on regional and on sectarian grounds.

The one obvious area where substantial savings were possible was security, for Ireland was severely over-policed. The RIC alone accounted for £1.4 million, nearly a quarter of the proposed block grant. The Cork rural radical William O'Brien had urged Asquith to hand control of the police to the home rule parliament immediately; he argued that the prospect of reducing the number of policemen, and with it the RIC pay bill, would give nationalists a vested interest in promoting 'the peace of the country.'[10] However, such an arrangement would have been anathema to unionists, especially the big landowners who were such a significant element within the movement's leadership in the south. The influence of that landowning clique was clear from the attendance at the Dublin rally, which included over twenty peers; apologies were received from sixteen more.[11]

The list of unionist businessmen who signed the economic indictment of home rule in Thursday's *Irish Times* was headed by the Earl of Kenmare, who was a director of Guinness's brewery; Lord Iveagh and three other members of the Guinness family were also among the signatories, along with another Guinness director, Chris Digges La Touche. Other leading businessmen who signed the list had less benign images with the working class. They included Sir William Goulding, George Jacob, and J. Sibthorpe, who had chaired the meeting of the Dublin Employers' Federation that endorsed Murphy's lockout strategy. The man who proposed the vote of thanks to William Martin Murphy at the Dublin Chamber of Commerce meeting on 1 September, Edward Andrews, was another signatory, along with J. D. Wallis, chairman of the Master Carters' Association, and John Jameson, chairman of the Dublin Coalowners' Association. Gerald Brunskill, a director of the City of Dublin Steam Packet Company, was also on the list.

How far was Larkin correct in his sectarian outburst at Cardiff the previous Sunday when he equated the southern unionist capitalist class with the leadership of the lockout on the employers' side? Inevitably the list of signatories to the anti-home-rule statement was composed predominantly of businessmen, but most of them were bank directors and financiers rather than employers. The largest group were the bankers. Twelve of the fourteen directors of the Bank of Ireland signed the letter, including the governor and deputy governor. However, only one director of the Royal Bank signed, and none of the directors of the Munster and Leinster. Already a parallel Catholic financial and rentier class was emerging and co-existing with the long-established—and still dominant—class of Protestant financiers. It would have been surprising if some of them did not share the concerns of the Bank of Ireland at the impact home rule would have on investment, returns on government stock, and interest rates; however, they were unlikely to voice them, for fear of offending the nationalist community that they served.

The signatories also included twelve members of the Dublin Stock Exchange. Like the bankers, many of them also held directorships in other companies—often firms run by relatives. However, these enterprises tended not to be firms directly involved in the lockout. Guinness's was the most notable example. The Pim dynasty, with interests spread among textiles, retailing, railways, and banking, was another good example of unionist businessmen who tried to avoid the conflict. And John Mooney of Johnston, Mooney and O'Brien was an advocate of compromise on the industrial relations front. Even employers such as the Goodbodys and the Dockrells, who had entered the fray reluctantly after their own employees walked off the job, were not among Murphy's core group of supporters within the Dublin Chamber of Commerce.

Of course there are degrees of involvement. Robert Goodbody was a director of Tedcastle McCormick and Company, whose chairman, Samuel McCormick, was the Shipping Federation representative in Dublin. Frederick Pim may have had good relations with his employees, but he was also chairman of the Dublin and South-Eastern Railway company, which allowed one of its managers, Charles Coghlan, to act as secretary to the Dublin Employers' Federation.

Protestant business families still dominated the railway companies, and the directors of these companies formed the third-largest category of signatories of the anti-home-rule declaration. It should not be forgotten that the quiescence of railway workers in 1913 was due in large part to the severe chastisement they received at the hands of Sir William Goulding in 1911, though with the support of his nationalist ally on the GSWR board,

William Martin Murphy. Business alignments may also explain why none of the three unionist directors of the DUTC signed the declaration: presumably they did not wish to embarrass the company chairman, William Martin Murphy, or his Catholic nationalist colleague, the Irish Party MP William Cotton, with public displays of loyalist fervour.

Nor did Murphy's politics, or his labour problems, prevent unionists from investing in the DUTC. One such investor was William Ireland, the wine and tea merchant who continued to carry the flag for the unionist cause on Dublin City Council. He was also a director of the Duke Shipping Company. Shipping was another industry that Protestant businessmen continued to dominate, along with the related coal-importing business.

However, whether by design or accident, the list of signatories of the unionist declaration did not include any of the leading protagonists in the dispute that had now closed the port. George Watson, the stockbroker, was a signatory, but not Sir William Watson or Edward Watson, who were leading figures in the City of Dublin Steam Packet Company and the British and Irish Steam Packet Company.[12] It could be, of course, that they were simply too busy with the dispute to be drafting, or even signing, political manifestos; or it could have been that they were genuinely concerned at Larkin's outburst four days earlier and did not want the dispute to exacerbate sectarian feeling in the city, already raised to a dangerous pitch by the activities of Dora Montefiore and her clerical opponents. The truth is that any member of Dublin's business class who could avoid involvement in Murphy's grisly battle probably did so. Historical factors determined that more Protestant capitalists and investors were in this fortunate position than Catholics; but in a business community as small as Dublin's, not many residents enjoyed the luxury of non-alignment.

*

Sir John Arnott, another signatory of the anti-home-rule declaration, facilitated a rapid response by the Dublin Employers' Federation to Larkin's sectarian claims in his newspaper, the *Irish Times*. On Wednesday 26 November it published a statement by the federation to the effect that Catholic employers comprised a majority of the membership. An unnamed spokesman pointed out not only that 'Protestants and Presbyterians and members of other religious persuasions' invested in the city's enterprises but that 'Roman Catholic charities and trusts' did so as well. Without naming Murphy, the spokesman said that 'several captains of Commerce in the city who are affected by the dispute … are Roman Catholics, including four of the 14 members of the federation's executive committee.' Larkin's outburst was ill-conceived and unfair. And yet there were too many Dublin businessmen's names on the anti-home-rule declaration to disarm the suspicions he had aroused.[13]

The unionist rally in the Theatre Royal on Friday 29 November was a far grander affair than the founding of the Irish Volunteers in the Rotunda three days earlier. The stage was 'a cave of Union Jacks,' the *Irish Times* reported, with the largest Union Jack ever made filling the back of the stage.

The closely packed parterre, platform, and galleries, were filled largely with businessmen, heads of great and small businesses, strong in the determination contained in the great motto over the stage, plain and uncompromising: 'We will not have Home Rule.' The ladies, who had the dress circle to themselves, were no less enthusiastic than the menfolk.

An orchestra entertained the crowd while it awaited the arrival of Carson and the leader of the opposition, Andrew Bonar Law, but the musicians could hardly be heard over the lusty voices singing 'Rule, Britannia' and 'The British Grenadier'. When the voices of the audience were finally exhausted, the orchestra switched to a ragtime selection. It was a remarkable demonstration of strength, and of weakness. Some counties were represented only by declarations of loyalty, or in the titles of the twenty-one peers present. Even some of these, such as Lord Cloncurry, had children who had deserted the defence of the Union for more radical causes.

Several of the speakers, including Bonar Law, did not hesitate to make capital out of Dublin's labour troubles. While conflicts between labour and capital were 'only too common' and 'always deplorable,' he could not remember a dispute more deplorable than the lockout. 'To me, ladies and gentlemen, the amazing thing ... is that no attempt to influence it has been made by the political leaders of Irish nationalism. (Cheers.)'

Carson's fellow-MP for Trinity College, John Campbell, made the most sustained attack on the Irish Party over the strike. He asked where John Redmond, 'the leader of the Irish race at home and abroad,' had been during the dispute. A voice from the audience answered, 'Abroad,' to loud laughter.

Where have been the Dublin Six? They are either in sympathy with the workers or with the employers. If they are in sympathy with the workers, why have they not the courage to come out and say so? If, on the other hand, their sympathies are with the employers, duty again requires and demands that they should come boldly and publicly forward and state their views.

Instead they had remained silent, while the dispute was 'paralysing and crippling the industries of your country. I have no sympathy with Larkin and his methods. (Hisses.)' He had 'denounced him from the platform in Dublin and from my seat in the House of Commons,' but the Irish executive had

feted him in Dublin Castle ... Jim Larkin would have been allowed ... to pursue his methods only he fell foul of Mr. John Redmond and the Ancient Order of Hibernians. (Hisses.) It was they who issued the order for his prosecution and arrest, and it is the knowledge of that which makes me so bitter. The English Radical papers, writing on this subject, say: After all, is it not a great opportunity for Dublin Unionists, now that in a Home Rule Parliament Redmond and Devlin will not have it all their own way, that they will have to deal with Jim Larkin and men like him? A nice prospect, ladies and gentlemen, for us, and a nice choice we have got between the devil and the deep sea. (Laughter.)

Though speaking for myself, I would rather suffer under the whips of Larkin than under the scorpions of Joe Devlin. I honestly believe that I would have a greater chance of liberty, of personal judgment and of conscience under Jim Larkin and the Irish Transport Union, than I would have under Joe Devlin and the Molly Maguires. (Cheers.)

Campbell's choice of 'devils' is an interesting one, as is his characterisation of the Joe Devlin school of industrial relations by association with the discredited methods of the Irish-American secret society.

Two leading Dublin employers also addressed the rally, Lord Iveagh and Sir Maurice Dockrell. Both stressed the threats to individual liberty, to freedom of expression and to the influence Protestants played in the 'commercial and professional life of the three provinces' posed by Home Rule. Neither of them mentioned the lockout.[14]

*

They may have felt that to do so would be to tempt fate, for Dublin that week was experiencing another spasm of the violence that periodically afflicted it during the lockout. Lord Iveagh had had personal experience of this only a few hours before the Theatre Royal rally. Carson and Bonar Law had been his guests at Iveagh House during their brief stay in Dublin. Earlier, Law had refused to meet local suffragists to discuss the Unionist Party's opposition to votes for women, and Lord Iveagh subsequently found his home under siege from members of the Irish Women's Franchise League and the more moderate Irish Women's Reform League. When the visitors emerged to pose for photographs before lunching at the Conservative Club, they were immediately accosted by Margaret Connery and Hanna Sheehy-Skeffington of the IWFL. The DMP swiftly bundled the women away, but not before an *Independent* photographer captured the scene. It published a picture on its front page the next day of Margaret Connery brandishing an *Irish Citizen* poster between the two stoic politicians. It was rare for Murphy's newspaper to give such prominence to the feminist cause; it was clearly a case of 'mine enemy's enemy.' In the commotion, a nationalist protester thrust a copy of the Irish Volunteer manifesto into Carson's hands. Being a mere man, he had escaped the attentions of the police.

Outside the Conservative Club, the Unionist leaders once more had to run the gauntlet of the suffragists, and Marguerite Palmer managed to grab Bonar Law by the arm and deliver a brief harangue before being dragged away. That afternoon suffragist hecklers managed to disturb the peace again briefly at the Theatre Royal rally before stewards ejected them. The hecklers included Francis Sheehy-Skeffington, who managed to enter the theatre disguised with a false beard.

Meanwhile Hanna Sheehy-Skeffington was in police custody, charged with attempting to 'molest' Bonar Law and Carson. She went on hunger strike next day after refusing to be bound over. The *Irish Citizen* found it 'satisfactory to note that, as in the recent case of Mr. Connolly, the ordinary privileges of a bail prisoner were not taken away from Mrs. Sheehy-Skeffington when she hunger-struck, as they were when she and others hunger-struck (also as bail prisoners) out of sympathy with Mrs. Leigh and Miss Evans last year.'[15] The latter two women had been involved in the suffragist disturbances that accompanied the visit of Asquith to Dublin for the monster home rule rally of 1912. Carson and Bonar Law could at least take comfort from reflection that, unlike Asquith, they had not had a hatchet thrown at them.

Hanna Sheehy-Skeffington became quite ill in prison and was released the following Thursday after her doctor, Elizabeth Tennant, made representations to Lady Aberdeen.

*

But the antics of suffragists were a comparatively minor irritation; the industrial conflict in the city and surrounding countryside threatened to take a more sinister turn. Bread supplies were under threat. Though Johnston, Mooney and O'Brien continued to operate normally, four other large bakeries requested heavy police escorts to protect 'free labourers' delivering flour. The Bakers' Union was too weak and disorganised to become involved in solidarity action with the ITGWU, but the refusal of ITGWU labourers to deliver 'tainted' flour from firms such as Shackleton's seriously affected supplies.[16] When union members at Merchants' Warehousing refused to handle flour, the company retaliated by obtaining ejectment orders against sixty employees and their families who lived in company houses at East Wall. In north County Dublin, agricultural workers were resorting once more to arson attacks on farms. At a meeting in Swords, P. T. Daly lamely denounced the burning of crops as 'the work of the police' and their agents.

In the absence of support from the railwaymen, the ITGWU attempted to hit Dublin's commerce by drawing bargemen with the Grand Canal Company into dispute. This initiative, which followed an unsuccessful attempt by Connolly to reach a settlement with the shipping companies on Monday, failed miserably. He proposed allowing ITGWU members to return if companies would undertake not to carry goods for Jacob's or Guinness's. The companies, having already gone to the trouble of recruiting so many 'free labourers', rejected the offer. Even employers who had tried to avoid confrontation were having to lay off workers. The tobacco firm T. P. and R. Goodbody let 150 employees go on Tuesday. Richard Goodbody (one of the signatories of the southern unionists' anti-home-rule statement) told the workers that either they must handle 'tainted' coal imports or the factory would close for lack of fuel. It closed, though apparently with 'good feelings' on both sides.

Connolly faced considerable criticism at a meeting of dockers later that day for his handling of the dispute in Larkin's absence. Some of the permanent men had been earning between £2 10s and £3 a week because of the extra work diverted from strike-bound lines. Now they were being asked to survive on strike pay of 10s a week, and strike-breakers were still ensuring that those cargoes were unloaded. There were calls for Larkin to come back from England to lead the strike; but there were no proposals for a return to work.

By Thursday 28 November the *Irish Times* was reporting that 'the congestion of goods is being rapidly overtaken' in the port, and that the NSFU had sent an English official to negotiate a return to work by its one hundred Dublin members: the local branch secretary, George Burke, was considered too much of a Larkinite by Havelock Wilson to be trusted with the job. The union had taken new offices in Commons Street, and evacuated Liberty Hall.[17]

*

The two labour renegades Billy Richardson and John Saturninus Kelly were also active. Richardson was seeking to revive the Irish National Workers' Union. He wrote a letter to the newspapers calling on workers to join this moribund body, and also put up recruiting posters. 'The thing called Larkinism should no longer be allowed to masquerade as trade unionism,' nor was the ITGWU 'an Irish organisation,' the poster declared; it was 'not led by an Irishman.' Kelly, who was still technically a Labour councillor, put down a motion for the next week's meeting of the city council condemning his fellow Labour representatives William Partridge and Thomas Lawlor 'for their usurping audacity ... going to England to support the socialistic candidates in opposition to ... Home Rule candidates ... pledged to support the present Government that has resolved to restore our long lost rights.' It was ruled out of order.

Kelly was prevented from reviving his own discredited Irish Railway Workers' Trade Union by the simple fact that it had been wound up because of insolvency six weeks earlier. Kelly had claimed 1,400 members for his union, but an investigation disclosed that there were never more than eighty-seven. It also found the administration costs 'excessive'.[18] The anti-Larkinite activities of Richardson and Kelly, like those of McIntyre, had no visible effect on the strike, but they served as another irritant in an increasingly explosive situation.

On Friday evening the violence erupted. It started at George's Quay at about 6:30 p.m. Denis O'Reilly and John O'Brien, two strike-breakers with Tedcastle McCormick's, were attacked by a mob as they drove a lorry to the firm's depot on the quays. Like many 'free labourers', they had been issued with licensed revolvers, and both men used them. O'Brien fired at least one round before being incapacitated by a missile, and O'Reilly fired seven. A fifty-year-old woman, Bridget Rowe of Waterford Street, was shot in the face as she stood watching on the steps of the Tivoli Theatre. The two men were subsequently arrested at the Tedcastle McCormick premises and charged with shooting the woman.

At about 11:30 p.m. more shots were fired by strike-breakers and by an off-duty DUTC conductor. This time the shots came from the top of a tram in Sackville Street. Two men had been recognised as 'scabs' and chased onto the tram. A large crowd, estimated at five hundred, surrounded the vehicle. Some of the pursuers boarded the tram, and when the conductor and ticket inspector tried to stop them they began wrecking the vehicle. A group of men tried to incapacitate the tram by pulling the trolley from the overhead wires. The police, who had been observing from a distance, intervened at this stage and took the gunmen into custody.

Rioting became general around Sackville Street and Rutland Square. The police cleared the main thoroughfares with a baton charge, and the crowds fled into side streets, from which they continued to throw stones. Every window in the Dublin County Council offices and at the Fowler Hall, where the Orange Order met, was smashed. Seven shops, most of the hotels and several private houses in the area also suffered damage. By the end of the night sixteen people had been arrested.

*

On Saturday morning Dublin's workers received a salutary lesson in the class nature of the criminal justice system. O'Brien and O'Reilly, the two men charged with shooting Bridget Rowe, were released on bail of £10. The charges were subsequently dropped, on the grounds that it could not be proved that either of them had fired the shot. In the Northern Police Court the Chief Magistrate, Swifte, accepted that they had been subjected to 'severe provocation'.

Swifte's colleague in the Southern Police Court, McInerney, heard the cases against the other men. John Roycroft, one of the strike-breakers who had fired from the top of the tram in Sackville Street, was discharged after the magistrate heard evidence from Sergeant Boyle of the DMP and the DUTC conductor that the lives of tram passengers were in danger. Thomas Murphy, an off-duty DUTC conductor who was a passenger on the tram and who fired the revolver he was carrying at the time, was discharged on the same grounds. Another 'free labourer', Michael Bowe, who had been seized by the crowd and accused of firing shots, was discharged for lack of evidence. By the time he had been handed over to the DMP, the alleged revolver had disappeared.

The chief witness for the prosecution against Bowe had been a man called Edward Byrne. He now found himself taken to the Northern Police Court and charged before Swifte with assaulting DUTC officials on the same tram. Detective-Sergeant McCabe of the DMP gave evidence that Byrne had been under observation 'for a considerable time' and was the ringleader of the crowd. Swifte fined Byrne £5 and sentenced him to a month in prison and a further month in default of paying the fine. Another man who boarded the bus with Byrne was brought before McInerney. He was fined 10s and ordered to pay damages to the DUTC of 13s or go to prison for fourteen days.[19]

As far as the strikers were concerned, there was one law for themselves and another for gun-toting strike-breakers. There would be more, and worse, incidents before the lockout ended. The rioting on Friday night, like the arson attacks on farms in the north county, suggest that the strikers were becoming increasingly desperate and demoralised and were losing faith in traditional forms of industrial action.

*

Union leaders must take some of the blame for fuelling the natural animosity against strike-breakers. Three days earlier a Belfast member of the ITGWU executive, Michael McKeown, who had come to Dublin to help Connolly run the strike, made a strong attack on them. He told a meeting in Beresford Place that 'free labourers' were being paid £1 15s a week, though it took them twice as long to unload a ship. At the same meeting Connolly used an unfortunate choice of phrase to tell the crowd that the 'sympathetic strike is like a revolver, which is a handy weapon … used by people who know how to use it, but when used recklessly, it is likely to do more harm than good.' However, he added that 'if the employers are prepared to give reasonable concessions, we are prepared to give a guarantee that the sympathetic strike will not be used recklessly and indiscriminately.'[20]

If Connolly emerged in the lockout as a militant with a bloodthirsty vision of the future, his militancy was not of the mindless variety. Indeed the Citizen Army he was helping to build was providing a useful outlet for the frustration of ITGWU members. Nevertheless, uncontrolled violence would continue to erupt from time to time.

37

CONNOLLY'S offer to 'check' the operation of sympathetic strikes if the employers were willing to 'give reasonable concessions' was seized upon by that idefatigable duo of Archbishop Walsh and James Seddon. Seddon was anxious to reconvene negotiations with the employers before the proposed special delegate conference of the TUC in London on 9 December. A settlement, even at this late hour, would avert a dangerously divisive debate that could only damage the British labour movement. Dr Walsh could see the corrosive effects of the lockout for himself, of which Friday's riot was the latest symptom. He could expect little help from Murphy, who was pursuing his offensive industrial strategy with zest. The *Sunday Independent* published a cartoon that weekend showing a worker pointing a gun, or a fuse, at a barrel of gunpowder marked *English Trade Unions*. The barrel explodes, leaving the heavily bandaged worker in bed under the slogan *To hell with contracts*. Given the shootings that weekend, it was a display of exceptionally poor taste, even by the *Independent's* standards.

Murphy had also written to the TUC newspaper, the *Daily Citizen*, congratulating it on its new editorial line.

> I welcome you as a convert to Murphyism, which is anti-Larkinism, but regret that while you are a Murphyite in England, you are still a Larkinite in Dublin. I am, however, hopeful, if Mr. Larkin continues much longer to exhibit himself before the British public, that your conversion will be complete, and that geographical boundaries to your new faith will disappear.[1]

The validity of Murphy's comments can only have added to the tensions within the trade union movement—as he intended.

But Dr Walsh had other contacts in the business community, and recent developments, besides Connolly's speech, gave some cause for hope. One of them was the decision of the Shipping Federation to unilaterally introduce 'strike expenses clauses' in its freight contracts. This was a very different situation from September, when the Dublin Chamber of Commerce had been able to appeal a similar move by the London Chamber of Commerce and the Institute of London Underwriters to the Board of Trade. The Shipping Federation was not attempting to change the terms unilaterally for all carriers, only for members and for those firms wishing to avail of the federation's services. In short, take it or leave it. An appeal to the Board of Trade was not an option.

The new terms stated that where the shipment of any cargo 'is hindered or prevented by strike, lockout, labour trouble, trade dispute, riot, civil commotion or any like circumstance, the captain, shipowner or agent shall have the right ... to take such measures as he or they think expedient' to ensure its delivery. Half the extra costs incurred were to be borne by the customer, while the clause exempted the shipping companies from damage or loss of cargo resulting from the special measures taken.

The decision had been taken on Monday 24 November and was now being transmitted to customers.[2] It was clearly intended to recoup from their customers some of the costs incurred by shipping companies as a result of the lockout. Apart from the additional costs that firms would face as a result, they would also be ceding a large measure of control over industrial relations to the federation. This was much further than most companies were prepared to go in following 'Murphyism', or the syndicalism of the Shipping Federation.

As it happened, a quarterly meeting of the Dublin Chamber of Commerce was scheduled for Monday 1 December. Edward Lee, the draper who had already publicly broken ranks with Murphy over how the dispute should be handled, tried to force a debate on the situation in the port. At a meeting of the council of the Chamber of Commerce on Saturday 29 November, Lee proposed a motion for Monday's general meeting that the chamber,

> whilst determinedly opposed to the principle of sympathetic strikes, with their attendant disastrous effects ... are of the opinion that the employers, in the interests of peace and good will, ought to withdraw the agreement they asked their workers to enter into in respect of the ITGWU, which the workers consider infringed their personal liberty.

The motion was regarded as a virtual capitulation by Murphy and his allies.

As president of the Chamber of Commerce, Murphy chaired council meetings and had prior notice of motions. It was hardly surprising, therefore, when one of his allies, Richard Jones, a butter merchant, submitted an alternative motion for Monday's meeting, stating that 'we the members of the D.C.C., in general meeting assembled, endorse the position adopted by the Employers' Executive Committee towards the I.T.G.W.U., that we do so on the proven grounds that the policy of the I.T.G.W.U. is destructive of all the principles that are usually regarded as directing the relations between genuine trade unions and bodies of employers.'

The council also received a letter from Sir William Goulding, who apologised for not being able to attend. He suggested that the Jones proposal not be put, 'as I consider that it would, at this present critical time cause a great deal of ill-feeling and division in the Chamber, which I think would be most hurtful to the interests of the employers.' Instead, 'it would be far better to meet the other [Lee's] resolution with a direct negative and with as little discussion as possible.' In the event, the council decided to go one better and unanimously agreed 'that discussion of the resolutions at the present time would be undesirable.' Neither motion would be put to Monday's meeting.[3]

While no record survives of the debate at the council meeting, or at the general meeting that followed on Monday, it seems clear that the employers were far from united. The DUTC, Jacob's, the coal importers and cross-channel shipping companies were committed to a fight to the finish, but several other large enterprises, most notably Guinness's and the railway companies, clearly preferred a speedy resolution. Companies dependent on supplies through the port, and those that enjoyed relatively good relations with their employees, such as Goodbody's, the tobacco firm, and Mooney and Morgan, the fertiliser manufacturers, cannot have been happy with the disruption taking place. The carters' position was even worse. Not only were they losing current business but the advent of the motor lorry was threatening their future livelihood. As we have seen, J. D. Wallis, chairman of the Master Carters' Association, had decided not to use lorries for strike-breaking purposes, in order to avoid further exacerbating the conflict. When Murphy was soliciting funds from Guinness's management three weeks earlier, it had been on the grounds that the dispute had left the smaller carters and coal merchants in dire straits.

Small builders were another group suffering hardship, and they had begun informal discussions with the unions on a return to work. However, without a resumption of building supplies any settlement would be inoperable. Lee himself may have reflected the concerns of retailers in general, who, unlike large companies such as Jacob's and Guinness's, lacked easy access to alternative shipping routes or the services of the Shipping Federation. They were also totally dependent on a now severely depressed domestic consumer market.

*

Dr Walsh would have been as well aware of the divisions in the employers' camp as he was of the much more publicised ones on the union side. He also kept in regular touch with Sir James Dougherty, the Irish Under-Secretary, and through him with Sir George Askwith. Dougherty was pessimistic about any new initiative succeeding. In a letter to Dr Walsh that week he said the reason Mitchell, one of Askwith's mediators, had not come to Dublin was lack of progress in informal consultations with the Dublin employers and British union leaders. Another obstacle to progress was Larkin's confidence that he could carry the special TUC delegate conference with him. Dougherty wrote:

> That would be a pretty kettle of fish. The Labour leaders think he is too sanguine. We must wait and see. Meanwhile Larkin is little likely to

agree to any settlement and allow his men to surrender. He will await the result of the pitched battle three weeks hence.[4]

It says much for Dr Walsh's commitment to finding a settlement that he was prepared to risk another rebuff from the intransigent duo of Larkin and Murphy. He was no doubt aware of Lee's motion and made a new plea for a settlement on Monday 1 December. As the members of the Dublin Chamber of Commerce made their way to its quarterly meeting, they could read in the newspapers the archbishop's injunction to pay less regard to 'extremist statements' and more to the clear indications 'that the course of events is gradually, though but slowly, shaping itself in the direction of peace.' He quoted Murphy and Connolly in support of his contention. In Murphy's case it was from his letter of the previous week in which he had stated: 'There are not five per cent of the men out … who may not return before their places are filled up, without any sacrifice of principle, or without any undertaking except to do the work they are paid for doing.' Dr Walsh deduced from this that Murphy was prepared to withdraw the requirement that workers sign the form renouncing the ITGWU. He then quoted Connolly's professed willingness to 'check' the operation of the sympathetic strike as evidence that the ITGWU was also willing to 'go a step forward in the direction of peace.'

> I ask, why should we turn our attention away from significant statements such as those that I have quoted, and fasten exclusively upon other statements, recklessly made, which, if they were to be taken literally, would amount to so many declarations of implacable and never-ending war?[5]

The answer was given instantly by the secretary of the Dublin Employers' Federation, Charles Coghlan. He was provided with far more space than Dr Walsh in the newspapers to explain why the war must go on. He began by deploring the way in which extraneous social and municipal questions had been dragged into the dispute to cloud the issue, as well as the false claim that Dublin employers were anti-union. The issue was the ITGWU, whose policy was to 'smash capital' and 'make the business of traders unworkable.' If this was the union's policy, 'the employers are surely entitled to say that if they are to be smashed, they may lawfully elect to die fighting rather than suffer extinction by being smothered.'

Employers found that their workers were no longer free agents

> but took their orders from Liberty Hall. Forced, willing or unwilling, to join the union they then became soldiers of labour, the employers the enemy. Threats and intimidation, and the weapon of the sympathetic strike, were freely used to coerce employers and workmen, farmers and factors, until a reign of terror was established in the city and surrounding districts—and *The Irish Worker*, as the official organ, spared neither man, woman nor child in pursuance of the official policy, which

aimed to make Mr. James Larkin Dictator of the City of Dublin … What the struggle has cost in wages alone … would be difficult to estimate, but it certainly would have gone a long way to rebuild the slum property of the city, about which we are hearing so much.

The 'charge of sweating' had also been levied against the employers, 'with as little foundation as the statement that out of the whole of the Dublin employers there are only two Roman Catholics.' The employers were not prepared, Coghlan said, to treat with a union that 'wants to dominate everyone,' that broke agreements, abused the sympathetic strike weapon, and followed an

avowed policy of destruction without any effort at construction. Borrowing from our opponents, employers are prepared to fight to a finish, or confer with those whom they can trust to see agreements arrived at carried out.

Nor was the archbishop's humiliation over, for the *Irish Times* that morning published an extraordinary letter from an anonymous employer, who had obviously been shown Dr Walsh's plea for peace. He took the archbishop sharply to task for thinking that Liberty Hall was run by 'honourable men'

… and the fact that a first lieutenant [Connolly] makes a sane remark or two in a speech out of about fifty vituperative utterances spread over 12 weeks is not, to say the least, a strong sign of willingness to settle. Moreover, I would remind His Grace, that it has been clearly stated from the first by the employers that they would not make any further terms with the present rulers of Liberty Hall under any circumstances.

Worse was to follow.

Now, as to the extract from Mr. Murphy's letter (which, by the way is not quite accurate as to percentage, 15 per cent would be nearer the mark. Mr. Murphy must have had only the Transport Union in his mind when writing). There is nothing in that letter implying or indicating a wish to make a settlement with the present rulers of Liberty Hall. It merely points out that 95 per cent, he says—I say 85 per cent—of those out of employment need only give an undertaking to carry out the instructions of their employers to enable them to resume work. The other 15 per cent are asked to sign out of the Transport Union because, I take it, the employers have found it quite impossible to carry on their business owing to the daily interference of that union.

This rewriting of Murphy's position, as he had given it a couple of weeks earlier to the press, must have stunned the archbishop. The anonymous employer continued in the same condescending vein.

What I would impress on these well-intentioned peace makers is that the employers quietly but firmly stated, and adhered to it all through, that they would not negotiate with the present rulers of the Irish Transport Union, and that, in my opinion the direction in which peace lies is through the men themselves. First they want to be taught what they are fighting about, for they do not know. Next, they want to take a little of the gospel preached by their leaders to the English rank and file (i.e. to tell their leaders what to do, and to make them do it) and apply it at home, where it is noteworthy that this policy is not being preached.

These remarks will apply equally well to the Dublin Trades Council, which is at present ruled by a few demagogues, hand in glove with Liberty Hall.

The anonymous letter-writer given such prominence went on to state his own view that the sympathetic strike

… finds no favour with the men. It hits them too hard, and in nine cases out of ten with no possible benefit to the individuals taking part in it. The sympathetic strike is, therefore, a leader's weapon only, used to get notoriety, and to impress those at a distance with their great power. When it is once understood by the men it will not be tolerated.

The men 'honestly think they have some great grievance to put right' but were victims of 'the clever confusing of things by their leaders.' The writer felt sure that

if the men could see the situation as it really is, they are manly enough to call a parley with their leaders. I would remind them that, if their leaders were men they would long ago have volunteered to step down and out, so as to allow some newly elected officers to make peace with honour, and so have saved so much suffering; for the leaders are the only obstacle to a permanent peace. This is further evidenced by their refusal to allow the English trades union delegates to negotiate a settlement.

The men were fighting 'for something that does not belong to them—i.e., the management of their employers' business.' This did not prevent the writer from enjoining the workers to ensure that their unions were 'termed and officered in a constitutional way' rather than 'run as a business in the interests of the secretary and committee only.'[6]

It is hard to think of another example of a Catholic prelate of the period being treated as shabbily as Dr Walsh was that morning by the leaders of Dublin's business community and by a national newspaper. What was most extraordinary about it was the way in which the anonymous employer was allowed to change the substance of Murphy's position without any challenge. His ability to read Murphy's mind was blindly accepted, as was his rewriting of the number and type of workers who would be reinstated. It is legitimate to ask why Murphy himself had not bothered to correct the record on such a crucial matter. The obvious explanation is that the real purpose of the original letter was to influence the outcome of the meeting between Larkin and the Parliamentary Committee of the TUC on 18

November. The new letter must have been written with Murphy's approval, if he did not actually write it himself. Both the letter and Coghlan's statement revealed clearly that, for the dominant forces within the Chamber of Commerce, the dispute was not fundamentally about pay or conditions but about power in the work-place and power in the city.

The one crumb of comfort for Dr Walsh was Coghlan's final veiled reference to the possibility of renewed talks with the TUC leaders, echoed in the letter of the anonymous employer. The archbishop has often been criticised for his handling of the Dublin 'kiddies' crisis, but against this should be put his persistent quest for peace in the face of blatant dishonesty, manipulation and condescension by the employers.

*

The Dublin Chamber of Commerce tried to maintain a discreet silence over its own dissensions. Murphy did not allow any discussion of the motions from Lee or Jones at Monday's general meeting; but Lee sent a copy of his resolution to the press regardless. He suggested that the chamber was in breach of its constitution, which required it 'to take cognisance and investigate such matters as, affecting the commerce, manufactures, shipping and carrying trade of Ireland generally, must necessarily influence those of the metropolis.'[7]

The TUC and Sir George Askwith were no more willing than Dr Walsh to allow Larkin or Murphy to set their face against further peace efforts. On 2 December, Larkin, Connolly and O'Brien were summoned to a meeting of the Joint Labour Board. This consisted of the TUC Parliamentary Committee, the Labour Party executive, and the General Federation of Trade Unions. The Dublin men reluctantly sanctioned a final effort by the British union leaders to reach a peace settlement before the special delegate conference. So tight was the schedule that the chairman of the Joint Board, Arthur Henderson MP, and the chairman of the GFTU management committee, James O'Grady, left immediately on the night train for Dublin to initiate contacts with the employers.[8]

There was also renewed public pressure on Murphy. One of the longest-serving members of the Chamber of Commerce, F. J. Usher, was a widely respected malt and grain merchant of long standing in the city; he had been one of the Chamber of Commerce's nominees to the Lord Mayor's proposed conciliation board earlier that summer. Usher wrote to the *Irish Times* suggesting that 'His Grace Archbishop Walsh, in his letter to the Press ... has indicated a movement towards peace and good will.' He did not go as far as renouncing Murphy, but he did suggest that employers should not insist on workers signing the form renouncing the ITGWU.

> Fifty years' experience has proved to me that the Dublin working man's word is his bond. I should ask none other, although a memorandum of employment might be necessary.

As if to challenge Murphy's hegemony, he addressed the letter from his offices in Commercial Buildings, which also housed the Chamber of Commerce, rather than his yard in Fumbally Lane.[9]

*

Many employers were as sick of the dispute as the workers and shared the growing public unease at the way violence was becoming endemic in the city. Particularly worrying was the frequency with which 'free labourers' were resorting to the use of firearms. The Civic League demanded that the government withdraw police protection from firms using strike-breakers. This measure would almost certainly have brought the city's trade to a standstill and led to a quick victory for the workers, unless the unions had abjured the right to use mass pickets. One of the league's more moderate members, Rev. R. M. Gwynn, dissociated himself from the proposal but added a rider that he might change his attitude if the employers persisted in using 'the "free" labourer who is a parasite on the sores of the state.'

In Britain the Fabian Society went as far as calling on the government to introduce a system of binding arbitration to resolve Dublin's intractable industrial relations problems. The arbitration body would have equal union and employer representation and would cover all workers earning less than £1 10s a week. While the society did not deny the right of employers to seek outside assistance during a dispute, it condemned the 'organised importation of strike-breakers' as 'a violation of public decency [which] ought to be made a criminal offence as conduct calculated to provoke a breach of the peace.' The society endorsed the call for police protection to be withdrawn from companies that used 'free labourers.'[10] The society's aims might be socialist, but it could not be written off as a marginal group of extremists. Not only the Labour Party but senior members of the British government, such as Winston Churchill, took its views seriously.[11]

*

Nevertheless, events suggested that the hard line adopted by the employers' leaders was beginning to pay off. On Tuesday 2 December they won an important psychological victory when a group of seventy ITGWU dockers not only returned to work but agreed to unload grain from the *Antiope*. It had been strike-bound for ten weeks, because it contained supplies for the Shackleton mills in Lucan, the first firm to lock its workers out. The *Irish Times* that day reported 'an unusually large number of vehicles ... waiting their turn to enter the docks, while there was a continuous stream of laden conveyances coming out, in the majority of cases under police protection.'[12] Some employers already believed that the threat of the TUC stepping up its action in support of the Dublin workers had passed; but, as so often happens in protracted disputes, even the most intransigent protagonists find it difficult to resist pressure to re-enter talks.[13]

When Henderson and O'Grady arrived in Dublin next morning they received a timely reminder that not all their problems lay with the employers. The *Irish Times* published a report of the previous night's proceedings at Beresford Place. In the absence of Larkin and Connolly in Britain, William Partridge put the best face on recent setbacks and promised to show the TUC delegates 'what a strike is like that is fizzling out.' The *Daily Citizen* might have joined the ranks 'of the corrupt capitalist Press' by printing Murphy's letter expounding 'Murphyism', but the TUC visitors would discover that 'however, and whenever, the strike is settled, it will be settled by no one else but Jim Larkin.' If the TUC should abandon them, Partridge assured his audience that the workers of France and America would close their ports to Dublin. Indeed he said they were already preparing to do so. He also held out the prospect of political victories for labour in the forthcoming municipal elections.[14]

The first step of the British advance party was to canvass the views of Dublin employers individually, and both talked of hopes of a settlement in their interviews with the newspapers.[15] By Wednesday evening they had agreed a procedure for resuming talks. It was, briefly, that the Joint Labour Board representatives would meet the employers on their own the next day. If the two groups failed to reach an agreement, further talks, involving direct negotiations with the strike leaders, could take place on Friday.

On Thursday morning Henderson and O'Grady met the rest of the British delegation and the strike leaders, including Connolly and O'Brien, who had just arrived back in the city. The Dublin men were reluctant to agree to procedures that in effect excluded them from the crucial initial discussions. Connolly drafted a face-saving motion that would allow the TUC men to meet the employers on the grounds that 'the interview will be preliminary to a conference with the local representatives.' It also stipulated—and Connolly printed the words in capital letters—'IF THE EMPLOYERS WILL SO EXPRESS THEMSELVES we will gladly notify the aforesaid men [the TUC delegation] of the advisability of consenting to their interview.'[16] Whether Connolly and his colleagues ever received the satisfaction of a formal notification from the employers that their interpretation of procedures was correct is not clear, but the 'interview' that followed between the Joint Labour Board members and the employers was to drag out over three days.

The reason for the protracted negotiations was of course the huge gap between the two sides. The brief that the strike leaders gave the British delegates entering the 'interview' was essentially the one they had been pursuing from the start of the lockout. They wanted an agreement that provided for the lifting of the employers' embargo on workers belonging to the ITGWU and the reinstatement of all the men laid off. In return, the unions would agree to a two-year truce and a guarantee that the sympathetic strike would not be used during that time against employers who agreed to new conciliation procedures. The strike leaders pointed out that their proposals were, in essence, those already recommended by Askwith and Sherlock.

The employers, on the other hand, wanted the unconditional abandonment of the sympathetic strike weapon and a recognition by the unions of the right of every employer to conduct his business 'in any way he considered advantageous … not infringing the individual liberty of the workers.' The employers' initial negotiating position was considered so unreasonable by the British delegation that its members refused to take it back to the strike committee. Eventually the employers agreed to enter discussions on 'a scheme or schemes for the prevention and settlement of future disputes,' but they refused to give any unconditional commitment to reinstate all the men in dispute. They further required a commitment from the Joint Labour Board that it would ensure that all Dublin trade unions conducted their business 'on proper and recognised Trade Union lines,' and that it would repudiate any union that broke the proposed agreement. The British delegates would have to guarantee that unions that misbehaved would receive no assistance, 'financial or otherwise,' from the TUC.[17]

It says much for the negotiating skills of the TUC delegation that it managed to bring the positions of the two sides close enough for them to engage in direct discussions by Saturday evening. There were a number of external factors in their favour. One was the fact that Larkin had decided to continue his 'fiery cross' crusade in Britain. However, this was a mixed blessing. While it may have made life easier for the British delegates, it left Connolly (who had now returned from Britain), a far less experienced negotiator, acting for the ITGWU. It also left open the possibility of Larkin reneging on any deal reached in his absence. He was already using his latest 'fiery cross' expedition to denounce British labour leaders such as Ramsay Macdonald and Philip Snowden for playing 'monkey tricks' on the rank and file.

To counter Larkin's latest outburst, the TUC published details of the number of strikers being supported with funds from Britain. At the end of November the total came to 14,968, of whom 12,829 were ITGWU members. However, it refrained from criticising Larkin, and it continued to condemn 'any body of employers attempting to dictate to their employees what union or form of union they shall belong to.' Of course publication of the figures revealed just how dependent the Dublin strike effort now was on British support. It was no wonder that the employers were seeking a commitment from the British delegation that the TUC repudiate the use of the sympathetic strike as part of any peace settlement.

*

British trade union support was not entirely in the gift of the Joint Labour Board or the TUC. As the talks dragged on in Dublin, 1,500 railway workers in Wales struck in support of two engine-drivers who had been sacked for refusing to handle 'tainted' good from Dublin. By Saturday thousands more NUR members had joined the unofficial action, 20,000 colliers were laid off because there were no trains to transport coal, and the whole south Wales region was plunged into chaos. Then, on Saturday evening, the trouble ended as quickly as it had begun. The men agreed to go back to work at the behest of Jimmy Thomas, on the basis of an agreement that could not be seen as anything but a defeat. The two drivers were not to be reinstated, the striking men were not offered any compensation for loss of earnings during the dispute, and they were guaranteed their own jobs only on condition that they resume work immediately.[18]

As in the previous action by dockers and railwaymen in the English midlands and north-west, the action of the few, some of whom had strong Irish connections, failed to translate into the solidarity of the many. The setback was in some ways more significant than earlier ones, for south Wales was home to one of the most influential syndicalist movements of the day, and the railwaymen had serious grievances of their own they wished to air. If these workers flinched from enforcing the 'tainted goods' doctrine in support of Dublin, who would implement it?[19] The outcome of the south Wales dispute settled the debate over whether there should be sympathetic action in Britain to support the Dublin workers three days before the TUC delegates met in London to formally consider the issue.

News of the collapse of the Welsh strike reached Dublin just as direct talks began between the employers and Irish trade union representatives at 6 p.m. in the Shelbourne Hotel. The Irish delegation was essentially the Trades Council strike committee, together with the vice-chairman of the ITUC Parliamentary Committee, Thomas Johnson, who had travelled down from Belfast to attend. Like Larkin, Johnson was a Liverpudlian, but there the similarities ended. Johnson, a future leader of the Irish Labour Party, was common sense and staidness personified.

The chances of success were recognised on all sides to be slim. An additional handicap was that the TUC delegation had been able to keep only in erratic contact with the Dublin strike leaders during the preliminary negotiations. They briefed the strike committee as best they could by telephone during the preliminary talks but only met them for the first time at 11:30 p.m. on Friday in the Trades Council hall.

They had resumed the preliminary negotiations on Saturday morning, and it was only at 1:30 p.m., when the 'interview' with the employers concluded, that the British were able to put the agreed terms for direct negotiations to the strike committee. Inevitably, much of the brief time left before formal talks opened with the employers at 6 p.m. was taken up with complaints from the Dublin men that they had been kept in the dark. Connolly appears to have been the leading critic.[20]

Larkin, who had kept in touch with Liberty Hall by telephone and telegrams, gave an even franker airing of his suspicions in that morning's *Irish Worker*.

> Certain well-disposed gentlemen that you and I have a bitter experience of are prepared to settle the present difficulty by hook or crook—mostly crook. The lines on which they are working is to get the blood-suckers to withdraw the ban against our Union: they will then go their way—the

victimisation of men and women they will minimise, the questions of the future ignore ... Be not confounded with the tactics of our friends in the Trade Union movement.[21]

Larkin was giving the Dublin employers credit for more subtlety than they possessed. It soon emerged at the Saturday evening meeting that they had no intention of giving any commitment to recognise the ITGWU or to reinstate workers. They even compromised the TUC delegation by insisting that Henderson chair the direct talks with the Trades Council, though the master builder John Good had chaired the preliminary negotiations. Murphy further undermined the British delegates by insinuating that they had gone further in the preliminary discussions than they were prepared to admit in front of the Trades Council members, a comment Henderson angrily rejected.

The employers refused to consider a request from the Dublin strike committee that, given the brief time available for discussions before the TUC conference, they should agree a provisional truce. The strike committee urged the employers to withdraw the lockout notices and reinstate all the workers. In return, the unions would guarantee that

no form of sympathetic strike or other strike will be entered upon until the matter in dispute has been the subject of investigation by a local conference of employers' and workers' representatives. The scheme or schemes to be completed not later than March 7th, 1914.

It was an honourable compromise; but after a brief adjournment to consider it, the employers said it was not acceptable. Any commitment by them to withdraw the lockout notices and reinstate the workers would have to be balanced on the union side by the abandonment of the sympathetic strike. John Good asked Connolly directly if he was willing to give such an undertaking on behalf of the ITGWU. Connolly said that the union 'could not absolutely undertake to put aside that weapon.' He suggested that the Lord Mayor's proposals, which the Trades Council supported, should be sufficient guarantee for the employers.

There was, of course, a significant qualification to the moratorium on industrial action contained in Sherlock's proposals. This provided for a two-year truce that would guarantee no strike action in companies that adhered to the peace formula. However, it left the unions free to take action against other employers. Further issues were then discussed; but it was obvious that no agreement could be reached on the central trade-off: full reinstatement for absolute guarantees of industrial peace.

By now it was well into Sunday morning. The employers' final offer on reinstatement was to make 'a *bona fide* effort to find employment for as many as possible and as soon as they can.' The final union position was that the employers must 'undertake that there will be no victimisation, and that employment will be found for the old workers within a period of one month from the date of settlement.' The gap was small but unbridgeable, and at 6 a.m. on Sunday, after twelve hours of continuous negotiation, the talks broke down.[22]

*

It is questionable whether the employers were serious about a settlement that was anything other than a complete and very public unconditional surrender by the unions. Even as the discussions were taking place, additional strike-breakers were being brought into the port, and Merchants' Warehousing had begun evicting the employees against whom court orders had been obtained earlier in the week. Such actions added substance to the fears of victimisation. Nor were most of the strikers at the end of their tether. The company tenants in Merchants' Road showed no sign of cracked morale, and they remained in the cottages until the sheriff's men kicked in the doors. As the families walked out into 'a bleak, blustering wind,' they 'cheered up their spirits ... by giving cheers for Larkin and singing strike choruses.'[23]

In the circumstances, it would have been rash of Connolly to give an unconditional commitment to abandon the threat of sympathetic action, as well as uncharacteristic. His was an invidious position, and it would have been difficult for him to respond positively even to a better offer. Although, in Larkin's absence, he was the *de facto* principal negotiator, he lacked Larkin's authority, and he knew that his leader was quite capable of disowning him if the agreement was not to his liking. Connolly's own authority was compromised by the public criticism he had had to endure from the dockers for closing the port.

The employers too were reluctant to make a deal in the absence of Larkin. His decision to pursue the mirage of a general strike in Britain when he was so sorely needed at the negotiating table was reckless, even by his own standards.

38

F EW people can have been more disappointed at the outcome of the
talks than Archbishop Walsh. He had told a confidant around this
time that he believed the trouble in Dublin was about to end. While
his prediction proved premature, the record of his views provides an
intriguing glimpse into the isolation Larkin faced within the official trade
union movement on the eve of the TUC conference. The archbishop's
confidant wrote in a memo shortly afterwards:

> I had a conversation with W—. It is evident the trouble in Dublin is
> nearing an end. He explained to me the machinery that was being set up
> for working in Dublin, and added you will not be troubled much more
> with Larkin. He said other trade union leaders would not be influenced
> by him, who knew what Larkin was ... All the money received from
> them, except what had been paid to the Co-Op for food, had been
> distributed by Larkin and his friends, fictitious names having been put
> down and no proper statement has been sent to the English unions, or
> appear to be in existence at all, and the leaders here are now beginning
> to realise they have been 'had' by Larkin and his friends. They doubt very
> much if the real workers received the half of the money put down to
> them ... Immediately Larkin comes out [against the agreement] W— is
> authorised by the Trades Council [TUC?] to publish Larkin's record, and
> the organised press of the English unions is to be ranged against him.
> W— believes Dublin will be working next week. I hope it may be so.[1]

Larkin's sympathisers were certainly becoming thin on the ground, but
even Dr Walsh would have been surprised at his latest indiscretion. Invited
to speak at Grimsby by the president of the British Socialist Party, Ernest
Marklew, Larkin cancelled the engagement at the last moment. When
pressed for an explanation, he told Marklew he would not speak at a
meeting chaired by a divorcee. The BSP had until then been to the forefront
in supporting Larkin's 'fiery cross' campaign; but Larkin's behaviour
resulted in Marklew (who was indeed divorced) denouncing him as 'an
absolute dictator'.

Larkin's decision would have come as no surprise to his fellow-Irishman
and radical socialist John Wheatley, who had recruited Larkin to the
Catholic Socialist Society in Scotland seven years earlier, nor to anyone

who had read Larkin's speeches closely. 'You don't know what we are fighting against, those of you who are not members of the church I belong to,' he told the crowd in Manchester when he made his 'divine mission' speech the previous September. 'The men I am fighting for have given sureties for their belief in their church, and the man who tells you that it is impossible to be a socialist and a Catholic is a liar.'[2] Judging by his treatment of Marklew, however, it does not seem that Larkin could divorce his religious beliefs from his political ones.

One wonders what Ben Tillet would have made of it. As it happened, he was in Dublin to address a meeting of the Irish Women's Franchise League. While Larkin denounced divorcees, Tillet described 'apostles of nationalism, patriotism, Romanism, the Non-conformist conscience and religion' as

> the greatest scoundrels and thieves who had ever cursed the earth. (Cheers.) … Now William Martin Murphy has lifted the stone in Ireland and exposed to view the dirty, wriggling and squirming things, the rascals who, in the name of patriotism and religion, are masquerading and exploiting the workers.

Larkin was still busy unmasking the 'scoundrels and thieves' in the labour movement. Inevitably the NUR leaders felt the lash of his tongue in the wake of the south Wales strike. 'We could have settled the Dublin strike thirteen weeks ago if we had allowed the employers to victimise their men,' he told a meeting in Wakefield. But if the Dublin dispute 'goes on twenty years there will never be a man of my union victimised.' Dublin was 'hell with the lid off,' and yet 'the labour leaders are working like devils to destroy this bigger movement.' All the same, he rejoiced that they were all living

> on the eve of great developments. It is good to be alive. You are living on a volcano which may burst out at any minute. You will get purified by fire, and by no other means.[3]

*

If Larkin was looking for railway leaders to tongue-lash, he did not have to look as far as Jimmy Thomas. In Dublin the *Irish Times* was able to reassure its readers that the city's merchants would be well stocked with Christmas fare, thanks to the railways, which had given 'every possible assistance' in beating the port blockade. Liverpool was the entrepot centre for Dublin, and the newspaper explained that deliveries from there had been rerouted through Drogheda, Dundalk, Newry, Belfast, Rosslare, and even Cork. There were still some shortages—asparagus and endives were not to be had at any price, and black grapes were as much as 150 per cent dearer than normal—but items such as apples and Jaffa oranges 'do not show any alarming increase in price, considering the fact that the cost of transit from the leading markets is now two-and-half to three times greater than they would be in normal times.' Some of the increases were also due to crop failures in North America, it explained.

Thanks to the 'determined action' of County Dublin farmers and the sentencing of several men for intimidation in the police courts, fresh vegetables were plentiful at the usual prices. However, the continuing strike by crews of the Dublin Steam Trawler Company meant that prime fish cost 25 to 30 per cent more than usual. Catches had to brought from the western and southern fishing ports.[4]

If readers had even more disturbing food for thought in the evidence being given to the inquiry by the Local Government Board into the city's slums, which had just opened, they could be comforted by the progress made by the Dublin Children's Distress Fund. The treasurer of the Society of St Vincent de Paul, the barrister William Ryan, was able tell the public that nearly ten thousand school meals were being served to the children of poor families, and more than fifteen thousand items of clothing had been distributed.[5]

*

On Tuesday morning nearly six hundred delegates, representing 350 unions with a combined membership of 2½ million workers, assembled for the special TUC conference in London. It was the first such conference since the congress was founded in 1868, but no special arrangements were made. It was left to Harry Gosling and William Roberts to organise the platform, appoint tellers, and make the general arrangements.[6] James Seddon, chairman of the Parliamentary Committee, would also chair the conference. Some historians of the dispute have made much of the fact that no special elections of delegates to the conference were held by the unions, the suggestion being that this was to stifle rank-and-file support for Larkin. But it was not normal practice then, or now, for most unions in Britain or Ireland to elect new delegates for special conferences held between the annual events. In any case, the delegates who arrived at the Memorial Hall on 9 December were the same ones who had voted so enthusiastically to support the Dublin workers in September, and who had helped provide them with the food, fuel and money to carry on the struggle ever since. There is no reason to think that new elections would have significantly altered the composition or the mood of the delegates. The events of the past three months had revealed differences between Dublin trade unionism and British trade unionism too deep to be attributed simply to the reactionary machinations of TUC officialdom.[7]

On the eve of the conference, William O'Brien inadvertently added to the mutual fear and loathing that now divided the Dublin strike leaders from the TUC. After the breakdown of talks with the employers in the Shelbourne Hotel he went home to get some sleep, only to have Francis Sheehy-Skeffington call. The two men were colleagues in the Socialist Party of Ireland and had campaigned together on many issues. As a special correspondent for the *Daily Herald*, Sheehy-Skeffington had also helped the struggle with his sympathetic reporting. Now, as a journalist, he wanted O'Brien's help with a background briefing on the negotiations. Like the other Dublin leaders, O'Brien was unhappy with Henderson's role in the negotiations and told Sheehy-Skeffington so.

Sheehy-Skeffington the journalist obviously had a stiff struggle that day with Sheehy-Skeffington the socialist confidant. Next morning's *Herald* published the outcome in a report that asked 'what truth there is in the rumour current in Dublin that the British delegation tried to jockey the Dublin men into an unfavourable settlement.' Connolly, who had been nominated to present the position of the Dublin strike leaders at the TUC conference, was furious. He rightly predicted that 'this thing will come up, and we will have a lot to do about it.'[8]

There was further embarrassment in store. To make the London conference in time, the strike leaders had to catch a ferry to Holyhead; because Dublin had been closed 'tight as a drum' by Connolly, the only way he and his comrades could reach their destination was on ships crewed by strike-breakers. The irony of the situation was not lost on D. P. Moran. The *Leader* expressed mock horror that Connolly, O'Brien and McPartlin had caught the LNWR steamer *Scotia* from Kingstown. 'If we remember rightly Connolly talked red in connection with the coming of "free" labourers, but alas he has gone to 'appy hEngland in the very boat that brought over some "frees" to Dublin.'[9] If the TUC delegates chose not to make capital of this lapse it was only because they were (literally) in the same boat themselves.

Bigger problems awaited the Dublin men in London. To their dismay, one of the staunchest allies they possessed, Robert Williams, was refused registration as a delegate at the conference. Despite his very public falling out with Larkin, Williams was still sympathetic to the general plight of the strikers. He was refused registration on an infuriating technicality. Though he was secretary of the NTWF, which consisted of twenty-nine unions affiliated to the TUC, the federation itself was not affiliated. Williams was outraged at being silenced and disfranchised, not only because of his close involvement in the Dublin dispute and his work in organising the delegate conference but because the TUC had agreed to grant representation to the Labour Party, the co-operative movement, and the Fabian Society; as Williams pointed out afterwards in the NTWF *Record*, some of the delegates of these organisations were not even members of a trade union.[10]

At least he was spared the ordeal of James Seddon, who, after all his work to engineer a compromise in Dublin and to maintain good relations with characters as disparate as Larkin and Archbishop Walsh, collapsed that morning with pleurisy. It was the vice-chairman of the Parliamentary Committee, W. J. Davies, the man who chaired the September congress, who had to take Seddon's place and open proceedings. He at least had the merit of not being identified with all the unseemly infighting since.

On the platform was an ill-assorted range of foes. Larkin, Connolly, O'Brien and McPartlin, representing Dublin Trades Council and the Dublin strike committee, sat immediately behind Davies. A chatty man on O'Brien's right began quizzing him about the situation in Dublin, and

O'Brien tried to be as helpful as he could, until Connolly leaned across and said, 'Young man, you will get into trouble.'

'For what?' O'Brien asked innocently.

'Consorting with the enemy,' Connolly replied, informing him that his inquisitive neighbour was the NUR leader Jimmy Thomas.[11]

Arthur Henderson was the first speaker.[12] He gave the congress a relatively straightforward account of discussions with the employers in Dublin over the previous few days; however, he could not resist adding, in an obvious reference to the previous day's *Herald* report, that there had been 'unworthy' suggestions that the delegation of the Joint Labour Board had attempted to impose a settlement on the Dublin men. Larkin immediately jumped up and shouted, 'I am not going to be insulted in that manner.' Uproar broke out, and it was several minutes before Davies could restore order.

Henderson concluded by stating his belief that, if the 'difficult corner' of reinstatement could be negotiated, 'a permanent settlement of this very troublesome dispute could be at once arranged.' He then moved his report of the dispute, which was a defence of the TUC record rather than an overt attack on Larkin and his Dublin colleagues. Harry Gosling, president of the NTWF, seconded the motion. He too had been part of the Joint Labour Board delegation to Dublin, and he tried to establish a semblance of unity by concentrating his fire on Murphy. He believed that even the difficult issue of reinstatement could have been resolved in the talks,

> were it not for Mr Murphy. ('Hear, hear.') Although there is an Employers' Federation in Dublin, it is Mr Murphy who is at the bottom of it. ('Hear, hear.') The other employers have got to pull Mr Murphy down and get a reasonable settlement, or dissociate themselves from him and get a settlement.

Connolly then rose to speak. He said there had been 'too much recrimination on both sides,' and then promptly added to it.

> An attempt has been made to represent Mr Henderson as endeavouring to jockey the workers. The suggestion of jockeying, however, did not originate with the workers, but the employers. I am sorry if anyone has fallen into the trap, and apparently Mr Henderson has been the first to fall into the trap. (Laughter.)
>
> Henderson: I did not fall into the trap. I read it in a newspaper.
>
> Connolly: How do you know the information was not supplied by the employers?
>
> Henderson: It is not likely that it would have been supplied by them between Sunday night and Monday morning to the *Daily Herald*. ('Hear, hear.')
>
> Connolly: That is an instance of the childlike faith in the guilelessness of the Dublin employer, which has amazed and amused us ever since. (Laughter.)

In a more conciliatory tone, Connolly accepted that the 'split' within the trade union movement might still be got over. But the damage had been done. After he spoke, Henderson's report was adopted unanimously.

There was worse to follow for the Dublin visitors. Ben Tillet, fresh from uncovering the 'dirty, wriggling and squirming thing' that was Murphyism in Dublin, moved a resolution deploring and condemning 'the 'unfair attacks made by men inside the trade union movement upon trade union officials.' He called on the congress to affirm its confidence in those officials 'so unjustly assailed, and its belief in their ability to negotiate an honourable settlement if assured of the effective support of all … concerned in the Dublin dispute.' This was not so much jockeying the Dublin men into a settlement as railroading them into it. Tillet said he had the 'greatest confidence in the men sent to Dublin,' and it was imperative for the congress 'to show the world it had every confidence in their leaders.' He reminded the Dublin men that the TUC had done more for them than for 'any other strikers' in its 45-year history.

Tillet's speech showed that even a radical union leader like himself was not prepared to indulge Larkin if it meant damaging relations with other unions. It was another brutal reminder that the British trade union movement anticipated major disputes in 1914 and did not want its funds bled off and its unity sapped by a peripheral row between unreasonable and unreasoning Irishmen.

Seconding the resolution, W. C. Anderson, another radical member of the NTWF, certainly saw things that way. He said that 'strong feeling has been aroused by unjustifiable attacks on trade union officials.' Union leaders in Britain 'had acted with great restraint … in the face of very real provocation.' Larkin's false allegations against Havelock Wilson of the National Sailors' and Firemen's Union, of supplying 'blackleg labour' in the Leith and Dublin strikes, had done 'infinite harm to the whole trade union movement.' Even when the dockers' leaders in Scotland had repudiated Larkin's attacks he had refused to apologise. 'That sort of thing is not going to help the Dublin workers,' Anderson concluded to loud cheers.

Jimmy Thomas received a more mixed reaction to his defence of the way the south Wales rail strike had been handled. He had not 'sold out' anyone, he said. 'Mr Larkin knows nothing of the history of the railway movement, and yet he has sown dissension in the ranks of the railway men, which is a most suicidal thing to do.' Warming to his theme, Thomas said he did not go around, 'as the "fiery cross" hero does, shouting "to hell with contracts" … but as a responsible man' who felt that, when a strike was a mistake, he should tell his members so.

A voice in the crowd, tiring of Thomas's self-serving speech, shouted: 'What has that to do with the Dublin strike?'

'What has that to do with the Dublin strike!' Thomas retorted angrily. 'Are we to stand silently by and allow ourselves to be libelled and slandered? I am not going to, for fifty Larkins. (Cheers.)'

Havelock Wilson then rose from the body of the hall and said that he had only been called 'a scab and a renegade because I have tried to impress privately a little common sense into the heads of those who have been mismanaging the business in Dublin. (Cheers.)' This brought Larkin to his feet, and once more there was 'a tremendous uproar.' When it subsided, Larkin began his address as only he could, with the phrase, 'Mr chairman and human beings.' Even Larkin's voice was drowned again in the contending shouts of sympathisers and opponents that followed.

'I am not concerned whether you let me go on or not, and can deal with you at any other time and at any place you like to name,' he said when the noise subsided. He simply wanted the opportunity to refute the 'foul, lying statements made against me.' A voice in the crowd shouted, 'Keep cool, Jim,' but Larkin, looking around the hall, seemed not to notice. 'There are men here who have no right to be here,' he said. 'I was told to come and meet men elected by the rank and file'; instead he could 'pick out a man who took my job and betrayed me as a friend. And I want to know who sent him here.' This attack on his old mentor, the ex-Fenian dockers' leader James Sexton, caused even greater uproar than before. There were shouts of 'That's a lie,' and calls for Larkin to retract his allegation.

Larkin said he was prepared to retract anything untrue, then turned his fire on Wilson. Casting his mind back to 1905 and his early days as a docks foreman in the NUDL, he said:

> Wilson has forgotten to tell you, and so has Sexton, that when the dockers went out in Liverpool I went out with the men with whom I was associated; but when Wilson tells me to sell my soul I will not do so. (Interruption.) Mr Wilson has said that he is a wise and statesmanlike gentlemen and that it is we in Dublin who have made mistakes. (Shouts of 'So you have.') It's not true. The mistakes have been made by the trades union leaders.

There was more disorder as Larkin pursued his vendetta against Wilson and the NSFU, for whom he had worked so hard in Dublin 'and never charged a damn cent.'

The noise from the hall was deafening, and Larkin, 'gesticulating violently,' shouted, 'I can see what it is: you are afraid to hear the truth.' He seemed to revel in the anger of his opponents, which totally failed to intimidate him. When the noise began to subside and hecklers complained, 'We've heard enough,' he answered, 'I am not responsible for your intelligence,' and provoked another outburst. A journalist reported him as pacing restlessly through the din. 'With perspiration streaming down his face and dropping from his chin, he almost frantically tried to make himself heard.'

Continuing undismayed, through 'a running fire of interruption,' Larkin concluded with a warning.

Neither you nor these gentlemen on the platform can settle this Dublin dispute. I challenge you to try it. I know, however, that the rank and file of British trade unionists will support the Dublin men ... and if we do not get that support we will do what we have done before—fight it out. (Cheers.) This is a game of war; it is not a game of beggar-my-neighbour. I know the men we have to deal with. All they want to do is delay the negotiations in order that they may weed the men out.

The ban against the union has not been withdrawn. The employers of Dublin are neither truthful nor honest, and the only way to deal with them is with a strong hand. We have always been able to do that. Take away your scabs out of Dublin, take away the men who are organised scabs, who are acting worse than the imported scabs. The men of Dublin will never handle tainted goods as long as I am with them as an official. (Cheers.)

Unrepentant, he repeated the point he had made to the Parliamentary Committee in London three weeks earlier, after his release from prison:

Your money is useful, but money never won a strike. (Cheers.) Discipline, solidarity, knowledge of the position, and the strength to carry out your will—these are the things you could win [with] in Dublin tomorrow if you mean to. If you do not mean to you should shut up. All the money and all the leaders will not beat the men we are fighting. I have said hard things, and you have said harder things and bitter things against me; but I have done according to my lights. I have given service for which I give no apology. (Cheers.)

Larkin will keep on fighting, and go down fighting.

Any hope that the morning session could end on a constructive note was dispelled when the Scottish NUDL leader, O'Connor Kessack, came to Sexton's defence. No-one had driven Larkin out of his job, he said; and when he was in it, 'Mr Larkin was drawing a bigger salary than any union organiser ever had,' while all the time secretly planning the formation of his own organisation.

The break for lunch did nothing to help tempers, and if the Dublin men used it for canvassing, it was to no avail. Davies put Tillet's motion condemning Larkin's 'unfair attacks ... upon trade union officials.' The vote was almost unanimous, with only six votes against.

Support for the Dublin strikers then came from an unusual quarter. John Ward, navvies' leader, hero of the Sudan War and Liberal MP, proposed a motion calling for 'continued help' for the strikers 'until the dispute is settled.' The situation in Dublin was

a disgrace to our civilisation and to our statesmanship. For trade unionists to withdraw their support to the Dublin workers because they could not support Mr Larkin's methods would be doing injury to their fellow-workers.

He hoped that 'the result of this congress will be to increase our support a hundredfold.' The motion was supported by Ben Turner of the Weavers' Association, which had subscribed heavily to the Dublin food fund, despite having to support several serious disputes of its own in the north of England that autumn.

Two further motions were put. The first, from the National Union of Labour and the Typographical Association, was relatively innocuous: it went no further than calling on the Joint Labour Board to 'continue their consultations with the Dublin Strike Committee' and to endeavour 'to resume negotiations with the Employers' Committee, with a view to a satisfactory and lasting settlement.'

The second motion was proposed from the platform. It called on the Joint Labour Board to convene a special conference in Dublin of the unions involved in the dispute. These were 'to consider the entire position, with a view to a united policy by which the dispute might be brought to a successful conclusion without the sacrifice of any trade union principle.' There were protests from the floor that it was not coming from a trade union, and that 'this is not a platform conference.' But Davies pushed it through without debate. It was, potentially, a useful bargaining chip for the Dublin strike leaders, as it continued to hold out the threat of sympathetic strike action by the British unions if the Dublin employers remained adamant. It was therefore a reasonable and even generous gesture from the TUC leadership.

However, Jack Jones, the militant leader of the Gasworkers' and General Labourers' Union, proposed going much further, and he tested the resolution of the congress to the utmost. His motion, while recording appreciation of the efforts made by the Parliamentary Committee to reach a settlement and its success in raising funds for the Dublin strikers, called for further action

> to uphold the right of combination and to resist the attempt of the Dublin employers to oppress the Transport Workers' Union.
>
> We therefore call upon all unions having members engaged in transport work, either on land or on sea, to notify the employers concerned that on a given date they will refuse to handle blackleg cargo or merchandise going to, or coming from firms which have locked out the workers of Dublin. We call upon all unions not connected with the transport trades to pledge themselves to support financially by a fixed monthly levy all workers who may be affected by the carrying out of the above proposed policy.

Jones further proposed that a special emergency committee of the TUC be appointed to work with the Joint Labour Board in establishing the blockade of Dublin. Finally, he called for the immediate withdrawal of all military and police protection for the city's employers. S. J. Davis of the Vehicle Builders seconded the motion.[13]

There was, of course, one fundamental weakness in the proposal, which its opponents were quick to point out. It was members of other unions who would be doing the fighting, while their members no doubt dutifully paid their monthly levies. J. E. Williams of the NUR said that if this motion were passed, members of his own union 'would never be at work.' He hoped the conference 'will not impose such tyrannical conditions upon a body of 250,000 trade unionists.' Tom Shaw of the Weavers warned the delegates against 'being led away by syndicalism.' Even 'Explosive' Joe Cotter, the self-proclaimed syndicalist leader of the Ships' Stewards', Cooks', Butchers' and Bakers' Union, baulked at the motion. It would involve his members and other transport workers in a general strike, he said. He turned Larkin's 'rank and file' argument on Jones and said that individual unions would have to consult their members before the TUC could embark on such a campaign.

T. E. Naylor of the London Compositors' Society argued that what Jones was calling for was 'a systematic, scientific strike,' not blind sympathetic action. But he suffered under the same handicap as Jones: there would not be many compositors engaging in 'scientific' action on behalf of Dublin, as Bob Smillie of the Miners' Federation was quick to point out.

The voice of the miners ought to be heard before there was any vote on sympathetic strikes, Smillie said. Like the railmen's and dockers' leaders, he had learnt about sympathetic action the hard way. At a Triple Alliance conference shortly afterwards he would state in more detail his objections to sympathetic action in support of isolated groups of workers.[14] For the moment, he asked

> what has been done by the organisations that are shouting for a general strike. The Miners' Federation is giving a thousand pounds a week towards the support of the Dublin strikers. It is a thousand to one that a great many of those who have been attending Mr Larkin's meetings are not trade unionists at all. ('Hear, hear.')

When the Jones motion to blockade Dublin was put, delegates representing 2,280,000 workers voted against it. Delegates voting for it only represented unions with a membership of 203,000. This was less than 10 per cent of the TUC membership; and yet, given Larkin's 'fiery cross' campaign, the wonder is that he still had that many supporters.

Further motions were passed, but they were only sops to the shattered Dublin leaders. The stance of the Dublin employers was condemned, and there was a call for legislation to ban 'the organised importation of strike-breakers' and another for the release of all Dublin workers imprisoned as a result of industrial action.

It was left to Connolly to respond on behalf of the strike committee; and it says something for the brutality of the debate that he began with uncharacteristic diffidence, even awkwardness. He said he was well aware of the responsibility that lay on him, and, 'having heard what I have heard during the day, I regret having to make the statement I am going to make.'

He was careful first to praise the co-operation of the British trade union movement.

> That co-operation is magnificent and, if you will allow me to say so, we are as proud of it as the English trade unions have a right to be. ('Hear, hear.') But I have heard speeches today that I can tell you make me, and those with me, question entirely the value of that co-operation. We have been told that those who pay the piper should call the tune. ('Hear, hear.') That might be so if we were selling something, but we from Dublin are not selling anything, and least of all selling our independence. (Laughter.)
>
> However, as a result there is to be vested in the British delegates some mysterious power to force the Dublin workers into a settlement. ('No!') I am not talking of the meeting, or of the action of the Joint Board delegates—they have never acted in such a manner. ('Hear, hear.') But I think that, for the sake of those whom I and those associated with me have to go back to, that we cannot allow such a phrase to pass without protesting hotly against it. ('Hear, hear.')

He then attacked Havelock Wilson and the NSFU for sending delegates to Dublin to negotiate a settlement with the shipping lines behind the back of the strike committee. Davies quickly called him to order. Connolly protested that 'it would have been better for the conference to have first endeavoured to try and settle the Dublin dispute and afterwards wash their dirty linen.' Davies pointed out that it was Larkin who had first 'gone into contentious matters.' He told Connolly he must accept the result of the conference. 'That cannot be altered.'

Connolly promised that he and his colleagues would acquaint 'the rank and file across the sea' with the outcome of the day. But he also warned the delegates that 'we in Dublin will not necessarily accept all the resolutions passed at this conference.'

It was, for Connolly, a feeble and disjointed effort. Larkin had addressed the conference at the height of the debate, which lent an incoherent fire to his speech. Connolly spoke in the aftermath of defeat. He spluttered out his words in the knowledge that Dublin was isolated.

*

That night Larkin headed north for Glasgow and another meeting to rally support, while the rest of the Dublin delegates caught the night train for Holyhead. At Crewe, Connolly bought an early edition of a morning paper and learnt that the NUR had already ordered its members back to work at the North Wall, on pain of forfeiting their strike pay.[15] Connolly's anger was still palpable two months later when he wrote in *Forward* that the NUR, 'whilst in attendance at the Special Conference in London on December 9th, had actually in their pockets the arrangements for the restarting of work on the London and North-Western boat at the North Wall of Dublin.'[16]

It was true. For fourteen weeks the LNWR terminal at the North Wall had been closed, as the NUR men had come out in solidarity with the ITGWU. On Wednesday, all 254 railwaymen agreed to return on the instructions of their union. Some of them returned immediately, to ensure that normal sailings between Dublin and Holyhead could resume from Wednesday morning. The *Irish Times* predicted that the City of Dublin Steam Packet Company would resume normal sailings following discussions with the NSFU; the report was premature, but there was a growing expectation in the business community that the worst was over. No less than five steamers entered the port that day for discharge. The cargoes included biscuit skips for Jacob's, empty barrels for Guinness's, and general goods for other firms.

In Swords, sixty-five farm labourers had turned up for a meeting called to organise the Independent Labour Union. Its founder was Joseph Early, a local farmer at Drynam. He appealed to the new members to show no hostility to their former comrades in the ITGWU—on the contrary, they should let them know that the farmers were willing to take back strikers who joined the new union on better terms than they had enjoyed 'previous to the outbreak of farm troubles.' The union had been some weeks in preparation and had acquired offices in Dublin and a rule book and disputes committee.[17]

*

On his return, Connolly moved quickly to forestall a return to work by the NSFU men with the City of Dublin Steam Packet Company. The union may have moved its offices to Commons Street, but the members' hearts remained in Liberty Hall, and it was there that Connolly arranged to meet them. The meeting began at 1 p.m. on Wednesday 10 December and lasted an hour. Despite some calls for a secret ballot, the men were prevailed upon by Connolly to stay out 'until the dispute was generally settled.' It was a crucial decision, because if the City of Dublin men had followed the LNWR back to work, it was widely believed that all the dockers would do so.[18]

Connolly described the hectic days that followed.

> The Seamen's and Firemen's Union men in Dublin were next ordered to man the boats of the Head Line of steamers, then being discharged by free labourers supplied by the Shipping Federation. In both Dublin and Belfast the members refused, and they were then informed that union men would be brought from Great Britain to take their places ... We were attempting to hold up Guinness' porter. A consignment was sent to Sligo for shipment there. The local Irish Transport and General Workers' Union official wired me for instructions. I wired to hold it up; his men obeyed, and it was removed from Sligo, railed to Derry, and there put on board by members of Mr. James Sexton's National Union of Dockers on ships manned by members of Mr. Havelock Wilson's National Union of Seamen and discharged in Liverpool by members of Mr. James Sexton's Union.[19]

*

It was no wonder that Connolly, like Larkin, had been so keen to expose the treachery of their traditional enemies at the London conference, and was so infuriated when those efforts were frustrated. He felt that a tremendous opportunity had been snatched from them, as he explained in *Forward.* In the same article in which he was to describe the help the British working class had given Dublin as 'its highest point of moral grandeur,' he went on to lament:

> Could that feeling but have been crystallised into organic expression, could we but have had real statesmen amongst us who, recognising the wonderful leap forward for our class, would have hastened to burn behind us the boats that might make easy a retreat to the old ground of isolation and division, could we have found labour leaders capable enough to declare that now that the working class had found its collective soul it should hasten to express itself as befitted that soul and not be fettered by the rules, regulations and codes of organisations conceived in the olden outworn spirit of sectional jealousies; could these things have but been vouchsafed to us, what a new world could now be opening delightfully upon the vision of labour? Consider what Dublin meant to you all! It meant that the whole force of organised labour should stand behind each organisation in each and all its battles, that no company, battalion or brigade should henceforth be allowed to face the enemy alone, and that the capitalist would be taught that when he fought a union anywhere he must be prepared to fight all unions everywhere … But sectionalism, intrigues and old-time jealousies damned us in the hour of victory, and officialdom was the first to fall to the tempter.
>
> And so we Irish workers must go down into Hell, bow our backs to the lash of the slave driver, let our hearts be seared by the iron of his hatred, and instead of the sacramental wafer of brotherhood and common sacrifice, eat the dust of defeat and betrayal. Dublin is isolated.[20]

It was the speech that Connolly had no doubt wanted to make in the Memorial Hall in London; and two months to reflect on defeat had only confirmed him in his analysis.

Robert Williams hadn't even been given the opportunity to speak at the special delegate conference. He considered himself no less a socialist than Connolly and was to be a founder of the Communist Party of Great Britain, but he had drawn different conclusions. In the issue of the NTWF's *Weekly Record* immediately after the conference he pointed out:

> The greater portion of the day was given up to the indulgence of sordid and petty recriminations and abuse, and it was for this—this!—that we and others strove sedulously for an international expression of solidarity. We have now to regret that an epoch-making movement has been temporarily stultified by Larkin's want of good judgement,

foresight, and tact. It is only on rare occasions that principles are able to transcend personalities. In this, a great occasion, need we say that personalities came before principles.

He did not absolve Larkin's enemies within the TUC leadership of their share of blame.

It is not altogether unsafe to say that the Agenda was deliberately and consciously rigged ... What possible need was there for men ... to pass resolutions congratulating one another? ... One is reminded of a mutual admiration society, where the almost unanimous opinions were confidence in and praise of one another, and extended denunciation of Larkin.

Unlike Connolly, who saw the London conference as a retreat into sectionalism, Williams wrote that

in spite of the fact that the main decision of the Conference was cowardly, in that it refused to accept its further obligation to settle the Dublin dispute, we are not without hope for the Future. The conference has established a precedent in industrial warfare. Although we move slowly, we do move. We are gradually forsaking the politics of the parish pump and are beginning to realise more and more that our industrial concepts must not be that of the shoemaker sticking to his last, nor, as Mr. Thomas and Mr. Williams of the Railwaymen would have it, the guard thinking only of his brake van and the signalman of his cabin and levers. A large and steadily-growing section of the rank and file are realising the interdependence of the modern labour movement. The members of their Unions, by their constant association with the machine process, know better than the officials that sectional Unionism must give way to the greater Class Unionism.[21]

*

The differences between Connolly and Williams, however, were not just about who was specifically to blame for the failure of the London conference, or whether sectionalism or class unity was in the ascendant within the trade union movement. The British trade union leaders did not have to be told of the need for greater working-class unity: the question was how to achieve it. Very few subscribed to Connolly's view that 'the whole force of organised labour should stand behind each organisation in each and all its battles, [so] that no company, battalion or brigade should henceforth be allowed to face the enemy alone.' It sounded fine, but that way led to permanent turmoil and potential revolution. Despite the barricade rhetoric of some union leaders, few within the ranks of the TUC subscribed to that school of thought. Experience had demonstrated unequivocally that the sympathetic strike did not work. According to Board of Trade strike statistics, unions were completely or partially successful in 79 per cent of disputes during 1913, but won only 5 per cent of those where sympathetic strike tactics were used.

It was hardly surprising that they looked to the solution Connolly scorned so much: promoting unity through amalgamation and organisational reform of the movement. They put their faith in the rules and regulations that Connolly denounced as 'fetters' on the revolutionary potential of the working class. As Bob Smillie of the Miners' Union had pointed out to such effect, it was those 'fetters' that had enabled his own federation to vote £1,000 a week to the Dublin strikers.

If Robert Williams represented a political and ideological 'half-way house' between traditional trade unionism and the full-blown syndicalism of Larkin and Connolly, Smillie was the thinking man's amalgamationist. At a Triple Alliance conference of miners, railwaymen and transport workers in April 1914 he spelt out the case against blind support for spontaneous militancy. While all three groups of workers had 'achieved a great deal by ... industrial struggles,' it had been at the expense of considerable suffering and privation.

> A strike on the railway system immediately affects the miners and transport workers, as well as others. Though these for the moment may not have any quarrel with their respective employers, yet within days they are ... idle and ... are thrown upon the funds of their unions ... When the miners struck in 1912 the cost to the railwaymen alone was about £94,000. Whenever any one of these three great sections have struck the others have had to stand by and suffer in silence.

Smillie did not advocate a formal amalgamation of the existing federations for miners, transport workers and rail workers but 'ways and means of working in common and so avoiding the evils of disjointed action.' The Triple Alliance would not mean that every time 'one section of the miners determines to strike they will receive the assistance of the new alliance. Action is to be confined to joint national action,' and

> no action will be taken until all three partners have met in conference and have agreed upon the course to be adopted. Sympathetic action, in fact, is no longer to be left to the uncontrolled emotions of a strike period, but is to be the calculated result of mature consideration and careful planning.[22]

This strategy was the one finally adopted by the alliance; and, far from using the sympathetic strike to bring the capitalist system crashing down, it proposed using it to transform the system gradually from within. Put in simple terms, it was British gradualism versus Irish impetuosity. The leaders of the syndicalist republic on the Liffey would not be allowed to rush the much bigger, more experienced and sober-minded TUC unions into an open-ended class war to the death. Events between 1910 and 1912 had taught them otherwise.

39

THE British trade unions had 'absolutely and emphatically repudiated' Larkin, a relieved *Irish Times* leader-writer crowed on Wednesday. 'Even Mr. Ben Tillet has turned against the folly and violence of the Celtic syndicalists.' The paper admitted that 'the question of reinstatement' remained an obstacle to peace but declared loftily that 'the reinstatement difficulty has never killed a strike settlement.' The dispute was capable of immediate resolution by men of good will. What this meant in practice was that the Dublin workers, if they wanted peace, 'must ... leave Mr. Larkin to his own devices.'[1]

Larkin and Connolly put the best face they could on their defeat. Larkin told the crowd in Glasgow the night before:

There is a great deal of humbug spat out by gentlemen who want jobs. Who are the men said to represent three million trade unionists? They are ... paid officials. The question at issue is the future of Labour in Great Britain. There is in the womb of labour a new birth, but foul abortionists have destroyed ... what should have been the greatest movement to bring under one control the whole forces of labour.

He promised his listeners that 'if I go down I will go down hand in hand with those I am fighting for.' At Edinburgh the following night he warned that

if Dublin goes down, everywhere goes down. All the leaders have said this, and yet some of them are out to pull Dublin down and degrade her.[2]

Connolly had referred to the TUC's betrayal as rejecting the 'sacramental wafer of brotherhood and common sacrifice.' The language they used betrayed the common confessional inheritance of the two Dublin strike leaders. Connolly quite deliberately conjured up nationalist emotions when he told workers in Beresford Place on Wednesday 10 December that 'Irishmen have been smashed up by Englishmen before, but they have always come up smiling.' The men who had 'framed the agenda for the London conference have made a mistake, and the evil consequences of their actions will set the labour movement back for at least the next ten years.' They had insisted on putting motions of confidence in English trade unions before discussing the 'Dublin trouble', which was the object of the conference. The English workers remained 'their brethren heart and soul,'

Connolly told the crowd; but he now numbered the TUC leadership with Ireland's enemies.

Returning to the dispute itself, Connolly confirmed bluntly that reinstatement had become the primary issue, rather than union recognition. Any settlement must ensure that 'not a single man, woman or child would be victimised.' He believed a settlement of the dispute was possible 'before Christmas,' if another conference could be arranged with the employers. But he did not suggest it was likely; instead he tried to cheer the crowd with the prospect January offered of an 'opportunity for regenerating the city and advancing another step towards industrial and political freedom by electing our own men to the Municipal Council.'[3] Only Connolly could have thought that such a simultaneously distant, challenging and chilling vista could warm the cockles of the heart.

*

It was understandable, given Connolly's public persona, that people did not warm to him. But there was a more human side to the man, as recently uncovered documents in the Guinness Archive reveal. On Friday 12 December, Connolly rang the brewery and asked to speak to one of the directors. Ernest Guinness took the call. He reported later that Connolly had asked the company to reconsider the 'slight trouble existing between us' over the dismissal of the six boatmen in October who had refused to handle 'tainted' goods. Two of the men in particular, Edward McCarthy, a boat skipper, and Patrick Donegan, who had come out in sympathy with him, had nearly forty years' service and had sixteen children between them. Connolly told Guinness that he was 'very wishful of having a Christmas gift of peace to people, and … he was very anxious that the port should now open.'

Ernest Guinness appears to have been a sympathetic enough listener for Connolly to follow up the conversation with a letter containing tentative proposals for a general settlement of the 'unfortunate dispute in Dublin.' Writing with the authority of the union's General Committee, Connolly said the ITGWU was lifting the embargo imposed on Guinness's goods

> as the result of the dismissal of a few of your men. Without at all making it a condition of our action, we desire to suggest to you that if your firm could see their way to the reinstatement of the six men in question, the act would help greatly to straighten out the tangle on the quays, and thus clear the way for the final greater settlement now being sought by all parties concerned.

It was an appeal to the heart very different from Connolly's usual platform utterances. The matter was considered serious enough to be referred to Lord Iveagh, and Ernest Guinness told his father that the situation was 'very hard on the [dismissed] men.' However, Lord Iveagh decided there would be no reinstatement: the example must stand, as a warning to others. Consequently, Colonel H. Renny-Tailyour wrote back to Connolly thanking him for 'the courteous tone of your communication' but reiterating the company's position that, while having no objection to employees being members of 'any Trades Union,' it reserved the right to dismiss them for 'insubordination'.[4]

With its access to Shipping Federation vessels and labour, by courtesy of the coal importers, Guinness's could afford to take such a stance. Indeed the company's vast resources allowed it to consider for this first time acquiring its own fleet of specialised tankers, to leave it less vulnerable to similar disputes in the future.[5]

Connolly, undeterred at his lack of success with the brewery, wrote a number of similar conciliatory letters to various shipping lines. He suggested that ITGWU members could return to work subject to only one proviso, that they would not handle any goods belonging to Jacob's biscuit factory.[6]

Connolly was desperately trying to prevent a defeat on the quayside from becoming a rout. Almost all the main shipping lines were operating a relatively normal service by the weekend. On Friday morning even the ITGWU members at the LNWR terminal had returned to work alongside NUR members and the strike-breakers who were bringing goods for shipment. The *Irish Times* reported: 'There was a complete absence of picketing and ... so far as the work of the port was concerned, it would be practically resumed in its entirety if the City of Dublin Steam Packet Company were in a position to sail their fleet of steamers.'[7] The company was in the unfortunate position of not yet having been readmitted to the fold of the Shipping Federation. While the NSFU had agreed a formula for returning to work, the union's Dublin crews were still refusing to accept it; and without access to the federation's 'free labourers', the company remained strike-bound.

Nevertheless the Shipping Federation members in Dublin met to consider the proposals outlined in Connolly's letter on Monday. The *Irish Times* went as far as to hail it as 'a wise, if belated, communication.' Connolly had gone 'a long way to conceding that the strike in the port is practically over.'

Hopes of peace were short-lived. Even at the City of Dublin line, where the men optimistically marched back in a body wearing the union's Red Hand badge on the strength of the Connolly letter, there was no settlement. Stuck as it was with continuing unofficial action by the NSFU men, the company presented the dockers with a form requiring them to load all goods tendered for transit and to give a month's notice of further industrial action. They refused, and returned to Liberty Hall.[8]

A request from the other shipping lines for clarification of Connolly's terms coincided with Larkin's return to the city, and in the afternoon he told the shipping lines in no uncertain terms that 'the strike is not half over.' His temper cannot have improved on discovering that his landlord had been given a decree that very morning to repossess the upstairs rooms of the house he rented in Auburn Street. Larkin had not paid the rent of 9s a week since 18 August. It could have been worse: the landlord had sought repossession of the whole building, but the ITGWU's solicitor had managed to have the order modified.

The consequences of sympathetic strikes were now being revisited with a vengeance on Liberty Hall. Connolly had pulled out the dockers to seal Dublin 'tight as a drum' in order to force employers such as Murphy and Jacob to the negotiating table. Most employers, including the shipping companies, now appeared willing to reinstate their employees, but Jacob's and the DUTC refused to budge. The dockers therefore had to stay out, and while the City of Dublin steamers lay idle at the North Wall as a result, Jacob's goods were being loaded at the nearby LNWR berth by NUR and ITGWU members. In fact the LNWR put on extra trains to handle the backlog of work.

On the south quays the situation was even worse. ITGWU dockers had begun discharging 3,000 tons of malting barley for Guinness's, in line with Connolly's peace initiative of the previous Friday, while carters left the union in order to return to work with contractors transporting the grain to James's Street.[9]

*

Despite the disarray of the ITGWU, the city's business community cannot have been happy at the contribution the dispute was making to the ineluctable atmosphere of violence that now gripped not alone Dublin but the whole country. Following a meeting of the Privy Council on 4 December, a royal proclamation had been issued reviving the ban on the importing of arms into Ireland. On the day after the TUC special conference in London, customs officers began intensive searches of ships and passengers bound for Belfast. Unionists denounced the move as a further threat to their civil liberties, while many other passengers treated the exercise as a joke until it proved disturbingly fruitful. On Thursday two cases containing fifty rifles and bayonets were seized in Heysham, Lancashire, bound from the Birmingham Small Arms Company for an address in Omagh. On Friday a consignment of 250 Continental rifles of 'recent design' were intercepted at the York Dock in Belfast as they were unloaded from the *City of Frankfort*, and several more cases of 'modern pattern' rifles were intercepted at Liverpool.[10]

Dublin too had its gunmen. On Thursday the business community was shocked at the news that one of the city's leading shipbrokers, John Hollwey, vice-chairman of Dublin Port and Docks Board and a member of Dalkey Urban District Council, had been shot in a street affray between a 'free labourer' and strikers. The incident occurred at about 5:30 p.m. when a group of men ambushed a cart belonging to the building firm of G. and P. Glorney in Poolbeg Street. The driver, James Lewis, drew a revolver and fired at a man who jumped on the back of the cart. The bullet missed the assailant and creased Hollwey's forehead; he managed to stagger into Mulligan's public house before he collapsed. Lewis was immediately taken into custody and held over the weekend. Another strike-breaker was taken into custody by the DMP on Saturday after firing shots in Sheriff Street.[11]

On Sunday the infection of violence spread to Cork. A meeting in the City Hall to found a local corps of the Irish Volunteers ended in fisticuffs and broken heads after Eoin MacNeill had asked the crowd to give three cheers for Sir Edward Carson. A more broad-minded assembly had obliged at the launch of the Volunteers in Galway, but on this occasion Professor MacNeill's request

> had an extraordinary effect upon the audience. The people became terribly excited, stood up on their seats, and roared themselves hoarse, hissing, groaning and uttering threats at the speaker, who blandly smiled.

Soon 'several men of powerful physique started to throw chairs at the speaker, and placed the reporters who were seated at the Press table beneath him in such an utterly untenable position that they had to beat a hasty retreat.' The chairman of the meeting, J. J. Walsh, who was also chairman of the GAA county board, was felled, and another platform member, Roger Casement, was jostled before the uproar subsided. The assailants appeared to be mainly Hibernians, who then left the hall in a body.[12]

Southern unionists must have found the violent ambiguities of nationalism disturbing. There was nothing ambiguous, however, about another Unionist by-election victory in Lanark at the weekend. Once again a large Liberal majority had been destroyed in a Scottish stronghold of radicalism. Again, intervention by a Labour candidate had ensured defeat for the government. 'The Ulster crisis has broken Scotland's adherence to the Radical tradition,' the *Irish Times* wrote. 'If Liberalism is not safe in a Scottish constituency … it is not safe anywhere.' As for the decisive Labour intervention, this showed that the dislike of socialists for the home rule government 'was a more powerful motive than the platonic affection which they are supposed to cherish for the Home Rule Bill.'[13]

The *Irish Times* was perhaps reading more into the by-election than the result warranted; its analysis of events in Cork was more perceptive.

> Irishmen are sometimes puzzled by the contradictions of their own politics. It is no wonder that British statesmen are so frequently disconcerted and disappointed by them. Mr. Birrell's one idea in the Government of Ireland is to gratify Mr. Redmond. With that object he has just prohibited the importation of arms into this country. He expected a paean of Nationalist applause for this blow at Ulster. Instead, he finds himself exceedingly unpopular. Ulster merely smiled at his edict; Nationalist Ireland resents it as an act of Saxon tyranny. It has crippled the operations of the new Nationalist Volunteers, who now find themselves without weapons, while Ulster appears to be well supplied. The incident will intensify Mr. Birrell's natural cynicism. Now the Irish

Volunteers have given him further cause for astonishment.

The response of the 'mixed audience of Nationalists—Hibernians, Redmondites and O'Brienites'—to Professor MacNeill's 'eulogy of the military movement in Ulster' was 'enthusiastic, but embarrassing.'

The remarkable thing about this incident is not that Professor McNeill's courageous request was so fiercely resented, but that he made it quite seriously, and that his catholic views about the armament movement in this country are shared by some other—perhaps, many educated—and enthusiastic Irishmen. Professor McNeill spoke at Cork for the advanced guard of the Gaelic League and for the 'Sinn Fein' party ... He sees in the Ulster Volunteer movement a declaration of independence against the British government in Ireland. He admires the high-spirited and resolute action of the men of Ulster. He wishes to infect the loquacious and excitable South with the same spirit of resolution. He wants all the manhood of Ireland to act together against what he regards as the common enemy. It is a bold and, in some respects, an alluring appeal. The call to arms is always attractive to the youth of a generous people.

However disconcerting, and even dangerous, the present spirit of militarism in Ireland may be, we all feel that it indicates ... the existence of a living patriotism. There is also an element of nobility in Professor McNeill's ideal of a united Ireland. It was for these reasons, no doubt, that, as he tells us, the young Nationalists of Galway gave three cheers for the Ulster Volunteers. But Professor McNeill and his friends are victims of at least three grave delusions.

The first is that the new Irish Volunteers want to co-operate with Sir Edward Carson. Their charter, promulgated last month at the inaugural meeting in the Rotunda states distinctly that the Unionist Party proposes to defeat Home Rule by 'the menace of armed violence,' and that the object of the Irish Volunteers is 'to take such measures as will effectively defeat this policy.' Professor McNeill seems to have forgotten his own manifesto.

His second delusion is, or, rather, was—that all Irish Nationalists share his admiration for the courage of Ulster and his desire for real national unity. That delusion was killed at Cork by the shouts and blows of the Ancient Order of Hibernians.

Professor McNeill's third and most fatal delusion consists in his entire misconception of the meaning and spirit of the Ulster Volunteer Movement. [Ulster] claims only to exercise her rights and enjoy her privileges under the Constitution of the United Kingdom. This we take to be a sound definition of Imperialism; it cannot be reconciled in any way with Professor McNeill's definition of nationalism. He would defy, and get rid of, all English political parties and all the influences of British government. Ulster's claim is to continue to be identified with British government. Ulster's ... present protest is against the unconstitutional tyranny of a particular British Government which seeks to impose its will upon her without the sanction of the people of England, Scotland, and Ireland. Professor McNeill's ideal of a self-contained and isolated Ireland is as hateful to the Ulster Unionists as it is, for very different reasons to Mr. Devlin's Hibernians.[14]

And yet southern unionists appear to have found the 'new' nationalism represented by the Irish Volunteers far less repellent than the old. When the MP for Galway North, Richard Hazleton, a rural radical, issued a public warning after the Cork affray for his constituents to keep MacNeill's movement at arm's length, the *Irish Times* took him, Redmond and Devlin to task for reducing nationalism to 'a mean sordid thing, concerned only with the lowest forms of political intrigue.' In the columns of the *Freeman's Journal*, Hazleton had denounced the folly of forming an armed movement in defiance of the British government's arms proclamation as 'ill-considered and muddle headed.' The *Irish Times* conceded that the Volunteers might be muddle-headed but said that the position of home-rulers such as himself was politically and morally bankrupt. Hazleton preferred a situation where,

> if Ulster must be crushed by force, the British Army will do it. It is to be the servant *ad hoc* of the men who cheered its defeats in South Africa. There is no need, therefore, for the youth of Nationalist Ireland to excite itself in the matter.
>
> From one point of view Mr. Hazleton is quite right. Mr. Redmond has made a bargain with the Government, and we suppose that the shooting down of Ulstermen, if that course should become necessary, is implied in the bargain ... Nevertheless, we doubt whether these teachings of common prudence will be very palatable to our young fellow-countrymen of the South and West. They mark a dramatic departure from the old ideals of Irish Nationalism. For Unionists those ideals were always tainted by an unreasoning bitterness against England. The rhetoric about 'the blood-stained Saxon shilling' was as foolish as it was false. But there was, after all, a breadth of vision and a strong spirit of patriotism in the ideals of Thomas Davis and his generation. For him all Irishmen were brothers. He was proud of the traditions and qualities of Ulster ... The young Nationalists of to-day seem to be sufficiently old-fashioned to cling to the theories of Thomas Davis. The idea of their Volunteer movement may be foolish, but it is not an ignoble folly. For them Ireland is still one family, and they want to keep this quarrel with Ulster a family matter. Mr. Redmond and his party have got well beyond that sentimental stage.

The *Times* was obviously delighted at any opportunity to embarrass the home rule leadership, but it had nailed the fatal weakness within the Redmondite position as accurately as it had that of MacNeill three days earlier. It described the Irish Party as 'the staunchest and most self-suppressing wing of the English Radical Coalition.' It told readers: 'There is no honour, no patriotism, no generosity in official Nationalist politics.'[15]

*

Few nationalists would have read, and fewer accepted, the verdict from Westmorland Street. They could argue that fisticuffs were unfortunately part of the rough and tumble of Irish politics; but with the country on a hair trigger, most Protestant employers in Dublin must have found the mood of the *Irish Times* leader-writers self-indulgently and dangerously whimsical. Besides, the Citizen Army that was now parading regularly through the streets of the city could not be endowed with the generosity of spirit of the Volunteers, at least not towards the property-owning classes. On Tuesday five thousand men spent the morning marching from Liberty Hall by different routes to Croydon Park. When they arrived, about a thousand were put through various military evolutions by Captain White and then marched in review past Larkin and Connolly. Ironically, the only violence recorded in the city that day came when a man entered the printing works where the *Irish Worker* was produced in Stafford Street and smashed a considerable quantity of type with a hammer. Apparently he objected to an article in the previous edition by the poet and writer James Stephens, who had called on the clergy to 'come down off that fence' in the dispute and learn that 'their business is not Mammon but God.' When a DMP constable arrived on the scene the man gave his name and was allowed to leave without being charged.[16]

Again, the contrast in the way different classes of lawbreakers were treated was not lost on the workers. That night in Beresford Place there were cries for arms. Larkin told the crowd that 'scabs' were not the only ones who could carry revolvers through the streets.

> Wait for a short time and you will be fully armed; and we'll see then who'll resist us. (Cheers.) We're at the start of a great fight, and when we have our brigades organised, we will control … all the means of wealth, so that the workers and the producers shall share equally in the wealth of the world.

Robert Williams, back in the city as part of a new TUC delegation trying to settle the dispute, gave a more prosaic promise. He said there would be no settlement until the embargo had been removed on the ITGWU and all the men reinstated. This would prove as unattainable as Larkin's grander design.[17]

The presence in the city of Williams and the other members of the Joint Labour Board was a reminder of the continuing imperative for a settlement. Business sources had told the *Irish Times* that the strike was still costing about £200,000 a week in lost income. The TUC was also saddled with the obligation of continuing financial support for the strikers, which was now running at over £10,000 a month; and even strike leaders like Larkin knew that this largesse would not continue indefinitely in the wake of the delegate conference dog-fight.[18]

It was not surprising, therefore, that both Dublin Trades Council and the Dublin Employers' Federation replied with some alacrity to an initiative from the Lord Mayor, Lorcan Sherlock, to resume talks. First, the Joint Labour Board, in keeping with the remit of the London conference, called together a meeting in Dublin of all the unions affected by the dispute, to be held in the Trades Council hall in Capel Street. All forty unions were invited to send three delegates each, regardless of the number of members directly involved in disputes with employers. Most of the unions involved were British, and Dublin employers hoped that their head offices would follow the lead of the NUR and NSFU in seeking a settlement regardless of the interests of the ITGWU. Their hopes proved ill-founded. When the hundred or so delegates turned up on Tuesday 17 December they agreed that full reinstatement of the workers in dispute remained the primary demand.[19]

On Wednesday afternoon the sub-committee mandated to present the workers' case to the employers met again at the Trades Council hall to draft more detailed proposals for peace. It took just two-and-a-half hours for them to agree a formula for returning to work. It contained four clauses. The first called for the withdrawal of the employers' agreement requiring workers to renounce the ITGWU. The second said that, in return, the unions would agree 'to abstain from any form of sympathetic strike, pending a Board of Wages and Conditions of Employment being set up by March 17th, 1914.' The third stated that no union member 'shall be refused employment on the grounds of his or her association in the dispute, and that no stranger shall be employed until all the old workers are re-engaged.' The fourth clause proposed that 'all cases of old workers not re-employed on February 1st, 1914, shall be considered at a conference to be held on February 15th, 1914.'[20] This represented a considerable movement from the union position of less than a fortnight earlier, when the immediate reinstatement of all the workers was sought and Connolly had refused to give the employers' representatives an unconditional commitment to suspend the use of the sympathetic strike weapon.

Any illusions that Larkin might accept the new concessions were destroyed when the *Daily Herald* published an appeal from him next morning calling on the 'rank and file' to repudiate 'a black and foul conspiracy' by the TUC to betray Dublin. 'Get busy, rebels in branches and lodges, and send us help direct at once. We will not bend.'[21]

There had always been direct contributions to the Trades Council strike fund, and these did increase following Larkin's appeal. Up to the end of November over £1,125 had been sent directly to the Trades Council, of which almost half came from the Co-Operative Bricklayers' Society in London. But in the next two weeks a further £1,700 was contributed by local union branches and trades councils in Ireland and Britain. Of this, £327 came from *Daily Herald* collections and another £161 from Cork Trades and Labour Council.[22] Yet, significant as these amounts were, only the continued support of the TUC 'traitors' could sustain the dispute.

*

Larkin's appeal did not augur well for the conference that opened in the Shelbourne Hotel, Dublin, on 18 December; nor did reports of more revolver shots in the city. The worst incident occurred as coal was being delivered to St Mark's Church in Great Brunswick Street (Pearse Street). A crowd made up primarily of women started shouting abuse at the strike-breakers and then grabbed coal scattered in the roadway as the frightened horse galloped off with its load. One of the men, Patrick Traynor, fired two shots at the crowd before the police intervened. A sixteen-year-old member of the Irish Women Workers' Union, Alice Brady, was hit in the wrist. Traynor was arrested.[23]

By now talks between the employers and union leaders had been under way at the Shelbourne Hotel for almost four hours. There must have been a sense of déjà vu about the proceedings, as most of the participants had attended the talks that collapsed in the early hours of Sunday 7 December. Even James Seddon managed to rise from his sick-bed and travel to Dublin to complete the trade union team. The only significant addition to the union representatives was Larkin. Across the table were familiar old adversaries, such as the master builder John Good, the wholesale book and newspaper distributor Charles Eason, the chairman of the master carters, John Wallis, the biscuit manufacturer George Jacob, and, of course, William Martin Murphy.

Direct discussions between the Dublin men was, however, limited. The negotiations were to prove rather like those of 6 December in reverse: they began with direct discussions between the strike committee and the Employers' Federation but were quickly replaced by indirect negotiations. As the hours drifted by, these in turn were reduced to written communications, with members of the Joint Labour Board conveying the views of each side to the other at an ever decelerating rate of shuttle diplomacy.[24]

It was left to Thomas McPartlin, president of the Trades Council, to open the workers' case, as Larkin and Connolly did not arrive until 11:15 a.m. and then decided to remain in a separate room with other ITGWU members for much of the time. When Larkin did attend the discussions it was to 'brush aside' Henderson, 'emphatically vetoing all suggestions by way of compromise,' according to employer sources.

The TUC record gives a somewhat different view: it shows the talks degenerating into a procedural wrangle.[25] The employers refused to entertain the unions' formula for a return to work and insisted that negotiations could only resume on the issue over which they had broken down almost a fortnight earlier: reinstatement. They wanted the most difficult issue resolved first. It is hard to see why they opted for this course, unless it was to force a breakdown in the negotiations.

Throughout the two-and-a-half days of negotiations that followed they would not budge from their position. They not only refused to give 'any approximate idea' of the number of trade union workers they would take back, even by the proposed Trades Council deadline of 1 February, but insisted on their right to retain suitable 'free labourers' recruited during the dispute. The union negotiators then tried to obtain a commitment based on Murphy's suggestion in his letter of 15 November that 'there are not more than five per cent of the men out of employment who may not return.' This also was not forthcoming.

The one important concession offered by the employers was that 'no worker shall be refused employment on the ground that he is a member of any particular trade union.' This meant that the formal ban on the ITGWU, the original cause of the lockout, was being withdrawn. In fact, as we have seen, most employers had never required their workers to sign the document of 19 July and had opted for a simpler declaration aimed at combating the sympathetic strike.

The abandonment of formal attempts to withdraw recognition from the ITGWU was of little value, however, if informal victimisation of union activists could still take place. In some respects the situation was worse than before, as victimisation might now apply to activists in other unions, locked out because of their support for the ITGWU. To agree a return to work and a suspension of the sympathetic strike weapon without guarantees on reinstatement would allow hard-line employers to victimise militants without even the threat of retaliatory sanctions being available.

And yet it is hard to believe that the gap could not have been bridged if there had been a willingness on both sides to do so. The employers could have agreed to fix a reinstatement target and included a formal non-victimisation clause in the return-to-work formula. The unions could have offered to extend the date for reinstatement and given stronger commitments not to engage in sympathetic strikes.

Instead the talks remained stalled on the reinstatement issue through Thursday and Friday, finally collapsing in the usual wave of mutual recrimination at 1 p.m. on Saturday. The TUC report subsequently blamed the employers unequivocally for the breakdown, but an unguarded remark by the Labour Party chairman, Tom Fox, on leaving the Shelbourne Hotel on Saturday afternoon probably summed up the real feelings of the British delegates. 'Neither side wants a settlement,' he told the *Irish Times*. 'They are both pugnacious. They are going to fight it out—there is no doubt about that.'

They did not disappoint. Within a few hours, employers and unions had given long recitals of each other's sins. Coghlan, for the Employers' Federation, cited Larkin's manifesto in the *Daily Herald* as conclusive evidence 'on the part of some at least of the workers' representatives [of] no real intention to seek a settlement.' For the Trades Council, McPartlin said that the federation's proposal to leave 'the question of re-employment … entirely to the … vindictiveness, the passions and the prejudices of the employers, who four months ago set out to starve us … back into slavery,' was unacceptable. 'The fight must go on.'[26]

The problem was that the British union leaders had no stomach left for a fight. It was their last attempt to resolve the Dublin dispute. Henderson had responded quickly to Larkin's appeal to the British 'rank and file' on the eve of the talks with a statement of unity issued on behalf of the TUC delegates and the Trades Council strike committee. But the employers had seen for themselves the bad blood between the two men at the meetings in the Shelbourne. They were also probably well aware by now of Dr Walsh's estimate of the depths to which relations between Larkin and the British leaders had sunk. At the same time, at least some of the more thoughtful employers, such as Edward Lee, must have been wondering whether total victory was either desirable or necessary. It is hard to dispute the view that the conflict was being driven by the hard-liners to what one historian of the dispute has described as 'a Carthaginian peace.'[27]

*

All that was left to the strike leaders was pugnacity, and that was something that Larkin, Connolly and their followers possessed in abundance. The Citizen Army continued to drill in Croydon Park, and dispensed rough justice to strike-breakers with hurleys. Carts continued to be attacked on the streets, and even some of the ITGWU dockers who had returned to work engaged in guerrilla tactics, refusing to unload cargoes for particularly objectionable employers, such as Jacob's and Shackleton's mills. Vessels belonging to the City of Dublin Steam Packet Company and to the smaller G. and J. Burns Line, which ran a ferry service to Glasgow, remained idle because of the refusal by members of the NSFU to obey union instructions to return to work. The Palgrave Murphy line also continued to be strike-bound, until the company's clerks undertook to do the dockers' work or face being sacked themselves.

Elsewhere in the port the 'free labourers' kept traffic moving.[28] Connolly now singled these out for special mention in the *Irish Worker* in terms not unlike those used to describe the Black and Tans a few years later.

During the progress of the present dispute we have seen imported into Dublin some of the lowest elements from the lowest depths of the criminal population of Great Britain and Ireland: this scum of the underworld have come here excited by appeals to the lowest instincts of their natures; these appeals being ... made by the gentlemen employers of Dublin. They have been incited to betray their fellows fighting against the imposition of an agreement denounced by the highest court of inquiry, as well as by public opinion ... as an interference with individual liberty ... To induce these Judases their lowest passions were catered to by the offer of wages higher than were ever paid to union men, and by the permission and encouragement to carry murderous weapons. Too much stress cannot be laid upon this latter encouragement. There are natures so low that permission to carry about the means whereby life may be destroyed has to them an irresistible appeal; the feeling that they carry in their pockets the possibility of destroying others has to these base creatures an intoxication all its own. To that feeling the employers of Dublin appealed. Deliberately, and with malice aforethought, they armed a gang of the lowest scoundrels in these islands, and after daily inflaming them with drink, sent them to and fro in the streets of the capital ... maddening all those upon whose liberties they were helping to make war. In one of those streets on Thursday afternoon, this cold-blooded policy of incitement to outrage had its effect. A few men jeered at the passing scabs and made a show of hostility. Immediately a scab drew a revolver, fired—and shot one of the employers principally responsible for bringing him here, and principally responsible for arming him and setting him loose, primed with drink, upon the streets of Dublin. That action of the employer in importing and arming such a scoundrel was a crime—an anti-social crime of the foulest nature—and surely never more dramatically did a crime bring its own punishment.[29]

In the same article, Connolly warned the British government, 'Landlords, ex-Crown Lawyers, ex-Ministers of the Crown, aspirants to be Ministers of the Crown, Ministers of the Gospel, smug-sweating capitalists and dear ladies living upon the sweated toil of poor women' that the Transport Union was organising its own 'regiments' to oppose them and was 'progressing nightly' in the task. Following the Citizen Army's example, the 'volunteer forces throughout Nationalist Ireland, and the young stalwart men who have ever cherished high dreams for Erin, commenced to learn the rudiments of drill.'

The militant mood on the streets cannot have been assuaged by the news that the two men who shot Bridget Rowe had been released. It seemed that the man who wounded the shipbroker John Hollwey would also escape unscathed; once his injuries were ascertained to be relatively minor, the initial zeal to prosecute James Lewis vanished, and the DMP corroborated his claim that he had been set upon and severely beaten on the same street three weeks earlier. He was released into the custody of his employer on a surety of £25. There was no sign of any urgency to prosecute Patrick Traynor, the strike-breaker who shot Alice Brady, though she had developed complications.

Even a strike-breaker who fired two shots for no apparent reason at pickets in Sheriff Street, and had been about to discharge a third when he was arrested, was only fined £2. Another strike-breaker who fired on a crowd that pelted him with 'cabbage stalks and stones' was ordered to find a surety of £20. In contrast, an ITGWU member before the same magistrate for tripping up a DUTC cleaner was imprisoned for a month, and another striker, arrested for stoning a tram in Talbot Street, received a month's imprisonment with hard labour.[30] Connolly's inflammatory language and exhortations to drill no doubt incited some of the violence on the streets, but without the gun-happy 'free labourers' and class-biased courts there would have been no drilling in the first place.

40

DUBLINERS were surprised by the collapse of the peace talks. 'The citizens were so anxious that the strike should be settled before Christmas that they had almost dismissed the possibility of failure,' said the *Irish Times*. 'Dublin is doomed to continued war for a reason of this one difficulty of reinstatement.'

Like the employers, Sir John Arnott's newspaper blamed this 'cruel … almost criminal' situation on 'Mr. Larkin's susceptibilities.' It suggested that, before agreeing to continue financing the struggle, the TUC leaders should at least demand a ballot of the strikers to 'satisfy themselves that the Dublin workers want the strike to be maintained.' While giving no credit to the union leaders, the newspaper, as always, was reluctant to see the men starved back; such a solution

> would furnish no guarantee against another and, perhaps, even fiercer conflict in the near future. It would embitter relations between our middle and lower classes, and would kill many of our brightest hopes of social reform.

Whatever the future held, the *Times* predicted that 'for thousands of Dublin workers the Christmas festival will be a cheerless season of hope deferred.' But this thought did not inhibit the newspaper's copious coverage of the shopping delights of Brown Thomas's, Andrews and Company, Switzer's, Barnardo's, and McBirney's.[1] In fact Christmas week was characterised by particularly wretched meanness towards the strikers. On Sunday 21 December, Lord Aberdeen demonstrated the extent of his Christmas spirit by directing that only seven prisoners serving sentences in Mountjoy for offences connected with the lockout be released on Christmas Eve; all seven were already due for release by 1 January.[2] It was a far cry from the general amnesty the special delegate conference of the TUC had sought.

William Martin Murphy had his own message for the strikers. The *Sunday Independent* published an interview with its owner on the front page in which he clarified his position on the reinstatement of the workers. The declaration in his letter of 15 November that 'there are not more than five per cent of the men out of employment who may not return, before their places are filled up, without any sacrifice of principle,' had been the subject of 'persistent and wilful misrepresentation.' What he had clearly meant was 'that not five per cent of those who could be re-employed would be asked to make any sacrifice of principles.' It was also clear that this referred to

> the condition requiring the renunciation of the Irish Transport Union, which many firms were insisting on. The five per cent in question had nothing whatever to say to the total number of workers out of employment, who could, or could not, be re-employed. Moreover I stated clearly that the men who could be re-employed at all were those whose 'places had not been filled up.'[3]

In other words, the tantalising hopes of peace entertained by Archbishop Walsh and the TUC leaders a month earlier had been based on a misconception. Murphy's clarification might have been more convincing if he had issued it immediately after the publication of his own letter on 17 November; instead it had been left to an anonymous 'Dublin Employer' to interpret it.

The front page of the *Sunday Independent* also published news that the latest peace attempt had failed. Wedged between the two stories was a cartoon entitled 'Christmas wishes,' in which Santa Claus scattered 'Good wishes' from an aircraft named *Sunday Independent*.[4] There was little danger of anyone mistaking the jolly bearded pilot for Murphy.

Nor was there much cheer on Dublin's streets next day, when a 'free labourer', Christopher O'Brien, was badly beaten and left for dead in the roadway. Such incidents discouraged some strike-breakers. On the weekend before Christmas, 150 of them left Dublin, their money made, to enjoy the festive season in a more congenial atmosphere; but 95 more came by the return sailing, and another 70 were shipped in before the new year. About 600 Shipping Federation hands worked the docks over Christmas, mainly in Alexandra Basin, which was relatively easy to protect. On the south quays there were about 200 strike-breakers, who were now co-existing with 150 returned ITGWU dockers. Elsewhere in the city another 200 strike-breakers were employed, most of whom had been recruited from the midlands.[5] But while employers seemed to have no difficulty recruiting 'free labour', the high turnover must have made it both inconvenient and expensive.

*

On Tuesday 23 December another attempt was made to evict the Larkin family from 27 Auburn Street. Larkin was out on union business at the time, and bailiffs used a ladder to force an entry through an upstairs window, after Elizabeth Larkin refused to let them in at the front door. The ITGWU solicitors managed to lodge an appeal before the family was physically ejected onto the street; but the incident may have prompted Larkin to announce unexpectedly at a strike meeting in Inchicore that evening that he would shortly be leaving for a lecture tour of America, France, and Germany.[6] Any celebrations on the part of the employers at the prospect of Larkin's departure were to prove several months premature.

In an effort to cheer supporters at home, Larkin had already threatened to rekindle his 'fiery cross' campaign in Britain. Supporters there had told the news agencies that they were planning a campaign to force a withdrawal of Labour Party support in the House of Commons for the Home Rule Bill. But employers canvassed by the *Irish Times* considered the battle won and predicted a general return to work after Christmas.[7]

Tuesday also witnessed the distribution of five thousand dolls at the Mansion House. The *Daily Sketch* had appealed to readers for dolls to distribute to the children of poor families in Britain. It received over 100,000, and the Lord Mayor, Lorcan Sherlock, who was running for re-election in January, requested that some be sent for distribution by himself in Dublin. From 11:30 a.m. on Tuesday until 3:30 p.m. in Dawson Street 'thousands of little girls were lined up in the queue system the whole length of the street.' They had been selected by 'clerical and lay friends' of the Lord Mayor from the poorer districts of the city.[8]

More essential items were in shorter supply. The families of most workers in dispute were now living on between 4s and 5s a week, together with the TUC food parcels. Women members had to get by on strike pay of 2s 6d a week. Between September and the end of the year an estimated £400,000 in wages had been lost to the city's working-class community. During the same period, £17,000 had been received from the TUC in strike pay and £50,000 in provisions; probably another £10,000 had been received in direct contributions by the Trades Council. Inevitably, small shopkeepers, tenement landlords and even pawnbrokers were 'feeling the pinch.'

And yet a few streets away the trade of the big city-centre shops seemed unaffected by the dispute. In an article on 'Shopping centre scenes,' an *Irish Times* reporter wrote:

> No stranger coming to Dublin at this time, and paying a visit to Grafton Street ... could believe that the city was beset by any deep industrial trouble. If one motor car was to be seen in Grafton Street yesterday afternoon, there must have been fifty. [Many were] of the very latest type, with resplendent bodywork and interiors, which were nests of luxury. Splendid furs, too, were to be frequently noticed, and every indication was of wealthy people out to do their Christmas shopping; left till the last minute, of course.

The leader-writer contrasted the scenes of opulence and destitution to be found within little more than a stone's throw of each other, and concluded:

> With all her religion, wealth, and charity, Dublin remains, in many essential respects, shockingly low in the scale of modern civilisation.[9]

In the circumstances, Christmas itself could not be expected to pass off peacefully. Larkin was as lacking in Christmas good will towards the enemy as Murphy. On Christmas Eve he attempted to disrupt parcel traffic in the city by calling out carters at the Post Office depot in Amiens Street. John Wallis, chairman of the Master Carters' Association, had the contract, and he had taken on extra workers to deal with the seasonal rush. Larkin may have been hoping for support from the Association of Irish Post Office Clerks, which had been threatening to strike in pursuit of a long-standing pay claim. However, the union was led by UIL activists close to William Field and Lorcan Sherlock. They criticised Larkin for attempting to drag a 'non-commercial' enterprise into the dispute, and only three workers at the sorting office, all members of the ITGWU, responded to the call. This helped confirm employers in their belief that the will to fight had gone out of the unions.

*

On Christmas Day, 'citizens of position' in the city visited the homes of the poor with presents, or helped with the traditional dinners provided by various charitable organisations. The Christian Union fed 550 men and women and the Mendicity Institution another 1,000 men, but numbers were down on previous years. Part of the reason may have been that the largest gathering of all that day was at Croydon Park. The ITGWU erected three marquees on the lawn, where as many as five thousand children may have been fed. Delia Larkin and the band of women who operated the food kitchens at Liberty Hall dispensed the food, and each departing child was given a toy and an apple or orange. When the children were finished, adults took their place. James Seddon, chairman of the TUC Parliamentary Committee, who had worked so hard to keep the food ships coming to Dublin, spent that Christmas in the city, supervising the arrangements.[10] It was a very different occasion from the summer tea party and temperance fete that had opened Croydon Park five months earlier; and few would have thought, after all that had happened, that the organiser of the Christmas treat would be the chairman of the Parliamentary Committee of the British TUC.

While the children at Croydon Park were in the middle of their Christmas dinner, a mob was stoning trams in High Street. There was also a distinctly unseasonal mood on the quays. Sergeant James Kiernan of the DMP was thrown into the Liffey after ordering a group of men away from a crane; when colleagues tried to rescue him there were angry scuffles, with onlookers, many of whom had just emerged from Mass in City Quay church, joining in. It took the police fifteen minutes to restore order and rescue McKiernan from the water. Later, twelve men were arrested in raids on tenements in the area, but they must have said little, for only two were subsequently charged. Both were ITGWU members. One was Robert Woods, a locked-out carter, who was fined £2 for breach of the peace. The other was James Montgomery, a striking labourer; he was charged with the attempted murder of McKiernan and with assaulting Constable James McGarry of the RIC while the latter was attempting to rescue the sergeant from the river. The murder charge was eventually dropped, and Montgomery received twelve months' imprisonment for the assault.[11] It did not augur well for a peaceful 1914.

41

ON Monday 29 December two hundred workers at Morgan Mooney's fertiliser plant in Alexandra Basin returned to work. They were the first large contingent of ITGWU members to abandon sympathetic strike action. Employers welcomed the news as the beginning of the end.

They were also heartened by reports that Transport Union dockers at a meeting on Sunday 28 December had criticised the handling of the dispute and had told officials that they could not survive on the reduced strike pay of 5s a week. But employer sources accepted that 'the men are breaking away from Liberty Hall in much smaller numbers than is usually the case with this class of worker.' The Morgan Mooney men had returned only with the agreement of Larkin, and it had been on the same terms and conditions that they had enjoyed before they walked off the job in early November.[1] It seemed that, if the ITGWU was not prepared to seek a general armistice, it was willing to allow members to make local settlements that provided peace with honour.

Larkin knew from his own gloomy predictions that it was only a matter of time before the financial support from Britain dried up. It was the Durham miners' MP John Wilson who first raised the issue publicly. The Miners' Federation was providing £1,000 a week to the Dublin Food Fund. Just before the new year, Wilson issued a circular to members asking how much longer the miners could be asked to subsidise Larkin's ego. Since Larkin had been released from prison by the efforts of the labour movement, Wilson told his members that he had become

> inflated with pride ... and ... threatened to stop the whole of our industries. There is no doubt but that Larkin convinced himself that he was able to bring such a thing about. He had been able to institute a strike covering the whole of Dublin, and by a process of fallacious logic ... he felt he could, with ease, extend the sympathetic strike.

Wilson denounced the sympathetic strike as

> a boomerang policy, in that the greatest suffering eventually falls on the workmen ... The strongest trades unions, with large resources within themselves, hold the strike in reserve as a last resort. How much more then a mass of unorganised or partially organised labour, who are ready to appeal to the charity of fellow-workmen and the public from the first

day of the stop. Mr. Larkin is a man brimful of energy: if he had discretion and tact commensurate he would make himself a useful man, and would save himself the regret and sorrow he is bound to feel as he looks upon the poverty and distress which is largely the result of his policy.[2]

It was hardly the sort of lecture to impress Larkin, and, far from using his discretion, he encouraged NSFU members in Dublin to continue their defiance of union instructions to return to work at the City of Dublin Steam Packet Company. When the union finally discontinued strike funds to its dissidents at the beginning of January, the Dublin strike committee adopted them. Though it could offer to pay only 5s a week, half the NSFU rate, they agreed to stay out. As secretary to the strike committee, William O'Brien promptly passed on the bill in the form of a request for an extra £80 a week from the TUC. This in turn led to enquiries to the TUC from both the NSFU and the Miners' Federation about the status of the strike fund.

When the Parliamentary Committee met on 7 January to consider the situation, its members agreed with the NSFU that the extra money was largely required to finance the union's 286 rebels in Dublin. Seddon and Gosling made a half-hearted defence of both O'Brien and John Farren, treasurer of the Trades Council, for the way they had administered the TUC funds so far; but they did not dissent from the majority view that O'Brien was seeking the extra funds to pay the NSFU dissidents. There was no real alternative for the TUC; the money was already beginning to dry up. There was only £1,500 in hand after outstanding bills were deducted. The committee decided to write to O'Brien and tell him that 'the remittances for this week would be the last one that could be forwarded to meet the strike pay of the Dublin workers unless the rank and file responded more generously than at the present time.'

It would be another month before the fund was formally wound up, but the bottom of the TUC's war chest was already in sight. When word of the decision reached Dublin next day, and it was clear that even the reduced strike pay was no longer available, the NSFU members decided to return to work.[3]

*

Trade union affairs in Dublin and London were still inextricably linked, but not the daily experience of trade unionists. Three days before the Parliamentary Committee met, the ITGWU buried its latest martyr, sixteen-year-old Alice Brady, who had died on 1 January from tetanus, two weeks after she had been shot in the wrist by a strike-breaker. The funeral was delayed because of the inquest, at which there was a strong clash of evidence between the police and strike-breakers on one side and local residents on the other about whether the gunman, Patrick Traynor, was justified in thinking his life was in danger when he fired. This was central to his defence against a threatened murder charge. He denied firing deliberately at Alice Brady, or realising she had been hit until after his arrest several minutes later. Medical evidence suggested that the bullet had indeed been a ricochet and that the tetanus infection may have been carried by it from the roadway into her hand.

Unlike the strike-breakers who shot John Hollwey and Bridget Rowe, Traynor had not been issued with his revolver by his employers but had acquired it himself from a gunsmith in the city. Small-calibre revolvers such as the one Traynor used were easily available from gunsmiths for as little as 2s 6d or 3s. After the inquest he was charged with wilful murder of the dead girl.[4] However, given the circumstances and what had happened in previous firearms cases involving strike-breakers, ITGWU members were rightly sceptical about the likely outcome of the case.

As usual, the union used the occasion of Alice Brady's funeral as a demonstration of strength. Thousands followed the cortege from her home at 21A Luke Street through the city to Glasnevin. Larkin, Connolly, Partridge, Delia Larkin and Constance Markievicz were among the mourners, as well as a contingent of five hundred members of the Irish Women Workers' Union. Larkin gave the oration, and he was uncharacteristically brief.

> It has pleased the all-wise Providence that our sister would be sacrificed on the altar of sweating misery and degradation. Though she was only a young girl she had shown great strength of character, and if she had been spared, she would, I believe, have been a great woman.

Connolly followed with an even briefer, and blunter, message. 'Every scab and every employer of scab labour in Dublin is morally responsible for the death of the young girl we have just buried.' Emotionally, the Dublin labour leaders were now operating on a very different plane from the men in the TUC's offices in London.[5]

*

Defeat had still not entered the ITGWU leaders' vocabulary, and they fastened their hopes of victory on a new mirage, the forthcoming municipal elections. As far back as November, Partridge and Connolly had been holding out the prospect of success at the polls as a way of breaking the industrial deadlock. Even at the height of his involvement with syndicalism, Connolly had never denied the primacy of politics in the class struggle. For almost twenty years he had sought an arena in which the political ground was left clear 'for the real battle of the Election betwixt the representative of the rankest Toryism and the representative of militant Social Democracy,' and always it had eluded him. Time and again, 'hundreds of men who would otherwise have voted Socialist, cast their votes reluctantly' for Liberals or nationalists 'to ensure the defeat of the Tory.' However, all the signs from the British by-elections had been that workers were at last voting for Labour candidates, even when this meant a victory in the short term for the Tories.[6]

Connolly believed that the struggles of the past four months had created conditions in which the illusions of Dublin workers about the national bourgeoisie could be destroyed. 'During the many cross-currents affecting the dispute in Dublin none are more perplexing than those caused by attempts to use the national traditions against the workers on strike,' he had written in the *Irish Worker* in November.

One would imagine that, as the great majority of the employers are Unionists ... and as the workers belong in the only militantly national organisation of labour in Ireland, the logical place of all true nationalists would be [at] the side of the locked-out workers. But if you imagine that you imagine a vain thing.

Practically every official element in Nationalist circles has striven hard all through this struggle to make capital against labour. At one time they were howling out for the workers to place their cause unreservedly in the hands of English delegates, and at another they are crying out that the English trade unions are making Dublin the cockpit of an English industrial struggle ... The Unionist Press, which denies the right of the Irish people to control their own destiny, and which insists that they are not fit to do so without the governing wisdom of the English to direct them, plays the same double game.

Connolly differentiated between the English government, which represented the master class, and English workers.

We are only concerned now with the fact—daily becoming more obvious—that the English workers, who have reached the moral stature of rebels, are now willing to assist the working class rebels of Ireland, and that those Irish rebels will, in their turn, help the rebels of England to break their chains and attain the dignity of freedom. There is still a majority of slaves in England—there are still a majority of slaves in Ireland. We are under no illusions as to either country.

For us and ours the path is clear. The first duty of the working class of the world is to settle accounts with the master class of the world— that of their own country at the head of the list. To that point this struggle is converging.[7]

What had prompted Connolly's article was the Manchester Martyrs commemoration in Dublin the previous weekend. Connolly had supported the decision by the Trades Council to participate in the parade. It had often marched in less controversial times, when any friction that arose was between rival nationalist groups for control of the committee. In 1913 the veteran Fenian Tom Clarke was chairman of the committee, and he had invited the unions, despite threats by the AOH and UIL to withdraw. Connolly saw it as an opportunity to isolate the nationalist political machine from its supporters, and he succeeded beyond expectation.

When the marchers assembled on 23 November, more than twelve thousand people participated, despite the boycott by the UIL and AOH.

The Lord Mayor, Lorcan Sherlock, and several other councillors had the political savvy to ignore the injunction from their party machine. Sinn Féin also attended, as did the usual contingents from organisations such as the Irish National Foresters, the GAA, and Fianna Éireann. But these were overshadowed by the huge Transport Union contingent. 'The whole demonstration might be described as a strike parade as those ... taking part in it outside of the Transport Workers' Union were in point of numbers of no account,' Birrell was told in an intelligence report from the DMP. The sources lamented that 'the good order which had hitherto been observed in connection with these processions did not prevail on this occasion, as on the return journey glass was broken in a number of tramcars, no doubt by the rowdies from Liberty Hall.'[8]

Connolly well knew the value of symbols, and he was as committed as any IRB man to seizing from the constitutionalists as many totems of national identity as he could. It would increase Labour's chances of extra representation on the city council and, in the process, help clear the political battleground for the final conflict between the workers and the master class in Ireland.

However, the gap between aspiration and performance proved enormous, as so often with socialist electoral campaigns. Though members of the Trades Council and the strike leaders had been talking about the coming electoral contest for two months, it was only on 12 January 1914, three days before polling and six days after the close of nominations, that the Trades Council formally endorsed ten labour candidates. It did not endorse one ITGWU member, Walter Carpenter, who was running on behalf of the Independent Labour Party of Ireland in Fitzwilliam ward. Nor did it endorse the candidature of John Lawlor, a member of the Trades Council, or William Chase, a wine merchant, both of whom ran as 'independent labour' candidates, Lawlor in Rotunda ward and Chase in Trinity ward.

The Trades Council belatedly appealed 'to the organised workers of the city to use every legitimate means in their power to secure the triumphant return of the Labour candidates, as we believe that their victory would tend towards a settlement of the present dispute and the uplifting of workers generally.' Thomas Murphy, the Carpet Planners' representative, warned his colleagues that 'considerable effort' would be required from all of them between then and polling day if the 'unscrupulous' tactics of their opponents were to be defeated.[9] But many delegates confused passing motions with electioneering and relied on what were to them the self-evident common interests of the workers with their trade union leaders to deliver seats.

One factor that undoubtedly boosted their confidence that this would happen was the proceedings of the Dublin housing inquiry. The commissioners of the Local Government Board were not to publish their findings until February, but their public hearings, begun in November, had proved highly embarrassing to the city's political establishment. The chief medical officer for the city, Sir Charles Cameron, tried to put the best face on things. 'In 8,914 of the 21,113 single-roomed tenements there is at least no overcrowding,' he told the commissioners.[10] The independent nationalist councillor Sarah Harrison had a different perspective. She told the commissioners that in the past ten years the number of people in bad housing in the city had risen from 104,251 to 118,461. Over 13,800 people lived nine or more to a room.[11]

Some of the most damning evidence came from Catholic priests who worked in the slums, such as the Franciscan Father Aloysius and Rev. T. J. Monaghan of Meath Street. Father Aloysius said that the condition of the housing in Church Street had deteriorated since the disaster in September. Father Monaghan recounted his twelve years of pastoral work in the slums of the Liberties and gave detailed descriptions of houses such as number 10 Francis Street, where 107 people had 'only two closets [toilets] to meet all sanitary needs.'[12]

It was a priest from one of the better-off districts, Rev. W. M. Farrell, who lifted the lid on political corruption in the city. He told the commission how two small tenements in Thomas Court, off Fitzwilliam Lane, had been reopened after being condemned, despite his representations to a nationalist councillor, Thomas Murty O'Beirne. O'Beirne was the owner of a temperance hotel and, more to the point, a tenement-owner himself.[13] It turned out that seventeen councillors owned or had interests in property, as had two of the city's own housing inspectors;[14] seven of these seventeen councillors would be running for re-election in January.[15] Father Farrell, who described himself as a 'strong home ruler,' had no doubt that the slums were a major factor in the city's current troubles. He could have been speaking for the Trades Council when he told the commission that 'the slum vote keeps the city in the slavery and servitude of slumdom.'[16]

One of the few members of the Trades Council to make a submission to the inquiry was Michael O'Lehane of the Drapers' Assistants; but his evidence served only to underline the different priorities of his members from those of the manual workers who comprised the great majority of the city's trade unionists. His principal complaint was not about the living conditions in the tenements but the rents in the suburbs. 'In Belfast, shop assistants have no difficulty in securing suitable houses at about £30 a year,' he said. 'The rent of houses of the same class in Dublin would range ... to £40.' He wanted a programme of local government reform introduced; this should allow for the extension of the city limits, the financing by the exchequer of low-cost housing schemes on new sites, and the introduction of cheap tram fares to enable workers to commute at reasonable expense to their places of work.[17]

Unfortunately, from the point of view of the Trades Council candidates, this was a programme to which Sinn Féin and progressive nationalist candidates could subscribe as well as their own. Indeed Lady Howth, Lady

Gormanston, Lady Fingall and other leading figures in Dublin society were so appalled at the evidence being given to the housing inquiry that they sponsored a centre for young working women, where they could socialise and find accommodation at reasonable rents between jobs. Not surprisingly, given the make-up of the committee, the centre was intended primarily for use by domestic servants.[18]

Nevertheless the nationalists entered the electoral contest as, in many people's minds, the landlords' party—and bad landlords at that. The largest slum landlord on the council was Alderman Patrick Corrigan, whose profession of undertaker gave rise to predictable jibes. All thirty-two of his properties were designated by the commission as being in the second and third, that is, the worst, categories. It also found that he was receiving rate rebates for repairs he had not carried out. The second-largest landlord was James Crozier, a vet by profession and, to the relief of the UIL, a unionist. All but one of his nineteen premises were 'in poor repair, and neglected.' The remainder of the landlords on the council were almost all nationalists and owners of properties categorised as 'very poor' and 'very decayed.' Ironically, Myles Murty O'Beirne, whose refusal to act on Father Farrell's complaints had first led to the investigation of councillors' property interests, was found to keep most of his properties 'in reasonable repair.'

The councillors concerned were no doubt relieved that their own evidence was taken immediately before the Christmas holiday, thus leaving a decent interval for the damaging newspaper reports to recede from public memory before polling day. But they did not help their cause with self-serving defences, such as corporation rules being too stringent, other cities having worse slums, or officials refusing to take account of the problems caused by bad tenants.[19]

Even the *Irish Times* accepted that the revelations changed the nature of the contest. In an editorial for the New Year it wrote: 'It matters nothing to what particular brand of Nationalism the Corporation owes allegiance if its municipal policy is to remain rotten and unchanged.' It accepted that unionist voters could not have a decisive impact on the outcome, and it urged them instead to vote for advocates of reform,

> whether Unionist, Nationalist, or Labour ... So long as the housing conditions of Dublin remain what they are, municipal reformers should regard the ownership of slum property as a disqualification for membership of the city council.

The 'same rule of exclusion should be applied to publicans, of whom already there are too many in the City Hall,' it added in a further spasm of reforming spirit.

> The problem of drunkenness is closely associated, if not quite identified, with the problem of the slums. Slum publicans cannot be slum reformers without waging war on their own interests as traders.

The voice of southern liberal unionism had 'nothing to say' about unionist candidates. 'Politics have been the curse of the Dublin Corporation ... The combination of educated Unionists and Nationalists with sincere reformers from the working class must create a new and beneficent power in Dublin.'[20]

However, the paper's appetite for full-blooded reform weakened by the time the nomination process closed on 6 January. While it accepted that 90 per cent of unionist voters 'will have to choose between voting for a Nationalist or Labour candidate and not voting at all,' it urged them, where possible, to vote for those who supported the programme of the Dublin Citizens' Association. This was a largely unionist ginger group whose manifesto emphasised the need to avoid any initiatives that might involve increases in the rates. In effect, the unionist strategy during the election was to support its own candidates and those nationalists who were least identified with the growing strength of the AOH faction; in the outlying townships of Pembroke, Rathmines and Kingstown the *Irish Times* openly advocated the re-election of Unionist councillors.[21] Its advice was as widely ignored by the voters in Kingstown as it was by those in the city, judging from the results.

*

The *Irish Worker* had no doubt what the issue was in the forthcoming election. On the front page of its first issue of the new year it ran the slogan 'Vote for labour and sweep away the slums.' The number of people 'who live in one room tenements with five or more occupants is 1,061 out of every 10,000 of the population in Dublin, but only 524 in Glasgow,' it told readers. The comparable figure for Edinburgh was 233, for London 70, and for Belfast 10.

> The houses of Dublin are infamously overcrowded ... their sanitary conditions are abominable ... Add to these the insufficient water supply, the dirty streets, the miles of uncleaned lanes and courts, the rickety stairways and murderous walls. Is it any wonder that the City Medical Officer of Health says, 'There is no city that I know ... which requires a more extensive system of housing improvement to be carried out than Dublin.'

It castigated the high death rate of the working class, and it tried to widen its appeal by warning:

> Even those who escape death from the slums still suffer from their curse. They are weakened by bad air and bad food, a prey of sickness, constantly falling out of work through weakness ... becoming paupers, dying in the end in hospital, workhouse or prison.

It did not pay the workers to tolerate such conditions, but it did pay

> the slum-owner and the publican, and so long as you elect slum owners and publicans the Corporation will make no serious attempt to get rid

of the slums. Therefore elect Labour candidates, whose interest it is to get rid of the slums. All the Labour candidates will insist on the full use of all the Corporation's present powers and will work to secure new and wide powers where necessary.

A Labour-controlled council would ensure that all streets, lanes and courts were cleaned regularly, the *Irish Worker* said. It would also demolish dangerous and insanitary buildings, force landlords to carry out repairs, take over derelict sites 'for use as gardens or for building,' provide new housing at low rents, 'and compel the Tramway Co. to give cheap workmen's fares, or else run a Municipal service so that workers can live farther away from their work.'

Inside, it published another election appeal. 'Vote for Labour and save your children's lives.'

> Every year 2,600 babies under five years of age die in Dublin. Nine out of every ten of them belong to the working class. In proportion to the population, for every baby that dies in an upper class home, and for every three babies that die in middle-class homes, no less than 14 die in the houses of labourers.

These babies died 'BECAUSE THEIR PARENTS ARE POOR.' Labour councillors would not only carry out housing reforms but would provide municipal milk, baby and school clinics, regular medical inspections for children, and school meals. They would also seek higher wages and shorter hours for as many workers as the corporation's influence could secure.[22]

The *Irish Citizen* lamented the lack of women candidates in the city but urged suffragists to support Walter Carpenter in Fitzwilliam ward. It pointed out that the ILP man was 'an associate' of the IWFL, had spoken at suffrage meetings, and had helped launch the school meals campaign in 1912.[23] Support from the *Irish Citizen* cannot have hurt Carpenter in a ward such as Fitzwilliam, which had a large middle-class vote. During the campaign he described himself as an insurance agent rather than as a union official, though how far this went towards allaying middle-class fears of an avowedly socialist candidate it is hard to judge. Carpenter made housing and municipal reform his main electoral planks.[24]

*

When nominations closed on Monday 5 January, ten 'Larkinites', as the press dubbed them, had entered the field. Despite the importance that strike leaders attached to the contest, hardly any of them were candidates. Larkin, Connolly and O'Brien all declined to run, and there were signs that the ticket was dictated more by internal Trades Council politics than by clarity of objectives. The three candidates with the highest public profile from the lockout were Thomas McPartlin of the Carpenters' Union and president of the Trades Council, P. T. Daly, secretary of the ITUC, and Thomas Foran, president of the ITGWU. McPartlin and Daly, who was also an ITGWU organiser, ran in North Dock ward; Foran ran in South Dock ward. In both areas they no doubt hoped to capitalise on the support of the dockers and other port workers. Apart from North Dock, the only other ward where two Trades Council candidates ran was Mountjoy.

Lorcan Sherlock was the target in Mountjoy ward. The Trades Council wanted to prevent his re-election if it could, but neither of its candidates was particularly well known outside trade union ranks. Arthur Murphy, who ran for alderman, was a prominent local member of the GAA and treasurer of the Tailors' Society, William O'Brien's union; the other candidate was James Campbell, secretary of the Irish Clerks' Union, a new union that admitted to having only fifty members. Campbell's candidature seemed to be as much for the purpose of recruiting clerical workers in the port as winning votes.

In North City ward the Trades Council candidate was Edward Harte, president of the Dublin Paviors' Society. In New Kilmainham, Henry Donnelly of the Society of Coachmakers had at least the merit of appealing to workers in the GSWR and to transport workers in general. Thomas Irwin, secretary of the Plasterers' Union, ran in Wood Quay. Two more craft union leaders were also nominated: Joseph Farrell of the Painters, and Andrew Breslan of the Carpenters. Despite the vaunted influence of the 'new unionism' and Larkin's 'dictatorship', six of the ten candidates endorsed by the Trades Council were leading members of craft unions; only two were members of the ITGWU, and one of these, Daly, was a former printer.[25]

*

The *Irish Worker* had at least a strategy. Besides stressing the issues of housing and health, it also published critiques of the different wings of the nationalist movement. Its issue of 3 January had made a concentrated attack on the Hibernians, and on 10 January it turned its fire on Sherlock and the more 'progressive' elements in the UIL. It paid Sherlock the compliment of a front-page cartoon, in which he was depicted attempting to whitewash a member of the DMP. Beside the beefy constable is a tombstone engraved *Sacred to the memory of Dublin citizens murdered by the police, 1913.*

Sherlock had offered himself as a suitable candidate to represent the people of Dublin on the Commission into the Dublin Disturbances. Birrell's decision to renege on his Bristol commitment to appoint a working-class representative to the inquiry into the riots had provoked widespread criticism. Even the *Irish Times* questioned his judgment; it believed that 'the police have absolutely nothing to fear' from an inquiry, which was all the more reason to have a 'really independent and impartial man' on it. It was on somewhat firmer ground when it predicted that radical nationalist and labour opponents of the Irish executive, with their 'desire to discredit the police at all costs,' would use the question of the inquiry team's composition to discredit its findings, and use them for electioneering purposes.[26]

No organ of public opinion was more outraged at Birrell's decision than the *Irish Worker.* The appointment of two Dublin barristers, Denis Henry

KC and Samuel Lombard Brown KC, as the only members of the inquiry team convinced the paper that the inquiry would indeed be a whitewash. It was a feeling widely shared. Henry was a Catholic unionist, Brown a Protestant convert to home rule. Both were perceived as lawyers whose hunger for judicial appointments was stronger than any political allegiances.

Of course it suited the *Irish Worker* to portray nationalist candidates such as Sherlock, who expressed public outrage at the composition of the commission, as secretly relieved that their own connivance at police brutality would not be investigated. This fitted in with Connolly's strategy of winning votes by proving that the only real nationalists were in the labour movement. When the inquiry began on Monday 5 January, the closing day for local government nominations, Larkin called on workers to boycott its hearings. They responded enthusiastically. Only 79 civilians— most of them middle class—testified, compared with 202 policemen. If the electorate responded as well to his call on polling day, then Labour would sweep the wards.

*

The highly personalised attacks on Sherlock appear to have been counter-productive. Whether Liberty Hall liked it or not, the Lord Mayor had strong support among the more 'respectable' class of worker, such as printers and clerks, as well as the lower middle class. Only the 'fierce conflict' in Mountjoy ward kept him away from the annual conference of the Association of Irish Post Office Clerks in the Mansion House on the day of the count. The local MP, William Field, stood in for the Lord Mayor and assured them of Sherlock's support in their long-standing pay claim against the British government. Michael O'Lehane of the Drapers' Assistants, who had been noticeably absent from the election platforms of Trades Council candidates, was also at the Mansion House to pledge his union's support to the postal clerks 'in every possible way.'[27]

Sherlock had, of course, the support of the Catholic Church. His regular visits to the archbishop's palace had won him the nickname of the 'Lay Pope'. Having the church's blessing was a powerful political asset, and many of Dublin's Catholic clergy needed little encouragement to dabble in local politics. Nor was their support invoked solely against the scourge of socialism: frequently they were asked to support one nationalist faction against another. In 1913 there was at least one complaint to Dr Walsh about his priests being enlisted to serve in such electoral civil wars.[28]

Perhaps it was the clerical factor that inspired one of the Larkinite slogans. In the last week of the campaign the *Irish Worker* advertised torchlight meetings and parades to be held in each of the wards under the heading 'Shame the devils and stir the angels up!' It also called to account nationalist candidates such as Patrick Shortall, a master builder, for locking their workers out. Shortall was sufficiently worried at the attacks to issue a leaflet in Rotunda ward denying the allegation; he was not helped by a decision of the Master Builders' Association to simultaneously issue a circular calling on unionised employees to accept 'free labourers' on sites, because of the labour shortages created by the lockout.[29]

On 14 January, the day before polling, the *Irish Worker* produced a special election edition, with photographs of the ten candidates endorsed by the Trades Council on its front page. 'Vote early,' it told electors. 'Don't wait for cars to call for you: walk to the polls.' The paper was no doubt worried that the nationalist party machine would nobble labour voters by offering them transport to the polling stations. Its message was brutally simple: 'Work for the Labour men ONE DAY, and they will work for you EVERY DAY they hold office.' In its call to arms the paper said:

> We work together, live together, and tramp together, we strike together, are locked-out together and are shot together. The time has come when we must learn to VOTE TOGETHER.

In contrast, 'Every vote given against the Labour candidates tomorrow is a stab at the heart of Labour and the worker.'[30]

*

Nevertheless, most candidates regarded association with Larkinism as a liability. The unionists in Pembroke went so far as to issue a leaflet claiming that the nationalist party organisation in the township had been 'captured' by Larkinites. Twelve nationalists retaliated with libel writs against their unionist opponents. Even the local Labour candidate, George Ganley, a bricklayer, was far from pleased at being associated with Larkin. He joined an eve-of-poll rally held by the outraged nationalist candidates on Sandymount Green and personally assured constituents that the allegation of Larkin controlling political machines in the area was 'an infernal lie!'[31]

A more substantial response to 'Larkinism' came from its main target in the city, Lorcan Sherlock. In his eve-of-poll address the outgoing Lord Mayor urged citizens who normally failed to vote to 'come to the poll, so that the real opinion of the citizens might be reflected.'

> Socialism is gradually making its way in Dublin; there is a growing feeling to disrespect even religious institutions, and clever Socialists are prostituting the labour movement and dragging it along the road to perdition.
>
> It is time for the tradesmen and working labourers of Dublin to end this wretched condition of affairs, while at the same time being loyal and true to … genuine trades unionism. Sooner or later Mr. James Larkin must be taught that he is but one man, and that he has no divine right to manufacture the opinions of the workers or intimidate those who differ from him.

Though Larkin was not a candidate, Sherlock continued to concentrate on Larkin's activities, his 'absolutely reckless' character and 'disordered imagination.' The future of the city's workers was too important to have it jeopardised by a campaign of lying, which will fail because it is built on an unsound foundation. Flouting the Archbishop's warning, insulting the priests, deporting the children, attacking the nuns, indifference to whether there are 39 gods or one; these are the means by which Mr. Larkin seeks to forward the workers' interest. For a time great numbers of reputable men were led astray by his wild talk, but the change is coming slowly. Common-sense, religion, nationalism are asserting themselves.

Larkin had isolated himself by

denouncing in foul and filthy language every man who differs from him in any way. Life-long trades union leaders, both in Ireland and England, are bespattered by his dirty tongue, because they do not recognise James Larkin as a heavenly-sent leader of men. It is true he can organise, but it is perfectly plain that he can break up and destroy whatever he has formed. One by one he has fought with everybody.

The only other strike leader Sherlock mentioned was Councillor William Partridge, whose 'truculent and stupid speeches' had helped defeat his own efforts to settle the dispute.[32]

*

On Thursday 15 January, when the votes were counted, only one of the candidates endorsed by the Trades Council had been elected: Henry Donnelly, the coachbuilder, who topped the poll in New Kilmainham. This was Labour's traditional electoral stronghold, where the strong organisation built by Partridge around the Inchicore engineering works always delivered a seat. But this could hardly be considered an endorsement for the Larkinite platform. New Kilmainham had the best working-class housing in the city, and its proletarian electorate was composed mainly of the same rail workers who had resolutely refused to join the sympathetic strike in the city. Donnelly defeated the nationalist candidate by a comfortable two hundred votes, and there was a small but sweet consolation prize: the third candidate in the field, Patrick Joseph McIntyre, editor of the *Toiler*, secured just eleven votes.

Sherlock's strategy of ignoring his electoral opponents and attacking Larkin, socialism and anti-clericalism paid off handsomely in Mountjoy ward. He won the councillorship with 1,672 votes to Campbell's 716. Indeed he had a bigger vote than his nationalist colleague J. J. Farrell (also a shopkeeper and former lord mayor), who was still comfortably elected alderman for the ward by 1,350 votes to 975 for Arthur Murphy, his 'Larkinite' opponent. Dr Walsh congratulated Sherlock publicly on his

notable victory over a combination of influences which, in addition to the havoc they have wrought in the industrial world of Dublin, have done no little harm in ... deadening the moral and religious sense of not a few amongst the working population.

Sherlock reciprocated by telling the archbishop: 'Your own parish and that of Canon Walsh [North William Street] have both struck a deadly blow against the insidious enemy, Socialism.'[33]

In North Dock ward, where the Trades Council had been so hopeful of victory, its president, Tom McPartlin, secured only 960 votes for alderman against the UIL candidate, the local publican Alfie Byrne, who received 1,425. In the same ward P. T. Daly ran for the council seat and came close to winning it, receiving 1,143 votes against 1,252 for James Higgins, the UIL candidate.[34]

But it was in South Dock ward that the Trades Council came closest to victory, with only thirteen votes separating Thomas Foran from the successful UIL candidate, Myles Keogh. It was a particularly creditable performance, given that Keogh was a respected local doctor. He received 795 votes to 782 for Daly. In Merchants' Quay ward the Trades Council candidate, Andrew Breslan of the Carpenters, did well, with 1,261 votes to 1,403 for John Scully, the High Sheriff and a senior UIL politician in the city.

In Wood Quay ward Thomas Irwin of the Plasterers' Union also polled well, with 1,089 votes, but it was not enough to defeat the outgoing UIL councillor, Peter O'Reilly, a local grocer and spirit merchant, who polled 1,332.

The remaining Trades Council candidate, Joseph Farrell of the Painters' Union performed well, but not well enough to defeat the UIL man, William O'Hara. Farrell polled 875 votes to 1,033 for O'Hara, who had the inestimable advantage of being nominated by the parish priest.

The independent labour candidates fared much worse than those with Trades Council endorsement. John Lawlor in Rotunda ward secured only 585 votes, and Walter Carpenter a mere 277. Though William Chase ran as an 'independent labour' candidate in Trinity ward, the victory of the publican over a UIL candidate could hardly be counted as a vote for either socialism or the lockout. Another publican, James Kelly, ran as a 'home rule labour' candidate in Usher's Quay ward but polled only 501 votes.

The extravagant hopes of victory inevitably made the outcome all the more demoralising. The Trades Council candidates had in fact come close to winning seats in most of the constituencies contested; but it is hard to understand at this remove why the strike committee placed such hopes in the municipal election. Even if they had won all ten seats it would not have overturned the nationalist majority on the eighty-member council. The powers of the council were in any case extremely limited. In some British boroughs, such as Leith, the Labour councillors had been able to use their influence on the watch committee to prevent police from being used to force a way through picket lines for 'free labourers';[35] but such a potentially powerful weapon was never within the grasp of Dublin councillors. Even those statutory powers they did possess could prove nebulous, as Labour councillors found when they tried to invoke them against the employers.

When William Partridge managed to have a motion passed to examine ways of revoking the licence of the DUTC, the Town Clerk and Law Agent responded with a detailed legal memorandum explaining why such an initiative would be futile unless it had the agreement of the company's board.[36] Similarly, the Labour councillors found it impossible to enforce by-laws requiring employers to use only unionised labour on corporation schemes. Attempts to cancel the North Lots drainage contract given to H. and J. Martin, because the firm had used strike-breakers, also proved futile. The company managed, through delaying tactics and a little help from senior officials, to hold on to the contract. Eventually Larkin wrote in exasperation to City Hall accusing 'all officers of the Council, the Mayor, Aldermen and Councillors, individually and collectively,' of 'conspiracy and collusion with Messrs. Martin.'[37]

Which raises the question, why did Larkin not run for election in 1913? One reason was probably his previous experience of being removed from the council in 1912 at the instigation of E. W. Stewart, the former socialist turned UIL election agent. Larkin's financial affairs remained parlous, but that did not prevent him from running successfully for Dublin City Council and Dáil Éireann in later years. A more significant factor, which probably applied also to other strike leaders, was that he was simply too busy with the dispute to contemplate becoming a candidate. He also appears at this stage in his career to have developed a marked antipathy towards electoral politics, preferring to confront capitalism industrially than at the polls. His hostility to electoral politics appears to have extended to the caucus of the Independent Labour Party of Ireland gathered around Connolly and O'Brien.[38] Larkin's attitude may have been a factor in the failure of both the Trades Council and the ITGWU to endorse Carpenter's candidacy in Fitzwilliam ward.

None of the strike leaders seemed to appreciate the importance of running themselves. Like so many ideologically driven political groups in modern Irish politics, the labour militants of 1913 expected people to vote for the self-evident virtues of their political programme. Provided the candidate was politically reliable, their political skills were a secondary consideration. As Thomas Murphy of the Carpet Planners had put it at the Trades Council meeting on 12 January, its candidates 'were proved men,' and that should be a good enough recommendation for working-class electors.

The fourth and most dangerous error of the strike leaders followed from their refusal to take a more pragmatic approach to electoral politics. They assumed that because the population of the areas they contested was predominantly working class, there was an automatic Labour majority in each ward. But fewer than 40,000 adult Dubliners had the vote in 1914. Property and residential qualifications ensured that the franchise remained weighted in favour of the middle class. To have a vote in a council election a tenement-dweller must in practice have had at least eighteen months' continuous residence in their flat—and they could still be disfranchised if the landlord failed to pay his rates on time. The Local Government (Ireland) Act (1898) had further weighted the franchise towards the middle class by giving the vote to women who were property-owners. Revision committees regularly updated the electoral lists, and the United Irish League had raised voter registration to an art. Young nationalist lawyers with political ambitions were expected to serve their time ensuring that as many party faithful were registered as possible and, conversely, as many potential voters for labour or unionist candidates were not. Even so, the cost of running registration societies was high, and the rival Unionist Registration Association had difficulty covering its expenses. Though trade unions provided some funds for labour candidates, they could not hope to compete with their better-resourced opponents in this area.[39]

The nationalists were no doubt relieved that Larkin did not contest a seat. In 1912, after his short-lived electoral victory, the secretary of the Mountjoy Ward Branch of the UIL wrote to John Dillon warning him that Larkin could pose a serious threat to both William Abraham and William Field in the next general election, 'as there is a very large number of his followers resident in both constituencies.'[40]

*

When the in-built handicaps of the electoral system are taken into account, the results of the municipal election can be seen as a notable achievement for the Trades Council. Its candidates had come within 150 votes of winning seats in four constituencies and within 13 votes in one. In general, Larkinite candidates had polled 12,026 votes to 16,627 for the nationalists, a ratio of seven to ten.[41] Naturally the unionists and nationalists depicted the failure to win seats as a defeat for Larkinism. This was especially so in Mountjoy ward, where Sherlock had romped home. Such an analysis helped these parties deflect attention from their own problems. For the unionists it was the collapse of the vote in their traditional stronghold of Kingstown, where the nationalists won seven extra seats; for the nationalists it was their own increasingly bitter civil war in the Dublin wards. The UIL may have faced a Larkinite challenge in eight constituencies, but it faced rival nationalist candidates in twelve.[42] In one instance, Drumcondra, the Unionist candidate was elected alderman after the UIL and AOH candidates split the in-built nationalist majority. Generally this danger was avoided by the UIL being left with a clear field in most constituencies where unionists or Trades Council candidates ran. This arrangement did not prevent the unionists from winning Clontarf West by the narrowest of margins: they recaptured the aldermanship from the UIL by 156 votes and retained the councillorship by just four votes.

Nor was it enough to win the UIL a seat in the labour stronghold of New Kilmainham, where P. J. McIntyre's campaign as an anti-Larkinite labour candidate barely registered. In Rotunda ward the Larkinite campaign against Patrick Shortall of the UIL, the master builder who had locked out his men, helped the independent radical nationalist Laurence O'Neill to retain the aldermanship by thirty-four votes.[43]

It was the high electoral expectations of the Trades Council, and the equally pessimistic forebodings of the nationalist and unionist political machines, that made the results so dramatic. The failure of the Trades Council to make the expected breakthrough brought home to the strike leaders their isolation and the reality of defeat on the industrial front.

Connolly, never a man to shun life's harsher realities, was the first to begin devising a strategy to cope with defeat. Perhaps it was his return to the less heady atmosphere of Belfast that reconciled him to the notion. Even before the election results were known he was writing to advise Larkin and O'Brien that they should announce that

> as the cross-channel unions … had definitely resolved not to assist us in fighting the battle against the Dublin sweaters in the only way they could be fought, viz: by holding up their goods … we are now prepared to advise a general resumption of work, and the handling of all goods PENDING A MORE GENERAL ACCEPTANCE OF THE DOCTRINE OF TAINTED GOODS BY THE TRADE UNION WORLD.

Such an approach 'would place the sole responsibility for our temporary check upon the cross-channel unions and also leave every employer free to act as he thought best, and I do not believe that the Murphy gang would be able to hold them any longer.'[44] The attempt to put the primary responsibility for defeat on the shoulders of the TUC was in line with Connolly's initial response to the London conference. It is clear that the new unionism was realigning itself with the new nationalism in his political firmament.

However, there were also sound tactical reasons for blaming the British. It would avoid a divisive debate within the Irish trade union movement about the basic soundness of the sympathetic strike tactic; it would help the ITGWU to retreat without having to sign 'an unsatisfactory GENERAL settlement,' Connolly stressed; and it could allow it to reserve the right to take industrial action against victimisation within individual firms after the lockout ended.[45]

*

Whatever Larkin thought of Connolly's advice, his anger at the election results in that Saturday's *Irish Worker* was directed at enemies nearer home. His political analysis was a heady mixture of despair and defiance. 'Labour's ranks have been broken, and we have been compelled to withdraw to our base,' he wrote. However, he also insisted that 'if the election had been held in November last, instead of holding our own … we would have had the satisfaction of chronicling at least eight victories.'

Having plumbed the depths, he typically soared upwards, urging his supporters to greater efforts.

> Our opponents are … proclaiming the fact that LARKINISM IS ROUTED. If that had been true, how is it that in every Ward we have increased our vote by hundreds; and you have to remember we had massed against us

every section of the employing class and every political party in the city. The press were united in this fight, the pulpits without an exception used as a platform to denounce us. The police as usual acting like jackals.

He explained Sherlock's vote by claiming, probably correctly, that

every public official, with a few brilliant exceptions, were abusing their offices … on behalf of our enemies. Practically two-thirds of the Corporation officials and staff were working for the chief wirepuller in Mountjoy Ward.

They were all part of a colourful alliance that Larkin depicted as 'slum landlords, scabs, prostitutes' bullies … Hibs, Orangemen, Temperance humbugs, and porter sharks,' of 'nice clean ladies and gentlemen (outwardly, but foul within),' of 'the shopkeeper … the brothel keeper, the white slave trafficker … the parson,' and many others, who had united to defeat labour.

What a combination! And they won by votes, some of them bona fide, many of them bogus. They beat Larkinism by votes: but they can never beat Larkinism by reason, by fact, by principles … I would suggest to those who pretend to look after the morals and uplifting of the people to pass the Verdon Bar, Talbot Street [Alfie Byrne's premises] today. I hope they have the courage to go in and shake hands with the brothers and sisters who associate there. Why should not the Freemen, the leaseholders, and those who call themselves respectable shopkeepers, and all those nice ladies who come up dressed in the newer fashions— why not all of you join your worthy alderman in the debauch which is now proceeding night and day? Why not join with Enright, the procurer … and his victims in the celebration of the rout of Larkinism? Why not invite the ghoul Murderer Murphy, Messrs. Drury and Swifte, Harrell, and Ross, Traynor the scab who shot an innocent girl or the brutes who murdered Byrne and Nolan. Birrell and the scabs who masqueraded as trade unionists … Why not have a loving feast, or better still, why not sacrifice as Abraham did by fire on an altar. Why not burn Larkin with prayer and incense, but don't forget the refreshing and stimulating porter which is the best friend the sweater, the slum landlord, and the politicians can call upon. But, friends, Larkinism is not routed. Friend Murphy and Sherlock … wait and see!

Larkin's biblical language contained a grain of truth, but it also betrayed a man at the end of his tether. On the same page the *Irish Worker* published a 'Notice to all workers in dispute!' to attend a mass meeting on Sunday in Croydon Park to 'consider such action as may be considered necessary.' Admission would be by union card only.[46]

Some did not wait until Sunday. On Saturday 17 January large numbers of strikers went to Croydon Park after rumours spread that Larkin intended making an important statement. There had been no distribution of food parcels in the city for two days, and many believed that the TUC had finally washed its hands of the Dublin dispute. The men at Croydon Park were eventually told to return next day. As they drifted back from Fairview towards the city, confused, disappointed, and fearful for the future, there were several attacks on carts driven by strike-breakers. The ugliest incident occurred in Amiens Street, where some twenty men surrounded a cart, pulled the driver to the ground, and kicked him unconscious.[47] Far worse would follow before the night was over.

42

17 Jan '14

ON Saturday evening two 'free labourers' left the protection of the Employers' Federation house, or the 'Barracks', as it was now popularly known, at number 2 Beresford Place for a drink. For the previous six weeks they had been living there while working for Tedcastle, McCormick and Company, the coal importers. They were George Maguire and Thomas Harten, farm labourers from Charleston, near Kells, County Meath, who had probably been attracted to the city by the high wages being offered to strike-breakers.

They knew they were taking a risk by going into the city centre, and they began their excursion with a trip to Samuel Slevin, a gun dealer on Eden Quay. They bought two revolvers and twelve rounds of ammunition; they told Slevin they wanted the guns to frighten off any would-be attackers. After that they went to the 7 p.m. show at the Tivoli Theatre. They left shortly before 9 p.m. and crossed O'Connell bridge for a drink in Keogh's pub. They left about 10:15 and decided to spend the night in the Iveagh Hostel. Ironically, they thought this would be safer than attempting to return to the federation house, which entailed passing Liberty Hall.

They recrossed O'Connell Bridge, only to be attacked a few minutes later by a gang of men at Wellington Quay. Maguire was grabbed by the arm and throat and knocked to the ground. He was kicked and beaten five or six times with 'some kind of instrument.' Harten managed to escape and fled across the Ha'penny Bridge. He seemed to be making for Beresford Place and had almost reached Butt Bridge when a group of four or five men caught up with him outside Liberty Hall. Like Maguire, he was beaten with some sort of weapon. The attack was particularly brutal, and an eyewitness later said that Harten's body 'spouted blood' as he was kicked along the quay. The assailants seemed to know who they were dealing with, for they subsequently searched him and took his revolver.

Harten was found lying in a pool of blood by two journalists at about 10:45 p.m. Onlookers refused to help, and one of the press men ran to the Abbey Theatre to telephone an ambulance. Harten died a few minutes after being admitted to Jervis Street Hospital. Maguire was already there; he saw his drinking companion of the night being brought in but did not recognise him, 'as he was covered in blood.'

The police began an immediate manhunt, and Thomas Daly, an unemployed coal labourer from Lower Gloucester Street, was charged with Harten's murder. Daly was already in custody for attacking two other strike-breakers that night. The first was James Reilly, who had been attacked in Ryan's pub in George's Quay by Brady and others after refusing to go with them to Liberty Hall. Reilly ran into the Tivoli Theatre, but Daly and his companions caught him in the foyer and beat Reilly so badly that he also ended up in Jervis Street. Daly was arrested shortly afterwards while administering similar treatment to another strike-breaker, James Mulvanny, in Tara Street. A revolver was found in his pocket, which the police claimed later was Harten's. They believed Daly was the leader of a group of ITGWU members who had spent the evening hunting for scabs in the city centre.[1]

The two journalists who had stumbled on the story of Harten's murder had been on their way back to their separate newspaper offices to report the final settlement of the dispute at the City of Dublin Steam Packet Company. The ITGWU dockers had at last agreed to return to work after two months out in sympathy with their locked-out comrades elsewhere in the city, the NSFU men having gone back on 8 January after their strike pay had finally been stopped. The company, on its side, had agreed to full reinstatement and the discharge of thirty-five strike-breakers.[2]

The contrasting events illustrate the underlying and conflicting strands that had emerged within the dispute during the election contest. On the one hand there were increasingly frequent attacks on strike-breakers and on the property of employers; on the other hand, settlements were being reached between the unions and those employers who no longer felt bound by the edicts of Murphy's executive committee.

*

The atmosphere on the streets was not helped by the fact that the Dublin Disturbances Commission was holding its public hearings into the riots of the previous August and September. The evidence not only revived memories of those events but led to angry exchanges at the city council. Partridge used the opportunity to allege 'a conspiracy between the murderous Liberal government ... and the professional nationalist members of this council to ... protect the police.'[3] In fact the government was now doing its best to allow both the riots controversy and the lockout to settle themselves. Lord Aberdeen had already turned his attention to sponsoring a much-needed city development plan. He 'felt so strongly the importance of doing what lay in his power in this direction' that he offered a prize of £500 'for the best plan for the reconstruction of Dublin.'[4]

The Disturbances Commission was left to its own gloomy devices, though some unexpected light relief was provided when the Liberal MP Handel Booth arrived to give evidence. As soon as the counsel for the police, J. B. Powell KC, had finished his opening address, Booth was on his feet demanding the 'opportunity of giving an answer to the extraordinary speech of Mr Powell—

Powell: Don't mind calling my speech extraordinary.

Booth: It was an extraordinary speech.

Powell: Address yourself to the court and don't mind describing my speech. Mind your own business and I'll mind mine.

Booth never did get around to dissecting Powell's 'extraordinary speech,' nor did he ever give evidence himself; after three days of being jibed by Powell, he stormed out of the 'tainted atmosphere' of the hearings. The two potentially most damaging witnesses against the police, a Liberal MP and his wife, had given not a jot of evidence. Larkin's boycott of the proceedings, and that of his supporters, was an added bonus for Powell.

The police counsel also managed to have a very damaging piece of photographic evidence disallowed. It consisted of two photographs taken by an *Evening Telegraph* journalist on 'Bloody Sunday'. One was taken a few moments before the baton charge, the second during the charge. The first photograph showed a throng of curious people in Sackville Street, but nothing to support police evidence of incipient disorder.

However, Powell's efforts were ultimately counter-productive,[5] as the *Evening Telegraph* published the two pictures on its front page later that day.[6] The very success of the police counsel's strategy at the hearings only helped convince the public that the inquiry was indeed a whitewashing exercise.

*

The same day that Handel Booth withdrew from the Disturbances Commission, the city sessions were inundated with insurance claims from farmers for incendiary attacks. Timothy Healy appeared for the largest claimant, and his fellow-parliamentarian J. J. Clancy, MP for North County Dublin, appeared for the county council. It was all in a day's work, but hardly an edifying spectacle for constitutional nationalism that two of its senior representatives could be seen feeding off a dispute that was crippling the city. In this case there was the added injury that the more successful Healy was in having his clients' claims allowed, the higher would be next year's rates.

Healy, who was no stranger to agrarian strife, has left us a vivid glimpse of conditions in the county with his description of events in the courts. One of his clients was Sarah Carey, who owned sixty acres at Baskin, Raheny. The lands were farmed for her by her two brothers. Healy told the court:

During the labour troubles the farm labourers had left and ... 'free' labour requisitioned. A large number of women were employed. On the night before the fire a meeting was held in Coolock to denounce the use of 'free' labour. It was a large and exciting meeting, and the farmers in the district and the 'free' labourers were denounced, booed, and groaned. At 11.30 p.m., on November 20th, Miss Carey retired, after having examined the farmyard, everything was all right. Within about

20 minutes afterwards her room became illuminated, and going to the window she discovered a large quantity of hay, oats, wheat, and straw, which had been stacked in a corrugated iron shed some distance from the house was on fire. She alarmed her brothers, and they, with the aid of the police ... did all they could to save as much of the property as they could. The shed was over one hundred feet long, and, though the fire occurred on a Thursday night, it was still burning on Saturday.

Sarah Carey's claim was for £789 3s 6d. The Recorder awarded her £700, 'to be levied off the rates.'[7]

Nor were incendiary attacks a thing of the past by January. Several serious incidents occurred, including one on 16 January at the Greenmount stables in Clonsilla. It was a serious blow to Maxwell Arnott, a director of the *Irish Times*, who lost a prize racehorse in the blaze; it had a stake value of £3,610 and was not insured. Fourteen other horses were rescued, with some difficulty. On the following Sunday another set of stables nearby were set alight. The damage to buildings alone from the two fires was estimated at over £2,000.[8] The fresh wave of arson in the county may have been related to the refusal of many farmers to pay the annual 'harvest money' or bonus to workers who had been locked out. The ITGWU had taken a test case at Raheny petty sessions against Charles Kettle, and lost.

*

But it was the violence in the city that most perturbed citizens. Feeling against the strike-breakers continued to run high. Coal deliveries were often made in convoy so that strike-breakers could offer each other some protection. This was not always effective. One of the worst attacks had occurred the day before Harten's murder, when five strike-breakers manning coal carts and lorries belonging to Heiton and Company were attacked by a mob in Abbey Street. All the men had been dragged from their vehicles and beaten 'unmercifully'. The attack stopped only when one of the men managed to draw his revolver and fire three or four shots in the air. The mob retired, taking one of the horses, a coal cart and a lorry with them.[9]

As coal merchants were the primary employers of 'free labour' in the city, it was inevitable that coal deliveries were in the front line of the brutal class warfare now being conducted. However, the sharp drop in temperature after a wet, mild autumn no doubt provided an added incentive for people to make an example of the coalmen—and acquire badly needed fuel in the process.

The continuing lack of zeal shown by the authorities in prosecuting strike-breakers for using firearms also fuelled working-class hostility. When Patrick Traynor, the man who shot Alice Brady, appeared again in the courts the murder charge was reduced to discharging a firearm at the dead girl. Even Drury, the magistrate, was appalled: he ordered that the charge be amended to manslaughter, and returned Traynor for trial by jury. The same day he sentenced a labourer, Daniel Keogh, to six months' imprisonment for beating his wife, and another six months for neglecting his children. The case received considerable publicity, because Keogh, who was on strike, had been demanding 2s from his wife for each food ship parcel he received. At a meeting of the South Dublin Union a fortnight earlier there had been several allegations of strikers selling food tickets wholesale for 2d each, but no hard evidence was produced. Despite the lavish attention given to Keogh's case, no other evidence emerged to support such claims. And Keogh, who had eight previous convictions, was hardly typical of the men locked out. This did not prevent the TUC from holding a formal investigation into the possibility of abuses in the food scheme. It was quickly satisfied that no racketeering was taking place; but its inquiries cannot have helped improve relations with Dublin.[10]

While the Dublin Employers' Federation continued to set its face against renewed negotiations, and the Shipping Federation continued to despatch 'free labourers' to the port, return-to-work settlements were being reached with a number of companies. Besides the City of Dublin Steam Packet Company, the men of the Burns shipping line returned, as did workers at Spence's engineering works in Cork Street. Some settlements went unreported, but an effort by James Seddon to transform this trickle into a formal general agreement failed miserably. After Seddon's failure the usually well-informed Labour Press Agency reported that the TUC leaders

> are almost unanimous in feeling that, by all the rules of industrial warfare known to them, the Dublin workers have been worsted in the struggle. But they cannot get away from the fact that the men themselves do not admit defeat, and many will continue the struggle until advised to give way by Mr. Larkin ... The only course left, therefore, is the not very dignified one of marking time.

The agency also noted that the promised new appeal for funds to support the Dublin strikers had yet to be issued by the TUC. It concluded that 'the obvious intention is that the financial support should be allowed to die a natural death.'[11]

In fact, after hearing Seddon's report on his latest ill-fated initiative, the TUC had decided to speak quite plainly to the Dublin strike leaders. The secretary of the TUC Parliamentary Committee, Charles Bowerman, wrote to Dublin Trades Council telling its members that 'the response to the appeal ... has weakened considerably ... Unless a more generous and general response is made than has been the case during the past few weeks, it will be impossible after the present week to continue the weekly remittance to your committee.'[12]

When the Trades Council met on Monday 12 January it was still preoccupied with the election campaign. Nevertheless it passed a vote of thanks to 'the Trades Unionists of Great Britain for their assistance in our present fight for existence.' It praised the 'brotherhood and generosity unequalled' of the British movement and decided that, besides sending the resolution to the Parliamentary Committee, it would despatch copies to the *Daily Citizen, Daily Herald* and *Irish Worker* to ensure that the message reached the rank and file. Quite separately, but simultaneously, a large batch of postcards arrived from Dublin at the TUC offices in London bearing the words 'Are you going to betray us?' None of these efforts softened the collective heart of the Parliamentary Committee. At the same meeting at which Bowerman had been instructed to write warning the Trades Council of the impending collapse of the strike fund, further deliberation on the Dublin dispute was restricted to a discussion about a suitable presentation for the captain of the *Hare*.[13] There was now almost as little meaningful communication between the TUC and Dublin Trades Council as there was between those bodies and the Dublin Employers' Federation.

*

Larkin's difficult personality, which had cost the strikers so much good will across the channel, almost cost them another ally that week. At a meeting on Sunday 11 January in Sackville Street, he turned on another speaker, Jack White, chairman of the Civic League and drill master of the Citizen Army. He described him as 'the son of Sir George White, who defended the British flag at Ladysmith, the dirty flag under which more disease and degradation had been experienced than anything else that I know of.' White immediately rose and left the platform. Larkin had apparently taken offence at a motion passed at a public meeting earlier that day, chaired by Captain White, which called for the Lord Mayor, Lorcan Sherlock, to conduct a new, independent inquiry into the behaviour of the police. Larkin was suspicious of White's motives in joining the Citizen Army and suspected him of wanting to 'influence or capture our organisation, or wean it from its first attachment to Labour Ideals.'[14] He may also have been a little jealous of the soldier's obvious popularity with the men. Other leading figures in the Citizen Army, such as Seán O'Casey and Connolly, managed to repair the breach for a time; but White and Larkin were both headstrong and highly strung, and the truce proved short-lived.[15]

Besides, Larkin knew that playing soldiers might keep idle hands busy but could not win the dispute. At the same Trades Council meeting that had sent the desperate vote of thanks for British support, building trade delegates told the strike leaders that their members could not hold out much longer. Some had already agreed to work alongside members of Richardson's 'scab' Irish National Workers' Union.[16] A delegate of the Iron-Moulders confirmed that some of his members were doing likewise. Over the next few days reports would come in of ITGWU men also trickling back to work. With speculation growing that the stopping of strike payments would soon be followed by the end of the food ships, the union had to make a decision before the trickle became a flood. By the time the strikers finally gathered at Croydon Park on Sunday 18 January there was little doubt about what that decision would be.

Only workers who could produce an ITGWU membership card were admitted to Croydon Park, and stewards kept reporters and police note-takers well out of earshot of the meeting. But it did not take long for word to drift back to the city that Larkin had advised his members to go back on the best terms available. His one injunction to them was not to sign the form renouncing the union.[17]

43

NEXT day, nearly a thousand men reported for work. Most of them were dockers, over five hundred of whom were taken back by the main shipping lines. It was heralded as the end of the dispute.

However, the numbers were deceptive. The dockers returning to work that Monday morning included employees of the City of Dublin Steam Packet Company and the Duke shipping line, where settlements had been reached less than twenty-four hours before the Croydon Park meeting. When two hundred men turned up at the Port and Docks Board, only forty were taken back immediately, and then only on condition that they begin on reduced rates as 'new hands'. The board said it would take on more men as vacancies arose. At the North Wall Extension and the terminal of the British and Irish Steam Packet Company on the South Wall, hardly anyone was taken back. In the city, a mere handful of carters were taken back by the main companies, John Wallis and Son and Pickford's; and Hammond Lane Foundry was the only significant engineering concern reported to be reinstating some of its workers.

The biggest return to work, surprisingly, was at the Dublin United Tramways Company. Sixty-eight of the 113 engineering workers who had walked out at Inchicore in August were taken back, and the remainder found work at the Ballsbridge depot; they had taken sympathetic strike action in support of coachbuilders who had refused to repair trams damaged in the lockout.[1] Their speedy return suggests that the DUTC had been less successful in finding 'free labourers' to replace these skilled men than the shipping lines had been in finding dockers.

In most employments, including the DUTC, the strikers found themselves having to work alongside strike-breakers and agreeing to handle 'tainted' goods. None of these firms appears to have asked the men to sign a form renouncing the ITGWU,[2] but the situation could hardly be described as a return to the *status quo ante*. For many dockers, especially those who were turned away at the gate, it must have been intensely demoralising to realise that their two months on the picket line in support of locked-out ITGWU members had achieved nothing.

*

On the same Monday morning that the great return to work began, the inquest on Thomas Harten was held. The dead man's companion, George

Maguire, appeared to give evidence with his head still wrapped in bandages. He was followed by Dr James Vaughan Ryan, the resident surgeon at Jervis Street Hospital, who gave gruesome evidence of the dead man's injuries. There was a two-inch cut at the side of the left eyebrow and three deep cuts beside the right eyeball, which had disintegrated. There was a puncture wound between the right eye and right ear, and the ear itself was partially shredded. There was a blood clot at the right side of the brain, and the base of the skull had been shattered. The injuries could not have resulted from a mere kicking: 'a heavy weapon must have been used with great violence.'[3]

Later that day Thomas Daly was charged with Harten's murder. He told the police magistrate, Drury: 'I know nothing at all about it.' In the early hours of Tuesday morning two more unemployed labourers, James Doyle and John Morrissey, were also charged with the murder.[4]

*

Despite continuing violence on the streets, some public figures were already putting the labour troubles behind them and addressing more traditional political concerns. Archbishop Walsh, hearing of the breakdown in talks between Asquith and Bonar Law to resolve the home rule crisis, preached a sermon on the dangers of civil war. While Larkin was telling his members to seek terms, Dr Walsh told his flock that an armed conflict with the unionists would 'open the abyss.' He besought all good Catholics 'to pray to God that that trouble may be averted, and that the words, often spoken carelessly, "God save Ireland," come true.'[5]

Unionists put their trust in more substantial manifestations of divine favour. On Monday night thousands of them flocked to the Ulster Hall in Belfast to be reassured by Carson and Lord Londonderry that the province stood in a high state of readiness for war. 'I only hope that at the last moment even the government may realise how false has been the advice given them by Mr Redmond,' Lord Londonderry said. 'Ulster is desperately in earnest, and is determined at all costs and at all hazards to resist being put under a parliament by means of which Mr Redmond, Mr Devlin, and men like Patrick Ford, the dynamiter, now dead, would control the destinies of this loyal, industrious, and prosperous province.' To underline the seriousness with which Ulster took the threat of a parliament peopled by dead Fenian dynamitards, Carson went next day to present colours to the 1st Battalion of the North Belfast Regiment of the Ulster Volunteers at Ewart's spinning mill on the Crumlin Road, accompanied by General Sir George Richardson, the UVF general staff and a mounted escort from the Ulster Despatch Riding Corps.[6] It was a far cry from the ragamuffin assemblies of Jack White in Croydon Park, and it is easy to see why Carson preferred the drama and colour of Belfast to the drab, primordial class warfare of his native Dublin.

*

While the Belfast men were waiting to be presented with their colours, Larkin was on his way to London, where the Parliamentary Committee of the TUC was meeting on 21 January to review the Dublin dispute. The overdue *Hare* had finally arrived in Dublin on Monday night, and huge queues gathered outside Liberty Hall on Tuesday for food tickets. The *Daily Herald* published a report that this would be the last food ship, and Larkin was desperately anxious that supplies should continue. He knew that however willing the workers were to return to work, many employers felt otherwise, and supplies were needed to tide the men over. The master builders, for instance, had rejected the initial approach of the building trade unions. Even in firms where workers had returned there were problems; after less than twenty-four hours the carters at Pickford's were again on the picket lines over a row about delivering eggs to Jacob's, which was still refusing to take back three hundred former employees in the ITGWU.

When Larkin arrived at the Aldwych Building in London on Wednesday afternoon with Tom Farren, the Stonecutters' representative on Dublin Trades Council, they received a frosty reception. When they asked about future financial support, Seddon told them that 'ample notice had been given ... that money has fallen off.' Larkin explained the difficulties in trying to secure return-to-work agreements, particularly with the building employers. The minutes record:

> Mr. Larkin then complained that no food had been sent on Friday or Saturday. Mr. Seddon replied that the 'Hare' was held up and explained the great difficulty he had had to get the food to Dublin. Nevertheless, the food had arrived in Dublin ... The warehouse was full of bread. The yard was full of potatoes, and the carts were bringing the stuff from the ship.
>
> Mr. Larkin: Last Friday and Saturday we got nothing at all. We got no information about the arrival of the food until Monday. Some of the men did not get their food at all. We got 8,000 tickets out of 14,000. The week the 'Hare' was held up we got no butter, no tea and sugar.

He then launched into an attack on the continued use of the *Hare*, which he now described as a 'blackleg boat', presumably because it was crewed by members of the NSFU. There were 'fifty other ways of delivering the food to Dublin,' he said. He asked where the 'four hundred packets of margarine' were supposed to be on the vessel; and he asked about newspaper reports that £12,000 worth of food had been despatched. 'It has not come forward to Dublin,' he said.

He received little satisfaction, and the members of the committee countered by asking about the postcards sent from Dublin accusing them of being about to betray the strikers. Larkin admitted telling people 'at a private meeting' to send postcards to the TUC if they wished; 'but he was not responsible for the form of words used.' He repeated his plea for supplies. There were over 9,000 people 'wanting food,' including 1,200 building labourers.

After Larkin and Farren left, the Parliamentary Committee decided it was time to send another delegation to Dublin 'to explain the situation.' Seddon and Gosling were charged with leading it. Bowerman was also authorised to issue a statement rebutting the *Daily Herald* report and confirming that there would be another shipload of food arriving in Dublin by the end of the week.[7]

*

As was so often the case when Larkin was absent from the scene, there was renewed violence in the city. On Wednesday morning several strikers were arrested by police after a group of fifty-three strike-breakers were ambushed at the junction of Townsend Street and Lombard Street. The attack was obviously planned and took place at 8 a.m., as the strike-breakers arrived in a body for work at Tedcastle McCormick's. They were apparently nervous, as (one of them said afterwards) they had only two revolvers between them. They were subjected to a shower of bricks, bottles, and stones; shots were fired on both sides, and then the strikers laid into the 'free labourers' with iron bars and hurleys. One strike-breaker was taken to hospital.

The police arrived within minutes, and twelve strikers were arrested. The speed and the strength of the police response suggest that they may have been forewarned of the attack. In a follow-up operation a further seven men were arrested. The lopsided arrest count was to be expected; and, unlike strike-breakers facing serious shooting charges, all the arrested strikers were refused bail while they awaited trial.

The chief witness against the men was a strike-breaker, Joseph Clarke, who admitted firing his gun twice in the melee but who had not been charged. He later told the court that he had been 'twice in the Portrane Asylum, and about twenty-four or twenty-five times in jail for street fights and "odd clouts" at the police.'[8] If Clarke matched in many respects the criminal profile Connolly had drawn of a strike-breaker in the *Irish Worker* five weeks earlier, he deviated from that description in one important respect: he was not the product of some British slum but Irish-born and bred. In fact a disconcertingly large number of the strike-breakers involved in the more serious clashes with the strikers were home-grown.[9] Arthur Griffith and D. P. Moran were not the only ones to wear green-tinted spectacles during the lockout.

The trouble outside Tedcastle McCormick's appears to have been sufficiently alarming for many dockland employers to soften their stance in the negotiations about a return to work. Tedcastle McCormick's, which had taken a lead in bringing the Shipping Federation into the port, opened negotiations with the men on a return to work the day after the clashes. Another factor influencing the employers was their increasingly difficult relationship with the Shipping Federation. On Thursday 22 January the Port and Docks Board received a letter from the Head Line complaining at the congested condition of the sheds and quays on the North Wall, the area of the port where strike-breakers had been most widely employed. There were also letters of complaint from city firms. The Shipping Federation itself was threatening to pull some of its men out of the port because of the chaotic state of affairs.[10] The ad hoc arrangements in the port during the strike were obviously beginning to crumble. The strike-breakers were not only proving more expensive to employ than the ITGWU men but also appeared to be less efficient. The timber and joinery trade was one of those worst affected by the chaos in the port; the firm of Norman McNaughten found it could not collect a consignment of pine because it was buried under grain.

On Wednesday these employers began direct negotiations with the British unions representing the bulk of the 1,500 or so workers involved. Engineering companies did likewise with the mainly British engineering unions. This did not necessarily augur well for the ITGWU. The Iron-Moulders' Union negotiated a return to work for a hundred employees with J. and C. McGloughlin, the construction and ecclesiastical engineers. This required the men not only to work alongside members of Richardson's 'scab' Irish National Workers' Union but to sign a form declaring that they would not join the ITGWU.[11]

*

Larkin no doubt heard of these examples of British perfidy when he returned to Dublin in advance of the TUC delegation. He was also just in time to witness the election of Lorcan Sherlock to a third term as Lord Mayor. It was a rowdy and acrimonious city council meeting, even by the standards of the day. Sherlock's supporters defended his decision to run again on the grounds that an experienced 'chief magistrate' was needed in the year when home rule was expected to make Dublin a capital city once again. On the other hand, David Quaid, a nationalist councillor from Drumcondra, suggested that they should elect 'one of the minority who has been excluded from preferment for the last thirty-two or thirty-three years.' This was a clear reference to Andrew Beattie, a long-serving councillor for South City ward. Beattie was a leading businessman in the city and a member of the National Liberal Club; however, he had begun his political life as a unionist and had become an independent only in the past couple of years. Quaid said that electing a Protestant mayor 'would show the people of England and Scotland that those people in the north of Ireland had nothing to fear from Irish nationalists.' His remarks provoked widespread laughter, and he could find no seconder.

Quaid had once been a Sinn Féin activist, and this may have affected his non-sectarian stance; but the fact that there was a significant unionist vote in his own ward was probably a more potent factor. He used the opportunity to attack the mass personation campaign by other nationalist candidates in Drumcondra, which had cost the popular Unionist alderman Francis Vance his seat. Quaid was joined by Dr James McWalter, the alderman for North City ward, in accusing Sherlock and the dominant UIL faction within the nationalist ranks of having already decided the outcome of the mayoral contest at a caucus meeting in 'a back room in some public house.' This led to general recriminations among the nationalist councillors over various caucus meetings to appoint a city engineer, a borough surveyor, and a tuberculosis officer, which provided great entertainment for readers of the following week's *Irish Worker.*

The lockout inevitably cast its shadow over the mayoral debate, and Quaid accused Sherlock of being 'immured in the Mansion House' on Bloody Sunday when 'as a courageous man he should have come down and protected the citizens.' Sherlock's main reason for seeking re-election on the eve of home rule was that 'there might be a visit of His Majesty to Dublin ... and that he would probably then receive the appreciation which he was always endeavouring to receive.' Sherlock was forced to deny that he was interested in a knighthood, and added vehemently that he would refuse one if offered. The two renegade labour councillors, William Richardson and John Saturninus Kelly, rallied to Sherlock's support and also defended him against the attacks of William Partridge and Richard O'Carroll, the two senior Labour councillors.

But Partridge's accusation that Sherlock had 'betrayed' the workers during the lockout was tame compared with the mutual bloodletting on the nationalist benches. Sherlock made a revealing response to the charge by colleagues that he had not done enough to resolve the tramway dispute.

> Who would believe that anything I could have done would move Mr. William Murphy? Didn't that man take the Corporation ... by the throat on the art gallery question, and beat them all by himself?

There was no response to that.

After Quaid's unsuccessful attempt to promote Beattie as a mayoral candidate, the Sinn Féin councillor for Usher's Quay ward, William Cosgrave, proposed another Sinn Féin member, Thomas Kelly, the alderman for Mansion House ward, to oppose Sherlock. He was seconded by William Dinnage, the new Unionist member for Glasnevin, who had won the aldermanship after the UIL and AOH candidates had split the nationalist vote. Obviously some unionists saw Sinn Féin, with its programme of municipal reform and its lack of direct ties with the Catholic Church, as preferable to traditional nationalism. Kelly secured the vote of seven Labour councillors, the four Sinn Féin votes (including his own), three unionist votes, that of Quaid, and the votes of four independent nationalists, including Sarah Harrison and William Chase, the newly elected 'Larkinite' publican. The great majority of nationalists on the council, including vehement critics of Sherlock such as Dr McWalter, voted for the outgoing mayor. So did two Unionists and the two Labour renegades, Richardson and Kelly.

In contrast, Belfast's mayoral election that day, when the unionist MP R. J. McMordie was re-elected unopposed, was a model of gentility. For the nationalists, Alderman Moore said that 'notwithstanding [that] there was electricity in the air and ... rumours of war,' McMordie had been fair in his decisions. The nationalist members looked forward to McMordie occupying 'a prominent place in the upper house in College Green' when home rule was established.[12]

*

Next morning there was no strike pay for ITGWU members in Dublin. Large-scale manoeuvres at Croydon Park were poor consolation, though Jack White had provided many of the men with new boots at his own expense. A worrying pattern had also emerged among a range of industries that boded ill for the future. Several groups of employers were happy enough to take back skilled and semi-skilled workers but temporised over the reinstatement of ITGWU men displaced by strike-breakers. The biggest sector affected was construction. Employers were demanding that members of the United Builders' Labourers' Trade Union sign an 'obnoxious agreement' not to work with ITGWU members. No such requirement was being put on craftsmen. The *Irish Times* reported that businessmen were of the opinion that 'many of the disaffected men will be unable to return, their places having been filled up.' It was no wonder there were further attacks on strike-breakers over the weekend.[13]

Meanwhile Dublin Trades Council met the TUC delegation in Capel Street to review the situation. The TUC men confirmed that any further strike money was out of the question, and there was little enough left for food. After Seddon, Gosling and A. Smith of the Vehicle Builders left to catch the midday boat from Kingstown to Holyhead, the Trades Council delegates held a post-mortem on the elections. Many of them took comfort in the high vote for strike candidates, but Councillor John Bohan of the ITGWU said they 'should be more alert next year and set about our work earlier, more especially in the revision courts.' John Sutton of the Plasterers suggested that they begin at once, and 'deprecated abuse of the clergy,' which had cost them votes.

Turning to the industrial situation, Tom McPartlin denied reports that the 'obnoxious document' presented by the building employers to their labourers demanding that they boycott the ITGWU had been signed by any of the craft unions. It would be 'foolish' for members of any union to sign, but building trade delegates cautioned that their members were coming under increasing pressure. The latest move by the employers had been to stop paying apprentices. No agreement could be reached, and the building dispute had to be referred back to the Trades Council executive.[14]

The slow collapse of the strike was good news in many quarters. That night Lord Aberdeen told the dinner of the Burns Club at the Gresham Hotel that the trade of the city was recovering rapidly, and the government's Irish securities were rising after a long slump. At the same time he conceded that Dublin had been

> passing through troublous times, and we are not yet free from such. And just now hearts are sore because of a horrible deed which will constitute a black spot in the history of Dublin. ('Hear, hear.') It is difficult to

abstain from expressing the feelings which we all share about such an occurrence.

He did abstain; but the fact that the only specific act of violence the Lord Lieutenant condemned during five months of class warfare on the streets of Dublin was the admittedly brutal killing of a strike-breaker confirmed for the city's working class that the sympathies of the Liberal administration were firmly on the side of the employers. Ever the maladroit exponent of good intentions, Lord Aberdeen blithely assured the Burns Club diners that he would now devote himself to countering those influences that promoted 'distrust and suspicion between one class and another.' A step in this direction would be his Civil Exhibition, and the accompanying competition for a new Dublin development plan. These would be held throughout July, August and September and would act as 'an antidote to any suggestion that a cold and unsympathetic attitude on the part of the comparatively well-to-do population has been manifested.'

*

Lord Aberdeen's belief that the worst was over, as far as Dublin's industrial problems were concerned, appears to have been shared by the leaders of the home rule movement. So far, at rallies throughout the country, Dublin's troubles had been passed over in silence; anything that detracted from the illusion of unity on all important issues in the southern part of the country was subversive of the cause. The outcome of the municipal elections in the capital gave the leadership of the Irish Party new confidence.

On Sunday 25 January at a rally in John Redmond's own constituency of Waterford, the skeleton of the lockout was at last allowed out of the home rule cupboard and rattled in public. The theme, as ever, was national unity. The leader of the northern nationalists, Joe Devlin, said that 'Mr Redmond can go back to the House of Commons with an Ireland united behind him, as Ireland was never united before.' Dublin's newly re-elected Lord Mayor was there to underline the point; if he was intimidated by his elevation to the premier league of nationalist politics, he did not allow it to show. He told the crowd that he had come

> from Ireland's capital to Waterford because I have recognised in English newspapers during the past few months many statements that the people of Ireland's chief city are not now loyally behind the Irish leader and the Irish cause. And there is, perhaps, unfortunately, some slight shadow of foundation for our enemies endeavouring to misinterpret the views of the people of Dublin, because we found men who had been elected under other cries to public representation on Boards in Dublin going to England and endeavouring to sell the National cause by splitting the Irish vote, and because also, amidst the cheers of a section of the people, rockets were let off when victories for the cause of Unionists were achieved.

This last comment was a blatant distortion of the facts. The rockets fired from the roof of Liberty Hall had been part of the successful campaign for

Larkin's release. In the circumstances it was probably inevitable that loyalty to a class by some Dubliners should be portrayed as treachery to the nation by another.

Sherlock was on stronger ground when he cited the municipal election results as evidence that 'the people of Ireland's capital have declared beyond doubt that they are behind Mr John Redmond and his party.' The enemy had 'only fought in the wards in which they had won victories in the last three years on a genuine ticket, but when they endeavoured to play false to the national aspirations of the city the manhood of the city rose and swept them away.'[15]

*

That same night Larkin gave a very different speech to the workers of Birmingham. It was one of his most sustained attacks on the TUC leadership and the traditional trade union concerns that they represented. 'In the past ten years there had appeared upon the horizon of labour a new hope,' he told the audience. But

> trade union leaders, on the whole … believe curfew has been tolled, and they are anxious to put out the newer light. I deny that I have any personal antagonism against any man, or any feeling of aggression. I am not out to improve my own status but to see an advance of the class to which I belong.

He asked the crowd if the men who claimed to be their leaders had succeeded in strengthening the trade union movement, and they responded with cries of 'No!'

> The present-day form of trade unions is absolutely obsolete. It is a blunted weapon, and the men who use it have blunted brains, if they have got any brains at all. (Laughter and applause.)

The National Union of Railwaymen 'is the best example of the brutal form of activity within the trade union movement,' and the Amalgamated Society of Engineers (Partridge's union), 'which includes in its ranks a higher form of intelligence than any other union, has done absolutely nothing for its members.' Until the 'ordinary form of trade union … has a bigger mission and a broader outlook it is a thing that has got to be fought.'

Larkin then turned on one of his favourite targets, Ramsay Macdonald. He quoted from a speech Macdonald had made in Dundee, where the chairman of the parliamentary labour party had compared Larkin to a blind Samson pulling down the pillars of the labour movement; it says something for the alienation that now existed that Macdonald should, consciously or otherwise, turn George Russell's description of the Dublin employers against the ITGWU leader. 'I only hope,' Larkin said to cheers and laughter, 'that when he does pull them down, all the trade union leaders may be buried under the ruins.' If the labour movement was 'going to send men to Parliament, let them pick the best men, and pay them enough to prevent them selling themselves and their class to the enemy.'

Macdonald 'is a clever man, and a clever man is always a danger.' Larkin showed considerable prescience when he said that the future prime minister was always

> trying to find excuses for the employing class. I do not say that Mr Macdonald can be bought by money, but he has been bought by what is more insidious—praise and flattery.

Larkin went on to defend the sympathetic strike tactic, and complained bitterly at the lack of support now being given to the Dublin workers. This was being put down to 'the unions ... getting apathetic and tired of Dublin; but, I respectfully suggest ... those who say so are telling a lie.' He denounced the failure of the British labour movement in allowing workers' rights to be suppressed by a government dependent on its vote.

> If the Labour Party cannot bring this cowardly, vicious government to heel, it is no good to us now or in future. We have proved sufficient against this Labour Party to damn them for ever.[16]

Larkin's comments were not mere recriminations in the hour of defeat. He was hoping to speak at the special conference of the Labour Party to be held in Glasgow the following Tuesday, where electoral and parliamentary strategy were to be discussed. The conference was taking place against an intensifying debate over the relationship between industrial and political action; Larkin's speech was intended to set the scene for that debate, and it is no accident that it was made in Birmingham, the heartland of Tom Mann's syndicalist Workers' Union.

Mann had been in America on a speaking tour during the critical weeks of the Dublin lockout. Now that he was back, he hastened to Dublin to show his support for the locked-out men, and their leader. Speaking 'as a convinced syndicalist,' he told a public meeting in the Antient Concert Rooms on Monday 27 January that 'trades unionism is syndicalism.' His object was 'to combine all workers in each industry, to raise them all nationally and internationally, so as to take over control of the whole economic system.' In that way the proletariat 'could fix the number of working days, the abolition of employers, capitalists and government— which latter is only a functionary of the employers.' The 'ideal of the co-operative commonwealth will be realised.'

Turning to the Dublin situation, Mann said that the success of the employers was due to

> the disorganised state of the British workers and the defection of some leaders ... A magnificent fight has been put up and carried on with great ability, especially by Mr Larkin. (Applause).

He predicted that current disputes in the British coal and building trades presaged titanic struggles in the months ahead. In the engineering industry, where Mann had organised many unskilled and semi-skilled workers, he predicted that the existing agreement would not be renewed when it expired in March. 'In April and May there will be a general strike of engineers, boilermakers, whitesmiths, blacksmiths and kindred trades, altogether comprising 750,000 men.' He doubted if it would end unless the employers conceded the six-hour day.

After Mann sat down to loud applause, Grace Neal, the organiser of the Domestic Workers' Union in Britain, who had assisted Dora Montefiore in her Dublin kiddies scheme, breathed a little reality into the gathering. It was a disgrace to the city of Dublin 'that the children are better fed and clothed during the strike than when their parents are working.' Employers and 'others' in Dublin were now doing something to address this situation, but it was only after 'English helpers came over to look after' the children. Her action had been 'described as proselytism, but if that is proselytism ... let us have more of it.'[17]

Mann's predictions of further labour troubles in Britain proved unduly bellicose and had a very different impact from the one he predicted. As the *Irish Times* shrewdly calculated, 'troubles in the English metropolis and elsewhere in Great Britain must hasten the final collapse of the strike in Dublin.' It would undermine the ability of the British unions to lend financial support to Irish ones.

However, there was one sector where British troubles were disrupting a return to normal working in Dublin: the building trade. On Monday the London Master Builders' Association locked out nearly fifty thousand craft workers, who had refused to sign a declaration that they would work alongside non-union labour. This reinforced the determination of the Dublin Master Builders' Association to insist on the United Builders' Labourers signing its own 'obnoxious document'. It was not made any more acceptable to the UBLTU by the fact that craft workers, many of whom had worked through the dispute, had still not been asked formally to sign the pledge.[18]

*

Despite the deadlock in the building trade, the lockout was dying on its feet. On Monday 27 January, Tedcastle McCormick's, one of the foremost employers of strike-breakers, had finally taken back most of its workers, on the same terms they had when they walked out two months earlier. That day large crowds continued to congregate outside Liberty Hall in the vain hope of strike pay, but the only help available was a limited number of food parcels, and one-way tickets to Glasgow. About a hundred ITGWU members availed of the free passage.[19]

On Tuesday, Will Thorne of the Gasworkers, the same union that supported the blacking of Dublin at the TUC special delegate conference, became the first British trade union leader to announce publicly that there would be no further subscriptions to the Dublin Food Fund. In a letter to the *Daily Herald* he explained that the union's executive council took its decision 'in consequence of the heavy demands upon our resources arising from the many disputes we have to contend with at the present time.' He said that 2,750 members were drawing strike pay, and the number could reach 5,000 if the London building dispute was stepped up.

Though the *Irish Times* had welcomed the effect that industrial strife in Britain would have nearer home, it now wondered whether Dublin

is not the only place where the system of collective bargaining has given evidence of collapse. The same spirit of irresponsibility in trade union ranks has displayed itself in England before. But it has never been revealed on so vast a scale as in the London building trade, or in circumstances so nearly identical with the circumstances in Dublin.

The *Times* cautioned the London employers against trying to 'smash trade unionism' by methods that would give justification to the sympathetic strike tactic. Collective bargaining was the only way forward, but it had been

made valueless by trade union irresponsibility … The whole structure of industrial life rests on the principle of collective bargaining, and it is threatened with destruction. The accredited leaders of British trade unionism will have to take an effective stand against the widespread spirit of wilful indiscipline, unless they are prepared to see our present industrial system lapse into utter anarchy.

*

The previous day, Larkin had been refused admission as a delegate to the special Labour Party conference in Glasgow. But there was no shortage of other critics of the Labour leadership.

As chairman of the Parliamentary Labour Party, Ramsay Macdonald was given the task of defending the movement's political strategy. His basic message was that the political system could not be changed until the working class sent 340 Labour MPs to London to represent them, rather than 40. Those forty members had 'to bet and gamble to get a place for their bills.' They had 'done as well [as], if not better than, any other forty men who could have been drawn from the trades unionist and socialist movement.' Macdonald also criticised the 'very extreme left wing of our party,' which insisted that no support should be given to either a Liberal or a Tory government; that in itself was an obstacle to winning the electoral support needed to give their own party a parliamentary majority. The argument about the need to win the middle ground would still be rehearsed at British, and Irish, Labour Party conferences over eighty years later.

The parliamentary party came in for particularly sustained criticism from the floor. One delegate from Macdonald's own constituency said that 'the Labour Party in Parliament pays far too much regard to etiquette, and are lacking in holy zeal.' They were 'helping the scab employer rather than trade unionists.' A Manchester delegate said that the MPs had

left their orange boxes at the street corners to sit on the soft cushions of the House of Commons, instead of doing the work of the party outside. (Laughter). There is too much of the garden party and lardy-dardy and doing the grand about them. I am afraid some members … neglect their work in order to ape the dukes. (More laughter and cheers.)

In defence of his colleagues, J. R. Clynes, the trade union representative on the ill-fated Askwith Inquiry in Dublin, replied testily:

The Labour Party in the House has been insidiously pursued by enemies who pretend to be friends, who find fault with every attempt and suppress every act of good work, and have mischievously spread abroad the worst and the vilest lies that could be invented against the party. It is hard to work as we do at drudgery in Parliament and then be told we are doing the grand. (Laughter.) I am not prepared to throw home rule and other measures into the melting pot. We … ought not to have indifferently and carelessly walked into the lobby to bring down the government on a point of irritation.

Clynes's speech was followed by a bitter dispute, involving several MPs, about whether Macdonald had used his position as chairman of the parliamentary party to do deals with Lloyd George.[20] The outcome of the debate was indecisive: no new parliamentary course was charted, and no attempt was made in the end to co-ordinate industrial with political strategy.

*

There was not even a hint of acrimony at the annual meeting of the Dublin Chamber of Commerce, held in Commercial Buildings the same day. There was an exceptionally large turn-out to congratulate the president, William Martin Murphy, on his climactic year. Despite the traumatic events of the previous six months, Murphy presented annual accounts that showed that the chamber's operating deficit had been reduced from £176 in 1912 to £81 in 1913. Similarly, the membership had risen to 738, an increase of 19 on the previous year. As so often in the past, Murphy had thrived on adversity and conflict, and so had his associates.

The main business of the day was of course the post-mortem on the great dispute. Murphy began both modestly and disingenuously.

I was not conscious that I was opening a fresh chapter in the history of labour disputes when I took what appeared to me to be the only and natural course of defeating, by every means at my disposal, a wanton attack on properties for which I was responsible.

This attack was easily repelled, but it soon became evident that it was but part of a plot to plunge the city into a state of anarchy, and to make all business impossible. This end was sought … by a system known as 'Syndicalism' or 'Sympathetic Strikes', with the object of bringing the trade of the city to a standstill. The history of this trouble is so recent that I need not dilate on it further than to record the utter failure of the Syndicalist system. Least of all was this system of any use as a means of improving the position of the working classes. Indeed, it was not intended by its authors to produce any such result. Their avowed objects were to destroy capitalists, to subvert the present order of things, and to establish what Mr Larkin called a 'Co-Operative Commonwealth,' of which he, no doubt, was to be the 'Cromwell.'

There is, however, a fatal defect in this scheme, as it makes no provision for maintaining the wage earner during the time which must elapse between the destruction of the employer and the setting up of the 'Co-Operative Commonwealth.' It is strange enough that even the most ignorant labourer should be caught by this claptrap, but it is amazing to think how the skilled tradesmen of the city, as represented by their Trades Council, came under the domination of Mr Larkin, and allowed themselves to be dragged at his tail.

The chief, if not the only cause of poverty and the slums of Dublin, is want of employment, especially for unskilled workmen. There are too many work-people and too few employers. The remedy of the new Social Reformers for this state of things is, by withdrawing labour from them, to destroy the employers, who to save themselves—were forced to import new hands, and thus further glut the labour market. This method of improving the position of the workingman seems to justify the derisive epithet of being an 'Irish way' of doing things. I have spoken to many men who went out on strike, and who applied for reinstatement, some of whom were re-employed, and some who could not be because their places had been filled up, and I have not met a single man who could give any intelligent reason why he threw up his job, or what advantage he ever hoped to gain by doing so.

Murphy turned from the hapless plight of former employees begging for their jobs back to the 'Buy Irish' issue. He reminded his listeners that not long before, word that a Dublin shopkeeper was importing a new shop front made in England would provoke

indignation meetings of the Trades Council ... and the offenders were duly denounced. Now it is the highest form of patriotism, according to the same Trades Council, to close up Jacob's biscuit factory, Dixon's Soap Factory, Paterson's Match Factory, Perry's Box Factory, and numerous others, and to drive out of the city all the industries we have left. If a determined stand had not been made against the would-be destroyers, not one of these industries would be alive today.

Like Connolly and Larkin, if for different reasons, Murphy blamed the TUC for Dublin's troubles.

The attempt to hold up the trade of Dublin would have been very short-lived indeed but for the intervention of certain leaders of the English Labour Party, who, with the most cynical and callous indifference to the losses of Irish employers or the suffering of Irish workmen, kept this trouble going for five months by doles of money and food provided by the whole trades union organisations of Great Britain. This was done, forsooth, to uphold the principles of trades unionism, as if the Irish Transport Union possessed any of the attributes of a legitimate trades union.

It was, perhaps, excusable that the English trades delegates should not at first have been able to understand the difference between the Irish Transport Union and a genuine trades union, but after 'Comrade' Larkin had carried his 'fiery cross' to England, where official trades unionism denounced himself and all his works, the same men, by continuing to support him in Dublin, gave colour to the suggestions which have been made—though I do not myself believe them—that a sinister design to crush Irish industry was at the back of the support given to the attacks on the employers of this city.

Murphy did admit, however, that he had

a shrewd suspicion that the English trades union delegates, when they have to consider on a future occasion the question of giving general support to a particular union, will have some regard to the manner in which it conducts its business, and take a lesson from the Dublin Employers' Federation.

He could not help returning to the bugbear of Larkin and 'Dublin syndicalism'. If Larkin had 'by any chance prevailed, it would be only a personal triumph for him, and not for trades unionism.' Nor could Murphy resist another favourite theme, that

working people … in 99 cases out of a hundred … will get more out of their employers in anticipation of a strike than after it takes place. The threat of a strike has much more terror for the employer than the strike itself, when he has his back to the wall and must fight for the existence of his business. If an object lesson to confirm this is wanting, it would be found in the action of the employers of this city, who stood together in such a remarkable manner for the last five months. ('Hear, hear.')

However, he told his audience that the victory they had won

should not … absolve employers from their obligation of seeing that their workpeople receive a wage which allows them to at least live in frugal comfort. Let us not be deterred by our recent experiences from acting on this principle, and from doing our best to develop the industries and trade of this city.

The speech showed that Murphy had a vision of Ireland not so different from many Irish-Irelanders: indeed his reference to the obligation on employers to keep their workers in 'frugal comfort' anticipated the greatest Irish-Irelander of them all, Éamon de Valera. Murphy's hatred of the ITGWU and its leader was clearly undiluted by the taste of victory: he saw them as carriers of foreign viruses that had to be destroyed; he obviously hoped that Dublin could return to the 'respectable' trade unionism of the old Dublin Trades Council.

Surprisingly, even in Murphy's moment of triumph there was a dissenting voice in the audience. It was not Edward Lee but a solicitor, James Brady, who questioned the wisdom of Murphy's strategy and who accused him, indirectly, of using the Dublin Chamber of Commerce for his own purposes. Brady was a well-known figure in nationalist and trade union circles who had been, by turns, a UIL and a Sinn Féin member of the city council. He had a large legal practice in the city, and had represented the United Builders' Labourers' Trade Union briefly at the Askwith tribunal.

Brady took up a point Murphy had made in passing, that the Chamber of Commerce had not been involved directly in the dispute but had left its conduct 'in the hands of a delegation of employers.' If the council of the Chamber of Commerce 'had not the courage' to grapple with the question itself, then Murphy should not have mentioned it at all in his presidential speech; nor should any reference to it appear in the annual report. Brady particularly objected to talk of 'anarchy' and 'sympathetic strikes'. These were

> a matter that should be left for report from the delegation of employers concerned. ('Hear, hear.') Why should the Chamber, without knowledge, proceed to chastise anybody of wrong-doing when they had no personal knowledge of the subject? [There have been] faults on both sides in connection with the dispute, and if better counsels had prevailed on both sides the city would have been saved from all the turmoil and trouble which it has gone through in the last few months. A little less anxiety to down everybody would have been of much service. I always admired the chairman for his great commercial capacity, but in reference to the recent dispute there are points on which we do not agree.

Brady asked the chamber 'to leave out all reference to the dispute' from its report

> and not have it paraded all over the world as denouncing anybody as anarchists and promoters of evil, when, perhaps, we are as much to blame as the others are.

Despite the vocal support some of these comments received, the chamber adopted Murphy's report with only one dissenting voice, that of Brady.

Murphy himself thought that 'most people in the city who have anything to lose, as well as the Chamber, will be in favour of the report.' So did Sir Robert Gardner of the city's leading accountancy firm, Craig Gardner, who was also chairman of Johnston, Mooney and O'Brien. He moved the vote of thanks to Murphy and the other officers of the council. He responded to Brady's comments by saying: 'When we find men of energy, ability, and position coming here week after week, considering with all the care and accuracy that they can bring to bear on different subjects— surely those men are deserving of our thanks?' He was met with loud applause.[21] The city's business community was in no humour to let self-doubt spoil its triumphalist mood.

44

WHILE Murphy was being lauded by his peers in Dublin, Larkin was publicly repudiated in Glasgow by his erstwhile allies of the National Transport Workers' Federation. It must have been a bitter experience, for the cause of his humiliation was Havelock Wilson.

Larkin had never replied to the letter from Robert Williams demanding that he either prove or retract the allegations of 'scabbing' against the NSFU leader. The executive of the NTWF met in Glasgow on 28 January; as no reply had been received to Williams's letter, it decided that Larkin's action 'be entirely repudiated; that he be dissociated from this federation, and that no member of this Federation shall support him in the future.'[1] Larkin was now a leper as far as the leaders of the British transport workers were concerned. It must have been music to Murphy's ears.

Larkin dismissed the NTWF's action as 'bluff and blow'; the federation 'had not given my supporters the slightest assistance' during the lockout. Far from being discouraged, he said the action of the NTWF executive had cleared the way for his own union to consider recruiting the thousands of workers in Britain who were seeking new leaders.

Despite the bluster, it is clear that the repudiation rankled with Larkin, and with Connolly. For weeks afterwards both men continued to justify their attacks on Wilson and to criticise the role of the NSFU in the lockout. As far as they were concerned, Wilson and his executive had ordered members in Dublin to 'scab', and the ITGWU would not apologise for telling the truth, whatever the cost. But in 1913 Wilson's stock in the trade union movement was still high, as one of its great pioneers. Even Tom Mann, the ablest and most consistent syndicalist leader, considered Wilson 'a straightforward, honourable and loyal comrade' at this time.[2] Larkin's statements could not pass unchallenged.

Further humiliation was in store for Larkin. He had stayed on in Glasgow after the special Labour Party conference on electoral strategy in the hope of addressing the fourteenth annual conference of the party, which was to follow. Despite angry appeals from the floor—to which Ramsay Macdonald responded with further attacks on syndicalism as the 'Delilah' of the labour movement—it was decided not to allow representatives of workers involved in current disputes to address the conference. Emotional addresses from workers in dispute were a party conference ritual; the decision to ban them on this occasion, in order to gag Larkin, showed how deeply the Dublin lockout had divided the British movement.[3]

*

While Larkin sat impotently listening to Ramsay Macdonald in Glasgow, the Dublin dispute was over in all but name. More than fifty vessels a day were entering and leaving the port, and trade was almost normal for the time of year. Even the 'accumulation of timber' that had caused complaints from the Shipping Federation a few days earlier was being 'gradually reduced.' The only threat of disruption to the traffic of the port came from an outbreak of foot and mouth disease in County Kildare.[4]

The only large groups of workers still in formal dispute with their employers were the IWWU members in Jacob's and the UBLTU members in the building trade. The IWWU members were in the unfortunate position that their employer could do without them indefinitely, partly because most had been replaced and partly because of the seasonal slump that always followed the Christmas trade. George Jacob had no intention of taking back the ingrates who had been the cause of appalling publicity for his factory and its products. In an effort to counteract the effects of that publicity he had invited church leaders, Poor Law guardians, representatives of local authorities and even the Royal College of Physicians to investigate working conditions at the factory in Bishop Street. Eventually he invited the press. Most of the papers took up his offer, and the *Irish Independent*, *Freeman's Journal* and *Irish Catholic* published large illustrated features that depicted happy, hard-working employees. The *Irish Catholic* was particularly enthusiastic in its description of this 'Hive of Work and Happiness.' It published photographs of a canteen packed for the one o'clock dinner, women dancing on the roof garden, girls drilling in the gym, and a group of the men's total abstinence association playing bagatelle in a recreation room. Its correspondent claimed to have seen 'all fashions in factories that prevail ... from the bleak snow-swept fishing sheds of Iceland to those palaces of industry in the rose gardens of Cairo where are made the dainty perfumed Egyptian cigarettes'; but he had no hesitation in placing Jacob's at the 'rose garden' rather than the 'fishing shed' end of the spectrum.[5]

Unfortunately the *Irish Catholic* commanded little attention in Britain, where George Jacob failed to convince the mass-circulation *Daily Herald* of the justice of his case. Eventually he sued the paper, and won considerable damages when the case was heard in July 1914.[6] One indirect achievement of the strikers had been a reduction in the working week for the 670 male workers, from 55 hours to 50, the same as those of female workers. Jacob's conceded the shorter hours rather than risk renewed strife at Bishop Street.[7]

Far more disruptive to the city's commerce was the continuing lockout of members of the United Builders' Labourers' Trade Union. Until they returned, thousands of craftsmen were also in effect locked out. There were 1,200 UBLTU members still eligible for strike pay at the end of January 1914 and about 2,000 in all who were refusing to sign the Employers' Federation renunciation of the ITGWU. But on Saturday 31 January, with no further strike pay in prospect, they accepted the inevitable. That afternoon over eight hundred members met in the union hall in Clanbrassil Street to vote on the latest settlement terms on offer from the Master Builders' Association. With such stalwarts of the Employers' Federation as Good, McLaughlin and Shortall representing the employers, they must have known that those terms would not be generous. The main provision was that UBLTU members would sign a new form confirming that they were not members of the ITGWU and would never become members in the future. They must also undertake not to participate in or support 'sympathetic' strikes; and they would carry out all instructions issued by their employers and 'work amicably with all other employees, whether they be members of a union or not.' The UBLTU was required to dismiss any member who broke this agreement. In return, the Master Builders' Association gave a vague commitment to re-employ such UBLTU members 'as they may require' in the coming months on the same wages and conditions as existed before the men walked off the job on 13 September.

The proposals represented a serious defeat for workers who had been out in sympathy with the ITGWU for four-and-a-half months rather than sign the original form of renunciation against the ITGWU. Nevertheless, the UBLTU leaders urged members to accept the terms of surrender. So did Father T. J. Monaghan, the Meath Street priest who had given such eloquent testimony to the Housing Inquiry; with his twelve years of work in the Liberties, he must have known many of the workers and the employers personally. He was now given leave to address the meeting, and he told the men that he had met the employers and had been given personal assurances that there would be no victimisation. After that the ballot should have been little more than a formality. Indeed, UBLTU members who worked for John Good had returned to work that morning without bothering to vote. In the event it was found that 112 building labourers out of the 812 who turned up for the ballot were prepared to carry on the fight regardless.[8]

They were not typical of the mood now prevailing in the city. ITGWU dockers unloading a grain ship, the *Marco Polo*, handed back their union cards rather than obey an instruction from Liberty Hall to stop because some strike-breakers were still being used in preference to idle trade union labour. At T. and C. Martin's, the first company in the city to import strike-breakers, 40 of its 130 'old hands' were taken back only after they agreed to sign an 'unconditional agreement' to carry out orders and work with non-union labour. The *Irish Times* told its readers that workers were practically begging for their jobs back throughout the city, and the only real obstacle to reinstatement in many firms was the fact that vacancies no longer existed. This was particularly so in the carting trade, where 'the necessity for ... re-employment is ceasing day after day, owing to the introduction of motor lorries.' Even so, a thousand carters were estimated to have been reinstated by Monday 2 February, and that night a meeting of coalmen at Liberty Hall decided to seek terms, even though the coal yards had made it clear that those accepted back must work with 'free labourers' and sign an agreement similar to that in force at T. and C. Martin's. By Wednesday an estimated four hundred coalmen had done so and received their jobs back.

Significantly, the declarations sought from workers by T. and C. Martin and by the coal merchants did not require workers to renounce the ITGWU, though in the case of the coal merchants the wearing of union badges was prohibited during working hours. In the Port and Docks Board, where elected representatives exercised some sway, no declarations of surrender were required. But even appeals by William Field MP and Councillor Alfie Byrne could not win reinstatement for workers for whom no vacancies existed. The most that could be achieved, on the motion of the nationalist councillor for South Dock ward, Thomas Murty O'Beirne, was that the question be kept under review.[9]

'We are at last able to record the definite end of the labour troubles which have afflicted Dublin for the better part of half a year,' the *Irish Times* felt it could report on 3 February 1914. The return to work of the builders' labourers and carters meant that 'all the work there is to be done in Dublin at present is being done ... The collapse of the strike is complete and certain.' It was an occasion for 'qualified satisfaction' and some bitterness, not against the workers but at

> the miserable part which the English trade union leaders have played in this weary dispute. We do not often enjoy the pleasure of being able to agree with Mr. Larkin, but there is considerable ground for his charge that these English leaders 'betrayed' the Dublin strikers. Either the Dublin strikers were, or they were not, engaged in upholding trade union principles and resisting an attempt to 'smash trade unionism.'

The English union leaders had two clear choices:

> they could have arrayed all the forces of organised Labour on the side of the Dublin strikers—a possibility the menace of which was scarcely appreciated, we think, by the employers of Dublin. They could have denounced the strike and had nothing more to do with it. They did neither of these obvious things. They sent money and food supplies to Dublin, and prolonged the dispute for months; they marked time until it became clear that the Syndicalist tail was not strong enough to wag the trade union dog; then they gradually threw away the Dublin strikers' cause.

Referring to the support the ITGWU members had given to the NUR and NSFU in 1911, the *Times* concluded that 'the education of Irish workmen in the advantages of English intervention, begun by the railway strike a few years ago, is vastly advanced by these sorry and cynical proceedings.' It was an inadvertent argument for a separate labour movement in Ireland; and the voice of southern unionist opinion had put it more succinctly than any separatist contributor to *Sinn Féin* or *Irish Freedom*.

*

The *Times* also had a word of censure and warning for the employers. They had achieved 'the worst kind of settlement—virtually "settlement by starvation".' Many of those who had gone back to work did so

> with the resentful feelings of hopelessly beaten men. There can be no element of finality about such a settlement.
>
> That is one reason why we find the end of the strike a matter less for rejoicing than for heart-searching. This must not be an ending; it must be a beginning—a beginning of applying the experience which we had so hardly learned during these disastrous months. The settlement of the strike has, in fact, settled nothing. The very necessary business of 'smashing Larkin' has been accomplished; but that is very far from being the same thing as 'smashing Larkinism.' There is no security whatever that the men who are now going about their work brooding over the bitterness of defeat will not endeavour to reorganise their broken forces, and, given another leader and another opportunity, strike a further and more desperate blow at the economic life of Dublin.
>
> It is the employers' first business to get on terms of permanent confidence and good will with their workmen. This is a business for which the deliberate cultivation of more human and more intimate relations between employer and employed is more important than any consideration of wages and conditions of employment. In the work of social reconstruction which now lies before us not only the employers, but the whole public of Dublin, have to play a part.

There is something surprisingly modern as well as sensible about the conclusions of the *Irish Times* leader-writer. But it was far too modern for the Dublin Employers' Federation.

While some individual employers no doubt sought to rebuild good relations with their workers, the federation decided to offer a reward of £100 'for such information as shall lead to the apprehension and conviction of those responsible for the brutal assault upon the man Thomas Harten, murdered on Eden Quay.' The offer was made in a letter sent to the press by the secretary of the Employers' executive committee, Charles Coghlan. He also announced that a fund was being opened for the dependants of Harten, and 'should the response of the public be such as to provide more than, in the Committee's judgement, is necessary for this immediate object, they will consider any surplus as a trust for meeting the needs of any similar case which might unhappily occur.' Coghlan announced that his own committee was donating £25 to the fund, and the Shipping Federation a further £10.[10] What dependants Harten, a single unemployed man, might have was never made clear. A week later a mere £16 9s 6d had been subscribed. Even William Martin Murphy had seen fit to subscribe only two guineas; after that the fund sank without trace.

The thinking behind the decision to offer a reward for information about Harten's murder when three men were awaiting trial for the same offence is hard to plumb. The most charitable interpretation is that the leaders of the lockout were so frightened by the recent increase in violence that fear overruled their better judgment. The more likely explanation is that Murphy hoped to uncover a conspiracy that would lead back to Liberty Hall and to Larkin. In his favour was the fact that the nineteen men arrested after the street battle with the strike-breakers in Townsend Street and the three men charged with Harten's murder were all represented by the ITGWU's solicitors; but as a veteran of the Parnell Commission inquiry, Murphy should have known that conspiracy was extremely difficult to prove, even by resorting to unscrupulous methods. Whatever else was motivating him and his colleagues, they were clearly not inspired by thoughts of reconciliation.

*

Murphy's lack of charity was probably due in part to the significant losses experienced by the DUTC as a result of the lockout. On Tuesday 3 February he presented the annual accounts for 1913 to the shareholders. The venue was the Imperial Hotel, scene of Larkin's dramatic appearance on Bloody Sunday and also a Murphy-owned establishment. The annual report showed that the company's net profit for the year was £119,871, compared with £142,382 in 1912, a drop of £22,511. This was despite greatly increased income, up from £218,821 in 1912 to £297,720 in 1913. Murphy freely admitted that the strike was the cause of the dramatic fall in profit.

Loss of receipts of £18,004 on the tramway service, and of £2,841 for the parcel service, was the main cause of the fall in profits. Some extra money had been earned from the use of trams to deliver coal, but this was more than offset by exceptional charges, such as legal fees for evicting striking employees, the hire of lorries, repairs to damaged vehicles, and special accommodation for strike-breakers, especially the vital power station workers. As a result of the labour troubles the board of directors decided to reduce the dividend on ordinary shares from 6 to 5 per cent for the second half of 1913, or 5½ per cent for the full year. The company still had almost £10,000 in hand, after £7,000 had been set aside for repairs to the permanent way and £3,000 to make good the trams lost in the strike. A drop of ½ per cent in dividends for the full year[11] must have seemed a small price to pay for total victory over the ITGWU.

A darker cloud was cast over the proceedings by a serious accident at Merrion Square on the previous Sunday. Twenty-four passengers were injured when the Dalkey tram jumped the points and toppled over. It was widely suspected that sabotage had been involved; if so, it was another worrying symptom of the dangerous regression towards naked class warfare that the lockout had provoked. Murphy alluded cryptically in his report to the possibility of sabotage; but this did not prevent him exulting once more at his victory over 'a certain Mr. Larkin, who claimed to have come with a divine mission [and] unfortunately selected this city a few years ago as the field of his missionary endeavours.' In the course of that summer

> it became abundantly evident that his ambition to become labour dictator of Dublin would not be fully satisfied until he had brought the Tramway Company under his subjection. It did not appear to me to be to the advantage of the shareholders that Mr. Larkin should control your property rather than the directors whom you appointed for that purpose, and I was determined that he should not. (Applause.)

Murphy recounted in detail how he had met the DUTC workers in the Antient Concert Rooms at midnight on 19 July with his fellow-directors. This approach had largely succeeded, but some dismissals of 'Transport Union emissaries' within the company for intimidation and assaults on non-striking employees proved necessary.

> The loyalty of a large proportion of our men … left no resource to Mr. Larkin's followers but violence and outrage. The net result of Larkinism during the last six months is, that after keeping the city in a state of turmoil and disturbance, and nearly ruining its trade, there is not a single Irish working man or woman in Dublin whose wages or conditions of employment have been improved in the least degree. So far from bringing any benefit to the working man, Larkin's campaign has brought nothing but untold misery on them and their families. I have no feeling of triumph over the utter defeat of the disruptionists, but I have the greatest commiseration for the victims of Mr. Larkin's ambition and their own folly.

To the end, Murphy acknowledged no blame for any of what had passed: it was all due to Larkin's ambition and the workers' folly. The shareholders fully agreed. Moving a vote of thanks on their behalf, J. J. Maguire said that they all owed 'a debt of gratitude to Mr Murphy for the bravery which he has shown in combating the conspiracy against the welfare and prosperity of their company.' The conspiracy was aimed not alone at the company but at 'the trade and industry of the city.' If the chairman had not confronted 'the machinery of intimidation and tyranny … I do not know where things would have ended.'[12]

There were other intimations for Dublin's workers that the wider world regarded them and their leader in a similar light. On the same Sunday that the Dalkey tram was derailed, the children 'exported' to Liverpool under

Dora Montefiore's 'kiddies scheme' returned home; a small, subdued crowd gathered at the North Wall to greet them. On Monday morning Larkin returned from Scotland equally unobtrusively. When he arrived at Liberty Hall at about 11 a.m. a few stalwarts called for 'three cheers for Jim Larkin' but met with little response from the crowd. Larkin made no speeches that day; however, some time later strike pay was issued, and there were a few food tickets. The lucky recipients of these found themselves entitled to just two loaves of bread each. The return to work by so many building labourers and carters had reduced the drain on resources, but the resources themselves were fast dwindling.

The last of the food ships had arrived in Larkin's absence; and when the Parliamentary Committee of the TUC met on Monday 9 February it decided to wind up the Dublin fund. The £1,000 remaining was to be disbursed 'among the bona fide Trade Unionists still out of work.' There were over four thousand ITGWU members alone in this category, so that the final disbursement must have been worth less than 5s to each worker.[13]

By coincidence, the Dublin Chamber of Commerce and Dublin Trades Council held their regular monthly meetings on the same day as the TUC fund was being formally wound up. Murphy had stood down as president of the Chamber of Commerce after giving his annual report a fortnight earlier, but there was no change in the chamber's mood of confident belligerence. The new president was R. K. Gamble, chairman of Brooks Thomas, honorary secretary of the Chamber of Commerce during the lockout, and a close ally of Murphy. The main business of the meeting was another tribute to Murphy. Richard Jones, the butter merchant who had so strongly opposed Edward Lee's attempt to end the lockout in November, proposed that the council constitute itself into a committee that would 'afford the citizens of Dublin and businessmen of Ireland an opportunity to express their appreciation of the great public services tendered by our Ex-President Mr. William Martin Murphy during the prolonged labour troubles.' The fund collected was used to commission a portrait of Murphy by Sir William Orpen, and this was presented by the employers of Dublin to their leader the following year. As it happened, Orpen was an admirer of Larkin and had sketched him at Liberty Hall during the lockout; the sketch shows a weary Larkin, surrounded by ghostly, famine-like figures. The painting of Murphy depicts a benign but sprightly-looking old gentleman reflecting on his life's achievements.[14]

The Trades Council meeting that evening was a tetchy affair dominated by the legacy of the lockout. It began with Larkin proposing that the council accept an invitation from Lorcan Sherlock to be represented on the Lord Mayor's fund for the families of Byrne and Nolan, the ITGWU men killed in the first weekend of rioting. Tom McPartlin, the vice-president, and John Farren, treasurer, normally allies of Larkin, said they had already refused Sherlock's invitation. They must have been surprised at Larkin's stance: he had denounced the fund and its sponsor repeatedly in the past, but now he insisted that the matter go to a vote, and won. The secretary, John Simmons, then proposed support for a 'ladies' committee' that was campaigning to have the school dinners legislation extended to Ireland. This time it was Larkin's turn to oppose the motion, which was passed. John Farren gave a largely positive and non-contentious report on his latest efforts to persuade the Insurance Advisory Committee in London to adopt a more positive approach to the unemployment benefit claims from locked-out workers.

Dissension broke out again when the Trades Council discussed the decision of the UBLTU members to return to work. Larkin accused the building labourers of having 'betrayed' the strikers 'at the insistence of a priest and a Jew,' who were 'in collusion with Freemasons.' The priest was Father Monaghan; the Jew was probably a builder called Ellion, who had been involved in the negotiations between the master builders and the construction unions. William O'Brien succeeded in having the issue referred back, but it showed how divided the experience of defeat had left Dublin's trade unionists.

Larkin's attack on Jews was not unique. Anti-semitism was not restricted to ultra-nationalists such as Arthur Griffith. Cartoons in the *Irish Worker* sometimes depicted capitalists with hooked noses, and Richard O'Carroll, the socialist leader of the Bricklayers, had already attacked Ellion as a Jew, rather than as an employer, during the lockout.[15] Larkin and O'Carroll could have claimed that they were lapsing into the idiom of the day: in working-class Dublin in 1914, and for many decades afterwards, the terms 'Jewman' and 'moneylender' were virtually synonymous. However, no-one at the meeting challenged the remarks. Instead, the normal preoccupations of the Trades Council began to reassert themselves. There was, for instance, unanimous support for the Tailors' Society in defending its traditional right to nominate members to fill vacancies in municipal workshops.

*

The consequences of the lockout pursued Larkin on a personal level. The courts had rejected his appeal against eviction from Auburn Street; with no alternative accommodation available for the penniless leader of a virtually bankrupt trade union, he solved the problem by the simple expedient of moving his family, including his sister, Delia, into Croydon Park.[16] But not all his problems could be solved as easily. As he had told the Trades Council on Monday night, he still had 'four thousand to five thousand men out fighting for trade union principles,' and no prospect of work for any of them. He could have added the five hundred IWWU members, mainly from Jacob's, who were in a similar plight.

A month later most of these workers were still out, and William O'Brien, newly elected president of the Trades Council in succession to McPartlin, estimated that 'more than half of these men and all the women and girls are permanently victimised.'[17] Once more Larkin decided to tour England. Now a well-known speaker and crowd-puller, he hoped to raise funds and rebuild the union's finances; he also needed to try to rebuild relations with the NTWF and other British unions, if only to obtain help in resolving various items of unfinished business with shipping companies such as the Head Line, which had locked out ITGWU dockers in Belfast for supporting their Dublin brethren.

In Larkin's absence the committee of the ITGWU's Number 1 Branch was once more the de facto executive, handling day-to-day business. In an effort to reduce costs, it decided there was no longer a requirement for a secretary to serve the needs of the DUTC section.[18] This was perhaps the greatest tribute of all to the effectiveness of William Martin Murphy's campaign. The branch also considered applications from members 'in a bad way' who wanted the fare to England to seek work there.[19]

We can only guess at the plight of many of those locked out. The letter from Brigid McCarthy to Colonel H. Renny-Tailyour, managing director of Guinness's brewery, gives some inkling of the fears for the future, as well as the immediate hardship, that many strikers' families experienced. She was the wife of Edward McCarthy, the Guinness boat skipper who had walked off the job in October 1913 rather than handle 'tainted' goods. Her husband had

> all his things ready to go away to sea, which is breaking my heart. Would you be so kind as to try and get him back, or would you try and get some money for me as I am very badly off with eight small children. I was talking to him today and he said if he was taken back he would give up all unions … I would not mind if he was put in some other part of the Brewery as he does not like the boats. Would you be so kind and let me know what can you do for me before he goes away.

Seven months later she was still writing letters pleading for her husband's reinstatement.[20]

McCarthy's fellow-striker Patrick Donegan had been eighteen years with the company, and also had eight children. He too was refused reinstatement. Donegan threw himself on the mercy of Lorcan Sherlock, who took up a collection 'to secure a horse and dray by which to earn a livelihood for himself and family.'[21]

Meanwhile the rest of the world was going about its business, and Dublin was returning to normality with astonishing speed. On Tuesday 3 February the first levee of the new season was held at Dublin Castle by Lord Aberdeen. The *Irish Times* correspondent blessed the changed situation, which made the circumstances of the levee 'more than usually favourable.' The weather was 'springlike in its mildness, while the sunshine which lent its brilliance to the scene was a pleasing change from the wintry weather of a recent period.' A high point of the evening was the changing of the guard by the King's Own Scottish Borderers. The state ball followed on Friday, and all seemed well for a world whose life had been severely disrupted since Horse Show Week.[22]

*

The return to normal was helped considerably by the good sense of Mr Justice Dodd. In the first two weeks of February he dealt with most of the outstanding charges arising from recent shooting incidents in the city. On 4 February, Patrick Traynor, the strike-breaker who shot Alice Brady, came before him at the City Commission. The charge was now one of causing the girl's death as a result of a revolver shot. However, the grand jury, made up of property-holders, found no bill against Traynor, even on the reduced indictment. In Traynor's favour was police evidence that he had been attacked by the mob, and that Alice Brady had, after all, died of tetanus. In discharging Traynor, Mr Justice Dodd used the opportunity to comment on what he called the labour situation. He said it would have been 'far better … left to the masters and men to come together themselves'; the 'interference' of 'outsiders and other busy people' had only aggravated the situation.

Later the same day James Lewis, the strike-breaker who shot John Hollwey, came before the commission. He was charged with maliciously wounding Hollwey and causing him grievous bodily harm. In many ways his defence was stronger than Traynor's: he had been ambushed in a narrow street where he had previously been badly beaten by strikers; he could not possibly have intended shooting Hollwey, who had been lucky enough to recover fully from his injuries. However, John Hollwey was a shipbroker, not a striking factory worker. Lewis had no legal representation in court and gave no evidence; it was up to Mr Justice Dodd to defend the man in his summary to the jury. He described Lewis as 'either a fool or a rogue,' but the circumstances that had brought him and other men into the dock at this time were 'heart-rending.' He said that 'free labourers were called upon in an emergency … to do something at the risk of their lives. One would think that, that being so, they deserved a little consideration, a little kindness, a little pity.' He then criticised the employers, G. and P. Glorney, for not having provided counsel for Lewis, 'who has apparently not much intelligence.' It was his employer who had supplied Lewis with a revolver, to use 'on his own responsibility.' The police were allowed weapons only 'on occasions of great disorder,' and the case 'raised the question of the advisability of the use of revolvers in the city by any person. Were the lives of citizens to be placed at the mercy of men like the man in the dock?' It was clear who Mr Justice Dodd would have preferred to see in the dock. He called for regulation to prevent employers issuing revolvers so that citizens could be shot at 'by a man of the class of the prisoner.'

The jury needed only a short recess to bring back a verdict of not guilty on the malicious wounding charge. It found Lewis guilty of causing grievous bodily harm, but requested clemency. Hollwey also spoke for the prisoner. Mr Justice Dodd allowed Lewis out on his own recognisances after a friend undertook to pay his fare to Wales. Though technically still liable to a sentence, Lewis could go home.[23]

All winter, magistrates in the police courts had been sending strikers to prison on less serious charges, and had been attacked in the columns of the

Irish Worker and from public platforms as agents of Murphy and the capitalist class. Two strike-breakers accused of serious shooting offences had walked free; yet Mr Justice Dodd was not lambasted by the labour movement. It was not that Dodd was particularly soft-hearted, as was shown in a domestic murder case later that week;[24] what marked him out from the magistrates was that he had taken the trouble to put the cases of the strike-breakers in their wider social and political context.

Also inhibiting trade union comment was the fact that nineteen members of the ITGWU were due up before Mr Justice Dodd the following week over the ambush of strike-breakers in Townsend Street. They appeared before him on Monday 9 February. Earlier in the day Dodd had heard a similar case against two ITGWU shop stewards accused of assaulting a strike-breaker named Philip Clerkin, who was, incidentally, a Dublin man. He claimed they were the ringleaders in a group of eighteen men who attacked him in Poolbeg Street. The two men in the dock were there purely on the strength of Clerkin's evidence, which was entertaining if not very credible. At one point he said that he was knocked down 'six times a minute inside fifteen minutes.' The defence counsel pointed out that this was 'ninety times you were knocked down.' 'Yes, sir,' Clerkin replied without hesitation.

Despite the flimsy evidence, the jury found the shop stewards guilty. Mr Justice Dodd then told them:

> Members of a guild union might succeed in hurting or injuring a free labourer, but every wound they gave a free labourer gave twenty wounds to their union. The freedom of the individual in this country must be maintained, and will be maintained, from the bench, and maintained, I hope, from the trade unions themselves.

Then, as in the case of Lewis, he deferred sentence.

When the nineteen members of the ITGWU appeared before Dodd for the fracas in Townsend Street on 21 January, all pleaded guilty to unlawful assembly. It was 'a most deplorable thing to see the prisoners in the dock,' Mr Justice Dodd said. 'They are all brothers, and I will try them as brothers.' He thought 'the justice of the case will be met by eighteen days' imprisonment, with hard labour, from the date of their arrest.' This meant in effect their immediate release; and the sentence was received with loud applause from the crowded public gallery.[25] By his handling of these cases, Mr Justice Dodd lanced an ulcer that could have aggravated the atmosphere in the city for months to come.

45

T HE great lockout had been called forth by William Martin Murphy to crush the ITGWU. It not only failed to do so but had called forth a host of new enemies.

Murphy had one small consolation prize: the dispute had breathed new life into the almost moribund Dublin Employers' Federation, and there was a huge attendance at its annual meeting on 9 February 1914. Like the ITGWU, it would go from strength to strength, eventually evolving in 1942 into the perversely named Federated Union of Employers. In 1990 the Federation of Irish Employers, as the FUE had been renamed, would amalgamate with the Confederation of Irish Industry to form the Irish Business and Employers' Confederation.

The meeting chaired by John Sibthorpe in February 1914 marked the beginning of that long road. He had chaired the meeting on 29 August at which the lockout tactic had been agreed in principle, and he could look back well pleased with the achievements of the past year. The fight against 'terrorism', as he termed the syndicalist enemy, had strengthened the federation. He told members that a 'body of volunteers' had also been formed during the struggle to assist traders who might experience difficulties in the future. 'The work of the past year encourages us to believe that, with adequate preparation ... we will not only be able to repel attacks but to secure immunity from them.'[1]

The lockout was quickly forgotten in the wider world. The opening of Parliament saw minds concentrate once more on the home rule crisis. The slow roll towards civil war had been in abeyance over Christmas; but on Tuesday 10 February, Austen Chamberlain, responding to the King's Speech, told the Liberal government that it must exclude Ulster from the bill, or 'war is certain.' Asquith's response was sufficiently confused to further alarm both unionists and nationalists. He said that 'exclusion, which, of course, always involves the possibility of future inclusion, would make Ulster a battleground for contending factions.' He assured the House of Commons that 'I shall be perfectly prepared to welcome ... the inclusion of Ulster, with the option of exclusion after a time.' This was a reference to a new compromise put forward by Sir Horace Plunkett;[2] and Asquith's eagerness to grasp at every new straw that drifted by did nothing to reassure friends or enemies of his commitment to the government's own programme. The only certainty was that the government would never accept the one precondition for a peaceful resolution of the crisis that the opposition was prepared to consider: a general election to be fought on the home rule issue.

Continuing defeats at by-elections in which the votes of Unionist and Labour candidates consistently rose were a compelling argument against going to the polls. The Liberals feared that their middle-class electorate would bolt to the Tories rather than vote for a government that must inevitably be even more dependent on Labour and Irish MPs.

The ghosts of the lockout were not quite banished; they were to be promenaded briefly through the House of Commons during the debate on the King's Speech over the coming days. Before that, however, they were the cause of a few shocks nearer home. The first came for the ratepayers of County Dublin when the annual estimates for the county council showed that the cost of extra policing and malicious damage claims would add over a penny in the pound to the rates.[3]

On 16 February the findings of the Dublin Disturbances Commission were published. The commissioners fully justified the fears of their critics.

> The officers and men of the Dublin Metropolitan Police and the Royal Irish Constabulary, as a whole, discharged their duties throughout this trying period with conspicuous courage and patience ... Had it not been for their zeal and determination, the outburst of lawlessness which took place in the months of August and September would have assumed more serious proportions, and been attended with far more evil results.[4]

Six policemen were charged with perjury arising from their evidence to the commission. However, the cases were dropped after a letter was published in the *Irish Times* from Rev. R. M. Gwynn on 18 February 1914 welcoming the prosecutions, suggesting that their conviction was little more than a formality. The Irish executive decided that the letter precluded the possibility of a fair trial. The cases were dropped, thus guaranteeing further public outrage.

Two days later the findings of the Local Government Board Inquiry into the Housing Conditions of Dublin's Working Class were published. The inquiry said that the 'existing conditions of tenement life are both physically and morally bad.' The conditions in many smaller houses were condemned, and the inquiry estimated that at least 14,000 new dwellings were needed to eradicate the slum problem. It criticised the corporation for lax enforcement of the housing by-laws, and it singled out the chief medical officer, Sir Charles Cameron, for particular criticism for granting rate rebates to councillors who owned slum property and made false renovation claims. The commissioners published the names of all the councillors and officials who owned slum properties, and it recommended that the task of rehousing the city's poor be taken out of the hands of the local authority. Finally, it recommended that the cost of making the tenements sanitary should be borne by the slum landlords rather than by the ratepayers.

Unfortunately, the report was too comprehensive, and too honest, to be effective; by attacking every vested interest in the city it guaranteed their combination in resisting its implementation. Within two weeks an alliance of nationalist, unionist and Sinn Féin councillors was at work in the Housing Committee to counter the threat it posed. By May they had produced a detailed critique of the report, which proved, at least to their own satisfaction, that the root of the housing problem lay with the Local Government Board. The councillors questioned the methods of the commissioners, deplored their attack on Cameron, and criticised the recommendations as expensive and impractical.[5]

The controversies generated by the police and housing inquiries helped inject new life into Dublin Trades Council. There had been a poor attendance at meetings since the lockout, and the new president, William O'Brien, described the mood as apathetic. However, defeat on the industrial battlefield did not affect the ascendancy that the advocates of the new trade unionism enjoyed. When the annual meeting took place on 23 February, O'Brien succeeded Tom McPartlin as president. McPartlin remained on the executive, which continued to be dominated by leading figures from the lockout, such as Thomas Foran, general president of the ITGWU, and Richard O'Carroll of the Bricklayers. John Farren of the Sheet Metal Workers was returned as treasurer, as was John Simmons of the Carpenters as secretary. Simmons had been secretary of the Trades Council since its formation and would continue in this position until his death in 1916.[6] He was a bridge between the old and the new, one of the labour movement's many quiet, devoted and neglected pioneers.

O'Brien's inaugural address concentrated not on the lockout but on the shortcomings of the Dublin Disturbances Commission. He attacked Birrell for failing to honour his promise that the commissioners would include an independent representative of the working class; he also defended the decision of the unions not to participate in the proceedings. He then criticised the attitude of the six Dublin MPs towards the commission's report when it had come up for debate in the House of Commons the previous Wednesday. He advised the members of the Trades Council to read the debate for themselves.[7]

*

It was good advice, for the debate revealed the immense gaps in the perception of events that had emerged between British Labour MPs and those of the Irish Party. In some ways it mirrored the bitter divisions between labour and nationalists in Dublin. No doubt Griffith's 'sleeping beauties' would have preferred that the report of the Dublin Disturbances Commission not be debated at all in the House of Commons. It was George Barnes who moved an amendment to the King's Speech regretting that no mention had been made of 'the recent deplorable events in Dublin' and Birrell's failure to hold 'an impartial and representative Commission of Inquiry into the conduct of the police.' Barnes's intervention was an interesting one. He had been one of the TUC speakers at the rally in Sackville Street the previous September; he was also a former general secretary of the ASE—William Partridge's union—and a leading activist in the co-operative movement. He would therefore have had good sources of information on the lockout.

His speech reflected the feeling of those in the leadership of the British labour movement who did not let their anger at Larkin deflect them from expressing concern at what they saw as the wider issues raised by the lockout. 'There has been a lurid light thrown upon Dublin during the last few months,' he said, 'and the efforts made by the poor of the city to better their conditions ought to have been met by sympathetic consideration on the part of the people in authority in Dublin … a city of low wages and very low conditions.' Referring to his trip to Dublin in September, he said:

> Dublin is a place where the forces of evil—and I am afraid I must include in them strong drink—makes havoc with people's lives. It was my lot to go through some of the slums there, and I am bound to say I never saw worse in my life. I have never seen such poverty anywhere else. Whatever else might be said of the Larkin movement, it has in Ireland, at all events, brought new life and new hope to these people, and from all I can gather it is a sober movement. [It] deserves sympathetic consideration … instead of which it meets with nothing but savage repression.

The commission appointed had 'not given any satisfaction to the people on the spot.' It had ignored the calls of Dublin Corporation for a full and impartial inquiry and was, in his view, 'a fraud upon the people.' The 'eminent lawyers' who comprised it 'know nothing at all about the working classes, or the views of organised labour in Dublin, or elsewhere. They are probably typical representatives of Dublin Castle rule.' He had spoken to victims of police brutality and read their evidence to the commission. 'That body of evidence against the police is of so serious and authentic a nature that the fullest and most representative inquiry is absolutely necessary for the sake not only of public confidence in the Government's good faith but also in the interests of the police themselves, and of their relations with the public.' Instead the public had been treated to a 'bean-feast of the policemen.' It had provided them with an opportunity to indulge in 'self-glorification' and 'put whitewash on themselves.'

These all appeared strong grounds to Barnes for holding a much more broadly based inquiry into the disturbances and into the circumstances in Dublin that had led to them. He appealed to members on the Irish Party benches to join him in supporting the amendment.

P. J. Brady replied for the Irish Party. He accepted that 'the state of things which obtained for five months in the City of Dublin is a matter for profound regret, and not a little disquiet.' If a stranger had visited Dublin he could have been forgiven for thinking himself 'in a beleaguered city,' whose trade was paralysed. However,

> no useful purpose could be served by entering now into any personal issues or analyses of motives. I have no desire to say anything harsh of men whose objects might have been good, but I feel … their methods, however well-intentioned, were wrong and … could only result … in disaster for those in whose cause they were adopted.
>
> During the recent troubles our enemies seized the opportunity of criticising the nationalist members of the city of Dublin and taunting them with their silence. We bore these criticisms and taunts in silence, because we knew they were unfounded. Throughout the struggle the attitude of the members for Dublin was that they conceived it to be no part of their duty to enter into the dispute till they were invited by the parties in dispute, and unless there was any likelihood of coming to a decision as a result of their intervention. (Nationalist cheers.) … Our attitude, if it has been misconstrued by our enemies, has not been misconstrued by our friends.

Speaking for himself, Brady said there was no reason to believe that any new inquiry 'would be better than that which had taken place.'

> *Barnes*: I assume that the working classes of Dublin would be represented on it.
>
> *Brady:* The Irish people have no confidence in such inquiries and commissions. The only inquiry in which they would have confidence would be one set up by the Irish executive of an Irish parliament responsible to the Irish people. (Nationalist cheers.) I do not blame the police. One has to go much deeper to get at the root of all the trouble that has happened in Dublin, and … the real culprits in this case are the authorities in Dublin Castle.

While Brady continued to simultaneously criticise the authorities for the shortcomings of the report and dismiss the need for another one, Handel Booth, the Liberal MP for Pontefract, made a telling intervention. He told the House of Commons that the insurance rate at Lloyd's against riots in Dublin had increased to 2s 6d in the pound, 'compared with 7s 6d per £100 against the risk of damage resulting from civil war in Ulster. (Laughter and cheers.)' Booth may have cut an absurd figure at the hearings of the commission, but he was an expert on the insurance business; it was an embarrassment bordering on insult to remind Irish MPs of all political hues that British investment specialists considered renewed class warfare in Dublin a much greater likelihood than the threat of civil war in Ulster.

The normally urbane Birrell made the poorest contribution to the debate. He said his commitment to appointing a working-class representative to the commission may not have been correctly reported.

That had certainly been my intention, if I could have found a High Court judge to preside over the commission; however, the Lords Chancellor of Ireland and Great Britain had both been unable to spare a judge of the experience and character required.

Therefore my whole scheme fell through. Of course I could not advertise for people of that character. (Laughter.) Therefore I was thrown back on the necessity of obtaining legal persons of high authority.

He defended the 'impartiality and ability of the commission, and ... [the] justice of their report.' Nevertheless, when the Labour Party amendment to the King's Speech was put to a vote, several Liberal MPs voted with the Labour Party, while the phalanx of Irish Party MPs was solid in its support for the government.

The Unionists abstained in a vote that could have inflicted an embarrassing and unexpected defeat on the government.[8] Why they did so is unclear. Perhaps they too had been caught unawares. The Ulster-born MP for Canterbury, Ronald McNeill, said that he felt that Barnes 'had made out a very strong case' against the findings of the Dublin Disturbance Commission, and he would have voted for the amendment if the Labour Party had 'seriously pressed it.' McNeill was not a typical unionist. He was keen to achieve a negotiated settlement that would allow home rule to be introduced, provided Ulster was excluded—though this had not prevented him from drawing blood when he struck Churchill over the head with the Speaker's copy of the House of Commons Standing Orders during a particularly rowdy debate on home rule.

The division may have caught them unawares, but the Unionists made no attempt to press for a vote when the Dublin riots controversy presented them with another opportunity to embarrass the government a few days later. This was the occasion of a supplementary estimate for the RIC, which had overrun its budget by £13,800—or more than 50 per cent—as a result of the extra duties in Dublin city and county. This time it was J. R. Clynes who spoke on behalf of the Labour Party. The former member of the Askwith tribunal criticised the use of 'vast sums ... bringing in either military or police' to subdue the workers. John Dillon made a testy response, most of which consisted of the traditional refrain about the Dublin ratepayers being saddled with bills for police forces over which they exercised no control.

It was not until 20 March that the Unionists mounted a formal vote of censure against the government over its handling of the home rule crisis. This was comfortably defeated by ninety-three votes, with Labour and Irish Party MPs rallying to the Liberals. At the end of the day the Unionists were clearly uncomfortable using a 'labour' issue to embarrass, let alone bring down, the government; that would send confusing signals to their own supporters.[9]

The lockout was even more embarrassing for the Irish Party. Brady, in his speech in the House of Commons, fell back on the old tactic of hiding divisions within the Irish nation by identifying the source of the problem as British rule, an approach that was wearing increasingly thin at home.

William O'Brien experienced no difficulty in having a resolution passed by the annual meeting of Dublin Trades Council condemning the city's Irish Party MPs for voting against the Labour amendment. The six members did not represent the opinions of the workers, or of the citizens generally, it declared. Before the Trades Council adjourned it agreed to hold a special meeting on 2 March to discuss the report of the Housing Committee.[10]

*

There was, however, one striking omission from the debate at the Trades Council's annual meeting. The day before, Sunday 22 February, the Catholic hierarchy issued a joint pastoral letter on Dublin's labour troubles. This was the most authoritative statement of the Catholic Church on the lockout, yet the Trades Council failed to discuss it, let alone make a response. It is one of the paradoxes of the Dublin labour movement at this time that the only union leader willing to regularly and systematically criticise the Catholic Church publicly was Larkin, who was a sincere Catholic socialist. Other members, such as O'Brien, who could be vehemently anti-clerical in private or in closet political discussions, avoided such confrontations. Some union leaders, such as Partridge, Daly, and McPartlin, even tried to cull scraps from Dr Walsh's pronouncements to prove that he was really on the side of the workers. There was, in short, a fundamental dishonesty about the individual and collective attitude of Dublin's union leaders towards the Catholic Church.

The question remains: why did the annual meeting of the Trades Council choose not to discuss or to respond to the most important pronouncement issued by the Catholic Church on the dispute? The answer probably lies in the document itself. If it was a somewhat lopsided analysis of the dispute, dwelling at length on the evils of syndicalism and socialism, it also criticised Dublin's employers and strongly recommended the establishment of conciliation boards to deal with future disputes. The Trades Council could hardly welcome the proposal for a conciliation board, which many of its members wanted, and ignore the condemnation of the political creed of its own leaders. Yet to challenge the hierarchy on ideological grounds was to engage in a confrontation the Trades Council could not possibly hope to win. The overriding need at that moment was to restore unity. It was fortunate that Larkin was on speaking engagements in Britain when the pastoral was issued.

The bishops' statement is worth quoting at some length. Though it appeared over the names of Cardinal Logue and the country's twenty-seven other bishops, and quarried deeply into *Rerum Novarum*, the author of the pastoral was clearly Dr Walsh. Its whole thrust was to promote a conciliation system that might avert another disastrous lockout in the future.

As pastors of the faithful children of St Peter we have deeply felt the pain and the sorrow which a prolonged labour dispute of singular mischief … has brought on our people.

Referring to the various abortive attempts by employers and union leaders since 1911 to establishment conciliation boards, the bishops pronounced that

whoever shares the responsibility in the past to set up Conciliation Boards in Dublin, for the prevention and settlement of labour disputes, has much to answer for. Had any reasonable system of arbitration and conciliation been in working order it is more than likely that the recent strikes and lockouts, with all their degrading consequences would not have taken place. A paralysis of employment, that was *altogether avoidable*, has left us the humiliating memory that in a year of plenty many thousands of the toiling masses in the capital city of our country were left for months in idle dependence on rations and strike-pay from England, and that large numbers of children had to be fed by charity away from their homes when not deported into strange fosterage across the channel.

The bishops then took a leaf from the Irish Party's bible of national unity.

The sense of misery caused by this deplorable strife, was deepened by the fact that, whatever is to be said about the instigation, the contest arose and went on between Irish employers and Irish workers, to the serious prejudice of the nation's interests at a time when the near prospect of native government should have raised the hearts of true Irishmen and drawn them together in harmonious and dignified relations. Had the healing influence of native rule been felt for even a few years we cannot believe that the bitter privations, the enormous waste, the loss, the shame, the sin of this insensate conflict, would have been entailed on a city, in which commerce and manufacture need to be fostered with tender care, instead of being recklessly endangered in a senseless war between workers and employers.

   The great lesson from this experience is the need of well-found Conciliation Boards, duly representative of both sides, to adjust their differences as they arise. Masters and men have a common interest in industry; and that is the way to maintain it for the common good.

The bishops accepted that, even with responsible and well-regulated trade unions and employer bodies, there would be disputes. But they suggested that conciliation boards would allow

a fair jury … a chance of bringing in its verdict before the protagonists on either side let loose the horrors of war.

They tried to paint a picture of the kind of happy if frugal future so beloved of nationalists of the era, with which they hoped their flock would be content. While we desire ardently to see suitable industries thrive—our desire is not for the enrichment of any class, but for such employment and remuneration of Irish labour at home as will afford our worthy people a worthy livelihood, and stem the tide of depopulating emigration.

The bishops then quoted from the papal encyclical to show that 'friendship for honest toil is seen from the first in the life of the Church.' The Pope had condemned the 'callousness of the employers and the greed of unrestrained competition.' However, in trying to remedy these evils, the socialists had worked on 'the poor man's envy of the rich ... to destroy private property.' The Pope had warned that 'capital cannot do without labour, nor labour without capital.' Unfortunately, the bishops said, more and more men were 'following the will o' the wisp into the quagmire of Socialism' and having recourse to 'ruinous strikes and lockouts.'

Coming largely from a rural background themselves, it was hardly surprising that the bishops seemed to pin their hopes for defeating the 'evils' of socialism on 'the beneficial effects of the land settlement in Ireland,' with its 'reasonably sized holdings owned by occupiers.' This would lead to a 'Christian comradeship between men and masters and [make] a sense of joint interest ... the rule and not the exception.'

The bishops saw the twin evils of British interference and alien ideology as the main threat to this dream.

> The trade unionists of Great Britain came to the aid of their Dublin fellow-workers with great liberality, in the belief, it may be assumed, that the right of combination was attacked. The great pity is, that the labour leaders, and still more the press in England were in such impatient haste to back in Ireland, about which they knew little, methods of action which they found would not answer in their own country. The subsequent efforts of the [British] leaders to make peace deserve all praise, but how came it to be their duty to cross over as peace missioners to settle a local dispute in a country on the eve of self-government where the race of capable men is not supposed to be extinct?

It was thus that 'this wretched, long-drawn out strife, like many another on Irish soil,' was due to outside influences and support.

The influence of unnamed syndicalists was even more malign, according to the bishops.

> Syndicalism wanted no employers in Ireland or anywhere else, and it prepared and took the field to use Irish workers and English unions for its own purposes ... If the Syndicalists must have a theatre for their operations they should find some other place than Ireland to experiment upon. Under Syndicalism the employer is compelled to disappear, and the workers are supposed to do everything and manage everything in an industrial federation away from state control.

It was not a bad summary of the syndicalist position; and in case it tempted any of their flock, the bishops added the warning that

> without capital from some quarter nothing can be done in the world of industry, even if the management were competent; and, to seize the property of employers would be wholesale robbery paving the way to anarchy.

Turning to the concerns of workers who might be seduced by the syndicalist siren, the bishops assured them that 'certainly the wage system should be so improved as nowhere to deserve the name of sweating or wage slavery.' They also assured workers that they understood that housing

> is not less important than the amount of their wages. What chance is there for health, or comfort, temperance or thrift, home education or a Christian life, if a married man has not a sanitary dwelling of three or four rooms to shelter his family?

The bishops endorsed the system of conciliation proposed by the Askwith Inquiry and stated that the work of setting it up 'seems to us so urgent as to brook no delay.' Perhaps sensing that they had dwelt too long on the evils of syndicalism and socialism, they then gave trade unions their blessing.

> Mainly through trade unions, with all their shortcomings, have the working classes secured something corresponding with the protection which, in a different industrial order, the church promoted in former times [a reference to the mediaeval guilds] their organisation as most desirable. If based on Christian principles the more widespread in industrial centres, and the more perfect it is, the better for all concerned.[11]

If there was an omission from the bishops' expressed concern it was over the plight of women workers; but then women never loomed large in their pastorals, at least not as an active social element. This was not an oversight that bothered the Dublin Chamber of Commerce when most of its quarterly meeting on 2 March was given over to discussion of the pastoral. The new president, R. K. Gamble, paid tribute to 'the theological, the metaphysical, the economic, and also practical point of view' of the bishops in their pastoral; it would be 'a valuable contribution to the discussion of one of the most important questions of the day.' He then went on to outline the history of the last attempt to set up a conciliation system in July 1913, before 'a vast sea of insurrection and insubordination ... burst its bonds.' He emphasised the considerable differences that existed between industrial relations in Britain, where conciliation and arbitration systems were well established, and Ireland. One of the essential differences was that British industry was large enough to accommodate conciliation systems designed to cater for single industries, or even individual firms; in

Ireland there were few such arrangements. The system envisaged for Dublin the previous summer had been to cater for all the trades in the city; and, as it was untried, it needed to be approached with caution.

Gamble was careful, having expressed his reservations about establishing a conciliation system, not to appear too intransigent or pessimistic about the future. 'The employers of Dublin will not be dismayed or deterred by what has happened, and … an honest attempt will be made to form Conciliation Boards to deal with disputes in the various trades,' he said to applause.[12] The reality, of course, was that a city-wide conciliation system had been considered only because of the effectiveness of Larkin's sympathetic strike tactic, and Murphy's temporary indisposition because of illness. Now that the sympathetic strike had been smashed, the employers had no further interest in such a scheme. Of course they dare not say so to the bishops.

*

A trade union response both to the bishops and to the employers did not come until June 1914, when Larkin addressed the ITUC at City Hall in Dublin, where he had just been elected president of the assembly by acclamation. It was still largely a talking-shop; but the election of Larkin was a timely reminder to the employers that the new unionism was very much alive, and kicking.

The best thanks they could offer the labour pioneers, 'who went before and who raised the Irish working class from their knees, is to press forward with determination and enthusiasm towards the ultimate goal of our efforts, a co-operative commonwealth for Ireland.' In the meantime 'the immediate work to hand is the establishment of a new party—a Labour Party—an industrial army; a political party whose politics would be the assurance of bread and butter for all.' It was a significant acknowledgment by Larkin, who had shown some hostility towards the efforts of people such as Connolly, O'Brien and Sheehy-Skeffington to build the political wing of the ITUC, that the syndicalist struggle on the economic front was not enough to overthrow capitalism on its own. However, he was still envisaging any political activity as complementary to, rather than superseding, class warfare in the work-place.

Turning to the home rule crisis, Larkin said that this issue, and 'what some people call religion, has been used to divide us in the past.' But he clearly shared the false optimism of many home-rulers when he went on to assure delegates that, 'now that the Government of Ireland Bill … is on the statute book, and will be law in the immediate future,' the home rule question would be 'settled once and for all.' The day had therefore arrived

> for us of the Irish working class to reconsider our position. Whatever other classes in Ireland might do, we must march forward to complete the reconquest of Ireland, not as representing sections, sects or parties but as representatives of the organised working class as a whole.

Inevitably he recalled the days of the lockout.

Looking back over the immediate past ... we see there was the attempt of an organised, unscrupulous capitalist class composed of men of different political parties and holding different sectarian views who had combined together for the purpose of destroying organised labour in Ireland. The lockout in 1913 was a deliberate attempt to starve us into submission, and met with well-deserved failure. The workers emerged from the struggle purified and strengthened, with fierce determination and a fixed purpose.

The 'direct attack upon the essential principles of trades unionism' by the employers had been met with

a new principle of solidarity inside the unions, and for the first time in the history of the world of labour the beautiful and more human principle has received universal recognition: 'An injury to one is the concern of all.' That motto will be emblazoned on the banner of labour the world over in the future.

Larkin dismissed the notion of the churchmen

that capital must be supplied by the employers, meaning by the present controllers of capital. That statement has only to be made to prove its absurdity. All capital is supplied by the working class: but to our undoing and our shame it is controlled by the capitalist class. As much as I respect the church to which I belong and the views of those who are interpreters of the dogmas of the church, and as much as I respect the opinions of members of any and every church, I make this claim: that as long as the working class allow any churchman to abuse his trust and interfere in our affairs in the industrial world, so long would we have to submit to hunger, privation, and wage-slavery ... I submit that the working class have as much right as any section or class in the community to enjoy all the advantages of science, art, and literature. No field of knowledge, no outlook in life and no book should be closed against the workers. We should demand our share in the effulgence of life and all that was created for the enjoyment of mankind. And here do I appeal to those who cannot see eye to eye with us—who feel they cannot come all the way—to come with us as far as their knowledge will permit. Come at least to the bottom of the boreen, and then if we must part, the pioneers will continue on and up the mountain to meet the dawning of the new tomorrow.

The working class must be free, not only economically but intellectually. [When I was] speaking to a priest some time ago he said: 'I agree with some of your views and believe that improvement and alteration is necessary in the world; but,' said he, 'we are determined to build a wall round Ireland and keep out the advanced ideas of western Europe.' I replied: 'As much as I respect your views, father, there is no power on earth can build a wall to keep out thought.' The men in this movement are determined to enjoy the fullness of life and the knowledge and power that the Creator ordained them for.

Turning to the struggle itself, Larkin praised the courage of 'women and men, aye, and little children ... Hunger, the jail, and death itself did not deter them.' While workers were

> murdered in the streets of this city by the hired hooligans of the capitalist class—the police—we found that no political party, no church, made a protest against the abuse of the laws by the capitalist class. While thirty-seven unions engaged in the struggle, each acting upon its own line of defence and attack according to its own methods, we had found there was neither unionist nor nationalist amongst the employing class ... We found no Redmondites, Carsonites, or O'Brienites then. The enemy were all employers, and every weapon they could wield—political, social, and administrative—they used unsparingly.

Larkin appealed for an end to working-class sectionalism. But this did not prevent him from attacking briefly the United Builders' Labourers and the NSFU, though he refrained from referring to them by name.

> The employers know no sectionalism. The employers give us the title of 'the working class'. Let us be proud of the term. Let us have, then, the one union, and not, as now, 1,100 separate unions, each acting upon its own. When one union is locked out or on strike, other unions or sections are either apathetic or scab on those in dispute. A stop must be put to this organised blacklegging.

Larkin summoned up the ghost of the 1907 general strike in Belfast and the unity of Catholic and Protestant workers in overcoming sectarian and sectional divisions to fight capitalism. But he immediately lapsed into nationalist symbolism and rhetoric to attack the contemporary 'law-breakers in Ulster', who seemed immune from prosecution, while Labour leaders who held meetings 'are arrested and cast into prison.'

> We must unite as Labourites in the three-leaved shamrock of fellowship; have faith in our cause, hope of its realisation, and charity of all men ... I hope we will see the day when we will take full advantage of our opportunities, cry 'finis' to our differences, and obliterate all jealousies from our ranks. Be truly Irish of the Irish. Give ear to all men who do worthy work ... Let us be comrades in the true sense of the word, and join with our brothers the world over to advance the cause of the class to which we belong ... We are entering upon a new era to do work worthy of the cause to which we are attached. Caitlín Ní Houlihan calls upon us to abolish old jealousies, old intolerances, that she may sit enthroned in the midst of the Western Sea.[13]

It was vintage Larkin, almost free of personal recrimination, and it was an unrepentant reassertion of socialist and syndicalist ideals. Only Larkin could have given such an unequivocal rebuff to the amateur political economists of Maynooth and been applauded for it. Only Larkin could have dressed the internationalist ideals of the socialist movement in such nationalist finery and been forgiven for it by representatives of the north's Protestant working class. But Larkin had a unique ability to move audiences by the spirit of his message rather than the mere words. It was because his dedication to the workers' cause was so total, his love of Dublin's most downtrodden class so obvious, his ability to convey ideas so magical, that he was received with such rapt attention. It was also because he gave his audiences an opportunity to escape the murky realities and mundane compromises of everyday trade unionism in his speeches that he was so loudly applauded. Even those immersed in trade union life as delegates, shop-floor activists or full-time officials needed to escape reality from time to time and be treated to a grander vision of the future they were striving to achieve.

*

Meanwhile, the real world marched on towards Armageddon. Irishmen were still preparing to fight one another—and might have done, if a Serbian nationalist had not assassinated an Austrian archduke in Sarajevo four weeks after Larkin made his address to the ITUC.

The dogs of war were happily ensconced in Liberty Hall. On 22 March, Larkin presided at a meeting of the executive of the Irish Citizen Army, held for the purpose of reconstituting the organisation. A new constitution had been drawn up by Constance Markievicz, James Connolly, and other militarily minded members of the ITGWU. It made provision for an Army Council, and included explicitly nationalist aims. Its first article stated:

> The first and last principle of the Irish Citizen Army is the avowal that the ownership of Ireland, moral and material, is vested of right in the people of Ireland.

Its second article declared:

> The Irish Citizen Army shall stand for the absolute unity of Irish nationhood, and shall support the rights and liberties of the democracies of all nations.[14]

Jack White had survived his earlier brushes with Larkin and was still in sufficiently high standing to be elected chairman of the first Army Council. The vice-chairmen were James Larkin, P. T. Daly, Constance Markievicz, William Partridge, Thomas Foran, and Francis Sheehy-Skeffington, who was the only pacifist on the committee. The secretary was Seán O'Casey, and the treasurers were Constance Markievicz and Richard Brannigan. The executive was composed mainly of ITGWU members but did not include Connolly, who had returned to Belfast to manage the union's affairs there.[15]

The meeting to reconstitute the Citizen Army on more formal military lines may have been inspired by the announcement two days earlier by General Hubert Gough, officer commanding the 3rd Cavalry Brigade at the

Curragh, and fifty-seven of its seventy officers that they would resign rather than accept orders to march on Ulster and enforce home rule.

March was a bad month for compromise in Ireland, and a good one for the militarists. The Liberal government had finally decided at the beginning of the month to accept the solution to the home rule crisis so strenuously promoted by Lloyd George and Churchill and to exclude Ulster initially from the provisions of the Government of Ireland Bill. Redmond reluctantly agreed to accept partition for five years, and then six; but Carson made it clear that the least the Unionists might settle for was permanent exclusion for Ulster, not 'a stay of execution for six years.' Asquith and Bonar Law resumed informal contacts to find a way out of the conflict; but the naturally bellicose Churchill decided it was time to counter Ulster intransigence with a show of force. Sending warships to Belfast Lough was not a problem, but the army proved a different matter. Its officer class had strong affinities, personal and spiritual, with the north. The Secretary of State for War, Colonel Jack Seely, woefully mishandled the situation, and the outcome was the 'Curragh Incident', as Gough's action was quickly named. That such a situation was allowed to arise was another symptom of the intractability of the home rule crisis and the seeping paralysis that seemed to have infected the British government.

If the officer class could mobilise in favour of Ulster's industrialists and landlords, it only made sense to Labour militants such as Connolly for the workers to mobilise in defence of their own class interests. Connolly also knew that outside Belfast there was little sympathy for the unionists among the organised working class, not alone in Ireland but in Britain as well. Labour and Liberal supporters were at one with Irish nationalists in seeing the Ulster Volunteers as simply a manifestation of Tory arrogance; a workers' army seemed a legitimate, even democratic, response

That feeling was amplified in Dublin, with its historic resonances as the country's deposed capital. The reputedly syndicalist-dominated Trades Council spent most of its meeting of 23 March debating the partition issue. It passed a resolution declaring that it 'views with dismay and anger the attempt to divide Ulster from the rest of Ireland.' The Parliamentary Committee of the ITUC followed suit and issued a manifesto in the following week's issue of the *Irish Worker*, calling on workers to 'Arouse! Awake! Arise!' The country faced a national crisis. 'The workers of Ireland have been kept asunder and divided in regard to political action during the past thirty years.' They had been 'utilised and humbugged.' Now they were faced with the 'unthinkable' prospect of partition.

> To us as Irishmen the cutting off of that Province or any part thereof which gave to our country such men as Shane O'Neill, Hugh Roe O'Donnell, Aodh Ruadh O'Neill, McCracken, Orr ... and the host of Northern men who have battled for freedom, and which from a Labour as well as a National point of view is of so much importance, is an act of pure suicide, and should not be persisted in. We claim Ulster in its

entirety, her sons are our brothers and we are opposed to any attempt to divide us.

The Parliamentary Committee, which contained such senior northern trade unionists as Thomas Johnson and David Campbell, incited soldiers in the British army to mutiny, on the grounds that they had as much right to exercise their convictions against shooting down 'brothers and sisters of the working class' as officers had to pursue their 'political and sectarian convictions.'[16]

From its wording, the manifesto could have been issued by Joe Devlin. If the ITUC stopped short of urging trade unionists to join the Irish Volunteers, that was in keeping with Irish Party thinking too.

Not all labour advocates were so moderate. On 6 April, Constance Markievicz addressed the Trades Council on behalf of the Citizen Army. She explained its aims and objects, and said that the organisation hoped to enrol five thousand members. 'There are a number of things to be learnt in a Citizen Army which may not be learnt elsewhere,' she told the delegates. The army's principles were those 'of Tone, Emmet, Mitchel and Fintan Lalor. We do not want enslavement as a class, or as citizens.'

Larkin spoke in support of Markievicz. The workers required an army if they were to be anything more than a mob, he said. 'If Carson and his men can have rifles, we must insist on them also.'

A few days earlier, a group of twelve leading Belfast trade unionists, all of them members of British unions, had issued a public appeal to their 'fellow trade unionists in Great Britain not to desert us. We are certain that the granting of Home Rule to Ireland must be fatal to the best interests of trade unionism in this country, and would be a deadly blow at the solidarity of the movement.' They predicted that home rule would lead to 'the setting up of rival ... Irish unions.' An Irish parliament dominated by 'agricultural constituencies' would deprive them of future improvements in social welfare.

These were serious and legitimate arguments against home rule; but bodies representing southern workers, such as Dublin Trades Council, were in no mood to give them serious consideration.[17]

*

For militant nationalists and socialists, the political agenda in Ireland was rapidly converging. In fact nationalists did not even have to be radical to feel a gut reaction against the developments of recent months. The doyen of clerical conservatism within the home rule movement, Timothy Healy, spoke for many Irish people when he denounced in the House of Commons the Ulster exclusion compromise. The government's proposals 'struck into the marrow of their hearts,' he said. Nationalist leaders 'had given their lives' to home rule, and

it is not to be measured by the half-leaf principle. We do not say half of Ireland—we insist on all Ireland. I prefer no bill to the bill declared for by the government.

The British government had capitulated to 'some drilling in Ulster, some refurbishment of firearms.' Ireland must remain 'a nation one and indivisible.'

Healy's position on the crucial issue of partition was not all that far from that of the labour men. In fact Connolly's objection to constitutional nationalists such as Healy was that they were poseurs and lacked the stomach for a real fight. In the *Irish Worker* he proclaimed that

> there are no real Nationalists in Ireland outside of the Irish Labour Movement. All others merely reject one part or another of the British Conquest—the Labour Movement alone rejects it in its entirety and sets itself to the re-conquest of Ireland.[18]

Within three weeks of Healy's speech to the House of Commons, the Ulster Volunteers' 'refurbishment of firearms' had reached a dramatic new plane. On 24 April they ran 35,000 German rifles and 2½ million rounds of ammunition into Larne, transforming the UVF overnight from a sparsely armed militia into one that could put on a respectable 'show' if Britain's officer class could ever be coaxed into moving against it. Meanwhile, militant nationalists, including members of the Citizen Army, became increasingly frantic in their own efforts to obtain weapons. They also became increasingly resentful and suspicious of the British government's embargo on the importing of firearms into Ireland, which seemed to work so much more effectively against nationalists than against unionists.

Of course the drudgery of daily life continued. Its participants slouched along resignedly, trying to keep in step with those caught up with the drama of military preparations and high politics. At the same meeting of the Trades Council at which Markievicz urged members to join the Citizen Army, O'Brien moved the nominations to a new conciliation panel to be presented to the employers. It consisted of Tom McPartlin, John Farren, Tom Murphy, Tom Farren, Richard O'Carroll, and James Larkin. All of them had been Trades Council nominees for the Lord Mayor's conciliation board the previous September.[19]

*

On the day that Healy was rejecting partition in the House of Commons and Markievicz was urging Trades Council members to join the Citizen Army, some unfinished business from the lockout was being taken care of in the courts. The trial of Thomas Daly for the murder of Thomas Harten finally began at the Dublin City Commission. The case against his co-accused had already been put back for lack of evidence, and the prosecution was relying on a conviction against Daly to mount a case against the others.

The evidence against Daly was largely circumstantial, though he had also been identified as one of Harten's assailants by a strike-breaker named Cunningham. Unfortunately for the prosecution, Cunningham's description of the clothes Daly was wearing did not match those Daly had on when arrested. Cunningham also admitted under cross-examination that he had been dishonourably discharged from the British army and had a string of criminal convictions. The circumstantial evidence against Daly was that he had been arrested in the act of attacking a strike-breaker, and had a revolver in his pocket. The prosecution claimed that the revolver was Harten's; Daly said he found it in Tara Street. The strongest point in Daly's favour was that Harten had been kicked by his attackers until the blood 'spouted out of him,' while there was not a speck of blood on Daly's clothing.

After a trial lasting two days it took the jury only half an hour to acquit Daly of the murder charge. However, he had pleaded guilty to assaulting two other strike-breakers that night, James Reilly and James Mulvanny. Mr Justice Moloney sentenced Daly to two years' imprisonment. It was a heavy sentence for a man whose own former employer testified that he had been an honest and hard worker for nineteen years. A *nolle prosequi* was entered against each of Daly's co-accused.

Daly's trial was overshadowed not just by political events but by another trial that day. Captain James Robert White DSO, late of the Gordon Highlanders, was charged with assaulting two policemen during a Citizen Army demonstration. White was twenty minutes late for his trial but was dealt with very differently from Daly by the Crown prosecutor, Serjeant McSweeny. He expressed

> some little sympathy with the prisoner, who is a person of a different social position from those who usually permit themselves to engage in a street brawl. He is the son of a very great soldier, and was himself a soldier of some distinction.

It is hardly surprising that this genteel attack ended also in a *nolle prosequi*. Mr Justice Molony entered into the spirit of things by giving 'both the police and Captain White ... an Easter benediction, with the hope that the peace and harmony which they are now inaugurating will long continue in the city of Dublin.'[20]

It proved a vain hope; but in May the most intractable lockout dispute of them all finally came to an end—of sorts. Jacob's was still refusing to take back its three hundred women strikers en bloc but agreed to accept a list of applicants for reinstatement presented through the ITGWU's solicitors, William Smyth and Son. Jacob's management informed Smyth that it would undertake to 're-employ the girls of good character when vacancies occurred.'[21]

*

A month later, Larkin and Connolly had to confront another poisoned legacy of the lockout. On 10 June they went to the conference of the National Transport Workers' Federation in Hull, only to be refused admission. They had hoped for a friendlier reception, as one of the main items on the agenda was the creation of an amalgamated trade union for transport and general workers in Britain and Ireland. The leaders of the British unions were in an unforgiving mood. In his address as president of the NTWF, Harry Gosling told delegates that the employers in Dublin had waged a 'bitter and unrelenting fight ... against the very principles of trade unionism.' But he also said that

> our greatest difficulty ... was the unwillingness of certain individuals to work amicably with those who desired to assist. The unions affiliated to this federation were amongst the most generous in proportion to their financial and numerical strength, and had it not been for the action of those individuals and their wanton attacks on all and sundry who did not agree with them, then the dispute might have been brought to a more successful issue than it ultimately reached.

Robert Williams, secretary of the NTWF, referred to the lockout in his annual report as 'the ill-starred Dublin strike.' He outlined its history, and assured the delegates that the NTWF executive had rendered 'all the assistance in its power' to the ITGWU, even though the latter was not affiliated to the federation.

> We now see, in retrospect, a magnificent movement, great in portent and far-reaching in ultimate effect, completely stultified by wretched and degrading personal abuse and vilification. In future, Larkin and others should realise that the whole edifice of democracy is built upon a spirit of toleration. Again, we attribute the disaster of Dublin to faulty methods of organisation, lack of discernment, and personal vanity.

It was Larkin's barbs that had cut deepest. Though Connolly had made a ferocious attack on the NTWF in *Forward* the previous April, there was considerable support from delegates for his admission to the conference. However, the motion from the floor was defeated.[22]

The British unions now had their eyes set on their own general offensive against the capitalist class, planned for later in the year. In the event, union affairs were to become suddenly irrelevant as political violence erupted onto the international scene with the advent of the First World War.

*

Before the war began, however, gunfire was heard in Dublin, which experienced the last act of political violence associated with the United Kingdom's own incipient civil war, and the first to be associated with the wider conflict of competing nationalisms and ideologies in the years ahead. It was appropriate too that the Citizen Army veterans of the lockout should play a minor role in the affair.

On 23 June the British government amended the Home Rule Bill to exclude the six north-eastern counties of Ulster from the legislation for six years. In late July a final effort to reach an acceptable compromise on partition took place between all the parties at Buckingham Palace. It broke down on 24 July; by then many advanced nationalists had already committed themselves to the Carsonite method of negotiation. On 26 July the Irish Volunteers carried out a minor Larne of their own by landing nine hundred German rifles and 29,000 rounds of ammunition at the County

Dublin fishing village of Howth. The Volunteers were assisted by the Fianna, which still enjoyed strong links with the ITGWU and the Citizen Army. The Volunteers proudly bore their trophies back to Dublin but were intercepted near Clontarf by a strong force of police and military. There were some serious scuffles, and one Volunteer officer was stabbed with a bayonet before the authorities gave up their attempt to seize the weapons. By then most of the rifles had been hurried away across fields and through the grounds of Croydon Park towards the city.

Inevitably, some weapons were 'gathered up' by Citizen Army men exercising in the park's grounds. The Volunteers never got them back. Colonel Maurice Moore, one of the Volunteer leaders, went to Croydon Park to demand their return. He later recounted: 'I was told that … I might clear out.' He had more success with the British authorities: nineteen rifles seized by police and military at Clontarf were duly returned to the Volunteers. None were in working order.

Citizen Army men still regarded the Volunteers with hostility, not least because they suspected that leaders such as Moore would never allow the Volunteers to use their weapons, a view no doubt confirmed by the alacrity with which the British authorities returned the seized rifles.

One reason for that alacrity was the subsequent events on Sunday. The King's Own Scottish Borderers, who had been the star attraction at Lord Aberdeen's February levee, marched back into the city to be greeted by jeers and stones for their failure to seize the Howth rifles. By the time they reached Batchelor's Walk they had had enough. When the soldiers finished firing there were three civilians dead and thirty-eight wounded. It was all very different from Larne.

There was another inquiry, and on this occasion a sacrificial lamb was offered up to nationalist opinion. This was the senior police officer on duty that day, Assistant Commissioner William Harrel of 'Bloody Sunday' fame. He was the first senior official to be dismissed by Dublin Castle to assuage nationalist anger. It was not enough. 'Remember Bachelor's Walk' would be a rebel catch-cry in Dublin for many years to come.[23]

EPILOGUE

I N August 1914 Tom Kettle was in Ostend trying to buy guns for the Irish Volunteers. The urbane and civilised professor made an unlikely gun-runner; there was probably no man on the Volunteer executive who hated war more. The political odyssey that took him there had begun in June, when John Redmond decided he had to stamp his authority on a movement that now boasted over 120,000 members. He issued an ultimatum to the Volunteer leadership: it must accept a raft of twenty-five Redmondites, or face denunciation.

Bulmer Hobson and his fellow IRB plotters cannily agreed to submit; they reasoned that the men who controlled the guns, and the militant minority prepared to use them, ultimately controlled the organisation. Thus Redmond's eminently respectable nominees, men such as Kettle and Maurice Moore, were co-opted onto the executive.[1]

Guns have a special significance for paramilitary organisations. They are not just instruments of war but a reason for being. The surrender of weapons is tantamount to castration; not to possess them in the first place is an absurdity. In 1914 the Volunteers had hardly any weapons, which made their acquisition all the more important. The IRB cabal within the organisation had stolen a march on the Redmondites with the Howth gun-running; and Kettle was in Ostend to prove that the Redmondites were every bit as committed to arming Irishmen as the Fenians were. Unfortunately, the German general staff put paid to Kettle's efforts, and he turned to the more congenial—and more dangerous—task of war correspondent.

The atrocities of the German army in Belgium in August 1914 appear no more than misdemeanours in the light of what our century would subsequently experience, but they genuinely shocked public opinion at the time. Kettle, an ardent Francophile, reacted with an outrage so strong that it robbed his writing of its usual seductive wit. In a report for the *Daily Mail* from Malines, where the Germans had shelled the cathedral, he wrote:

> I am not ashamed to confess that when I, an Irish Catholic, walked into the Grand Place and saw the stamp of Berlin imprinted on those grey walls I did not think at once of material injury, or money, or subscriptions. What came was anger against the desecration of a holy

place. My mind said to me: 'This is how Nietzsche had, from the grave, spat, as he wished to spit, upon Nazareth.'[2]

Kettle fully supported Redmond's fateful decision to give unreserved support to the British war effort: a stand for the 'rights of small nations' in Flanders could only help the cause at home, and show that nationalists were as committed in their way to the empire as the unionists. The sanctity of a common blood sacrifice in Europe would heal the bickering at home. Besides, any attempt at neutrality, let alone support for the Germans, would vindicate the stand taken against home rule by Carson and the Ulster Volunteers.

Kettle decided he would rather be 'a sixth rate soldier than a first rate man of letters.' The War Office thought otherwise. Kettle's health was poor, and it was decided that he was much too valuable to the war effort as an orator and recruiting agent to be wasted at the front. Recruiting men to die in his place was not a task Kettle enjoyed, and it revolted him after the Easter Rising of 1916. Several friends died either during or in the aftermath of the rising, including MacDonagh and Plunkett, fellow-members of the Dublin Industrial Peace Committee, and Francis Sheehy-Skeffington. The latter's death particularly affected him, for Kettle's diminutive, opinionated and totally fearless brother-in-law had not even taken up arms against the empire.

Sheehy-Skeffington's death proved a serious embarrassment for the British government, for it took place in bizarre and sordid circumstances. As a pacifist, Sheehy-Skeffington was opposed to the Rising; but Sheehy-Skeffington the socialist appears to have played a more ambiguous role.[3] At Connolly's request, he tried to establish a Citizens' Committee that might form the basis for a civilian government in the event of the rising being successful; in the meantime it could ensure that no looting or other criminal activities dishonoured the infant republic proclaimed at the GPO. It was in this capacity that Sheehy-Skeffington was arrested by Captain J. C. Bowen-Colthurst, a southern unionist officer deeply disturbed at the outbreak of fighting in the city. By a strange chance of war, Bowen-Colthurst also arrested two other journalists that day. One was P. J. McIntyre of the defunct *Toiler*; the other was Thomas Dickson. McIntyre was now editing *Searchlight*, a nationalist newspaper that was rabidly anti-German, while Dickson was editing the *Eye-Opener*, an equally rabid loyalist journal. Both were found sheltering in a pub belonging to James Kelly, the unsuccessful 'Home Rule Labour' candidate in the 1914 municipal elections. Kelly had subsequently succeeded in being elected to the city council, and Bowen-Colthurst mistook him for his Sinn Féin namesake Tom Kelly. The three journalists were taken to Portobello Barracks, and shot on Bowen-Colthurst's orders. What form their final, doomed conversations took we can only guess at.

Another leading figure in the lockout was to die at the hands of Bowen-Colthurst. This was the Bricklayers' leader Richard O'Carroll. A lieutenant in the Irish Volunteers, O'Carroll was captured in Camden Street. Bowen-Colthurst shot him casually in the stomach; it took O'Carroll two weeks to die from his wounds.[4] William Partridge, who fought with the Citizen Army in St Stephen's Green, survived only to be sentenced to fifteen years' imprisonment. He was released from prison in April 1917, seriously ill; he was taken to his brother's home in Ballaghaderreen, also the home of John Dillon, to die. It was perhaps fitting that Partridge's funeral was an early demonstration of strength by the resurgent rebels. Constance Markievicz gave the oration.[5]

*

The most prominent Labour martyr of Easter week was of course Connolly. Though he was elected president of the Irish Neutrality League in 1914, Connolly continued the journey down the road to militant nationalism that his character and ideological proclivities had to some extent ordained. From the beginning of the war, Connolly planned for insurrection, arguing that 'Ireland may yet set the torch of a European conflagration that will not burn out until the last throne and the last capitalist bond and debenture will be shrivelled on the funeral pyre of the last warlord.' However, in the same article that contained this internationalist hyperbole he also advised readers that 'should a German army land in Ireland tomorrow we should be perfectly justified in joining it, if by doing so we could rid this country once and for all from its connection with the Brigand Empire that drags us unwillingly into this war.'[6] Such a position had a long and honourable place in the separatist tradition, but it had little to do with that of revolutionary socialism, let alone the pacifism that inspired many socialist opponents of the war. Connolly justified his call to arms by stating that 'no general uprising of the forces of Labour in Europe could possibly carry with it, or entail a greater slaughter of socialists than will their participation as soldiers in the campaigns of their respective countries.'[7] It was an increasingly powerful argument as the casualties mounted and the twin gods of nationalism and socialism battled for Connolly's soul.

It was also an unequal struggle. Connolly's thoughts about Germany quickly moved from giving qualified support to an invasion of Ireland to contrasting the achievements of the well-educated German workers' movement with the backwardness of the 'half-educated working class of England,' which had been 'trained to a slavish subservience' to imperialism.[8] By March 1916 Connolly was also telling readers of the *Workers' Republic* that German imperialism was superior to British imperialism. 'The German Empire is a homogeneous Empire of self-governing people; the British Empire is a heterogeneous collection in which a very small number of self-governing communities connive at the subjugation, by force, of a vast number of despotically-ruled subject populations.'[9] It is easy to see how Connolly was able to sign the 1916 proclamation, which described imperial Germany and the Austro-Hungarian empire as the Irish revolutionaries' 'gallant allies in Europe.'

Connolly had been asked to contest the Harbour constituency in 1915, when William Abraham died, but his mind was already set on armed revolt. He told William O'Brien that Labour could win the seat at any time, and declined to support calls for him to fight it during Larkin's absence in America. He did so on the grounds that an election campaign would distract workers from the real struggle, which was at the barricades, not the Palace of Westminster. The publican Alfie Byrne won the seat in a three-cornered fight between nationalist candidates; he would represent the area for most of the next forty years. It was not a result that could have pleased Larkin; it was less than two years since the exiled union leader (and teetotaller) had denounced Byrne's public house as a sink of political and other corruption in the aftermath of the municipal elections debacle.[10]

Byrne's victory came less than twelve months before Connolly attained immortality in the Easter rising. The labour leader's involvement in this radical nationalist putsch left Irish socialists with a conundrum that would confuse them for the rest of the century.

Because he was seriously wounded in the fighting, Connolly was the last signatory of the 1916 proclamation to be put to death. There had been hopes that his life would be spared, because of mounting public revulsion at the executions. Connolly had to be strapped in a chair to face the firing squad. Father Aloysius, president of the Workmen's Temperance Committee, gave him the last sacraments. When he asked if Connolly would say a prayer for the men about to shoot him, Connolly replied: 'I will say a prayer for all brave men who do their duty according to their lights.'[11]

One wonders whether that benediction extended to William Martin Murphy. The *Irish Independent* had expressed concern at the 'indiscriminate demand for clemency' towards the insurgents. In words Murphy could never eradicate from the public memory, his newspaper demanded that 'the worst of the ringleaders be singled out and dealt with as they deserve.' That was on 10 May. On 12 May, Connolly was shot.[12]

Inevitably, Murphy was accused of hounding one of his principal opponents in the lockout to his death, and using a British army firing-squad to achieve it. Murphy asserted ever afterwards that the editorial calling for Connolly's death appeared without his knowledge or approval. However, it was not out of character, and his evidence to the Royal Commission into the 1916 rising showed that he believed the seeds of rebellion had been sown in 1913.

Public opinion believed what it chose to believe, and who can blame it if it chose to think the worst of Dublin's 'financial octopus'. At a time when politicians from John Dillon to Sir Edward Carson were counselling moderation by the British government in its reaction to rebellion, and British liberals were calling for an end to the executions, it required a rare vindictiveness to persist in a demand for the execution of a badly wounded man. That was a quality people attributed to William Martin Murphy in plenty.[13]

The blame for Connolly's execution haunted Murphy until his own death at his home in Dartry on 26 June 1919, aged seventy-four. His last years were overshadowed by the death of a son at the front, and this may have influenced the increasingly bitter attitude of his papers towards the British government and the Irish Party. Any remaining sympathy he had for the Irish Party leadership evaporated when Redmond accepted partition for Ulster, though as a temporary measure. John Dillon blamed the party's electoral rout by Sinn Féin in 1918 on the editorial policy of the *Irish Independent*.

However, in the immediate aftermath of the rising Murphy was preoccupied with compensation claims for the damage suffered by his commercial empire. With characteristic energy he set up the Dublin Fire and Property Losses Association, which brought together many of the protagonists of the lockout on the employers' side. Another long-term associate of Murphy's, Sir William Goulding, headed the commission subsequently established to assess claims. Like Murphy, Goulding lived long enough to see the electoral triumph of Sinn Féin in 1918, when the remnants of the 'Dublin Six' were swept away. He quickly adjusted to the new dispensation and became an important link in the nineteen-twenties between the Free State government and the Protestant business community.

Like many of the older generation of parliamentary nationalists, the AOH leader, John Dillon Nugent, was less adaptable. He won John Nannetti's seat on the latter's death in 1915 in a bitterly fought contest with the Labour candidate Thomas Farren. The lockout debate was rehearsed once more, and the vote, in which Nugent polled 2,445 to Farren's 1,816, mirrored that between nationalists and 'Larkinites' in the 1914 municipal elections. Nugent's victory was short-lived: he was left stranded by the Sinn Féin revolution in the south. He subsequently became a nationalist MP in the Northern Ireland parliament for his native County Armagh, where the electorate was more in tune with his Hibernianism. The Hibernian Insurance Company continued to prosper under his leadership. He died in 1940.[14]

The veteran William Field, 'friend of labour', was defeated by Constance Markievicz in 1918, another friend of labour who was campaigning on a Sinn Féin ticket. In the aftermath of the Rising, Sinn Féin swept up all the other Dublin seats, except for Trinity College and Rathmines. The Unionist victor in Rathmines was another veteran of 1913, the businessman Maurice Dockrell.

Murphy's old ally Timothy Healy had the wit to stand aside and allow Sinn Féin a clear field. He acted as an adviser and go-between for both the Sinn Féin leadership and the British government in the troubled years ahead. He was ultimately rewarded with the Governor-Generalship of the Irish Free State.

*

Another man who came to terms with the Sinn Féin revolution was Archbishop Walsh. Like Murphy, most members of the Catholic hierarchy were totally opposed to Redmond's acceptance of partition. Already disillusioned by the Irish Party's inability to deal with the lockout, or even to assist his own efforts to end it, Dr Walsh had no difficulty recognising the dynamism inherent in the separatist leadership. He worked hard to cultivate and to channel constructively the more moderate wing within the revolutionary movement. As so often in the past, the archbishop took the lead among his fellow-bishops in adjusting to the new political realities, and he remained unapologetically patriotic in his dealings with the British. Despite continuing ill-health, he worked hard for peace right up to his death on 9 April 1921, three months before the truce that ended the 'Tan' war.

Walsh's beloved conciliation plan for dealing with industrial disputes would not bear fruit for another twenty-five years, with the establishment of the Labour Court. This courageous, canny and conscientious bishop must have found the lockout and all the troubles that came after a trying experience at a time when he had expected to lead his flock into the peaceful pastures of home rule. A fellow-bishop wrote to commiserate with him on the 'troubles and sorrows of one kind or another … that have arrived only after nigh thirty years in the episcopacy, when your vigour and health to combat them is not now what it was in years gone by.'[15]

*

One wonders how poor Tom Kettle would have survived the coming decade. He was at least spared witnessing the rout of constitutional nationalism in 1918. After the Easter Rising he insisted on joining his regiment, the Dublin Fusiliers, at the front. He left Ireland for active service on Bastille Day, 1916, an appropriate date for a Francophile. Medically unfit, it must have taken considerable effort on his part to be allowed serve at the front and, when he reached it, to survive the horror of the trenches. 'Physically I am having a heavy time,' he wrote to his wife. 'I am doing my best, but I see better men than me dropping out day by day and wonder if I shall ever have the luck or grace to come home.' In another letter he complained:

> The heat is bad, as are the insects and rats, but the moral strain is positively terrible. It is not that I am not happy in a way—a poor way—but my heart does long for a chance to come home.

He never did. On 9 August 1916 he was killed leading a group of Dublin Fusiliers in an attack at Ginchy, on the Somme. His remains were never recovered.[16]

It is unlikely that there were any survivors of the 'Dockers' Company' of the Dublin Fusiliers to witness his death. In 1914 a group of ITGWU men, unable to win reinstatement on the docks, had joined the regiment en bloc. They were part of the regular army that held the line in Flanders while

Kitchener's mass volunteer army was training in Britain. On 24 April 1915 they took part in an attack on Saint-Julien, near Ypres. They advanced 'in faultless order' to within a hundred yards of the village, then their line was swept away by machine-gun fire. The handful who crawled back gave 'three cheers for Jim Larkin,' just as if they were once more outside Liberty Hall.[17]

The Easter Rising took place exactly one year after the fighting at Saint-Julien, in which almost three thousand Irishmen, many of them Dublin Fusiliers, had been killed or seriously wounded. It was one reason why so many 'separation women' (wives and widows of soldiers receiving War Office payments) showed such hostility to the rebel prisoners as they were marched through the streets of Dublin.

*

No doubt Larkin, if he had been there to see it, would have depicted the scene as another example of capitalism's innate power to divide the working class. But Larkin was in America. He had gone there in November 1914, shortly before the suppression of the *Irish Worker* for its anti-war views, partly to recuperate from the nervous and physical exhaustion he felt in the wake of the lockout and partly to speak about the struggle and to raise funds for his shattered union. He did not return for nine years.

The ITGWU proved remarkably resilient. At the end of 1913 it had £2,381 6s 9d in hand, compared with £1,798 18s 8d at the beginning of the year. Larkin was like an impresario who could conjure money out of any spectacle, even a lockout. He was never a man to worry about financial niceties, and the figures may well have been doctored to pass muster with the Registrar of Friendly Societies. Even so, they bear testimony to the remarkable strength of the young union, especially when it is remembered that the ITGWU had paid £5,500 for Liberty Hall in the summer of 1913.

Significantly, the returns for 1913 show that only £3,842 6s 4d was paid out under the heading of 'unemployment benefit, travel and emigration pay chargeable to the Union's own funds,' suggesting that the union succeeded in extracting large amounts not only from the TUC's Dublin Fund but also from the new state social insurance scheme in order to finance its industrial war. In contrast, almost as much was spent on 'management expenses,' which totalled £3,398 18s 11d.[18] How real these figures are is hard to say. For instance, they do not include a loan of £2,000 raised by mortgaging Liberty Hall, and there may have been other hidden transactions.[19]

The union was certainly not awash with liquid funds, as evidenced by Larkin's own eviction and reports that Liberty Hall itself was so dilapidated that the union was seriously considering renting temporary premises early in 1914.[20] It also owed William Smyth and Son £1,422 3s 10d in legal fees, which arose largely out of the lockout. Four hundred members had been defended on charges ranging from intimidation to malicious damage, riot, assault, and murder. During the lockout the union fought sixty-three ejectment proceedings for members, sixteen cases of wrongful dismissal, and two cases under the Workmen's Compensation Act. The largest fees were £83 18s 4d for Larkin's defence in the October sedition trial, and £31 2s 2d for Daly's defence in the Harten murder case.

Besides defending its own members, the ITGWU paid for the legal representation of other Trades Council leaders, such as William O'Brien, and for sympathisers such as Dora Montefiore, Lucille Rand and Francis Sheehy-Skeffington when they fell foul of the law because of their activities in support of the workers.[21] While the union lost the majority of cases, Larkin believed fighting them was important. Before the lockout, workers who had the misfortune to be arrested during industrial disputes were treated as if they were already convicted criminals. After the lockout they were treated in the courts as citizens—not always as first-class citizens, but citizens nevertheless, entitled to a fair hearing.[22]

Ultimately, the financial well-being of the union would depend on membership. At the end of 1913 the ITGWU had 22,935 members, compared with 24,135 in January. Two thousand members were admitted during the year, and 3,200 left.[23] National membership records for the period 1914 to 1916 are incomplete. The period was necessarily one of recovery and recuperation, not made any easier by the ITGWU becoming a prime target of repression before, during and after the Easter Rising, largely because of the leading role Connolly and other union figures played in the separatist movement.

The membership rolls for the Number 1 Branch of the union, which was in the cockpit of the lockout, suggest that by the end of 1915 the union had made good its losses in some employments. At Morgan Mooney's fertiliser plant and the City of Dublin Steam Packet Company, for instance, the number of ITGWU members was as high as in 1913. However, in two of the leading coal merchants, Tedcastle McCormick's and Heiton's, the union had only twenty-one members and ten members, respectively. At Brooks Thomas there were just eleven members, and at Palgrave Murphy, where the clerks had gone out to unload cargoes, there were five. At T. and C. Martin's, the first company to bring strike-breakers into the port, there were ten ITGWU members. At the Dublin Steam Trawler Company, whose workers stayed out in sympathy until early 1914, there were two members. Not surprisingly, the bulk of the branch membership was now composed of casual dockers, carters, and coalmen, rather than permanent workers.[24]

Though Connolly has been cast by some of his admirers as the hard-headed revolutionary who rebuilt the union after the more temperamental Larkin had left for America, there is little evidence of this in the records for the years preceding 1916. If anything, Connolly's growing preoccupation with the Citizen Army and insurrectionary plots suggests that he neglected the more mundane tasks involved in revitalising the union.

It was not until 1917 that national membership began to grow significantly. It was 14,500 at the beginning of the year, and crept up to

14,920 by its end.[25] The lean times would soon end: by 1920 it would soar to a peak of 120,000.[26] This was due to many factors, including growing trade union militancy, political radicalisation during the 'troubles', and above all the labour shortages created as a result of the war and a booming domestic economy. It was also in large measure due to the stewardship of William O'Brien. He took no part in the Rising, a deformed foot having made him ineligible for service in the Volunteers or the Citizen Army and also giving rise to the nickname 'Hoofy', with which P.J. McIntyre baited him in the *Toiler*. During the Rising, Connolly had asked O'Brien to undertake various 'civilian' duties similar to those of Sheehy-Skeffington. O'Brien was able to do little before he was arrested and interned, but after his release he took an increasing interest in the ITGWU. He joined it in 1917, was elected to the executive in 1918, and became the union's first full-time treasurer in 1919.[27]

O'Brien proved to be the cuckoo in the ITGWU nest. Larkin found on his return to Dublin in 1923 that the new organisation was firmly in the new man's hands. When the inevitable clash came, the prophet Larkin was driven into the wilderness by the tailor O'Brien. Larkin took much of the Dublin membership with him to found the Workers' Union of Ireland, which became in time the second-largest union in Ireland. In 1990 the two unions founded by Larkin amalgamated to form SIPTU, which at the time of writing had 40 per cent of unionised workers in the Republic enrolled as members.

O'Brien, to legitimise his own regime, portrayed himself as a disciple of Connolly—even going to the extent of having the dead leader's selected writings published. He was undoubtedly a gifted union organiser and a committed socialist; but he shared the fate of many who toil to build and sustain a large organisation. The union, supposed to be the means to the socialist millennium, became the end of his endeavours.

*

The question arises, why did Larkin spend so long in America? One reason was simply the difficulty of wartime travel; and the British government was in no hurry to facilitate his return to Ireland. Besides, he was soon distracted by the need to fight new battles. He clashed with Irish-American Fenians and conservative labour leaders; he attacked celebrities such as the tenor John McCormack for his support of the British war effort; and when the Russian Revolution erupted, he became one of its most committed supporters.

During his stay in America, Larkin's contact with his family was minimal. His wife visited him briefly in 1915 and again in 1919; but shortly after his return to Ireland in 1923, the couple separated permanently. Whether he would have returned to Ireland at all that year if he had not been deported is doubtful. In November 1919 he had been charged with 'criminal anarchy'. As usual, he mounted his own defence. It was brilliant, it was wounding to the American establishment, and it led to a prison sentence of five to ten years. He was released from Sing Sing, a 'grimly mediaeval' prison, by the newly elected Governor of New York, the Irish-American Al Smith, and deported. Smith said he was releasing Larkin 'not because of agreement with his views, but despite disagreement with them … Full and free discussion of political issues is a fundamental of democracy.'[28]

It may be that Larkin preferred America to Ireland, at least until he landed in Sing Sing. In America he may have felt less of an outsider than in Ireland. It is one of the peculiarities of Irish labour history that its two seminal figures, Larkin and Connolly, were outsiders: Connolly was born in Edinburgh, Larkin in Liverpool. Both were the children of Irish emigrants; both prided themselves on their Irish heritage and were defensive when their nationality was attacked, even giving the impression that they had been born in Ireland. Both laid claim to a Fenian tradition in the family, which made little sense in a socialist context but a great deal of sense if they wanted acceptance by nationalists.

Nevertheless, the nationalism of Larkin was very different from that of Connolly. Larkin did on occasion react emotionally to nationalist issues, particularly when partition loomed in 1914. 'Ireland is one and indivisible,' he wrote in the *Irish Worker*.[29] He told trade unionists that if they

> stand idly by whilst they are being betrayed, they get what they deserve … Our fathers died that we might be free men. Are we going to allow their life sacrifice to be as naught? Or are we going to follow in their footsteps at the Rising of the Moon?[30]

Similarly, when the First World War broke out, he appealed to

> Irishmen, dear countrymen … Stop at Home. Arm for Ireland. Fight for Ireland and no other land.

Nor did he stop at words. He contacted his old comrade Fred Bower in Liverpool, who had helped look after the Dublin 'kiddies' on Merseyside, and asked him to smuggle arms for the Citizen Army. The syndicalist stonemason dutifully packed the guns between slabs in a crate labelled *Tombstone—With care*, and despatched them to Dublin.[31] Larkin's response to the war was not that of most European revolutionary socialists: it was firmly locked in an Irish psyche.

When Larkin travelled to America he continued to campaign vigorously against support for the British war effort. Yet when a German military attaché offered him $200 a week to co-operate with his government's sabotage operations, Larkin angrily rejected the offer. He told the Germans that he would disrupt the British war effort through the collective action of the organised working class; he was nobody's pawn, least of all a pawn of a capitalist power.

Connolly had a very different relationship with the German war effort. Through his membership of the military council of the IRB he not only laid claim to a family tradition but became a Fenian himself. He was, in fact, an adherent of the same school of political activism as the Clan na Gael representatives who introduced Larkin to the Germans in America. It was a tradition that included Lenin and the Bolsheviks as well as Pearse, the founder of the IRB, James Stephens, and the political godfather of them all, the French revolutionary conspirator Louis-Auguste Blanqui. It was a tradition that even predated Blanqui in Ireland, reaching back to the militant wing of the United Irishmen, to Theobald Wolfe Tone, Robert Emmet, and Connolly's particular hero, the weaver Jemmy Hope.

Connolly believed, as the IRB believed, in the sovereignty of a political elite. It was Connolly, not Pearse, who wrote, a month before the 1916 Rising: 'It is not the will of the majority which ultimately prevails; that which ultimately prevails is the ideal of the noblest of each generation.'[32] It was a political outlook with which Larkin profoundly disagreed. Despite his platform swagger, his association with the Comintern, and his use of bloodcurdling language, Larkin saw socialism as essentially a democratic movement. He believed that the working class could and would emancipate itself once the right conditions had been created. His beliefs were far closer to those of the British labour left, from which he had sprung, than to those of Irish social radicalism. Indeed a fellow-Liverpudlian and future leader of the Irish Labour Party, Thomas Johnson, who knew Larkin well, probably gave the most accurate assessment of the ITGWU leader when he placed him with the 'anarchist syndicalists.'[33]

Paradoxically, Connolly's greater sense of political reality and his longer experience of Irish politics made him despair of creating the right conditions for the establishment of socialism by democratic means in a country dominated by nationalist and religious sentiment. In time of war particularly, other methods were necessary. These two very different men therefore bequeathed political testaments to the Irish left that were deceptively similar in terminology but conflicted profoundly in substance.

Those differences, and their ultimately divergent destinations, were not obvious in 1913, and they have remained largely obscured since. Paradoxically, the idiosyncratic nature of their socialist beliefs ensured that neither man left a viable strategic programme for Irish labour to pursue but could inspire a range of political activists within the broader left and nationalist movements. It suited the future political leadership of a wide range of interests, including the radical wings of Fianna Fáil and the republican movement, the Labour Party, the trade unions, and elements within the voluntary and community sectors, to leave the ideological lines blurred. The task was made easier by the fact that, despite their very different personalities and perspectives, the collective memory of the two men is of them working together during the lockout. The sheer ferocity of the enemy's onslaught in 1913 left little time for internal wrangles.

*

The lockout itself was unquestionably a tragedy, and an unnecessary one. And yet, like all tragedies, it was almost inevitable. Connolly was surely right when he said that syndicalist methods were the only way to win concessions for Dublin's unskilled workers in the early years of the twentieth century. There was such a surplus of labour that any strike could easily be defeated by Dublin's employers recruiting new workers from the huge reservoir at their door. Only by convincing those workers that 'an injury to one is the concern of all'[34] could the ITGWU counter the employers' tactic with the sympathetic strike. It proved highly successful, particularly in the first half of 1913, when Larkin had the employers on the run. However, it was susceptible to a counter-strategy, though a fairly drastic one, and that was the sympathetic lockout. This was precisely the plan adopted by William Martin Murphy.

It was only Murphy's ill-health in the summer of 1913 that allowed the Lord Mayor, Lorcan Sherlock, to promote his conciliation plan. Both the Dublin Chamber of Commerce and Dublin Trades Council had gone as far as considering the composition of panels for the conciliation body when the tramway strike began, and Murphy was able to retrieve the initiative. In retrospect, it is clear that Murphy's purge of ITGWU members in the DUTC, and at the *Irish Independent*, was aimed at provoking a wider confrontation, or at least at ensuring that his own commercial empire was free from Larkinite contamination before any conciliation system was established.

For Larkin, the unionisation of the DUTC was essential to his strategy of creating a powerful union of transport workers. The tramway system was a vital commercial artery, and control of its work force would immensely increase the industrial muscle of the ITGWU everywhere in the city. To use a military metaphor, the lockout was an 'encounter battle', where two commanders with larger strategic objectives stumbled into each other and had little option but to fight it out, or allow their opponent a decisive advantage.

And it was a war that was fought in Dublin that year. Like most intractable industrial disputes, the tramway strike, and the huge conflict that grew out of it, was not primarily about money or working conditions. It was about power. The employers were ready to accept Murphy's leadership because they felt they were losing control over their own businesses to the twin-headed monster of socialism and syndicalism. Similarly the Trades Council, and subsequently the British TUC, were willing to back Larkin because they saw the dispute as being about fundamental trade union rights. The right to union recognition, the right to freedom of association and even the right to freedom of expression and assembly were under threat.

It was fortuitous for Larkin that Bloody Sunday occurred on the eve of the TUC congress in Manchester. Not even his bitterest opponents in the British trade union movement, such as James Sexton, could refuse to support him. Of course when they had time to reflect, most of the British union leaders made honourable withdrawal from Ireland a priority. But there is no reason to doubt the good faith of men like James Seddon, Harry Gosling and Robert Williams in trying to resolve the Dublin dispute.

It is certainly a mistake to portray the TUC's action as some form of betrayal of the Dublin men. What divided the two groups was not just ideology but experience. The leaders of the British transport unions, including the railway unions, had learnt the hard way that the use of the sympathetic strike was not only costly and risky but frequently ineffective. It might be possible to argue that sympathetic action tended to be less successful because it was most commonly resorted to in the most difficult situations; but that was hardly a defence likely to endear it as a tactic to the TUC, the National Transport Workers' Federation, or the National Union of Railwaymen. They saw conciliation as a more viable strategy—as indeed Larkin and Connolly admitted in calmer moments. In the end, the Board of Trade statistic that sympathetic strikes were sixteen times less likely to succeed than traditional sectional disputes spoke louder than any theory.[35]

Ideological disputes aggravated and complicated this fundamental divide. Men such as Bob Smillie of the Miners and Robert Williams of the NTWF began as allies of the Dublin men and ended up as enemies. The divide was also cultural. The Dublin strike leaders were extremely jealous of both their nationality and their operational autonomy. Some of the more conservative British leaders were extremely insensitive on both counts. However, to the extent that there was any explicit chauvinism, it appeared to emanate mainly from the Irish side. Connolly in particular tended to depict the TUC leaders towards the end of the dispute as new recruits to the perfidious English ruling class that had always oppressed Ireland. They therefore provided convenient scapegoats in defeat; and by demonising them, Connolly was forwarding his own increasingly nationalist political agenda, one in which primacy should go to the Irish working class because it was the most patriotic class, as well as the most socially progressive class, in the country.

It is certainly true that the TUC leadership rigged the debate at the special delegate conference on 9 December 1913 to isolate Larkin. But given his ferocious 'fiery cross' campaign of the preceding weeks, it is hard to blame them.

*

Ultimately it was what happened in Dublin that decided the course of the dispute. Before, during and after the lockout, both the employers and the strike leaders had a tendency to underestimate their opponents' ability and to overestimate their own ability to achieve their objectives. Once the TUC joined the fray, the lockout became a war of attrition. As we now know, the unions came close to winning, until the Shipping Federation agreed to throw its weight behind the coal importers and other cross-channel operators. Between October 1913 and April 1914 the TUC provided the Dublin strikers with £93,673 13s 9¼d in food, clothing, and money. Dublin Trades Council received another £13,338 10s 10d from other sources; and some of the unions, including the ITGWU, had considerable resources of their own.

Over the same period the Shipping Federation invested only £9,967 10s 2d in support of the employers. In other words, for every pound spent by the British employers to help their Irish counterparts keep Dublin port open, it cost the British trade unions £10 to support their Irish brethren who were on strike in order to close it.

It was the strikers' misfortune that the dispute coincided with the advent of motorised transport. This militated particularly against carters and workers handling bulk goods such as grain, beer, and coal; it is no coincidence that it was in these categories that the highest numbers of strikers failed to win reinstatement. Ironically, the car and motor lorry would also ultimately drive Murphy's trams off the streets of Dublin.

The employers also had the support of the state in the dispute. There was a massive police and military presence on the streets to ensure that the tram service and other businesses were not disrupted. In the courts there was a two-tier justice system: strikers often received prison sentences for comparatively minor offences, while gun-toting strike-breakers were released on bail or even discharged after shooting people. Apart from the police baton charge in Sackville Street on 'Bloody Sunday', accounts of 1913 have tended to ignore the lockout's violent aspects. We should not forget that it was a battle fought as much in the pubs, back streets and gutters of the city as on the picket lines or in the newspaper columns. The sanitising of the lockout presaged similar historical treatment of the 'Tan' war: indeed the depiction of the strike-breakers as the scum of English slums (though at least a quarter of them were probably Irish) anticipated similar characterisation of the Black and Tans. Dark forces were already stirring.

Nationalists were understandably aggrieved at being the victims of the proxy war between the Shipping Federation and the TUC. It was as if the two sides were experimenting in new forms of industrial conflict before renewing their own struggles at home. Nor did the fact that the TUC sent most of its aid in the form of foodstuffs endear it to Dublin's shopkeepers and publicans, who happened to be particularly influential in municipal politics.

The proposal to send children to England in October had no real bearing on the outcome of the strike, but it did reveal the huge gap in cultures and understanding between Irish and British society. British trade unionists were revolted by what they saw as a poverty-stricken, priest-ridden society opposing a humanitarian project to help the children; Irish nationalists saw crusaders such as Dora Montefiore as at best condescending and at worst arrogant in the time-honoured British way. What both the British and Irish labour movements failed to perceive was that the mass mobilisation by the AOH and others to 'save' the children was an early manifestation of the alliance between the Catholic Church and the rising urban middle class that was to dominate the culture of the nascent Irish state. George Russell's immortal depiction of the employers as 'an oligarchy of four hundred masters deciding openly upon starving one hundred thousand people, and refusing to consider any solution except that fixed by their pride,' may have awoken some of the readers of the *Irish Times* to the enormity of what was taking place, but it has been misleading us ever since. Russell had been outraged at the behaviour of the employers, as were the TUC, British public opinion, and even some members of the British government; but he had little impact on the sensibilities of Dublin's solid middle class, or their country cousins. These people gave very little financial, material, political or moral support to the strikers. Appeals for the families of the Fethard lifeboat men, survivors of the *Titanic*, and even the 'Loyal Tramway Men', found a readier response among them than the plight of the strikers' families. Even the explicit exclusion of the strikers' themselves from relief failed to attract the largesse of middle-class donors to Marie Sherlock's distress fund. It seems that when Murphy denounced Larkin and the strikers he was speaking for more people than we might like to think.

*

The British government and its Irish executive did not come well out of the crisis either. They were understandably preoccupied with industrial strife at home and the danger of civil war in Ulster. But no British city, least of all the capital, would have been left for five months with its industry paralysed and a third of its population on the bread-line. The inaction of the British government over the lockout was a powerful argument in favour of Irish independence. Birrell reinforced it by his laziness and indecision; at the same time he resented the efforts of more forceful and ambitious colleagues, such as Churchill and Lloyd George, to sort out Irish problems.

The DMP, the courts and authority in general were discredited by the lockout. The damage was not repaired by the time the Tan war broke out. After 1916 the majority of DMP members made their accommodations with the IRA, though a few of the 'diehards' in the G Division did precisely that. The Aberdeens left Ireland, unmourned, shortly after the First World War broke out, to be replaced by a series of increasingly unsympathetic and remote symbols of authority—usually authority in a military uniform. They may have been figures of fun, but they were the last occupants of the Viceregal Lodge to show any real concern for, or knowledge of, the social problems that beset the Irish people.

It is hard to overestimate the influence that the incipient revolt of Ulster unionists had on political behaviour throughout Ireland, and indeed Britain. Intransigence and violence replaced discourse and compromise. If the Ulster crisis had exposed the hidden dangers connected with the introduction of home rule, the lockout revealed those that lay ahead if the British government abandoned its project for greater Irish autonomy. Dublin strikers and Irish Volunteers, armed with hurleys, were less flamboyant than the Ulstermen, but many young nationalists in Dublin came to see the lockout in retrospect as a dress rehearsal for 1916 and for all that followed.

*

Larkin may have had an international syndicalist agenda when he launched his 'fiery cross' campaign in Britain, but his defeat gave a strong impetus to separatist tendencies within Irish labour. As the Trades Council strike leaders repeatedly said during the lockout, they welcomed financial support from the British movement, but that did not give the TUC ownership of their dispute: it would be settled by Irishmen.

For men such as James Seddon, Harry Gosling and Robert Williams the lockout experience must have been deeply frustrating. They devoted a huge amount of time and effort, not to mention the physical discomfort of regular crossings of the Irish Sea, to try to settle the dispute. Seddon even spent the Christmas of 1913 in Dublin with the strikers and their families. It must have been all the more frustrating to know that the dispute was eminently capable of resolution and that failure to resolve it was giving syndicalists and other radicals in the trade union movement a stick with which to beat the TUC leadership. At the same time it was a dangerous drain on the British movement's resources and a distraction at a time when it was trying to rationalise and strengthen its own structures.

If Larkin and Connolly despised the penchant of the TUC and NTWF for amalgamations—and predicted that these would be self-defeating, because they would kill the natural militancy and spontaneity of the movement—British leaders could retort that the Dublin men's own brand of sympathetic strike had achieved little. However, from the time of the Askwith Inquiry onwards it was clear that the Trades Council was willing to come to terms. It was willing to offer an industrial truce to the employers if they would agree to the establishment of a conciliation system. The employers refused. One reason was undoubtedly their distrust of Larkin: they no longer believed he could keep an agreement; but an even more potent factor was the ascendancy Murphy had over his colleagues. Once he had shown them they could win, his authority was never seriously challenged.

*

If Larkin was deluding himself in thinking that the sympathetic strike could turn Dublin into the birthplace of a syndicalist revolution, Murphy was equally deluded by his admittedly more modest dream of destroying the ITGWU. He is, of course, one of capitalism's great villains. The twinkling, good-humoured face with its almost boyish expression, and the sanctimonious piety in which he usually wrapped his sordid schemes, served only to underline the inner vindictiveness of his soul. Anyone who could leave thousands of workers on the bread-line, and tens of thousands of women and children under the threat of starvation, to wring from his opponents a 'Carthaginian peace' deserves all the obloquy that posterity has bestowed on him.[36] His final victory proved short-lived: it was snatched away by the labour shortages that arose after the outbreak of the First

World War. The ITGWU and the Dublin trade union movement rebuilt themselves stronger than ever.

The major companies also appear to have emerged from the dispute relatively unscathed. The DUTC suffered a sharp drop in operating profits, and this was reflected in other firms heavily involved in the dispute; but these losses were short-lived. Some shipping companies had to provide indemnities against losses caused to customers by future industrial disputes. Companies based primarily on exports to the buoyant British market, such as Guinness's, suffered a short-term loss of sales, but not on a significant scale.[37]

The real damage inflicted by Murphy's strategy was its undermining of whatever moral authority Dublin employers had in a society about to undergo dramatic political change. As a class, they would play no part in the coming nationalist revolution. Of course an accommodation would quickly be reached with the political elite of the new Irish state; but for the oldest elements in Dublin's business community, the Protestant unionists, it was the beginning of the end. It was ironic that it was a rabid Catholic nationalist businessman who helped them dig their own grave.

As for Larkin and Connolly, if they failed to storm the gates of Heaven, they taught the Dublin working class one valuable lesson, which it took to its collective heart: 'An injury to one is the concern of all.' In the peculiar way that only the bitterest and most hard-fought defeats can impress a lesson on the soul, the lockout impressed that lesson on the soul of Ireland's working class. It still echoes down the years, and the memory of 1913 is routinely invoked whenever there is a dispute over union recognition, or indeed any other form of social injustice.

*

When Larkin returned to Ireland in 1923 he had almost a quarter of a century more of service to give to the working class. By turn syndicalist, socialist, communist, union organiser, agitator, member of Dublin City Council, of Dáil Éireann and of the Comintern, he never ceased to preach the doctrine behind the sympathetic strike: the brotherhood of man. If his family life, like so much else, had been a casualty of the struggle, he had at least the satisfaction of seeing his sons follow in his footsteps. Young Jim and Denis Larkin would each in turn be general secretary of the Workers' Union of Ireland. 'Young Jim' would emerge in many respects as a greater and certainly a more mature trade union leader than his father.

Shortly before Christmas 1946, Larkin slipped and fell while inspecting repairs to the WUI hall. He ignored advice to have his injuries seen to, and in the early hours of 30 January he died in his sleep at the Meath Hospital. On Monday 2 February 1947 the city he loved came to a standstill. Leaders of church and state and thousands of the workers he had led came out to pay their homage. The ageing iconoclast Seán O'Casey, now a celebrated writer and exile in England, wrote a tribute for the *Irish Times*.

> There was a man sent from God whose name was Jim, and that man was Larkin. Jim Larkin is not dead, but is with us, and will be with us always.[38]

NOTES

DDA   Dublin Diocesan Archive
MRC   Modern Records Centre, University of Warwick
NA   National Archives, Dublin
NLI   National Library of Ireland, Dublin
PRO   Public Records Office, London
TCD   Trinity College, Dublin

PROLOGUE (p. xvii–xxx)

1. British army intelligence notes, 1913, Military Archives, Dublin; *Irish Times*, 13–19 Aug. 1913.
2. *Irish Times*, 5 Aug. 1913. In 1990 the Irish Transport and General Workers' Union amalgamated with the Federated Workers' Union of Ireland, which had been founded by Larkin in 1924, to form the Services, Industrial, Professional and Technical Union (SIPTU).
3. *Irish Worker*, 2 May 1914.
4. Schedule of fees and charges from William Smyth and Son to the ITGWU, NLI, ms. 27,504. Smyth and Son were the union's solicitors. Liberty Hall was in fact in Beresford Place, at the junction with Eden Quay. See Sweeney, 'The oul' spot by the river.'
5. Bew, *Ideology and the Irish Question*, 24–5; Stewart, *The Ulster Crisis*, 65–8. The nationalist majority in Derry had been 57 votes in a 95 per cent turnout.
6. For Protestant predominance in the professions see Joseph O'Brien, *Dear, Dirty Dublin*, 40; also the *Leader*, 21 and 28 Feb. 1914. For Dublin's Protestant working class see Maguire, 'A socio-economic analysis of the Dublin Protestant working class'; Maguire, 'The organisation and activism of Dublin's Protestant working class'; and Maguire, 'The Dublin working class, 1870s–1930s.'
7. Stewart, *Edward Carson*, 20. Despite his grief at the death of his first wife, Annette Kirwan, Carson married his second wife, Ruby Frewen, within two years. Both women were from strong unionist backgrounds.
8. Dangerfield, *The Damnable Question*, 70.
9. Bond, *War and Society in Europe*, chap. 2 and 3, gives a pan-European treatment of this phenomenon. See also Keegan, *A History of Warfare*, 347–59. The British authorities had baulked at extending the Territorial Army to Ireland, for security reasons; see Muenger, *The British Military Dilemma in Ireland*, chap. 6.

10. Quoted by Joseph O'Brien, *Dear, Dirty Dublin*, 9.
11. Wright, *Disturbed Dublin*, 3–4. The claim that Wright was paid £500 (ten times the annual wage of a labourer in 1913) was made by Desmond Ryan in an editorial note to a review of Wright's book by Connolly. Connolly's review appeared in the *Irish Worker* on 18 November and was republished by the ITGWU in 1951 in *The Workers' Republic*, a selection of his writings edited by Ryan. The source of Ryan's information was probably his father, William P. Ryan, a close friend of many leading Irish and British socialists, who also knew Wright. From 1911 until his death in 1942 W. P. Ryan was assistant editor of the *Daily Herald* in London and was responsible for its detailed coverage of the lockout. Wright was commissioned to produce his book after a series of articles he produced for the *Westminster Gazette* was reprinted in pamphlet form by the Shipping Federation, a leading employers' organisation. Wright's account of events in *Disturbed Dublin* is generally accurate, if selective.
12. Address by D. A. Chart to Statistical and Social Inquiry Society of Dublin, 6 Mar. 1914, *Irish Times*, 7 Mar. 1914. The old pound consisted of 240 pence, with 12 pence comprising a shilling. A shilling (1s) was the equivalent of five new pence, and six pence (6d) was the equivalent of 2½ new pence. Half a crown, or 2s 6d, was the equivalent of 12½ new pence.
13. *Irish Times*, 7 Mar. 1914.
14. *Irish Times*, 7 Mar. 1914.
15. *Irish Times*, 7 Mar. 1914. The price of coal is based on that prevailing in August 1913. This rose sharply during the early phases of the lockout, more because of racketeering and panic buying than because of real shortages. However, it subsequently fell again. Prices are taken from market reports in the *Irish Times*, Sep.–Dec. 1913.
16. *Irish Times*, 7 Mar. 1914.
17. *Irish Times*, 7 Mar. 1914. Chart's speech, 'Unskilled labour in Dublin: its housing and living conditions,' was subsequently published in the *Irish Social and Statistical Bulletin*, part 4, 1914.
18. The science of statistics was still in its infancy before the First World War, as Tom Kettle soon discovered when he became professor of national economics at University College, Dublin. The Board of Trade introduced uniform cost-of-living indices partly as a result of the wave of strikes that swept Britain in 1911 and 1912. The figures given here for Dublin in the twenty years before 1913 are based on those cited by Joseph O'Brien, *Dear, Dirty Dublin*, 204–6; Cody et al., *The Parliament of Labour*, 47–51; Daly, *Dublin: The Deposed Capital*, 64–76; a 'Cost of living' survey in the *Leader*, 13 Sep. 1913; *Irish Worker*, 24 Jan. 1914.
19. Wright, *Disturbed Dublin*, 106–7, 305–7; *Report of the Dublin Disturbances Commission* (Cd. 7421), Parliamentary Papers, vol. 67 , 1914, 430.
20. *Irish Times*, 9 July 1913.
21. Dublin Chamber of Commerce minutes, 18 Aug. 1913, NA; Dublin Trades Council minutes, 2 and 8 Sep. 1913, NLI, ms. 12,779–85; Guinness Archive, Board memoranda, 2144–431. The Dublin Trades Council went ahead and appointed its members to the proposed conciliation board on 8 September, even though full-scale industrial warfare had broken out by then.
22. Emmet Larkin, *James Larkin*, xii–xiv. Emmet Larkin and other biographers of James Larkin believed their subject was born in 1876. In fact he was born in 1874. I have given his correct age at the relevant points in this narrative.
23. Howell, *A Lost Left*, 232–6.

24. Coates and Topham, *The Making of the Transport and General Workers' Union,* 167; Sexton, *Sir James Sexton,* 203–4.

25. Greaves, *The Irish Transport and General Workers' Union,* 24–7; William O'Brien, *Forth the Banners Go,* 56. There had been earlier attempts to introduce the 'new unionism' to Dublin: see, for example, Cody et al., *The Parliament of Labour,* 16–18, and Keogh, *The Rise of the Irish Working Class,* 89–103. O'Brien's claim to have suggested adding the word 'General' to the union's title has been disputed: see William O'Brien, *Forth the Banners Go,* 56; for an opposing view see Francis Devine, 'Larkin and the ITGWU, 1909–1912,' in Nevin, *James Larkin,* 31.

26. Greaves, *The Irish Transport and General Workers' Union,* 26–7, 50–51; Eric Taplin, 'Liverpool: The Apprenticeship of a Revolutionary,' in Nevin, *James Larkin,* 21–2; Wright, *Disturbed Dublin,* 46–9; Francis Devine, 'Larkin and the ITGWU, 1909–1912,' in Nevin, *James Larkin,* 33.

27. Emmet Larkin, *James Larkin,* 163. One contemporary who knew Larkin well was Thomas Johnson, who saw similarities in personality and speaking style between Larkin and Adolf Hitler: see J. Anthony Gaughan's *Thomas Johnson.* In appendix 20, 476, he quotes from a letter by Johnson in which he recalls reading 'a character sketch of Hitler' by the Berlin correspondent of the *Guardian.* 'I cut it out and kept it for a long time, thinking how accurately it portrayed the man we knew as Jim Larkin.' Johnson accepted that Larkin was a very different political animal from 'the Hitler of later years'; nevertheless he let the comparison of the two men as orators stand.

28. Francis Devine, 'Larkin and the ITGWU, 1909–1912,' in Nevin, *James Larkin,* 33.

29. Samuel Levenson, *James Connolly,* 217–23.

30. Samuel Levenson, *Maud Gonne,* 180.

31. Appreciation of Larkin by Seán O'Casey, *Irish Times,* 1 Feb. 1947.

32. Tom Kettle, 'Labour: war or peace,' in *The Day's Burden,* 1937 edition.

33. Grigg, *Lloyd George: From Peace to War, 1912–1916,* 23. For production days lost and unemployment rates see *Strikes and Lockouts, 1913* (Cd. 7658), Parliamentary Papers, vol. 36, 1914. For a good overview of the international setting of the 1913 lockout see Kenneth Brown, 'The strikes of 1911–1913: their international significance,' in Nevin, *James Larkin,* 56–63. For what is still the best account of the British experience see Dangerfield, *The Strange Death of Liberal England.*

34. Quotation from *Sinn Féin,* 30 Sep. 1911, in Davis, *Arthur Griffith and Non-Violent Sinn Féin,* 138. Griffith was attacking Larkin over a union recognition dispute at Jacob's biscuit factory in Dublin. This factory would later feature significantly in the 1913 lockout.

CHAPTER 1 (p. 1–15)

1. Details of events on 26 August 1913 are based mainly on reports in the daily papers, especially the *Irish Times* and *Freeman's Journal,* which were less partisan than the Murphy titles. For the origin of the Red Hand badge see Francis Devine, 'ITGWU Red Hand badge,' in Nevin, *James Larkin,* 151.

2. Wright, *Disturbed Dublin,* 78.

3. Morrissey, *William Martin Murphy,* 32.

4. Morrissey, *William Martin Murphy,* chap. 2 and 4; Dublin Chamber of

Commerce reports, 1912 and 1913, and minutes of quarterly meeting, 2 Mar. 1914, NA; *Irish Times*, 20 Aug. 1913; half-yearly reports of Great Southern and Western Railway, 1904. I am indebted to Clifton Flewitt and Brendan Pender of the Railway Society for drawing my attention to Murphy's investment in British electrical engineering companies, such as BECC.

5. Wright, *Disturbed Dublin*, 77–8.
6. 'Office Window,' portrait in *Daily Chronicle*, quoted by Morrissey in *William Martin Murphy*, 77.
7. Callanan, *T. M. Healy*, 464–89, 711, n. 31; Morrissey, *William Martin Murphy*, 32; Healy, *Letters and Leaders of My Day*, vol. 2, 601; G. K. Chesterton, *Irish Impressions*, London: Collins 1919, 75. Public recriminations did not prevent O'Brien and Healy working frequently together when it suited them politically: see Maume, *The Long Gestation*.
8. O'Connor, *Memoirs of an Old Parliamentarian*, vol. 2, 58.
9. Callanan, *T. M. Healy*, 363.
10. Wright, *Disturbed Dublin*, 77.
11. Callanan, *T. M. Healy*, 503.
12. Morrissey, *William Martin Murphy*, 16.
13. Guinness Archive, Board memoranda, 2144–431.
14. 'Dublin Tram Men's Grievances,' undated, Walsh Papers, laity file, DDA, 1913.
15. 'Dublin Tram Men's Grievances,' undated, Walsh Papers, laity file, DDA, 1913.
16. Details of the meeting in the Antient Concert Rooms are taken largely from evidence to the Askwith Inquiry, 3 and 4 Oct. 1913; also the annual report of the DUTC in the *Irish Times*, 4 Feb. 1914. For the full text of Murphy's speech see Nevin, *1913*, 21–2.
17. *Irish Times*, 18 Aug. 1913.
18. Emmet Larkin, *James Larkin*, 119; *Leader*, 27 Sep. 1913.
19. For Murphy's attitude to the conciliation scheme see the minutes of his meeting with C. E. Sutton, assistant managing director of Guinness, 21 Sep. 1913, Guinness Archive, Board memoranda, 2144–431; Greaves, *The Irish Transport and General Workers' Union*, 95–6; *Irish Times*, 22 Aug. 1913; Irish Worker, 27 Aug. 1913.
20. For details of street traders see quarterly reports of the Children's (Street Trading) Court in Dublin Corporation reports for 1913; also *Irish Times*, 18 Aug. 1913.
21. Greaves, *The Irish Transport and General Workers' Union*, 95–6.
22. *Irish Times*, 20 Aug. 1913; William O'Brien, *Forth the Banners Go*, 51–2.
23. *Irish Worker*, 27 Aug. 1913; *Irish Times*, 20 Aug. 1913.
24. The first report of Murphy's 'secret' meeting at City Hall with the police authorities was given in the *Irish Worker*, 27 Aug. 1913; it was subsequently confirmed at the proceedings of the Dublin Disturbances Commission.
25. *Irish Times*, 21 and 22 Aug. 1913; Greaves, *The Irish Transport and General Workers' Union*, 96
26. The name of Dublin's main thoroughfare, originally called Sackville Street, was a highly political issue at this time. The nationalist-dominated city council had attempted to rename it O'Connell Street in 1884, but the predominantly unionist residents and business proprietors obtained an injunction preventing any change. Nationalist and labour leaders frequently referred to it as O'Connell Street, but legally its name was Sackville Street until 1925.

27. *Freeman's Journal* and *Irish Times*, 23 and 26 Aug. 1913.
28. The background information on Stewart and Richardson is based on a variety of sources, including Cody et al., *The Parliament of Labour*, 36–70, and Mitchell, *Labour in Irish Politics*, 28–30. There is a copy of the 'History of Larkinism' in O'Brien Papers, NLI, LO, 92. The employers' historian of the lockout, Arnold Wright, relied on it heavily and appears to have met Stewart while researching his book.
29. O'Brien Papers, NLI, LO, 108.
30. John S. Kelly to Dr Walsh, 22 Aug. 1913, Walsh Papers, laity file, DDA, 1913; *Freeman's Journal* and *Irish Times*, 11 Oct. 1913.
31. *Freeman's Journal* and *Irish Times*, 26 Aug. 1913.
32. Wright, *Disturbed Dublin*, 118–19; Emmet Larkin, *James Larkin*, 129–30. See also *Irish Times*, 4 Sep. 1913. The (British) Shipping Federation considered giving support to its members in Dublin over the *Lady Gwendolen* incident.
33. Greaves, *The Irish Transport and General Workers' Union*, 96; *Irish Times* and *Freeman's Journal*, 26 Aug. 1913.
34. Joyce, *Ulysses*, chap. 7, part I.
35. Cody et al., *The Parliament of Labour*, 11–29; Clarkson, *Labour and Nationalism in Ireland*, 252.
36. Dublin Trades Council minutes, 25 Aug. 1913, NLI, ms. 12,779–85; *Irish Worker*, 27 Aug. 1913.
37. Father Curran to Dr Walsh, 26 Aug. 1913, DDA.
38. *Freeman's Journal* and *Irish Times*, 20–26 Aug. 1913; *Irish Worker*, 27 Aug. 1913.

CHAPTER 2 (p. 16–21)

1. *Freeman's Journal* and *Irish Times*, 27 Aug. 1913. Murphy told the newspapers that only 150 employees left work at the DUTC to join the strike, while the ITGWU claimed a figure of 800. Murphy was probably counting only those who physically abandoned their trams that day, while the ITGWU would have included employees already dismissed or suspended for union activities, such as workers in the parcels section and labourers on the permanent way. Even so, the ITGWU figure is almost certainly a gross exaggeration. While Murphy's scrupulousness inclined him to use fairly accurate figures in pursuit of his often devious objectives, Larkin tended to invoke statistical fictions to prove an underlying truth.
2. Schedule of fees from William Smyth and Son, solicitors, to ITGWU, NLI, ms. 27,054.
3. *Evening Herald*, 26 Aug. 1913; *Irish Times*, 27 Aug. 1913.
4. David Garnett, recalling Larkin's oratory in 1938, quoted by Fox in *The History of the Irish Citizen Army*, 2.
5. O'Casey, 'The Story of the Irish Citizen Army,' 182–4. O'Casey's memory did not play tricks, at least as far as the weather was concerned. Average maximum temperatures in August 1913 were 18°F (10°C) higher than in August 1914: see *Irish Times* weather reports and Dublin Chamber of Commerce annual report for 1913.
6. *Irish Times*, 27 Aug. 1913.

CHAPTER 3 (p. 22–26)

1. *Irish Times*, 27 Aug. 1913.
2. *Irish Times*, 27 Aug. 1913.
3. Cody et al., *The Parliament of Labour*, 57.
4. Father Curran to Dr Walsh, 28 Aug. 1913, DDA.
5. *Irish Worker*, 27 Aug. 1913.
6. Greaves, *The Irish Transport and General Workers' Union*, 64.
7. Figures for the *Irish Worker* are based on the evidence of the printer, William Henry West, and Larkin at the bankruptcy proceedings: *Evening Herald*, 26 Aug. 1913, and *Irish Times*, 27 Aug. 1913. Figures for the Murphy publications are taken from Callanan, *T. M. Healy*, 484.
8. *Irish Worker*, 27 Aug. 1913.

CHAPTER 4 (p. 27–46)

1. *Evening Herald*, 26 Aug. 1913; letter from Father Curran to Dr Walsh, 26 Aug. 1913, on Employers' Federation. For Shackleton's relationship with Sinn Féin see Davis, *Arthur Griffith and Non-Violent Sinn Féin*, 141, 173–5 ; also Greaves, *The Irish Transport and General Workers' Union*, 100.
2. *Irish Times*, 27 Aug. 1913.
3. *Irish Times*, *Freeman's Journal* and *Evening Herald*, 27 Aug. 1913.
4. *Evening Herald*, 27 Aug. 1913.
5. Father Curran to Dr Walsh, 26 Aug. 1913.
6. *Evening Herald*, 27 Aug. 1913.
7. *Irish Times*, 27 Aug. 1913.
8. See Daly, *Dublin: The Deposed Capital*, 67–76, for a discussion of wages and prices; also Cody et al., *The Parliament of Labour*, 49–50. A good example of wage statistics in the *Irish Worker* is in the issue of 24 Jan. 1913. Dangerfield, *The Strange Death of Liberal England*, chap. 4, gives a good synopsis of British labour problems in the years to 1914 and the underlying causes of industrial unrest.
9. Joseph O'Brien, *Dear, Dirty Dublin*, chap. 1, 2, and 8; also Daly, *Dublin: The Deposed Capital*, 64–76.
10. Daly, *Dublin: The Deposed Capital*, 76; *Board of Trade Report on Industrial Disputes* (Cd. 7658), Parliamentary Papers, vol. 36 , 1914–16; D'Arcy, 'Wages of labourers in the building industry, 1667–1918,' and 'Wages of skilled workers in the building industry, 1667–1918'; Redmond, The Irish Municipal Employees' Trade Union, chap. 4.
11. *Irish Times*, 28 Aug. 1913.
12. Quinn's testimony at the preliminary hearing of the case against Larkin and others at the Bridewell, as reported in the *Irish Times*, 29 Aug. 1913.
13. *Freeman's Journal*, *Irish Times* and *Evening Herald*, 28 Aug. 1913.
14. *Irish Times*, 28 Aug. 1913.
15. William O'Brien, *Forth the Banners Go*, 83.
16. Ó Broin, *Revolutionary Underground*, 132–5; Cody, 'P. T. Daly.'
17. The allegation was made at a Socialist Party of Ireland rally by Walter Carpenter on 15 September 1913 and was never denied by Swifte: DMP report, NA, CSO, CR 17597. Many of the city's middle class, including public representatives, held shares in Dublin's most successful company. Carpenter, an English sweep, was a long-standing friend of Connolly and a member of the

ITGWU; he was later to serve as a captain in the Citizen Army.

18. *Irish Times*, 29 Aug. 1913.
19. *Irish Times* and *Freeman's Journal*, 29 Aug. 1913.
20. *Irish Times* and *Freeman's Journal*, 29 Aug. 1913.
21. *Irish Times*, 29 Aug. 1913.
22. *Saturday Herald*, 30 Aug. 1913; Nevin, *James Larkin*, 465–6.
23. *Evening Herald*, 29 Aug. 1913; Eric Taplin, 'Liverpool: the apprenticeship of a revolutionary,' in Nevin, *James Larkin*, 17.
24. *Evening Herald*, 29 Aug. 1913.
25. *Irish Times* and *Freeman's Journal*, 29 and 30 Aug. 1913.
26. *Irish Times*, *Freeman's Journal* and *Evening Herald*, 30 Aug. 1913.
27. *Irish Times*, 18 Aug. 1913.
28. *Irish Times*, 20 Aug. 1913.
29. Samuel Levenson, *James Connolly*, 24, 42–3.
30. Dudley Edwards, *Patrick Pearse*, 177.
31. *Irish Worker*, 30 Aug. 1913.
32. Callanan, *T. M. Healy*, 484.
33. Hepburn, *A Past Apart*, 165. For an acute summary of the AOH's role see Hepburn, chap. 9; on the wider Catholic middle-class agenda see Maume, *D. P. Moran*.
34. For a concise summary of the problems facing Redmond, and the reasons why the Irish Party and United Irish League failed to develop a strategy for dealing with the new situation they confronted in the early nineteen-hundreds, see Philip Bull, 'Land and politics, 1879–1903,' in Boyce, *The Revolution in Ireland*.
35. *Evening Herald*, 30 Aug. 1913; *Irish Times*, 1 Sep. 1913; William O'Brien, *Forth the Banners Go*, 88–9; Greaves, *The Life and Times of James Connolly*, 249; Emmet Larkin, *James Larkin*, 124, n. 2. It was the vice-president of the Dublin Trades Council, William O'Brien, who had warned Larkin of the arrest warrant after hearing about it from Francis Sheehy-Skeffington. Sheehy-Skeffington's source within the Dublin Castle establishment is not known. Neither person seems to have known that a similar warrant had been issued for Connolly. When Larkin fled he gave O'Brien a note stating that in the event of his apprehension, Connolly should take charge of the ITGWU; consequently Connolly was at Liberty Hall when the DMP arrived.

CHAPTER 5 (p. 47–57)

1. Ó Faoláin, *Constance Markievicz*, 92–6; van Voris, *Constance de Markievicz*, 72; Norman, *Terrible Beauty*, 67–8.
2. Van Voris, *Constance de Markievicz*, 99–100; Norman, *Terrible Beauty*, 83
3. Marreco, *The Rebel Countess*, 159.
4. *Irish Times*, 1 Sep. 1913.
5. See, for instance, *Irish Times* and *Freeman's Journal*, 1 Sep. 1913; *Report of Dublin Disturbances Commission* (Cd. 7269, Cd. 7272), Parliamentary Papers, vol. 18, 1914. (Unless otherwise stated, the account of the riots given here and the quotations used are based on the evidence given to the commission.)
6. From a letter sent by Father Curran to the Commissioner of the DMP, Sir John Ross, 1 Oct. 1913. He later gave permission for the police to submit it in evidence to the Dublin Disturbances Commission.
7. *Report of Dublin Disturbances Commission*, appendix, 5.

8. *Irish Times*, 1 Sep. 1913. Figures for the numbers in Liberty Hall are based on the testimony of P. T. Daly at the Nolan inquest, as reported in the *Irish Times*, 6 Sep. 1913.
9. Nevin, *1913*, 30; Maguire, *Servants to the Public*, 34.
10. Neligan, *The Spy in the Castle*, 37.
11. Monteith, *Casement's Last Adventure*, 6.
12. Statistical Returns of DMP for 1900–14. For a detailed discussion of prostitution in Dublin see Prunty, *Dublin Slums*, 263–70; Joseph O'Brien, *Dear, Dirty Dublin*, 191–4; Maria Luddy, 'Prostitution and rescue work in nineteenth-century Ireland,' in Luddy and Murphy, *Women Surviving*. For local attitudes to prostitution see Kearns, *Dublin Tenement Life*, 54–5.
13. Joseph O'Brien, *Forth the Banners Go*, 116–17.
14. Statistical Returns of the DMP, 1912 and 1913.
15. Monteith, *Casement's Last Adventure*, 6.
16. *Report of Dublin Disturbances Commission*, appendix, 6.
17. Figures are based on those given by various police representatives at the hearings of the Dublin Disturbances Commission. The cry of 'Come on, ye whores,' was sanitised in press reports to 'Come on, ye curs,' to spare the sensitivities of readers.
18. *Report of Dublin Disturbances Commission*, appendix, 7.
19. *Irish Times*, 1 Sep. 1913.

CHAPTER 6 (p. 58–75)

1. The accounts given here are based primarily on William O'Brien, *Forth the Banners Go*, 88–91, and on the evidence of Inspector Willoughby and Assistant Commissioner Harrell to the Dublin Disturbances Commission. While all these sources are hostile to Larkin, they are borne out by others, including Fox in *Jim Larkin*, 88–9, which is a very sympathetic biography.
2. Quoted by Keogh in *The Rise of the Irish Working Class*, 200.
3. Details of police activity on 31 August 1913 are largely drawn from the report of the Dublin Disturbances Commission and the evidence given to it by eye-witnesses. Other sources used are referred to either in the text or in the notes.
4. Walsh Papers, laity file, DDA, 1913. The view of Sir John Ross as an independent-minded defender of traditional unionist values is taken from a private memorandum by Arthur Hamilton Norway, secretary of the Irish Post Office, in Ó Broin Papers, NLI. Following his victory at Bladensburg, Sir Robert Ross, grandfather of the DMP Commissioner, burnt Washington; when it was renovated the presidential residence was repainted, becoming the 'White House'. Ross was subsequently killed at the siege of Baltimore, which inspired 'The Star-Spangled Banner'. Thus his career linked this British military family with two major American institutions.
5. See Harrel's evidence in the appendix to the *Report of Dublin Disturbances Commission*. Mac Giolla Choille, *Chief Secretary's Office*, 46, says that during the strike the DMP was augmented by 5 district inspectors, 13 head constables and 137 men of the RIC. However, he gives no breakdown for this; the strengths of the RIC contingents clearly varied from time to time. Harrel was in a position to give detailed figures. He had no reason to falsify them, and they are borne out by figures published in the *Irish Times* from time to time on police strengths in the city during the lockout.
6. *Report of Dublin Disturbances Commission*, appendix.

7. Joseph O'Brien, *Dear, Dirty Dublin*, 178 et seq., for details of DMP pay and conditions in the years before 1913; see also the debate on DMP pay and conditions in the *Irish Times* in December 1913 and early January 1914. Though pay may have been slipping, a young member of the force was still considered a good catch by the likes of Mrs Makebelieve: see Stephens, *The Charwoman's Daughter.*

8. William O'Brien, *Forth the Banners Go*, 91.

9. *Irish Times*, 1 Sep. 1913.

10. Ó Faoláin, *Constance Markievicz*, 114; van Voris, *Constance de Markievicz*, 105.

11. *Report of Dublin Disturbances Commission*, appendix, 104.

12. Nevin, *1913*, 33–4.

13. Nevin, *1913*, 34–5.

14. *Report of Dublin Disturbances Commission*, appendix, 64–5.

15. Nevin, *1913*, 34–5.

16. *Report of Dublin Disturbances Commission*, appendix, 126.

17. O'Casey, *Drums under the Windows*, 205, 223.

18. Based on lists of people arrested and patients treated in Jervis Street Hospital, *Irish Times*, 1 Sep. 1913.

19. *Irish Times*, 1 Sep. 1913; Father Curran to Dr Walsh, 2 Sep. 1913, DDA.

20. *Report of Dublin Disturbances Commission*, 421; *Irish Times*, 1 Sep. 1913.

21. Wright, *Disturbed Dublin*, 145.

22. O'Casey, *Drums under the Windows*, 193.

23. Father Healy to Dr Walsh, 1 Sep. 1913, DDA.

24. Tony Gregory, the independent socialist TD for Dublin Central during the nineteen-eighties and nineties, is a grandson of Robert Gregory.

25. *Report of Dublin Disturbances Commission*, appendix, 235.

CHAPTER 7 (p. 76–98)

1. *Irish Independent*, 1 Sep. 1913.

2. The rats story is from Eugene Sheehy, *May It Please the Court*, Dublin: C. J. Fallon 1951, 34, quoted by Akenson in *Conor*, 15.

3. See Ward, *Hanna Sheehy-Skeffington*, 20.

4. Ward, *Hanna Sheehy-Skeffington*; Caffrey, 'Jacob's women workers during the 1913 lockout.'

5. *Irish Times*, 2 Sep. 1913.

6. Dublin Chamber of Commerce records.

7. Dublin Chamber of Commerce records.

8. See Michael Foot, *Aneurin Bevan: A Biography*, London: Davis-Poynter, 1973, vol. 1, 27–8, on the perception of Larkin and indeed his deputy, James Connolly, within the TUC; Coates and Topham, *The Making of the Transport and General Workers' Union*, chap. 13; *Daily Herald*, 1 Sep. 1913; *Board of Trade Report on Industrial Disputes* (Cd. 7658), Parliamentary Papers, vol. 36, 1914–16.

9. *Irish Times*, 2 Sep. 1913.

10. *Irish Worker*, 8 Feb. 1913. Grigg, *Lloyd George: The People's Champion, 1902–1911*, chap. 11, has a good account of the National Insurance Act (1911) and the politics behind it.

11. Joseph O'Brien, *Dear, Dirty Dublin*, 80, 90, 93. See also Dublin Corporation Reports, 1913, vol. 1. The occupations of councillors are taken largely from

Thom's Directory, 1912–14.

12. See Cody et al., *The Parliament of Labour*, especially 30–47; Boyle, *The Irish Labour Movement in the Nineteenth Century*, chap. 10. See Murray, 'Electoral politics and the Dublin working class before the First World War,' for a detailed analysis of the effect of the electoral laws. Figures on domestic servants are taken from Hearn, *Below Stairs*, 9. Information on Partridge is from Geraghty, 'William Partridge.'

13. Lysaght, 'The rake's progress of a syndicalist'; Geraghty, 'William Partridge.' For details of ITGWU expenditure in 1913 see returns to Registrar of Friendly Societies, NLI. Details of ITPS membership and capitation fees are taken from the *Irish Times* court report of 8 Oct. 1913.

14. Hepburn, *A Past Apart*, 166–7; ITGWU returns to Registrar of Friendly Societies for 1913; DMP police reports, NLI, Pose 8173; obituary of J. D. Nugent, *Irish Independent*, 1 Mar. 1940.

15. Minutes of Dublin City Council, 1 Sep. 1913, Dublin City Archives, supplemented by reports in the *Irish Times* and *Freeman's Journal*, 2 Sep. 1913. Though the newspaper reports say that McWalter's addendum called for 'a withdrawal of the police and military from the streets of Dublin,' and most of the speakers in the debate, including McWalter, seem to have understood it as meaning this, the wording in the minutes is 'extra Police and Military.' This would imply that only the RIC and military reinforcements drafted in to help the DMP to deal with the disturbances would have been affected by the motion. Whether McWalter was misunderstood by his fellow-councillors and the newspaper reporters present, or whether the minute was doctored, we will never know.

16. *Irish Times*, 4 Sep. 1913.

17. *Irish Times* and *Freeman's Journal*, 2 Sep. 1913.

18. DMP Statistical Returns, 1912–14; Wright, *Disturbed Dublin*, 313; report of the Visiting Committee of City Prisons, 1914–15; Dublin Corporation Reports, 1914.

19. DMP Statistical Returns, 1912–14.

20. *Irish Times*, 20 Feb. 1914, for damage caused in the lockout. The Easter Rising figure is taken from Joseph O'Brien, *Dear, Dirty Dublin*, 273.

CHAPTER 8 (p. 99–105)

1. *Freeman's Journal*, 3 Sep. 1913.

2. *Freeman's Journal*, 3 Sep. 1913; Cody et al., *The Parliament of Labour*, 95–106; Greaves, *The Irish Transport and General Workers' Union*, 101; Dublin Trades Council minutes, 2 Sep. 1913.

3. *Freeman's Journal* and *Irish Times*, 3 Sep. 1913.

4. *Freeman's Journal* and *Irish Times*, 3 Sep. 1913; *Dublin Transport Workers' Dispute: Report of the Parliamentary Committee of the TUC*, 23 Sep. 1913.

5. *Freeman's Journal*, 3 Sep. 1913.

6. Father Curran to Dr Walsh, 2 Sep. 1913, DDA.

7. *Irish Times*, 2 Sep. 1913.

8. Stephen Gwynn to Dr Walsh, 29 Oct. 1913, DDA.

9. *Thom's Directory*, 1914; Bew, *Ideology and the Irish Question*, 14; O'Connor, *A Labour History of Ireland*, 58; Lyons, *Ireland since the Famine*, 270; Maume, *The Long Gestation*, 6, 228; Mandle, *The Gaelic Athletic Association and Irish Nationalist Politics*, especially 96–7; Horgan, *From Parnell to Pearse*, 151.

10. Bew, *Ideology and the Irish Question*, 16, 47; O'Day, *Irish Home Rule*, 210; Cody et al., *The Parliament of Labour*, 13.
11. *Thom's Directory*, 1914; *Irish Times*, 18 and 26 Aug. 1913.
12. Dillon to T. P. O'Connor, 16 Oct. 1913, Dillon Papers, TCD.
13. Various letters of Dillon's during this period bear out this view: see for instance his correspondence with Richard McGhee, MP for Mid-Tyrone, quoted in chap. 17 below.

CHAPTER 9 (p. 106–109)

1. For instance the *Freeman's Journal*, 3 Sep. 1913, reported that sixteen families lived in the houses, while the *Evening Herald* of the same date said there were ten families. The correct figure was eleven, comprising forty-six individuals, almost a third of whom were killed or injured in the collapse.
2. *Evening Herald*, 3 Sep. 1913.
3. *Irish Times*, 4 Sep. 1913.
4. *Freeman's Journal*, 3 Sep. 1913.
5. Wright, *Disturbed Dublin*, 30.
6. Prunty, *Dublin Slums*, 174–5.
7. Joseph O'Brien, *Dear, Dirty Dublin*, 25–6, 310, n. 24.
8. *Report of the Departmental Committee into the the Housing Conditions of the Working Classes in the City of Dublin*, appendix 15.
9. *Irish Worker*, 8 May 1913.
10. Quarterly report of Dublin chief medical officer, Sir Charles Cameron, for the end of 1913, Dublin City Archives.
11. Joseph O'Brien, *Dear, Dirty Dublin*, 28.
12. *Irish Times*, 6 Sep. 1913. Derham was not one of the inspectors who owned slum property.

CHAPTER 10 (p. 110–117)

1. *Irish Times*, 4 Sep. 1913.
2. *Irish Times*, 4 Sep. 1913.
3. *Irish Times*, 4 Sep. 1913.
4. *Irish Times*, 4 Sep. 1913.
5. See Dublin Chamber of Commerce Report for 1913; Wright, *Disturbed Dublin*, especially chap. 9–11.
6. *Irish Times*, 4 Sep. 1913.
7. Charles M. Coghlan to Arthur Henderson MP, 6 Dec. 1913, in *Dublin Transport Workers' Dispute: Report of the Parliamentary Committee of the TUC*, Dec. 1914.
8. *Irish Times*, 4 Sep. 1913.
9. *Irish Worker*, 6 Sep. 1913; *Freeman's Journal*, 4 Sep. 1913; Dublin Disturbances Commission, appendix, 309 and 383.
10. *Freeman's Journal*, 4 Sep. 1913.

CHAPTER 11 (p. 118–128)

1. William O'Brien, *Forth the Banners Go*, 93–4.
2. Morgan, *James Connolly*, 92.
3. Dublin Trades Council minutes, 2 Sep. 1913.
4. William O'Brien, *Forth the Banners Go*, 10.
5. William O'Brien, *Forth the Banners Go*, 95.

6. *Evening Herald*, 4 Sep. 1913.
7. *Irish Times*, 5 Sep. 1913.
8. *Irish Times*, 5 Sep. 1913.
9. *Irish Times*, 5 Sep. 1913; Morgan, *Labour and Partition*, 157; Greaves, *The Life and Times of James Connolly*, 250.
10. *Irish Times*, 5 Sep. 1913.
11. William O'Brien, *Forth the Banners Go*, 95–6.
12. William O'Brien, *Forth the Banners Go*, 95–6.
13. Wright, *Disturbed Dublin*, 162.
14. Frederick Wookey to Archbishop Walsh, 24 Oct. 1913, DDA.
15. See Wright, *Disturbed Dublin*, 162–3, for a fairly frank summing up of the employers' position; also the *Irish Times* and *Freeman's Journal*, 5 Sep. 1913.
16. *Irish Times*, 6 Sep. 1913.
17. *Irish Times*, 6 Sep. 1913.
18. *Irish Times*, 6 Sep. 1913; *Liberator*, 6 Sep. 1913.
19. Memorandum of Norway in Ó Broin Papers, NLI.
20. Memorandum of Norway in Ó Broin Papers, NLI.
21. I am indebted to Fergal Tobin of Gill and Macmillan for this item of Dubliniana.
22. *Freeman's Journal*, 24 Sep. 1913.
23. Norway memorandum in Ó Broin Papers, NLI; *Irish Times*, 6–9 Sep. 1913.
24. The memorandum in the Ó Broin Papers, NLI, refers to the telephone problem. Birrell to Dillon, 14 Sep. 1913, Dillon Papers, TCD.
25. NA, CSO, 16540–748.
26. Ó Broin, *The Chief Secretary*, 74–5; Birrell to Dillon, 14 Sep. 1913, Dillon Papers, TCD.

CHAPTER 12 (p. 129–148)

1. Wright, *Disturbed Dublin*, 161–2; *Irish Times*, 5 Sep. 1913.
2. NA, Chief Secretary's Office, CR 16580, for file marked 'Immediate' from Attorney-General.
3. Ó Broin, *The Chief Secretary*, 47.
4. Maye, *Arthur Griffith*, 318.
5. Quoted by Keogh in 'William Martin Murphy and the origins of the 1913 lockout,' 31.
6. *Sunday Independent*, 7 Sep. 1913.
7. *Sunday Independent*, 7 Sep. 1913; *Irish Times*, 9 Sep. 1913.
8. Father Curran to Dr Walsh, 6 Sep. 1913, DDA.
9. *Sunday Independent*, 7 Sep. 1913; *Irish Times*, 8 and 10 Sep. 1913.
10. This interpretation of the employers' attitude is based on their own historian's assessment of their strategy at this stage: see Wright, *Disturbed Dublin*, chap. 15. Further evidence that the employers were not interested in a settlement at this stage comes from Father Curran. In his letter of the previous day to Dr Walsh, he confided that some builders intended locking out employees on Tuesday 'unless some extraordinary change comes about.' In the event the builders did as Curran predicted.
11. Accounts of speeches are based largely on the *Irish Times*, 8 Sep. 1913, supplemented by the *Freeman's Journal*.
12. Wright, *Disturbed Dublin*, 164–5; *Irish Times*, 9 Sep. 1913.

13. Based on a report by Francis Sheehy-Skeffington to a strike meeting, 16 Sep. 1913, NA, CSO CR 17232.
14. *Irish Independent*, 17 Jan. 1913; *Irish Times*, 18 Aug. 1913; Dublin Corporation minutes, 8 Sep. 1913; Dublin Chamber of Commerce minutes, Mar. and 12 Aug. 1913. For a good summary of the controversy and its wider implications see Joseph O'Brien, *Dear, Dirty Dublin*, 56–60, and Lyons, *Culture and Anarchy in Ireland*, 75–6.
15. *Irish Times*, 11 Jan. 1913; R. F. Foster, *W. B. Yeats: A Life, vol. 1: The Apprentice Mage*, 479–81.
16. Cullingford, *Yeats, Ireland and Fascism*, 78.
17. Lyons, *Culture and Anarchy in Ireland*, 76.
18. Cullingford, *Yeats, Ireland and Fascism*, 78.
19. Cullingford, *Yeats, Ireland and Fascism*, 78–9.
20. 'September 1913,' in *Collected Poems of W. B. Yeats*, 120–121. See also Conor Cruise O'Brien, *Passion and Cunning: Essays on Nationalism, Terrorism, and Revolution*, New York: Simon and Schuster, 1988, 22–8, for a less charitable interpretation of Yeats's motivation in supporting the lockout, i.e. his antipathy towards the clerical, business and political establishment.
21. Dublin Chamber of Commerce annual report, 1913.
22. *Irish Times*, 10 Sep. 1913.
23. *Irish Times*, 10 Sep. 1913.
24. *Irish Times*, 10 Sep. 1913.
25. *Irish Times*, 10 Sep. 1913.
26. Wright, *Disturbed Dublin*, 165–6; *Irish Times*, 13 Sep. 1913.
27. NA, CSO CR 17587 1913; Father Curran to Dr Walsh, 13 Sep. 1913, DDA.
28. NA, CSO CR 17657, 1913.
29. *Irish Times*, 12 Sep. 1913.
30. *Irish Times*, 12 and 13 Sep. 1913.
31. *Irish Times*, 23 Sep. 1913.
32. Father Curran to Dr Walsh, 13 Sep. 1913. See meteorological reports for July and August 1913 in NA, CSO CR 16515, and weather résumé in the annual report of the Dublin Chamber of Commerce for 1913. While the weather became more broken in September, it remained mild until November, thus easing the hardship on strikers.

CHAPTER 13 (p. 149–158)

1. Connolly O'Brien, *James Connolly*, 146.
2. See NA, CSO CR 17232, and attached DMP documents for a report of the Socialist Party of Ireland meeting.
3. Based on reports of the speech in Emmet Larkin, *James Larkin*, 128, Wright, *Disturbed Dublin*, 172–3, and *Irish Times*, 15 Sep. 1913.
4. *Irish Times*, 15 Sep. 1913; Moran, '1913, Jim Larkin and the British Labour movement.'
5. Board memoranda, 2144–431, Guinness Archive.
6. *Irish Times* and *Freeman's Journal*, 15 Sep. 1913; *Irish Worker*, 13 Sep. 1913; Moriarty, 'Larkin and the women's movement,' in Nevin, *James Larkin*, 93–101.
7. NA, CSO CR 17232; *Irish Times*, 16 and 17 Sep. 1913.
8. NA, CSO CR 17232.
9. *Irish Times*, 16 Sep. 1913.

10. *Irish Times*, 17 Sep. 1913.
11. *Irish Times*, 18–20 Sep. 1913.
12. *Irish Times*, 18 Sep. 1913.
13. The figures are based on the returns of the ITGWU to the Registrar for Friendly Societies for 1913, with additional information in O'Brien Papers, NLI.
14. *Irish Times*, 18 Sep. 1913.
15. *Irish Times*, 18 Sep. 1913.
16. *Irish Times*, 18 Sep. 1913.
17. See especially Father Curran to Dr Walsh, 13 Sep. 1913, DDA
18. Father Curran to Dr Walsh, 23 Sep. 1913, DDA.

CHAPTER 14 (p. 159–180)

1. Father Curran to Dr Walsh, 18 Sep. 1913, DDA.
2. The figures for religious denominations are from Joseph O'Brien, *Dear, Dirty Dublin*, 39–40. Biographical details of J. J. Hughes are from Morrissey, *A Man Called Hughes*, 4–24.
3. Morrissey, *A Man Called Hughes*, 29–31.
4. This is certainly the view of Dermot Keogh in *The Rise of the Irish Working Class* and in 'William Martin Murphy and the origins of the 1913 lockout.'
5. *Irish Times*, 19 Sep. 1913; Father Curran to Dr Walsh, 23 Sep. 1913, DDA.
6. *Irish Times*, 19 Sep. 1913.
7. *Irish Times*, 6 and 19 Sep. 1913; Dublin Chamber of Commerce Annual Report, 1913; Guinness Archive, Board memoranda, 2144–431; *Thom's Directory*, 1913.
8. Wright, *Disturbed Dublin*, 174.
9. Father Curran to Dr Walsh, 23 Sep. 1913, DDA.
10. Father Curran to Dr Walsh, 23 Sep. 1913, DDA.
11. *Sunday Independent*, 21 Sep. 1913; Father Curran to Dr Walsh, 23 Sep. 1913, DDA; *Irish Times*, 22 Sep. 1913. The general Larkin referred to was Sir George Richardson, who was not officially appointed to command the Ulster Volunteer Force until 25 September.
12. *Irish Times*, 22 Sep. 1913.
13. *Irish Times*, 22 Sep. 1913; Father Curran to Dr Walsh, 23 Sep. 1913, DDA; Dublin Disturbances Commission, 1914. Details of Sergeant Morris are in the *Irish Times*, 2 Feb. 1914.
14. NA, CSO CR 17743, and attached reports.
15. Birrell to Asquith, 30 Aug. 1913, quoted by Ó Broin in *The Chief Secretary*, 68.
16. Ó Broin, *The Chief Secretary*, 71; *Irish Times*, 23 Sep. 1913.
17. *Irish Times*, 22 Sep. 1913.
18. *Freeman's Journal* and *Irish Tiimes*, 23 Sep. 1913.
19. From the statement of the Parliamentary Committee of the TUC, reproduced in the *Freeman's Journal*, 24 Sep. 1913. See also the annual report of the TUC, 1913, 350–351.
20. *Freeman's Journal*, 24 Sep. 1913.
21. *Irish Times*, 23 Sep. 1913, and *Freeman's Journal*, 25 Sep. 1913. Quaid had also been a Sinn Féin activist, before becoming a nationalist member of the city council.

22. See *Irish Times*, 22 and 30 Sep. 1913, and *Freeman's Journal* for the same dates to compare subscription lists.
23. See, for example, *Irish Times*, 18–23 Sep. 1913. Sherlock's optimism is understandable. That there remained significant support for this type of settlement is shown by the fact that the same terms were still being proposed by well-wishers to Birrell as late as November 1913: see, for example, NA, CSO CR 21594.
24. *Freeman's Journal*, 24 Sep. 1913.
25. Guinness Archive, meeting of Dublin Employers' Federation with Guinness, 16 Sep. 1913, Board memoranda 2144–431.
26. Dublin Trades Council minutes, 22 and 23 Sep. 1913.
27. *Irish Times* and *Freeman's Journal*, 25 Sep. 1913.
28. *Irish Times*, 23 Sep. 1913.
29. *Irish Times*, 26 Sep. 1913.
30. *Irish Times*, 24, 25 and 26 Sep. 1913.
31. Asquith Papers, Bodleian Library, Oxford, f. 210; Ó Broin Papers, NLI; Ó Broin, *The Chief Secretary*, 75.
32. NA, CSO CR 17597; Mac Giolla Choille, *Chief Secretary's Office*, 46–7.
33. *Irish Times*, 23 Sep. 1914.
34. *Freeman's Journal*, 24 Sep. 1913. See Bew, *Ideology and the Irish Question*, 81–2, for Meehan's family and political background.
35. *Freeman's Journal*, 23 Sep. 1913.
36. *Irish Times*, 25 and 27 Sep. 1913.
37. *Irish Times*, 25 Sep. 1913.

CHAPTER 15 (p. 181–191)

1. Dangerfield, *The Strange Death of Liberal England*, 206.
2. Wright, *Disturbed Dublin*, 185.
3. Birrell to Asquith, 26 Sep. 1913, cited by Ó Broin, *The Chief Secretary*, 75–6.
4. *Irish Times* and *Irish Worker*, 27 Sep. 1913.
5. See, for instance, *Sunday Independent*, 28 Sep. 1913, *Irish Times*, *Daily Sketch* and *Daily Mirror*, 29 Sep. 1913.
6. Based mainly on the comprehensive report in the *Irish Times*, 29 Sep. 1913, supplemented by the *Sunday Independent*, 28 Sep. 1913, and *Freeman's Journal*, 29 Sep. 1913. Unless otherwise stated, quotations are from the *Irish Times*.
7. *Irish Times*, 29 Sep. 1913. The food parcels provided by the TUC may seem meagre but they reflect the basic diet of the Dublin worker at that time. A study carried out in 1904 by the city's chief medical officer, Sir Charles Cameron, showed that working-class families rarely ate meat, except on Sundays. Breakfast and supper consisted of tea or cocoa, with bread and jam, butter, or margarine. The dinner menu was potatoes and cabbage, occasionally supplemented by other vegetables, fish, or bacon, as means allowed. Subsequent food consignments from Britain included significant amounts of bacon but relatively little beef. I am indebted to Theresa Moriarty of the Irish Labour History Society for making available to me her notes of Cameron's study, entitled 'How the Poor Live,' and also those on Sir John Robert O'Connell's 'The Problem of the Dublin Slums.' Both documents are available in the NLI.

8. See, for instance, Prunty, *Dublin Slums*, chap. 7, for the role of competition in Dublin charities of the period.
9. See all the daily papers for 20 September 1913. For Inghinidhe na hÉireann see Ward, *Unmanageable Revolutionaries*, chap. 2. The article in the *Labour Leader* is cited by Moran in '1913, Jim Larkin and the British Labour Movement.'
10. *Irish Times*, 29 Sep. 1913. On the role of the *Hare* in the port see Guinness Archive, Board memoranda, 2144–431.
11. A variety of sources were used for this account of the Askwith Inquiry, including the Parliamentary Papers, but the quotations are taken from either the *Irish Times* or the *Freeman's Journal*, unless otherwise indicated.
12. *Irish Times*, 2 Oct. 1913.
13. *Irish Times*, 3 Oct. 1913.
14. Jones, *These Obstreperous Lassies*, 10–11; Fox, *Jim Larkin*, 151; Moriarty, 'Larkin and the women's movement,' in Nevin, *James Larkin*, 93–101; van Voris, *Constance de Markievicz*, 109.
15. O'Casey, *Drums under the Windows*, 211–12.

CHAPTER 16 (p. 192–213)

1. This account of events in County Dublin is based on the *Irish Times* and *Freeman's Journal*, 1–6 Oct. 1913.
2. John Eglinton [William Magee], *A Memoir of Æ: George William Russell*, London: Macmillan, 1937, 86, quoted by Emmet Larkin in *James Larkin*, 133.
3. The speech extracts are based mainly on the *Freeman's Journal*, 6 Oct. 1913, which contains more detailed and more direct quotations than the *Irish Times* of the same date; but the latter has been used in places to supplement it.
4. William O'Brien, NLI, Pos 6989.
5. *Irish Times*, 6 Oct. 1913.
6. *Report of the Government Court of Inquiry, Oct. 5th, 1913*.
7. Wright, *Disturbed Dublin*, 211. See chap. 18 and 19 for a good overview of the employers' attitude towards the Askwith Inquiry. Details of Healy's speech are from the *Irish Times*, 7 Oct. 1913.

CHAPTER 17 (p. 214–230)

1. *Freeman's Journal*, 7 Oct. 1913; Dublin Trades Council minutes, 6 Oct. 1913.
2. From the extract in the *Irish Times*, 8 Oct. 1913.
3. *Irish Times*, 7 Oct. 1913.
4. West, *Horace Plunkett*, 87–9, 96.
5. *Irish Times*, 7 Oct. 1913.
6. Clarkson, *Labour and Nationalism in Ireland*, 281–2; O'Casey, *Drums under the Windows*, 164–5.
7. *Irish Freedom*, Oct. 1913. Daly's identification with the conservative wing of the IRB is based on Kevin Nowlan, 'Tom Clarke, MacDermott, and the IRB,' in Martin, *Leaders and Men of the Easter Rising*, 113. Ó Broin, *Revolutionary Underground*, chap. 9, plays down the conflict between Daly and Clarke, pointing out that Daly was expelled from the Supreme Council of the IRB for financial irregularities not long after Clarke's return to Ireland from America in 1907.

8. Ward, *Hanna Sheehy-Skeffington*, 35–6, 84.
9. See the *Irish Citizen* for 1913–14.
10. Ward, *Hanna Sheehy-Skeffington*, 65.
11. *Irish Citizen*, vol. 2, no. 13.
12. *Irish Citizen*, vol. 2, no. 14; *Freeman's Journal*, 3 Oct. 1913.
13. *Irish Citizen*, vol. 2, no. 15 and 16.
14. *Irish Citizen*, vol. 2, no. 17.
15. *Irish Citizen*, vol. 2, no. 18. Louie Bennett is a sadly neglected figure. R. M. Fox wrote a sympathetic biography, now more than forty years out of print. For the best modern assessment see Hazelkorn, 'The social and political views of Louie Bennett.'
16. *Irish Citizen*, vol. 2, no. 18.
17. *Irish Citizen*, vol. 2, no. 18.
18. *Freeman's Journal*, 6 Oct. 1913.
19. *Freeman's Journal*, 7 Oct. 1913.
20. The quotation is from a memoir by Kettle's widow, Mary Kettle, first published with a posthumous collection of his essays in 1917, taken here from the 1968 edition of Kettle, *The Day's Burden*, 31.
21. *Freeman's Journal*, 8 Oct. 1913.

CHAPTER 18 (p. 233–246)

1. Guinness Archive, secretary's annual report for 1913, Board memoranda, 2144–431; ITGWU Correspondence, 1913, NLI, box 6. See also Dennison and MacDonagh, *Guinness, 1886–1939*, 144–6, which provides a concise summary of relations between the company, the ITGWU, and the employers' federation.
2. Guinness Archive, Board memoranda, 2144–431.
3. *Irish Times*, 10 and 11 Oct. 1913.
4. S. Leslie, 'Archbishop Walsh,' in Cruise O'Brien, *The Shaping of Modern Ireland*, 101.
5. S. Leslie, 'Archbishop Walsh,' in Cruise O'Brien, *The Shaping of Modern Ireland*, 101.
6. Walsh, *William J. Walsh*, chap. 14; see also Cruise O'Brien, *Parnell and His Party*, 305, and Callanan, *The Parnell Split*, 55–7.
7. Walsh, *William J. Walsh*, 595.
8. S. Leslie, 'Archbishop Walsh,' in Cruise O'Brien, *The Shaping of Modern Ireland*, 104.
9. Walsh, *William J. Walsh*, 577–83.
10. Walsh, *William J. Walsh*, 568.
11. There are frequent references to photography in the Walsh-Curran correspondence.
12. I am indebted to David Sheehy, Dublin Diocesan Archivist, for drawing my attention to Dr Walsh's views on industrial relations and his informal but highly effective conciliation service.
13. Aberdeen to Walsh, 9 Oct. 1913, DDA.
14. Walsh to Aberdeen, 10 Oct. 1913, DDA.
15. Timothy Healy to Maurice Healy, 14 Oct. 1913, quoted by Callanan in *T. M. Healy*, 489 and 742.
16. Timothy Healy to Maurice Healy, 10 Oct. 1913, quoted by Callanan in *T. M. Healy*, 489, 742.

17. Timothy Healy to Maurice Healy, 10 Oct. 1913, quoted by Callanan in *T. M. Healy*, 489, 742.
18. Timothy Healy to Maurice Healy, 10 Oct. 1913, quoted by Callanan in *T. M. Healy*, 489, 742. Callanan makes a strong case for Healy's underlying sympathy being with the strikers, as opposed to their leaders. See Maume, *The Long Gestation*, 140–2, for the efforts of William O'Brien and the *Cork Free Press* to exploit the lockout to embarrass Redmond.
19. Lyons, *John Dillon*, 322–3, 330.
20. *Irish Times*, 1 Sep. 1913.
21. Coates and Topham, *The Making of the Transport and General Workers' Union*, 79–85, 110, 166–7, 367.
22. Richard McGhee to John Dillon, 2 Sep. 1913, Dillon Papers, TCD.
23. Richard McGhee to John Dillon, 15 Sep. 1913, Dillon Papers, TCD.
24. Richard McGhee to John Dillon, 11 Sep. 1913, Dillon Papers, TCD.
25. Richard McGhee to John Dillon, 11 Sep. 1913, Dillon Papers, TCD.
26. John Dillon to T. P. O'Connor, 1 Oct. 1913, Dillon Papers, TCD.
27. *Irish Times*, 9 Oct. 1913.
28. See the correspondence of John Dillon and T. P. O'Connor, 3–8 Oct. 1913, Dillon Papers, TCD.
29. *Irish Times* and *Freeman's Journal*, 9 Oct. 1913.
30. *Freeman's Journal*, 10 and 11 Oct. 1913; *Irish Times*, 13 Oct. 1913.
31. *Freeman's Journal*, 15 Oct. 1913. In 1885, when Parnell had been anxious to build stronger links between the Irish Party and the Catholic Church, he had expressed a wish to have a priest on every party platform; he could hardly have hoped to have his prayers answered so lavishly.
32. T. P. O'Connor to John Dillon, 15 and 16 Oct. 1913, Dillon Papers, TCD
33. John Dillon to T. P. O'Connor, 16 Oct. 1913, Dillon Papers, TCD.
34. John Dillon to T. P. O'Connor, 15 Oct. 1913.
35. See D. P. Moran of the *Leader*, below, who brought the argument of blaming the lockout on British trade unionists to a fine art.
36. Coates and Topham, *The Making of the Transport and General Workers' Union*, 58–9, 167.
37. O'Day, *The English Face of Irish Nationalism*, 122–5; O'Day, *Irish Home Rule*, 229; Maume, *The Long Gestation*, 10, 238.
38. Lyons, *John Dillon*, 336.
39. Timothy Healy to Maurice Healy, 10 Oct. 1913, quoted by Callanan in *T. M. Healy*, 489, 742.
40. Art O'Brien to Dr Walsh, Oct. 1913, DDA.

CHAPTER 19 (p. 247–256)

1. *Times* (London), 11 Oct. 1913, quoted by Emmet Larkin in *James Larkin*, 137–8.
2. *Irish Times*, 11 Oct. 1913.
3. Montefiore, *From a Victorian to a Modern*, 156; *Irish Times* and *Freeman's Journal*, 11 and 13 Oct. 1913.
4. For this information and much of the other material used here on Montefiore's involvement in the dispute I am indebted to Theresa Moriarty, archivist of the Irish Labour History Society.
5. Montefiore, *From a Victorian to a Modern*, 159.

6. *Irish Times* and *Freeman's Journal*, 10 and 11 Oct. 1913.
7. James Lawlor to Dr Walsh, written *c.* 17 October but posted later, DDA; Dublin Trades Council minutes, 14 Oct. 1913.
8. *Irish Times* and *Freeman's Journal*, 14–22 Oct. 1913.
9. *Irish Times* and *Freeman's Journal*, 15 Oct. 1913.
10. *Irish Times* and *Freeman's Journal*, 15 Oct. 1913.
11. According to a statement issued by the secretary of the Parliamentary Committee of the TUC, Charles Bowerman, on 14 October 1913 and published in all the newspapers the next day.
12. *Irish Times*, 14 and 16 Oct. 1913.
13. *Irish Times*, 16 Oct. 1913.
14. Birrell to Asquith, 3 Oct. 1913, Asquith Papers, Bodleian Library, Oxford, ms. 38, f. 220.
15. Lady Pirrie to Birrell, 1 Aug. 1913, Asquith Papers, Bodleian Library, Oxford, ms. 38, f. 116.
16. Birrell to Asquith, 16 Oct. 1913, Asquith Papers, Bodleian Library, Oxford, ms. 38, f. 236.

CHAPTER 20 (p. 257–272)

1. The *Irish Times* estimated the crowd at 4,000, while the *Freeman's Journal* put the number at 8,000. The figures for the number of ITGWU members in dispute are based on Dublin Trades Council figures for strike pay disbursements contained in O'Brien Papers, NLI, Pos 6989.
2. *Irish Times*, 24 Oct. 1913; *Evening Herald*, 20 Oct. 1913.
3. *Irish Times*, 21 Oct. 1913; *Freeman's Journal*, 22 Oct. 1913.
4. Montefiore, *From a Victorian to a Modern*, 160.
5. 'ICM Story,' 178, quoted by Prunty in *Dublin Slums*, 255.
6. St Brigid's Order, sixth annual report, 1862, 19, quoted by Prunty in *Dublin Slums*, 238–9.
7. *Leader*, 11 Oct. 1913.
8. Document in Walsh Papers, laity file, DDA. There is no reference to the group in the annual reports of the Society of St Vincent de Paul, though it is clear from the document that it was intimately involved with the Dublin Council of the society. Father Finlay was a close collaborator with Moran and worked with him on various editorial projects; he was also the priest who responded to D. A. Chart at the historic meeting of the Statistical and Social Inquiry Society on 16 March 1914 to discuss the lockout.
9. Document in Walsh Papers, laity file, DDA.
10. *Daily Express*, 16 Apr. 1913.
11. Society of St Vincent de Paul sub-committee report, Walsh Papers, laity file, DDA. The report includes details taken from published annual reports of the Irish Church Mission's Dublin institutions.
12. Society of St Vincent de Paul Annual Report for 1913, Walsh Papers, DDA.
13. *Freeman's Journal*, 22 Oct. 1913.
14. *Evening Herald*, 22 Oct. 1913; *Freeman's Journal* and *Irish Times*, 23 Oct. 1913.
15. Montefiore, *From a Victorian to a Modern*, 160–161.
16. Montefiore, *From a Victorian to a Modern*, 160–161; *Evening Herald*, 22 Oct. 1913; *Freeman's Journal*, 23 Oct. 1913.
17. Montefiore, *From a Victorian to a Modern*, 160–161.

18. Montefiore, *From a Victorian to a Modern*, 162–3.
19. *Irish Times*, 23 Oct. 1913.
20. *Irish Times*, 23 Oct. 1913. The newspapers all refer to a group of fifteen children, but Montefiore says in her memoirs that there were eighteen, as does Canon Pinnington, a Catholic priest who met the group at Liverpool. Generally where there is a discrepancy between Montefiore's chronology and newspaper reports I have opted to go with the newspapers' version, as they were contemporaneous. However, in this instance it is clear that there were eighteen children: see Montefiore, *From a Victorian to a Modern*, 168, and letter from Canon William Pinnington to Father Flavin, 23 Oct. 1913, Walsh Papers, laity file, DDA.
21. *Evening Herald*, 22 Oct. 1913; *Freeman's Journal* and *Irish Times*, 23 Oct. 1913.
22. *Evening Herald*, 22 Oct. 1913.
23. *Freeman's Journal*, 22 Oct. 1913.
24. *Freeman's Journal*, 22 Oct. 1913.

CHAPTER 21 (p. 273–279)
1. All these details are taken from the *Evening Herald*, 23 Oct. 1913, and *Freeman's Journal* and *Irish Times*, 23 and 24 Oct. 1913.
2. Fred Bower, *Rolling Stonemason*, 1937, 174–5, quoted by Coates and Topham in *The Making of the Transport and General Workers' Union*, 482–3.
3. Canon William Pinnington to Father Flavin, 23 Oct. 1913, Walsh Papers, laity file, DDA.
4. *Freeman's Journal* and *Irish Times*, 24 Oct. 1913; Montefiore, *From a Victorian to a Modern*, 169–70.
5. Minutes of the Parliamentary Committee, 15 Oct. 1913.
6. *Irish Times* and *Freeman's Journal*, 24 Oct. 1913.
7. *Irish Times* and *Freeman's Journal*, 24 Oct. 1913.

CHAPTER 22 (p. 280–284)
1. *Freeman's Journal* and *Irish Times*, 25 Oct. 1913.
2. *Freeman's Journal* and *Evening Herald*, 24 Oct. 1913.
3. *Evening Herald*, 24 Oct. 1913; Montefiore, *From a Victorian to a Modern*, 171.
4. *Freeman's Journal*, 25 Oct. 1913. For the Foresters see Pollard, *The Secret Societies of Ireland*, especially appendix G, 274–6.
5. *Freeman's Journal*, 25 Oct. 1913.
6. *Irish Times*, 25 Oct. 1913.
7. *Freeman's Journal*, 25 Oct. 1913.

CHAPTER 23 (p. 285–291)
1. *Evening Herald*, 25 Oct. 1913.
2. *Sunday Independent*, 26 Oct. 1913; *Irish Times*, 28 Oct. 1913.
3. Leah Levenson, *With Wooden Sword*, 147.
4. *Sunday Independent*, 26 Oct. 1913; *Irish Times*, 28 Oct. 1913.
5. *Evening Telegraph*, 5 Nov. 1913; Sheehy-Skeffington Papers, NLI, ms. 22,256; ITGWU file, NLI, ms. 27,054 (1); *Irish Times*, 28 Oct. 1913.
6. *Sunday Independent*, 26 Oct. 1913; *Irish Times* and *Freeman's Journal*, 27 Oct. 1913.

7. The letter from Wookey was written on 24 October and that from McGloughlin on 23 October 1913.
8. *Sunday Freeman*, 26 Oct. 1913; *Irish Times*, 27 Oct. 1913.
9. *Freeman's Journal*, 28 Oct. 1913.
10. Minutes of the Parliamentary Committee of the TUC, 15 Oct. 1913.
11. Minutes of the Parliamentary Committee of the TUC, 28 Oct. 1913; *Irish Times* and *Freeman's Journal*, 27 Oct. 1913.
12. Charles Coghlan to Dr Walsh, 27 Oct. 1913.
13. Gwynn to Walsh, Oct. 1913, DDA.
14. *Irish Times*, 27 Oct. 1913.
15. Redmond to Dillon, 1 Nov. 1913, Dillon Papers, TCD.
16. Birrell to Asquith, 28 Oct. 1913, Asquith Papers, Bodleian Library, Oxford, ms. 38, f. 243.

CHAPTER 24 (p. 292–299)

1. *Freeman's Journal*, 28 Oct. 1913.
2. *Freeman's Journal*, 28 Oct. 1913.
3. Wright, *Disturbed Dublin*, 228–9.
4. *Irish Times*, 27 Oct. 1913.
5. Quoted by Coates and Topham in *The Making of the Transport and General Workers' Union*, 483.
6. *Freeman's Journal* and *Irish Times*, 28 Oct. 1913. Partridge wrote to Dr Walsh on 21 November stating that he had never referred to priests as 'corner boys': he had only referred to 'the people who followed the priests through the streets as having acted like corner boys.' However, he does not seem to have demanded a public correction from any of the newspapers.
7. *Freeman's Journal* and *Irish Times*, 28 Oct. 1913; *Irish Citizen*, 1 Nov. 1913; Morrissey, *Introduction to the Social Teachings of James Connolly*, 17, 91–2, n. 13.
8. Minutes of the Parliamentary Committee of the TUC, 28 Oct. 1913; *Irish Times*, 29 Oct. 1913.
9. *Irish Times*, 21 Oct. 1913.
10. *Irish Times*, 28 Oct. 1913.
11. *Evening Herald*, 29 Oct. 1913.
12. Lillian Scott Troy to Dr Walsh, 29 Dec. 1913, Walsh Papers, laity file, DDA; *Irish Times*, 28 Oct. 1913.

CHAPTER 25 (p. 300–304)

1. *Irish Times* and *Freeman's Journal*, 28 and 29 Oct. 1913.
2. Minutes of the Parliamentary Committee of the TUC, 28 Oct. 1913.
3. *Irish Times*, 29 Oct. 1913. Contrary to popular legend, Connolly did not close the Liberty Hall food kitchens in retaliation for the clerical and AOH opposition to the 'kiddies scheme'.
4. *Irish Times*, 29 Oct. 1913.
5. *NTWF Weekly Record*, 25 Oct. 1913, quoted by Coates and Topham in *The Making of the Transport and General Workers' Union*, 480–481.
6. *Irish Times*, 1 Nov. 1913.
7. *Irish Times*, 30 Oct. 1913.
8. DMP Statistical Returns for 1913 and 1914. Court returns, which might allow

for a more precise analysis of cases, have yet to emerge from the National Archives or from the vast amount of material now being sorted by the Archives Section of the Garda Síochána.

9. See the memorandum of the meeting between Guinness management and a Shipping Federation representative on 5 November 1913 and the report of the General Purposes Committee of the Shipping Federation's Executive Council of 12 November 1913; *Irish Times*, 31 Oct. to 4 Nov. 1913.
10. *Irish Times*, 31 Oct. 1913.

CHAPTER 26 (p. 305–317)

1. *Irish Times*, 31 Oct. 1913.
2. Coates and Topham, *The Making of the Transport and General Workers' Union*, 481–2; Daily Herald, 17 Sep. 1913, quoted by Howell in *A Lost Left*, 117. Howell offers a very different perspective on Connolly's role in the early British and Irish labour movements from that of other biographers.
3. Coates and Topham, *The Making of the Transport and General Workers' Union*, 481.
4. Helen Hayes, 'Feeding the children,' in *Irish Citizen*, 18 Oct. 1913; Ward, *Unmanageable Revolutionaries*, 80–83.
5. *Irish Times*, 23 Oct. 1913. She voiced similar fears about the non-unionised workers and their families in a letter to W. B. Yeats; she told him she was selling the last of her jewellery to send money to the distress fund.
6. Minutes of ITGWU No. 1 Branch committee, 15 Oct. 1913.
7. *Irish Times*, 23 Oct. 1913.
8. *Irish Times*, 30 Oct. 1913.
9. *Irish Times*, 28 Oct. 1913.
10. *Irish Times*, 28 Oct. 1913.
11. *Irish Times*, 25 Oct. 1913.
12. *Irish Times*, 10 Jan. 1914.
13. NSPCC annual reports for 1911/12, 1912/13, 1913/14, 1914/15.
14. Dr Walsh to Countess Plunkett, 23 Oct. 1913, Walsh Papers, laity file, DDA.
15. Countess Plunkett to Dr Walsh, 24 Oct. 1913, Walsh Papers, laity file, DDA.
16. Reports of the Society of St Vincent de Paul to Dr Walsh, 1 July 1913 and 11 Feb. 1914, Walsh Papers, laity file, DDA; Bolster, *The Knights of St Columbanus*, chap. 1 and 2.
17. *Irish Citizen*, 13 Dec. 1913.

CHAPTER 27 (p. 318–332)

1. *Irish Times* and *Freeman's Journal*, 29 Oct. to 4 Nov. 1913.
2. *Irish Times*, 31 Oct.
3. Minutes of the United Irish Societies Relief Fund Committee, 22 Oct. 1913 to 1 Jan. 1914, NLI, ms. 1,563; correspondence from Dr Peter Amigo, Bishop of Southwark, and Lord Ashbourne to Dr Walsh, Nov. 1913, DDA.
4. This estimate is based on the location and type of school listed by the *Irish Catholic*, 1 Nov. 1913; it is obviously open to other, and more generous, guesstimates. Dr Walsh had given a figure of 2,045 children in his address to the Society of St Vincent de Paul on 27 October. The figures of 7,259 and 4,253 are given in the report of the School Meals Committee to Dublin Corporation, 20 November 1914.

5. Redmond, *The Irish Municipal Employees' Trade Union*, chap. 3–5, gives an excellent account of what it was like organising a union of the unskilled in Dublin at the time. Particular details cited are from p. 26–8, 42, and 60–1. The rates for drapers' assistants ran from 5s (25p) a week for apprentices to 50s (£2.50) for senior employees, but the average income was 30s (£1.50). See the evidence of M. J. O'Lehane to the Inquiry into the the the Housing Conditions of the Working Classes, 2 Dec. 1913, for details.

6. Minutes of Executive Committee, Drapers' Assistants' Association, 3 Sep. 1913 to 7 Jan. 1914.

7. For details of the composition of the Drapers' Assistants' Association see the evidence of M. J. O'Lehane to the Inquiry into the Housing Conditions of the Working Classes, 2 Dec. 1913. For the special tribute to Dublin drapers see minutes of the Parliamentary Committee of the TUC, 15 Oct. 1913. It was made by James Seddon, who may have been biased, as he was leader of the Shopworkers' Union in Britain.

8. *Draper's Assistant*, Oct. 1913.

9. *Draper's Assistant*, Oct. 1913.

10. See Emmet Larkin, 'James Larkin: labour leader,' in Nevin, *James Larkin*, 6, for details of porters at Hickey's drapery shop in North Earl Street. The minutes of the Executive Committee of the Drapers' Assistants' Association contain several references to correspondence and telephone calls from the ITGWU complaining of the activities of shop assistants: see particularly 22 October 1913. The association may have suffered unduly from the fact that its records (now in the possession of Mandate) were kept so scrupulously. The contribution of Clery's employees to Dr Walsh's appeal was reported in the *Irish Catholic*, 8 Nov. 1911.

11. Figures are taken from the subscription lists in the report of the Parliamentary Committee of the TUC on the Dublin Food Fund, 1914. The TUC report, which runs to thirty-five pages and contains nearly seven thousand individual entries, is a very useful but largely untapped source of information on the state of the British labour movement of the time. See the pioneering document study by Jimmy Sweeney, 'The Dublin lockout, 1913: the response of British Labour.' Other sources used here include the audited accounts of the Dublin Trades Council strike fund, 1914, O'Brien Papers, and the memoranda drawn up by the Dublin Trades Council strike committee in January 1914, O'Brien Papers, NLI.

12. Statement of accounts, Dublin Children's Distress Fund, Feb. 1914, Walsh Papers, laity file, DDA; correspondence of Dr McHugh and Father William Lockhart with Dr Walsh, 29 Oct. 1913, Walsh Papers, laity file, DDA. Dr McHugh always had a strong interest in social and political issues; he went on to found the Irish Nation League in 1916 to oppose the Irish Party's acceptance of partition.

13. Dr Logue to Dr Walsh, 6 Nov. 1913, Walsh Papers, laity file, DDA.

14. 'Statement of the Work,' Dublin Children's Distress Committee, Feb. 1914.

15. Keane, *Ishbel*, 207–9.

16. Father Stafford to Dr Walsh, 7 Dec. 1913, Walsh Papers, laity file, DDA.

17. Jones, *These Obstreperous Lassies*, 11.

18. *Irish Citizen*, 4 Oct. 1913.

CHAPTER 28 (p. 333–337)

1. Society of St Vincent de Paul, Annual Report, 1913; *SVP Bulletin*, May 1914.
2. *SVP Bulletin*, May 1914.
3. *SVP Bulletin*, May 1914.
4. Society of St Vincent de Paul, Annual Report, 1913.
5. Parliamentary Committee of the TUC, Dublin Food Fund.
6. Dublin Trades Council minutes, 2 Nov. and 1 Dec. 1913. Difficulties over obtaining unemployment benefits for locked-out members were first raised at the November meeting. Some improvements were achieved by December, but the problem of obtaining benefits was a recurring theme at the trades council for the rest of the lockout.
7. The quotation is from the Society of St Vincent de Paul annual report for 1913. The figures used in this paragraph for estimating expenditure per capita are based on the total collected by the TUC, together with the £13,338 that came in to Dublin Trades Council in direct donations. As both the trade union and St Vincent de Paul totals combine cash payments and relief in kind, they appear to be directly comparable.
8. Society of St Vincent de Paul, annual report, 1913; 'St Vincent de Paul and Proselytism,' report sent to Dr Walsh on 11 Feb. 1914, Walsh Papers, laity file, DDA.
9. Society of St Vincent de Paul, annual report, 1913.
10. *Irish Times*, 28 Oct. 1913.
11. Joseph O'Brien, *Dear, Dirty Dublin*, 212.
12. *Irish Times*, 24 Feb. and 3 Mar. 1914; *Irish Catholic*, 8 Nov. to 6 Dec. 1913.
13. *Leader*, 21 Feb. 1914. The collection for the Home Rule Fund was so good in 1913 that a moratorium was called for 1914, the 'Year of Home Rule'.

CHAPTER 29 (p. 338–368)

1. *Irish Times*, 31 Oct. and 4 Nov. 1913. The city of Dublin had by far the highest policing bill to meet. It would have to pay £6,300 for the five hundred RIC men on duty since August; these cost 4s 6d each a day in subsistence money. The other £980 was for a hundred men deployed in County Dublin on a daily subsistence rate of 3s 6d. There was £131 5s due for the five district inspectors in charge, at a daily rate of 15s each.
2. Records of the South Dublin Union, NA, BG 79 G 130–137; also Chief Secretary's Office, NA, box 5277.
3. Joseph O'Brien, *Dear, Dirty Dublin*, 172–3, argues that the British legislation had little impact on the Dublin poor before the First World War. Details of the difficulties experienced by unions in securing insurance payments for members locked out are contained in Dublin Trades Council minutes, 2 Nov. 1913 to 9 Feb. 1914.
4. Connolly, 'The Reconquest of Ireland,' in *Labour in Ireland*, 204.
5. Dublin Corporation Health Reports of Sir Charles Cameron, 1912–14.
6. A press cutting of the *Irish Worker* item in the O'Brien Papers bears the comment *Not by Larkin*. The general tone suggests that Larkin may have left a rough draft behind him, but other aspects, not least the military metaphors, suggest that it was at least 'tidied up' by Connolly. So does the inclusion of Michael McKeown, the Belfast activist and close associate of Connolly's, in the all-important reference to Larkin's mantle passing to 'men such as Daly, Partridge, McKeown and Connolly.'

7. Russell to Yeats, undated, published by Yeats in *Tribute to Thomas Davis*, 20.
8. Nevin, 'Æ and the Dublin lock-out,' in *James Larkin*, 211–14.
9. *Irish Times*, 11 Nov. 1913.
10. Letter to F. S. Oliver, 18 Dec. 1913, quoted by West in *Horace Plunkett*, 250, n. 1.
11. *Sunday Independent*, 9 Nov. 1913; *Irish Times*, 3 Nov. 1913.
12. *Leader*, 8 and 15 Nov. 1913.
13. Russell to Yeats, 5 Nov. 1913, from Alan Denson (ed.), *The Letters of Æ*, 91, reproduced by Nevin in *James Larkin*, 216.
14. *Leader*, 6 Sep. 1913.
15. *Leader*, 13 Sep. 1913.
16. *Leader*, 20 Sep. 'The lock-out and the strike' criticises the employers' stance in some detail. The quotation criticising the Irish Party is taken from the *Leader*, 8 Nov. 1913.
17. *Leader*, 4 and 11 Oct. 1913.
18. *Leader*, 1 and 8 Nov. 1913.
19. *Irish Catholic*, 8 Nov. 1913. Eviction cases in the Southern Police Court on 21 October 1913 involving five priests were highly publicised in the *Irish Worker* of 1 November; it was not the sort of opportunity it would let pass easily. Many more priests in the city—including Dr Walsh—were landlords, but the absence of similar reports suggests that most of them did not follow the example of the DUTC and several other employers in ordering evictions.
20. Quotations in this paragraph are from *Sinn Féin*, 6 September, 18 October and 8 November 1913. Good summaries of Griffith's attitude to the lockout are given by Davis in *Arthur Griffith and Non-Violent Sinn Féin*, chap. 9, and, less critically, by Maye in *Arthur Griffith*, part 6, chap. 1–3.
21. *Sinn Féin*, 28 Nov. and 5 Dec. 1908, quoted by Clarkson in *Labour and Nationalism in Ireland*, 268–9. See also below, chap. 12.
22. *Sinn Féin*, 27 Sep. 1913.
23. *Sinn Féin*, 4 and 11 Oct. 1913.
24. *Sinn Féin*, 25 Oct. 1913.
25. See Howell, *A Lost Left*, chap. 5, for a detailed analysis of Connolly's views on this topic.
26. *Sinn Féin*, 25 Oct. 1913.
27. *Sinn Féin*, 25 Oct. 1913.
28. *Sinn Féin*, 1 Nov. 1913.
29. *Sinn Féin*, 1 Nov. 1913.
30. *Sinn Féin*, 11 Oct. 1913.
31. *Irish Freedom*, Nov. 1913.
32. *Irish Citizen*, 13 Sep. 1913.
33. *Irish Citizen*, 27 Sep. 1913.
34. *Irish Citizen*, 27 Sep. 1913.
35. *Irish Citizen*, 27 Sep. 1913.
36. *Irish Citizen*, 4 Oct. 1913. Little Denmark Street no longer exists: the ILAC Centre was built over it.
37. *Irish Citizen*, 11 Oct. 1913.
38. *Irish Citizen*, 11 Oct. 1913.
39. *Irish Citizen*, 18 Oct. 1913.
40. *Irish Citizen*, 18 Oct. 1913.

41. *Sinn Féin*, 21 Sep. 1907, quoted by Cullen Owens in *Smashing Times*, 122; *Freeman's Journal*, 12 Aug. 1907, quoted by Emmet Larkin in *James Larkin*, 41.
42. *Irish Citizen*, 25 Oct. 1913.
43. *Irish Citizen*, 15 Nov. 1913.
44. *Irish Citizen*, 15 Nov. 1913.
45. *Irish Citizen*, 15 Nov. 1913.
46. See the reports of Dublin Corporation's School Meals Committee, no. 268–.
47. See L. Priestly, 'The unionist women,' in *Irish Citizen*, 23 Aug. 1913, for a good summary of the preoccupations of this group at the time. The summary of developments in the British suffrage movement relies heavily on Dangerfield, *The Strange Death of Liberal England*, especially 121–77 and 293–312.
48. *Forward*, 9 Feb. 1914, reprinted by Ryan in *The Workers' Republic*, 142.

CHAPTER 30 (p. 371–383)

1. Evidence of Cuthbert Laws, general manager of the Shipping Federation, quoted in *Report of the Industrial Council of Inquiry into Industrial Agreements* (Cd. 6953), Parliamentary Papers, vol. 28, 1913, 568–75; annual report of the Shipping Federation for 1913, MRC, ms. 367.
2. *Report of the Industrial Council of Inquiry into Industrial Agreements* (Cd. 6953), Parliamentary Papers, vol. 28, 1913, 568–75.
3. Reports of the General Purposes Committee, Shipping Federation, 16 May and 19 Sep. 1913, MRC, ms. 367.
4. Annual Labour Report of the Shipping Federation for 1913–14, MRC, ms. 367, 3. This verdict is shared by Emmet Larkin, *James Larkin*, 115; Timothy Healy in his submission to the Askwith Inquiry; and Arnold Wright, *Disturbed Dublin*, 101–11. Greaves, *The Irish Transport and General Workers' Union*, 84–7, gives a more qualified assessment.
5. Annual Labour Report of the Shipping Federation for 1913–14, MRC, ms. 367.
6. Annual Labour Report of the Shipping Federation for 1913–14, MRC, ms. 367.
7. *Irish Times*, 4 Nov. 1913.
8. *Irish Times*, 5 Nov. 1913.
9. *Irish Times*, 4 Nov. 1913
10. *Irish Times*, 4 and 5 Nov. 1913; A. P. Magill to G. A. Touche MP, 21 Nov. 1913, quoted by Murray in 'A militant among the magdalens?' Jacob's had ceased advertising for new workers on 11 October 1913: see McCaffrey, 'Jacob's women workers during the 1913 Lockout.'
11. *Irish Times*, 4 Nov. 1913. Father Patrick Flavin was a curate in Kingstown (Dún Laoghaire) and should not be confused with Father James Flavin, administrator of the Pro-Cathedral in Dublin, who had also been active in opposing Dora Montefiore's 'kiddies scheme'.
12. *Irish Times*, 5 Nov. 1913. I am also indebted to Séamus Fitzpatrick of IMPACT for making available material on James Byrne prepared by FÁS trainees for Dún Laoghaire and Rathdown Heritage Society. Union activists in IMPACT and SIPTU are discussing plans with the society for the erection of a memorial at Byrne's grave.
13. *Irish Times*, 5 Nov. 1915.
14. Report of meeting between Shipping Federation representatives and Guinness, 5 Nov. 1913, Guinness Archive, GDB/COOP/24.

15. Report of meeting between William Martin Murphy and Charles Sutton, 7 Nov. 1913, Guinness Archive, GDB/COOP/24. Renny-Tailyour to Lord Iveagh, 24 Dec. 1913. See also Dennison and MacDonagh, *Guinness, 1886–1939*, 241.
16. The complaint of the British and Irish Steam Packet Company was on 20 September 1913. For this and the subsequent investigation see NA, CSO 17697.
17. NA, CSO 20410–21326.
18. The free labourers' rates are taken from the *Irish Times*, 6 Nov. 1913. The Dublin rates are taken from the copy of the agreement between the ITGWU and the Dublin shipping companies of 26 May 1913, published as an appendix by Wright in *Disturbed Dublin*, 306–7.
19. *Irish Times*, 6 Nov. 1913.
20. Chief Secretary's Office, 1913, NA, CSORP 20538. Captain Vane de V. M. Vallance to his mother, 26 Oct. 1913, Vallance Papers, NLI, quoted by D'Arcy in 'Larkin and the Dublin lockout,' in Nevin, *James Larkin*, 44.
21. Chief Secretary's Office, 7 Nov. 1913, NA, CSORP 20538.
22. Chief Secretary's Office, 8 Nov. 1913, NA, CSORP 20538.
23. Chief Secretary's Office, 11 Nov. 1913, NA, CSORP 20538.
24. Bew, *Ideology and the Irish Question*, 31–4.
25. *Irish Times*, 14 Nov. 1913.
26. *Irish Times*, 20 Nov. 1913.
27. *Irish Times*, 26 Nov. 1913.
28. *Irish Times*, 14 Nov. 1913.
29. *Irish Times*, 18 Nov. 1913.

CHAPTER 31 (p. 384–392)

1. Annual Report of Shipping Federation, 1913–14; *Irish Times*, 8 Nov. 1913.
2. Annual Report of Shipping Federation, 1913–14; report of the Financial Committee of the Shipping Federation, May 1914; *Irish Times*, 8 and 11 Nov. 1913.
3. *Irish Times*, 8 and 11 Nov. 1913.
4. *Irish Worker*, 8 Nov. 1913.
5. *Sunday Independent*, 9 Nov. 1913.
6. Joe Devlin to Percy Illingworth, 7 Nov. 1913, copy in Dillon Papers, TCD, 6729–30/164.
7. Clarkson, *Labour and Nationalism in Ireland*, 254.
8. *Daily Citizen*, 12 Nov. 1913, quoted by Emmet Larkin in *James Larkin*, 142.
9. Dr Christopher Addison to David Lloyd George, 10 Nov. 1913, and reply, 11 Nov. 1913, Lloyd George Papers, PRO, C/10/2/24 (*a*). Far from feeling betrayed by his electorate, Isaacs took the title of Lord Reading when he was eventually appointed to the House of Lords.
10. Cabinet Papers, PRO, 41/34/33.
11. Asquith Papers, Bodleian Library, Oxford, ms. 38, f. 196, 243.
12. *Irish Times*, 30 Oct., 1, 5 and 6 Nov. 1913.
13. Asquith Papers, Bodleian Library, Oxford, ms. 38, 236
14. Asquith Papers, Bodleian Library, Oxford, ms. 38, f. 198.
15. Asquith Papers, Bodleian Library, Oxford, ms. 38, f. 220, 236, 243.
16. Cabinet Papers, PRO, 41/34/34. The idea of partition had been in the air for some time. It was first proposed on a county-by-county basis by a Liberal MP,

T. C. Agar Robartes, during the second reading of the Home Rule Bill. 'I have never heard that orange bitters will mix with Irish whisky,' he told the House of Commons on 11 June 1911. The notion of partition had been toyed with by some Irish-Irelanders, for instance D. P. Moran, who believed that the exclusion of Ulster might speed up the 'Catholicisation' of Irish society: see Maume, *The Long Gestation*, 134–8.

17. Asquith Papers, Bodleian Library, Oxford, ms. 38, f. 20, 22.
18. Cabinet Papers, PRO, 41/33/51–6.

CHAPTER 32 (p. 393–400)

1. *Irish Times*, 14 Nov. 1913.
2. *Freeman's Journal* and *Irish Times*, 14 Nov. 1913.
3. Eric Taplin, 'Liverpool: the apprenticeship of a revolutionary,' in Nevin, *James Larkin*, 17–19.
4. Nevin, *James Larkin*, 465–6.
5. 'A rebel's wife,' Daily Sketch, 15 Nov. 1913, reprinted by Nevin in *James Larkin*, 469–70.
6. *Freeman's Journal* and *Irish Times*, 14 Nov. 1913.
7. *Freeman's Journal* and *Irish Times*, 14 Nov. 1913.
8. *Irish Times*, 11 Nov. 1913.
9. *Irish Times*, 7 and 11 Nov.
10. *Irish Times*, 12 Nov. 1913.
11. *Irish Times*, 12 Nov. 1913; letter of Jack Carney, 1 May 1948, reproduced by Nevin in *James Larkin*, 399.
12. *Irish Times*, 12 Nov. 1913.
13. *Irish Times*, 12 Nov. 1913.
14. Minutes of the Executive Council of the Shipping Federation, 14 Nov. 1913.
15. *Irish Times*, 13 Nov. 1914.

CHAPTER 33 (p. 401–415)

1. *Irish Times*, 14 Nov. 1913.
2. Minutes of General Council of Shipping Federation, 14 Nov. 1913; financial statement of accounts for Shipping Federation, 1 Oct. to 31 Dec. 1913, and annual report for the years ending 31 Mar. 1913 and 31 Mar. 1914.
3. Newsinger, 'The Devil it was who sent Larkin to Ireland.' Newsinger appears to accept that Doyle's venture was initially a *bona fide* effort to oppose Larkin from within the Dublin trade unions. Doyle's views probably did reflect those of many of his fellow-printers at the time.
4. *Liberator*, 6–27 Sep. and 22 Nov. 1913.
5. Greaves, *The Irish Transport and General Workers' Union*, 33, 37, 48–9, 51–3, 58, 72, 79; Morrissey, *A Man Called Hughes*, 356, n. 40.
6. Morrissey, *A Man Called Hughes*, 30.
7. *Toiler*, 27 Dec. 1913.
8. *Toiler*, 17 Jan. 1914.
9. A thorough discussion of Larkin's birthplace is given in Nevin, *James Larkin*, 133–6.
10. Emmet Larkin, *James Larkin*, 144.
11. Nevin, *James Larkin*, 134.
12. Greaves, *The Irish Transport and General Workers' Union*, 117.

13. *Irish Times*, 15 Nov. 1913.
14. *Irish Times*, 15–18 Nov. 1913.
15. *Irish Times*, 15 and 17 Nov. 1913.
16. *Irish Times*, 17 Nov. 1913.
17. William O'Brien, *Forth the Banners Go*, 53; Wright, *Disturbed Dublin*, 159.
18. Report no. 1 of the West Coast Short Traders' Committee of the Shipping Federation, 7 Nov. 1913.
19. *Irish Times*, 18 Nov. 1913.
20. O'Brien Papers, NLI, Pos 6989.
21. *Irish Times*, 18 Nov. 1913.
22. 'Old wine in new bottles,' *New Age*, 30 Apr. 1914, reprinted by Beresford Ellis in James Connolly, *Selected Writings*, 176.
23. 'Old wine in new bottles,' *New Age*, 30 Apr. 1914, reprinted by Beresford Ellis in James Connolly, *Selected Writings*, 178–9.
24. *Irish Times*, 17 Nov. 1913.
25. *Irish Times*, 17 Nov. 1913; NA, CSORP 21491; report of the Visiting Committee of City Prisons, 1914–15, Dublin City Archives. An excellent detailed study of the Mary Murphy controversy is given by Murray in 'A militant among the magdalens?' The figures for the number of women arrested for incidents arising from the lockout are based on the DMP Statistical Returns for 1912 and 1913. No women were charged with riot or intimidation in 1912, but sixteen charges were brought against women under these categories in 1913. There were 458 charges brought against women for various assault offences in 1912, and 499 under the same headings in 1913. This comes to 57 additional offences, but they may not all have related to the labour troubles, and some of the women may have been charged with more than one offence. 'Over forty' seems to me, therefore, a reasonable number to attribute to the lockout.
26. *Irish Times*, 17 Nov. 1913; Emmet Larkin, *James Larkin*, 144–5; Nevin, *James Larkin*, 200–201.
27. *Irish Times*, 17 Nov. 1913.

CHAPTER 34 (p. 416–430)

1. *Irish Times*, 19 Nov. 1913.
2. Minutes of the Parliamentary Committee of the TUC, 18 Nov. 1913.
3. *Irish Times*, 19 Nov. 1913.
4. *Irish Times*, 19 Nov. 1913.
5. Minutes of the Parliamentary Committee of the TUC, 19 Nov. 1913.
6. Minutes of the Parliamentary Committee of the TUC, 20 Nov.
7. *Irish Times*, 20 Nov. 1913.
8. *Irish Times*, 20 Nov. 1913.
9. *Irish Times*, 15 and 17 Nov. 1913.
10. *Irish Times*, 17 Nov. 1913.
11. DMP Report to Chief Secretary, 17 Nov. 1913, NA, CSORP 21406.
12. The quotation from Rev. R. M. Gwynn is given by Fox in *The History of the Irish Citizen Army*, 45. See also Samuel Levenson, *James Connolly*, 239–40, and Greaves, *The Life and Times of James Connolly*, 262, for details of the origins of the Citizen Army. Fox's history, first published in 1943, remains by far the best account.

13. *Irish Times*, 19 Nov. 1913.
14. *Irish Freedom*, Nov. 1913.
15. Fox, *The History of the Citizen Army*, 38–9, 49–51.
16. *Irish Times*, 19 Nov. 1913.
17. *Irish Times*, 19 Nov. 1913.
18. *Irish Times*, 20 Nov. 1913.
19. *Irish Times*, 20 Nov. 1913.
20. *Irish Times*, 19 Nov. 1913.
21. *Irish Times*, 20–26 Nov. 1913. For details of the Workers' Union see correspondence between Dublin Trades Council, Dr Walsh, Father Curran and Father Flavin, Jan. 1914, DDA.
22. Shipping Federation, report of General Purposes Committee, 12 Nov. 1913, Guinness Archive, ms. 367. See also references in Board memoranda, Guinness Archive, 2144–431, and in ITGWU related correspondence, box 6.
23. Wright, *Disturbed Dublin*, 238.

CHAPTER 35 (p. 431–436)

1. *Daily Herald*, 22 Nov. 1913.
2. *Daily Citizen*, 22 Nov. 1913.
3. *Irish Times*, 24 Nov. 1913.
4. *Sunday Independent*, 23 Nov. 1913.
5. *Irish Times*, 24 Nov. 1913.
6. See, for instance, Tom Mann, *Memoirs*, quoted by Coates and Topham in *The Making of the Transport and General Workers' Union*, 342.
7. Coates and Topham, *The Making of the Transport and General Workers' Union*, 486–7.
8. Connolly, *Selected Writings*, 179.
9. O'Brien Papers, NLI, Pos 6989.
10. *Irish Times*, 27 Nov. and 1 Dec. 1913.
11. *Irish Times*, 24 Nov. 1913.
12. *Freeman's Journal*, 4 Dec. 1913.
13. *Irish Times*, 25 Nov. 1913.
14. *Irish Times*, 1 Dec. 1913.
15. A. J. Davies, *To Build a New Jerusalem*, 163–7. The Guinness quotation is from the *Irish Times*, 26 Nov. 1913. In the thirties Lansbury's pacifism and appeasement policies lost him the Labour leadership again. He cut a rather pathetic figure as he ended his political career by making a series of visits to Hitler and Mussolini, urging them to see the error of their ways.
16. *Irish Times*, 27 and 29 Nov. 1913.
17. *Irish Times*, 27 Nov. 1913.
18. *Irish Times*, 28 Nov. 1913.

CHAPTER 36 (p. 437–449)

1. *Irish Times*, 28 Nov. 1913.
2. Bulmer Hobson, 'Foundation and growth of the Irish Volunteers, 1913–1914,' in Martin, *The Irish Volunteers*, 23.
3. Eoin Mac Neill, 'The north began,' *An Claidheamh Soluis*, 1 Nov. 1913, reprinted by Martin in *The Irish Volunteers*, 59.
4. Bulmer Hobson, 'Foundation and growth of the Irish Volunteers, 1913–1914,' in Martin, *The Irish Volunteers*, 24.

5. Patrick Pearse, 'The coming revolution,' *An Claidheamh Soluis*, reprinted in *Political Writings and Speeches*, 98–9.
6. Bulmer Hobson, 'Foundation and growth of the Irish Volunteers, 1913–1914,' in Martin, *The Irish Volunteers*, 24, 29.
7. *Irish Times*, 26 Nov. 1913.
8. See Bond, *War and Society in Europe*, chap. 2 and 3, for a pan-European treatment of this phenomenon. See also Keegan, *A History of Warfare*, 347–59.
9. *Irish Times*, 27 Nov. 1913.
10. Strauss, *Irish Nationalism and British Democracy*, chap. 20, still gives the best summary of the underlying economic arguments. William O'Brien made his suggestion to Asquith in a letter of 4 Nov. 1911, Asquith Papers, Bodleian Library, Oxford, ms. 36.
11. *Irish Times*, 29 Nov. 1913.
12. The directorships of the companies that were signatories to the list are largely taken from *Thom's Directory* for 1913 and 1914 but also from a number of other sources, including the Guinness Archive, contemporary newspaper files, Dublin Chamber of Commerce reports, and references in Wright, *Disturbed Dublin*.
13. *Irish Times*, 26 Nov. 1913.
14. *Irish Times*, 29 Nov. 1913.
15. *Irish Citizen*, 6 and 13 Dec. 1913.
16. See Swift, *John Swift*, 18, for an informed view of the role of the Bakers' Union in the dispute.
17. *Irish Times*, 24–8 Nov. and 6 Dec. 1913.
18. *Irish Times*, 11 Oct., 17 and 27 Nov. 1913.
19. *Irish Times*, 29 Nov. to 5 Dec. 1913.
20. *Irish Times*, 26 Nov. 1913.

CHAPTER 37 (p. 450–462)

1. *Sunday Independent*, 30 Nov. 1913; *Irish Times*, 27 Nov. 1913.
2. International Shipping Federation circular, 24 Nov. 1913, and attached documents, MRC, ms. 367.
3. Dublin Chamber of Commerce council minutes, 29 Nov. 1913.
4. Sir James Browne Dougherty to Dr Walsh, 22 Nov. 1913, Walsh Papers, laity file, DDA.
5. *Irish Times*, 1 Dec. 1913.
6. *Irish Times*, 1 Dec. 1913.
7. *Irish Times*, 2 Dec. 1913.
8. *Irish Times*, 3 Dec. 1913; *Dublin Transport Workers' Dispute: Report of the Parliamentary Committee of the TUC*, Dec. 1914. The GFTU was set up in 1899 to provide a fighting fund for locked-out workers. However, it had never been very effective and was almost moribund by 1913.
9. *Irish Times*, 3 Dec. 1913.
10. *Irish Times*, 3 Dec. 1913.
11. Churchill's interest in the Fabians is well documented: see, for instance, Martin Gilbert, *Churchill: A Life*, London: Heinemann, 1991, and N. Rose, *Churchill: An Unruly Life*, London: Simon and Schuster 1994, 71. Typically, Churchill was as much attracted to the personality of the Fabian leader Beatrice Webb as to her ideas. She considered him 'egotistical, bumptious, shallow-minded and reactionary.'

12. *Irish Times*, 3 Dec. 1913.
13. For a good summary of the employers' attitudes see Wright, *Disturbed Dublin*, 242–3.
14. *Irish Times*, 3 Dec. 1913.
15. *Irish Times*, 4 Dec. 1913.
16. *Dublin Transport Workers' Dispute: Report of the Parliamentary Committee of the TUC*, Dec. 1914; O'Brien Papers, NLI, Pos 6989; Wright, *Disturbed Dublin*, 243–5.
17. *Dublin Transport Workers' Dispute: Report of the Parliamentary Committee of the TUC*, Dec. 1914; Wright, *Disturbed Dublin*, 243–5; *Irish Times*, 5, 6 and 8 Dec. 1913.
18. *Irish Times*, 8 Dec. 1913.
19. Howell, *A Lost Left*, 116–22.
20. *Dublin Transport Workers' Dispute: Report of the Parliamentary Committee of the TUC*, Dec. 1914.
21. *Irish Worker*, 6 Dec. 1913.
22. *Irish Times*, 8 Dec. 1913; *Dublin Transport Workers' Dispute: Report of the Parliamentary Committee of the TUC*, Dec. 1914.
23. *Irish Times*, 5 Dec. 1913.

CHAPTER 38 (p. 463–477)

1. Anonymous and undated memorandum in pencil in Dr Walsh's laity file for 1913. The document could relate to any period from the initial peace efforts by the TUC in September up to the end of the year; however, the contents suggest that it probably coincided with Dr Walsh's peace efforts in late October or December. December seems more likely. Of course the 'W' could refer to someone other than the archbishop, but there are no obvious candidates. The memorandum was presumably written by someone who had been briefed by Dr Walsh, possibly a journalist, for a third party; somehow or other it found its way back to the archbishop—an indication of the incestuous nature of Dublin society.
2. *Irish Times*, 15 Sep. and 6 Dec. 1913; Howell, *A Lost Left*, 229–37. Howell provides a useful summary of Catholic socialism and the attitude of émigré Irish radicals like Wheatley towards Catholicism, socialism, and nationality.
3. *Irish Times*, 8 Dec. 1913.
4. *Irish Times*, 4 Dec. 1913.
5. *Irish Times*, 9 Dec.
6. Minutes of the Parliamentary Committee of the TUC, 8 Dec. 1913.
7. This was the view put forward by C. Desmond Greaves and accepted by many others. It is partly based on the role that men like Wilson, Thomas, Macdonald, Snowden and others were to play subsequently; it also suited the left wing of the British labour movement to prove that their conservative opponents were always rotten to the core.
8. William O'Brien, *Forth the Banners Go*, 98–9.
9. *Leader*, 13 Dec. 1913.
10. Coates and Topham, *The Making of the Transport and General Workers' Union*, 489–90.
11. William O'Brien, *Forth the Banners Go*, 99.
12. *Irish Times*, 10 Dec. 1913. Unless otherwise stated, the quotations from the TUC debate are from the *Irish Times* of that day.

13. *Dublin Transport Workers' Dispute: Report of the Parliamentary Committee of the TUC*, Dec. 1914. The *Irish Times* report describes Jones's motion as an amendment to that from the National Union of Labour and the Typographical Association; however, the TUC report carries it as a motion in its own right, and the reports suggest that it was debated exclusively on its own merits, or lack of them.

14. At a Triple Alliance meeting in April 1914 Smillie said that sympathetic action could 'no longer be left to the uncontrolled emotions of the strike period': it had to be 'the calculated result of mature consideration and careful planning': Coates and Topham, *The Making of the Transport and General Workers' Union*, 550.

15. Greaves, *The Life and Times of James Connolly*, 268–9.

16. *Forward*, 9 Feb. 1914, reprinted by Ryan in *The Workers' Republic*, 144.

17. *Irish Times*, 10 Dec. 1913.

18. *Irish Times*, 11 Dec. 1913.

19. *Forward*, 9 Feb. 1914, reprinted by Ryan in *The Workers' Republic*, 144–5.

20. *Forward*, 9 Feb. 1914, reprinted by Ryan in *The Workers' Republic*, 142–6.

21. *NTWF Weekly Record*, 13 Dec. 1913, quoted by Coates and Topham in *The Making of the Transport and General Workers' Union*, 489–90.

22. *Board of Trade Reports on Industrial Disputes* (Cd. 7658), Parliamentary Papers, vol. 36, 1914–16; Robert Smillie, *Labour Year Book, 1915*, quoted by Coates and Topham in *The Making of the Transport and General Workers' Union*, 550–551.

CHAPTER 39 (p. 478–490)

1. *Irish Times*, 10 Dec. 1913.

2. *Irish Times*, 11 and 12 Dec. 1913.

3. *Irish Times*, 11 Dec. 1913.

4. Board Memoranda, 2144–431, and ITGWU correspondence, Guinness Archive, box 6.

5. *Irish Times*, 15 Dec. 1913.

6. *Irish Times*, 13 and 15 Dec. 1913.

7. *Irish Times*, 13 Dec. 1913.

8. *Irish Times*, 16 Dec. 1913.

9. *Irish Times*, 16 Dec. 1913.

10. *Irish Times*, 10, 11, 12 and 13 Dec. 1913. The ban on the importing of arms was lifted in 1906 at the request of John Redmond. See above, Prologue.

11. *Irish Times*, 12, 13, 15 and 16 Dec. 1913.

12. *Irish Times*, 15 Dec. 1913.

13. *Irish Times*, 15 Dec. 1913.

14. *Irish Times*, 16 Dec. 1913.

15. *Irish Times*, 19 Dec. 1913.

16. *Irish Times*, 17 Dec. 1913; *Irish Worker*, 13 Dec. 1913.

17. *Irish Times*, 17 Dec. 1913.

18. *Irish Times*, 13 Dec. 1913; TUC Dublin Food Fund, 8.

19. *Irish Times*, 17 Dec. 1913.

20. *Irish Times*, 18 Dec. 1913.

21. Wright, *Disturbed Dublin*, 250.

22. See lists in *Irish Worker*, 29 Nov. and 13 Dec. 1913. There were also large

numbers of small individual donations, inspiriting to the strikers if of no great financial value.

23. *Irish Times*, 19 Dec. 1913, 3 and 6 Jan. 1914.
24. *Dublin Transport Workers' Dispute: Report of the Parliamentary Committee of the TUC*, Dec. 1914.
25. *Dublin Transport Workers' Dispute: Report of the Parliamentary Committee of the TUC*, Dec. 1914. See Wright, *Disturbed Dublin*, 250–251, for the employers' perspective; also the *Irish Times*, 19 Dec. 1913.
26. *Dublin Transport Workers' Dispute: Report of the Parliamentary Committee of the TUC*, Dec. 1914; *Irish Times*, 19, 20 and 22 Dec.
27. The phrase is that of Professor Dermot Keogh, a historian not unsympathetic to Murphy, from his essay 'Clash of Titans: James Larkin and William Martin Murphy,' in Nevin, *James Larkin*, 55.
28. *Irish Times*, 15–22 Dec. 1913.
29. *Irish Worker*, 13 Dec. 1913.
30. *Irish Times*, 16–19 Dec. 1913.

CHAPTER 40 (p. 491–495)

1. *Irish Times*, 22 Dec. 1913.
2. *Irish Times*, 22 Dec. 1913.
3. *Sunday Independent*, 21 Dec. 1913. See also the text of a letter by William Martin Murphy in the *Irish Times*, 26 Dec. 1913.
4. *Sunday Independent*, 21 Dec. 1913.
5. *Irish Times*, 23 Dec. 1913 and 1 Jan. 1914.
6. *Irish Times*, 26 Dec. 1913. Immediately after Christmas, Larkin announced that he had no intention of going on a lecture tour for the moment.
7. *Irish Worker*, 20 Dec. 1913; *Irish Times*, 22–4 Dec. 1913.
8. *Irish Worker*, 20 Dec. 1913; *Irish Times*, 22–4 Dec. 1913.
9. ITGWU Accounts, O'Brien Papers, NLI, Pos 6989; *Irish Times*, 23 and 24 Dec. 1913.
10. *Irish Times*, 16 and 26 Dec. 1913. Sherlock chaired the conference of the Association of Irish Post Office Clerks that considered the Holt Report on postal clerks' pay. The figures for the number of children fed in Croydon Park on Christmas Day vary from a minimum of 2,000 in the *Irish Times* to 5,000 in the *Daily Herald*. I have opted for the second figure, as the *Daily Herald* would have had access, through Francis Sheehy-Skeffington, to the most detailed information.
11. *Irish Times*, 26 and 27 Dec. 1913, 3 Jan. 1914; schedule of legal fees, William Smyth and Son, NLI, ms. 27,054 (1).

CHAPTER 41 (p. 496–514)

1. *Irish Times*, 30 Dec. 1913.
2. *Irish Times*, 30 Dec. 1913.
3. Minutes of the Parliamentary Committee of the TUC, 7 Jan. 1913; O'Brien Papers, NLI, Pos 6989; *Irish Times*, 9 Jan. 1914.
4. *Irish Times*, 3 Jan. 1913. By coincidence, there was a death remarkably similar to Alice Brady's that weekend in the city. Michael Keelty, a barman in a pub on Eden Quay, died of tetanus the Sunday after the inquest on Alice Brady. He too had been shot: another barman, who had bought a small pistol for 5s from a

city gunsmith, hit Kielty in the foot when the weapon accidentally discharged. Again the small-calibre bullet had caused only a minor wound, which was dressed in a hospital. Two such fatalities so close together are an indication not just of the proliferation of small arms in the city but of just how dirty and disease-ridden the Dublin of the day was. At another inquest two weeks later evidence was given that a fifteen-year-old fitter's apprentice accidentally shot himself with a revolver he had bought for 2s 9d. The evidence at both inquests emphasised how cheaply and easily revolvers could be acquired. The barman who shot Kielty told the inquest he had decided to buy a gun after seeing so many 'free labourers' carrying them.

5. *Irish Times*, 5 Jan. 1913.
6. James Connolly, *Edinburgh Labour Chronicle*, 5 Nov. and 1 Dec. 1894, quoted by Howell in *A Lost Left*, 21.
7. *Irish Worker*, 29 Nov. 1913.
8. Dublin Trades Council minutes, 19 Nov. 1913, and NLI, CO 904, Pos 8170.
9. Dublin Trades Council minutes, 12 Jan. 1914.
10. *Irish Times*, 22 Nov. 1913.
11. *Irish Times*, 25 Nov. 1913.
12. *Irish Times*, 26 Nov. 1913.
13. *Irish Times*, 27 Nov. 1913; *Thom's Directory*, 1914; *Report of the Departmental Committee into the the Housing Conditions of the Working Classes in the City of Dublin*, appendix 15 and 16, 344.
14. *Report of the Departmental Committee into the the Housing Conditions of the Working Classes in the City of Dublin*, appendix 15 and 16, 344.
15. *Irish Times*, 16 Jan. 1914.
16. *Irish Times*, 27 Nov. 1913.
17. *Irish Times*, 2 Dec. 1913.
18. *Irish Times*, 10 Dec. 1913.
19. *Irish Times*, 23 Dec. 1913.
20. *Irish Times*, 31 Dec. 1913.
21. *Irish Times*, 6 Jan. 1914.
22. *Irish Worker*, 3 Jan. 1914.
23. *Irish Citizen*, 10 Jan. 1914,
24. *Irish Worker*, 5 Jan. 1914.
25. *Irish Times*, 6 Jan. 1914; *Irish Worker*, 10 Jan. 1914.
26. *Irish Times*, 20 Dec. 1913.
27. *Irish Times*, 17 Jan. 1913.
28. See O'Brien Papers, NLI, LO P116, item 7, for an example of a priest's endorsement of a nationalist candidate in 1907. The priest was Father Monaghan of Francis Street, who gave evidence to the Inquiry into the the Housing Conditions of the Working Classes. For the 1914 election see J. E. Lyons to Dr Walsh, 11 Jan. 1914, complaining at attempts to depict an independent nationalist candidate as a 'socialist': Walsh Papers, laity file, DDA; also letters from Sherlock to Dr Walsh in the same file. He forwarded progress reports to the archbishop on the Distress Fund as well as a copy of the final report. The *Irish Times*, 16 Dec. 1913, illustrates Sherlock's links with the Assocation of Irish Post Office Clerks and his views on industrial relations. At an election rally in Ballybough on 13 January, William Partridge acknowledged Sherlock's support for the workers, and even the ITGWU, in the

past but accused him of treachery: see the report in the *Irish Times*, 14 Jan. 1913.

29. *Irish Worker*, 10 Jan. 1914; *Irish Times*, 6 and 12 Jan. and 19 Feb. 1914.
30. *Irish Worker*, 14 Jan. 1914.
31. *Irish Times*, 15 Jan. 1914.
32. *Irish Times*, 15 Jan. 1914.
33. *Irish Times*, 17 Jan. 1914.
34. Daly would win the North Dock seat in 1915.
35. Report of General Purposes Committee to the General Council of the Shipping Federation, 12 Nov. 1913, MRC, ms. 367.
36. Dublin Trades Council minutes, 18 Aug. and 6 Oct. 1913; letter from Law Agent's office, 25 Aug. 1913, Dublin City Archives.
37. Report of the Improvements Committee of Dublin Corporation, Feb. 1914, Dublin City Archives.
38. Mitchell, *Labour in Irish Politics*, 36–7.
39. Murray, 'Electoral politics and the Dublin working class before the First World War'; Maguire, 'The organisation and activism of Dublin's Protestant working class, 1883–1935,' *Irish Historical Studies*, vol. 29 (1994), no. 113.
40. Murray, 'Electoral politics and the Dublin working class before the First World War'.
41. When the *Irish Worker* published its own analysis of the polls on 24 January 1914 it segregated the votes for Dr McWalter and Laurence O'Neill from those of other nationalists and categorised them as 'Nationalists in Sympathy with Labour'. I have included them with the nationalist total. While both men were relatively progressive on social issues, McWalter was a leading member of the Dublin Catholic Association, and O'Neill ran on an independent nationalist ticket. I have also included William Chase, the self-proclaimed independent labour candidate, and James Kelly, the 'Home Rule-Labour' candidate, with the nationalists. Neither had the backing of Dublin Trades Council, and the *Irish Worker* included their votes with the total cast for mainstream nationalist candidates. The *Irish Times*, for reasons that are unclear, insisted on labelling Chase as a Larkinite and thus declaring that the candidates endorsed by Dublin Trades Council had won two seats.
42. This figure ignores challenges to candidates of the United Irish League posed by 'labour' mavericks such as Kelly, Chase, and McIntyre.
43. *Irish Times*, 16 Jan. 1914; *Irish Worker*, 17 Jan. 1914.
44. James Connolly to William O'Brien, 15 Jan. 1914; William O'Brien, *Forth the Banners Go*, 240–241.
45. James Connolly to William O'Brien, 15 Jan. 1914; William O'Brien, *Forth the Banners Go*, 240–241.
46. *Irish Worker*, 17 Jan. 1914. In fairness to Larkin, it should be said that his allegations of public officials campaigning for the lord mayor and other nationalist candidates were probably true. The great majority of appointments, from that of Henry Campbell, town clerk, downwards, were political. Campbell had been a former secretary to Parnell.
47. *Irish Times*, 17 and 19 Jan. 1913.

CHAPTER 42 (p. 515–521)

1. *Irish Times*, 10, 19 and 27 Jan. 1914.
2. *Irish Times*, 9 and 19 Jan. 1914.
3. *Irish Times*, 6 Jan. 1914.
4. *Irish Times*, 8 Jan. 1914.
5. *Irish Times*, 8–10 Jan. 1914.
6. *Evening Telegraph*, 10 Jan. 1914.
7. *Irish Times*, 8 Jan. 1914.
8. *Irish Times*, 17 and 19 Jan. 1914.
9. *Irish Times*, 7–17 Jan. 1914.
10. *Irish Times*, 1, 6 and 8 Jan. 1914; *Evening Herald*, 6 Jan. 1914.
11. *Irish Times*, 7–12 Jan. 1914.
12. Charles Bowerman to William O'Brien, O'Brien Papers, NLI, Pos 6989, ms. 13913.
13. *Irish Times*, 12 Jan. 1914; Dublin Trades Council minutes, 12 Jan. 1914; minutes of the Parliamentary Committee of the TUC, 7 and 21 Jan. 1914.
14. O'Casey, 'The Story of the Irish Citizen Army,' 190–93.
15. On 15 January 1914 the *Irish Times* reported White to be back drilling the men at Croydon Park, but not on speaking terms with Larkin. For the relationship of White with the ITGWU leaders in the early days of the Citizen Army see O'Casey, 'The Story of the Irish Citizen Army,' and Fox, *The History of the Irish Citizen Army*, 49.
16. Dublin Trades Council minutes, 12 Jan. 1914.
17. *Irish Times*, 19 Jan. 1914.

CHAPTER 43 (p. 522–538)

1. *Irish Times*, 20, 21 and 23 Jan. 1914.
2. *Irish Times*, 20, 21 and 23 Jan. 1914.
3. *Irish Times*, 20 Jan. 1914.
4. *Irish Times*, 21 Jan. 1914.
5. *Irish Times*, 19 Jan. 1914.
6. *Irish Times*, 20 and 22 Jan. 1914.
7. Minutes of the Parliamentary Committee of the TUC, 21 Jan. 1914.
8. *Irish Times*, 22 and 23 Jan. 1914.
9. *Irish Times*, 24 and 26 Jan. 1914. Two 'free labourers' seriously assaulted over that weekend were Dublin men.
10. *Irish Times*, 23 Jan. 1914.
11. *Irish Times*, 23 Jan. 1914.
12. *Irish Times*, 24 Jan. 1914; *Irish Worker*, 31 Jan. 1914.
13. *Irish Times*, 24 and 26 Jan. 1914.
14. Ibid. 26 Jan. 1914; Dublin Trades Council minutes, 24 Jan. 1914.
15. *Irish Times*, 26 Jan. 1914.
16. *Irish Times*, 26 Jan. 1914.
17. *Irish Times*, 27 Jan. 1914. Tom Mann's absence in America has been considered by some labour historians to be critical to the failure of the ITGWU to mobilise more support: see Coates and Topham, *The Making of the Transport and General Workers' Union*, 490. But Larkin's capacity to alienate allies should never be underestimated. Mann's support could well have gone the way of Tillet's and Williams's.

18. *Irish Times*, 27 and 28 Jan. 1914. Claims for strike pay by building craft workers in the O'Brien papers show, for instance, only 12 plumbers seeking relief, 40 slaters, 65 carpenters, and 74 plasterers. The list for plasterers specifically states that 120 members were working in Dublin. The largest group of craft workers involved in sympathetic action with the United Builders' Labourers and the ITGWU were Richard O'Carroll's bricklayers, 540 of whom were 'idle' at one point. It must also be remembered that some craft workers had been locked out from non-construction employments.
19. *Irish Times*, 27 Jan. 1914.
20. *Irish Times*, 28 Jan. 1914.
21. *Irish Times*, 28 Jan. 1914; Dublin Chamber of Commerce minutes, annual general meeting, 27 Jan. 1914; Dublin Chamber of Commerce, Annual Report, 1914; *Thom's Directory*, 1914.

CHAPTER 44 (p. 539–550)

1. *Irish Times*, 29 Jan. 1914.
2. Coates and Topham, *The Making of the Transport and General Workers' Union*, 342.
3. *Irish Times*, 29 and 30 Jan. 1914.
4. *Irish Times*, 27–9 Jan. 1914.
5. *Irish Catholic*, 6 Dec. 1913.
6. McCaffrey, 'Jacob's women workers during the 1913 lockout,' 128, n. 13.
7. *Irish Catholic*, 6 Dec. 1913.
8. *Irish Times*, 31 Jan. and 2 Feb. 1914.
9. *Irish Times*, 31 Jan. to 5 Feb. 1914.
10. *Irish Times*, 31 Jan. 1914.
11. *Irish Times*, 4 Feb. 1914.
12. *Irish Times*, 4 Feb. 1914.
13. *Irish Times*, 2–4 Feb. 1914; minutes of the Parliamentary Committee of the TUC, 9 Feb. 1914. The figures for the number of ITGWU members still locked out are based on a statement by Larkin to Dublin Trades Council on 9 February 1914 and an undated memorandum for the same year in the O'Brien Papers. The O'Brien memorandum probably dates from March 1914. He estimates the total number of locked-out ITGWU members then at 4,000, so that the numbers locked out in February must have been at least as high: O'Brien Papers, NLI, Pos 6989.
14. Dublin Chamber of Commerce, Council report, 9 Feb. 1914; Dublin Chamber of Commerce, annual reports, 1914 and 1915.
15. Dublin Trades Council minutes, 9 Feb. 1914. Regarding Richard O'Carroll and Ellion see the letter to William O'Brien, 31 Jan. 1914, O'Brien Papers, NLI, Pos 6989.
16. Greaves, *The Irish Transport and General Workers' Union*, 120.
17. Dublin Trades Council minutes, 9 Feb. 1914; O'Brien Papers, NLI, undated memorandum, Pos 6989.
18. Greaves, *The Irish Transport and General Workers' Union*, 122–3; Emmet Larkin, *James Larkin*, 170.
19. Minutes of No. 1 Branch, ITGWU, 10 Mar. 1914, NLI.
20. Mrs B. McCarthy to 'Mr. Taylor', 4 Jan. 1914, ITGWU Correspondence, Guinness Archive, Box 6.

21. Guinness Archive, Board memoranda, 2144–431; subscription list in Walsh Papers, laity file, DDA.
22. *Irish Times*, 4 and 7 Feb. 1914.
23. *Irish Times*, 5 Feb. 1914.
24. *Irish Times*, 7 Feb. 1914.
25. *Irish Times*, 10 Feb. 1914.

CHAPTER 45 (p. 551–570)

1. *Irish Times*, 10 Feb. 1914.
2. *Irish Times*, 10 Feb. 1914.
3. *Irish Times*, 14 Feb. 1914.
4. *Report of the Dublin Disturbances Commission* (Cd. 7421), Parliamentary Papers, vol. 67 , 1914.
5. See *Irish Times*, 18 Feb. 1914, for a useful summary of the findings of the Inquiry into the the Housing Conditions of the Working Classes. The response of the Housing Committee of Dublin Corporation can be found in Dublin Corporation Reports, vol. 3, 1914.
6. Minutes of Dublin Trades Council, 23 Feb. 1914.
7. Minutes of Dublin Trades Council, 23 Feb. 1914.
8. *Irish Times*, 19 Feb. 1914.
9. See Bew, *Ideology and the Irish Question*, 84 and 100, for details of Ronald McNeill, 110–11, for evidence of serious reservations senior unionists had about an armed conflict; *Irish Times*, 27 Feb. and 20 Mar. 1914.
10. Dublin Trades Council minutes, 23 Feb. 1914.
11. *Irish Catholic*, 28 Feb. 1914.
12. *Irish Times*, 3 Mar. 1914.
13. Nevin, *James Larkin*, 266–71, gives the full text of the speech.
14. Fox, *The History of the Irish Citizen Army*, 63–4.
15. Fox, *The History of the Irish Citizen Army*, 63–4. O'Casey and White would not be members of the Citizen Army for much longer. Both resigned because of differences of opinion about the relationship the Citizen Army should have with the Irish Volunteers. White resigned in May when he was foiled in his efforts to work more closely with the Volunteers; he subsequently approached Roger Casement, who recommended him to Maurice Moore as 'useful from a military point of view … provided no questions of "policies" are permitted': Redmond Papers, NLI, ms. 10,561. O'Casey considered the Volunteers to be 'reactionary' and class enemies. Having helped to force White's resignation, he also sought to remove Constance Markievicz from the Citizen Army executive because of her joint membership of the two military groups. However, Markievicz was made of sterner stuff than White and also enjoyed the support of both Larkin and Connolly. In end it was O'Casey who resigned. The upshot of the faction-fighting was that the Citizen Army lost a clerk and Ireland gained a playwright.
16. *Irish Worker*, 28 Mar. 1914.
17. *Irish Times*, 7 Apr. 1913; Dublin Trades Council minutes, 6 Apr. 1914.
18. *Irish Times*, 7 Apr. 1914; *Irish Worker*, 30 May 1914; Fox, *The History of the Irish Citizen Army*, 72. Fox, who knew many of Connolly's contemporaries, argues that from this point on Connolly was 'completely and militarily national.'

19. Dublin Trades Council minutes, 6 Apr. 1914 and 8 Sep. 1913. William O'Brien was precluded from military service by a deformed foot. He was nominated by Connolly, along with Francis Sheehy-Skeffington, to look after 'civilian matters' in 1916.
20. *Irish Times*, 7–9 Apr. 1914.
21. Correspondence of William Smyth and Son with ITGWU, 6–11 May 1914, NLI, ms. 27,054.
22. Annual report of the National Transport Workers' Federation, 1914.
23. Hardinge Commission on the causes of the rebellion, as reproduced in the *Irish Times Sinn Féin Rebellion Handbook*, 1916, 182–7, Macardle, *The Irish Republic*, 112–15; Fox, *The History of the Irish Citizen Army*, 74–6. The Commissioner of the DMP, Sir John Ross, resigned in protest at the way Harrell had been treated.

EPILOGUE (p. 571–587)

1. For Kettle's views on war see the memoir by his widow, Mary Kettle, in the 1968 edition of his collection of essays, *The Day's Burden*, 20. For a particularly scathing view of Redmond's nominees to the Volunteer executive see Bulmer Hobson, 'Foundation and growth of the Irish Volunteers, 1913–1914,' in Martin, *The Irish Volunteers*, 45–53.
2. Tom Kettle, 'The Ways of War,' quoted by Lyons in *What Did I Die Of?*, 183. The guns acquired by Kettle were handed over to the Belgian government to protect the 'rights of small nations.'
3. I have largely followed the interpretation of Sheehy-Skeffington's role in the Rising taken by Conor Cruise O'Brien in his recent memoir, *My Life and Themes*, chap. 1.
4. Caulfield, *The Easter Rising*, 202, 218, 243–4.
5. Greaves, *The Irish Transport and General Workers' Union*, 185.
6. *Irish Worker*, 8 Aug. 1914. It should be remembered that up to the outbreak of war it was the unionists who made up most of Ireland's German sympathisers. The most prominent of these was Sir James Craig, who became the first Prime Minister of Northern Ireland in 1921.
7. *Irish Worker*, 8 Aug. 1914.
8. *Forward*, 15 Aug. 1914, quoted by Howell in *A Lost Left*, 131.
9. *Workers' Republic*, 29 Aug. 1915 and 18 Mar. 1916, quoted by Ryan in *Socialism and Nationalism*, 139, 143–4. See also Howell, *A Lost Left*, chap. 8, for a good summary of Connolly's reasons for participating in the Rising. The *Workers' Republic* replaced the *Irish Worker*, which was one of a number of radical publications suppressed by the British authorities in November 1914.
10. Mitchell, *Labour in Irish Politics*, 63–7; Cody et al., *The Parliament of Labour*, 111–16; William O'Brien, *Forth the Banners Go*, 71, 262–4. The other candidates were J. J. Farrell, a former lord mayor sponsored by the United Irish League, and Pierce O'Mahony. Despite O'Mahony's stand during the lockout, he laboured under the handicap of supporting the British war effort at a time when it was rapidly losing its appeal because of high taxes, rising casualty figures, and growing fears of conscription.
11. Samuel Levenson, *James Connolly*, 325. I have also followed Tom Morrissey (in his introduction to the 1991 edition of *The Social Teachings of James Connolly* by Lambert McKenna SJ) in accepting that Connolly was a sincere Catholic at the end of his life and that his confession was not a ruse to convince Irish

workers that it was possible to be a Marxist and a member of the Catholic Church.

12. Callanan, *T. M. Healy*, 517; Morrissey, *William Martin Murphy*, 63–4.

13. Morrissey, *William Martin Murphy*, 64; Lyons, *Ireland Since the Famine*, 375, 777, n. 15. See also 'Hardinge Commission on the Causes of the Irish Rebellion' in *Irish Times Sinn Féin Rebellion Handbook*, 191.

14. Mitchell, *Labour in Irish Politics*, 63–7; Cody et al., *The Parliament of Labour*, 111–16; Maume, *The Long Gestation*, 168.

15. Dr Abraham Brownrigg, Bishop of Ossory, to Dr Walsh, 7 Nov. 1913, DDA.

16. Mary Kettle, 'Memoir,' in Kettle, *The Day's Burden*, 38.

17. Johnstone, *Orange, Green and Khaki*, 74–5.

18. William Smyth and Son, schedule of fees for services to ITGWU, NLI, ms. 27,054; returns of ITGWU to Registrar of Friendly Societies for the year ending 31 Dec. 1913.

19. Greaves, *The Irish Transport and General Workers' Union*, 140.

20. *Irish Times*, 2 Feb. 1914.

21. William Smyth and Son, schedule of fees for services to ITGWU, NLI, ms. 27,054.

22. Greaves, *The Irish Transport and General Workers' Union*, 120.

23. Returns of ITGWU to Registrar of Friendly Societies for year ending 31 Dec. 1913.

24. Membership Roll, 1915, NLI, ms. 3097; Greaves, *The Irish Transport and General Workers' Union*, 152–3.

25. Returns of ITGWU to Registrar of Friendly Societies for year ending 31 Dec. 1917.

26. O'Connor, *A Labour History of Ireland*, 98.

27. Lysaght, 'The rake's progress of a syndicalist,' 49.

28. Details of Larkin's life in the United States are taken mainly from Manus O'Riordan, 'Larkin in America: the road to Sing Sing,' in Nevin, *James Larkin*, 64–73; details of Larkin's marriage are taken mainly from 'The Larkin family' in Nevin, *James Larkin*, 486.

29. *Irish Worker*, 11 July 1914, quoted by Emmet Larkin in *James Larkin*, 180.

30. *Irish Worker*, 11 July 1914, quoted by Emmet Larkin in *James Larkin*, 180.

31. *Irish Worker*, 8 Aug. 1914, quoted by Emmet Larkin in *James Larkin*, 181. See also McCarthy, 'Larkin and the Working Class,' for a more reflective assessment.

32. *Workers' Republic*, 8 Mar. 1914, quoted by Howell in *A Lost Left*, 141.

33. Gaughan, *Thomas Johnson*, 475; see also McCarthy, 'Larkin and the working class.'

34. See Connolly, 'The Reconquest of Ireland,' in *Labour in Ireland*, 206–9, for a detailed exposition of the principle of the sympathetic strike.

35. *Board of Trade Reports on Industrial Disputes* (Cd. 7658), Parliamentary Papers, vol. 36, 1914–16.

36. The term appears in a generally sympathetic treatment of Murphy by Dermot Keogh, 'Clash of Titans: James Larkin and William Martin Murphy,' in Nevin, *James Larkin*, 47–55.

37. Dublin Chamber of Commerce, annual reports, 1913 and 1914; Guinness, annual report, 1913, Guinness Archive; Palgrave Murphy shipping records, 1913–14, NA.

38. *Irish Times*, 31 Jan. 1947. 'Young Jim' Larkin remains an undeservedly neglected figure. The seminal work on him is Manus O'Riordan, 'The Voice of a Thinking, Intelligent Movement: James Larkin Junior and the Ideological Modernisation of Irish Trade Unions,' paper read to Irish Labour History Society, Dublin, 1995.

BIBLIOGRAPHY

PRIMARY SOURCES

Guinness Archive, Board memoranda, Dublin.

British army intelligence notes, donation of Capt J. Mortell, Military Archives, Dublin.

Cabinet Papers, Public Records Office, London.

Chief Secretary's Office files, National Archives.

Drapers' Assistants' Association records, Mandate, Dublin.

Dublin Chamber of Commerce, annual reports and minutes, 1912–14, National Archives.

Dublin Corporation, minutes and reports, 1912–14, Dublin City Archives.

Dublin Trades Council, minutes, National Library of Ireland.

Great Southern and Western Railway, half-yearly reports, 1900–14, Railway Society, Heuston Station, Dublin.

ITGWU records, National Library of Ireland.

National Federation of Transport Workers, records, National Records Centre, Warwick University, Coventry.

National Society for the Prevention of Cruelty to Children, annual reports, 1911–15.

Registrar of Friendly Societies, returns, 1909–14, National Library of Ireland.

Shipping Federation records, Modern Records Centre, Warwick University, Coventry.

Society of St Vincent de Paul, national records, 1900–14, Dublin.

Trades Union Congress, annual reports, 1911–1915; minutes of Parliamentary Committee, 1913–1914; Dublin Food Fund report.

United Irish Society, London, records, National Library of Ireland.

PERSONAL PAPERS

Herbert Henry Asquith Papers, Bodleian Library, Oxford.

Augustine Birrell Papers, Bodleian Library, Oxford.

John Dillon Papers, Trinity College, Dublin.

Rosamund Jacob Papers, National Library of Ireland, Dublin.

David Lloyd George Papers, House of Lords Records Office, London.

William O'Brien Papers, National Library of Ireland, Dublin.

León Ó Broin Papers, National Library of Ireland, Dublin.

John Redmond Papers, National Library of Ireland, Dublin.

Francis Sheehy-Skeffington Papers, National Library of Ireland, Dublin.

Dr William Walsh, laity files, 1913–14, Dublin Diocesan Archives.

PARLIAMENTARY PAPERS

DMP Statistical Returns, 1912–14.

Board of Trade Reports on Industrial Disputes (Cd. 4254), Parliamentary Papers, vol. 48, 1908.

Board of Trade Reports on Industrial Disputes (Cd. 4680), Parliamentary Papers, vol. 44, 1909.

Board of Trade Reports on Industrial Disputes (Cd. 5325), Parliamentary Papers, vol. 58, 1910.

Board of Trade Reports on Industrial Disputes (Cd. 5850), Parliamentary Papers, vol. 41, 1911.

Board of Trade Reports on Industrial Disputes (Cd. 6472), Parliamentary Papers, vol. 47, 1912–13.

Board of Trade Reports on Industrial Disputes (Cd. 7089), Parliamentary Papers, vol. 48, 1914.

Board of Trade Reports on Industrial Disputes (Cd. 6953), Parliamentary Papers, vol. 36, 1914–16.

Board of Trade Reports on Industrial Disputes (Cd. 7658), Parliamentary Papers, vol. 36, 1914–16.

Askwith Inquiry (Cd. 6953, Cd. 7658), 1914.

Report of the Departmental Committee into the Housing Conditions of the Working Classes in the City of Dublin (Cd. 7273), Parliamentary Papers, vol. 19, 1914; *Evidence and Appendices* (Cd 7317), vol. 19, 1914.

Report into the Causes of the Rebellion in Ireland [Hardinge Commission] (Cd 8279), Parliamentary Papers, vol. 11, 1916; *Evidence and Appendices* (Cd 8311), vol. 11, 1916.

Report of the Dublin Disturbances Commission (Cd. 7269), Parliamentary Papers, vol. 8, 1914; *Evidence and Appendices* (Cd. 7272) vol. 8 , 1914.

NEWSPAPERS AND PERIODICALS

Draper's Assistant, 1913–14.
Evening Herald, 1913–14.
Freeman's Journal, 1913–14.
Irish Independent, 1913–14 and 1943.
Irish Times, 1913–14.
Irish Worker, 1908–14.
Leader, 1912–14.
Thom's Directory, 1912–14.

BOOKS AND ARTICLES

Aberdeen, Lord and Lady, *We Twa: Reminiscences*, London 1936.

Akenson, Donald, *Small Differences: Irish Catholics and Irish Protestants, 1815–1922*, Dublin: Gill and Macmillan 1988.

Akenson, Donald, *Conor: A Biography of Conor Cruise O'Brien* (two vols.), Montréal and Kingston: McGill-Queen's University Press 1994.

Anderson, William, *James Connolly and the Irish Left*, Dublin: Irish Academic Press 1994.

Andrews, C. S., *Dublin Made Me*, Cork: Mercier Press 1979.

Bew, Paul, *Ideology and the Irish Question: Ulster Unionism and Irish Nationalism, 1912–1916*, Oxford: Oxford University Press 1995.

Bew, Paul, *John Redmond*, Dundalk: Dundalgan Press (for Historical Association of Ireland) 1996.

Bolster, Evelyn, *The Knights of St Columbanus*, Dublin: Gill and Macmillan 1979.

Bond, Brian, *War and Society in Europe, 1870–1970*, London: Fontana 1983.

Boyce, D. G. (ed.), *The Revolution in Ireland, 1879–1923*, Dublin: Gill and Macmillan 1988.

Boylan, Henry, *A Dictionary of Irish Biography*, Dublin: Gill and Macmillan 1978.

Boyle, John, *Leaders and Workers*, Cork: Mercier Press n.d. [1986].

Boyle, John, *The Irish Labor Movement in the Nineteenth Century*, Washington: Catholic University of America Press 1988.

Brady, Thomas, *The Historical Basis of Socialism in Ireland*, Cork: Saor Éire Press 1969.

British and Irish Communist Organisation, *Was Connolly a Bourgeois Intellectual?* Belfast: BICO n.d.

Caffrey, P., 'Jacob's women workers during the 1913 strike,' *Saothar*, no. 16, 1991.

Callanan, Frank, *T. M. Healy*, Cork: Cork University Press 1996.

Cameron, Charles, *How the Poor Lived*, privately printed.

Caulfield, Max, *The Easter Rebellion*, London: Frederick Muller 1964.

Clarke, Kathleen, *Revolutionary Woman*, Dublin: O'Brien Press 1991.

Clarkson, J. Dunsmore, *Labour and Nationalism in Ireland*, New York: AMD Press 1978.

Coates, Ken, and Topham, Tony, *The Making of the Transport and General Workers' Union: The Emergence of the Labour Movement, 1870–1922*, Oxford: Basil Blackwell 1991.

Cody, Séamus, *May Day in Dublin, 1890–1986*, Dublin: Dublin Council of Trade Unions n.d. [1986].

Cody, Séamus, 'P. T. Daly,' unpublished monograph.

Cody, Séamus, O'Dowd, John, and Rigney, Peter, *The Parliament of Labour: 100 Years of the Dublin Council of Trade Unions*, Dublin: DCTU 1986.

Connolly, James, *Socialism and Nationalism* (ed. Desmond Ryan), Dublin: Three Candles 1948.

Connolly, James, *Labour and Easter Week* (ed. Desmond Ryan), Dublin: Three Candles 1949.

Connolly, James, *The Workers' Republic* (ed. Desmond Ryan), Dublin: Three Candles 1951.

Connolly, James, *Erin's Hope and the New Evangel*, Dublin: New Books 1968.

Connolly, James, *Revolutionary Warfare*, Dublin: New Books 1968.

Connolly, James, *Selected Writings* (ed. Peter Berresford Ellis), Harmondsworth (Middx): Penguin 1973.

Connolly, James, *Socialism Made Easy*, Dublin: Labour Party 1982.

Connolly, James, *The Lost Writings* (ed. Aindrias Ó Cathasaigh), London: Pluto 1997.

Connolly, James, *Labour in Ireland* (ed. Desmond Ryan), Dublin: Three Candles n.d.

Connolly, James, *Yellow Unions in Ireland and Other Articles*, Belfast: British and Irish Communist Organisation n.d.

Connolly, James, Russell, C., and Sigerson S., *Sinn Féin and Socialism*, Cork: Cork Workers' Club n.d.

Connolly, James, and Walker, William, *The Connolly-Walker Controversy on*

Socialist Unity in Ireland, Cork: Cork Workers' Club n.d.

Connolly O'Brien, Nora, *James Connolly: Portrait of a Rebel Father*, Dublin: Four Masters Press 1975.

Costello, Peter, *Dublin Churches*, Dublin: Gill and Macmillan 1989.

Crossman, Virginia, *Local Government in Nineteenth-Century Ireland*, Dublin: Institute of Public Administration 1994.

Cruise O'Brien, Conor (ed.), *The Shaping of Modern Ireland*, London: Routledge and Kegan Paul 1960.

Cruise O'Brien, Conor, *Parnell and His Party*, Oxford: Oxford University Press 1968.

Cruise O'Brien, Conor, *My Life and Themes*, Dublin: Poolbeg 1998.

Cullen Owens, Rosemary, *Smashing Times: A History of the Irish Women's Suffrage Movement, 1889–1922*, Dublin: Attic Press 1984.

Cullingford, Elizabeth, *Yeats, Ireland and Fascism*, London: Macmillan 1981.

Curriculum Development Unit, City of Dublin VEC, Trinity College, and Department of Education, *Dublin, 1913: A Divided City*, Dublin: O'Brien Press 1982.

D'Arcy, Fergus, 'Wages of labourers in the building industry, 1667–1918,' *Saothar*, no. 14, 1989.

D'Arcy, Fergus, 'Wages of skilled workers in the building industry, 1667–1918,' *Saothar*, no. 15, 1990.

Daly, Mary, *Dublin: The Deposed Capital: A Social and Economic History, 1860–1914*, Cork: Cork University Press 1984.

Daly, Mary, *Women and Work in Ireland*, Dundalk: Dundalgan Press (for Economic and Social History Society of Ireland) 1997.

Dangerfield, George, *The Damnable Question*, London: Constable 1979.

Dangerfield, George, *The Strange Death of Liberal England*, London: Serif 1997.

Davies, A. J., *To Build a New Jerusalem*, London: Abacus 1996.

Davis, Richard, *Arthur Griffith and Non-Violent Sinn Féin*, Dublin: Anvil Books 1974.

Dawson, Richard, *Red Terror and Green*, London: New English Library 1972.

de Búrca, Séamus, *The Soldier's Song: The Story of Peadar Kearney*, Dublin: P. J. Bourke 1957.

Dennison, Stanley, and Mac Donagh, Oliver, *Guinness, 1886–1939: From Incorporation to the Second World War*, Cork: Cork University Press 1998.

Doherty, E., *Matt Talbot*, Milwaukee: Bruce 1953.

Dudley Edwards, Ruth, *Patrick Pearse: The Triumph of Failure*, London: Victor Gollancz 1977.

Enright, Michael, *Men of Iron: Wexford Foundry Dispute, 1890 and 1911*, Wexford: Wexford Council of Trade Unions 1987.

Farmar, Tony, *Ordinary Lives: Three Generations of Irish Middle-Class Experience*, Dublin: Gill and Macmillan 1991.

Farrell, Brian (ed.), *Communications and Community in Ireland* (Thomas Davis Lectures), Cork and Dublin: Mercier Press 1984.

Fox, R. M., *The History of the Irish Citizen Army*, Dublin: Duffy 1943.

Fox, R. M., *Jim Larkin: The Rise of the Underman*, London: Lawrence and Wishart 1957.

Gaughan, J. Anthony, *Thomas Johnson, 1872–1963*, Dublin: Kingdom Books 1980.

Geraghty, H., 'William Partridge,' unpublished manuscript.

Gilbert, Martin, *Churchill: A Life*, London: Heinemann 1991.

Gonne MacBride, Maud, *A Servant of the Queen*, London: Victor Gollancz 1974.

Greaves, C. Desmond, *The Life and Times of James Connolly*, London: Lawrence and Wishart 1961.

Greaves, C. Desmond, *The Irish Transport and General Workers' Union: The Formative Years*, Dublin: Gill and Macmillan 1982.

Griffith, Arthur, *The Resurrection of Hungary*, Dublin: Whelan and Son 1918.

Grigg, John, *Lloyd George: The People's Champion, 1902–1911*, London: Harper-Collins 1997.

Grigg, John, London: Harper-Collins 1997.

Hazelkorn, Ellen, 'The social and political views of Louie Bennett, 1870–1956,' *Saothar*, no. 13, 1988.

Healy, Timothy, *Letters and Leaders of My Day*, London: Thornton Butterworth n.d. [1928].

Hearn, Mona, *Below Stairs: Domestic Service Remembered in Dublin and Beyond, 1880–1922*, Dublin: Lilliput 1993.

Hepburn, A. (ed.), *A Past Apart: Studies in the History of Catholic Belfast, 1850–1950*, Belfast: Ulster Historical Foundation 1996.

Horgan, J. J., *Parnell to Pearse*, Dublin: Browne and Nolan 1948.

Howell, David, *A Lost Left: Three Studies in Socialism and Nationalism*, Chicago: University of Chicago Press 1986.

Hyland, James, *Life and Times of James Connolly*, Dundalk: Dundalgan Press (for Historical Association of Ireland) 1997.

Irish Times, *Sinn Féin Rebellion Handbook, Easter 1916*, Dublin: Irish Times 1916.

Irish Transport and General Workers' Union, *Fifty Years of Liberty Hall*, Dublin: Three Candles 1959.

Johnston, A., Larraghy, J., and McWilliams, E., *Connolly: A Marxist Analysis*, Dublin: Irish Workers' Group 1990.

Johnstone, Tom, *Orange, Green and Khaki: The Story of the Irish Regiments in the Great War, 1914–1918*, Dublin: Gill and Macmillan 1992.

Jones, Mary, *These Obstreperous Lassies: A History of the IWWU*, Dublin: Gill and Macmillan 1988.

Joyce, James, *Dubliners*, Harmondsworth (Middx): Penguin 1961.

Joyce, James, *Ulysses: The Corrected Text* (ed. Hans Gabler, Wolfhard Steppe, and Claus Melchior), London: Bodley Head 1986.

Keane, M., *Ishbel: Lady Aberdeen in Ireland*, Dublin: Colourpoint Books 1999.

Kearns, Kevin, *Dublin Tenement Life: An Oral History*, Dublin: Gill and Macmillan 1994.

Keegan, John, *A History of Warfare*, London: Pimlico 1994.

Keogh, Dermot, 'William Martin Murphy and the origins of the 1913 lockout,' *Saothar*, no. 4, 1978.

Keogh, Dermot, *The Rise of the Irish Working Class: The Dublin Trade Union Movement and Labour Leadership, 1890–1914*, Belfast: Appletree Press 1982.

Kettle, Andrew, *The Material for Victory* (ed. Laurence Kettle), Dublin: C. J. Fallon 1958.

Kettle, Tom, *The Day's Burden*, Dublin: Browne and Nolan 1937; reissued Dublin: Gill and Macmillan 1968.

Laffan, Michael, *The Partition of Ireland, 1911–25*, Dublin: Dublin Historical Association 1983.

Laffan, Michael, *The Resurrection of Ireland: The Sinn Féin Party, 1916–1923*, Cambridge: Cambridge University Press 1999.

Lane, Fintan, *The Origins of Modern Irish Socialism*, Cork: Cork University Press 1997.

Larkin, Emmet, *James Larkin, 1874–1947: Irish Labour Leader*, London: Routledge and Kegan Paul 1965.

Larkin, James [Junior], *In the Footsteps of Big Jim: A Family Biography*, Dublin: Blackwater Press n.d. [1996].

Leslie, John, *The Irish Question* (Historical Reprints, no. 7), Cork: Cork Workers' Club 1974.

Levenson, Leah, *With Wooden Sword: A Portrait of Francis Sheehy-Skeffington, Militant Pacifist*, Dublin: Gill and Macmillan 1983.

Levenson, Leah, and Natterstad, Jerry, *Hanna Sheehy-Skeffington: Irish Feminist*, Syracuse (NY): Syracuse University Press 1986.

Levenson, Samuel, *James Connolly: A Biography*, London: Martin Brian and O'Keeffe 1973.

Levenson, Samuel, *Maud Gonne*, London: Cassell 1977.

Luddy, Maria, and Murphy, Clíona, *Women Surviving: Studies in Irish Women's History in the 19th and 20th Centuries*, Dublin: Poolbeg 1990.

Lyons, F. S. L., *John Dillon: A Biography*, London: Routledge and Keegan Paul 1968.

Lyons, F. S. L., *Ireland since the Famine*, London: Weidenfeld and Nicolson 1971.

Lyons, F. S. L., *Culture and Anarchy in Ireland, 1890–1939*, Oxford: Oxford University Press 1979.

Lyons, J. B., *The Enigma of Tom Kettle*, Dublin: Glendale Press 1983.

Lyons, J. B., *What Did I Die of?*, Dublin: Lilliput 1991.

Lysaght, D. R. O'Connor, 'The rake's progress of a syndicalist: the political career of William O'Brien, Irish labour leader,' *Saothar*, no. 9, 1983.

Macardle, Dorothy, *The Irish Republic*, Dublin: Irish Press 1951.

McCamley, Bill, *The Third James: The Story of the Irish Labour Pioneer James Fearon*, Dublin: Labour History Workshop 1984.

McCarthy, Charles, 'Larkin and the Working Class, 1907–1913,' paper read to conference of Irish Labour History Society, Dublin, Sep. 1980.

Mac Giolla Choille, Breandán (ed.), *Chief Secretary's Office, Dublin Castle: Intelligence Notes, 1913–1916*, Dublin: Stationery Office 1966.

McKenna, Lambert, *The Social Teachings of James Connolly* (ed. Thomas Morrissey), Dublin: Veritas 1991.

Maguire, Martin, *Servants to the Public: A History of the Local Government and Public Services Union, 1901 to 1899*, Dublin: Institute of Public Administration 1998.

Maguire, M., 'The Dublin working class, 1870s–1930s: economy, society, politics,' in Thomas Bartlett (ed.), *History and Environment*, Dublin: University College 1988.

Maguire, M., 'A socio-economic analysis of the Dublin Protestant working class, 1870–1926,' *Irish Economic and Social History*, vol. 20 (1993).

Maguire, M., 'The organisation and activism of Dublin's Protestant working class,' *Irish Historical Studies*, vol. 29 (1994), no. 113.

Mandle, William, *The Gaelic Athletic Association and Irish Nationalist Politics, 1884–1924*, Dublin: Gill and Macmillan 1987.

Mann, Tom, *Memoirs*, London: McGibbon and Kee 1967.

Marreco, Anne, *The Rebel Countess: The Life and Times of Constance Markievicz*, London: Weidenfeld and Nicolson 1967.

Martin, F. X. (ed.), *The Irish Volunteers, 1913–1915: Recollections and Documents*, Dublin: James Duffy 1963.

Martin, F. X. (ed.), *Leaders and Men of the Easter Rising: Dublin, 1916*, London: Methuen 1967.

Martin, G., *Churchill: A Life*, London: Heinemann 1991.

Maume, Patrick, *D. P. Moran*, Dundalk: Dundalgan Press 1995.

Maume, Patrick, *The Long Gestation: Irish Nationalist Life, 1891–1918*, Dublin: Gill and Macmillan 1999.

Maye, Brian, *Arthur Griffith*, Dublin: Griffith College 1997.

Mitchell, Arthur, *Labour in Irish Politics, 1890–1930*, Dublin: Irish University Press 1974.

Montefiore, Dora, *From a Victorian to a Modern*, London: E. Archer 1917.

Monteith, Robert, *Casement's Last Adventure*, Dublin: Michael F. Moynihan 1953.

Moran, B., 1913, 'Jim Larkin and the British labour movement,' *Saothar*, no. 4, 1978.

Morgan, Austen, *James Connolly: A Political Biography*, Manchester: Manchester University Press 1988.

Morgan, Austen, *Labour and Partition: The Belfast Working Class, 1905–1923*, London: Pluto Press 1991.

Morrissey, Thomas, *A Man Called Hughes: The Life and Times of Séamus Hughes, 1881–1943*, Dublin: Veritas 1991.

Morrissey, Thomas, *William Martin Murphy*, Dundalk: Dundalgan Press 1997.

Muenger, Elizabeth, *The British Military Dilemma in Ireland: Occupation Politics, 1886–1914*, Dublin: Gill and Macmillan 1991.

Murray, P., 'Electoral politics and the Dublin working class before the First World War,' *Saothar*, no. 6, 1980.

Murray, P., 'A militant among the magdalens?' *Saothar*, no. 20, 1995.

Neligan, David, *The Spy in the Castle*, London: McGibbon and Kee 1968.

Nevin, Dónal (ed.), *1913: Jim Larkin and the 1913 Lockout*, Dublin: Workers' Union of Ireland 1964.

Nevin, Dónal (ed.), *Trade Union Century*, Cork and Dublin: Mercier Press 1994.

Nevin, Dónal (ed.), *James Larkin: Lion of the Fold*, Dublin: Gill and Macmillan 1998.

Newsinger, John, 'The Devil it was who sent Larkin to Ireland: the Liberator, Larkinism, and the Dublin lockout of 1913,' *Saothar*, no. 18, 1993.

Norman, Diana, *Terrible Beauty: A Life of Constance Markievicz*, Dublin: Poolbeg 1987.

O'Brien, Joseph, *Dear, Dirty Dublin: A City in Distress, 1899–1916*, London: University of California Press 1982.

O'Brien, William, *Forth the Banners Go* (ed. Edward MacLysaght), Dublin: Three Candles 1969.

Ó Broin, León, *Dublin Castle and the 1916 Rising*, Dublin: Helicon 1966.

Ó Broin, León, *The Chief Secretary: Augustine Birrell in Ireland*, London: Chatto and Windus 1969.

Ó Broin, León, *Revolutionary Underground: The Story of the Irish Republican Brotherhood, 1858–1924*, Dublin: Gill and Macmillan 1976.

O'Casey, Seán, 'The Story of the Irish Citizen Army,' in *Feathers from the Green Crow: Seán O'Casey, 1905–1925* (ed. Robert Hogan), London: Macmillan 1963.

O'Casey, Seán, *Drums under the Windows*, London: Pan Books 1973.

O'Connell, J., *The Problem with Dublin Slums*, Dublin: Hodges, Figgis n.d.

O'Connor, Emmet, *A Labour History of Ireland, 1824–1960*, Dublin: Gill and Macmillan 1992.

O'Connor, T. P., *Memoirs of An Old Parliamentarian*, London: Ernest Benn 1929.

O'Day, Alan, *The English Face of Irish Nationalism: Parnellite Involvement in British Politics, 1880–86*, Dublin: Gill and Macmillan 1977.

O'Day, Alan, *Parnell and the First Home Rule Episode*, Dublin: Gill and Macmillan 1986.

O'Day, Alan, *Irish Home Rule, 1867–1921*, Manchester: Manchester University Press 1998.

Ó Faoláin, Seán, *Constance Markievicz*, London: Jonathan Cape 1934.

O'Halpin, Eunan, *The Decline of the Union: British Government in Ireland, 1892–1920*, Dublin: Gill and Macmillan 1987.

O'Riordan, Manus, 'The Voice of a Thinking, Intelligent Movement: James Larkin Junior and the Ideological Modernisation of the Irish Trade Unions,' Dublin: Irish Labour History Society 1995.

Paseta, Senia, *Before the Revolution: Nationalism and Social Change*, Cork: Cork University Press 1999.

Patterson, Henry, *Class Conflict and Sectarianism: The Protestant Working Class and the Belfast Labour Movement, 1868–1920*, Belfast: Blackstaff Press 1980.

Pearse, Patrick, *The Letters of P. H. Pearse* (ed. Séamus Ó Buachalla), Gerrards Cross (Bucks): Colin Smythe 1980.

Pearse, Patrick, *Political Writings and Speeches*, Dublin: Talbot press 1962.

Phillips, W. Alison, *The Revolution in Ireland, 1906–1923*, London: Longman 1926.

Plunkett, James, *Strumpet City*, St Albans: Panther Books 1973.

Pollard, Hugh, *The Secret Societies of Ireland: Their Rise and Progress*, London: P. Allan 1922; reprinted Kilkenny: Irish Historical Press 1998.

Prunty, Jacinta, *Dublin Slums, 1800–1925: A Study in Urban Geography*, Dublin: Irish Academic Press 1998.

Prunty, Jacinta, *Margaret Aylward, 1810–1889: Lady of Charity, Sister of Faith*, Dublin: Four Courts Press 1999.

Redmond, Seán, *The Irish Municipal Employees' Trade Union, 1883–1983*, Dublin: IMETU n.d.

Robbins, Frank, *Under the Starry Plough: Recollections of the Irish Citizen Army*, Dublin: Academy Press 1977.

Rose, N., *Churchill: An Unruly Life*, London: Simon and Schuster 1994.

Ryan, Frederick, *Socialism, Democracy, and the Church*, Dublin: Labour History Workshop 1984.

Ryan, Frederick, *Sinn Féin and Reaction*, Dublin: Labour History Workshop 1984.

Ryan, William P., *The Irish Labour Movement: From the 'Twenties to Our Own Day*, Dublin: Talbot Press n.d. [1919].

Services, Industrial, Professional and Technical Union, *Tribute to James Larkin: Orator, Agitator, Revolutionary, Trade Union Leader*, Dublin: SIPTU 1997.

Sexton, James, *Sir James Sexton, Agitator: The Life of the Dockers' M.P.*, London: Faber and Faber 1936.

Stephens, James, *The Charwoman's Daughter*, London: Macmillan 1923.

Stewart, A. T. Q., *Edward Carson*, Dublin: Gill and Macmillan 1981.

Strauss, Erich, *Irish Nationalism and British Democracy*, London: Methuen 1951.

Sweeney, Jimmy, 'The Dublin lockout, 1913: the response of British labour,' *Saothar*, no. 6, 1980.

Sweeney, Jimmy, 'The oul' spot by the river,' *Liberty*, no. 75.

Swift, John [Junior], *John Swift: An Irish Dissident*, Dublin: Gill and Macmillan 1991.

van Voris, Jacqueline, *Constance de Markievicz in the Cause of Ireland*, Amherst (Mass.): University of Massachusetts Press 1967.

Walsh, Patrick, *William J. Walsh, Archbishop of Dublin*, London: Longman Green 1928.

Ward, Margaret, *Unmanageable Revolutionaries*, London: Pluto Press 1983.

Ward, Margaret, *Hanna Sheehy-Skeffington: A Life*, Cork: Attic Press 1997.

West, Trevor, *Horace Plunkett: Co-Operation and Politics*, Gerrards Cross (Bucks): Colin Smythe 1986.

Wright, Arnold, *Disturbed Dublin: The Story of the Great Strike*, London: Longman Green 1914.

Yeats, William B., *Collected Poems*, London: Macmillan 1963.

Yeats, William B., *Tribute to Thomas Davis*, Cork: Cork University Press 1965.

INDEX